Public Administration

PUBLIC ADMINISTRATION
The State of the Discipline

Edited by

NAOMI B. LYNN
Georgia State University

and

AARON WILDAVSKY
University of California, Berkeley

CHATHAM HOUSE PUBLISHERS, INC.
Chatham, New Jersey

PUBLIC ADMINISTRATION
The State of the Discipline

CHATHAM HOUSE PUBLISHERS, INC.
Box One, Chatham, New Jersey 07928

Publisher: Edward Artinian
Production supervisor: Chris Kelaher
Cover design: Lawrence Ratzkin
Composition: Bang, Motley, and Olufsen
Printing and Binding: Port City Press

LIBRARY OF CONGRESS CATALOGING-IN-PUBLICATION DATA
Public administration : the state of the discipline / edited by Naomi
B. Lynn and Aaron Wildavsky.
   p. cm.
  Includes bibliographical references.
  ISBN 0-934540-62-4
  1. Public administration. 2. Public administration—United
States. I. Lynn, Naomi B. II. Wildavsky, Aaron B.
JF1351.P8185   1990
350—dc20   89-29690
                                                      CIP

Manufactured in the United States of America
10 9 8 7 6 5 4 3 2 1

For the next generation
ARI and YONI
JESSICA, JOSHUA, HILARY, ADAM
and more to follow

Contents

Preface

NAOMI B. LYNN

This is the first book to be sponsored jointly by the American Society for Public Administration (ASPA) and the American Political Science Association (APSA). Although a large number of members belong to both organizations, there has been minimal official contact between the two groups. There are several reasons for this segregation, some of which are discussed by the authors in this book.

In 1985 I served as president of ASPA and Aaron Wildavsky was president of APSA. Wildavsky and I found ourselves discussing ways of bringing political scientists with a specialty in public administration into a more active role in APSA. We were encouraged by the large number of APSA members who had joined the newly organized Section on Public Administration. I mentioned to Wildavsky the unfortunate lack of a chapter on public administration in *Political Science: The State of the Discipline,* which had been published by APSA in 1983, and told him that in response to that omission I had commissioned a number of papers on the state of the discipline of public administration when I served as program chair of the 1984 annual meeting of ASPA. He and I agreed that it would be valuable to put these and other commissioned papers together and prepare a volume to be sponsored jointly by ASPA and APSA. This volume would meet the need for public administration to do some stock taking of its intellectual development, help the two associations identify some mutual interests, and serve as an important resource for students and practitioners who seek a better understanding of the administration process.

The authors whose work is included in this book are all members of both ASPA and APSA and have agreed that all royalties would be owned equally by the two associations. All papers were reviewed by anonymous peer reviewers. Some authors also received the benefits of comments by panelists at the national meetings. Not all subjects and areas of public administration can be covered in a single volume. The editors have attempted to include the most prominent facets of the discipline. As always, this must be a somewhat subjective decision. A number of individuals who helped with the editing and preparation of this volume at Georgia State University merit special words of appreciation: Claudette Parrish, Reggie Foster, Regina Brandt, and Angie Jackson. The executive directors of ASPA and APSA, Keith Mulrooney and Thomas Mann, were most enthusiastic, as were their successors, Shirley Wester and Catherine Rudder.

The late Charles Levine, a past chair of ASPA's Publication Committee, supported this book from its inception and was instrumental in bringing Chatham House into discussion of the project. His help with this book was just one of many contributions he made to our field. His family, friends, and colleagues, as well as the discipline of public administration, suffered a tragic loss with his untimely death at the age of 49.

It is our trust and hope that this book will help develop a new generation of committed scholars. That would please Charles Levine and would be a most appropriate tribute to a life devoted to scholarship. The field of public administration owes much to his work and his enthusiasm, and the next generation of scholars, for whom this volume is intended, are beneficiaries of his legacy.

A number of other colleagues and scholars in public administration made thoughtful and valuable contributions to this book. We want to thank the following persons for their comments and help:

Howard Ball, University of Utah

Carolyn Ban, State University of New York at Albany

Don Bowen, University of Arizona

James Bowman, Florida State University

Barry Bozeman, Syracuse University

Bayard Catron, George Washington University

Joseph Cayer, Arizona State University

Alfred Diamant, Indiana University

William B. Eddy, University of Missouri-Kansas City

George M. Guess, Georgia State University

Michael Harmon, George Washington University

Steven Hays, University of South Carolina

Edward T. Jennings, University of Kentucky

Rita Mae Kelly, Arizona State University

Laurence Lynn, University of Chicago

Cynthia McSwain, George Washington University

Daniel Mazmanian, Claremont Graduate School

Kenneth J. Meier, University of Wisconsin Madison

H. Brinton Milward, University of Arizona

Theodore H. Poister, Georgia State University

William Richter, Kansas State University

Charles Sampson, Sangamon State University

Richard Schorr, Long Island University

Kenneth Shepsle, Harvard University

Richard Stillman, George Mason University

Dwight Waldo, Syracuse University
Mylon Winn, Miami University (Ohio)
Deil Wright, University of North
    Carolina

Tinsley E. Yarbrough, East Carolina
    University
Richard Zody, Virginia Polytechnic In-
    stitute and State University

It is my sincere hope that this volume will serve as a guide to some of the more salient features of public administration and, especially, that it will inspire students and scholars in this discipline to turn their attention and talent to the task of furthering the study of this relatively young but very important academic subject.

Introduction:
Administration without Hierarchy?
Bureaucracy without Authority?

AARON WILDAVSKY

It cannot be said that we are self-satisfied. Perry and Kraemer tell us our research fails to cumulate into greater understanding, is poorly supported financially, and is little valued professionally. Rainey refers to "a widely perceived insufficiency in relevant research." Studies of public administration, Caiden advises, are fragmented. Worse still, efforts to unify the discipline through public-choice theory could well lead to "environmental degradation and social disintegration." Given to more gentle remonstration, Fried patiently explains "why universal theory remains elusive." For Nigro, public personnel administration is an impossible subject: Where performance criteria can be followed, they are rejected (the traditional model for managers); where they are accepted (the human relations approach by managers), they are too vague to be implemented. Although viable alternatives exist, Golembiewski promises, the "schizoid character" of opinion on administration, which results in contradictory recommendations, makes progress difficult. Kaufman worries that the fortuitous alliance of the movements for executive leadership and neutral competence, which bolstered the public service, has declined without a new alliance to take its place. And while Goodsell is prepared to advocate a new and imposing role of the public "administrator as teacher of governance to society," he is concerned, as we all are, about the teacher's credibility. I am concerned, as will become evident, about what we will teach.

The positive message is that we collectively know a good deal more about public administration than we used to know, without being able to say exactly what we know. Those who delimit the scope of their inquiry find it more manageable—the only indispensable quality of formal theory, Bendor assures us, is deduction—at the expense, possibly, of applicability. Those whose aspirations know few bounds risk replacing the discipline they have come to save. Intergovernmental Management (IGM), according to Marando and Florestano, claims new territory; networking by entrepreneurial managers joins private, public, and intrapublic policy. IGM is prescriptive, reformist, result oriented.

There are other optimists. And they have a message for the rest of us. The flaw, as Stewart sees it, is the disproportionate constraint on opportunity faced by women in public administration caused by an excess of paternalism. The remedy is to improve the status of women. Research fits in by continuous studies of the status of women. The metaphor of diminishing differences among people—men and women, black and white, experts and laypeople, superiors and subordinates—that suffuses these inquiries serves as a paradigm for the removal of other obstacles to opportunity that affect public administration as a whole.

The shifts in the subject matter of writing on public administration that Denhardt chronicles all move in the same direction. People who trust in authority do not write endlessly about the ethics of those who wield authority. If you trust your own motives as public managers, you do not need depth psychology. If you do not feel that contemporary discourse puts people down, or hides more than it reveals, there is less reason for you to explore rival epistemologies. The concern of formal theorists with "principal-agent" models suggests all is not well with agents, the bureaucracy, who do not necessarily represent their principals, the elected officials. Nor would one satisfied with the status quo blame the system of relationships that apparently constitutes public administration. Were bureaucracy human, there would be no need to humanize it any more than if managers managed appropriately there would be a need for talk about managing without managers. When Rainey speaks of the "growing skepticism over the efficiency and effectiveness of large public agencies," and about candidates who "campaigned as aggressively against the governmental bureaucracy as against political opponents," we know trouble is among us.*

Denhardt lays it on the line: Public administration, he feels, has been limited by business values (*read* efficiency) and by hierarchy (*read* bureaucracy). What is left for administration, we may ask, if its hierarchical form of organization and its search for efficiency are rejected? Why, indeed, would practitioners and scholars want to rid the field of exactly those features that have made them famous? What would a public administration without a hierarchical form of organization have to offer the nation? What appeal would a bureaucracy without authority have to its members? How, in sum, can we explain the lack of confidence in prevailing doctrine that is perhaps the most evident feature of public administration in our time?

When Max Weber provided the classical definition of bureaucracy, he em-

---

* Running for office against the bureaucracy is not new. Andrew Jackson was the prime exemplar. He dethroned "King Caucus" and increased mass participation through his political party. In office, he fought the "monster bank" of the United States. Like Ronald Reagan, Jackson used the presidential office to try to reduce the size and scope of central government. In a system within which hierarchy is disparaged, even the chief executive may oppose "his" government. See Richard Ellis and Aaron Wildavsky, 1989.

phasized two features: security of tenure and monopoly of expertise. In the United States, this monopoly, although it never existed entirely in a system of checks and balances,* has been shattered by the rise of policy analysis. All around the country, in think tanks, consultant firms, schools of policy analysis, state and local governments, congressional staffs, and elsewhere, there are rival teams of analysts who have recently been or expect soon to be in government. They know as much as those in the bureaucracy know or used to know. Virtually everything that officials can say based on their expertise can be contradicted with conviction by these analysts in (temporary) exile. Consequently, public officials can no longer say with confidence that their views should carry special weight because they know more than their critics.

Security of tenure has also been weakened. The legal rights of civil servants are now counterbalanced by the rights others have against them. When their units go, so may they. As the size of the public service comes under attack, so do its prerogatives, especially the salaries and travel of the upper echelons. Not a happy prospect. What accounts for the defensive position of the public service?

In days gone by, the divisions among and within the two major political parties were more supportive of public servants. Republicans wanted a smaller domestic government and Democrats wanted a larger one. At least under the Democrats, then, public servants could expect support, perhaps even sympathy, for they were the ones who carried out the programs. Even under the Republicans there was respect for their authority, if not agreement on their size and scope. No longer. Now both parties contain elements antithetical to the bureaucracy.†

The Republican party is an alliance between social conservatives and economic libertarians. Social conservatives are prepared to support government on their own terms—intervention abroad and in private life in defense of patriarchal values. But such intervention leaves the public service queasy; for them, hierarchy has its limited rationale in public, not private, life. Sensing resistance, social conservatives do not view the public service as an ally whose authority deserves support; to these conservatives, government exerts both too little authority in support of patriarchy and too much against it, as when it opposes prayer in schools. Economic liber-

---

* In the 1930s, and even the 1950s, it seems to me, the federal government had a much larger share of the available expertise about social security, defense, housing, health, and down the list of major programs than it does today.

† I do not wish to exaggerate. Hierarchical forces, as the demise of the Federalist and Whig parties should show us, have been weak from the beginning. Why, in America, should one trust a person who has not "met a payroll" or "carried a district," i.e., met the tests of economic or political competition? This has always been true. My sense is that it is even " truer" now.

tarians, who want a much smaller and less intrusive domestic government, view public servants as opponents. For these supporters of competitive individualism now have doctrines that tell them bureaucrats are expansionists. Thus the support for existing authority that conservative parties bring to government elsewhere is not found in America.

Well, there are always the Democrats, the party of government, as they once happily called themselves. No more. For one thing, they think the defense budget is too large and often buys the wrong weapons. For another, by far the largest programs are entitlements, mostly payments to individuals, which involve check-writing more than detailed administration. Hence there is less dependence on large numbers of public servants. More important than either of these factors, however, is the increasing ambivalence on the part of Democratic party liberals, its largest faction, about the role of government.

Liberals would like government to do more to help classes of people they deem disadvantaged. These liberals do have a positive view of government as redressing existing inequalities. But precisely because of their desire to move from formal to substantive equality of opportunity (they believe that the government in which the federal bureaucracy is embedded is unfair to disadvantaged groups), they question bureaucratic authority. After all, authority—the expectation that people who occupy positions should be followed because their power is legitimate—is a prima facie case of inequality. Thus there arises the by now familiar category of bureaucracy without authority, namely a desire for policies that increase the need for bureaucracy on the part of people who are reluctant to cede to its members the necessary authority.

An important consequence of the desire for egalitarian policies is that more and more groups are included: minorities, women, the poor, the elderly, children, on and on. This speaks well of social conscience. But it also speaks poorly of priorities. Because there are now so many categories of the deprived and their numbers have grown so large, it becomes difficult to choose among them or to find the resources to aid them all. The bottom line is that the seemingly bloodless category—nondefense discretionary expenditure—amounts to some 11 percent of the budget. And this, outside of defense, is where almost the entire public service is found.

Belonging to the nonentitled, the bureaucracy finds itself under attack from numerous directions. Conservative Democrats and Republicans want to get the deficit down. Gramm-Rudman-Hollings tells the story: General government and defense bear the brunt because they are what is left after entitlements, veterans, and interest on the debt. Looked at another way, the symbols of government, the national defense and the public service, are required to sacrifice. Moderate Democrats and Republicans, the informal party of stability and balance, are caught between saving essential services and despairing over deficits and budget deadlocks. Reluctantly but inevitably, for want of agreed-on alternatives, moderates agree to savage nondefense discretionary spending, that is, the general government of the United States.

Civil servants do not have to be told these are hard times. Whichever way they turn, however political fortunes change, they will get the short end of a hard stick. At one end, told to do more with less, they get clobbered by spending cuts; at the other end, their lives are made difficult by requirements for open meetings, so it is harder to get agreement, restrictions on hiring, so it is more difficult to find the right people or to fire the wrong ones, and controls designed to make sure no wrongful act occurs by making it difficult to do anything at all.

Learning how to live amid opposing demands will not be easy. What, in the spirit of this volume, can students of public administration do by way of research that will help practitioner and theorist alike understand why life in public service is bound to be difficult and what, if anything, can be done about it?*

Know thine enemy. We will never understand the problems of public service, I am persuaded, so long as we suffer from a poverty of organizational forms. In addition to hierarchy cum bureaucracy, to which I shall return, we should study at least two other types—competitive individualism and egalitarian collectivism. Individualists wish to substitute self-regulation for authority, yet they are dependent on an external source of authority for sufficient stability to maintain market relationships and adjudicate differences. What has been the experience of political regimes that value self-organization over central authority? How do individualists behave within organizations? Will they stand for the accouterments of hierarchy—rules, forms, decorum, a belief in procedures as essential for orderly administration? Can accommodation be made with them?

Egalitarians reject authority as coercive and unfair. Group decisions, they believe, should be binding on members, but only if they participate fully and give

---

* An excellent beginning would be to read and ponder Herbert Kaufman (1981, 4). Especially relevant is his identification of bureaucrats from their point of view: "From where they [senior bureaucrats] stand, the proposition that they are becoming the dominant power in the political system seems not only incomprehensible but downright ludicrous. What impresses them is their own comparative weakness. In part, this may be attributed to what I call the Law of Perceptions of Power, which holds that the power an observer believes another person or a group wields is directly proportional to the square of the distance of the observer from the observed. Thus, the closer the observer comes to the observed, the more limited the power of the observed seems. And when the distance is zero—that is, when the situation is seen through the eyes of the holder of power—what stand out are the fragility and limits of power, not its greatness. That is why presidents and the people close to them tend to bewail their inability to get things done, while people far removed frequently talk of the presidency as the strongest office on earth. The law also applies to bureaucrats."

their consent freely. Each individual is her or his own (and only) authority. Yet egalitarians need organizational authority to redistribute resources. What has been the experience of egalitarian organizations? Do their members stay together without authority? If people are born good but corrupted by evil institutions, as egalitarians believe, how do they explain internal conflict? Beset by individualists and egalitarians, bureaucrats need to know what they are up against.

Know thyself. There are different types of hierarchies, and hence bureaucracies, that matter. Hierarchical collectivism (or hierarchy, for short), with its strong group boundaries and its numerous and detailed prescriptions binding on members, is a system that supports central leadership. Authority inheres in position. Where egalitarians blame misfortune (say, poverty) on the system, and individualists fault the unsuccessful, hierarchies blame the deviant for not following the rules. How hierarchies behave, however, depends on how they are structured, and on the context within which they operate. Inclusive hierarchies (my father's house has many mansions and there is room for all—rich and poor, gay and straight, black and white) differ from exclusive hierarchies (there is no room at the inn for anyone who does not conform). Hierarchies that compete with others differ from those that have a monopoly of power. Caste hierarchies that exert power by moving away from lesser people differ from class hierarchies that stand over them. *If there is a single research priority for public administration, it is to study the organizational forms on which bureaucracies are based.*

The question must be faced: *Can we denigrate hierarchy (from which bureaucracy derives) while still honoring public service?* Can there be an effective bureaucracy without respect for authority? Coming at the question the back way —is hierarchy the only or the best form of organization for most tasks?—while better than neglect, is ultimately an evasion. For if we give the self-evident answer ("No, it isn't"), we have still not asked whether hierarchy can and should be done away with. Yet much recent writing implies just that. Shall we say, then, that public officials are just folks, on an equal plane with others, who should count for just one person, one voice? If they are persuasive, so be it, but if not, that's just too bad. Or shall we say that the bureaucracy deserves the benefit of the doubt because it is so constituted as to be considered authoritative until proven otherwise?

Kicking around a strawman, or so I expect to be told, is easy work. No one, presumably, wants or proposes to abandon hierarchy cum bureaucracy, only to modify its more oppressive features. True, but false. No one quite says so, but many believe bureaucracy is an unadulterated bad. How else can we explain why there is virtually no defense of hierarchical principles? If defending hierarchy would be to belabor the obvious, students of public administration are working hard to avoid it.

If hierarchy is necessary, why won't we say so? If it is in part desirable, why don't we teach so? Why does one hear so little now about the virtues (as well as the vices) of hierarchy—stability, continuity, predictability—with enthusiasm and with pride? My guess is that validating hierarchy would mean approving of inequality, that is, saying that some people deserve more deference than others.

If all inequalities are bad, why should there be (and why should we support) bureaucracy? Of course, there is some support for individual bureaucrats. But that is not the same as supporting principles of hierarchy—specialization, division of labor, expertise, authority, the view that different people are fitted for different tasks—that alone make bureaucracy defensible.

The message society gives to public servants is ambivalent. On the one hand, public service is the highest aspiration a citizen can have; on the other hand, bureaucracy is the problem, not the solution. When society is basically agreed, that is, when disagreements are limited, then bureaucrats become public servants; they are honored as implementors of an agreed-upon creed. There is criticism, too, as is appropriate, but it largely concerns how well they perform the agreed-upon task, not that they are doing the wrong thing. When relative consensus is replaced by relative dissensus, however, public servants revert to being bureaucrats. They become the scapegoats for other people's quarrels. Anyone can do the possible. Public service is the highest service because it is the hardest service there is. Public service is also the most necessary service, for without respect for community, there can be none for individuals.

References

Ellis, Richard, and Aaron Wildavsky. 1989. *Dilemmas of Presidential Leadership: From Washington through Lincoln.* New Brunswick, N.J.: Transaction.

Kaufman, Herbert. 1981. "Fear of Bureaucracy: A Raging Pandemic." *Public Administration Review* 41(1):1–9.

PART ONE

Professional History and Theory

1

Root and Branch:
Public Administration's Travail
toward the Future

Nicholas L. Henry

"Root and branch" is defined by one particularly ponderous dictionary as "utterly, entirely." I have no ambitions in this chapter to describe the field of public administration utterly and entirely, but I do harbor thoughts about the field's lineage (its roots) and future (its branches).

I also prescribe. To quote a now deceased Soviet public administrator, "What must be done?" What must be done if public administration is to retain and institutionalize its still shaky identity as an independent field of study in the towers of those who teach, and as a viable profession in the domains of those who do? Before we can know what to do, however, it is helpful to know where we have been—to unearth our roots before we clamber our branches.

Roots: Assessing the Impact of Public Administration's Parentage

It is said that public administration is a field with two parents: political science and management. Perhaps a more accurate description is that public administration has had a parent and a foster parent. The mother discipline is political science; the field's foster parent is management. The kinds of adults that progeny become is a product of many forces, but the influence of parents and foster parents is not the least of them.

Political Science, Democracy, and the Distressing Dilemma of "Hands-On" Education

The relationship between political science and public administration, at least since the 1930s, has been one of tension. On occasion, this tension has been creative; more frequently, it has been destructive.

3

In the 1930s, public administration dominated the fields of both political science and management. Public administration scholars got the research grants; public administration faculty got the students; and public administration consultants got the contracts. But by the early 1950s, primarily because of new intellectual and political developments, public administration, both as a discipline and as a profession, was on the skids. Intellectually, the principles of administration— one of the field's two conceptual pillars—had been demolished by the writers of the late 1940s (Dahl 1947, 1–11; Simon 1946, 53–67; 1947a, 201–4; 1947b; Waldo 1948), and public administration as a scholarly enterprise began a long, downward spiral that lasted well into the 1960s. Politically, the advent of a Republican administration in the White House after two decades of uninterrupted Democratic rule abruptly called into serious question that other conceptual cornerstone of the field, "the politics/administration dichotomy," the notion that politics and public administration were separate beasts kept in separate cages in the nation's social zoo. The transition in 1952 to a new political philosophy in the Presidency brought with it new public administrators who shared that philosophy; no longer could the myth be maintained that the nation's bureaucrats were value neutral (Gaus 1950, 168; Long 1954, 23; Marx 1946; Schick 1975, 152).

Even before the change in administrations in 1952, practitioners of public administration were beginning to wonder about the validity of the politics/administration dichotomy. Several of them expressed their concerns in Fritz Morstein Marx's book of readings (1946). And by 1950, a distinguished scholar could note that the dichotomy between politics and administration was sufficiently unclear that "a theory of public administration means in our time of theory of politics also" (Gaus 1950, 168). But the real (and ultimately unresolved) debate over the proper relations between policy makers and implementors appeared in 1955 in the form of a massive federal report titled *Personnel and Civil Service* (Commission on Organization 1955). Although the commission found it useful to maintain the illusion of a politics/administration dichotomy in its report (on its first page, the report states, "One requirement ... is that the officials responsible for establishing ... government policies ... should be selected by the successful party. ... The other requirement is that there must be numerous, trained, skilled and nonpartisan employees in the Federal service to provide continuity in the administration of the Government's activities"), the academics had dropped the notion with a resounding thud. As Norton E. Long wrote in 1954, "However attractive an administration receiving its values from political policy makers may be, it has one fatal flaw. It does not accord with the facts of administrative life" (p. 23). Oddly, the field of public administration (or any other field) has never resolved the problem of the relations between politics and administration, and the old, abandoned dichotomy currently seems to be enjoying an intellectual resurrection, or at least a partial resurrection (see, for example, Schick 1975, 152).

Writers in the field of public administration have since decried the eagerness with which many political scientists used these developments to reassert the continued "dominion of political science over public administration" (Martin 1952, 665) and to keep public administration in a position of "second-class citizenship" (Waldo 1968, 8). But two, perhaps more lasting developments in public administration emanating from its experience with political science seem worthy of attention here: the inculcation of democratic values among public administration scholars and practitioners that was likely facilitated by political science, and the problematic role of public policy research in both fields.

Political Science and the Inculcation of Democratic Values. Political science, the parent of public administration, clearly has had more profound affects on the field than has management, its foster parent. Public administration was born in the house of political science, and its early rearing occurred in its backyard. The fundamental precepts of American political science—the self-evident worth of democracy, a pluralistic polity, political participation, equality under law, and due process —continue to hold sway among even the most independently minded of the public administrationists. While it can be convincingly argued that the American civic culture inculcates these values among all its intellectuals and that American public administrationists would cherish democratic values regardless of their experiences in political science, it nonetheless seems valid that the environment of political science sharpened and deepened the commitment of public administrationists to the country's core constitutional concepts. If public administration had been born and bred in the nation's business schools, would we have the same kind of academic field that we have today? Perhaps not. In any event, one can argue that political science was a salutary former of the field in laying its philosophic and normative foundations.

Political Science, Public Administration, and the Persistent Problem of Public Policy. But if public administrationists could hop on the bandwagon of democracy with enthusiasm, there was less gusto in their ranks about boarding the battered bus of public policy. The subfield of public policy, or policy studies, began to form during the same period when public administration was reasserting its identity as a field. Public administration has defined its identity as something apart and distinct from both political science and management. Not so, however, in the case of public policy, which claims adherents from both political science and public administration.

Public policy as a subfield emerged for many of the same reasons that motivated public administration to secede from political science, particularly the concern shared by some political scientists that their field was far more concerned with science than politics. One of the early contributors to the public policy subfield, Austin Ranney (1986b) said it well: "At least since 1945 most American political scientists have focused their professional attention mainly on the processes by which public policies are made and have shown relatively little concern with their contents" (p. 3). Ranney and his colleagues took issue with this emphasis and believed that a more substantive approach was needed. From its beginnings, public policy has been an effort to apply political science to public affairs; its inherent sympathies with the practical field of public administration are real, and many scholars who identify with the public policy subfield find themselves in a twilight zone between political science and public administration, pirouetting in the shadows of both disciplines.

Perhaps the first formal recognition by political scientists of the importance of public policy was a small meeting held in 1965 under the auspices of the Committee on Governmental and Legal Processes of the Social Science Research Council. Out of this meeting emerged "a consensus that the most timely and urgent question . . . is: What professional expertise and obligations, if any, have political scientists to study, evaluate, and make recommendations about the contents of public policy?" (Ranney, 1968a, vii). Two committee-sponsored conferences on the question followed in 1966 and 1967, and the papers presented at them were published the following year (Ranney 1968a, vii).

Also in 1967, the American Political Science Association's annual conference featured a panel on public policy under its American Politics section, and four papers on public policy were presented at the meeting. In 1970, the association granted public policy its first section at its annual conference; by now the number of papers on the topic exceeded 30. By 1982, 140 papers on public policy analysis were presented at the annual meeting, involving thirty-six panels (Hansen 1983, 217–45).

Public policy was even more popular among political scientists than the proliferating presentations of papers on the topic indicate. During this period, the Policy Studies Organization was founded (in 1972), and it provided additional outlets for political scientists interested in public policy—within a decade of its creation, the organization had more than 2000 members. The Policy Studies Organization publishes *Policy Studies Review,* which reflects a more public administration hue, and *Policy Studies Journal,* which casts a longer shadow in political science. But the organization's membership appears to be dominated by political scientists—more than two-thirds are political scientists (Hansen 1983, 239). In 1979, 68 percent of the members of the Policy Studies Organization were political scientists, although this figure may include academics who identify with public administration as well.

The Policy Studies Organization, of course, is not the only association of scholars with an interest in public policy. The Association for Public Policy Analysis and Management, the American Institute for Decision Sciences, and the Public Choice Society are examples of others, and there are more. But most of these groups have an intellectual cast that is distinctly economic or operations research in nature. Political scientists who belong to such associations seem to be repentant about their original choice of a field and often are found delivering papers at professional conferences on the subject of how they really wanted to be economists.

An important component of the public policy subfield is comparative, or cross-national, public policy. The specialization began to emerge in the early 1970s, and in 1975 a book on the topic received the Gladys M. Kammerer Award from the American Political Science Association (Heidenheimer, Heclo, and Adams 1975). More than a quarter of the public policy papers presented at the annual conferences of the American Political Science Association are in the comparative area (Hansen 1983, 219). In 1982, 27 percent of the public policy papers took a comparative approach.

Public policy as a subfield can be viewed as bisecting along two, increasingly distinct, intellectual branches. One is the substantive branch. The dominant mode of public policy as a subfield of political science has always been and continues to be substantive issues—what Ranney called "contents," and what Herbert Simon, years earlier, called "prescribing for public policy" (Simon 1947a, 202). Roughly half the papers presented at the American Political Science Association's annual conferences in any given year deal with substance, such as the environment, welfare, education, or energy. The journals and papers published by the Policy Studies Organization also reflect this substantive bias. Paramountly, the substantive branch of public policy means a paper, article, book, or course on "The Politics of" some current issue.

The other, less leafy but nonetheless supple branch of public policy is the theoretical branch. Susan B. Hansen (1983) has usefully categorized the literature comprising this branch (which she calls "three promising theoretical trends") in terms of political economy, organization theory, and program evaluation and implementation (pp. 220–29).* There are, of course, other ways in which this literature may be categorized. The problem of public policy as a subfield is what it symbolizes for both political science and public administration.

First, political scientists and public administrationists seem to have different definitions of what they are doing in the subfield and why. Public policy researchers who identify primarily with political science seem to be those who, by and large, work on the subfield's substantive branch ("The Politics of" something), while those who identify with public administration seem to be found more frequently on its theoretical branch and are more concerned with problems of research design, public choice, strategic planning, implementation, organization, program evaluation, efficiency, effectiveness, productivity, and public policy questions that are only incidentally related to matters of substance and content. The differences in these two

---

* Some license has been taken with Hansen's categories. Hansen calls the literature of program evaluation and its attendant case studies "changing conceptions of policy failure," which strikes me as a somewhat idiosyncratic description.

approaches parallel the differences that the field of public administration has with political science: Public administrationists have always preferred studying questions of public policy that relate to "knowledgeable action" as opposed to an "intellectualized understanding" of public issues (Caldwell 1965, 57).

Of these two approaches to the study of public policy, the future seems fairer for that preferred by public administrationists. While there will always be both room and need for each tack, the substantive one has a deadly deficiency in the longer haul: It is, by dint of its structure, essentially atheoretical. One cannot build theory on the basis of ultimately transitory public events. True, there will always be public policies for health, energy, environment, welfare, or whatever, but how does understanding these issues as discrete phenomena get us very far in understanding the process of public policy—its formulation, execution, and ongoing revision—so that we can develop ideas that enable us to make more responsive policies in all areas and deliver them more effectively? Individual studies of individual public issues often yield us an appreciation of the issues involved, and this is important and useful; but aside from their utility as case histories, these studies cannot really address the larger theoretical questions, the answers to which can, one hopes, be of use to public decision makers regardless of the policy arena in which they find themselves.

A more worrisome aspect of political science's preference for the substantive approach to policy studies is that its intellectual evolution will parallel the experience of comparative public administration, in that it will try to do too much, and end up, to quote Robert T. Golembiewski on the dilemma of comparative public administration, creating a "self-imposed failure experience . . . an unattainable goal" (Golembiewski 1977, 147). Certainly this dreary prospect at least seems possible when we appreciate the number of public policies extant, all of them fairly panting to be analyzed, and the problem is especially evident in the area of comparative public policy. The literature of comparative public policy is heavily substantive (Ashford, Katzenstein, and Pempel 1978; Peters 1981), but as Elliot J. Feldman (1978, 287–305) points out, the specialty has yet to develop a "guiding" theory of its own to focus research.

A second problem of public policy analysis in its political science mode is that it smacks of an effort by political scientists to fill the vacuum created by the departure of public administration—a last gasp, croaked in the general direction of hands-on political science and, of course, relevance. In this fashion, political science, symbolically at least, retains public administration without admitting it. The fact that the explosive growth of the public policy subfield correlates remarkably in time (i.e., the 1970s) with the secession of public administration, lends some credence to this notion. Figure 1.1 illustrates some rough measures of this relationship.

There is nothing sinister in this effort to reestablish within political science a concern with what is applied and relevant under a new guise called public policy, but if this is the motivation, then it seems unlikely to succeed. Public policy in its sub-

Number

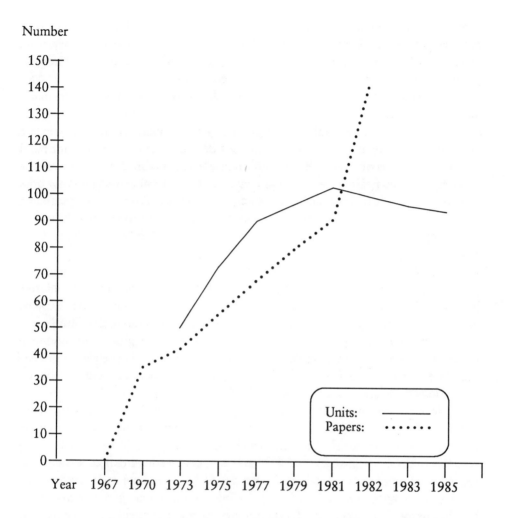

FIGURE 1.1
Growth in Numbers of Autonomous Public Affairs/Public Administration
Academic Units,[a] 1973–85, and of Public Policy
Papers Presented at ASPA Conferences, 1967–82

SOURCES: National Association of Schools of Public Affairs and Administration (1973, 1975, 1977, 1979, 1981, 1983) and Hansen (1983).

a. Departments and schools of public affairs or public administration that report to a dean or vice president in a university.

stantive mode may not be, as I have noted, a vehicle ready for long journeys. It is no replacement for public administration. An understanding of education policy, for example, is no substitute for an understanding of human resource administration, public budgeting and finance, organization theory, intergovernmental management, program evaluation and the several other interrelated areas that constitute the public administration field.

One of the more notable achievements of public administration in its new, "self-aware" paradigm (to borrow Dwight Waldo's 1979 expressive description) is that it has motivated many of its younger academics to build workable, usable theories of public policy—theories that could be helpful to practitioners in all fields of public policy. It is this branch of public policy that the profession of public administration should encourage with particular care, for it is the theoretical branch of the subfield that likely will contribute the most to the larger field of public administration.

Destroying Domesticus? The subfield of public policy highlights the ambivalence of attitudes that many political scientists hold about addressing problems of action, practice, and the grass roots. But the opinions held among political scientists about these values—which can be encapsulated in the phrase *education for knowledgeable action*—may actually be stronger than mere ambivalence. Although I can state this only with considerable tentativeness, at root the field of political science may be hostile to such concerns.

It is noteworthy in this respect that political science has accepted the secession of public administration with remarkably good grace. A review of the discipline published by the American Political Science Association in 1983 contained no discussion of public administration as a subfield in a compendium that covers nineteen chapters and more than 600 pages (Finifter 1983).* The volume itself stands as testimony not only to the reality of public administration's emergence as a separate field but to the quiet acceptance (perhaps relief) by political scientists over its departure.

Despite the equanimity of political scientists, the effects of public administration and its subsequent secession from political science are both profound and disquieting. A recent assessment of the state of the discipline conducted by political scientists made the following points: "The growth of Masters in Public Administration programs also drained off some of the bright career oriented students. About a third

---

* One could contend, and some will, that I am overstating the case, and some may cite as evidence the emergence of a strong and viable section devoted to public administration in the American Political Science Association. But I would suggest that the recent formation of this group is due considerably more to the initiative of public administrationists than of political scientists.

of political science departments had reported a decline in the quality of new Ph.D.s ... " (Lynn 1983, 102). The assessment further concluded that public administration was one of only two "pockets of optimism" among political science faculty. Most political scientists had experienced a "statistically significant deterioration in career satisfaction from 1963 to 1976" (Roettger 1977, 33).

I do not necessarily ascribe to the assertion that the departure of public administration from political science has resulted in a lower quality of graduate students and an emotionally depressed faculty in political science departments, but the existence of such a possibility may not stretch the bounds of reason. What may stretch the bounds of reason is the apparent determination of political scientists to disassociate themselves from programs that have long been central in subsidizing political science departments through high enrollments and that increasingly are evidencing renewed intellectual vitality and a sense of academic purpose. Public administrationists should not forget that they were not, and often are not, the only ones who want them to get out of political science departments; typically, political scientists also want public administrationists to get out of political science departments. In fact, in many instances, particularly in the 1970s, public administrationists and political scientists mutually decided that separation was in the best interest of both fields.

If public administrationists thought it was in their best interest to disassociate themselves from political scientists, then a remaining question is why political scientists also agreed—often readily. I do not know the answer, but there seems to be more to the eagerness among political scientists to divest themselves of public administration than merely their desire to distance themselves from a field that has always taken pride in having a practical turn of mind. This eagerness seems to stem also from an inclination among political scientists to put daylight between themselves and any kind of academic enterprise that deals with domestic concerns. After all, not only has public administration been bid a fond adieu by political scientists, but so have related fields that have a distinctly American cast, such as urban politics and criminal justice.

Now we are beginning to hear reports that such baseline courses (certainly insofar as student enrollments are concerned) as American government and state and local politics are being given increasingly short shrift within the nation's major political science departments. If these reports are at all accurate, then they constitute impressive evidence indeed to the capacities for self-destruction among America's political scientists.

Management and the Clarification of Issues

Leaving aside its ambivalent experience with public policy and hands-on education in general, political science nonetheless was profoundly influential on the evolution of public administration. Management was less so. But, in many ways, the impact of management on public administration was more positive. In part, this was because management entered into the upbringing of public administration when the field was beginning its adolescence, and, unlike political science, it was not a blood relative; consequently, public administration was granted more independence and breathing room to grow and develop on its own. This is not to say that the household environment created by the field of management for public administration was one of warmth and succor. It was not. But instead of treating public administration like an abusive parent, as political science occasionally did, management let public administration stay in its house like an absent-minded aunt who was never quite sure who was living in which room, and who often forgot to serve meals.

Management had at least three distinct influences on public administration: It forced public administration to examine more closely what the public in public administration meant; it convinced many public administrationists that a whole new set of methodologies was needed; and it provided public administration with a model of how to assess what, as a field, it was teaching and why.

Understanding the Public in Public Administration. One of the principal effects of the management field on public administration concerned the distinction between public and private administration. When public administrationists had thought about this distinction at all, public administration was defined largely in institutional terms—that is, the government bureaucracy. But the experience of public administrationists who were situated in schools of business, particularly in the 1960s and 1970s, forced them to reconsider what the public in public administration really meant.

These public administrationists saw, perhaps more clearly than did others whose experiences related more to political science, that the field had to be defined in something other than institutional terms. Real-world phenomena were and are making the public/private distinction an increasingly difficult one to define empirically. The research and development contract; the military-industrial complex; the roles of regulatory agencies and their relations with industry; the emergence of third-sector organizations; and the developing awareness of what one author has called "the margins of the state" (Sharkansky 1979, 11) in reference to such phenomena as the expansive growth of government corporations and the privatization of public policy, all have conspired to make public administration an elusive entity.

To deal with these problems, public administrationists began in the 1960s to desert the traditional paradigms that defined public administration in terms of institutional locus and to cast the field into terms of philosophic, normative, and ethical concepts. In this new, more dynamic approach, the public in public administration became those phenomena that affected the public interest. Thus, rather than concentrate on the Department of Defense, for example, as its proper public locus, and leave, say, Lockheed Corporation to students of business management, public administrationists began to understand that the department's contractual and political relationships with Lockheed should now be their central object of study, since these relationships clearly involved the public interest. This new, noninstitutional, and normative definition of the public in public administration was brought about in large part by the difficulties encountered by public administrationists who were working within the confines of generic schools of management in explaining their field to their academic colleagues—who, on occasion, were somewhat less than sympathetic to the role of government in society and even to the notion of the public interest.

An admittedly unfair (and possibly fictitious) example of this problem is provided by my former university, which, it is alleged, houses the largest business school in the free world. (It has some 12,000 students.) The story goes that a lone student stood up in the back of a lecture hall containing several hundred business administration students and asked the instructor, "Sir, what is the social responsibility of business?" The professor replied unhesitatingly, "Son, business has no social responsibility." On hearing the answer, the class burst into applause.

The New Methodologies. A second impact that management had on public administration was methodological. Public administrationists associated with political science departments had long known (or at least it was dawning on them with accelerating speed) that the methodologies of political science were inappropriate to the concerns of public administration. Often these scholars looked to management schools for illumination and guidance. In many cases, because public administrationists (usually those who were associated with departments of political science) did not fully understand the methodologies employed by management scientists, they put great (and frequently inappropriate) stock in their potential utility. In other instances, public administrationists rejected the methodologies of management out of hand because they found them threatening or were ignorant of them.

The combined consequence of these reactions to the management methodologies was the ultimate recognition by the more committed public administrationists (whether they were found in political science departments or in management schools) that wholly new methodologies were needed for the field. Indeed, the development of these methodologies was central to the emergence of self-aware public administration.

In some instances, adapting on a selective basis existing methodologies of both political science and management was appropriate, such as survey research (from political science) and operations research (from management). But, by and large, new methods were needed, and evaluation research or program evaluation has become the term we currently associate with many of the developing bundles of methodologies that public administration calls its own (Weiss 1972). The emphasis

13

on these methodologies is on whether public programs are effective, efficient, and, increasingly, whether they are needed. They borrow techniques from a variety of disciplines and have a clearly applied research cast. Closely related to evaluation research are the continually evolving methods of budgeting, ranging from line item to zero base. Increasingly, these budgetary concepts are becoming management-control strategies that use the methodologies of program evaluation in determining budget allocations (Heclo 1983; White 1985, 623–30).

Finally, a plethora of existing quantitative techniques fall under the general (and unsatisfactory) rubric of public decision making or public management and are being increasingly transformed and adapted to a governmental context. These include probability theory, statistical comparisons, linear correlations and linear programming (particularly sensitivity analysis and the simplex method), critical path method, benefit-cost analysis, decision trees, queuing theory, public-choice theory, simulations, and management information systems, among others. A number of recent works have done a fine job in applying these and other methods to problems of the public sector (Bingham and Etheridge 1982; Gohagan 1980; Henry 1982; McKenna 1980; Quade 1982; Welch and Comer 1983).

Learning How to Take Oneself Seriously. A final area in which the field of management influenced the evolution of public administration as a field of study was the relatively serious way in which business schools took their enterprise. Compared to political science departments, at least, the process of educating students in generic schools of management and in business schools was and is far more focused, self-analytical, systematic, and serious. This is not to say that individual political scientists or public administrationists take their classroom responsibilities lightly; by and large, they do not. But as a field, political science has never put itself through the long-term self-examination and critical assessment that business education has.

During the 1950s, business educators inflicted on themselves a well-financed and searching examination of their curricula and instructional programs. The resulting reports—two thick volumes often containing sharp criticism of current practices—had profound effects on business education (Gordon and Howell 1959; Pierson 1959). By contrast, the only comparable effort conducted by political science during this period resulted in a book (Committee for the Advancement of Teaching 1951) that has been dismissed by political scientists themselves as one whose "very triteness and superficiality ... made it important" (Somit and Tanenhaus 1967, 188). A later attempt to redress this problem focused more specifically on public administration education, but still as it was conducted within the environment of political science. The results were much the same (Honey 1967, 301–19). Public administrationists criticized the report as dealing with "venerable and eminently fatiguing issues" (Savage 1968, 391; see also Bowman and Plant 1982, 40).

These reports on education for the public service appeared in 1951 and 1967, when public administration was dominated by political science. Their superficiality in dealing with the problems they sought to address was rendered all the more stark when compared to the reports of 1959 that had been prepared by business educators. This lesson has not been lost on public administrationists of the 1980s. A proliferating number of analyses of all aspects of public administration education by individual scholars has appeared since the mid-1970s (Adams 1983, 443–46; Daniels, Darcy, and Swain 1982, 55–65; Downs et al. 1982; Morgan et al. 1981, 666–73; Morgan and Meier 1982, 171–73; Sorg and Laverty 1981; Thai 1981b; Turnbull, Zuck, Fry, and Weinback, 1985), indicating a renewed concern with the problem. More significantly, the National Association of Schools of Public Affairs and Administration (NASPAA) has grown since its founding in 1970 into a body of more than 220 member institutions: it is well-funded and is maturing into an organization that has the greatest likelihood of producing a self-evaluation of public administration education that parallels in scope and quality the analyses of business education conducted in the 1950s. Perhaps the model of a searching and systematic self-assessment that has been provided by the business education community may become the single most constructive effect that management ultimately has on the field of public administration.

As I noted at the beginning of this chapter, to know where we are, we sometimes must know where we have been. Most public administration faculty know only too well and too ruefully where the field has been, for growing up in the backyard of political science and in the garret of management was not easy (Henry 1986, 19–47). But both political science and management added important and integral components of what we now know as the field of public administration. To recognize those components is to capitalize on them.

Out of the Swamp: The Blossoming of Public Administration

The formation of NASPAA in 1970 represented not only an act of secession by public administrationists but a rise of self-confidence as well. NASPAA's origins lay in the Council on Graduate Education for Public Administration, which had been founded in the 1950s by a small number of graduate programs in the field. The decision in 1970 dramatically to expand the scope of this unusually cozy group and the decision in 1983 to become a formal professional accrediting agency for public administration programs indicated a determination by public administration educators to take public responsibility for upgrading the educational backgrounds and technical competence of the nation's government managers. By 1970, as represented by the founding of NASPAA, public administration could properly call itself, and increasingly be recognized as, a separate, self-aware field of study.

The profile of public administration as a self-aware field shows that considerable progress has been made in refining the applied techniques and methodologies of public administration, particularly in the area of information science, and a renewed interest is evident about public organization theory. Public administration appears to be emphasizing such areas as state and local government, executive management, administrative law, and all those questions that seek to explain what the public interest is in a technobureaucratic "Big Democracy."

The emerging curriculum of graduate public administration education reflects these emphases. A more or less agreed-upon core curriculum seems to have developed for public administration education at the graduate level, and it centers on the environment of public administration (i.e., general introductory courses that focus on the role of the bureaucracy in a democracy), quantitative methods, public budgeting and financial management, organization theory, and personnel administration. The average number of required hours in these core areas grew from fewer than thirty-nine in 1974–75 to more than forty-one in 1980–81, with the primary expansion being quantitative methods and public budgeting and financial management. It appears that this increase in the required number of hours taken in the core curriculum occurred at the cost of electives that students might otherwise take (Thai 1981a, 7, 11).

The increases in certain required courses in the M.P.A. degree curriculum reflects to some degree the growing clout of NASPAA, which has worked toward the establishment of a common core curriculum in M.P.A. programs. But there was more to the rising influence of NASPAA than alterations in the M.P.A. curriculum. A national survey of public administration program directors found that M.P.A. programs that had been granted the functional equivalent of accreditation by NASPAA (a practice, initiated in 1978, that has approved more than eighty programs as in compliance with its standards) were thought to be more prestigious programs by about two-thirds of these educators, and a plurality of the respondents believed that NASPAA-approved programs were in a better position to recruit higher-quality faculty and higher-quality students, and to offer a higher-quality curriculum (Daniels 1983). Another survey of this same population found that NASPAA's influence had altered not only the curricula of M.P.A. degrees across the country (at least in the views of most of the public administration educators who responded) but had exercised a favorable impact on problems of programmatic jurisdiction, independence, and authority that confronted M.P.A. directors as well (Uveges 1985, 18–23). That is, NASPAA and its M.P.A. standards were seen as a somewhat effective instrument for enhancing the administrative and intellectual autonomy of public administration programs within universities: "A relationship may be suggested [by the data obtained in this survey] between perceived impact [of

TABLE 1.1
Organizational Patterns of Public Administration Programs, 1973–85

Organizational pattern	1973 N	1973 %	1975 N	1975 %	1977 N	1977 %	1979 N	1979 %	1981 N	1981 %	1983 N	1983 %	1985 N	1985 %
Separate professional schools	25	25	29	21	32	21	29	16	32	17	26	14	27	14
Separate departments in large units	23	23	35	25	49	31	64	34	63	33	64	34	65	34
P.A. programs combined with another professional school or department (e.g., business administration)	17	17	23	16	13	8	14	8	20	10	26	14	29	15
P.A. programs within political science	36	36	53	38	62	40	70	38	74	39	70	38	60	31
Unclassified organization[a]	0	0	0	0	0	0	8	4	3	1	0	0	12	6
Total	101	100	140	100	156	100	185	100	192	100	186	100	193	100

SOURCE: NASPAA 1986, xix. Percentages have been rounded.

a. Includes interdisciplinary programs and institutes reporting to the central university administration and other organizational structures.

NASPAA's standards] and the degree to which the [public administration] program ... was in a position to effectively initiate and carry out [its agenda] ... with limited interference ... by others" (Uveges 1985, 23).

Trends within the nation's universities lend credence to this finding. Table 1.1 details the organizational pattern of (mostly graduate) public administration programs from 1973 through 1985, as determined by surveys conducted of institutional members of NASPAA. The number of public administration programs that were members of NASPAA nearly doubled during those twelve years; programs organized as separate professional schools or separate departments also nearly doubled.

The year 1985 was the first in which national surveys were conducted in which public administration programs within political science departments did not constitute a plurality among the possible organizational patterns available for public administration programs in universities. For the first time, separate departments of public administration constituted a plurality (one-third of all member programs of NASPAA are separate departments), and their number had nearly tripled since 1973. Between them, separate schools and departments of public administration amount to nearly half of all university public administration programs that are members of NASPAA. The secession, in short, is real.

There are nearly 23,000 students enrolled in master's degree programs in public administration across the country, up from fewer than 11,000 a dozen years earlier. Forty-three percent are women, 13 percent are black, and 4 percent are of Hispanic origin (National Association 1986, xix–xx).

Students in M.P.A. programs are an unusual group. Seventy percent have jobs, 20 percent are taking courses at off-campus sites, 63 percent are part-time students (National Association 1986, xx), and more than half the students are twenty-five years of age or older (Young and Eddy 1982, 59–61). There are also approximately 8000 undergraduates registered as public administration majors, of whom 24 percent are part-time students (National Association 1982, iv), in contrast to the nearly two-thirds of graduate students who attend M.P.A. programs on a part-time basis.

Meeting the educational needs of these students and, in the process, supplying the public with capable managers of its business is no easy task. As the president of Harvard University, which houses the John F. Kennedy School of Government, put it:

> The universities have a major opportunity and responsibility to set about the task of training a corps of able people to occupy influential positions in public life. What is needed is nothing less than the education of a new profession. . . . I can scarcely overemphasize the importance of this effort. . . . Since universities are primarily responsible for advanced training in our society, they share

a unique opportunity and obligation to prepare a profession of public servants equipped to discharge these heavy responsibilities to the nation. (Bok 1975, 4–5, 10)

Branches: Forecasting the Future
of Public Administration

Harvard president Derek Bok phrases the challenge well. But a vitally important question remains unanswered: Who will train Bok's "corps of able people to occupy influential positions in public life?" (1975, 4). Who will teach the classes? Professors of public administration, naturally, is the forthcoming answer. Herein lies our dilemma.

As shown in table 1.2, political scientists with Ph.D.s increased by 500 in 1982, while the field of business and management churned out more than 850 new doctorates, more than half (485, or 57 percent) of them in subfields that have a

TABLE 1.2
Earned Doctorates Conferred in Political Science, Business and
Management, and Public Affairs, 1971, 1977, and 1982,
and Selected Subfields, 1982

Field	1971	1977	1982
Political science and government	700	641	513
Business and management	807	863	857
Business management and administration	—	—	424
Operations research	—	—	40
Personnel management	—	—	4
Labor and industrial relations	—	—	17
Other[a]	—	—	372
Public affairs and services	185	316	429
Public administration	—	—	134
Other[b]	—	—	295

SOURCES: Grant and Snyder 1986, table 112; and U.S. Bureau of the Census 1985, table 273.

a. Includes business and commerce, general (155 doctorates granted in 1982); accounting (61); business statistics (11); banking and finance (35); investments and securities (0); hotel and restaurant management (2); marketing and purchasing (24); transportation and public utilities (2); real estate (2); insurance (4); international business (5); secretarial studies (0); business economics (55); and "other" (18).

b. Includes community services, general (36 doctorates granted in 1982); parks and recreation management (33); social work (198); law enforcement and corrections (24); international public service (0); and "other" (4).

reasonably direct bearing on public administration, namely, business management and administration (which accounted for more than 49 percent of the larger category), operations research, personnel management, and labor and industrial relations. A total of 134, or 7 percent of the doctorates awarded in 1982 in political science, business and management, and public affairs combined, were D.P.A.s and Ph.D.s in public administration.

The numbers of doctorates awarded in public administration are fractional compared to the doctoral productivity of fields that have in the past claimed (and occasionally still claim) public administration as one of their subfields. This low production of doctorates in public administration is dangerous to the field's continued identification as a self-aware, separate academic and professional enterprise, and this danger intensifies when we combine it with a few other facts.

First, a disproportionately high number of newly minted doctorates in public administration will likely enter (or already are in) professions other than higher education. Although we cannot pinpoint this ratio, recall that 70 percent of all graduate students (master's and doctoral students combined) in the field are inservice, 63 percent are part-time students, and a fifth are students taking courses at sites other than the campus (National Association 1986, xx). These figures highlight a pool of doctoral graduates that has little interest in pursuing an academic career.

Second, many of the new doctorates in public administration may be of questionable academic quality. Although we have no hard data on this, the high levels of part-time, off-campus students nonetheless imply that doctoral programs in the field may not be providing the intense, intimate, scholarly experience that is the hallmark of graduate education for students wishing to become professors. Moreover, at least in the recent past, about 30 percent of all the new D.P.A.s and Ph.D.s in public administration were awarded by a single institution, Nova University, and although Nova's impressive productivity in this sphere has since slipped, it nonetheless remains the single largest producer of public administration doctorates in the nation (Klay 1982, 2–3; Universities Award 1986, 11, 21, 23).* Since 1973, Nova University has conducted D.P.A. classes at fifteen sites across the country, relying on nine full-time faculty, a host of adjunct faculty, and intensive course formats to do so (Wolf 1982, 118, 120). Few, if any, of Nova's graduates enter an academic career, but its rank as number one (at least quantitatively) among the nation's doctoral programs is at best disquieting to those of us who view as essential the education of new faculty in public administration.

---

* In 1986, Nova University awarded 16 D.P.A. degrees (it does not offer the Ph.D.), or 13 percent of all the D.P.A.s and Ph.D.s in public administration awarded that year. It was followed by the University of Pittsburgh (14 Ph.D.s) and the University of Southern California (11 D.P.A.s and Ph.D.s). The average number of public administration doctorates granted per institution in 1986 was about 4.

Third, of the estimated 5000 faculty members teaching in public administration programs, fewer than a fifth teach public administration courses on a full-time basis (Wolf 1982, 119), and about three-fourths have terminal degrees in fields other than public administration (National Association 1986, xx). There are nearly as many political scientists teaching courses in public administration (20 percent of the total) as there are faculty who are public administrationists (26 percent) (National Association 1986, xx).

What do these data amount to? A great deal, if one believes (as do I) that public administration ultimately will fail as a professional field unless it succeeds as an academic one. And it will not succeed as an academic field unless it can assure itself of an ongoing transfusion of new intellectual blood. Currently, new blood is not being infused at the levels needed.

Nor will public administration succeed as a field if it continues to cling, as most public administration programs still do, to its interdisciplinary model. Sad as it may seem, interdisciplinary programs in universities are at best transitional periods marking a field's evolution from its status as a subfield of another discipline into a field of scholarly rigor, intellectual independence, administrative autonomy, and entrenched professionalism; at worst, interdisciplinary programs are token efforts by university administrators to look relevant, to be problem solving, to position their institutions more favorably temporarily as a prospective recipient of more students, grants, or endowments, or to isolate troublesome and sometimes mediocre faculty.

Public administration cannot afford to remain interdisciplinary much longer. As the founding director of an interdisciplinary School of Public Affairs and as the founding dean of an interdisciplinary College of Public Programs, my commitment to the value of interdisciplinary learning is clear. The point I am advocating is that it is past time for public administration as a field to stop borrowing faculty from other disciplines. Public administration must begin to develop itself as a discipline; doing this requires that public administrationists grow their own faculty, not pluck them from other fields. This maturation in no way should inhibit public administration as an interdisciplinary enterprise in an intellectual sense (indeed, it should strengthen it); it will, however, be essential in assuring public administration's survival in universities. The academic landscape is littered with the corpses (or stalked by the walking dead) of interdisciplinary programs that ultimately transitioned nowhere. Some of these programs are close to home and have had a heavy influence on the development of public administration itself; urban affairs, science and public policy, environmental studies, and business and society are examples. But where are these and other interdisciplinary programs now? In most of the universities that initiated them, they are gone or are going fast.

This fate still lurks in the shadows of academe's groves, and could be waiting to consume public administration, particularly public administration units that use in their titles such words as center, institute, division, or program (in contrast to department, school, or college), or, in all too many instances, have no title at all. How do we avoid this end? Three mutually reinforcing possibilities present themselves.

What Must Be Done?

The first concern is organizational. If public administration is to survive in universities, it must gain control over the careers of its own faculties. Split appointments (in which a professor answers to the heads of two academic units), special public service responsibilities for public administration faculty with no diminution of research and teaching expectations, and the farming out of the public administration curriculum to sundry relevant departments should be actively resisted. Promotion, tenure, teaching load, and merit pay for professors of public administration should lodge primarily in the hands of other professors of public administration. Much progress has been made over the past fifteen years in achieving these goals, but in more than half of the nation's major public administration programs some or all of these objectives have yet to be attained. Only when the careers of public administration faculties are rationally secured can the curricula and research agenda of public administration education be rationally developed.

Second, the improvement and expansion of doctoral education in public administration are necessities. How can a professor of public administration claim that he or she even has a field when only a quarter of his or her colleagues, on the average, identify their academic field as public administration?

Finally, more of those few doctoral students in public administration should be channeled into academic careers. Although we do not have information on the number of part-time doctoral students in public administration, as a proportion of the total the number is doubtlessly many times higher than the rates found in political science and management. This means that public administration faculties must devote more of their energies to finding normal graduate students (i.e., talented undergraduates in their early twenties who are interested in pursuing an academic career full-time) and the means of supporting their advanced educations.

References

Adams, William C. 1983. "Reputation, Size, and Student Success in Public Administration/Affairs Programs." *Public Administration Review* 43:443–46.

Ashford, Douglas E., Peter J. Katzenstein, and T.J. Pempel, eds. 1978. *Comparative Public Policy: A Cross-National Bibliography*. Beverly Hills: Sage.

Bingham, Richard D., and Marcus E. Ethridge, eds. 1982. *Reaching Decisions in Public Policy and Administration: Methods and Applications*. New York: Longman.

Bok, Derek. 1975. "The President's Report, 1973–74." *Harvard Today* 18:4–5, 10.

Bowman, James S., and Jeremy F. Plant. 1982. "Institutional Problems of Public Administration Programs: A House without a Home." In *Public Administration Education in Transition,* edited by Thomas Vocino and Richard Heimovics. New York: Marcel Dekker.

Caldwell, Lynton K. 1965. "Public Administration and the Universities: A Half-Century of Development." *Public Administration Review* 25:57.

Commission on Organization of the Executive Branch of the Government. 1955. Personnel and Civil Service. Washington, D.C.: Government Printing Office.

Committee for the Advancement of Teaching. American Political Science Association. 1951. *Goals for Political Science.* New York: Sloane.

Dahl, Robert A. 1947. "The Science of Public Administration: Three Problems." *Public Administration Review* 7:1–11.

Daniels, Mark R. 1983. "Public Administration as an Emergent Profession: A Survey of Attitudes About the Review and Accreditation Programs." Presented at the National Conference of the American Society for Public Administration, New York.

Daniels, Mark R., Robert Emmet Darcy, and John W. Swain. 1982. "Public Administration Extension Activities by American Colleges and Universities." *Public Administration Review* 42:55–65.

Downs, Bryan. 1982. *Undergraduate Public Administration Education: An Empirical Analysis with Options for Program Review by the Undergraduate Section of the National Association of Schools of Public Affairs and Administration.* Washington, D.C.: National Association of Schools of Public Affairs and Administration.

Feldman, Elliott J. 1978. "Comparative Public Policy: Field or Method?" *Comparative Politics* 10:287–305.

Finifter, Ada W., ed. 1983. *Political Science: The State of the Discipline.* Washington, D.C.: American Political Science Association.

Gaus, John Merriman. 1950. "Trends in the Theory of Public Administration." *Public Administration Review* 10:168.

Gohagan, John Kenneth. 1980. *Quantitative Analysis for Public Policy.* New York: McGraw-Hill.

Golembiewski, Robert T. 1977. *Public Administration as a Developing Discipline, Part I: Perspectives on Past and Present.* New York: Marcel Dekker.

Gordon, Robert Aaron, and James E. Howell. 1959. *Higher Education for Business.* New York: Columbia University Press.

Grant, W. Vance, and Thomas D. Synder. 1986. *Digest of Education Statistics, 1985–86.* Washington, D.C.: Government Printing Office.

Hansen, Susan B. 1983. "Public Policy Analysis: Some Recent Developments and Current Problems." In *Political Science: The State of the Discipline,* edited by Ada W. Finifter. Washington, D.C.: American Political Science Association.

Heclo, Hugh. 1983. "Executive Budget Making." Presented at the Urban Institute Conference on Federal Budget Policy in the 1980s, Washington, D.C.

Heidenheimer, Arnold J., Hugh Heclo, and Carolyn Teich Adams. 1975. *Comparative Public Policy: The Politics of Social Choice in Europe and America.* New York: St. Martin's.

Henry, Nicholas, ed. 1982. *Doing Public Administration: Exercises, Essays, and Cases.* 2d ed. Boston: Allyn and Bacon.

Henry, Nicholas. 1986. *Public Administration and Public Affairs.* 3d ed. Englewood Cliffs, N.J.: Prentice-Hall.

Honey, John C. 1967. "A Report: Higher Education for Public Service." *Public Administration Review* 27:301–19.

Klay, William Earle. 1982. "Innovations and Standards in Public Administration Education." In *Public Administration Education in Transition,* edited by Thomas Vocino and Richard Heimovics. New York: Marcel Dekker.

Long, Norton. 1954. "Public Policy and Administration: The Goals of Rationality and Responsibility." *Public Administration Review* 14:23.

Lynn, Naomi B. 1983. "Self-Portrait: Profile of Political Scientists." In *Political Science: The State of the Discipline,* edited by Ada W. Finifter. Washington, D.C.: American Political Science Association.

McKenna, Christopher K. 1980. *Quantitative Methods for Public Decision Making.* New York: McGraw-Hill.

Martin, Roscoe. 1952. "Political Science and Public Administration—A Note on the State of the Union." *American Political Science Review* 46:665.

Marx, Fritz Morstein. 1946. *Elements of Public Administration.* New York: Prentice-Hall.

Morgan, David R., and Kenneth J. Meier. 1982. "Reputation and Productivity of Public Administration/Affairs Programs: Additional Data." *Public Administration Review* 42:171–73.

Morgan, David R., Kenneth J. Meier, Richard C. Kearney, Steven W. Hays, and Harold B. Birch. 1981. "Reputation and Productivity Among U.S. Public Administration and Public Affairs Programs." *Public Administration Review* 41:666–73.

National Association of Schools of Public Affairs and Administration. 1973. *1973 Directory: Programs in Public Affairs and Administration.* Washington, D.C.: The Association.

National Association of Schools of Public Affairs and Administration. 1975. *1975 Directory: Programs in Public Affairs and Administration.* Washington, D.C.: The Association.

National Association of Schools of Public Affairs and Administration. 1977. *1977 Directory: Programs in Public Affairs and Administration.* Washington, D.C.: The Association.

National Association of Schools of Public Affairs and Administration. 1979. *1979 Directory: Programs in Public Affairs and Administration.* Washington, D.C.: The Association.

National Association of Schools of Public Affairs and Administration. 1981. *1981 Directory: Programs in Public Affairs and Administration.* Washington, D.C.: The Association.

National Association of Schools of Public Affairs and Administration. 1983. *1983 Directory: Programs in Public Affairs and Administration.* Washington, D.C.: The Association.

National Association of Schools of Public Affairs and Administration. 1986. *1986 Directory: Programs in Public Affairs and Administration.* Washington, D.C.: The Association.

Peters, B. Guy. 1981. "Comparative Public Policy (Bibliography)." *Policy Studies Review* 1:183–97.

Pierson, Frank. 1959. *The Education of American Businessmen.* New York: Carnegie Corporation.

Quade, E.S. 1982. *Analysis for Public Decisions.* 2d ed. New York: Elsevier.

Ranney, Austin. 1968a. "Preface." In *Political Science and Public Policy,* edited by Austin Ranney. Chicago: Markham.

Ranney, Austin. 1968b. "The Study of Policy Content: A Framework for Choice." In *Political Science and Public Policy,* edited by Austin Ranney. Chicago: Markham.

Roettger, Walter B. 1977. "I Never Promised You a Rose Garden: Career Satisfaction in an Age of Uncertainty." Presented at the Iowa Conference of Political Science, Des Moines.

Savage, Peter. 1968. "What Am I Bid for Public Administration?" *Public Administration Review* 28:391.

Schick, Allen. 1975. "The Trauma of Politics: Public Administration in the Sixties." In *American Public Administration: Past, Present, Future,* edited by Frederick C. Mosher. Syracuse: Maxwell School of Citizenship and Public Affairs and the National Association of Schools of Public Affairs and Administration.

Sharkansky, Ira. 1979. *Wither the State? Politics and Public Enterprise in Three Countries.* Chatham, N.J.: Chatham House.

Simon, Herbert A. 1946. "The Proverbs of Administration." *Public Administration Review* 6:53–67.

Simon, Herbert A. 1947a. "A Comment on 'The Science of Public Administration.'" *Public Administration Review* 7:201–4.

Simon, Herbert A. 1947b. *Administrative Behavior: A Study of Decision-Making Processes in Administration Organizations.* New York: Macmillan.

Somit, Albert, and Joseph Tanenhaus. 1967. *The Development of Political Science.* Boston: Allyn and Bacon.

Sorg, James D., and Edward B. Laverty. 1981. *The Computer and Graduate Instruction in Public Administration and Public Affairs Curricula: A National Survey.* Orono: University of Maine.

Thai, Khi V. 1981a. "Does NASPAA Peer Review Improve the Quality of PA/A Education?" Manuscript.

Thai, Khi V. 1981b. *Public Administration Education: The Current Status and Perceived Needs.* Orono: University of Maine.

Thai, Khi V. 1984. "Toward a Curriculum Design for Future PA/A Education Problems and Some Suggested Mathematical Models." Presented at the National Conference of the American Society for Public Administration, Denver.

Turnbull, Augustus B., III, Alfred M. Zuck, Brian R. Fry, and Robert Weinback. 1985. *The M.P.A. Degree: A Forum.* Columbia: University of South Carolina.

"Universities Award 123 Doctoral Degrees." 1986. *Public Administration Times Supplement,* 15 October, 11, 21, 23.

U.S. Bureau of the Census. 1986. *Statistical Abstract of the United States, 1986.* Washington, D.C.: Government Printing Office.

Uveges, Joseph A., Jr. 1985. "Identifying the Impacts of NASPAA's M.P.A. Standards and Peer Review Process on Education for the Public Service: 1975–1985." Presented at the Southeast Regional Meeting of the American Society for Public Administration, Charleston.

Waldo, Dwight. 1948. *The Administrative State: A Study of the Political Theory of American Public Administration.* New York: Ronald.

Waldo, Dwight. 1968. "Scope of the Theory of Public Administration." In *Theory and Practice of Public Administration: Scope, Objectives, and Methods,* edited by James C. Charlesworth. Philadelphia: American Academy of Political and Social Science.

Waldo, Dwight. 1979. "Introduction: Trends and Issues in Education for Public Administration." In *Education for Public Service: 1979,* edited by Guthrie S. Birkhead and James D. Carroll. Syracuse: Syracuse University.

Weiss, Carol H. 1972. *Evaluation Research: Methods of Assessing Programs.* Englewood Cliffs, N.J.: Prentice-Hall.

Welch, Susan, and John C. Comer. 1983. *Quantitative Methods for Public Administration: Technique and Applications.* Homewood, Ill.: Dorsey.

White, Joseph. 1985. "Much Ado About Everything: Making Sense of Federal Budgeting." *Public Administration Review* 45:623–30.

Wolf, James F. 1982. "Careers in Public Administration Education." In *Public Administration Education in Transition,* edited by Thomas Vocino and Richard Heimovics. New York: Marcel Dekker.

Young, Deborah J., and William B. Eddy. 1982. "Adult Learning Methods in Public Administration Education." In *Public Administration Education in Transition,* edited by Thomas Vocino and Richard Heimovics. New York: Marcel Dekker.

2

Blacks in Public Administration: An Endangered Species

MICHAEL B. PRESTON AND MAURICE C. WOODARD

In America today, one of the principal sources of individual and group mobility is education. The more education one has, the more likely one will be able to attain decent employment and increase one's chances for economic and social mobility. Increasingly, individuals and groups who lack this key resource will find themselves at an extreme disadvantage in the marketplace. A high school education, while still important, offers limited opportunities in today's highly technological society. Indeed, even the bachelor's degree, which some consider the culmination of their education before entering the job market, now only meets the needs of entry-level requirements for most jobs and is increasingly becoming more restrictive as one seeks upward mobility. In today's society, then, the measure of a person's worth is dictated by his or her educational achievements.

Most white Americans have long recognized the need for advanced degrees as a way to improve their chances for upward mobility. As higher education has become more accessible to blacks, they too have come to see the advantages of an advanced degree. The problem for blacks is this: While more are aware of the need to pursue graduate education, fewer are doing so. This is especially true in the fields of political science and public administration. As a result of the decline, fewer black faculty or administrators will be available in public administration in the near future. More important, given the paucity of blacks in the field and the decline in enrollments, blacks are rapidly becoming an endangered species in the field of public administration.

The decline of blacks in public administration is ironically coming at a time when more opportunities for employment are likely to be available. According to a recent article in the *Chronicle of Higher Education,* the decline is occurring when one-third or more of the current professors in the field are expected to retire by the end of this century (Heller 1986). In the same issue, Reginald Wilson, director of the Office of Minority Concerns of the American Council on Education, stated, "We

27

have the potential for achieving parity for minority faculty members, but if we don't have the faculty there to hire, then the chance will be lost" (Heller, 1986, 1, 24).

The current number of blacks in graduate schools is discouraging. According to the Department of Education's Center for Statistics, blacks constituted 6 percent of graduate school enrollments in 1976. This percentage had dropped to 4.8 percent by 1984 (Heller 1986). As table 2.1 shows, blacks were the only minority group to experience a numerical decline in graduate enrollments.

TABLE 2.1
Minorities and Women in Graduate School[a]

	1975–77	1984–85	Percent change
Blacks	65,352	52,834	−19.2
Hispanics	20,274	24,402	20.4
Asians	18,487	28,543	54.4
Women	467,155	503,525	7.8

SOURCE: "Minorities and Women in Graduate School" (1986).
a. Figures include U.S. citizens only.

The purpose of this chapter is to examine the state of blacks in public administration from 1934 to the present. In order to understand more about these scholars, we need to seek answers to the following questions: How many of the early black scholars listed public administration as an area of specialization and at what institutions did they receive their degrees? Which universities have been the top producers of black Ph.D.s in public administration? What has been or is being done, if anything, to reduce the enrollment decline of blacks in public administration? And what are the consequences for the profession if the decline in black faculty and students is not reversed? We begin by briefly describing the linkages between political science and public administration. Today, as in the past, most public administration programs are found within the departments of political science.

Political Science and Public Administration: The Linkages

Dwight Waldo, Albert Schweitzer Distinguished Service Professor Emeritus of the Maxwell School of Citizenship and Public Affairs, has documented the early linkages between the fields of political science and public administration. He points out that public administration emerged as part of the discipline of political science and was considered a field or subdiscipline along with political theory, parties and politics, comparative governments, and international relations (Waldo 1981). Other scholars (Somit and Tanenhaus 1967; Stone and Stone 1976) have described in detail the connections between the fields. They cite budgeting and municipal and state governments as some of these linkages. These interconnections are important because according to the National Association of Schools of Public Affairs and Administration (NASPAA), public administration programs in departments of political science are the second most popular organizational arrangements for graduate programs (American Political Science Association, 1985a, 1985b, 1986). (It was the most popular organizational pattern as late as 1984.) In addition, the American Political Science Association (APSA) *Directory* lists 1312 departments of political science that offer the bachelor's degree up to the Ph.D. All offer courses and training in public administration. Thus, any attempts to locate the origins of black Ph.D.s in the field of public administration must of necessity begin with the discipline of political science.

Black Ph.D.s in Political Science and Public Administration

From 1934 to the early 1950s, many black Ph.D.s did not specialize in public administration. Traditional areas in the discipline were better established. Nevertheless, public administration was widely discussed in courses in American government, political theory, municipal and state governments, international organization, and comparative government. The following seven black pioneers did list public administration as a major area of academic specialization: Vincent Browne, Jewel Prestage, Robert Gill, Earl M. Lewis, G. James Fleming, J. Errol Miller, and John Davis. An eighth, Lucius Barker, listed public policy as his specialty. Thirty-eight percent of the early doctoral recipients specialized in public administration. Ralph Bunche, the first black American to receive the Ph.D. in political science, graduated from Harvard in 1934. He went on to a distinguished career and is the only black to be elected president of the APSA. Jewel L. Prestage was the first black American female to receive the doctorate. She graduated from the University of Iowa in 1954. Twenty-two blacks had received the doctorate by that time (see table 2.2).

In the late 1960s, Jewel Prestage and a Ford Foundation committee compiled the first list of black American Ph.D.s in political science for a conference focusing on the political science curriculum at predominantly black institutions. The conference was held at Southern University in April 1969. The list contained the names of sixty-four persons. Of these, twenty-five were teaching at predominantly black educational institutions; twenty-three were teaching at majority white educational institutions; six held administrative positions in black colleges and universities; seven were employed at governmental agencies and foundations; one was a secondary

TABLE 2.2
Black Ph.D.s as of 1954

University	Number of graduates	Name	Year degree received
Harvard	3	Robert Brisbane	1948
		Vincent Browne[a]	1946
		Ralph Bunche	1934
Iowa	3	Rodney Higgins	1940
		Jewel Prestage[a]	1954
		Alexander Waller	1940
Michigan	3	William Boyd	1944
		Robert Gill[a]	1942
		Thomas R. Solomon	1939
Chicago	2	Earl M. Lewis[a]	1951
		Robert Martin	1947
Ohio State	2	William Nowlin	1950
		Samuel D. Colk	1954
Pennsylvania	2	G. James Flemming[a]	1948
		J. Errol Miller[a]	1945
Columbia	1	John Davis[a]	1950
American	1	Emmett Dorsey	1953
Illinois	1	Lucius J. Barker	1954
Minnesota	1	William McIntosh	1953
New York	1	William Robinson	1952
Pittsburgh	1	George Davis	1951

SOURCE: Prestage, 1984.
a. Listed public administration as an area of specialization.

school principal; one was retired; and the affiliation of one was unknown. In October 1969, further research by the committee discovered eight more doctorates, bringing the total to seventy-two.

The original Prestage list did not indicate where the Ph.D.s had been received. Further inquiry revealed that seventy of them had been completed in the United States. The totals for the leading universities are listed in table 2.3. In addition, several departments or specialized schools had graduated at least one Ph.D.: Colorado, Howard, Idaho, Johns Hopkins, Massachusetts, Maryland, Michigan State, Minnesota, Missouri, North Carolina, Northwestern, Pittsburgh, University of

TABLE 2.3 Top Producers of Black Ph.D.s as of 1969		TABLE 2.4 Top Producers of Black Ph.D.s from 1969 to 1977[a]	
University	Number	University	Number
Harvard	6	Claremont	15
Illinois	5	University of California— Berkeley	9
Michigan	5		
Chicago	4	Chicago	9
New York	4	Illinois	7
Columbia	4	Ohio State	7
Iowa	4	Howard	6
Ohio State	4	Northwestern	5
Wisconsin	3	University of Southern California	5
Indiana	3		
American	2	Florida State	4
Denver, Graduate School of International Studies	2	Indiana	4
		Massachusetts	4
Pennsylvania	2	University of Washington	4
Princeton	2		
Southern Illinois	2		
Kansas	2		

SOURCE: Prestage, 1977.

SOURCE: American Political Science Association, 1977.

a. Includes only those persons who graduated from departments of political science. Specialized schools are not included.

Southern California, St. Louis, the Fletcher School of Law and Diplomacy at Tufts, and the University of Texas.

Of the seventy-two black American doctorates in 1969, the following additional persons listed public administration as their primary area of specialization in one or more of the American Society for Public Administration (ASPA) directories: Harry Bailey, Kansas (1964); Tyrone Baines, Maryland (1969); Charles Harris, Wisconsin (1960); Matthew Holden, Northwestern (1961); Lawrence Howard, Harvard (1956); Tobe Johnson, Columbia (1963); Willard Johnson, Harvard (1965); James T. Jones, Illinois (1965); W. Astor Kirk, Texas (1958); E.W. Miles, Indiana (1962); Leroy Oliver, Indiana (1955); Ernest Patterson, St. Louis (1968); George C. Robinson, New York (1965); Tandy Tollerson, Missouri (1962); William J. Williams, University of Southern California (1960); and Maurice C. Woodard, Kansas (1969).

The above list increases the number of black Americans with doctorates in political science who claim public administration as their primary area of specialization to twenty-three. This amounted to 31 percent with a specialty in public admin-

TABLE 2.5 Top Producers of Black Ph.D.s from 1978 to 1980[a]		TABLE 2.6 Top Producers of Black Ph.D.s in 1983[a]	
University	Number	University	Number
Howard	10	Atlanta	9
Atlanta	8	Michigan	5
Yale	6	Howard	4
University of California—Berkeley	5	Wisconsin	4
Ohio State	5	Harvard	3
Chicago	4	Indiana	3
Florida State	4	Yale	3
Illinois	4	Claremont	2
Claremont	3	Florida State	2
Harvard	3	Iowa	2
MIT	3	MIT	2
Miami	3	State University of New York—Buffalo	2
Michigan	3	South Carolina	2
Purdue	3	Tennessee	2
University of Washington	3	Washington University—St. Louis	2
		Wayne State	2

SOURCE: American Political Science Association, 1980.

a. Includes only those persons who graduated from departments of political science. Specialized schools are not included.

SOURCE: American Political Science Association, 1984.

a. Includes only those persons who graduated from departments of political science. Specialized schools are not included.

istration. In the 1977 APSA *Directory of Black Americans in Political Science,* 202 black American Ph.D.s are identified. The leading universities are listed in table 2.4. In addition, three Ph.D.s apiece were produced by Atlanta, Columbia, Michigan, New York, Oregon, and Princeton. Brandeis, UCLA, Harvard, MIT, Michigan State, North Carolina, and Notre Dame each produced two.

The 1977 APSA *Directory* contains entries from 370 black Americans as well as an index by field of specialization and research interest. The public administration index listed 153; 74 with doctorates were listed. Of seven fields, public administration was second only to American politics. The list contained entries from all active persons teaching, conducting research, or in public service. Virtually all those listed received their graduate training in departments of political science. Six graduated from the Graduate School of Public and International Affairs at the University of Pittsburgh; two each graduated from the School of Public Administration at the University of Southern California and Florida State University. The following specialized schools graduated one each: Maxwell and the University of California at Berkeley.

The departments graduating the largest number of Ph.D.s in political science with a concentration in public administration from 1969 to 1977 included Claremont (seven), Howard (four), Michigan (four), California–Berkeley (four), and Illinois (four). These departments are included in the totals presented in table 2.4.

The 1980 APSA survey of graduate departments revealed that 133 black Americans received their doctorates in political science from 1978 to 1980. The leading universities are presented in table 2.5. Forty-four departments produced the others.

It is estimated that 44 persons, or 33 percent of the new doctorates, were in the field of public administration. The APSA Committee on the Status of Blacks in the Profession is currently compiling an up-to-date directory of individuals with public administration backgrounds.

The 1984 *Guide to Graduate Study in Political Science* (APSA, 1984) indicates that eighty doctorates were earned by black Americans between 1981 and 1983. Atlanta and Howard were again at the top of the schools listed (see table 2.6, page 32).

An estimated thirty-four black Americans received a Ph.D. in political science in 1984. The cumulative totals (1934–84) for universities graduating black American Ph.D.s are presented in table 2.7 (page 34).

The optimism that flowed from the increased enrollment of blacks in Ph.D. programs in the late 1960s and 1970s has been replaced in the 1980s by the harsh reality that black enrollment in political science is decreasing. In truth, the number of black students entering advanced degree programs in political science has dropped steadily since 1980. Even more alarming is the fact that it shows no sign of rebounding. Indeed, all available evidence indicates that enrollments are likely to decrease further before they increase.

The Rise and Decline of Black Political Scientists

The Committee on the Status of Blacks in the Profession of the APSA organized a conference of a select number of political scientists to discuss the reasons for the declining enrollments of blacks in political science and public administration. A key part of the discussion focused on what could be done to improve the situation (Preston and Woodard 1984).

According to the committee, the problem was twofold and had both short- and long-range consequences: (1) How to increase the number of minorities, especially blacks, with Ph.D.s in political science; and (2) how to improve the rate of promotion and tenure among young black faculty who get jobs in their fields. The committee viewed the initial conference as a fact-finding and educational meeting, believing that specific problems needed to be identified before attempts were made to fashion solutions to the broader questions. The committee's plan was to have a small group of people attend the initial session and involve significant others at regional and other meetings.

The initial discussion focused on the problem of recruiting and retaining black graduate students. Using data provided by the committee, participants made several important observations. First, they noted that there has been a sharp decline during the last decade in the number of blacks entering Ph.D. programs. In 1974, for example, 131 blacks entered Ph.D. programs in political science (9 percent of all new students); by 1985, the number of blacks dropped to 52 (6 percent of all new students). During this same period, the number of blacks enrolled in doctoral programs was halved—from 435 in 1974 to 277 in 1983 (see tables 2.8 and 2.9).

Second, because of the long and highly variable time it takes to complete the Ph.D. (the average time between the bachelor's degree and the Ph.D. in political science is eleven years), the decline in black graduate students is not yet fully reflected in the number of Ph.D.s

TABLE 2.7

Sixteen Top Producers of Black American Ph.D.s, 1934–84[a]

University	Number
Howard	21
Claremont	20
Illinois	19
Chicago	18
Atlanta	17
Michigan	16
University of California—Berkeley	14
Harvard	14
Ohio State	14
Florida State	10
Indiana	10
Wisconsin	10
Yale	10
Columbia	8
New York	8
Northwestern	8

a. Includes only those persons who graduated from departments of political science. Specialized schools are not included.

awarded. The National Research Council reported the following numbers of Ph.D.s awarded to blacks in political science, international relations, and public administration (including both U.S. citizens and non-U.S. citizens with permanent visas): 1977 (47), 1978 (48), 1979 (36), 1980 (26), 1981 (34), and 1982 (45).

The recruitment and retention problem is significant. If we assume that of the fifty-two blacks receiving Ph.D.s in political science over any three-year period, fifteen decide not to go into teaching but into nonacademic areas, we are left with thirty-seven. Of the thirty-seven, if ten fail to get promotions, we have twenty-seven. And if fifteen of the twenty-seven decide to teach in predominantly black colleges and universities, that leaves only twelve for hiring in other major universities. Predominantly white institutions cannot hire black faculty if they are virtually non-

TABLE 2.8
Students Beginning Ph.D. Study in Political Science

Fall of	Total	Women		Black	
		N	%	N	%
1985	933	286	31	52	6
1984	936	264	28	48	5
1983	838	230	27	51	6
1982	772	208	27	39	5
1981	1042	299	29	76	7
1980	1068	301	28	104	9
1979	1100	305	28	101	9
1978	1051	255	24	102	10
1977	1182	270	23	111	10
1976	1064	274	26	100	9
1975	1174	270	23	129	11
1974	1443	342	24	131	9
1973	1414	N.A.		N.A.	
1972	1576	N.A.		N.A.	
1971	1695	N.A.		N.A.	
1970	2138	N.A.		N.A.	
1969	2487	N.A.		N.A.	

SOURCE: American Political Science Association, various years.
NOTE: N.A. = not available.

existent. Yet it is also true that these same universities are the bottlenecks through which most faculty must pass if their numbers are to increase.

The conferees concluded that a very serious problem exists and that the profession must think of new ways to recruit and retain black graduate students. The intense competition among graduate departments for a handful of outstanding black undergraduates does little to increase the number of blacks entering graduate study in political science. Other factors are also involved, including the number of blacks receiving undergraduate degrees (it has actually declined in recent years in the Chicago area); the fact that political science is not considered an attractive undergraduate major (the trend among blacks appears to be toward business and communication); and the fact that law and business schools are more popular than graduate schools (however, the expected shifts among blacks from graduate schools to law and business schools have not materialized, which may mean that qualified blacks are opting for jobs instead).

The conference explored several ideas for increasing the number of blacks entering graduate programs in political science. They recommended that a prestigious APSA body call attention to the problem and then begin to work through the

TABLE 2.9
Graduate Student Enrollments in Ph.D.
Programs in Political Science

Year	Total	Women		Black		Foreign	
		N	%	N	%	N	%
1985–86	4894	1349	28	277	7	1292	26
1984–85	4994	1353	27	273	5	1346	27
1983–84	4171	1105	26	207	5	1075	26
1982–83	N.A.	N.A.		N.A.		N.A.	
1981–82	5491	1505	27	315	6	1181	22
1980–81	5756	1415	25	373	6	1212	21
1979–80	5888	1384	24	406	7	1146	21
1978–79	5742	1258	22	432	8	948	17
1977–78	5737	1278	22	413	7	819	14
1976–77	5462	1209	22	402	7	813	15
1975–76	6150	1475	24	435	7	N.A.	
1974–75	6450	N.A.		N.A.		N.A.	

SOURCE: American Political Science Association, various years.
NOTE: N.A. = not available.

network of department chairs. The APSA should develop materials that make a positive case for the profession of political science and how it is linked with the world of public affairs and public policy; APSA should work with the National Conference of Black Political Scientists (NCOBPS) to develop an "Introduction to Quantitative Methods" course for black undergraduates (the lack of such a course was seen as one of the major weaknesses of most black undergraduates); APSA should develop a network of teachers at historically black colleges to identify potential graduate students; and conferences similar to that of the committee should be held at regional and state political science association meetings.

Participants also addressed the problem of retaining minority graduate students after they are recruited. Black students suffer from having few black colleagues in the student body, few black faculty members to serve as mentors and role models, and difficulty with the methodology courses for which they are ill prepared. It was suggested that APSA might develop and publicize models for departments to assist minority students and that Ohio State University, with its minority graduate student visitation day, one hundred minority fellowships, and an office of minority affairs that continually monitors minority students, might serve as such a model.

It should be pointed out that the committee and the APSA have followed up on four of the items listed above. The most significant accomplishment has been a Summer Institute held during 1986 in Baton Rouge, Louisiana. Southern University and LSU co-sponsored the institute for twenty-five undergraduates from predominantly black institutions. The results of a survey at the end of the summer showed that over half the students became more interested in political science and public affairs instead of a career in law. Eight of the students applied for APSA black fellowships to enter graduate school in 1986–87. The Summer Institute was clearly a success; it exposed students to some of the top black and white professors in the field and taught them quantitative analysis. Should they choose to enter graduate school, they will have a better chance for success.

TABLE 2.10
Full-Time Faculty in Political Science Departments

	Total Faculty	Black Faculty	
		Number	%
Political Science Departments, 1982–83 (N = 619)			
Tenure-track faculty	5089	168	3
Full professors	2213	40	2
Associate professors	1578	44	3
Assistant professors	1161	59	5
Instructors / lecturers	137	25	18
Nontenure-track faculty	266	15	6
Total faculty	5355	183	3
Political Science Departments, 1975–76 (N = 623)			
Tenure-track faculty	4862	141	3
Full professors	1652	26	2
Associate professors	1451	30	2
Assistant professors	1536	65	4
Instructors / lecturers	224	20	9
Nontenure-track faculty	252	16	6
Total faculty	5114	157	3

SOURCE: American Political Science Association, various years.

Black Faculty

The current number of black faculty in political science and public administration is disquieting. Data from ASPA Surveys of Departments reveal that blacks composed about 3 percent of all political science faculty in 1975–76; the number was still at 3 percent in 1982–83 (see table 2.10). In public administration, a recent publication of NASPAA vividly described the lack of faculty diversity:

This issue of Public Enterprise, sponsored by NASPAA's Diversity Committee, is devoted to a consideration of several of the most serious and longstanding challenges confronting NASPAA and its member institutions; most notably, the need to increase the representation of minorities and women at all levels of faculty and administrative staff and among the student body in both MPA and Ph.D. programs. The point of view expressed by individual contributors may not represent, in toto, the perspective of every member of the committee. The intent, however, is to heighten awareness of the problems, to initiate widespread discussion and debate within NASPAA, and, most importantly, to suggest some of the many ways NASPAA and its member schools can work together to create an academic environment truly responsive to the achievement of equal opportunity. (National Association 1986)

In bemoaning the lack of faculty diversity, the Diversity Committee stated that minority faculty had increased from 4 percent in 1974–1975 to 9 percent in 1982–1983. Blacks represented 4 percent, Asian/Pacific Islanders 3 percent, and Hispanics 2 percent. The preliminary data in 1986 indicate that blacks have shown a slight increase since 1982–1983. Currently, blacks make up 5 percent; Asian/Pacific Islanders 2 percent; Hispanics 1 percent; American Indians 1 percent; and foreign faculty 1 percent (see table 2.11, page 39).

The 1986 survey also indicates that of the NASPAA member schools responding, thirty-six programs had no female faculty; eighty-one had no minority faculty; and seventeen programs have neither female nor minority faculty. Thus, the total minority faculty is only 146 (7.4 percent), out of a total of 1966 full-time faculty. If one looks at total numbers, there are 79 blacks and only 18 Hispanics as of April 1986. If diversity is a goal of both ASPA and NASPAA, these figures suggest that both organizations have a long way to go before faculty diversity becomes a reality.

William Harvey (State University of New York at Stony Brook) recently discussed the deleterious effects of the absence of faculty diversity.

Obviously, a decreasing black faculty presence means not only that less assistance and support will be available for black students, but also that there will be fewer role models for those students to pattern their own performance and career aspiration after. The situation is particularly compelling regarding black graduate students, since it has been shown that the number of blacks on graduate school faculties is the most significant predictor of success in recruiting black students for graduate and professional schools. (Harvey 1986, 96)

In an era of retrenchment, especially at the federal level, the number of blacks going to graduate school has declined steeply. The reasons for the decline are numerous. But it is probably fair to say that the poor economic position of blacks and other minorities over the last five years has led to a lack of applicants. At the same time, the cost of education has increased by over 50 percent and financial aid under President Reagan declined by over 21 percent. Thus, even though minority graduation rates from high school are up, the financial situation surely is one major reason why college enrollments are down (Heller 1986). If we also assume that blacks and other minorities are being excluded from some institutions because of restrictive GRE scores and the racial attitudes of some faculty members, then the magnitude of the problem becomes clearer and finding solutions becomes less problematic.

TABLE 2.11
Faculty Characteristics in NASPAA Member Schools,
Preliminary Data, 1986

	Number	%
Sexual composition of faculty		
Male	1660	84
Female	306	16
Ethnic / racial composition of faculty		
Black	79	5 [a]
Asians / Pacific Islanders	47	2
Hispanics	18	1
American Indians	2	
Foreign	22	1
Total faculty	1966	
Number of responding schools	166 [b]	
Average faculty size (range = 1–79)	11.9	

SOURCE: National Association, 1986.
a. Twenty-one of the total number are located at Howard University.
b. Required information for graduate programs; some undergraduate programs voluntarily submitted data.

Conclusion

The facts are inescapable. Blacks are as underrepresented on the faculties and in the student bodies of public administration schools and programs as they are in top decision-making positions in other segments of American society. Trends in enrollments over the past ten years are very discouraging; what is even more discouraging is that the decline in students and thus black faculty is coming at a time when opportunities for more parity are possible. Since blacks in 1982–83 were only 3 percent of total full-time faculty, the decline in enrollments, along with faculty retirements, deaths, and other factors, may well drop the percentage of black faculty below the 3–5 percent mark. This would not only be undesirable but would have long-range consequences for the future of blacks in the profession. What can be done?

One of the most effective short-term strategies is the approach taken by NASPAA. According to Charles Sampson of the Conference of Minority Public Administrators (COMPA), NASPAA has urged its affiliate schools to increase their efforts to recruit black faculty and students. Some of the suggestions made by NASPAA to affiliate schools include demonstration of an active outreach effort, within the traditional vehicles of professional recruitment but also beyond—within related professions, within doctoral programs, and within minority/women's organizations; and development of a systematic program to recruit minority students from the undergraduate to the master's-level program, and from the master's program to the doctoral level. Institutions without a doctoral program would be encouraged to enter into cooperative agreements with doctoral programs at nearby institutions.

In addition, the NASPAA guidelines also suggested the use of part-time, adjunct, half-time, and/or visiting appointments to enhance faculty diversity. Affiliates were encouraged to use internships as a way to expose minority students to people beyond the university and to diversify their curriculums to include work done by minority faculty and/or use materials showing minorities as part of the school and work environment. Finally, NASPAA urged affiliates to be more active in the recruitment of minority undergraduates to ensure diversity. Strategies for recruitment included networks with predominantly black institutions, more advertisements in regional and national journals, and recruitment of minorities from public agencies. If the NASPAA affiliates actively pursue these strategies, the short-term picture may not be as dismal as it now looks.

In an era of diminishing resources, the solution to the problem becomes a bit more difficult, but that is no reason to abandon the effort. What is needed is a commitment by people in authority at ASPA and NASPAA to making this a top-priority item on their agendas. The profession has made progress toward its goal of faculty diversity; to allow that progress to be lost is unpardonable. One of the major goals of leadership is to protect goals that are precarious until such time as they become as secure as other values we cherish. If we in the profession believe that diversity is a value worth preserving, and I believe we do, then leadership must make a serious commitment to making it a top priority. It is clear that leadership cannot do the job alone, but it can create the conditions that make it possible.

The NASPAA's Diversity Committee is in the process of completing a survey of all NASPAA institutions to gather more detailed information on the problem. They also will be making a series of recommendations on ways to help solve the problem. These reports should provide the leadership with more objective information on which to base their decisions. If this report stimulates a wide-ranging discussion of the situation, it may well be the first important step in finding a solution.

Acknowledgment

The authors wish to thank Charles Sampson of Sangamon State University for survey data that he thoughtfully provided.

References

American Political Science Association. 1977. *The 1977 Directory of Black Americans in Political Science.* Washington, D.C.: APSA.

American Political Science Association. 1980. *Guide to Graduate Study in Political Science.* Washington, D.C.: APSA.

American Political Science Association. 1984. *Guide to Graduate Study in Political Science.* Washington, D.C.: APSA.

American Political Science Association. 1985a. *The 1985–1986 American Political Science Association Directory.* Washington, D.C.: APSA.

American Political Science Association. 1985b. *The 1985–1986 Directory of Department Chairpersons.* Washington, D.C.: APSA.

American Political Science Association. 1986. *The 1986 Directory of Programs in Public Affairs and Administration.* Washington, D.C.: APSA.

Harvey, William. 1986. "Where Are the Black Faculty Members?" *Chronicle of Higher Education,* 22 January, 96.

Heller, Scott. 1986. "Women Flock to Graduate Schools in Record Numbers but Fewer Blacks Are Entering the Academic Pipeline." *Chronicle of Higher Education* 33(2):1, 24.

"Minorities and Women in Graduate School." 1986. *Chronicle of Higher Education,* 10 September, 1.

National Association of Schools of Public Affairs and Administration. 1986. *The Public Enterprise.* Washington, D.C.: The Association.

Prestage, Jewel. 1977. "Report of the Conference on Political Science Curriculum at Predominantly Black Institutions." In *Blacks and Political Science,* edited by Maurice C. Woodard. Washington, D.C.: APSA.

Prestage, Jewel. 1984. "The Role of Black Colleges and Universities in Graduate Education." In *Black Colleges and Universities,* edited by Antoine Garibaldi. New York: Praeger.

Preston, Michael B., and Maurice C. Woodard. 1984. "The Rise and Decline of Black Political Scientists." *P.S.* 17:787–92.

Somit, Albert, and Joseph Tanenhaus. 1967. *The Development of American Political Science.* Boston: Allyn and Bacon.

Stone, Alice B., and Donald Stone. 1976. "Early Development of Education." In *Public Administration: Past, Present, Future,* edited by Frederick C. Mosher. University, Ala.: University of Alabama Press.

Waldo, Dwight. 1981. *The Enterprise of Public Administration.* New York: Chandler and Sharp.

Woodard, Maurice C., and Michael B. Preston. 1989. "Black Political Scientists: Where Are the New Ph.D.s?" *P.S.* 18:80–88.

3

Public Administration Theory: The State of the Discipline

ROBERT B. DENHARDT

Generally speaking, public administration is concerned with managing change in pursuit of publicly defined societal values. In the definition of the field are implied serious theoretical issues. What is the role of the public administrator in shaping and executing public policy? How might public organizations best be designed and managed? What are the proper roles and responsibilities of the public manager? In an effort to answer such questions, students and practitioners of public administration over the years have developed a variety of theoretical approaches. Yet all have been bound together in their attempt to conceptualize and to understand the management of public programs.

While having common interests, theorists have ranged widely in their approaches to developing theories of public organizations. Even the briefest listing of efforts in public administration theory would have to include work by public administrationists in empirical theory, normative theory, ethical theory, public-choice theory, phenomenology, critical theory, psychoanalytic theory, and so on. In addition, one might wish to include theories related to public administration growing out of political science, management, sociology, anthropology, and a host of other disciplines. Public administration theory is contributed to by social scientists engaged in specific research projects and seeking to contribute to theory, but also by a small group of scholars who identify themselves as public administration theorists.

In my view, public administration theory draws its greatest strength and its most serious limitation from this diversity. On the one hand, public administration theorists are required to understand a broad range of perspectives relevant to their theory-building task. There is a tremendous richness and complexity built into public administration theory. On the other hand, the diversity of public administration often means that the field lacks a sense of identity. Many even question whether it is possible to speak of building a coherent and integrated public administration theory.

Under these circumstances, a review and assessment of public administration theory is timely.

Recent periodical literature and a large number of recent books in the field have been examined in preparing this chapter. Specifically, the major public administration journals from 1980 to 1985 have been reviewed, and articles that contributed most directly to public administration theory have been identified. An impressive accumulation of material on such diverse topics as democratic responsibility, democratic governance, the politics of bureaucracy, ethical concerns, citizenship, organizational dynamics, and political economy has resulted. The diversity and richness of public administration theory were both surprising and encouraging. Next, a listing of books published in the 1980s that seemed to be self-consciously theoretical in their presentation was developed. Again, the collection of material was impressive, though diverse in content and approach.

In reading the recent articles in public administration theory, one is struck by the diversity of topics being considered by public administration theorists; in reading recently published books, one gets more of a sense of trends in the field. For this reason, the diversity of topics in public administration theory is illustrated using the collection of journal articles as a base, then shifts that are occurring in our approach to public administration theory are explored using recently published books as a base. Following this review, several developments that set an agenda of topics needing further exploration by public administration theories are discussed.

The Content of Public Administration Theory: The Articles

The current periodical literature in public administration theory illustrates a vast range of topics including the role of the public bureaucracy in the governance process, the ethics of public service, citizenship and civic education, alternative epistemologies, organizational dynamics, interorganizational policy implementation, and political economy and public choice. Although it is not possible here to review all the current work in public administration theory, representative work in each of the topical areas is examined.

The Role of the Public Bureaucracy in the Governance Process

Recent public administration theorists have continued to explore many familiar issues, such as the relationship between politics and administration or between bureaucracy and democracy. Indeed, Grosenick (1984) draws from the American Society for Public Administration's Centennial Agendas project to identify eleven topical areas currently being examined through research in democratic governance. These include such concerns as basic political values, responsibility and accountability, and checks and balances—all topics long considered the core of the study and practice of public administration.

One noteworthy treatment of these issues is provided by Thompson (1983), who explores various ways in which the public bureaucracy can be reconciled with a democratic political system. Among these approaches, he identifies the hierarchical model of administrative responsibility, reliance on the professionalism of the civil service to achieve responsiveness, a pluralist model of citizen involvement, and the participatory model. Thompson argues that the participatory model provides the best starting point for reconciling bureaucracy and democracy, but that it needs to be supplemented by the best features of the other models.

David Rosenbloom (1983) treats the same general issue in a different fashion, suggesting three approaches to public administration theory: the "managerial," the "political," and the "legal." Each approach corresponds to a particular branch of government and each carries a distinctive set of values. Rosenbloom argues that in the modern administrative state, these three sets of values have permeated the administrative agencies of government, placing administrators in the unenviable position of having to balance the various interests represented by the three approaches. One illustration of these difficulties is provided in Lerner and Wanat's (1983) discussion of the fuzziness of legislative mandates and the ways in which bureaucrats seek to minimize the problems arising from mismatched intentions and understandings.

Hart and Scott (1982) offer the view that American public administration has been taken over by the values of American business management, values they consider inappropriate to the conduct of public affairs. In contrast, they assert that the field of public administration must recover from its dependence on business values and develop both a philosophy and an approach to education for the public service that will emphasize the inherent uniqueness and strength of the field. The conduct of public affairs, they argue, should be guided by the natural-law values of our constitutional foundation. Hart (1984) carries the argument further by applying the philosophical principles underlying the American system to an analysis of virtue among citizens and honor among bureaucrats. Seen in this light, "public administration is not a kind of technology but a form of moral endeavor" (p. 116), one requiring what Frederickson and Hart (1985) term a "patriotism of benevolence."

In addition to these general philosophical statements concerning the role of public organizations in a democratic society, several theorists have taken a historical approach to the field, seeking to understand more clearly some of the traditional values associated with the public organizations. O'Toole (1984), for example, examines the reform tradition in public administration, arguing that administrative thinkers over the past hundred years have remained remarkably true to the tradition from which the field evolved. He suggests, however, that certain problems are so deeply rooted in our political culture that a field primarily concerned with reform will have great difficulty in addressing them. Similarly, whether the image or presentation of the field to the larger political culture can be altered is the topic addressed by Killingsworth (1982), who argues for a new style of presentation.

Finally, we should note several articles that attempt to conceptualize more precisely notions of responsiveness (Saltzstein 1985) or efficiency (Goodin and Wilenski 1984), or to develop empirical tests of the correspondence between bureaucratic action and public demands (Gaertner, Gaertner, and Devine 1983; McEachern and Al-Arayed 1984; Romzek and Hendricks 1982).

Related to these discussions of the role of public organizations are a number of articles stimulated by recent attacks on the public service by politicians and others. Drucker's (1980) discussion of the deadly sins of public administration suggests several errors agencies make in implementing programs that undermine their success. More positively, Kaufman's (1981) discussion of the fear of bureaucracy suggests that whatever the validity of recent attacks on the public bureaucracy, the fear itself deserves some explanation. Kaufman conjectures that the fear may be stimulated by a need on the part of the public to assign specific blame for problems that may be far more systemic than they appear. He suggests that we should look for deeper explanations rather than scapegoats. This same sentiment is echoed by Wriston (1980) and Adams (1984), both of whom acknowledge certain weaknesses in public organizations but underscore their positive contributions to society.

From this brief review, it is clear that the traditional concerns of public administration theory continue to occupy the attention of major theorists in the 1980s. Notable in its philosophical tone, this material suggests a field continuing to search for an adequate expression of its role in democratic governance. While such a search is informed by historical developments in the field, it recognizes that the changing demands placed on public organizations in modern society require a redefinition of such notions as *responsiveness*. The image of the public administrator of the future is still being formed, but not in the minds of contemporary theorists; the new administrator is likely to be one active in the policy process, highly sensitive to notions of the public interest, and always mindful of the moral and political context of administrative action.

The Ethics of Public Service

If there is one striking shift in the priorities of public administration theorists in the 1980s, it is surely the extensive attention now being given to ethical concerns. Although we might speculate on the reasons for this new attention (Watergate certainly being a prime candidate), there is no question that theorists have assigned great emphasis to ethical concerns. The ethics of public service is discussed more fully in chapter 5 of this book, but we should at least indicate here the range of materials now being developed by public administration theorists.

The territory is well laid out by Willbern (1984), who identifies six kinds of morality for public officials: (1) basic honesty and conformity to law, (2) conflicts of interest, (3) service orientation and procedural fairness, (4) the ethic of democratic responsibility, (5) the ethic of public policy determination, and (6) the ethic of compromise and social integration. This list is elaborated on by Brady (1981), Lilla (1981), and Thompson (1985), each of whom considers the range of ethical studies and the way this study should be approached. Especially important is Thompson's demonstration that two major arguments against the possibility of developing ethical administration are not compelling.

Specific discussions of the relationship between law and public administration include Foster's (1981) argument in behalf of an "intermediate legalism"—law as if people mattered—that would complement and foster moral behavior in public agencies. Similarly, Rohr (1985) presages his recent book on ethics in the administrative state by comparing the political theory of the Constitution with the constitutional theory of Wilson (1887) and Goodnow (1900).

The question of individual responsibility in public organizations has been discussed even more frequently. Representative articles include those by Brady (1983), Scott (1982), and Thompson (1980). Stewart (1985) illustrates the flavor of these discussions well in her assessment of ethics and the profession of public administration.

A special condition affecting the ethical behavior of officials is the influence of professional values, values that may clash with the ethics of public service. Bell (1985), for example, studies the interplay between professional values and organizational purposes in housing policy, while Yarwood (1986) concludes more generally that "science and the professions must share the blame for any ethical problems caused by formal organizations" (p. 483).

Finally, several authors have considered the dissemination of ethical standards throughout the profession, with Chandler (1983) providing an analysis of arguments both in favor of and in opposition to a Code of Ethics for the American Society for Public Administration, and with Koritansky (1982), Mayer and Harmon (1982), and Schorr (1983) considering the teaching of ethics in professional programs in public administration. Mayer and Harmon (1982) summarize this work well in their comment: "The role of the administrator is to mediate, not merely to judge or to solve problems. . . . Performing this essential role requires that the administrator be responsible in each of three senses: professionally, politically, and personally. Moral education for public administrators requires an understanding of each and an understanding of their relationship" (p. 222).

Citizenship and Civic Education

One important area combining studies of the governance process with studies of administrative ethics has been citizenship and civic education. Fredrickson's (1982) article on the "recovery of civicism" sets the tone for these discussions by arguing that, in de-emphasizing the public aspect of public administration, we have lost sight of the importance of democratic values as they affect the work of individual administrators. A similar conclusion, though one arrived at through different means, is reached by McSwain (1985), who argues that we do not now have an adequate grounding for a fully developed notion of citizenship and that the liberalist legacy of the Constitution has undermined notions of community and the public interest with rational individualism. Under such circumstances, she argues, the administrator is left with little guidance in making responsible decisions concerning public values.

In addition to these independent works, a special symposium on citizenship in the *Public Administration Review* included several important theoretical articles (including the article by Hart discussed earlier). In contrast to other theorists interested in ethics who take a more legalistic approach, Cooper (1984) argues that the ethical obligations of the public administrator are derived from the fact that administrators are citizens, "professional citizens," or "citizen-administrators." Among the administrator's obligations, argues McGregor (1984), is that of educating the citizenry, something that Gawthrop (1984a) finds difficult in a time in which the meaning of citizenship has become devoid of significance. Finally, Rohr (1985) discusses limitations on the administrator's political activity as instructive with respect to the language of citizenship.

Alternative Epistemologies

The questioning of traditional positivist approaches to research in public administration that characterized much of the theory work during the 1970s continued in the early 1980s; however, more recent work is not merely critical of earlier approaches but also seeks to outline alternative perspectives. (Many of these are discussed in Morgan 1983, especially the entries by Forester and White, and McSwain.) Among these, several theorists approached their topic from perspectives growing out of phenomenology and literary criticism. Ostrom (1980) expressed the flavor of these new approaches: "I have gradually come to conclude that the study of public administration should not be treated as strictly natural phenomena. The methods of the natural sciences are not fully appropriate to the study of public administration. Instead, we need to look upon administrative tasks and administrative arrangements as works of art or as artifacts" (p. 309).

Sederberg (1984) suggests that we examine the metaphors underlying various research traditions. In contrast to the more traditional machine, organic, and dramatic metaphors, he offers an explanatory metaphor, one he claims is more sensitive to the subjective nature of organizations. Since all organizations are based on the experience of individual actors involved in explaining their actions and their participation, clarifying the structure of knowledge acquisition might well provide clues to the understanding of organizational structures and behavior. Killingsworth (1984), in contrast, employs Speech-Act philosophy as a framework for investigating idle talk in administrative organizations, noting both the ideological and fictional nature of what occurs in organized life. Finally, Fischer (1983) seeks a way of integrating empirical and normative judgments through a logic of questions that might aid in understanding decision making, while Jung (1982) provides a detailed application of phenomenology to public affairs.

Other theorists have focused on critical social theory as a source of inspiration for their studies. Denhardt (1981a, 1981b), for example, has outlined a critical theory of public organization, based on the work of the Frankfurt School of social philosophy. In such an approach, self-reflection and self-critique on the part of the administrator become central to organizational transformations. Similarly, Forester (1981) has applied Habermas's theory of communicative competence to the work of planners and administrators, emphasizing the administrator's contribution to enhanced public discourse in a society characterized by systematically distorted patterns of communications. Forester (1984) has also applied this perspective to an analysis of the concept of administrative rationality.

The process of developing new approaches to public administration theory has itself been a subject of some speculation. Both Morgan (1984) and Lovrich (1985) have written articles indicating opportunities that might arise from a diversity of paradigms in a field such as public administration, while White (1981) has explored some of the difficulties encountered by those seeking to develop alternative approaches. Finally, several recent articles in the *Public Administration Review,* including contributions by Cleary and McCurdy (1985) and White (1986), have discussed various approaches to research in public administration.

Organizational Dynamics

Several theorists identified with the field of public administration have effectively contributed to organization theory generally over the past several years, while others have adapted models of organization theory to public organizations. For example, Cohen (1984) has discussed the influence of conflicting subgoals on organizational search effectiveness, while Scholl (1981) has proposed an alternative to the goal model of organization, one he terms a political model. More broadly, McGregor (1981) has reviewed the work of Charles Lindblom in terms of its impact on the study of organized systems, especially as it emphasizes authority, exchange, and persuasion.

Adaptation of more general approaches to organization theory to the field of public administration has included Bozeman's (1981) discussion of organization design and Korten's (1984) development of the concept of strategic organization. Korten's work suggests that traditional models of organization are not well suited for the future and that strategic management represents a positive alternative, one that carries with it "a proactive commitment to the ideal that the purpose of organization is to serve the needs of people, while facilitating the human growth of all participants" (p. 341).

The possibility of reordering complex organizations for the future is also addressed by Cleveland (1985), who suggests that information is now our most basic resource, but that the models of organization now employed were based on resource scarcities of other kinds. Such models, emphasizing influence and control, may be inappropriate to an information society, thus suggesting the possibility of major shifts in our approaches to organizing complex tasks. Under such conditions, hierarchy is likely to be an early victim.

One striking development among public administration theorists interested in organizational dynamics is an increased attention to psychological issues. In part, this work has been stimulated by new approaches to organizational learning developed by Argyris (1980) and others, but it also includes attention by Romzek (1985) to psychological linkages between work and nonwork involvements, and by Agor (1985) to managerial intuition.

Most interesting is the use of psychoanalytic constructs to understand organizational life. Baum (1982, 1983a, 1983b) has investigated the psychological relationship between advisers and their clients, as well as the psychodynamics of the bureaucratic lives of planners. Diamond (1984) has described bureaucracy as "an externalized self-system" and has outlined various psychological responses to stress in complex organizations (Diamond and Allcorn 1985). The later work suggests several distinct managerial styles that seem to characterize managers under stress. For example, one response growing from a fragmented self-image is trying to control events and feelings through rigid, perfectionist behavior.

Interorganizational Policy Implementation, Political Economy, and Public Choice

Several other approaches to public administration theory, most notably an increased attention to the development and operation of interorganizational networks, have been of great importance. Following the theoretical position outlined by Aldrich and Whetten (1981), several scholars have examined the patterns that emerge when several agencies interact regularly with respect to specific policy developments. O'Toole and Montjoy (1984) focus on situations in which two or more agencies are asked to work together toward implementation of a particular program, finding that with certain structures of interdependence, the chances of successful implementation are improved. Keller (1984) employs a political economy approach—considering both politics and economics—to the analysis of networks involved in groundwater management. The study of interorganizational networks is one among many uses of the political economy approach proposed by Goodsell (1984), who suggests such an approach be applied as well to administrative histories, business-government comparisons, program evaluation, and policy analysis. It should be noted, with respect to interorganizational networks, that Goodsell proposes a more subjectivist approach than normally assumed by interorganizational theorists. Finally, we should note that several theorists, such as Alexander (1985) and Springer (1985), have proposed revised approaches to policy analysis and implementation.

Relatively few articles appearing in the 1980s have extended the public-choice approach prominent during the 1970s, although both Berg (1984) and Butler (1983) have provided critiques of certain work in this area. An important and related body of work, however, growing out of the economic approach to bureaucratic behavior proposed by Niskanen (1971), has appeared. The broadest application of this work is Bendor and Moe's (1985) proposal for an adaptive model of bureaucratic politics, a model based on what they see as a circular flow of influence characteristic of representative government. "Citizens pressure legislators through elections, legislators influence the bureau through budgets and oversight, the bureau affects citizens through the costs and benefits generated by regulatory enforcement—and the circle is closed when citizens link their electoral support to legislators' positions on agency-relevant issues" (p. 757). (In the actual model, interest groups replace citizens as actors in the system.) The result is a model emphasizing decision making and adaptation under conditions of limited information, one that is claimed to conform certain aspects of pluralist and incrementalist thought.

More specific applications of this work, primarily centering on the relationship between bureaus and legislatures, have also been developed. Miller and Moe (1983) suggested limitations in the budget-maximizing capacities of bureaus, emphasizing instead the legislature's decision-making process; Eavey and Miller (1984) have similarly suggested that bureaucratic agenda control does not lead to monopolistic influence over legislatures but a process of bargaining that eventually determines budgetary outcomes. Bendor, Taylor, and Van Gaalen (1985) extend this work by analyzing the strategic behavior of bureaus and the ways in which legislatures detect and counter bureaucratic efforts to increase budgetary support.

Concluding Comments

The periodical literature in public administration theory over the past six years demonstrates the diversity and complexity of the theoretical enterprise. Certainly public administration theorists have continued to address many traditional concerns of public administrationists, such as the role of public organizations in the governance process. In terms of shifting areas of emphasis, the increased attention now being paid to the ethics of public service (along with related topics such as citizenship) is dramatic. Additionally, the more positive (not positivist) approach of epistemologists and the new interest of public administration theorists in psychological studies are noteworthy. Finally, interest in interorganizational networks and economic models of bureaucratic behavior has been strong. The picture of public administration theory that emerges from the periodical literature is one of a dynamic and changing field; whether that characterization should be read as a lack of coherence or as an indicator of the breadth and complexity of the field is considered later.

Approaches to Public Administration Theory:
The Books

In terms of the substantive areas covered by the representative articles reviewed here, public administration theory in the 1980s has much in common with the work of previous generations of scholars. In terms of approach, however, public administration theory today is strikingly different from that of earlier years. In order to illustrate the difference, the major books in public administration theory published in the 1980s are discussed in terms of a classification scheme similar to that used by Burrell and Morgan (1979) in their important work, *Sociological Paradigms in Organisational Analysis.*

Burrell and Morgan (1979) argue that "all theories of organisation are based upon a philosophy of science and a theory of society" (p. 1), an assumption that leads them to suggest two dimensions on which theories of organization can be arrayed. The first dimension focuses on assumptions about the nature of social science and includes questions related to ontology, epistemology, human nature, and methodology. They maintain that each of these questions can be answered in two ways and that the resulting sequence of responses can be grouped to form a single dimension, which they call "the subjective-objective dimension." This dimension ranges from German idealism, which emphasizes the subjective nature of human affairs, to the more familiar sociological positivism, which seeks to apply the natural science procedures to the collection and analysis of human behavior.

Their second dimension focuses on assumptions about the nature of society, essentially differences concerning the principal issue in the field of sociology—what they term the order-conflict debate. A slight reworking of this debate leads them to postulate a second dimension, ranging from "the sociology of regulation" to the "sociology of radical change." The former, again the more familiar, emphasizes the underlying order to cohesiveness of human systems, while the latter seeks explanations for radical changes in society.

The juxtaposition of these two dimensions provides a way of classifying various paradigms in sociological analysis, a classification Burrell and Morgan (1979) later applied to a review of works in organization theory, as illustrated in figure 3.1.

While one dimension of the Burrell and Morgan (1979) scheme is well suited to an analysis of public administration theory, the other needs substantial revision. Certainly the subjective-objective dimension would seem relevant to the study of public administration. Although those in public administration have rarely articulated the ontological issues as clearly as those in sociology (probably preferring to borrow these materials from others), public administration theorists certainly have debated epistemological and methodological issues in great detail over the years. Thus, we might join Burrell and Morgan in defining the subjective viewpoint as focusing on "an understanding of the way in which the individual creates, modifies, and interprets the world in which he or she finds himself" (p. 3). Similarly, we might define the objective dimension as searching for "universal laws which explain and govern the reality which is being observed" (p. 3). Moreover, those in public administration have differed with respect to questions about human nature, specifically raising questions concerning whether the individual acts voluntarily or deterministically. Some theorists have offered a concept of the individual as creating the social world, while others see the individual more as a

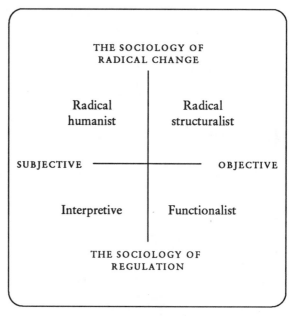

FIGURE 3.1

product of the environment. In public administration, these assumptions have led some to focus on the role of values in personal change and others to focus on structural devices capable of influencing individual behavior. In this way as well, there would seem to be some justification in employing the subjective-objective dimension in a review of public administration theory.

The other dimension, however, must be changed to fit the field of public administration. Burrell and Morgan (1979) developed this dimension by attempting to identify what they saw as the key issue in sociology. But, as we would expect, the key issue in sociology is not necessarily the key issue in public administration. For this reason, we should drop the regulation-change dimension, replacing it completely with the key issue in the study of public administration.

The most logical candidate for that dimension, I would suggest, is "politics and administration," not the old politics-administration dichotomy, but the continuing tension between political and organizational concerns. Theorists in the field of public administration have tended to focus their work either on political questions, such as responsiveness and accountability, or on organizational questions, such as efficiency and effectiveness. Indeed, while one might argue that political and organizational interests are not mutually exclusive, the particular tension that exists between the two defines the central problem of public administration today. Again, it is important to note that this dimension is not an adaptation of Burrell and Morgan but is one based on work in public administration.

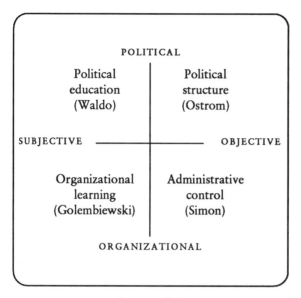

FIGURE 3.2

Using a subjective-objective dimension and a political-organizational dimension, one arrives at the classification scheme in figure 3.2. For the most part, theorists in public administration who have based their work on objectivist assumptions and have primarily focused on organizational issues have been most interested in administrative control mechanisms. (Simon's rational model of administration would belong in this group.) In contrast, theorists who have proceeded on subjectivist assumptions and have focused on organizational issues have been interested in organization development or organizational learning. (Golembiewski's work on organization development would be included here.)

Another group, employing subjectivist assumptions but more interested in political questions, shows an interest in political education. (Waldo's discussion of the administrative state would be illustrative.) A final group, using objectivist assumptions and interested in political questions, has tended to focus on structural approaches to politics. (Ostrom's work in public choice might be included here.) While it is clear that the categories are not rigid and many authors span several categories in their work, the classification scheme does seem helpful in illustrating the variety of approaches public administration theorists employ and in indicating shifting patterns of emphasis over time.

These changes are illustrated in figure 3.3. I argue that public administration theory during the 1950s and 1960s was dominated by studies that, for the most part, fell in the circle marked 1. In contrast, the majority of books in public administration theory in the 1980s fell in the area encompassed by circle 2. This would indicate a distinct and important shift in public administration theory, not a shift we should call paradigmatic, but certainly a shift in focus, a shift that is dramatic in its movement toward the subjective end of the horizontal dimension and one that is fairly marked on the other dimension as well. The following review of major publications by public administration theorists during the 1980s illustrates this shift.

Works in the Objectivist Tradition

In previous decades, the objectivist tradition in public administration theory boasted such major contributions as Herbert Simon's (1957) *Administrative Behavior,* Vincent Ostrom's (1973) *The Intellectual Crisis in Public Administration,* Allison's (1971) *Essence of Decision,* Downs's (1967) *Inside Bureaucracy,* Selznick's (1949) *TVA and the Grass Roots,* Kaufman's (1960) *The Forest Ranger,* Wamsley and Zald's (1973) *The Political Economy of Public Organizations,* and Wildavsky's (1970)

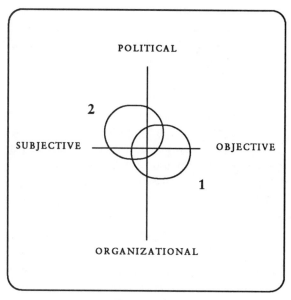

FIGURE 3.3

Speaking Truth to Power. The 1980s produced relatively few distinctive contributions within this tradition.

Of the objectivist treatments of public administration theory that appeared in the 1980s, more focused on political structure than administrative control. (Such a finding is perfectly understandable inasmuch as the objectivist tradition supports a generic approach to the study of complex organizations, a point later examined in more detail.) Objectivist studies of the political role of public organizations in the 1980s include three second editions of important general approaches to public administration theory.

Charles T. Goodsell's (1983) *The Case for Bureaucracy* is admittedly a polemic in defense of the public bureaucracy; nevertheless, it is a work with important theoretical implications as well. The book, written as a response to recent attacks on the public bureaucracy by political leaders and academics alike, paints a far more positive picture of the public bureaucracy than that portrayed in the popular media or in many scholarly publications. According to Goodsell, the public bureaucracy, despite its admitted flaws, performs many important functions and is far less oppressive to its members and clients than the conventional wisdom in public administration contends. (It should be noted, in addition, that Goodsell and several colleagues at Virginia Tech have been circulating a paper they refer to as the

"Blacksburg Manifesto" that seeks to develop a more positive role for the bureaucracy in a pluralist system of governance.)

Guy Peters's (1984) text, *The Politics of Bureaucracy,* is distinguished from other texts in the field by two important theoretical perspectives. First, Peters argues that public administration is "an integral part of the political process" (p. 5) and that the traditional dichotomy between politics and administration has eroded and will erode further as the public bureaucracy plays a greater role in the policy process. Second, Peters forcefully argues for a comparative approach to public administration, an approach almost completely absent from most similar treatments. Finally, Seidman and Gilmour (1986) have provided an updated version of Seidman's *Politics, Position, and Power,* emphasizing the expanded role of third parties in the delivery of domestic services and examining in some detail the increased role of the federal courts in regulatory activities.

Other recent works in the objectivist tradition have focused on the public bureaucracy and the policy process. Although a wide variety of policy studies have appeared in recent years (and are treated elsewhere in this volume), the theoretical underpinnings of the study are well represented in William Dunn's (1981) *Public Policy Analysis.* Dunn describes policy analysis as an applied social science oriented toward developing information in such a way that it will be of use in resolving policy problems. Especially important for our purposes is the general reliance of the field on the objectivist methods of the natural sciences; in Stuart Nagel's (1980) words, "Policy analysis is not something new methodologically" (p. 16). (In a related vein, the absence of major books dealing with issues of public choice during this period should be noted, although a variant of that tradition appears to be continuing in the periodical literature.)

While much of the recent literature in policy analysis has focused on the theoretical problem of agenda building and policy development (see John Kingdon's [1984] *Agendas, Alternatives, and Public Policies*), one recent focus in policy studies has been the implementation process. Mazmanian and Sabatier (1983), for example, consider in *Implementation and Public Policy* the variables that affect the achievement of legal objectives, such concerns as the tractability of the problem, the ability to structure implementation, and other variables affecting support for a particular program. Similarly, Ripley and Franklin (1982), writing in *Bureaucracy and Policy Implementation,* examine the implementation of public policy in a variety of areas, such as protective, competitive, or redistributive programs. Finally, some scholars have chosen to make specific recommendations for the conduct of agencies so as to ensure more effective implementation.

One noteworthy edited volume by Hall and Quinn (1983) examines the relationship between *Organization Theory and Public Policy* with most, although not all, of the contributions falling in the objectivist tradition emphasizing the importance of organizational environments in the policy process. Especially interesting is the section in their book that describes the increasing importance of interorganizational networks built around specific public programs. Under such conditions, the authors suggest, loosely linked networks, built around bargaining and negotiation rather than hierarchical structures, may become the primary unit of analysis for theorists in public administration.

Finally, several works that would fall roughly in the political/objectivist category focus on ethical behavior in the field of public administration. In a rather broad-ranging essay, Louis Gawthrop (1984b) examines *Public Sector Management, Systems, and Ethics*. In the light of the increasing environmental uncertainty and complexity faced by public organizations, Gawthrop suggests that "the preeminent purpose of public management . . . is the maintenance and enhancement of an ethical perspective that inspires the amplification of managerial innovation and creativity and, at the same time, facilitates the integration and convergence of social values" (p. 6). Although Gawthrop remains obscure with respect to his proposed redesign of public organizations, his approach seeks to combine general systems theory with a somewhat more personalized ethic than would ordinarily be associated with such an approach.

In two recent books, John Rohr (1978, 1986) has made important contributions to the understanding of the ethics of public service. In the earlier *Ethics for Bureaucrats,* Rohr argued that the fundamental ethical problem facing public administrators was that involved in exercising discretionary authority, a problem that could be overcome by clearly understanding the values of the regime, especially as amplified by the Supreme Court. More recently, in *To Run a Constitution,* Rohr performs a detailed objective analysis of the constitutional legitimacy of the administrative state as a prelude to a normative theory of public administration in a constitutional context. Rohr sees the agencies of government as subordinate to the three branches of government but simultaneously able to balance the various interests expressed there. Public administrators, key actors in this pluralistic balancing act, are to uphold the Constitution—to use "their discretionary power in order to maintain the constitutional balance of powers in support of individual rights" (p. 181).

Another book sharing much of the pluralistic orientation of Rohr's work is Douglas Yates's (1982) *Bureaucratic Democracy.* Yates is concerned with the tension that seems to exist between pluralist democracy and the desire for administrative efficiency in public organizations. Arguing that decisions are increasingly made in a bureaucratic democracy by administrative officials away from the public eye, Yates seeks mechanisms of political control over the bureaucracy that would provide public review of administrative activities while not impeding efforts to improve efficiency.

In addition to these works in the objectivist tradition, works seeking solutions to political issues through mechanisms for institutional control, the small number of books by public administration theorists that use the objectivist approach in trying to understand organizational behavior should be noted. The small number here is surprising, for objectivists have always supported the viewpoint that all organizations—whether public or private—are essentially the same and can best be approached through a generic study of management and organization. Thus, for the objectivist interested in organizational behavior, public administration theory does not exist; what is most important is the development of general studies of organizational behavior.

But those trained in public administration do contribute to such a generic study. Two such contributions are noteworthy, one for its contribution to the generic study of organizations and the other for its curious adaptation of traditional studies of organizational control to the implementation of public policy. The first, Herbert Kaufman's (1985) *Time, Chance, and Organizations*, presents a theory of the life cycle of organizations based on social and even biological theories of evolution. Kaufman uses this approach not only in analyzing the rise and fall of organizations but also in predicting increasing levels of organizational complexity. George Edwards (1980), in contrast, is concerned with *Implementing Public Policy* and, in that sense, is representative of a larger group interested in implementation processes. What is most striking about Edwards's work is his rediscovery of organizational mechanisms long familiar to students of public organization. Not surprisingly, the implementation of public policy requires successful administration.

The Subjectivist Treatment of Organizational Issues

Public administration theorists produced relatively few books before the 1970s that would be considered primarily subjective in orientation; Waldo's (1948) *Administrative State* and Golembiewski's (1967) *Men, Management, and Morality* were notable exceptions. Theorists in the 1980s generated an impressive list of publications written from this perspective. Although covering a wide variety of topics, these books share an interest in viewing political and organizational issues from the perspective of those involved. Their concern is with the meaning of their experience rather than with the behavioral data of the natural sciences. In a sense, this work may represent an emerging orthodoxy in public administration theory, one consistent with trends in many social sciences today, but perhaps more advanced in public administration than in others.

Many of these works by scholars in public administration deal with organizational issues somewhat independent of political concerns and apply to organizations beyond those in the public sector. For example, several are explicitly critical of the effects of an organizational society—not only public organizations—on human growth and development. Denhardt (1981a) argues that modern life is carried out *In the Shadow of Organization*, that is, bounded by a new and encompassing ethic of organization that extends to many different aspects of social life. Through developments in phenomenology, critical theory, and depth psychology, he suggests a reordering of priorities that would give primacy to the growth of the individual rather than the productivity of the organization. Many of Denhardt's themes are illustrated in an edited work by Fischer and Sirianni (1984), *Critical Studies in Organization and Bureaucracy.*

Ralph Hummel (1982) pursues a similar line of argument in *The Bureaucratic Experience,* suggesting that "bureaucracy is a new society and a new culture. Bureaucratic functionaries represent a new personality type and speak a new language. Bureaucracy is a new way of exercising power" (p. vii). By examining the various ways different people—members, clients, and so on—interact with bureaucracy, Hummel hoped not only to facilitate our adaptation to the new bureaucratic culture but, more important, to help us transcend that culture.

In a similar but more specific fashion, Kathy Ferguson (1984; see also 1983) builds *The Feminist Case Against Bureaucracy,* arguing that bureaucratic subordination parallels the subordination of women and that lessons learned from the experience of efforts at women's liberation might aid in reconstructing patterns of domination in complex organizations. For example, the efforts of feminine discourse to move beyond the submerged discourse of women's experience might suggest ways to open to question the more public but more constrained system of bureaucratic discourse in our society.

In *The New Science of Organizations,* Alberto Guerreiro Ramos (1981) argues that the market-centered society has engendered a particular kind of organization, what he calls the "economizing organization." This type of organization, based on the idea of instrumental rationality (the coordination of means to given ends), has been insensitive to both psychological and ecological concerns. In contrast, Ramos proposes a new science of organizations that would delimit the influence of economizing organizations and lead to new organizational designs. The result would be a new multicentric or reticular society in which different forms of organization would be applied to different purposes, always with a view toward maintaining environmental stability.

Two other books go directly to the question whether hierarchically structured organizations can be fundamentally reordered. Fredrick Thayer (1981) argues for *An End to Hierarchy and Competition,* in which the alienating effects of hierarchy would be reduced as the artificial distinctions that cause some to be designated leaders and others followers were eliminated. Similarly, Scott and Hart (1979) describe the ills of *Organizational America,* concluding with a plea for organizational reform, one in which the existing organizational imperative would be challenged primarily by professionals operating out of an interest in individualism.

In addition to these efforts in the critique of organizations, other books provide special analyses of the way in which organizational operations might be improved. Harmon and Thayer (1986), for example, provide a textbook review of many approaches to *Organization Theory for Public Administration,* concluding that organizational action is both a behavioral and a moral problem. More specifically, Robert T. Golembiewski (1985) continues his analysis of theories of organization development in a new book, *Humanizing Public Organizations*. Although much of this work is familiar to students of organization development, its theoretical importance to the field of public administration lies in its analysis of the relationship between bureaucracy and democracy, a moral and political question central to Golembiewski's (1967b) *Men, Management, and Morality*. Criticizing formulations of Democracy and Administration or Democracy vs. Administration, Golembiewski argues for Democracy within and through Administration. In contrast to others who have made the same point in abstract terms, Golembiewski attempts to specify exactly how such an arrangement might be brought about.

Another work of substantial importance to the field is Michael Lipsky's (1980) *Street-Level Bureaucracy*. Lipsky first brought the term "street-level bureaucrat" to the attention of the field by pointing out that public policy is determined not merely by legislators and managers at high levels of government but by the police officer, the nurse, and the welfare worker (among others), who engage in the direct delivery of services. Lipsky writes that "the decisions of street-level bureaucrats, the routines they establish, and the devices they invent to cope with uncertainties and work pressures, effectively become the public policies they carry out" (p. xii). Finding that systemic constraints on the professional practices of street-level bureaucrats result in confusion and conflicting demands, Lipsky offers several important suggestions for reform, suggestions addressed to the concerns of street-level bureaucrats but not without relevance to those at all levels of public agencies.

Works by other public administration theorists interested in organizational topics have ranged widely. Shan Martin (1983), for example, proposes *Managing without Managers,* that is, creating autonomous work groups in lieu of today's over-supervised structures. Howell Baum (1983b, 1987), in contrast, in both *Planners and Public Expectations* and *The Invisible Bureaucracy* has explored the psychodynamics of organizational involvement, arguing that both conscious and unconscious intentions and motives affect the individual's understanding of, and activity in, complex organizations.

Subjectivist Treatments of Political Issues Facing Public Organizations

A number of interesting treatments of political issues facing the field of public administration have been developed from the subjectivist stance. In each case, the role of public administrators in the governance process is the central issue, with matters of accountability and responsibility considered essential. And, in each case, the values and intentions of the individual administrator are seen as the basis for understanding and altering existing patterns of administrative action. Among these works, several derive from the New Public Administration of the early 1970s and some related concerns for ethics and citizenship, several are noteworthy for their applications of alternative epistemological stances, and several provide broad reinterpretations of the literature of public administration from a value-critical perspective.

The movement generally referred to as the New Public Administration is primarily associated with theoretical developments in public administration in the late 1960s and early 1970s. Nevertheless, several books published during the 1980s are closely tied to that movement. Without question, George Fredrickson's (1980) *New Public Administration* should be considered one of these. Indeed, Frederickson's book, based on a series of lectures at the University of Alabama, draws heavily from previously published materials dating back to the original Minnowbrook conference proceedings (Marini 1971).

A related contribution is Carl Bellone's (1980) edited volume of essays, *Organization Theory and the New Public Administration.* Of the essays, those by Frederick Thayer, Alberto Guerreiro-Ramos, and Michael Harmon are of special interest, as is the introduction by Luther Gulick, who describes the New Public Administration as engaging in a missionary zeal, "an inspired but sophisticated declaration of faith in a new humanity in a new society" (p. vii). The spirit of the New Public Administration was certainly contagious; there are more questions about its substance.

Although not explicitly associated with the New Public Administration, a recent book sharing many of the same concerns for ethics and citizenship is Terry Cooper's (1982) *The Responsible Administrator.* Cooper focuses on the question of administrative responsibility, as executed within the structure of public organizations. Noting the need to balance objective methods of achieving responsibility (Rohr) with those more subjective in nature, Cooper ultimately seeks an integration of the two through a matrix of responsible conduct drawing from important themes in the New Public Administration. "Only a deeply internalized set of moral qualities, mental attitudes, and regime values can maintain congruence with the organization's goals and . . . consistency with the obligations of citizenship in a democracy" (pp. 130–31).

Another set of works is distinctive in its use of alternative epistemologies to approach questions of political responsibility. Just as Hummel (1982) used phenomenology and Denhardt (1981a, 1981b) employed critical theory in examining the limits of modern organizational life, others have pursued similar viewpoints in assessing more political questions. In *Action Theory for Public Administration,* for example, Michael Harmon (1981) explores the possible implications of phenomenology for work in public organizations. As a phenomenologist, Harmon sees the individual as an intentional being, suggesting that individual action is both normatively based and socially executed. This position leads to a conceptualization of the "proactive administrator," one who institutionalizes and facilitates consensual decision making both within the organization and with the clientele served. A similar viewpoint characterizes a recent and theoretically distinctive text by Jong Jun (1986), *Public Administration: Design and Problem-Solving*. Jun develops an image of the field of public administration marked by a proactive view of change, a marked sensitivity to public values, and the skill and creativity for administrators to operate effectively within a turbulent environment.

Related applications of phenomenology to policy studies include Frank Fischer's (1980) *Politics, Values, and Public Policy* and David Schuman's (1982) *Policy Analysis, Education, and Everyday Life*. Fischer focuses on methodological problems in policy analysis, suggesting a way of bringing together factual and valuative elements of evaluation. Schuman enjoys a similar perspective in an evaluation of the effect of education on the everyday life of individuals in our society. In this view, the evaluation of public policy must ultimately be based on an understanding of the meaning of the everyday lives of individuals and the interaction of their intentions with the social and political forces that surround them.

Finally, two books provide critical interpretations of the literature of public administration. Robert Denhardt (1984), in *Theories of Public Organization*, reviews the most prominent approaches to the field of public administration, discovering great consistency in the literature of public administration, especially in its dependence on the notion of instrumental rationality and its view of democratic accountability implicitly based in the old politics-administration dichotomy. Denhardt outlines a broader view of the work of public organizations, seeking to integrate the requirements of efficiency and effectiveness with an enhanced sense of democratic responsibility. In such a view, the administrator assumes an active but responsive role in discovering and articulating the public interest.

Similarly, in *The Enterprise of Public Administration*, Dwight Waldo (1980) summarizes several decades of important theoretical work in public administration, considering such themes as education for the public service, politics and administration, bureaucracy and democracy, and public administration and ethics. In addition to its careful synthesis of theoretical work on these important topics, Waldo's enterprise is important for the set of issues it outlines as emerging and prospective (chap. 11). From a subjective standpoint, one recognizes implicitly in this work an admonition that the values and intentions of theorists in public administration will play an important role in our shaping of the field over the coming years.

Concluding Remarks on Shifts in Public Administration Theory

The categories defined by our classification scheme should not be taken as distinct or unchanging. Many theorists move in and out of various categories, especially along the political-organizational dimension. For example, both the Golembiewski and Lipsky books discussed earlier focus primarily on organizational operations, yet they have important implications for the political question of how public policy is to be determined. Some care must be exercised in using the categories; however, the classification scheme enables us to see rather dramatically the extent of the shift in public administration theory from objectivist to subjectivist thought, and perhaps less distinctly the increasing interest in political questions as opposed to organizational questions. Clearly, material that was very much out of the mainstream only a decade ago is now very much in the mainstream. In the following section, the implications of this finding is considered, including the question whether work that is integrative of material from all categories is necessary in order to build a more coherent and integrated theory of public organizations.

Framing an Agenda for the Future

Given recent developments in public administration theory, where might we expect the field to move in the future? What are the issues that will frame the agenda for public administration for the next several years? Several possibilities present themselves.

The first question is whether there can be a coherent and integrated theory of public organizations, a question that has been most often approached through commentary on the potential for our achieving disciplinary status. I argue that a discipline, in both the academic sense and the practical sense, is formed by the possibility of developing theoretical coherence within a given field. A discipline requires rigor and perspective—although not necessarily a paradigm. What hopes do we have of such an achievement?

At various points in our history, other disciplines have been eager to embrace public administration under their own theoretical banner. Many early writers in the field and some still today argue that public administration is made distinctive by its relationship to the governmental process. In contrast to this position, others have argued that the behavior of individuals within organizations and the behavior of organizations themselves is much the same regardless of the kind of organization being studied.

Somewhere between these positions is the view that I suspect is most popular among theorists today—that public administration is best viewed as a profession drawing from many different theoretical perspectives. Since no single discipline can currently provide the range of knowledge needed by administrators in the public sector, it seems reasonable to bring coherence to programs through their professional orientation.

Unfortunately, this view of public administration as a profession, perhaps even more than the other views presented here, precludes the possibility that we shall achieve a distinctive theoretical orientation or that we shall fully satisfy the needs of practitioners in the field. While information from other disciplines may indeed be of use from time to time, if there is something distinctive about public organizations, none of these disciplines will directly capture that difference. By taking the position that public administration must merely draw from other disciplines, we are in danger of enhancing the periphery of work in public organizations while neglecting the core.

If we take the position that political science fails to comprehend the full range of concerns of those in public organizations by failing to give full consideration to organizational and managerial concerns; if we take the position that organizational analysis is also limited through its failure to comprehend adequately the moral and political context of work in public organizations; and if we take the position that a view of public administration as a professional field of study fails because it must always borrow from other disciplines and never address our own concerns directly—is there any hope of developing a discipline around the concerns of those in public organizations? I think the answer is yes. But I think that answer must wait until we address a second question, one related to what is acceptable, or even proper, in terms of academic research.

For those in the field of public administration, the answer to this question has been intimately bound up with the question of the proper relationship between theory and practice, but more profoundly it has to do with the validity of various approaches to knowledge acquisition. In my view, the shift toward a more subjectivist position in public administration theory holds forth considerable promise for establishing a better connection between theory and practice, an issue I have addressed elsewhere (Denhardt 1984). This is not merely to say, however, that researchers in the field of public administration should always address their work primarily to practitioners. Although I hesitate to use the terms *pure* and *applied* to refer to two different modes of research practice, I do feel that public administration theorists, as well as other researchers in the field, have a dual obligation: to enhance the state of knowledge of public organizations generally and to transmit our understanding of the world of public organizations to those active in that world.

But however we resolve the theory-practice issue, that issue is related to more general controversies surrounding the appropriate basis for knowledge acquisition in our field and in the social sciences generally. Typically, this argument has been waged in terms of contending epistemological positions, with positivism, phenomenology, and critical theory being most prominent. As we have seen, there have been well-defined shifts in emphasis over the past decades. In my view, however, the relationship between various modes of knowledge acquisition and various patterns of human action has not yet been fully explored, nor have we sought ways of integrating the various approaches now available to us.

In addition to questions we might raise about the proper modes of knowledge acquisition, we must also consider more carefully some fairly basic substantive issues in our field. Students of public administration recall that the most important issue in the early days of public administration was the question of how to run a constitution, that is, how to manage public agencies honestly and efficiently (and, one hopes, in a way consistent with the public interest). The question was perfectly appropriate to that time, a time of corruption and inefficiency, but it may no longer hold such centrality in the field of public administration. Certainly we complain about the occasional public scandals and the apparent inefficiency of such areas as military procurement practices. Those are important concerns, but they may not be central. Instead, the central issues of public organization today are probably better expressed in terms of the quality of the public service and the responsiveness of the public bureaucracy in a democratic society.

In my view, public administration in the past has been limited by two important positions deeply rooted in the history of the discipline: (1) a view of moral and political accountability conceived in hierarchical terms, in terms of responsiveness of agencies to elected officials; and (2) a transposition of business values or at least managerial values into the conduct of public agencies.

While such views may have been responsive to the concerns of the nineteenth century, they may not be appropriate to the concerns of the late twentieth century and beyond. Now, with the massive growth of public bureaucracy and the inevitable discretion that must be given administrative officials, we must recognize that those in public organizations have a direct impact on the lives of individuals, not only as they execute orders handed down from the legislature, but also as they act on their own in pursuit of public purposes. Whether we like it or not, the proper moral and political basis for public organizations can no longer be encapsulated in the hierarchical relationship between agencies and legislatures.

We should also call into question the wholesale adoption by public agencies of the values of private organizations. Indeed, I would propose that just the opposite should occur. Certainly, major aspects of public policy are being decided or seriously affected by so-called private agencies. Many of these private organizations far exceed in their size and complexity governments in other countries and previous governments in this country. Modern organizations of all kinds have an enormous impact on the personal lives of individuals in society, a trend that suggests that all organizations in a democratic society should be evaluated by the degree of their publicness, the degree to which they express values defined publicly rather than privately. In such an effort, public administration theories, especially theories of democratic administration, might come to be models for organization theory in general.

All of this leads toward a new approach to defining the field of public administration, an approach that has been outlined elsewhere (Denhardt 1984), that we are students not merely of public administration but students of public organizations, that our concern is with managing change in pursuit of publicly defined societal values. Around such a definition, one that focuses on action rather than agencies, I think we have a chance of building a new theory of public organizations, one that recognizes the diversity of our field but also acknowledges our common purposes. There is something distinctive about administrative action in public organizations, and that distinctiveness should provide the basis for a coherent and integrated theory of public organizations.

One final question has to do with the roles and responsibilities of theorists themselves. In my view, the connection between thought and action, theory and practice, demands that public administration theorists share a moral obligation with practitioners in public organizations. This responsibility, the responsibility of the theorist, is especially well illustrated if we consider developing what might be called a normative theory of practice. To the extent that theorists participate in the normative design of institutions and processes, they share a responsibility for outcomes as well. A final challenge to theorists in the field of public administration is to understand the moral implications of their own work, for this defines the vocation and obligation of the theorist.

References

Adams, Bruce. 1984. "The Frustrations of Government Service." *Public Administration* 44:5–14.

Agor, Weston H. 1985. "Managing Brain Skills to Increase Productivity." *Public Administration Review* 45:864–69.

Aldrich, Howard, and David A. Whetten. 1981. "Organization-Sets, Action-Sets, and Networks: Making the Most of Simplicity." In *Handbook of Organizational Design,* vol. 1, edited by P.C. Nystrom and W.H. Starbuck. Oxford: Oxford University Press.

Alexander, Ernest R. 1985. "From Idea to Action: Notes for a Contingency Theory of the Policy Implementation Process." *Administration and Society* 16:403–27.

Allsion, Graham T. 1971. *Essence of Decision: Explaining the Cuban Missile Crisis.* Boston: Little, Brown.

Argyris, Chris. 1980. "Making the Undiscussable and Its Undiscussability Discussable." *Public Administration Review* 40:205–14.

Baum, Howell S. 1982. "The Advisor as Invited Intruder." *Public Administration Review* 42:546–52.

Baum, Howell S. 1983a. "Autonomy, Shame, and Doubt: Power in the Bureaucratic Lives of Planners." *Administration and Society* 15:147–84.

Baum, Howell S. 1983b. *Planners and Public Expectations.* Cambridge, Mass.: Schenkman.

Baum, Howell S. 1987. *The Invisible Bureaucracy: Problem Solving in Bureaucratic Organizations.* New York: Oxford University Press.

Bell, Robert, 1985. "Professional Values and Organizational Decision Making." *Administration and Society* 17:21–61.

Bellone, Carl, ed. 1980. *Organization Theory and the New Public Administration.* Boston: Allyn and Bacon.

Bendor, Jonathan, and Terry Moe. 1985. "An Adaptive Model of Bureaucratic Politics." *American Political Science Review* 79:755–74.

Bendor, Jonathan, Serge Taylor, and Roland Van Gaalen. 1985. "Bureaucratic Expertise Versus Legislative Authority: A Model of Deception and Monitoring in Budgeting." *American Political Science Review* 79:1041–60.

Berg, Bruce. 1984. "Public Choice, Pluralism, and Scarcity: Implications for Bureaucratic Behavior." *Administration and Society* 161:71–83.

Bozeman, Barry. 1981. "Organization Design in the Public Bureaucracy." *American Review of Public Administration* 15:107–18.

Bozeman, Barry. 1983. "Strategic Management and Productivity: A 'Firehouse Theory.'" *State Government* 56:2–7.

Brady, F. Neil. 1981. "Ethical Theory for the Public Administrator: The Management of Competing Interests." *American Review of Public Administration* 15:119–26.

Brady, F. Neil. 1983. "Feeling and Understanding: A Moral Psychology for Public Servants." *Public Administration Quarterly* 7:220–40.

Burrell, Gibson, and Gareth Morgan. 1979. *Sociological Paradigms and Organisational Analysis.* London: Heinemann.

Butler, Richard. 1983. "A Transactional Approach to Organizing Efficiency: Perspectives from Markets, Hierarchies, and Collectives." *Administration and Society* 15:323–62.

Chandler, Ralph Clark. 1983. "The Problem of Moral Reasoning in American Public Administration: The Case for a Code of Ethics." *Public Administration Review* 43:32–40.

Cleveland, Harlan. 1985. "The Twilight of Hierarchy: Speculations on the Global Information Society." *Public Administration Review* 45:185–95.

Cohen, Michael. 1984. "Conflict and Complexity: Goal Diversity and Organization Search Effectiveness." *American Political Science Review* 78:435–51.

Cooper, Terry L. 1982. *The Responsible Administrator: An Approach to Ethics for the Administrative Role.* New York: Kennikat Press.

Cooper, Terry L. 1984. "Citizenship and Professionalism in Public Administration." *Public Administration Review* 44:143–49.

Denhardt, Robert B. 1981a. *In the Shadow of Organization.* Lawrence, Kan.: University Press of Kansas.

Denhardt, Robert B. 1981b. "Toward a Critical Theory of Public Organization." *Public Administration Review* 41:628–35.

Denhardt, Robert B. 1984. "Theories of Public Organization." Monterey, Calif.: Brooks/Cole.

Denhardt, Robert B. 1985. "Strategic Planning in State and Local Government." *State and Local Government Review* 17:174–79.

Diamond, Michael A. 1984. "Bureaucracy as Externalized Self-System: A View from the Psychological Interior." *Administration and Society* 16:195–214.

Diamond, Michael A., and Seth Allcorn. 1985. "Psychological Responses to Stress in Complex Organizations." *Administration and Society* 17:217–39.

Downs, Anthony. 1967. *Inside Bureaucracy.* Boston: Little, Brown.

Drucker, Peter F. 1980. "The Deadly Sins in Public Administration." *Public Administration Review* 40:103–6.

Dunn, William N. 1981. *Public Policy Analysis.* Englewood Cliffs, N.J.: Prentice-Hall.

Eavey, Cheryl L. and Gary J. Miller. 1984. "Bureaucratic Agenda Control: Imposition or Bargaining?" *American Political Science Review* 78:719–33.

Edwards, George C. 1980. *Implementing Public Policy.* Washington, D.C.: CQ Press.

Ferguson, Kathy E. 1983. "Bureaucracy and Public Life: The Feminization of the Polity." *Administration and Society* 15:295–322.

Ferguson, Kathy E. 1984. *The Feminist Case Against Bureaucracy.* Philadelphia: Temple University Press.

Fischer, Frank. 1980. *Politics, Values, and Public Policy: The Problem of Methodology.* Denver: Westview Press.

Fischer, Frank. 1983. "Ethical Discourse in Public Administration." *Administration and Society* 15:5–43.

Fischer, Frank, and Carmen Sirianni. 1984. *Critical Studies in Organization and Bureaucracy.* Philadelphia: Temple University Press.

Forester, John. 1981. "Questioning and Organizing Attention: Toward a Critical Theory of Planning and Administrative Practice." *Administration and Society* 13:161–207.

Forester, John. 1983. "Critical Theory and Organizational Analysis." In *Beyond Method,* edited by G. Morgan. Beverly Hills: Sage.

Forester, John. 1984. "Bounded Rationality and the Politics of Muddling Through." *Public Administration Review* 44:23–32.

Foster, Gregory D. 1981. "Law, Morality, and the Public Servant." *Public Administration Review* 41:29–34.

Frederickson, H. George. 1980. *New Public Administration.* University, Ala.: University of Alabama Press.

Frederickson, H. George. 1982. "The Recovery of Civism in Public Administration." *Public Administration Review* 42:501–8.

Frederickson, H. George, and David K. Hart. 1985. "New Public Service and the Patriotism of Benevolence." *Public Administration Review* 45:547–53.

Gaertner, Gregory H., Karen N. Gaertner, and Irene Devine. 1983. "Federal Agencies in the Context of Transition: A Contrast between Democratic and Organizational Theories." *Public Administration Review* 43:421–32.

Gawthrop, Louis C. 1984a. "Civis, Civitas, and Civilitas: A New Focus for the Year 2000." *Public Administration Review* 44:101–7.

Gawthrop, Louis C. 1984b. *Public Sector Management, Systems, and Ethics.* Bloomington: Indiana University Press.

Golembiewski, Robert T. 1967. *Men, Management, and Morality.* New York: McGraw-Hill.

Golembiewski, Robert T. 1985. *Humanizing Public Organizations.* Mt. Airy, Md.: Lomond Publications.

Goodin, Robert E., and Peter Wilenski. 1984. "Beyond Efficiency: The Logical Underpinnings of Administrative Principles." *Public Administration Review* 44:512–18.

Goodnow, Frank. 1900. *Policy and Administration.* New York: Macmillan.

Goodsell, Charles T. 1983. *The Case for Bureaucracy: A Public Administration Polemic.* Chatham, N. J.: Chatham House.

Goodsell, Charles T. 1984. "Political Economy as a Research Focus." *Public Administration Quarterly* 8:288–301.

Grosenick, Leigh E. 1984. "Research in Democratic Governance." *Public Administration Quarterly* 8:266–87.

Hall, Richard H., and Robert E. Quinn. 1983. *Organizational Theory and Public Policy.* Beverly Hills: Sage.

Harmon, Michael M. 1981. *Action Theory for Public Administration.* New York: Longman.

Harmon, Michael M., and Richard T. Mayer. 1986. *Organization Theory for Public Administration.* Boston: Little, Brown.

Hart, David K. 1984. "The Virtuous Citizen, the Honorable Bureaucrat, and Public Administration." *Public Administration Review* 44:111–20.

Hart, David K., and William G. Scott. 1982. "The Philosophy of American Management." *Southern Review of Public Administration* 6:240–52.

Hummel, Ralph P. 1982. *The Bureaucratic Experience.* 2d ed. New York: St. Martin's Press.

Jun, Jong S. 1986. *Public Administration: Design and Problem Solving.* New York: Macmillan.

Jung, Hwa Yol. 1982. "Phenomenology as a Critique of Public Affairs Education." *Southern Review of Public Administration* 6:175–87.

Kaufman, Herbert. 1960. *The Forest Ranger.* Baltimore, Md.: Johns Hopkins University Press.

Kaufman, Herbert. 1981. "Fear of Bureaucracy: A Raging Pandemic." *Public Administration Review* 41:1–10.

Kaufman, Herbert. 1985. *Time, Chance, and Organizations.* Chatham, N.J.: Chatham House.

Keller, Lawrence F. 1984. "The Political Economy of Public Management: An Interorganizational Network Perspective." *Administration and Society* 15:455–74.

Killingsworth, James R. 1982. "War Stories, Principles, and Public Administration." *Southern Review of Public Administration* 6:227–39.

Killingsworth, James R. 1984. "Idle Talk and Modern Administration." *Administration and Society* 16:346–84.

Kingdon, John W. 1984. *Agendas, Alternatives, and Public Policies.* Boston: Little, Brown.

Koritansky, John C. 1982. "Prudence and the Practice of Government." *Southern Review of Public Administration* 6:111–22.

Korten, David C. 1984. "Strategic Organization for People-Centered Development." *Public Administration Review* 44:341–53.

Lerner, Allan W., and John Wanat. 1983. "Fuzziness and Bureaucracy." *Public Administration Review* 43:500–509.

Lilla, Mark T. 1981. "Ethos, Ethics, and Public Services." *Public Interest* 63:3–17.

Lipsky, Michael. 1980. *Street-Level Bureaucracy.* New York: Russell Sage.

Lovrich, Nicholas P., Jr. 1985. "Contending Paradigms in Public Administration: A Sign of Crisis or Intellectual Vitality?" *Administration and Society* 17:307–30.

Lynn, Laurence E., Jr. 1981. *Managing the Public's Business.* New York: Basic Books.

McEachern, A.W., and Jawad Al-Arayed. 1984. "Discerning the Public Interest." *Administration and Society* 15:439–54.

McGregor, Eugene B., Jr. 1981. "Administration's Many Instruments: Mining, Refining, and Applying Charles Lindblom's Politics and Markets." *Administration and Society* 13:347–75.

McGregor, Eugene B., Jr. 1984. "The Great Paradox of Democratic Citizenship and Public Personnel Administration." *Public Administration Review* 44:126–32.

McSwain, Cynthia J. 1985. "Administrators and Citizenship: The Liberalist Legacy of the Constitution." *Administration and Society* 17:131–49.

Marini, Frank, ed. 1971. *Toward a New Public Administration.* San Francisco: Chandler.

Martin, Shan. 1983. *Managing without Managers: Alternative Work Arrangements in Public Organizations.* Beverly Hills: Sage.

Mayer, Richard T., and Michael M. Harmon. 1982. "Teaching Moral Education in Public Administration." *Southern Review of Public Administration* 6:217–26.

Mazmanian, Daniel A., and Paul A. Sabatier. 1983. *Implementation and Public Policy.* Glenview, Ill.: Scott, Foresman.

Miller, Gary, and Terry M. Moe. 1983. "Bureaucrats, Legislators, and the Size of Government." *American Political Science Review* 77:297–322.

Morgan, Gareth. 1983. *Beyond Method.* Beverly Hills: Sage.

Morgan, Gareth. 1984. "Opportunities Arising from Paradigm Diversity." *Administration and Society* 16:306–28.

Nagel, Stuart, ed. 1980. *Improving Policy Analysis.* Beverly Hills: Sage.

Niskanen, William A., Jr. 1971. *Bureaucracy and Representative Government.* Chicago: Aldine-Atherton.

Ostrom, Vincent. 1973. *The Intellectual Crisis in American Public Administration.* University, Ala.: University of Alabama Press.

Ostrom, Vincent. 1980. "Artisanship and Artifact." *Public Administration Review* 40: 309–17.

O'Toole, Laurence J., Jr. 1984. "American Public Administration and the Idea of Reform." *Administration and Society* 16:141–66.

O'Toole, Laurence J., Jr., and Robert S. Montjoy. 1984. "Interorganizational Policy Implementation: A Theoretical Perspective." *Public Administration Review* 44: 491–504.

Peters, B. Guy. 1984. *The Politics of Bureaucracy.* 2d ed. New York: Longman.

Ramos, Alberto Guerreiro. 1981. *The New Science of Organizations: A Reconceptualization of the Wealth of Nations.* Toronto: University of Toronto Press.

Riggs, Fred W. 1980. "The Ecology and Context of Public Administration: A Comparative Perspective." *Public Administration Review* 40:107–15.

Ripley, Randall B., and Grace A. Franklin. 1982. *Bureaucracy and Policy Implementation.* Ontario: Dorsey Press.

Rohr, John A. 1978. *Ethics for Bureaucrats: An Essay on Law and Values.* New York: Marcel Dekker.

Rohr, John A. 1984. "Civil Servants and Second Class Citizens." *Public Administration Review* 44:135–40.

Rohr, John A. 1985. "Professionalism, Legitimacy, and the Constitution." *Public Administration Quarterly* 8:401–18.

Rohr, John A. 1986. *To Run a Constitution.* Lawrence, Kan.: University Press of Kansas.

Romzek, Barbara S. 1985. "Work and Nonwork Psychological Involvements: The Search for Linkage." *Administration and Society* 17:257–81.

Romzek, Barbara S., and J. Stephen Hendricks. 1982. "Organization Involvement and Representative Bureaucracy: Can We Have It Both Ways?" *American Political Science Review* 76:75–82.

Rosenbloom, David H. 1983. "Public Administrative Theory and the Separation of Powers." *Public Administration Review* 43:219–27.

Saltzstein, Grace Hall. 1985. "Conceptualizing Bureaucratic Responsiveness." *Administration and Society* 17:283–306.

Savas, E.S. 1982. *Privatizing the Public Sector.* Chatham, N.J.: Chatham House.

Scholl, Richard W. 1981. "An Analysis of Macro Models of Organizations: The Goal and Political Models." *Administration and Society* 13:271–98.

Schorr, Philip. 1983. "Learning Ethics: The Search for an Ideal Model." *Public Administration Quarterly* 7:323–45.

Schuman, David. 1982. *Policy Analysis, Education, and Everyday Life: An Empirical Reevaluation of Higher Education in America.* Lexington, Mass.: Heath.

Scott, William G. 1982. "Barnard on the Nature of Elitist Responsibility." *Public Administration Review* 42:197–202.

Scott, William G., and David K. Hart. 1979. *Organizational America*. Boston: Houghton Mifflin.

Sederberg, Peter C. 1984. "Organization and Explanation: New Metaphors for Old Problems." *Administration and Society* 16:167–94.

Seidman, Harold, and Robert Gilmour. 1986. *Politics, Position, and Power: From the Positive to the Regulatory State*. 4th ed. New York: Oxford University Press.

Selznick, Philip. 1949. *TVA and the Grass Roots*. New York: Harper & Row.

Simon, Herbert A. 1957. *Administrative Behavior*. New York: Macmillan.

Springer, J. Fred. 1985. "Policy Analysis and Organizational Decisions: Toward a Conceptual Revision." *Administration and Society* 6:475–509.

Stewart, Debra W. 1985. "Ethics and the Profession of Public Administration: The Moral Responsibility of Individuals in Public Sector Organizations." *Public Administration Quarterly* 8:487–95.

Thayer, Frederick C. 1980. "Organization Theory as Epistemology." In *Organization Theory and the New Public Administration,* edited by Carl Bellone. Boston: Allyn and Bacon.

Thayer, Frederick C. 1981. *An End to Hierarchy and Competition: Administration in the Post-Affluent World*. 2d ed. New York: Franklin Watts.

Thompson, Dennis F. 1980. "Moral Responsibility of Public Officials: The Problem of Many Hands." *American Political Science Review* 74:905–16.

Thompson, Dennis F. 1983. "Bureaucracy and Democracy." In *Democratic Theory and Practice,* edited by G. Duncan. Cambridge: Cambridge University Press.

Thompson, Dennis F. 1985. "The Possibility of Administrative Ethics." *Public Administration Review* 45:555–62.

Waldo, Dwight. 1948. *The Administrative State*. New York: Ronald Press.

Waldo, Dwight. 1971. *Public Administration in a Time of Turbulence*. Scranton, Pa.: Chandler.

Waldo, Dwight. 1980. *The Enterprise of Public Administration*. Novato, Calif.: Chandler and Sharp.

Wamsley, Gary, and Mayer Zald. 1973. *The Political Economy of Public Organizations*. Lexington, Mass.: Lexington Books.

White, Jay D. 1982. "Public Policy Analysis: Reason, Method, and Praxis." Doctoral dissertation, George Washington University.

White, Orion F., Jr. 1981. "Communication-Induced Distortion in Scholarly Research—The Case of Action Theory in American Public Administration." *International Journal of Public Administration* 5:119–50.

White, Orion F., Jr. 1983. "Improving the Prospects for Heterodoxy in Organization Theory: A Review of Sociological Paradigms and Organizational Analysis." *Administration and Society* 15:257–71.

Wholey, Joseph S., Mark A. Abramson, and Christopher Bellavita. 1986. *Performance and Credibility: Developing Excellence in Public and Nonprofit Organizations*. Lexington, Mass.: Heath.

Wildavsky, Aaron. 1979. *Speaking Truth to Power: The Art and Craft of Policy Analysis*. Boston: Little, Brown.

Wildavsky, Aaron, ed. 1984. *The Politics of the Budgetary Process*. 4th ed. Boston: Little, Brown.

Willbern, York. 1984. "Types and Levels of Public Morality." *Public Administration Review* 44:102–9.

Wilson, Woodrow. 1887. "Study of Administration." *Political Science Quarterly* 2:197–222.

Wriston, Michael J. 1980. "In Defense of Bureaucracy." *Public Administration Review* 40:179–83.

Yarwood, Dean L. 1986. "The Ethical World of Organizational Professionals and Scientists." *Public Administration Quarterly* 8:461–86.

Yates, Douglas. 1982. *Bureaucratic Democracy*. Cambridge, Mass.: Harvard University Press.

4

A Theory of Public Administration Means in Our Time a Theory of Politics Also

Dwight Waldo

The title of this chapter, appropriate to the occasion, is the final sentence of an essay by John Gaus. The essay appeared in *Public Administration Review* in 1950 and was a survey of and reflection on "Trends in the Theory of Public Administration." Now, four decades later, many of the references are dated. But Gaus's description of the problem and his statement of the need for a solution are as relevant today as at midcentury.

A gap between the political and the administrative seemed to Gaus to have created a historical situation comparable to that created by the decline of the city-state or the feudal system and had created a comparable need for new thought and new institutions. Observing the development of varied respectable theories, but the lack nevertheless of a credible theory that could create a sociopolitical universe, he hoped—symbolically at least—for a Jeremy Bentham, Edmund Burke, or Adam Smith. He made no claim that the hoped-for synthesis of politics and administration could be created by practitioners and students of administration. But he was firmly of the opinion that administration would be an "essential constituent to any social theory that has purposes other than decorative. . . . I do not see how any advance in a reasonable explanation of political life can be made in our time without this kind of humble turning to a first-hand observation of government in action, of the functions which people perform collectively through its use, of how they are best organized throughout the community. A theory of public administration means in our time a theory of politics also" (Gaus 1950, 167–68).

Have we made progress in closing the gap, in repairing what is often referred to as the politics-administration dichotomy? Opinions on this vary; some may deny that there has been a troublesome cleft in our public world. While much excellent work has been done in the intervening decades, the cleft remains a prominent feature of our institutional and intellectual world.

This chapter addresses some aspects of the matter in a discursive manner. How the politics-administration dichotomy in our conceptual world, the troubled relationship of political science and public administration in academia, and the problematic identity and role of administration in American government are connected is explained. This is a synthesis of information that has previously been published but warrants continued attention.

First, a discussion of the relationship of political science and public administration. Public administration in the United States was brought to self-awareness by political scientists and in political science departments. But a sense of estrangement, both on the part of public administrationists and of their disciplinary colleagues has since developed. In some instances, good intradisciplinary and interpersonal relations were and are maintained. In other instances, this was not so, and in a substantial number of cases public administration programs have become located outside political science departments.

The word *estrangement* is perhaps too mild to characterize the relationship of public administration to other fields of political science. Woodrow Wilson's lament in 1887 that administration was "put aside as a 'practical detail' which clerks could arrange after doctors had agreed on principles" (p. 199) seems not greatly changed in some quarters today. In the perception of most political scientists down to this day, I judge, public administration concerns the lower things of government, details for lesser minds. Two decades ago, it was observed that "the lower things with which public administration is now deeply engaged are such matters as the common defense, education, safety and health, economic development and the elimination of poverty, problems of freedom and equality, law enforcement and the administration of justice, the preservation and development of resources, social and physical mobility, population planning, recreation and the amenities, the development of science and the use of technology; and with the interactions of all such matters with governmental theories, institutions and processes, at all levels of government at home and abroad" (Waldo 1968, n. 3). It is interesting to note that a political scientist, describing his graduate education in the early 1970s, documented the low esteem of public administration. It was treated with "particular disdain" by professors and "in" graduate students. "Those who chose to devote their graduate careers to the study of public administration were deemed simply benighted" (Postbrief 1982, 573).

So it then seemed to a public administrationist. So it still seems to a public administrationist, with side glances at titles in recent issues of *History of Political Thought,* such as "Greek States and Greek Oracles" and "Nicholas of Cusa and the Tyrolese Monasteries." As a sometime would-be political theorist, such pieces are interesting, but as a public administrationist, they are certainly no more relevant to the conduct of government and the future of society than run-of-the-issue pieces in the journals of public administration.

I argue that to ask which side of the politics-administration dichotomy is right is to ask a rather meaningless, if not a contentiously diverting question.

There are several reasons for public administration's low esteem (Waldo 1986). One factor is the liberal arts ethos. To the extent this survives and colors political science, it creates a bias against occupationally useful subjects. Properly conceived, it holds, education has as objectives the enriching of the mind, the refinement of the sensibilities, the growth of the spirit, the attainment of balance and wisdom, not training for employment—this is philistine.* Studying the Peloponnesian War, listening to Bach, reading Plutarch—such pursuits are simply better than counting manhole covers. Who but a philistine would disagree? On the other hand, a certain sympathy is due the administrator whose would-be assistants could parse verbs in four languages but could not run a lemonade stand.

One aspect of the liberal arts ethos has been the fact that despite the prominence of business, the historic disdain of trade has largely persisted. "The field of administration is a field of business," Wilson declared (1887, 209), and public administration has often, openly and liberally, drawn on business sources for its concepts and techniques. Given the historical circumstances, this is understandable, perhaps inevitable. But it should be noted here that skepticism also became a part of the "mix," as indicated by the currency of Wallace Sayre's *mot*: Business organizations and public organizations are fundamentally alike in all unimportant respects.

Another reason for the low esteem of public administration—in some respects the opposite of the liberal arts ethos—was its failure to participate importantly in the behavioral movement dominant in political science in the 1950s and 1960s. Public administrationists could plead that their behavioral research was being conducted for them in such areas as social psychology and organization behavior, and that they were fully occupied with the task of preparing persons for administrative careers, no apologies necessary. Relevant considerations, but not fully responsive and strategic. Public administrationists should have been more sensitive to the issue of empirical research in public organization and administration. Although classification is difficult, the important work of some deserves note. Examples are Robert Golembiewski, Herbert Kaufman, Norton E. Long, Frederick C. Mosher, Robert Presthus, Harold Seidman, Victor Thompson, and Aaron Wildavsky.

In recent years, the amount of work that is both methodologically respectable and theoretically significant has increased. And by coming later to careful empirical research, there have been some advantages. In both the failures and successes of the behavioral wave, there have been lessons.

---

* Gaus once observed to me that a complimentary exemption is made for political theorists who train other political theorists for the occupation of training other political theorists.

Somewhat related is the failure of public administration to address the area of policy early and decisively. For something like two decades after it became well recognized that public administrators are inevitably substantively engaged in policy matters, few significant responses were forthcoming. When policy study, policy science, policy analysis, policy evaluation— choose your term—developed rapidly in the late 1960s and 1970s, the attention, energy, ideas, and techniques came largely from economics and other sources. In the 1980s, of course, there was something of a rapprochement. Typically, instructional programs in public administration included a policy component, and policy programs included an administrative component, although almost certainly under the less contaminated term management.

Public administration's problems of definition and image have from the beginning been complicated by something that relates to political science but also has a massive outside referent: the law—the entire complex of laws, courts, and lawyers. What is administration as something apart from the law?

In public administration's early period of self-awareness, this problem was so prominent that the first textbook—L.D. White's—dealt with it in the preface. White (1948a) "assumed"—his word—that administration is a single universal process and the study of administration "should start from the base of management rather than the foundation of law" (p. xii).

It was not easy to establish an identity independent of the legal process and its organs; nor was the attempt completely successful. But in later years, roughly after midcentury, the matter was put aside. Problems of definition and relationship remained, but public administrationists presumed that they had established a function and identity apart from the law.

An obvious point is that several, if not all, the aspects of the enterprise of public administration I have identified have a relationship to the architecture and terminology of the Constitution. I refer of course to the creation of the executive, the legislative, and the judicial, and to the absence of the term *administration*. The framers (of the Constitution) left it for history to determine, with only a few referents, how what we regard as public administration be empowered, organized, operated, and controlled. Public administrationists have also tried to legitimate their function by arguing that public administration is the same as, or an extension of, the executive branch. This can be argued impressively, but hardly conclusively (Waldo 1986).

A not so obvious but very relevant point is that it is proper to think of the judicial organs and apparatus as constitutionally privileged and functionally specialized instruments of public administration. The task or role of the public administrator is to interpret and apply the law. The task or role of the judicial organ is to interpret and apply the law. There are of course modal differences, and at the extremes—say an undercover police officer and a justice of the Supreme Court —differences that are great indeed. But not just logic supports the view that courts are administrative organs. Plainly, courts historically have been organs of governmental administration, often important to and sometimes central to the governmental process. Plainly, they now are organs of administration and, increasingly, centers of administrative activity.

I now suggest a perspective that aids in understanding the politics-administration dichotomy, the troubled status of public administration in the discipline that gave it birth, and the problem of the identity and role of administration in American government.

Government in the West is usefully conceived as the rise and mingling of two traditions, the Greek and the Roman. The two traditions, designated the "Civic Culture" and the "Imperial," have been added to and altered by the medieval and the modern experience and, of course, by the variety of regional, ethnic, and national histories. But both have been and remain influential. Modern Western states or countries combine the Greek and Roman traditions in varying proportions, however much history and circumstances, in particular cases, add ingredients that are neither.

The Roman, or Imperial, tradition originated in the ancient empires of the Near East and the Mediterranean. Imperial Rome was the latest and greatest of these, and its legacy of centuries-long rule over a large part of three continents has been determinative for much that has followed. For present purposes, this: When the modern state was created by reassembling the pieces of government distributed about in the feudal system, the Roman idea and aura provided inspiration and the Roman law a sort of guidebook. The slogan "The king is emperor in his own realm" sums it nicely. Most of the Continent has inclined toward the Imperial tradition.

The Civic Culture tradition arose in the experience and writings of the *polis* and was added to by such things as the experience of the Roman republic and early modern city-states. By several means, it was infused into English-British constitutional development, mingling with a Roman-Imperial component introduced by the Conquest and the Church, and with indigenous Saxon, feudal, and other components. Our framers created a government very much in the Civic Culture mode.

In an ideal-typical or paradigmatic presentation of Civic Culture, citizenship in the political entity is broadly based, and citizenship—membership—is positively valued. There is a widely held belief that the advantages of citizenship are accompanied by obligations of service to and participation in the political entity. In ideal-typical terms: In a Civic Culture entity, every citizen is a public official. Citizens have legal equality and a substantial amount of liberty. Both equality and liberty, whatever their compatibility or incompatibility, have a high value in the political culture. In the making of policy decisions for and by the administrative apparatus, there is a comparatively high component of amateurism as against professionalism/expertise. The exercise of power in the political entity is restrained by theoretical-constitutional factors.

There is a weak sense of *state*. The boundary between society and the state is indistinct, shifting, porous. *De jure* or *de facto,* or both, there is considerable regional-local autonomy for government activities and functions. The organization of the administrative apparatus tends to be untidy in appearance, more organic or pragmatic, less logical or formally rational. The functions of government are to an important degree performed through secondary groups or intermediate associations between the family on the one hand and official state bureaucracies on the other (Waldo 1981).

Agreement with all items in the characterization of Civic Culture administration is not essential. It is enough if you agree that the schema is, in general, on target. An ideal-typical depiction of the Imperial is not attempted.* It is enough to say that some of the descriptors would be similar, but that others, notably the sense of state, would be different.

If the argument has made sense in a rough sort of way, how might it help in understanding government operation and problems in the United States? The framers conceived and put into operation a scheme largely in the Civic Culture mode. But in two centuries the government of the United States has moved significantly in the Imperial direction. Some of our problems can be understood in the light of this paradigm shift or paradigm friction that has created lacunae, conflicts, and conundrums. The framers hardly envisaged a United States with a military presence around the world.

The argument, at its broadest, is that to understand the politics-administration dichotomy and its reflection in intra- and interdisciplinary tensions and divisions it is revealing to see it not simply as a parochial and petty quarrel among American academics. Instead, in significant measure what is involved is a divergence and tension between Grecian and Roman influences. In Greece and Rome, the Civic Culture and Imperial modes have their origin, and the two modes are deeply matrixed in subsequent Western history and culture. The argument is simplified. Much else is involved—for example, Hellenic philosophy, Judeo-Christian theology and institutions, and varieties of modern theory and philosophy. The simplification is asserted to make a point: Our politics are Greek, but our administration is Roman. This is meant in two senses. One is historical, cultural, and causal. The other is symbolic, analogical, and heuristic.

That Greece and Rome have been influential, but differently so, in Western development is hardly a new theme. Nor is the thought that the differing influence extends to the political-governmental; this has been the subject of considerable scholarly treatment. To explore that literature is not the present concern. The pres-

---

* The use of the term *Imperial* is intendedly denotative, descriptive, not pejorative. Perhaps *continental* would serve as well or better to designate the states strongly influenced by the Roman experience: France is the paradigm state.

ent concern is the political governmental complex in the United States and self-aware political science and public administration in relation thereto.

The argument begins with etymology. Politics and political, of course, derive from *polis*. Government derives from the Latin *gubernare,* though it in turn derived from the Greek root that gives us cybernetics. Administration and management, of course, have Latin roots. We have an American Political Science Association and an American Society for Public Administration. We do not have an American Government Association.

The Greek *polis* was, at maximum, the size of a medium-size American city. Small in population and simple in technology, it had no need of a large or complex administrative apparatus. Administration at the top was typically amateur and unpaid, both a duty and an honor for the citizen. Some administration was remunerated, but most of the work was done by slaves.

As Roman rule expanded, administration became large and complex. On a Weberian scale for bureaucracy, it never scored very high. But it worked and left a legacy for church and state.

Among the brilliant Greek achievements was bringing the political-governmental to self-awareness. Government, by any reasonable definition, had preceded classical Greece by two millennia, but it remained for the Greeks to see it and philosophize about it.

But what they saw and addressed was the Greek mode; the then contemporary empires were monstrous creations of lesser people. (In polite terms, the Greeks were ethnocentric.) In defining government in terms of the *polis,* the Greeks importantly influenced the course of Western political-governmental history. They influenced the way we think about government down to the present day.

My personal library contains several weighty histories of political theory, thought, or philosophy—choose your term. Not one of them has an entry in the table of contents or index for administration, public administration, or management. Only one has an entry for bureaucracy and only one for organization.

This is revealing—and astounding. An administrative component is necessary for there to be a government, and since it is quantitatively the largest part of a government, how can it be ignored?

I came to realize that the term *administrative state,* which I may have helped to give currency, is pleonastic, rather like a six-sided cube. The expression is perhaps useful as a matter of emphasis. But all states are administrative, else they are not states. Three times I have written about American political science in the round—its origins, concepts, interests, methods, and so forth. Each time I puzzled over a certain rootlessness. American political science, as it gained self-awareness, could be related to various antecedents, such as the history of political theory, college courses in moral philosophy, the yeast of reformism, or the rise of science. And, of course, the formal beginning was an offshoot from the American Historical Society.

But the history on which it centered in its origins was rather parochial—some of it indeed fanciful and ethnically biased. Where was the history of government as a general enterprise, its role in what we call civilization? Shouldn't political science have this kind of foundation? Why should there be a *History of Political Thought* journal and not a *History of Government* journal?

The history of some governments has been well treated, and there is a rich literature on the rise of the modern state, written largely by historians and sociologists. But the history of government as such, its functions, institutions, and operations, as far as I know, is a nonsubject, and I have questioned historians on the matter. The closest thing to a general history of government with which I am familiar is E.N. Gladden's (1972) two-volume *A History of Public Administration,* and the closest thing to a history of government in the United States is L.D. White's (1948, 1951, 1954) multivolume history of our public administration—a statement that, at this point, will not surprise you.

A growth area in social science for several decades has been organization theory—and it continues to grow. There are hundreds of books and various journals partially or completely devoted to the subject. Any master's curriculum in public administration or public policy will, allegedly, ensure that students learn about several of the varieties of conceptualization and theory.

Twice, once in the early 1960s and again in the late 1970s, I reviewed a cluster of organization theory books. Both times, I commented on what struck me as a significant fact: No brand of organization theory could be identified as arising from or supplied by political science. Perspectives, theories, and schools had been contributed—thrust forward, if that seems more accurate—by anthropologists, business administrationists, economists, legalists, philosophers, sociologists, sociobiologists, systems theorists, and theologians. But not by political scientists. Why not?

In the early 1970s a book with the title *The Political Process in Modern Organizations* (Rogers 1971) was advertised. I ordered it with some eagerness. The book was rewarding, but the conceptual apparatus was taken from systems theory and anthropology. In the obligatory bibliography, two works by political scientists were cited but not used in the analysis.

Allowance must be made for the possibility that there is an organization theory—other than justificatory for polity or regime—that I do not properly credit because I am too familiar with it to recognize it as organization theory or lack objectivity. Candidates to be discussed include decision theory, power theory, and democratic organization theories of various kinds. This is a subject worthy of discussion. By what criteria are such theories political science theories? By what criteria are they organization theories? Empirical or normative? What is their relationship to constitutional provisions, more generally regime values? And so forth. These questions cannot be pursued here.

But if I am correct, or even largely correct, what does this signify? About political science? And now, it must be added, about public administration?

I feel that I should be seeking to understand, not to assign blame for the estrangement of public administration, and that it is rather meaningless to argue about which side of the politics-administration dichotomy is right. In a sense, plenty of blame might be attributed, on both sides or across the spectrum, for ignorance, arrogance, obtuseness, and so forth. I accept a double portion. But if my central thesis is correct, our problems of communication, cooperation, and industry are not just personal and disciplinary. Their source is a cleft in Western history and culture, arguably one widened or deepened by the American experience. Certainly, the Iran-*contra* imbroglio has demonstrated how far we are from a meshing of the political and the administrative that is generally understandable and acceptable.

In the essay that gave me the title for this piece, Gaus expressed the opinion that we are in a period of discontinuity and transition comparable to the ones that came with the decline of the city-state and feudalism. In this opinion, of course, he has much—and varied—company. If it is a correct opinion, then dealing with it better than we have in our part of the intellectual-institutional field will surely play a part in finding our way forward. It will not be easy. It requires time and effort, as well as luck and—if Gaus is right—a touch of genius.

When, in my mind, I construct a list of those who have addressed some aspect of the problem creatively or insightfully—to name only some no longer living: Appleby, Follett, Friedrich, Gaus, Sayre, White—I observe that most were trained as political scientists. Perhaps this is only an accident of timing and career opportunities. But perhaps it is a significant datum and, if so, raises the question whether I have been unfair to political science. Perhaps so. Perhaps it should not be taxed with a failure to solve insoluble problems. In any event, the matter is relevant to the future of programs in public administration—under whatever name academic fashions and strategies may dictate, whether in or out of political science departments.

During the 1960s and 1970s, at least, I think the better case was for separation. Lucky was the program in public administration that suffered no worse than disdain in those times. In the preface to his *The Development of the Modern State*, in 1978, Gianfranco Poggi observed, "As for political science, over the past thirty years or so it seems to me to have gone to incredible lengths to forget the state . . ." (p. xiii). As if reminded, a few years later the American Political Science Association took "The State" as the theme of its annual meeting. While this was rather like the American Medical Association devoting its annual meeting to "The Body," the move was welcomed. There are other hopeful signs, notably including the size and vitality of the recently re-created Section on Public Administration in the association.

If institutional or programmatic separation is to continue and become decisive, then those in public administration programs will have to become their own political scientists. They will, that is, if the cleft is not to widen and if they are to discharge successfully their educational function. I can at least hope that those on the other side of the cleft will become increasingly aware of, and knowledgeable about, administration to give it highly informed and serious attention.

A final note. That we are the beneficiaries as well as the victims of the cleft between politics and administration is recognized. The cleft gives room for maneuver. Its tensions, lapses, confusions, and contradictions can and do sometimes serve ends we value. Arguably, indeed, some of the ends we value have been created by the existence of the cleft.

If one searches for a term to designate a human collectivity in which politics and administration are well integrated, two of the terms considered certainly would be *totalitarian* and *utopian*. Patently, we are not currently at risk for totalitarianism or within sight of utopia. But if and as we seek to move toward the latter, we must be aware of the former.

Acknowledgment

This chapter is a revised version of the John M. Gaus Lecture delivered at the annual meeting of the American Political Science Association on 3 September 1987.

References

Gaus, John. 1950. "Trends in the Theory of Public Administration." *Public Administration Review* 10(3):161–68.

Gladden, E.N. 1972. *A History of Public Administration*. Vols. 1 and 2. Totowa, N.J.: Biblio Distribution Center.

Poggi, Gianfranco. 1978. *The Development of the Modern State*. Stanford, Calif.: Stanford University Press.

Postbrief, Sam. 1982. "Review of Waldo: *The Enterprise of Public Administration*." *Ethics* 92(3):573–74.

Rogers, Rolf E. 1971. *The Political Process in Modern Organizations*. New York: Exposition Press.

Waldo, Dwight. 1968. "Public Administration." *Journal of Politics* 30:443–49.

Waldo, Dwight. 1981. "Civic Culture Administration." In *Encyclopedia of Public Administration—An International and Integrative Concept*, edited by Klaus König and Michael Protz. Speyer, Germany: Hochschule für Verwaltungswissenschaften.

Waldo, Dwight. 1986. "Afterword." In *A Search for Public Administration*, edited by Brack Brown and Richard J. Stillman. College Station: Texas A&M University Press.

White, Leonard D. 1948a. *The Federalists: A Study in Administrative History*. New York: Macmillan.

White, Leonard D. 1948b. *Introduction to the Study of Public Administration.* New York: Macmillan.

White, Leonard D. 1951. *The Jeffersonians: A Study in Administrative History, 1808–1829.* New York: Macmillan.

White, Leonard D. 1954. *The Jacksonians: A Study in Administrative History, 1829–1861.* New York: Macmillan.

Wilson, Woodrow. 1887. "The Study of Administration." *Political Science Quarterly* 2:197–222.

5

The State and Its Study:
The Whole and the Parts

JAMES W. FESLER

John Gaus gave me my first job as a political scientist, one with the National Resources Committee (later rechristened the National Resources Planning Board). His group's report, *Regional Factors in National Planning and Development,* included two chapters that constituted my first professional publication. Our frequent contacts thereafter were marked by the kindness and generosity on his part that so many of my generation found inspiriting. His scholarly perspective and reflectiveness shaped the work of younger scholars. He defined the horizons of public administration so as to invite us to be political scientists and social scientists, not just narrow specialists in our subdiscipline.

He would be surprised, I believe, by the current tendency to view bureaucracy as dominant in the state, which would worry him on two grounds. First, it misperceives the real-world situation. Second, it unduly magnifies the role of students of public administration at a time when the prospect of divorce from the field of political science threatens to narrow their concern for the state as a whole. He would also fear that talented political scientists in other fields would neglect administration, leaving it to the specialists.

This may be a propitious time in which to address these concerns. We are now commemorating the origin and adoption of the United States Constitution. Inevitably our attention is turned to the State that the Constitution and the doctrine of independence created, to the governmental institutions that act for the State, to the Preamble's commitment "to promote the general welfare," and to the history through which the Constitution, its State, our governmental institutions, and the general-welfare concept have evolved. None of these topics has been fashionable among political scientists for several decades. Current attention to them may be merely an aberrant departure from regnant style, bound to last only during the brief celebratory period. My hope is that this is not the case. This hope is buoyed by the work of a number of thoughtful political scientists who, independent of the celebratory mood, have proposed bringing the State, its history and institutions, and the public interest back into the purview of political science (Evans, Rueschemeyer, and Skocpol 1985; Krasner 1984; March and Olsen 1984g, 1986; Smith 1988; Stepan 1978; White and Wildavsky 1989).

Herein I venture to explore the grounds for this hope. After a preliminary look at the supposition that the United States system is distinctively dominated by the bureaucracy, I reflect on the reintroduction of the State and its institutions and history, and to examine more fully the relation of bureaucracy to the other institutions. Then I shall invite your consideration of the public interest as a concept that the revival of the State entails. Finally, I shall attempt to explore the symbiotic relationship between political science and the study of public administration.

The scope of administration is determined by the scope of governmental functions, which is decided politically. One measure of what a government does is its share of the society's gross domestic product (GDP). A little over a third of our society's GDP is accounted for by American governments at all levels. Contrast that to the roughly half to two-thirds of GDP accounted for by the governments of Canada, West Germany, the United Kingdom, France, Belgium, Italy, and the Scandinavian countries. That ranks us tenth (Organisation for Economic Cooperation and Development [OECD], 1987). Another measure of the scope of administration is the number of governmental employees. Here, again, comparative data are instructive. In 1982, American governments employed about 17 percent of the country's work force. That was about the same proportion shown by the governments of France and Germany, and it was lower than the United Kingdom's 22 percent, Norway's 23 percent, and Sweden's 32 percent (Saunders and Klau 1985). Another calculation reveals a larger gap between the United States and the European democracies, for in the latter countries public employment increased from 11 percent to 23 percent over a period of 30 years, while an increase of 1 percent occurred in the United States (Rose, Parry, Page, Schmidt, Pignatelli, and Peters 1985).

During the last twenty years, employment by our national executive branch has been almost constant, wavering within the narrow range of 2.8 million to 3 million. In the last ten years, an increase of almost 200,000 has been more than accounted for by the Postal Service, the Defense Department, and the Veterans Administration. The expansion of these departments, exceeding the total increase and only marginally related to claims of a bureaucratic state, have been largely counterbalanced by cuts in domestic departments, with Health and Human Services the biggest loser (U.S. Congressional Budget Office 1987). If these data tell us anything, it is that among modern democracies the American government least warrants designation as a dominantly bureaucratic state. I shall return to this issue after addressing some broader concerns.

My interest is twofold, with both the real world of governance and the analytical world of political science. The two worlds should not be far apart. Both the practice and the analysis of government involve the relation of the whole to the parts and, by necessary implication, the relations among the parts. This is obvious in American government. I think it is equally obvious in the sphere of political science, where the centrifugal pull of subdisciplines threatens to negate our common responsibility.

To be sure, our discipline has enjoyed—if that is the right word—a succession of paradigms: pluralism, behavioralism, structure-functionalism, public choice. Each was introduced with fanfare and broad claims that it was the master design of public life that all political scientists should adopt. Each eventually moderated its claims and was absorbed into our discipline as one more alternative way of pursuing analysis.

Public-choice theory is at this time in an early stage of moderation:

> To the extent that the individual reckons that a constitutional rule [i.e., one "within which ordinary politics is to be allowed to operate"] will remain applicable over a long sequence of periods . . . choices among rules will . . . tend to be based on generalizable criteria of fairness. . . . [Furthermore] it is almost impossible to construct a contractual calculus in which representatives of separate generations would agree to allow majorities in a single generation to finance currently enjoyed public consumption through the issuance of public debt that ensures the imposition of utility losses on later generations of taxpayers. (Buchanan 1987, 1433–36)

The parallel of these cycles with the cycles of real-world government is striking. Planning-Programming-Budgeting, Zero-Based Budgeting, Management-by-Objectives, and other massive reforms were similarly trumpeted as nostrums for the body politic. Each failed to fulfill its exaggerated claims. Yet each left a legacy that continues to inform the conduct of public affairs. So, too, in political science each grand model has helped to integrate our subfields into a vision of the whole. No doubt, there is yet another paradigm waiting to be born. My hope is that it will not focus so intently on inputs to the system that it will neglect output and, consequently, administration.

It is in administration that complexity imposes the most familiar example of relations between whole and parts. Division of labor on the one hand, and the need for coordination and bureaucratic responsibility on the other, require a hierarchy that nests smaller units within larger ones. All governments in America and abroad recognize the dual demands, and they choose hierarchy, tight or loose, as an organizational necessity. Much of my own work, I tardily realize, has focused on the relations of the administrative whole and its parts, whether manifested in centralization and decentralization, field administration, executive branch organization, or interaction between the political- and career-executive echelons. Such standard concerns of public administration I leave aside now, preferring to reflect on administrative agencies' and other institutions' interactions as parts of the whole that is the State.

Bringing the State back into the domain of political science is not universally applauded. Let me distance myself from some of this controversy. I am not invoking an image of the State in any mystical sense, nor reviving sovereignty as a concept. What I have in mind is a shorthand term representing the political system in a restricted sense or the government in a broad sense. The State is distinguished from the society despite extensive interplay between the two. I use the term "the State" simply to stand for a whole, composed of a multitude of large and small parts, whose articulation is a problem for effective government and for political science teaching and scholarship.

In the case of both the State and its institutions one can reasonably hypothecate five interrelated characteristics. First, they take actions; this is a given in international relations and, I would argue, an observable fact in domestic affairs. This is not to reify either the State or governmental institutions. Individual officials make the decisions. They do this, however, within constraints imposed by their trusteeship of values, by history, by organizational cultures, and by power structures. The second characteristic is the distinctive set of values that inhere in the concept of public office as public trust. Third, the State and its institutions have a history whose impact on the present we too often ignore. Fourth, both major and minor institutions of the State have organization cultures, themselves the products of history, which through recruitment and socialization of their members assure a continuity of outlook that canalizes individual behavior. Finally, the State and its institutions have power structures, reinforced by sanctions, generally expressed as hierarchy and authority. I should not like to be misunderstood; if these be norms, they are sometimes violated. But our capacity to identify violations and to distinguish gross violations from minor ones is itself acknowledgment of the norms.

Bringing the State back into political science means also bringing history back in. Our custom is to use the terms "the political system" and "the government" in a strictly contemporaneous sense. Each nation-state, though, has a history of development marked by both continuity and change. "The State" appears to be the proper term to express the nation's continuity, while acknowledging as well the changes that it and its institutions have undergone. In any contemporary nation-state having a century or more of history, the present, if properly examined, reveals the persistence of traditions—some of normative orientations, some of institutional arrangements, some extending to societal orientations about such matters as competent young people's aspirations for public service. A long perspective reveals, too, such alterations as shifts in the class origins of recruited public servants, as is notably demonstrated in the administrative histories of France, Britain, and Germany. Both these phenomena of time—continuity and change—are more readily captured, I think, by a sense of the State as an entity with a past and a future, as well as an intervening present.

The constitution of a modern nation seems legitimately described as a constitution for the State, as it indeed seeks to legitimate the State. A large part of any such document or set of documents establishes the major governmental offices and institutions. Another important part, though, establishes individual rights, protecting them from impairment by government or, as with the abolition of slavery and the on-again, off-again treatment of intoxicating beverages, from impairment by individual persons.

The great parts of the American State are the three branches of government. Their intricate interrelations are mapped by political scientists, though often from the confining perspective of subfields primarily concerned with individual branches. Whether from a broad or narrow perspective, our task is daunting. James Madison anticipated our problems:

> Experience has instructed us that no skill in the science of Government has yet been able to discriminate and define, with sufficient certainty, its three great provinces, the Legislative, Executive, and Judiciary; or even the privileges and powers of the different Legislative branches. Questions daily occur in the course of practice, which prove the obscurity which reigns in these subjects, and which puzzle the greatest adepts in political science. (Madison 1961, no. 37)

I do not propose a lengthy tread along these well-worn paths. Each branch is an institution, has a history rich in traditions, and enjoys a distinctive organizational culture. This I take to be indisputable in the case of Congress, in each of its houses, and in the Supreme Court.

Curiously, the Presidency seems least attentive to institutional history, in contrast to much of our current scholarship. The neglect is a result, I suspect, of the other branches' continuity of membership and, therefore, of memory. Memory is an asset of "the permanent government," which comprises most members of Congress, some long-serving congressional staff aides, many members of congressional staff agencies, judges, civil servants, and military officers. (Beyond the State, there are Washington law firms, interest groups, think tanks, and some individual lobbyists and consultants who also have long memories.) In sharp contrast is the temporary incumbency of the President, the White House staff, and members of the Cabinet and subcabinet. Rapid turnover at the top levels of the executive branch deprives the institution of memory unless the resources of senior career civil servants are tapped. This condition has not been satisfied of late.

The agencies engaged in public administration have an ambiguous status. They are certainly not "a fourth branch of government," as some have proposed.

They are parts of the executive branch, but they depend on Congress for their existence and for their functions, appropriations, staff, and procedures. And they are subject to judicial nay-saying when they stray beyond constitutional and statutory limits, as those limits are perceived by the courts. They are parts of a whole, but the whole is not just the executive branch but the government itself and, if you will permit, the State. That is to say, the best of them derive much of their tradition from the premises of democracy, the higher authority of the major institutions of the State, and the obligation to pursue the public interest. They socialize their staff members according to such State-based premises, which by definition are other-regarding rather than self-regarding.

Administrative discretion, some argue, has become so swollen as to threaten the State as Americans have conceived it. The point that this charge misses is that the expansion of administrative discretion parallels the expanded exercise of discretion by legislative bodies and courts, which reflects legislatures' and courts' efforts to relate public expectations of ameliorative action to new, obdurate, technically freighted, and future-oriented problems of public policy. Many of these efforts are egalitarian in spirit and seek internalization of the costs of externalities.

Administrators perceive their discretion to be tightly restricted. Though some respected scholars take a different view, Congress, the President, and the courts all impose constraints which in earlier periods were less, not more, in evidence. In economic regulation, Congress has vested authority in independent regulatory commissions, providing only such statutory guidelines as "fair and reasonable rates," "public interest, convenience and necessity," and "fair methods of competition." In the newer social regulation statutes, such as those protecting the environment and workers' health and safety, Congress incorporates an astonishing amount of details in a practice characterized as micromanagement. Congress specifies priorities for investigation of specific, suspected pollutants, it sets zero-tolerance levels for substances inducing cancer in man or animal, it specifies fuel-economy standards to be applied to automobiles, and it sets deadlines for administrative elimination of named evils and for intermediate actions. The laws for the Environmental Protection Agency contain 38 mandatory deadlines for issuance of rules and regulations and 36 deadlines for completion of studies, guidelines, and reports (Thomas 1986). Congress has imposed on agencies a total of 3300 requirements of recurring reports to itself, four times those of 1970 (U.S. General Accounting Office 1988).

Congress and the courts have required that agencies' new regulatory initiatives be accompanied by extensive consultation with affected interests, opportunity for individual citizens to register their views, and full documentation of the agencies' responses to all significant comments received. Sunshine, Sunset, and Freedom of Information laws all change the setting of administrative discretion. Congressional committees and especially subcommittees, reinforced by large staffs, provide more substantial oversight than they did in earlier periods. Riders on appropriation acts and committees' reports accompanying bills give enhanced opportunities for control. Statutes and implementation regulations on budget administration, procurement, personnel, printing, and travel so confine administrative discretion that, it is said, managers can no longer manage (National Academy of Public Administration 1983).

The judicial as well as the legislative branch has, despite some oscillation, greatly expanded opportunities for citizens and public interest groups both to challenge actions that agencies have taken and to force agencies to act. In some areas such as schools, prisons, and mental institutions, the courts have occasionally taken over administration from the authorized agencies.

Presidents during the last fifteen years have instituted review mechanisms over regulatory agencies' proposed actions. The power now exerted in this field by the Office of Management and Budget is unprecedented. Whatever one may think of its virtues and defects, it unquestionably limits agency discretion. In the meantime, White House staff members have eagerly implemented their principal's conviction that a rampant bureaucracy must be brought to heel. Much of this activity reflects a belief in a president's electoral mandate which is, however, a myth, as Robert Dahl has recently demonstrated (Dahl 1988).

These many external controls of discretion are supplemented by self-regulating mechanisms within the bureaucracy itself and reinforced by organizational incapacities to embrace contemporary policy problems. "The bureaucracy" is itself a misnomer, for what we have is a multiplicity of bureaucracies. We have no government-wide elite administrative corps such as those in Britain and France; the Senior Executive Service has failed to promote interagency career paths. Though, as a result, civil servants tend to identify with their individual agencies instead of the executive branch or of the government as a whole, their agencies rarely enjoy autonomy. Concerns of policy intermingle domestic fields and interlink domestic fields with international fields. Defense contracts shape a large part of the nation's industrial sector and absorb much of our scientific and engineering talent. Acid rain results domestically from regional flows, but it is also a high-priority feature of Canadian-United States relations. Much of the domestic economy is hostage to foreign trade and foreign investments. The result for bureaucracy is that fragmentation is now the fact, interpenetration of jurisdictions the commonplace, and reciprocal watchfulness the mode. More significantly, the overlaps among agencies and among their bureaus force decision making upward, from bureaucrats to the agencies' political appointees and the White House. Thus the altogetherness of everything reinforces external control of the bureaucracy.

A consequence of the readmission of the State and its institutions to our vocabulary is the revival of the concept of the public interest. In international relations, we have little difficulty with the concept of the national interest (see Krasner 1978). But the public interest in domestic affairs has long been under a cloud—a myth, it is called, and here the usage is meant to suggest falsity, the incapacity of proponents to specify the content of the term. Even among neo-institutionalists the term is often displaced by a proxy such as "community interest" or "common good" or "general welfare."

The simple fact is that the public interest is an ideal. It is for administrators what objectivity is for scholars—something to be strived for, even if imperfectly achieved, something not to be spurned because performance falls short of the goal. If there is not a public interest then we must denounce the idea of ideals. The public interest is not something you pick up in your hands. It is not something whose height and breadth and weight can be measured. If it is illusory, so are justice, liberty, and integrity. If these and other ideal values cannot be absolutes but must be reconciled when in conflict in concrete cases, it is the public official's responsibility to seek the balance among them that most nearly approaches the public interest so far as he can perceive it.

Sir Isaiah Berlin has elegantly summarized the problem that confronts the responsible official:

> Both liberty and equality are among the primary goals pursued by human beings through many centuries; but total liberty for wolves is death to the lambs, total liberty of the powerful, the gifted, is not compatible with the rights to a decent existence of the weak and the less gifted. (Berlin 1988, p. 11)

Yet the problem is not insoluble:

> We must not dramatize the incompatibility of values— there is a great deal of broad agreement among people in different societies over long stretches of time about what is right and wrong, good and evil. . . . In the end it is not a matter of purely subjective judgment; it is dictated by the forms of life of the society to which one belongs, a society . . . with values held in common, whether or not they are in conflict. (Berlin 1988, 11 ff.)

If we cannot precisely define the public interest, we do know when it is flouted. Does anyone doubt that corruption is against the public interest, however sophisticatedly we explain its transactional advantages in developed societies or its cultural rooting in developing societies? On the positive side, as recent events suggest, a good place to start is the oath taken by every federal employee, "that I will bear true faith and allegiance to the Constitution of the United States." The President's constitutional mandate "to take care that the laws be faithfully executed" might well be read as incorporated in employees' oaths. The public interest goes beyond this, of course. The people's confidence in the State and its institutions requires not only that officials avoid unethical conduct but that they avoid the appearance of such conduct. No one who has served in the government, as I have been privileged to do, could suppose that the behavior of career civil servants can be summed up as simply self-regarding. Some is, and it varies with individuals and settings, but it is a narrow vision indeed that disregards public servants' commitment to the search for the public interest and its reflection in their actions. The best of them have, in Cato's words, "capacities large enough to judge the Whole of Things ... and superior minds, elevated above private interest and selfish views" (quoted in Schmidt 1988).

The search for the public interest is not simply a task performed by individual officials in isolation. There are ways to organize the bureaucracy and to establish procedures that enhance decision making in the public interest while simultaneously reinforcing bureaucratic responsibility to the President and his appointees, to the Congress, and to the courts. Decisions of moment, instead of being left to specialized units, can be drawn upward in the hierarchy so that other relevant units' information and analyses can be folded in and the conclusion can be reached by an official with a capacious view and a responsibility to political executives and to Congress. (This is no argument for centralization of decision making in the Executive Office of the President. For a sophisticated demonstration of my main point, see Hammond 1986.) The exceptions that prove the rule are agencies subject to capture by single-interest groups. Confirming cases are the Office of Price Administration and the War Production Board of the World War II era; they succeeded in establishing organizations and procedures that countered any industry divisions' impulses to serve their industries more than the State.

In the study of the State, public administration and other fields of political science have a symbiotic relationship. We may well start with the disturbing definition of symbiosis—"the relationship of two or more different organisms in a close association that may be but is not necessarily of benefit to each." Some public administration students have concluded that our relationship with political science is not of benefit to our field. That conclusion, in many cases, rests on entrancement with generic administration, public and private, and on a related belief that other disciplines contribute more than political science to understanding this genus. Other factors enter as well. The position, it seems to me, reflects too much the unhappy relations that some colleagues have experienced on their campuses. It fails to acknowledge parallels with other fields' troubles in the political science community; it confuses professional training for public service careers with the scholarly and pedagogical task of developing an understanding of the administrative province as a part of the governmental world; and it assumes that public administration is unique in features that are in fact common to other fields.

Allow me to put aside the graduate-level, professional training of public administrators. Schools of public affairs and administration are comparable to the law schools that train even more of our discipline's recent undergraduate majors, many of whom are destined to devote all or parts of their careers to public service as judges, legislators, and administrators. My concern is not with professional schools but with the subfield of political science that, though incidentally educating some students for administrative careers, seeks primarily to develop a grasp of the theory and practice of public administration.

There is a complaint that political science wants to expel public administration and a proposal, in the nature of a preemptive strike, that public administration should secede from political science. Political science departments exclude or disdain public administration, I understand, because it is practical in focus, out of phase with the behavioral, quantitative, and other regnant modes of the mother discipline, and often disconcerting to the balance of a department because it attracts too many students, some of them career-motivated. It is not, I would agree, central to the discipline; and if it is not central, it is thought to be dispensable.

If we can put aside the emotional traumas—though their costs to colleagues are not minor—much of that rationale is shared by other fields of political science. Though international relations courses are not so "practical" as public administration courses, their enrollments, I dare say, are not unrelated to students' improbable aspirations for entry to the Foreign Service; only 200 of the 18,000 examined in a year are appointed (Spiers 1987). Not all teaching and research are in the behavioral and quantitative modes. They cannot be. Only certain fields are blessed with readily available measures—of elections, congressional votes, public opinion, Supreme Court votes, and others. Students of the Presidency confront the $N = 1$ barrier to quantitative analysis (sometimes expanded to $N = 9$ for the last half-century; see, however, King and Ragsdale 1988). So do students of administration sensitive to situational variables, including agencies' cultures, external environments, and leadership. Students of political philosophy, certainly not "practical," have endured traumas of rejection and disdain.

The secessionist argument, if freed from its rejectionist pique, rests heavily on the proposition that the field of public administration draws on many disciplines. True, public administration as a field draws on social psychology, sociology, economics, law, history, business management, and other scholarly disciplines. In this, though, it is not distinctive. Surely the same disciplines (save perhaps that of business management) enrich the work of students of public opinion, electoral behavior, Congress, the Presidency, the judiciary, international relations, and comparative government.

The winds of change bring fresh connections between past and present and between public administration and political science. We are broadening the grooves of academe. The growth of political scientists' interest in the evolution of regimes and their administrative institutions, in the role of critical elections, and in public opinion's constancy and variation over time signify an openness to the historical dimension. No longer need the historical be disguised under such rubrics as "diachronic," "longitudinal," "time-sequence," and "developmental." The "rediscovery" of the State and the "new institutionalism" are scarcely conceivable as enterprises without incorporation of the administrative operations of government. The Constitution bicentennial and public awareness of illegality in high places have been accompanied by, and have perhaps prompted, a fresh interest in the relation of public law to public administration. The same phenomena have sparked a spirited effort to explore the ethical dimensions of administration, an undertaking that must call on political philosophers for help.

I may be misjudging what is happening in the discipline. I am impressed by the decade's yield of studies by comparative-government scholars on comparative administration and bureaucracy; well done as most of them are, they contribute not only to the subdiscipline of public administration but also to our understanding of states and of relations among their component institutions. That positive view, however, is not helped by the current offering of graduate-level core courses in comparative politics. Only a sixth of such courses include "bureaucracy" or "administration" in their syllabi (McHenry 1988). I worry that this neglect may influence the agenda of the next generation of scholar-teachers.

Let me put it simply. Administration is an integral, interactive, and subordinated part of the government, a part of the whole. As such, it cannot be understood apart from government. Understanding government is the task of political science. It follows that the study of public administration is a part of the larger political science enterprise.

Let me reassure you that I am not just peddling another paradigm. I do not propose that we repeat the errors of the past. Bringing back the State, its institutions, the public interest, and history does not mean displacement of all that we have learned from other approaches. Rather, it invites broadening of our sense of relevancies. It means fresh awareness that the State and its institutions are not simply dependent variables of interest groups, public opinion polls, purely self-regarding motivations of political actors, and other societal-based influences. Yet it does not deny that the directional arrow frequently points that way.

The suggested reorientation means that, just as in the real world the State and its institutions invite attention to the relation of the whole and the parts, so we as political scientists need to rise above our subdisciplinary fractionation; we need to foster flexible linkages and to conceive ourselves as engaged in a common enterprise. It seems not too much to ask that we do as the other large-brain animals do. These, the dolphins and chimpanzees, "live in an extremely fluid and flexible community, referred to as a 'fusion-fission society,' where individuals may join temporary parties of varying sizes, instead of operating in one relatively closed or rigid group" (Booth 1988).

References

Berlin, Isaiah. 1988. "On the Pursuit of the Ideal." *New York Review of Books* 35:11–16.

Booth, William. 1988. "The Social Lives of Dolphins." *Science* 240:1273–74.

Buchanan, James M. 1987. "The Constitution of Economic Policy" [article based on his lecture delivered upon receiving the Nobel Prize in Economics]. *Science* 236:1433–36.

Dahl, Robert A. 1988. "The Pseudodemocratization of the American Presidency." In *The Tanner Lectures on Human Values X,* edited by Grethe B. Peterson. Salt Lake City: University of Utah Press.

Evans, Peter B., Dietrich Rueschemeyer, and Theda Skocpol, eds. 1985. *Bringing the State Back In.* Cambridge: Cambridge University Press.

Hammond, Thomas. 1986. "Agenda Control, Organizational Structure, and Bureaucratic Politics." *American Journal of Political Science* 30:379–420.

King, Gary, and Lyn Ragsdale. 1988. *The Elusive Executive: Discovering Statistical Patterns in the Presidency.* Washington, D.C.: CQ Press.

Krasner, Stephen D. 1978. *Defending the National Interest: Raw Materials Investments and U.S. Foreign Policy.* Princeton: Princeton University Press.

Krasner, Stephen. 1984. "Approaches to the State: Alternative Conceptions and Historical Dynamics" [review article]. *Comparative Politics* 16:223–46.

Madison, James. 1961. *The Federalist,* edited by Jacob E. Cooke. Middletown, Conn.: Wesleyan University Press.

March, James G., and Johan P. Olsen. 1984. "The New Institutionalism: Organizational Factors in Political Life." *American Political Science Review* 78:734–49.

March, James G., and Johan P. Olsen. 1986. "Popular Sovereignty and the Search for Appropriate Institutions." *Journal of Public Policy* 6:341–70.

McHenry, Dean E., Jr. 1988. "Summary and Analysis of a Survey of Graduate Core Courses in Comparative Politics." *Political Science Teacher,* 5–6.

National Academy of Public Administration. 1983. *Revitalizing Federal Management: Managers and Their Overburdened Systems* [panel report]. Washington, D.C.: National Academy of Public Administration.

Organisation for Economic Cooperation and Development (OECD). 1987. *OECD Economic Outlook,* 42, table R 14 at p. 187.

Rose, R., R. Parry, E. Page, K.-D. Schmidt, A.C. Pignatelli, and B.G. Peters. 1985. *Public Employment in Western Nations.* Cambridge: Cambridge University Press.

Saunders, Peter, and Friedrich Klau. 1985. "The Role of the Public Sector." *OECD Economic Studies* 4:63.

Schmidt, Benno C., Jr. 1988. "A Republic of Virtue" [baccalaureate address, Yale University].

Smith, Rogers M. 1988. "Political Jurisprudence, the 'New Institutionalism,' and the Future of Public Law." *American Political Science Review* 82:89–108.

Spiers, Ronald I. 1987. *Perspectives on the Public Management Challenge.* Washington, D.C.: National Academy of Public Administration.

Stepan, Alfred. 1978. *The State and Society: Peru in Comparative Perspective.* Princeton: Princeton University Press.

Thomas, Lee M. 1986. Address to the National Academy of Public Administration.

U.S. Congressional Budget Office. 1987. *Federal Civilian Employment.* Washington, D.C.: Government Printing Office.

U.S. General Accounting Office. 1988. *Congressional Reporting Requirements Need Improvements.* Washington, D.C.: Government Printing Office.

White, Joseph, and Aaron Wildavsky. 1989. "Public Authority and the Public Interest: What the 1980s Budget Battles Tell Us About the American State." *Journal of Theoretical Politics* 1:7–31.

6

Ethics in Public Administration:
A State-of-the-Discipline Report

JOHN A. ROHR

It will come as a surprise to no one to learn that the field of ethics is chaotic. The term is undefined; the inquiry, unbounded. Yet there is vitality in the ethics literature—a vitality no one should extinguish with unsolicited declarations of premature closure. For example, as a National Association of Schools of Public Affairs and Administration (NASPAA) Fellow with the General Management Training Center of the old Civil Service Commission eleven years ago, one of my tasks was to prepare an annotated bibliography on "Ethics in Public Administration." An ever-expanding definition of both ethics and public administration had to be justified to make any pretense at having done the job—or, more precisely, to make any pretense that there was a job to be done.

Today the problem is just the opposite. I find myself looking for reasons to cut the topic back to manageable proportions. Because Robert Denhardt presents a report on administrative theory, I have drawn a distinction between ethics and administrative theory—a distinction that I am sure is about as convincing as the distinction between policy and administration. This distinction is the basis for the decision to exclude the works of such prominent administrative theorists as Denhardt, Michael Harmon, Orion White, Fred Thayer, and Ralph Hummel. Clearly there is considerable overlap between ethics and administrative theory; but there is also an overlap between ethics and just about everything else in the field—personnel, budgeting, administrative law, and so on. As a result of this overlap, many topics, themes, and authors that one might reasonably expect to find included have been excluded.

The report is composed of five sections: highlights, correspondence, the literature, personal observations, and conclusion. In these the concentration is on developments from 1981–87 inclusive.

Highlights

In thinking about the state of the discipline, one's attention is drawn to books, journals, research ideas, bibliographies, and the other trappings of the academic enterprise. As far as ethics is concerned, however, there is one event of a nonacademic nature that is of paramount importance—the adoption of the American Society for Public Administration's (ASPA) Code of Ethics in 1984. The twelve statements of the code are supplemented with detailed explanatory guidelines.

The development of the code has not been without controversy. Ralph Chandler (1983) has written a severe but perceptive critique of a 1981 decision by ASPA's National Council to adopt a statement of principles instead of a real code of ethics. Douglas Morgan (1985) offered a close examination of some of the wording of the code at the 1985 meeting of the American Political Science Association. I feel confident in predicting that we can look forward to many more articles on the code in the future. This is certainly as it should be.

If we look to our colleagues in the International City Managers Association (ICMA), we discover that they have had five revisions of their code of ethics, which was originally approved in 1924. The various versions of their code show how the influence of scientific management and the politics/administration dichotomy waxed and waned throughout this century. The influence of both the civil rights movement and the women's movement is apparent in more recent editions of the ICMA code.

Perhaps the same development awaits ASPA's code. If, twenty-five years from now, the code is unchanged, we will be certain that it has had little or no influence on either the theory or practice of public administration. The academic journals are the likely starting point for improving or defending the code, but journals are only the starting point. To make changes in the code, or to resist them, will require lively debate that will engage the best and the brightest of ASPA's practitioners and academics.

The fact that we have a code of ethics in place is an important achievement for ASPA. It would be a serious error, however, to look upon it as a definitive utterance of timeless truths. It is, instead, an effort to focus our public argument which is now well underway.

Other highlights of a somewhat official nature can be found in NASPAA's requirement that accredited public administration curricula "shall develop in the students a demonstrated ability to . . . implement an effective and ethical course of action" (National Association 1981, 3); in the appearance of the second edition of ASPA's Ethics Workbook (Mertins and Hennigan 1982); in the cluster of ethics panels at ASPA's 1986 national conference; and in the frequent coverage given to ethics in the pages of *Public Administration Times* (e.g., Denhardt 1985; White 1985).

The abundance of literature on public administration ethics is perhaps the best indication of the vitality and intellectual interest in the field. Nearly every publication that might reasonably be considered a public administration journal has carried at least one article on ethics since 1980 and most have carried many more. Interestingly, *Public Administration Review* and the *Bureaucrat,* two journals that are widely read by practitioners (Vocino and Elliott 1982), took the lead in publishing articles related to ethics suggesting that questions of ethics might provide a useful means of keeping ASPA's practitioners and academics in touch with one another.

In addition to public administration journals, journals devoted exclusively to ethical issues that have published articles pertinent to public administration include *Business and Professional Ethics Journal,* published by the Rensselaer Polytechnic Institute of Troy, New York; *Environmental Ethics,* published by the John Muir Institute for Environmental Studies, Inc. and the University of New Mexico–Albuquerque; *Ethics in Science and Medicine,* published by Pergamon Press;* the *Hastings Center Report;* and the prestigious philosophical journal, *Ethics,* published by the University of Chicago Press. Closely related to these journals are *Philosophy and Public Affairs,* published by the Princeton University Press, and the *Report from the Center for Philosophy and Public Policy* at the University of Maryland. The scope of these two publications, as their titles indicate, extends beyond questions of ethics. Most of the articles that have appeared in these journals, however, are related to ethics, and many of them to ethical questions pertinent to public administration.

Since 1980, a number of books have been published that deal directly with public administration ethics. Coming readily to mind are Frank Fischer's (1980) *Politics, Values and Public Policy;* Terry Cooper's (1982) *The Responsible Administrator;* Louis Gawthrop's (1984) *Public Sector Management, Systems, and Ethics;* William Louthan's (1981) *The Politics of Managerial Morality; The Fraud Control Game* by John Gardiner and Theodore Lyman (1984); and John P. Burke's (1986) *Bureaucratic Responsibility.*

There is, of course, an overwhelming literature on ethics in government in general that touches only in passing on questions of public administration. Michael Johnston's (1982) *Political Corruption and Public Policy in America* is a good example of literature of this sort and is beyond the scope of this report (see also Bowie 1981; French 1983). Questions of accountability through external control (Rosen 1982), representative bureaucracy (Krislov and Rosenbloom 1981), and democracy versus bureaucracy (Yates 1982)—important and timeless as these topics are—cannot be included in this report.†

In addition to books and articles, several collections of essays are or soon will be available. These include *Public Duties* edited by Joel Fleishman, Lance Leibman, and Mark H. Moore (1981); *Essentials of Management: Ethical Values, Attitudes*

---

* Since 1982, this publication has appeared under the title *Social Science and Medicine.*

† For a review of these three books, see Burke (1984).

and Actions edited by James Bowman (1983); *Political Ethics,* a collection of essays by Dennis Thompson (1987); *Confronting Values in Policy Analysis: The Politics of Criteria,* edited by Frank Fischer and John Forester (1987); and *Politics, Ethics, and the Public Service,* six essays on ethics in the United Kingdom published by the Royal Institute of Public Administration (1985). The essays from the UK are particularly interesting because, despite the important formal differences between American and British government, the ethical problems of the respective civil services are remarkably similar. The main theme that unifies the essays is the struggle to state the proper relationship between the career civil service and the government of the day.

The international study of questions of ethics in public administration will be strengthened by the appearance of a symposium on this topic in a forthcoming issue of the *International Journal of Political Science.* The editors of the symposium are O.P. Dwivedi of Guelph University in Canada and Dele Olowu of Ife University in Nigeria.*

Teachers of public administration ethics were pleased to note the publication of what I believe is the first casebook on ethics that is suitable for public administration classes—*Ethics and Politics,* edited by Amy Gutmann and Dennis Thompson (1984). Despite the broad wording of the title, all the cases are suitable for public administration courses.

Bibliographies on public administration ethics are also readily available. James Bowman of Florida State University has clearly taken the lead in this area with his annotated bibliography on professional dissent (Bowman, Elliston, and Lockhart 1984) and his earlier bibliography, part of an ethics symposium published in the *Public Personnel Management Journal* (Bowman 1981). Leigh Grosenick of Virginia Commonwealth University has also compiled a bibliography that is thorough and up to date. Another good source is the Center for the Study of Ethics in the Professions at the Illinois Institute of Technology. This center has published a " 'compilation' of statements relating to standards of professional responsibility and freedom." A bibliography prepared by Peter J. Bergerson and Brian P. Nedwek (1986) divides its entries conveniently into nine categories—e.g., state and local government, government and business.

In recent years, state and federal agencies have made a steady stream of useful publications available. At the federal level, the Office of Government Ethics (OGE) publishes a quarterly newsletter titled *Ethics Newsgram,* a brief but informative source of recent developments in ethics enforcement policy, court cases, and important publications. The OGE also makes available a digest of selected letters written in response to inquiries on the interpretation of the Ethics in Government Act of 1978. This is an invaluable source for persons interested in questions concerning

---

* For a discussion of ethics in developing nations, see Ajvogu (1983).

financial disclosure, conflict of interest, and postemployment restrictions on federal workers.

Correspondence

Once I agreed to undertake this project, I wrote to twenty-seven scholars and teachers whom I knew had given serious thought to public administration ethics. I asked them to assist in the preparation of this report by giving a brief statement of their own ethics research interests and projects, both past and present, and by giving a fuller statement assessing the present position of ethics research in the field. I also asked that they identify others who might be interested in this project. The original twenty-seven letters yielded six more contacts, for a total of thirty-three. All but nine of the thirty-three responded. Five of the nine had colleagues at their own universities who did reply, so they may have made some contributions to the responses I actually received. Following is a series of excerpts from this correspondence. A bright graduate student who is thinking about writing a dissertation in the area of ethics might receive some encouragement from seeing that a distinguished social scientist such as Frank Fischer believes that "one of the next steps in ethical research should be an attempt to ground the concerns of ethics in a substantive political context (perhaps a kind of sociology of knowledge)." Perhaps the graduate student is thinking along similar lines and will contact Fischer for further guidance and direction. Such contacts create a community of disciplined discourse.

In presenting these excerpts, I also hope to contribute to a sense of community among mature scholars already active in the field. Many of the letters complained that the field of administrative ethics is badly fragmented. So it is, but a careful reading of the excerpts may show more harmony of interest than initially expected.

Del Dunn and Terry Cooper both see a need for more empirical work, but John Gardiner, who comes closer to being an empiricist than anyone else in the field, has some serious reservations about empiricism. Bayard Catron and Justine Mann see a serious problem arising from the shallow philosophical underpinnings in much of the ethics in public administration literature. Phil Schorr, Dwight Kiel, and Jeremy Plant find themselves turning to history for an understanding of ethics. Leigh Grosenick, Kathryn Denhardt, and Lewis Mainzer see the interaction between person and organization as a central concern in the field.

Dennis Thompson and Jerry Pops are interested in the connection between administration and the democratic process with reference (explicit for Thompson and implicit for Pops) to the welfare state. Jeremy Plant and Jerry Pops share a common view on the importance of the relation between law and ethics. Kathryn Denhardt and Phil Schorr have both noted the recent emphasis on public administration as a calling—Schorr rather favorably, Denhardt less so. Jerry Pops and Bayard Catron agree on the importance of legitimating administrative institutions as well as seeing ethical questions as pervasive in public administration rather than simply as a part of it. Justine Mann agrees on the second point.

The previous statements are my interpretations of the replies I received. They are examples of what we can learn from others' comments in this field. The comments from the correspondents follow.*

Bayard Catron (George Washington University)

Work is fragmented, poorly understood, quite idiosyncratic, and lacks a common theoretical grounding—and even a common vocabulary. Second, much current work centers around rather specialized issues in professional ethics (e.g., whistleblowing, conflict of interest, etc.), or is done from the vantage point of particular policy issues and/or disciplines, like biomedical ethics. Third, it seems that there are quite a few new players in the game—public administrationists (organization theorists, personnel people, etc.) who have come to it for idiosyncratic reasons without any particular background in ethics as an historical field of study, and philosophers drawn by a concern for relevance or operating out of a particular socio-political orientation.

From a pedagogical and curricular standpoint, I think we need more attention to the ethical dimension in public decision making. The practical aim, it seems to me, should be to legitimize the dimension as co-equal in importance with the political, economic, organizational, and legal dimensions of public administration.

Viewing ethics as a dimension of everyday conduct and a type of concern in deciding and acting helps as a practical matter in decompartmentalizing it and appreciating its pervasive importance. From a theoretical standpoint, the concern with ethics can be seen as part of the post-behavioral, post-positivist revolution—or alternatively, as the re-emergence of a dimension of organization theory which has been largely latent since Barnard and Selznick.

Terry Cooper (University of Southern California)

As I see it ethics research has received increasing attention during the last ten years, but I believe we are rapidly approaching a critical juncture. Most of the work to date has been theoretical, both descriptive and normative, with either

---

* Fuller excerpts from these letters were presented in the original version of this paper presented at the 1986 American Society for Public Administration conference at Anaheim, California.

no clear empirical underpinning or empirical support which is systematic only to a very limited extent. Although I am clearly not an empiricist in the limited sense, I find myself feeling increasingly uncomfortable with the lack of empirical research on administrative ethics. If more empirical work were being undertaken I would feel easier about focusing my own work in a normative theoretical direction.

In my judgment, empirical research in public administration needs serious attention if the subject is to continue to receive significant attention from both practitioners and scholars. Those of us who prefer to work on normative theory need this empirical referent and an ongoing scholarly dialogue with those who would develop it.

Kathryn Denhardt (University of Missouri–Columbia)

In terms of ethics research in general, I see an abandonment of any detailed discussion of the moral principles which should guide public administration. Perhaps this is appropriate given the lack of consensus around specific moral precepts. But at the same time it seems to represent an avoidance of concerns in political thought and ideology which ought to influence the ethical nature of public administration. Recent conference papers have dealt with issues such as public administration as a calling, and this I take as a sign that researchers recognize the need to explore more fully the moral groundings of the field, but aren't certain how to approach doing so.

Another aspect of the current state of ethics research which I see as important is the significant attention being given to the impact of organizations on public administration ethics. This is an area I have long been concerned with, and I am seeing more and more attention being given to it by others as well. Both defenders and critics of bureaucracies at some point address the question of bureaucracies' impact on decisions, especially the moral aspects of those decisions. I see this as enormously important since ethics research in general often maintains a focus on the individual and the culture, but not so much on the institutions in which the individual operates. This might set the study of public administration ethics apart from the study of ethics in other fields such as medicine and law.

Delmer Dunn (University of Georgia)

Another observation is that many who presently write in the area are closely akin to the earlier generation [i.e., Appleby et al.] in that they approach the subject from a normative rather than an empirical frame of reference (Gardiner and Bowman are notable exceptions). One need I feel is for more empirical grappling with the actual ethical dilemmas which confront the public administrator. I don't know whether the best approach for this is to follow managers around for a while (like Mintzberg, but with a focus on ethics) or to use a survey approach.

Frank Fischer (Rutgers University–Newark)

With John Forester I am also co-editing a book titled *Social Values in Policy Analysis.* In some ways the focus of the book addresses part of question two. In my view, one of the next steps in ethical research should be an attempt to ground the concerns of ethics in a substantive political context (perhaps a kind of sociology of knowledge). To some extent the essays in the book try to deal with ethical issues in this context. In this regard, I am presently writing a chapter on the relation of policy analysis to the values of the liberal state.

John Gardiner (University of Illinois–Chicago)

To the best of my knowledge, every attempt to measure misbehavior has been useless; the numbers of reported incidents, as I discuss in the beginnings of *Decisions for Sale* and *The Fraud and Control Game,* are simply artifacts of how many people are sent to look for booboos and whether they decide to report what they've found. Most organizations, even with the most ethical of leaders, have little incentive to go looking for impropriety (in the absence of current or incipient scandal) and no incentive to keep statistics on errata. (There is one exception to the last statement—headhunters such as auditors and inspectors-general will amass and publish very meaningless figures on excess payments or payments disallowed. They are useless for research and, I would assume, for administrators as well, although I am occasionally curious as to whether someone wants to project an agency image as having a lot or very few problems.)

Leigh Grosenick (Virginia Commonwealth University)

As for trends, problems, strengths and weaknesses—here are some issues that may interest you:
Professional ethical relativity as the major cause of ethical ambivalence and low standards of the public service. The client orientation of the professional often conflicts with public duties and the citizen-serving obligations of the professional public manager. Individual professions engaging in some common pursuit of the public good can conflict professionally. How do we solve this problem of the trained incapacity of the professional to serve the public?

Or, can the lawyer, doctor, social worker, policeman or engineer ever become a professional or competent citizen?

Dwight Kiel (University of Kansas)

I am now working on the Progressive Era in an attempt to decipher the role of religious influence on urban reform. What strikes me here is that ethical urban administration depended upon the promise of a new urban social contract which was supposed to include the poor and the immigrants. Yet, once in power, the urban reformers depoliticized the city in the name of ethics and created a city with honest administrators but without ethical action. Equity decisions (the true test of an ethical life) were obscured and depoliticized by urban reform.

Lewis Mainzer (University of Massachusetts–Amherst)

My own interests: some years ago some writing of mine dealt with the problem of being a good person with a large, formal (bureaucratic) organization. The possible corruption of having power over others and the possible corruption of subjection to the authority and power of others concerned me. The issues were utterly real and important to me, not vaguely interesting academic research possibilities. I have sustained concern in this area through an annual graduate course, now essentially populated by MPA candidates, on public administration responsibility, including individual ethics as a dimension, along with institutional forms of securing responsibility.

Justine Mann (Georgia Southern College)

It seems to me that far too many of the people writing in the field evidence a woefully inadequate background in moral philosophy. I end the article or book knowing the writer has no comprehension, in MacIntyre's sense, of morality.

We do not need more research. The blind leading the blind is a sorry spectacle. We ought to stop to look at the assumptions we use. I put no trust at all in industrial morality.

Jeremy Plant (Pennsylvania State University at Harrisburg)

I became interested for a variety of reasons in the three-way connection between law, statistics, and public administration and through it, ethical questions tied to the intersection of the three. This led me to some research on discrimination/Equal Employment Opportunity (EEO) more as a means to understand the implications of a rule of law that was almost entirely statistical in nature, devoid of a concern for anything nonquantifiable. (Interestingly, the research also showed that the best statisticians might be penalized, since the legal decision making processes were themselves dominated by nonstatistically oriented actors.) This led me to consider the ethical problems of traditional legal reasonableness doctrines in the context of current public administration. . . .

Needless to say from the above, I haven't solved the theoretical problem, and I am still trying to learn more about what is out there to fit to some framework. I find most of the work in the field to be narrow, either in the phenomena illustrated/studied or the possible theoretical frameworks tested. Or perhaps ideological, as in some public choice and new public administration stuff. Unlike most of my colleagues, when I find myself in a state of confusion, I rarely go to theoretical works, but immerse myself in history and/or applied research; I wish I could say it has worked, but I'm still groping for coherence. So, my writing for the near future that has any connection with ethics is thus: a paper generally on statistical proofs as an avoidance device of the modern governing process for moral argumentation, and a paper looking specifically at EEO/workplace discrimination policy to pinpoint the implications of statistical reality in that policy arena. This [paper] looks at statistical arguments in the litigation process, and the impact of managing a large backlog of cases using statistical performance indicators to guide the application of scarce resources in the EEO Commission.

Jerry Pops (West Virginia University)

In the work that Tom Pavlak and I are doing on administrative justice, we argue that looking at public organizations as devices for making justice decisions is at least as good a notion as seeing them as rational bureaucracies. When we think about the consequences were this heresy to be taken seriously, we could expect a fundamental reordering of the role of public administration in the American polity. As of now, justice is the legal profession's business, process is public administration's domain and ethics is either irrelevant or the business of politics. Public organizations, given system volume, get to play with justice, but are heavily scrutinized at points of system change lest they screw up due process or, God forbid, invoke ethical questions. In the reordering, the courts and legal profession would be reduced to the role of partner in justice and, worse, an agonizing reappraisal of the myth of individuality and the nature of our system of private law in the U.S. would ensue. I have really struggled over the past months to respond to your letter calling for help. I would look at it, try a reply, then put it away dissatisfied. Now I know why. It was the implicit assumption . . . that ethics is a topic within public administration, rather than about public administration, that I resisted. I still do. Strongly.

Phil Schorr (Long Island University). After discussing methods of teaching ethics, Professor Schorr continues:

> Following this investigation I received from your school a jointly written article, the "Blacksburg Manifesto," on the need for reconfirming our values in public administration. I was especially attracted by the use of the term *calling,* which was not too clearly defined or elaborated. I then decided to do some research on the nature of the calling. This issue took me back to the Old Testament, the Koran, the Monastery Movement, the Crusades, the Conquistadores, the Protestant Reformation, the Puritans, the Unitarians (who indeed seem to have secularized the calling), and into the present. The term has been modified, bent, misapplied, abused, and used. But nevertheless, to this writer, it still has significance as an ethical construct for public administrators.

Dennis Thompson (Harvard University)

> You should know about a two-year project in which I am currently involved since it is focused partly on administrative ethics. The project is centered at Princeton under the leadership of Professor Amy Gutmann, and is part of a national "Project on the Federal Social Role," sponsored by the Carnegie Foundation, among others. The Princeton section begins this fall and will concentrate on the relationship between the democratic process, especially administration, and the social values underlying the welfare state. Invited speakers and local scholars will present papers, which will later be published as a book.

The Public Administration Journals

Journals are the life blood of any academic discipline. The only comprehensive statement I can make is that there is just too much to summarize neatly. The problem is compounded by the difficulty in defining what we mean by ethics in public administration. I believe Jerry Pops was correct when he said it is a mistake to think "that ethics is a topic within public administration, rather than about public administration." I am sure we could pick up any issue of *Public Administration Review* and with a little ingenuity discover an ethical question lurking in even the darkest positivist recesses. Ethical matters are and should be pervasive.

This is not to say that all administrative questions are of equal ethical significance or are equally amenable to ethical analysis. Nor is it to say that it is futile to try to define what one means by an ethical issue. It is to say that any review of the literature will necessarily be incomplete.

My review is no exception.* One clear trend is a careful attention to the use of language in moral argument. There are several first-rate articles on this point (Chandler 1983; Fischer 1983; Killingsworth 1984; Scott 1985). Another trend is to place considerable emphasis on administrative discretion as a central and perhaps the central problem in public administration ethics (Brady 1983; Chandler 1983; Foster 1981; Hetzner and Schmidt 1986; Koritansky 1982; Lilla 1981; Mayer and Harmon 1982; Morgan 1987; Warwick 1981). I return to this point later. One frequently finds articles on the teaching of ethics in the literature. There is no other topic in the field of public administration that has so many articles about teaching in refereed journals.

The point made by Delmer Dunn and Terry Cooper in the previous section about the dearth of empirical work is empirically verified by glancing through articles with such words as *moral, ethical,* or *responsible* in the titles. It is not altogether clear that authors writing in the field of ethics would make use of empirical work if there were more from which to choose. For instance, there is one fine empirical study on the espoused values of nearly seven hundred students and alumni from four graduate programs at the University of Kansas (public administration, law, business administration, and social welfare) (Edwards, Nalbandian, and Wedel 1981). The study shows that program affiliation accounts for differences in value preferences. This strikes me as a very significant finding, but the article is rarely cited in the ethics literature. This information would be particularly helpful for those who are of the business-is-different persuasion.

In view of the importance the media give to questions of conflict of interest and waste, fraud, and abuse, there is surprisingly little said about these matters in the public administration journals. For the most part, articles that do appear are written by practitioners (Dempsey 1984; Kusserow 1983; Walter 1981). As one might expect, these articles are quite effective in integrating ethical issues and management practice. For example, the best article on the Ethics in Government Act of 1978 was written by the first director of the Office of Government Ethics (Walter 1981).

---

* In deciding what journals I would examine, I followed the lead of David R. Morgan (Morgan et al. 1981). I read or reread every article related to ethics in the ten journals he selected for productivity analysis. Some have changed their names—e.g., *The Southern Review of Public Administration* is now *Public Administration Quarterly*. My starting date was 1981. I have also included other articles I read before starting to work on this report, even though they appeared in journals other than the ten selected by Morgan et al.

Most journal articles tend to paint with a broad brush and favor discussion of public administration ethics in general rather than specific areas of administrative activity. An important exception is the area of policy analysis, which has provided three particularly thoughtful articles. Each goes off in a different direction, but together they show that policy analysis yields interesting and important normative themes (Amy 1984; Beneveniste 1984; Davis and Portis 1982).* Debra Stewart's (1984) article on an "Ethical Framework for Human Resource Decision Making" also bucks the ethics in general trend. Stewart's article provides an excellent example of how an author can make a serious contribution to the ethics literature by addressing a carefully defined topic. There is a desperate need for articles with the sort of limited objectives Stewart addresses so skillfully.

My efforts to comment on the state of the discipline have been anticipated in several journal articles that offer broad, overall comments on certain aspects of ethical inquiry in public administration.† There are four such articles. The first is by John Worthley and Barbara Grumet (1983); it deals with teaching ethics. The authors provide some data from a survey in which they contacted one of every three programs affiliated with NASPAA—71 programs in all. Of the 71 programs, 31 replied. Of the 31 replies, 21 provide for some study of ethics in the curriculum; 15 of these 21 programs offer separate courses in ethics, and 9 of the 15 courses are required.

What I found most surprising in the article was the response to the authors' query "on which topics were included in the school's coverage of ethics. . . . The most frequent topic mentioned was discussion of values, including values clarification" (Worthley and Grumet 1983, 55). This was surprising because in reviewing the academic journals for this report, I noticed values clarification was rarely mentioned. I noted this absence with some satisfaction because I recently became critical of values clarification as a method of teaching. Although it can be effective when handled well, I have seen it too often reduced to mere propaganda for dogmatic relativists. I was eagerly looking forward to announcing the demise of values clarification on the basis of my review of the literature when I came upon the Worthley and Grumet finding of its salience in the classroom. Their finding suggests that there is quite a disparity between what one reads in the journals and what is going on in the classroom.

A second article with a state-of-the-discipline flavor bears the disconcerting

---

* A survey of teaching practices in schools of public policy is provided by Brown (1986).

† More recent information on ethics education may soon be available. There are at least two research projects under way. One is being conducted by April Dennis at the University of Southern California and the other by Dalton S. Lee and Darrell L. Pugh at San Diego State University.

title "The Possibility of Administrative Ethics" (Thompson 1985). Even more disconcerting than the title is the opening sentence: "Is administrative ethics possible?" (p. 555). The author replies in the affirmative. The point of the article is to show that it is impossible to discuss administrative ethics seriously unless one rejects

> two common views of administration. The first asserts that administrators ought to act neutrally in the sense that they should follow not their own moral principles but the decisions and policies of the organization. This is the ethic of neutrality. The second asserts that not administrators but the organization (and its formal officers) should be held responsible for its decisions and policies. This is the ethic of structure. (Thompson 1985, 555)

Thompsons's article attacks these two ethics. In the attack on the ethic of neutrality, Thompson preaches to the choir. It is a fine sermon, but there are few, if any, administrative theorists writing on ethics who are in need of repentance.* The recent literature in public administration journals emphatically rejects anything like the ethic of neutrality (Catron 1981; Fredrickson and Hart 1985; Hart 1983; Kerneghan 1984). It is somewhat ironic that the most valuable part of Thompson's measured and nuanced criticism of the ethic of neutrality is that it may serve as a wholesome corrective against intemperate and excessive rejections of the very position Thompson rejects. Excessive rejections of the ethic of neutrality come close to denying any moral value at all to any form of authority.

Thompson's attack on the ethic of structure is a major contribution to public administration ethics. The ethic of structure "asserts that not administrators, but the organization (and its formal officers) should be held responsible for its decisions and policies." This is a central problem in public administration ethics and, indeed, in any normative reflection on organizational life. In 1980, the *American Political Science Review* (APSR) carried an article by Thompson titled "Moral Responsibility of Public Officials: The Problem of Many Hands." This article succeeds in demonstrating how it is possible for an individual to be held morally responsible for an organizational decision. It is the best example of clear and careful moral reasoning that I have seen in a political science journal. Had it been published in *Public Administration Review* instead of the *American Political Science Review,* it would be cited much more frequently in public administration journals. Thompson's 1985 article, which does appear in *Public Administration Review,* restates the main line of the argument in the earlier article but is no substitute for the earlier article. For anyone interested in the important question of personal accountability in collective decision making, "The Problem of Many Hands" is required reading.

A third state-of-the-discipline comment appeared in an article by M.S.

---

* The only author cited directly is George Graham (1974).

Jackson (1984) in the *Australian Journal of Public Administration*. The article, titled "Eichmann, Bureaucracy, and Ethics," began with a review of the many academic references to Eichmann as the archetypal bureaucrat. Jackson argues that these references fail to understand both Eichmann and bureaucracy. He maintains (correctly, I believe) that the SS was not a Weberian bureaucracy, nor was it just another government department. Jackson is certainly correct when he says the SS was "no model of bureaucratic functioning either internally or externally" (Jackson 1984, 304).

As for Eichmann, Jackson maintains those who describe him as one who followed orders mindlessly have been taken in by Eichmann. This, after all, was his defense in a capital trial—a rather inept defense as events revealed, but perhaps his best chance to escape justice. Hannah Arendt took Eichmann seriously, but saw more deeply into his character—or more precisely into his lack of character. She argues that "Eichmann was neither the demonic anti-Semite asserted by the prosecution nor the archetype of the bureaucrat asserted by Eichmann himself. Rather, he was a man devoid of the ability to make judgments or even to see that a judgment was needed. This is the banality of evil" (Jackson 1984, 303).

Following Arendt, Jackson (1984) maintains that there is no evidence to support the claim that it was "the bureaucratic system that had prevented him [Eichmann] from exercising what Immanuel Kant had called reflective judgment to distinguish right from wrong. He lacked that ability in the first place"(p. 303).

Jackson offers a serious challenge to scholars prone to make facile comments on Eichmann as symptomatic of the evils of bureaucracy. One even hears the term "petit Eichmann" used to describe stodgy, rigid, rule-bound, time-serving bureaucrats in a welfare agency or an educational bureaucracy. Such language is ill advised. It calumniates the stodgy bureaucrat who, despite his or her failings, may well be a decent person—something Eichmann was not. Petit Eichmann suggests that the difference between bureaucratic rigidity and mass murder is simply one of degree. It strikes me as an insensitive use of language that trivializes the Holocaust.

I hope that future articles linking Eichmann (grand ou petit) to bureaucracy take Jackson seriously. I cannot believe that the case against bureaucracy is so weak that it must subpoena Eichmann as a star witness.

Jackson (1984, 306) makes two other points that are pertinent to the purposes of this report. The first is a rather sweeping statement that "books on public administration now have a mandatory chapter on ethics." (I think he means textbooks.) He continues: "In these perfunctory discussions all too often moral relativism or subjectivism is assumed and all ethical terms are qualified in some unspecified way by the liberal use of quotation marks, italics, or rhetorical questions" (Jackson 1984, 306).

Jackson cites only one book to support his assertion. I regret that I have not examined textbooks closely enough to hazard a judgment on the accuracy of

Jackson's remark. I note it only because if Jackson is correct, we may have an explanation for the anomaly on values clarification I mentioned above—values clarification is prevalent in the classroom but ignored in refereed journals. Perhaps the textbooks account for the survival of values clarification.

Jackson's second point concerns the heavy reliance on John Rawls in the public administration literature. He points out that one of the reasons for the popularity of Rawls's *Theory of Justice* is that it rests on an exposition of liberal democratic values. He continues: "But surely, there is something fundamentally wrong in being asked to accept those values because they are ours" (Jackson 1984, 306). Jackson is correct; this is a most unphilosophical reason for accepting a philosophical position. If we are going to accept Rawls's philosophy, we should do so not because it flatters our prejudices but because it is true. Before we decide whether it is true, however, it would seem reasonable to ask authors who follow Rawls to give evidence of some familiarity with the serious body of literature critical of Rawls —more than the fashionable juxtaposing of Rawls and Nozick. Literature that challenges Rawls on the most fundamental questions (see Bloom 1975; Burke 1986; Schaefer 1979) should be examined.

The final article in the state-of-the-discipline mode is Mark Lilla's (1981) "Ethos, Ethics, and Public Service," which appeared in the *Public Interest.** Lilla is not a professor of public administration, so his comments provide something of an outside view of our efforts to teach and write about ethics in public administration.

Lilla (1981) is quite critical of what he finds. The gist of his argument is captured in his observation that our students "are learning a rather peculiar sort of philosophical discourse which allows them to make sophisticated excuses for their actions without preparing them to act responsibly in a democracy" (p. 8). Much of Lilla's article is devoted to a discussion of what he sees as the unfortunate influence of philosophers on schools of public policy. Lilla (1981) maintains that, across the nation, "programs in public administration were changed in the 1960s to graduate programs in public policy and this change in appellation signified a great shift in what was taught and the spirit in which it was taught" (p. 8). The new emphasis provided more sophisticated analytic techniques. What he criticizes is that the change from public administration to public policy signaled a loss of "an ethic which prepares the student, through an informal moral education to take his place within a democratic government" (Lilla 1981, 8).†

He fondly reviews the literature of an earlier era and mourns the passing of such men as Paul Appleby, whose writings he cites to warn against the blandish-

---

* A discussion of Lilla's article is found in Mayer and Harmon (1982).

† For a further criticism of the emphasis on public policy, see Dennis Hale (1988).

ments of philosophy. He quotes approvingly from Appleby's 1952 book, *Morality and Administration in Democratic Government:* "We therefore beg the more general questions which philosophers ruminate; we begin by assuming democracy" (Appleby 1952, 28).

Lilla discusses with respect the venerable debate between Carl Friedrich and Herman Finer on the responsible use of administrative discretion and reminds us that we have lost something terribly important:

> Rereading these old debates, one is struck with how deeply an unquestioned ethos penetrated the ideas and writings of the time. No matter how much debate there was over the nature of administrative responsibility in a democracy, there was no question but that democracy in the U.S. was itself legitimate; the only question was how the moral public official could best serve that democracy when government agencies and programs become large and complex and administrators found themselves with discretion. Like Talmudic scholars, students and teachers of public administration pored over the Constitution and American legal history to find the proper interpretation of "duty" and "responsibility." That its character was so seriously debated shows that the democratic administrative ethos was alive and well. (Lilla 1981, 6–7)

Lilla is right. We have lost some of the public-spiritedness of the men and women who led our field in the past. Part of the problem is that we have lost touch with our past. It was disappointing but hardly surprising to find in my review of the literature precious few references to the works of Paul Appleby (1952), Carl Friedrich (1940), Herman Finer (1941), Stephen Bailey (1964), and Wayne Leys (1943). The one notable exception was a thoughtful article by York Willbern (1984). The problem with Willbern's article, however, was that he had no references to works published after 1966. Thus, his essay, thoughtful as it was, did little for maintaining a continuity in the professional ethics discussion.*

Indeed, so weak is our sense of continuity that the current ethics literature has only a few passing references to a movement as recent as the "new public administration." This is fair enough, perhaps, in view of the new public administration's cavalier treatment of its own predecessors. Fair or not, it is certainly unfortunate and potentially disastrous to carry on our normative reflections in isolation from our past. Ethical principles that are effective in influencing behavior do not spring full-blown from the minds of philosophers. They grow within traditions.

---

* In addition to pre-1967 literature, Willbern cites an unpublished lecture that Dwight Waldo delivered at Indiana University in 1977.

Personal Observations

In thinking about the state of the discipline, I found several concerns recurring at different points in the work. These concerns took the shape of complaints, suggestions, and ideas for further research. This section describes some of those concerns.

Word, Words, Words

Three terms should be used with greater circumspection than we often find in literature and conversation about ethics. They are *rhetoric, prudence,* and *following orders.* All three are frequently used with pejorative connotations that are inappropriate.

Rhetoric is the art of persuasive speech or writing. One of the hallmarks of a free society is that persuasion, as opposed to coercion, is supposed to play an important role in governmental decision making. If we burden rhetoric with overtones of cheap gimmickry, we degrade our politics.

Prudence is the name of a virtue, not a vice. It is a virtue in which those who govern should excel. Unfortunately, the word is often used as though it were synonymous with crass expediency. Eugene Miller (1979) and John Koritansky (1982) have written well on prudence in a way that is pertinent to public administrators.

Following orders is another expression with undeservedly pejorative overtones. The expression, of course, is redolent of Eichmann's defense at his Jerusalem trial. What is often overlooked, however, is that we despise Eichmann, not because he followed orders, but because of the orders he followed. The American soldiers who died at Normandy were also following orders. We rightly revere them as heroes. There is nothing abject or craven about following orders when one has freely chosen to obey the legal commands of those who govern a fundamentally just regime. For the most part, when government officials follow orders, they are simply putting into practice their fidelity to the rule of law. Before we condemn those who follow orders, we should first look at the nature of the orders they follow. The Watergate thugs went to jail, not because they followed orders, but because the orders they followed were illegal.

Case Studies

A common criticism of the public administration ethics literature is that it is too abstract. This criticism is surely understandable. It should be taken seriously, but not too seriously. There is simply no point in trying to please those who want to take their ethics in anecdotal capsules. This is not to say, however, that no effort should be made to accommodate those who see our work as excessively abstract.

Case studies are one way of making the accommodation. Many teachers of public administration ethics use various kinds of case studies in their classrooms. This would seem to be a sensible way to make abstract principles come alive. Unfortunately, case studies play a very minor role in ethics research and writing. The reason for this is that case studies provide a rather fragile basis for generalizations.

Case studies should be used to test and apply principles rather than simply collect them to support a general proposition. One difficulty with this suggestion is that it would make journal articles terribly long. Before an author applies his principle to a case, he must first explain the case. Ordinarily, this cannot be done in a paragraph or two. The strength of the case study often lies in its gothic and arcane detail.

We could solve the problem if we could take it for granted that everyone writing in the field of public administration ethics knew the details of certain cases. Lawyers do this when they refer to elaborate mixtures of law and fact by case title (e.g., *Brown* v. *Board of Education*, the *Schecter* case, the *Bakke* decision). Common literary allusions fill the same shorthand function. Authors weave into the fabric of their arguments the names of Sampson, Achilles, Lady Macbeth, Huckleberry Finn, Mr. Micawber, and Holden Caulfield without tedious explanations. The same is true of references to historical periods: classical antiquity, the Renaissance, the Reformation, the Napoleonic era, the New Deal, and so on. Indeed, similar laconic expressions are not unknown in our own field. In a journal article, the author is not obliged to explain what he means by the Hawthorne Effect, the politics/administration dichotomy, scientific management, or the *Literary Digest* poll.

There is readily available a good collection of case studies selected specifically with ethical questions in mind: *Ethics and Politics: Cases and Comments*, edited by Amy Gutmann and Dennis Thompson (1984). Would it be possible for people writing for publication in public administration journals to apply their principles and arguments with brief references to certain persons or situations in these cases? To do this, persons writing in the field (and journal referees) would have to reach some sort of informal understanding on what might be an acceptable technique in this matter. All the cases in the Gutmann and Thompson casebook touch on public administration, but some are more useful than others for bringing out ethical principles.* Whatever quarrels one might have with particular selections in the Gutmann and Thompson book, the great advantage of the book is that it exists. If we were to become accustomed to using the same cases as points of reference, we might take a step toward remedying the defect Bayard Catron noted when he described our work as "fragmented, poorly understood, quite idiosyncratic, and lack[ing] a common theoretical grounding—and even a common vocabulary."

---

* The cases I have found most helpful are: Henry L. Stimson, "The Decision to Use the Atomic Bomb"; Dennis Thompson, "The Denver Income Maintenance Experiment"; Gary L. Greenberg, "Revolt at Justice"; Taylor Branch, "The Odd Couple"; Fred G. Leebron, "Ellsberg and the Pentagon Papers"; Marion Smiley, "Legalizing Laetrile"; and Joseph A. Califano, "Abortion."

In making this suggestion, I do not intend to confer canonical status on the Gutmann and Thompson casebook. To be sure, many (and perhaps most) journal articles require no reference to case studies of any kind. Other articles will find other case studies more helpful. When this is the case, the author will be obliged to explain the case as fully as necessary. My point has been to address the situation in which one of the Gutmann and Thompson cases would illustrate or test adequately the principle an author had in mind. In those circumstances, it would seem to represent an advance in our work if an author could analyze an argument advanced by a leading character in, say, the Laetrile case without feeling obliged to give the full factual background of the argument.

Management of Governmental Ethics Programs

These have received little attention in the literature. The Office of Governmental Ethics (OGE), created by the Ethics in Government Act of 1978, would seem to be a likely candidate for close scrutiny by academics interested in questions of ethics. Jeremy Plant and Harold Gortner (1981) published a good article on OGE in 1981.* An article in *Public Administration Review* by J. Jackson Walter, the former director of OGE, was mentioned earlier (Walter 1981). Despite these efforts, much remains to be learned about the management of ethics programs at both state and national levels.

The OGE is a particularly interesting organization because it is part of the Office of Personnel Management (OPM). Recall that one of the main purposes of the Civil Service Reform Act of 1978 (CSRA) was to separate the management and watchdog functions of the old Civil Service Commission. The Merit System Protection Board (MSPA) was to police the merit system, while OPM was to serve as a managerial arm of the President.

The fact that OGE was housed in OPM suggests that Congress saw ethics as a function of presidential management. As it turned out, however, one of the most important functions of OGE was to be sure that the financial affairs of presidential appointees were in compliance with the Ethics in Government Act of 1978. This meant that OGE had a somewhat adversarial relationship to the President and to OPM. Interestingly, this development put pressure on the distinction between policing the President and managing on his behalf—the distinction that was at the heart of the CSRA.

The plot thickened when OGE faced its five-year review for renewal in 1983. The Senate passed a bill that would have permitted the President to remove the director for cause only. The Justice Department strenuously objected to this provi-

---

* In the same volume, see also James S. Bowman, "The Management of Ethics: Codes of Conduct in Organizations."

sion on consitutional grounds. In a letter to Congressman William Ford, chairman of the House Committee on Post Office and Civil Service, Assistant Attorney General Robert A. McConnell developed a straightforward managerial view of the President's relationship to OGE. McConnell maintained that the function of the director of OGE was purely executive and that therefore it would be unconstitutional for Congress to impose a cause-only condition on the President's power to remove such an officer (U.S. Congress, Senate Committee 1983). This interpretation ignored the director's need for independence when he must make difficult decisions on financial affairs of men and women the President wishes to appoint to high executive office.

Thus the old problem of the defunct Civil Service Commission—the fusion of managerial and watchdog functions in one agency—seems to have resurfaced in OGE. *Plus ça change, plus la même chose.* This is a subject that is ready for serious research.

Politicizing the Civil Service

The politicization of the federal civil service is a serious and constant theme in public administration literature. The topic has important implications for ethics as well as for the field of public administration as a whole. A central aspect of the problem is that much of the politicization is legal. If we deplore this trend, as most of us do, we find that the high ground of our argument has been cut out from under us by the Civil Service Reform Act of 1978. I believe it is accurate to say that this legislation was intended, at least in part, to politicize the civil service. If this is true, then charges of abuse and corruption must be made with some caution.

If career civil servants must make their peace with a politicized professional environment, we must rethink the proper role of the civil service. Such thinking, of course, takes us far beyond questions of ethics. One ethical issue we might consider, however, is to help the career civil servant develop a new ideal of what a public administration professional ought to be. At the higher reaches of the career service, it may no longer be reasonable to talk about nonpartisanship as an ideal. Perhaps we should rethink the traditional norm in terms of bipartisanship rather than nonpartisanship. That is, the high-ranking career civil servant is one who can serve both Democrats and Republicans. He can do this, not because he is indifferent to both parties (the old ideal of nonpartisanship), but because he can be committed to each of them (the new ideal of bipartisanship).

For decades, public administration journals have provided a steady drumbeat attacking the politics/administration dichotomy. To mix the metaphor, these chickens have now come home to roost. We were right. The administrative process is inherently political, as we said all along. We might wish that the CSRA had recognized this reality in a way that was more subtle and less threatening to the integrity of administrative institutions, but the work of politics is never that tidy. The CSRA is a terribly significant piece of legislation. It requires a rethinking of the normative foundations of our field.

In suggesting that bipartisanship replace nonpartisanship, I direct the attention of the career civil servant to the Constitution that he or she has sworn to uphold. One can then look on our bipartisan politics as a concrete expression of the constitutional order, albeit an expression somewhat at odds with what the framers of the Constitution had in mind. The ideal for the high-ranking civil servant would be to carry out his or her program like a loyal Democrat in a Democratic administration and like a loyal Republican in a Republican administration. Such chameleon-like behavior does not demand that a person abandon all principles. On the contrary, it suggests that a person develop a principle much deeper than the partisan principles that motivate Democrats and Republicans.* The civil servant's commitment is to the preservation of the constitutional order, which is now in the hands of one party and now in the hands of another. Questions such as affirmative action, deregulation, a nuclear freeze, and the Strategic Defense Initiative would be taken seriously, but they would be seen as questions of a second level of seriousness for the civil servant. The preservation of the constitutional order would always come first. The American civil servant would revere the Constitution the way the British civil servant reveres the Crown.

As a behavioral consequence of this bipartisan way of looking at the civil service, we could deduce an ethical obligation to study carefully the platforms of both major parties during a presidential campaign. This would apply especially to those aspects of the platforms and the candidates' speeches that affect a particular civil servant's program. There would be a further obligation to consider seriously what one might do at one's own level to help the successful candidate put his or her campaign objective into effect. The practice in the British civil service of studying the partisan manifestoes during an election campaign might serve as a model.

These ideas are sketchy but are offered as a positive way of coming to terms with what we may someday look upon as a new era of public administration that began with CSRA. It is not terribly helpful to wring our hands over the politicization of the civil service when the law is on the side of the politicizers. These ideas have been more fully developed elsewhere (Rohr 1986).

---

* Because of the commitment to the Constitution, I can parry the thrust that my ideal bureaucrat is an American version of the Vicar of Bray, "who kept his job 'no matter what King may rule, sir'—shifting from allegiance to allegiance, from prayer book to prayer book, with not a thought for God, conscience or national interest " (Ridley 1985, 31).

Conclusion

Throughout this report, I have stressed the diversity in the ethics field; a diversity that comes close to chaos. I do not want to leave the impression that there is no consensus. On the contrary, there is an emerging consensus on the precise nature of the ethical problem that is peculiar to the career civil servant—as opposed to the judge or the elected official. That problem is the responsible use of administrative discretion.

My reason for saying this is somewhat personal; it rests primarily on the reviews of my book *Ethics for Bureaucrats* (Rohr 1978). Many faults were found with that book, but on one major point I escaped unscathed. In the first chapter, I argued that the way a bureaucrat uses discretion is the central ethical problem for the career civil servant. This is because through administrative discretion a career civil servant participates in governing a democratic society without being directly accountable to the electorate. As far as I can recall, no reviewer questioned that point. Nor have I ever been challenged on this point in question periods following lectures I have given on ethics and public administration. I have been boxed about the ears on just about everything else I have to say about ethics, but not on the centrality of discretion.

I will not claim that it was pellucid reasoning on my part that has led to a general acquiesence in this position. It is more likely that no one disagreed with me because I had belabored the obvious. There was certainly nothing original in what I had to say. Wayne Leys noted the connection between ethics and discretion as early as 1943, and his argument was anticipated by Carl Friedrich in his famous debate with Herman Finer in 1939–40. Many contemporary authors continue to make the same point in a variety of ways.* Indeed, so prevalent are the references to discretion in the public administration ethics literature that I am prepared to assert that a consensus has settled around the proposition that the responsible use of administrative discretion is the central ethical problem for the career civil service. I do not intend this assertion to be provocative. If it is provocative, then it is false; for if it provokes, no consensus exists. I hope it will be received as the bland truism I think it is. Truisms are dull, but they have the advantage of being true. If it is true that a consensus has settled around the centrality of administrative discretion, we have made some progress since the bleak days of Vietnam and Watergate when so many academics found themselves embarrassed by their inability to know where to begin to think and to write seriously about moral issues in public adminstration.

---

* For contemporary articles linking ethics and discretion, see Chandler 1983; Foster 1981; Lilla 1981; Warwick 1981; Koritansky 1982; Mayer and Harmon 1982; Brady 1983; Hetzner and Schmidt 1986; and Morgan 1987. I have stressed the centrality of discretion in several of my own articles (see Rohr 1980, 1982, 1983). The link between ethics and discretion is quite clear in several books and collections of essays (see Burke 1986; Handler 1986; Hibbeln and Shumavon 1986).

References

Ajvogu, M.O. 1983. "Ethical Dilemmas of Public Sector Executives in a Developing Economy." *International Review of Administrative Sciences* 49:386–92.

Amy, Douglas J. 1984. "Why Policy Analysis and Ethics Are Incompatible." *Journal of Policy Analysis and Management* 3:523–91.

Appleby, Paul. 1952. *Morality and Administration in Democratic Government.* Baton Rouge: Louisiana State University Press.

Bailey, Stephen K. 1964. "Ethics and the Public Service." *Public Administration Review* 24:234–43.

Beneveniste, Guy. 1984. "On a Code of Ethics for Policy Experts." *Journal of Policy Analysis and Management* 3:561–72.

Bergerson, Peter J., and Brian R. Nedwek. 1986. "Ethics and Public Policy: Toward an Understanding of a Research Tradition." Presented at the annual meeting of the American Society for Public Administration, Anaheim, Calif.

Bloom, Allan. 1975. "Justice: A Spectrum of Responses to John Rawls's Theory." *American Political Science Review* 69:585–674.

Bowie, Norman E. 1981. *Ethical Issues in Government.* Philadelphia: Temple University Press.

Bowman, James S. 1981. "Ethics and the Public Service: A Selected Annotated Bibliography." *Public Personnel Management Journal* 10:179–99.

Bowman, James S. 1983. *Essentials of Management: Ethical Values, Attitudes, and Actions.* New York: Associated Faculty Press.

Bowman, James S., F. A. Elliston, and Paula Lockhart, eds. 1984. *Professional Dissent: An Annotated Bibliography and Research Guide.* New York: Garland.

Brady, Neil F. 1983. "Feeling and Understanding: A Moral Psychology for Public Servants." *Public Administration Quarterly* 7:220–40.

Brown, Peter G. 1986. "Ethics and Education for Public Service in a Liberal State." *Journal of Policy Analysis and Management* 6:56–68.

Burke, John P. 1984. "Squaring the Circle: Making Bureaucracy Accountable." *Polity* 17:179–91.

Burke, John P. 1986. *Bureaucratic Responsibility.* Baltimore: Johns Hopkins University Press.

Catron, Bayard L. 1981. "Ethical Postures and Ethical Posturing." *American Review of Public Administration* 17:155–58.

Chandler, Ralph Clark. 1983. "The Problem of Moral Reasoning in American Public Administration: The Case for a Code of Ethics." *Public Administration Review* 43:32–39.

Cooper, Terry L. 1982. *The Responsible Administrator: An Approach to Ethics for the Administrative Role.* Port Washington, N.Y.: Kennikat Press.

Davis, Dwight F., and Edward B. Portis. 1982. "A Categorical Imperative for Social Scientific Policy Evaluation." *Administration and Society* 14:175–93.

Dempsey, Charles L. 1984. "Managerial Accountability and Responsibility." *Bureaucrat* 12:17–23.

Edwards, Terry, John Nalbandian, and Kenneth R. Wedel. 1981. "Individual Values and Professional Education." *Administration and Society* 13:123–44.

Finer, Herman. 1941. "Administrative Responsibility in Democratic Government." *Public Administration Review* 1:335–50.

Fischer, Frank. 1980. *Politics, Values, and Public Policy: The Problem of Methodology.* Boulder, Colo.: Westview Press.

Fischer, Frank. 1983. "Ethical Discourses in Public Administration." *Administration and Society* 15:5–42.

Fischer, Frank, and John Forester, eds. 1987. *Confronting Values in Policy Analysis: The Politics of Criteria.* Beverly Hills: Sage.

Fleishmann, Joel, Lance Leibman, and Mark H. Moore. 1981. *Public Duties: The Moral Obligations of Government Officials.* Cambridge, Mass.: Harvard University Press.

Foster, Gregory D. 1981. "Law, Morality, and the Public Servant." *Public Administration Review* 41:29–34.

Frederickson, H. George, and David K. Hart. 1985. "The Public Service and the Patriotism of Benevolence." *Public Administration Review* 45:547–54.

French, P.A. 1983. *Ethics in Government.* Englewood Cliffs, N.J.: Prentice-Hall.

Friedrich, Carl J. 1940. "The Nature of Administrative Responsibility." In *Public Policy,* edited by Carl J. Friedrich. Cambridge, Mass.: Harvard University Press.

Gardiner, John, and Theodore Lyman. 1984. *The Fraud Control Game: State Responses to Fraud and Abuses in AFDC and Medical Programs.* Bloomington: Indiana University Press.

Gawthrop, Louis. 1984. *Public Sector Management, Systems, and Ethics.* Bloomington: Indiana University Press.

Graham, George. 1974. "Ethical Guidelines for Public Administrators." *Public Administration Review* 34:90–92.

Gutmann, Amy, and Dennis Thompson, eds. 1984. *Ethics and Politics: Cases and Comments.* Chicago: Nelson-Hall.

Hale, Dennis. 1988. "Just What Is Policy Anyway? And Who's Supposed to Make It? A Survey of the Public Administration and Policy Texts." *Administration and Society* 19:423–52.

Handler, Joel F. 1986. *The Conditions of Discretion: Autonomy, Community, Bureaucracy.* New York: Russell Sage.

Hart, David K. 1983. "The Honorable Bureaucrat among the Philistines: A Reply to 'Ethical Discourse in Public Administration.'" *Administration and Society* 15:43–48.

Hetzner, C., and V.A. Schmidt. 1986. "Bringing Moral Values Back In: The Role of Formal Philosophy in Effective Ethical Public Administration." *International Journal of Public Administration* 8:429–53.

Hibbeln, Kenneth, and Douglas Shumavon. 1986. *Administrative Decision and Public Policy.* New York: Praeger.

Jackson, M.S. 1984. "Eichmann, Bureaucracy and Ethics." *Australian Journal of Public Administration* 43:301–7.

Johnston, Michael. 1982. *Political Corruption and Public Policy in America.* Monterey, Calif.: Brooks/Cole.

Kerneghan, Kenneth. 1984. "The Conscience of the Bureaucrat." *Canadian Public Administration* 27:576–91.

Killingsworth, James R. 1984. "Idle Talk and Modern Administration." *Administration and Society* 16:346–83.

Koritansky, John C. 1982. "Prudence and the Practice of Government." *Public Administration Quarterly* 6:111–22.

Krislov, Samuel, and David H. Rosenbloom. 1981. *Representative Bureaucracy and the American Political System.* New York: Praeger.

Kusserow, Richard P. 1983. "Fighting Fraud, Waste, and Abuse." *Bureaucrat* 12:19–23.

Leys, Wayne A.R. 1943. "Ethics and Administrative Discretion." *Public Administration Review* 3:10–23.

Leys, Wayne A.R. 1952. *Ethics for Policy Decisions.* New York: Prentice-Hall.

Lilla, Mark T. 1981. "Ethos, Ethics, and Public Service." *Public Interest* 63:3–17.

Louthan, William C. 1981. *The Politics of Managerial Morality.* Washington, D.C.: University Press of America.

Mayer, Richard T., and Michael M. Harmon. 1982. "Teaching Moral Education in Public Administration." *Southern Review of Public Administration* 6:217–26.

Mertins, Herman, Jr., and P.J. Hennigan, eds. 1982. *Applying Professional Standards and Ethics in the Eighties: A Workbook and Study Guide for Public Administrators.* 2d ed. Washington, D.C.: American Society for Public Administration.

Miller, Eugene. 1979. "Prudence and the Role of Law." *American Journal of Jurisprudence* 24:181–205.

Morgan, David R., Kenneth J. Meier, Richard C. Kearney, Steven W. Hays, and Harold B. Birch. 1981. "Reputation and Productivity among U.S. Public Administration and Public Affairs Programs." *Public Administration Review* 41:666–73.

Morgan, Douglas. 1985. "Centennials and Bicentennials: The Moral Foundation of American Administrative Discretion." Presented at the annual meeting of the American Political Science Association in New Orleans, La.

Morgan, Douglas. 1987. "Varieties of Administrative Abuse: Some Reflections on Ethics and Discretion." *Administration and Society* 19:267–84.

National Association of Schools of Public Affairs and Administration. 1981. *Standards for Professional Master's Degree Programs in Public Affairs and Administration.* Washington, D.C.: The Association.

Plant, Jeremy, and Harold Gortner. 1981. "Ethics, Personnel Management and Civil Service Reform." *Public Personnel Management* 10:3–10.

Rawls, John. 1971. *Theory of Justice.* Cambridge, Mass.: Harvard University Press.

Ridley, F. 1985. "Political Neutrality in the British Civil Service." In Royal Institute of Public Administration compilation, *Politics, Ethics and the Public Service.* London: Royal Institute of Public Administration.

Rohr, John A. 1978. *Ethics for Bureaucrats: An Essay on Law and Values.* New York: Marcel Dekker.

Rohr, John A. 1980. "Ethics for the Senior Executive Service." *Administration and Society* 12:203–16.

Rohr, John A. 1982. "The Problem of Professional Ethics." *Bureaucrat* 11:47–51.

Rohr, John A. 1983. "Administrative Decision Making and Professionalism." *Review of Public Personnel Administration* 11:61–70.

Rohr, John A. 1986. *To Run a Constitution: The Legitimacy of the Administrative State.* Lawrence, Kan.: University Press of Kansas.

Rosen, Bernard. 1982. *Holding Government Bureaucracies Accountable.* New York: Praeger.

Royal Institute of Public Administration. 1985. *Politics, Ethics, and the Public Service.* London: The Institute.

Schaefer, David L. 1979. *Justice or Tyranny: A Critique of John Rawls' A Theory of Justice.* Port Washington, N.Y.: Kennikat Press.

Scott, William G. 1985. "Organization Revolution: An End to Managerial Orthodoxy." *Administration and Society* 17:149–70.

Stewart, Debra. 1984. "Managing Conflicting Claims: An Ethical Framework for Human Resource Decision Making." *Public Administration Review* 44:14–22.

Thompson, Dennis. 1980. "Moral Responsibility of Public Officials: The Problem of Many Hands." *American Political Science Review* 74:905–16.

Thompson, Dennis. 1981. "The Private Lives of Public Officials." In *Public Duties: The Moral Obligation of Government Officials,* edited by Joel Fleishman, Lance Liebman, and Mark H. Moore. Cambridge, Mass.: Harvard University Press.

Thompson, Dennis. 1985. "The Possibility of Administrative Ethics." *Public Administration Review* 45:555–61.

Thompson, Dennis. 1987. *Political Ethics and Public Office.* Cambridge, Mass.: Harvard University Press.

U.S. Congress, Senate Committee on Governmental Affairs. 1983. *Reorganization of the Office of Governmental Affairs.* S. 461 Report #98-59. Washington, D.C.: Government Printing Office.

Vocino, Thomas, and Robert Elliott. 1982. "Journal Prestige in Public Administration: A Research Note." *Administration and Society* 14:5–14.

Walter, J. Jackson. 1981. "The Ethics in Government Act, Conflict of Interest Laws, and Presidential Recruiting." *Public Administration Review* 41:659–65.

Warwick, Donald P. 1981. "The Ethics of Administrative Discretion." In *Public Duties: The Moral Obligations of Government Officials,* edited by Joel Fleishman, Lance Liebman, and Mark H. Moore. Cambridge, Mass.: Harvard University Press.

Willbern, York. 1984. "Type and Levels of Public Morality." *Public Administration Review* 44:102–8.

Worthley, John, and Barbara Grumet. 1983. "Ethics and Public Administration: Teaching What Can't Be Taught." *American Review of Public Administration* 17:54–86.

Yates, Douglas. 1982. *Bureaucratic Democracy: The Search for Democracy and Efficiency in American Government.* Cambridge, Mass.: Harvard University Press.

PART TWO

Issues of Organization and Management

7

Public Sector Organization Behavior and Theory: Perspectives on Nagging Problems and on Real Progress

Robert T. Golembiewski

The complex and often contradictory body of analysis and practice referred to as Public Sector Organization Behavior and Theory (PSOBT) has developed over an extended period of time but still has far to go. Hence, this chapter has a dual focus —on nagging problems as well as on real progress in public-sector organization behavior and theory.

This field of analysis/practice has been with us since ancient times. Consider how Plato approached the practical/theoretical/philosophical issues of staffing the just polity, recommending what amounted to a set of stress interviews to assess the "real selves" of candidates by getting them to overindulge in strong drink. Moreover, we have long had a reasonable sense of the conceptual expanse covered by public-sector organization behavior and theory, as Plato again illustrates. He in effect relied on an empirical theory of the complex personality—with levels of consciousness, including defenses that serve to camouflage or distort but that can be relaxed, thus revealing the core attitudes and values of the real person. At the same time, Plato raised the normative and ethical issues that must dominate in organization behavior and theory. Is alcohol an appropriate aid in selection processes? This presages latter-day innovations in thought control, such as lie detectors, and the mind control suggested by experiments with brain stimulation.

Mapping Two Major Perspectives

No single approach can adequately assess the state of PSOBT, and this effort no doubt neglects something. But so it must be. This analysis focuses on two major perspectives on PSOBT: *problems* in development and *progress* in development.

Problems in Development

The focus on problems may be misleading in two ways, and may induce counterproductive defensiveness. Problems might well be labeled "challenges" due to their inherent complexity, or even "opportunities" because of their leverage for personal and collective empowerment. This wording may change the mind-set of some readers. Moreover, the problems in the developmental history sketched below are not all unique to the public sector. Proponents of PSOBT need not feel that the problems, challenges, or opportunities are theirs alone to bear.

These caveats aside, the present view of PSOBT developmental problems is trinitarian. Major sections focus on (1) the schizoid character of opinion about the role of values in political and organization arenas, (2) the confusion about kinds of theories and their various relevancies to PSOBT, and (3) the forms in which PSOBT has manifested itself over time.

The Uneasy Tension between Political and Organizational Values

This chapter can only begin to detail the major issues highlighting the relevance of values for organizations within a political system of representative democracy, but some primitive points need to be made. In an elemental and simplified spirit, values are defined as an individual's concept of an ideal relationship or state of affairs, which a person uses to assess the goodness or badness, the rightness or wrongness, of actual conditions observed or contemplated (Scott 1964, 3). This analysis first deals with the general case, then focuses on values in PSOBT.

Some General Issues Involving Values. Humans vest all things and relationships with value. Indeed, humans are perhaps essentially characterized by their ubiquitous value-infusing proclivities. This investing with value involves both the "desired" and the "desirable," which can be identical in some cases but very different in others.

The "desired" relates to that variety of preferences having naturalist or humanist roots, and these may be substantially variable or even contradictory over time. Thus the desired may appear in conventional social agreements reinforced by pressure toward conformity or by a need for approval, or it may derive from postulated human needs such as those described by Maslow, Herzberg, or Argyris (e.g., Eddy 1981, 99–101). Conveniently, the desired is often reflected in means-oriented ways—as in guidelines for behavior, in statements of ethics to guide professionals, and so on. These have a basic weakness: Their relative specificity often cannot contain human ingenuity, particularly in complex and changing environments.

In contrast, the "desirable" emphasizes ends-oriented approaches, following Walter's useful distinction (1984, 424). Basically, an ends-orientation proposes general principles—of morals as well as "goods" or "shoulds." The ethical task involves deciding in specific cases which particular practices or policies contribute to these ends and which detract from them. Walter focuses on three such goods—individual freedom, privacy, and self-esteem. Similarly, Golembiewski (1965, 64–65) derives five goals from the Judeo-Christian moral tradition that should characterize life in organizations (e.g., work should not generally threaten the individual, and the organization should not be the sole and final arbiter of behavior).

Neither organizational analysis nor praxis can avoid dealing with values as both desired and desirable, because the very act of organizing utilizes resources in some ways for some purposes. These ways and purposes involve choice, and choice presupposes judgments concerning the desired and the desirable. But both organization analysis and application have complicated the straightforward. For example, contemporary social science methodology often has aspired to value-free status, or at least to value neutrality. That tradition variously confounds and confuses what seems direct (Sjoberg, Vaughan, and Sjoberg 1984).

The confounding and confusing of value issues derives from complex sources, but the mischief is always substantial. One simply cannot conduct organization analysis, and especially application, that way. Values in fact have an impact on organization analysis and application, and must do so in principle. First, as to the fact, consider these illustrations.

Utilitarianism has explicitly influenced the behavioral and social sciences, covering the range from the Supreme Court decision in *Brown* v. *Board of Education* (1954, 1955) about racial segregation in education to typical survey/feedback intervention. Utilitarianism proposes that each individual performs hedonist pleasure/pain calculations, and the greatest good for the greater number becomes the criterion for collective choice between alternatives.*

Nation-state morality has affected the behavioral sciences generally (Prewitt 1984), and international relations specifically (Beer 1984). Nation-state moral imperatives emphasize patriotism, legal and civil order, and so on.

Cultural relativism has a pervasive influence not only in disciplinary contexts but especially in the broad prescription that the moral orientations of some cultures (especially dominant ones) should not be imposed on either the analysis of other cultures or on their practices. This prescription often has been coupled with the notion that there is nothing to choose between sets of cultural standards—that is, that the desired is only conventional and that even seeking the desirable is a pointless exercise because no appropriate standards exist (Sjoberg et al. 1984, 313–16).

Second, as to the need in principle for values to influence organizational analysis and action—whether implicitly or explicitly—consider the contemporary clamor for participation, often by organizational elites as well as by ordinary members. But participation for what? All forms of participative management remain

---

* For an elaboration of the point, and a technology for an alternative approach to survey/feedback interventions in organizations, see Golembiewski and Hilles (1979).

devices or techniques that can be fully evaluated only in connection with the goals in whose service they are used. Thus, while participative management can help approach greater responsible freedom in political republics (e.g., Golembiewski 1985), it can also be put into effective service in totalitarian states for polar-opposite ends, which have included genocide as well as global war (e.g., Singer and Wooton 1976; Speer 1970).

Specific Value Issues in PSOBT. From the earliest days of the republic, value issues concerning administrative processes were front-and-center. Gawthrop (1970), Stillman (1982), and others make the point fully. For example, Alexander Hamilton favored a strong and highly centralized system of management (Gawthrop 1970, 70). In Hamilton's words: "Only through centralization of administrative regulation and operating efficiency can [citizens be] truly liberated" (Gawthrop 1970, 69). In direct contrast, Thomas Jefferson focused on a popular counterbalance to a possibly tyrannical executive, which dictated prominent and persistent involvement of the citizenry in daily administration, complemented by thoroughgoing decentralization of a management system that was both simple and legally constrained (Stillman 1982). For Jefferson, democracy's main bulwark was "an enlightened, responsible and fully participating citizenry," a role rooted in "the human dignity of man" (Gawthrop 1970, 67–68). James Madison offered a pluralistic prescription for safeguarding the individual's private interest: The basic threat to democracy "could best be eliminated," he proposed, "simply by ensuring that no single group in society would ever presume to speak as a majority" (Gawthrop 1970, 69). Congenial to Madison is a public service limited enough to be just another small group seeking its own interest, and perhaps further hedged as "politically neutral" (Stillman 1982, 27–28).

Many variations exist on these central themes, and they all have influenced public management. Parsimoniously, Kaufman (1969) proposes a cyclicality of three basic prescriptions for how government should be organized. He envisions regular shifts, "brought about by a change in emphasis among three values: representativeness, politically neutral competence, and executive leadership" (p. 3). These shift-positions more or less mirror the views of Jefferson, Madison, and Hamilton, respectively. The shifts were never absolute, but amounted to powerful ebbs and flows in the relative prominence of the three values.

While this circularity among values did occur at the macro level over the years, a basic stability persisted in the dominant organization theory. The bureaucratic model conceptually tied political officials to the permanent bureaucracy and prescribed the pattern for the internal workings of the public officialdom. And, curiously, that dominant theory—perhaps better to call it a prevailing orthodoxy, if not doxology or even mythology—was antidemocratic and autocratic.

There are no easy answers to the question of how the antidemocratic or autocratic organization theory came to be put in the service of representative democratic values (see, e.g., Golembiewski 1985, 133–93). Perhaps only two reasonable things can be said about this curious paradox: that it came largely by definition rather than via analysis, and that the same organization theory came to dominate in a very short period of time, and literally everywhere—in capitalist and communist societies, in both Western and Eastern civilizations. Some observers refer to it as the bureaucratization of the world. Specifically, this bureaucratic theory of organization prescribes a well-defined chain of command that vertically channels formal interaction; a division of labor based on specialization by major function or process that vertically fragments a flow of work; a system of procedures and rules for dealing with contingencies at work that reinforces the reporting insularity of each unit; promotion and selection based on technical competence, which is defined consistently with the first three items; and impersonality in relations between organization members and between them and their clients.

Despite deep questions about why the quick, broad dissemination of the bureaucratic principles occurred, there is no question about their being patched awkwardly, if enthusiastically—and all but universally—to all of the versions of the democratic vision sketched above. Four points provide detail supporting this significant conclusion.

First, a single-and-solitary-organization metaphor underlies the traditional bureaucratic model, the assumption being that responsibility is enhanced when authority is centralized at a single point (Ostrom 1973). This reflects simple and sovereign advice to citizens: Put all your eggs in one basket, and then watch that basket.

This dominant view implies a major conceptual problem with our basic separation of powers, but a magnum assumption is usually relied on to finesse facing this problem. Consider what Redford (1969) calls "a simple model of overhead democracy" (p. 70), a kind of direct-line model superimposed on a fragmented world. Redford explains that this view

> asserted that democratic control should run through a single line from the representatives of the people to all those who exercised power in the name of the government. The line ran from the people to their representatives in the Presidency and the Congress, and from there to the President as chief executive, then to departments, then to bureaus, then to lesser units, and so on to the fingertips of administration. Exceptions to the single line were acceptable only for the judiciary, and perhaps also for certain quasi-judicial and quasi-legislative functions and the auditing function. (1969, 70–71)

Second, the politics/administration dichotomy provided simple and long-lasting conceptual support for the bureaucratic model, and vice versa. After a fashion, the politics/administration dichotomy explained in two quite distinct ways the autocratic bureaucratic model being put in the service of a representative system. Thus, if the two spheres are distinct, and if the latter has little or no impact on the former, then those careless with concepts could at once accept organizational autocracy while breathing a sigh of relief that their cherished ideals of political democracy would not be overtly challenged. From another vantage point, the distinction between politics and administration, and the subordination of the latter to the former, would superficially allay fears that public managers could use their large numbers and their knowledge of the intricacies of policies, procedures, and technologies to steal sovereignty from the people. Allaying this fear became increasingly relevant, practically as well as conceptually, because the people had become more and more docile figures in prevailing political thought (e.g., Thompson 1975).

Third, most observers saw no viable alternative to the bureaucratic model, a perception with self-fulfilling features. That is, the belief became both reason and excuse for not learning the literatures which were beginning to develop increasingly comprehensive networks of theory and experience that provided just such alternatives.

At one time, both the reason and the excuse made some practical sense, but that time has long since passed. Thus only the glimmer of an alternative existed when Simon (1946) destroyed the bureaucratic model with logic, and not even that glimmer was apparent in earlier critiques of the deficient methodology of bureaucratic principles (e.g., Coker 1922). But the empirical literatures have accumulated at a rapidly accelerating pace, first establishing that the bureaucratic model had major, and growing, unexpected consequences (e.g., Golembiewski 1965), which added practical force to the neglect of values that some excused in the name of the assumed necessity of the bureaucratic model. And now, accumulating organizational prescriptions not only provide viable alternatives to the bureaucratic model but also provide a more comfortable fit with representative political ideals (e.g., Golembiewski 1985).

Fourth, most major historical figures in the public management literature have in the main supported and reinforced the bureaucratic model—albeit in various ways and degrees, and with variable consciousness of the conflict between bureaucratic and democratic values. Consider only a small sample of such writings: "I do not see how we can stretch the meaning of 'democratic' to include the hierarchy of administration ... rule by the people requires not only democratic forms but also nondemocratic forms of delegated authority" (Dahl 1975, 94); "Autocracy during hours [at work] is the price of democracy after hours. ... I accept bureaucracy not so much as desirable as necessary—as instrumental to many goods, including democratic goods, but also as [leading to] many bads" (Waldo 1980, 90).

The Confused View of Theories

This curious acceptance of sharp value incompatibilities between political and organization arenas had a profound impact on the empirical work going on in PSOBT, and this is no trivial point. A good organization theory will model reality and provide a map of how we may reasonably go about getting what we consider desirable and desired.

But the term "organization theory" is imprecise. Indeed, at least four kinds of such theories populate the literature; their properties are detailed in table 7.1.

This inventory of theories provides a foundation for several interpretive conclusions. Globally, a comprehensive PSOBT should emphasize the last three kinds of organization theory, but in practice much existing effort can be classified as utopian theory. This point gains ample support from the analysis-by-definition underlying politics/administration and from the fixation on the bureaucratic model as the prescription for all conditions. Note also that values require explicit attention in all four kinds of theory, but especially in goal-based empirical theory and in action research. Nevertheless, much public management literature is either not sufficiently specific about values, or assumes that only bureaucratic forms are compatible with efficiency and effectiveness. Finally, PSOBT has often been unclear as to the kind of theoretic enterprise in which it is engaged and in which it should be engaged. The results of such ambiguity are not sanguine. Golembiewski (1986) concludes: "The appropriate scrupulosity seldom exists, with consequences that trend towards confusion, obfuscation, and even unredemptive conflict" (p. 293).

Theories as Manifest in Schools or Approaches

Table 7.1 is abstract, of course, and can benefit from some illustrations of the four theoretical perspectives as they became manifest in major schools or approaches to PSOBT. Table 7.2 labels four major foci for thought and action in PSOBT and briefly describes them. Five sections follow. The first four provide further content for each school or approach, and a fifth section provides some sense of the interfaces between the four traditions of analysis and application. At times, the interfaces are reinforcing and supportive; but the junctions have generated more heat than light.

Organization Analysis and Theory (OA&T). OA&T refers to a vast and complex literature, which differs in many particulars while sharing a core of significant features. This is the classic management tradition. It requires little attention here. It is well known and has already received substantial notice in this chapter. It includes among many others: Taylor (1947) and his followers in Scientific Management, who were major carriers of the bureaucratic model; and Gulick and Urwick (1937), who helped to popularize the approach to management as "functions," often expressed in the mnemonic POSDCORB, which refers to Planning, Organizing, and so on. Generally, OA&T includes the nonquantitative rational sys-

TABLE 7.1
Differences in Central Tendencies between Four Kinds of Theoretical Orientations

	Utopian theory	Empirical theory	Goal-based empirical theory	Action research
Primary task	Elaborate an ideational system relating a set of definitions and axioms.	Describe existing realities, identify causal relations.	Focus on limited causal relations relevant to specific goals.	Define and realize targeted realities, often nonexisting or low-probability realities that are desirable.
Range of applicable values	No limits, but values often unrecognized.	Only the values of scientific process apply to generating theory: disinterestedness as to specific outcomes, honesty in reporting, and so on.	Goal-bases define desired or desirable states, with the outcomes of the theoretical effort consequently being explicitly targeted.	Targeted realities are defined by generic values—e.g., increasing responsible freedom and enhancing growthful feedback—blended with an emphasis on local values and definitions of reality.
Primary approach	Increase specificity of underlying definitions and axioms, and extend reach of derivative system.	Reduce threats to validity and reliability as by distancing observer from observation or by random assignment to experimental and control groups.	Increase applicability of fragments of empirical theory to specified goals.	Focus on applications of relevance to specific publics, which often require close contact between publics and researchers and preclude random assignment of subjects as "normal science" prescribes.

Dominant emphasis	Explore what might exist under specified definitions and axioms.	Replicate patterns of relations in multiple settings in order to test and extend networks of covariants.	Test fragments of empirical theory in terms of their ability successfully to guide approaches to desired/desirable states.	Heighten local involvement and ownership, even at the cost of failure to produce knowledge of broader applicability.
Overarching goal	Develop relations between a set of definitions and axioms into an ideational system.	Develop even broader and even universal networks of covariants in nature.	Enrich theoretical networks relevant to specific goal-bases in a widening range of settings.	Produce knowledge applicable in specific local settings, and perhaps exportable to others.
Core abilities/skills	Insight in stating definitions and axioms, and logical rigor in exploring their derivatives.	Conceptual and analytic.	Identifying fragments of existing empirical theory relevant to specific goal bases, and linking these theory fragments in expanding networks.	Develop individual and group relationships; intervening in systems at multiple levels.

NOTE: Elaborates and extends Golembiewski (1986b, 294).

TABLE 7.2

Four Schools or Approaches to Organization Phenomena

Organizational analysis and theory (OA&T)	Classical organization (Micro OB)	Contingency theory (Macro OB)	Organization development (OD)
Emphasis on application of general, even universal, principles.	Emphasis on description.	Emphasis on description.	Emphasis on application via "action research" that is primarily responsive to local needs.
Firmly, if often implicitly, loaded with "one best way" values.	Determinedly scientific, and often presented as value-free and universal.	Values enter mostly because any regularities are restricted to specific environments, cultures, and so on: culture-bound theory.	Explicitly value-laden.
Emphasis on macro and structural features—coordination via unity of command, line-staff relations, etc.	Emphasis on micro and psychological features, often in small groups.	Includes macro as well as micro features.	Emphasis on micro and psychological features, but with systemic and macro ambitions.
Broad socioeconomic focus, carefully reflected in concern about "causal textures" of external environments, or carelessly in "economic man" assumptions.	Focus on concerns internal to an organization.	Focus on external context as well as internal features, at times involving several organizations and their contexts.	Usually focuses on concerns internal to target group or organization.
Structural emphasis, with a rational and even deductive character.	Affective and immediate emphasis, as in focus on feelings, satisfaction, or morale.	Structural and technological emphasis, often with longish time frames but with some attention to affective and immediate features.	Affective and immediate emphasis, but with some search for congenial structures and policies.

NOTE: Expanded from Golembiewski (1986b, 283).

tems theorists, who focus on roles, structures, and technologies (Bolman and Deal 1984, 2–3).

OA&T focuses on applications, for which it prescribes principles offered as broadly appropriate, if not in fact universal. Consistently, OA&T exponents often see management as generic and draw few or no distinctions between public and business administration. Historically, many exponents also accept the politics/administration dichotomy (e.g., Wilson 1887), boldly proposing that the latter is a field of business. In addition, much of the work has strong overtones of utopian theory.

Classical Organization Behavior (Micro OB). Micro OB represents a long and clearly established tradition of research, and in effect trades breadth of coverage for scientific precision. Hence the focus typically is on an organization, or some part thereof; the focus is often on specific behaviors, attitudes, and feelings, as contrasted with the rational/technical aspects of organization life.

In terms of the table 7.1 typology of theories, Micro OB clearly aspires to an empirical theory. The literature on leadership, typically in the small work unit, typifies this line of research.

Contingency Theory (Macro OB). The term Macro OB takes some liberties as a descriptor of work in this tradition, but the imprecision is bearable. Commonly, such work seeks to provide empirical propositions of greater specificity and coverage than Micro OB by taking into account the differentiating features of an organization's context or environment (e.g., Miles 1980). Different outcomes and relationships, in effect, can be expected in different milieux.

More commonly, work in this tradition is labeled "contingency theory." Outcomes or relationships depend on the specific field of observation, in terms congenial both to modern physical as well as much behavioral research. To illustrate, Macro OB prescriptions for appropriate managerial structures or techniques differ, depending upon such factors as different cultures, whether narrowly organizational (e.g., Schein 1985) or associated with some broad society (e.g., Hofstede 1980); different arenas, such as the public sector or business (e.g., Allison 1980); different technologies (e.g., Woodward 1958); different phases of growth (Chandler 1959); the "causal textures" of environments distinguished in terms of their turbulence or placidity (Emery and Trist 1965); cutback or decline as a stage of economic growth, which first appeared in public-sector research (e.g., Levine 1978, 1980) and later in work concerned with business (e.g., Whetten 1980); stages or phases of organizational development or maturation (e.g., Kimberly, Miles, and associates 1980); and stages or phases of development in various specialized contexts—such as a plant start-up intended to be participative (e.g., Perkins, Nieva, and Lawler 1983), as contrasted with a bureaucratic start-up.

Macro OB has firm roots in empirical theory, like Micro OB, but it also has a "best fit" orientation that inclines such work toward separate goal-based empirical theories. For example, consider the range of work focused on decline and retrenchment, which began with description but has branched out into prescriptions of what to do and how to do it under conditions of resource scarcity.

Macro OB has many attractions, as in the case of focusing on decline as a contingency. Globally, organizational decline, down-sizing, and death usefully complement most organization analysis, which in the main is oriented toward growth (e.g., Whetten 1980). Specifically, the focus has a patent and potent relevance (e.g., Slote 1977); decline's etiology can be described in ways that enrich both theory and practice (Whetten 1980); the associated activities relate to both managerial strategy (Cameron and Zammuto 1983) and implementation; some designs have been developed that permit amelioration of decline's effects (e.g., Golembiewski 1982–83); and organizational decline forces attention to environmental features, not only in theory but especially in praxis (Price and D'Aunno 1983; Taber, Walsh, and Cooke 1979).

Organization Development (OD). OD represents the most prominent form of action research developed over the past few decades. After getting its start in moderate-to-high technology business contexts, it penetrated into public management (e.g., Zawacki and Warrick 1976; Manley and McNichols 1977; Golembiewski and Eddy 1978; Morrison and Sturgess 1980; Golembiewski 1985).

In a nutshell, OD seeks to increase responsible freedom at the work site for individuals and groups. OD's core technology develops around values and skills to guide interaction and form a specific culture having properties such as that associated with "regenerative" systems of communication for dealing with ideas and especially with feelings (Golembiewski 1979a, vol. 1, chaps. 1–3) (see figure 7.1).

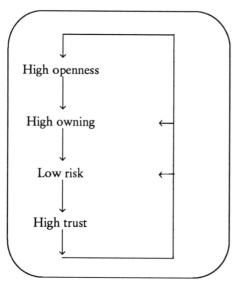

FIGURE 7.1

This simple model is viewed as cyclical and self-heightening, whereas much of the world is "degenerative" —with low openness, low owning of ideas and feelings, high risk, and low trust. In degenerative interaction, the wrong decisions tend to get focused on, relevant information is likely to be withheld, and individuals feel a sense of psychological failure because their central interests and needs are not likely to be expressed and hence will not be built into the decision processes. Even decisions that seem firmly made will have a tendency to come undone in degenerative systems.

OD's focus on developing regenerative interaction both derives from and rests on the high degrees of participation by, and commitment of, organization members, who become intimately involved in the diagnosis of their own systems as well as in problem solving. Hence the terms "action research" or "action theory" describe much OD effort. Unlike straight science (e.g., Susman and Evered 1978), the person is not only the object of research but in various ways is also the subject.

Not all OD is restricted to interaction, nor do all OD decisions rest on consensus only. That would condemn action research to perpetually seeking to rediscover the wheel. Especially with reference to structure and to policies and procedures, OD has developed a growing inventory of designs or interventions that serve basic OD values via increasing organization members' responsible freedom, while those designs also build on as well as reinforce regenerative interaction. Flexible work hours, or flexi-time, is one of the simplest of such interventions (e.g., Golembiewski 1985; Rainey and Wolf 1981). But a broad and growing family of related designs also exists. As for forms of organizational structure, for example, the following designs can serve OD values at various levels of organization: job enrichment, group decision making, autonomous groups, flow-of-work structures emphasizing purpose vs. function, and matrix structures (Golembiewski 1979, vol. 2, 1987b).

Early OD proponents warned that the specific texture of public-sector work poses difficult and even unique challenges, but that fact has not precluded a large volume of applications in government as well as business. If anything, indeed, public-sector applications are overrepresented in a panel of 574 cases (Golembiewski, Proehl, and Sink 1981). Notably, also, several approaches to estimating success rates do not show major differences between public-sector OD applications and those in business; success rates in both arenas are high by any standards. In effect, on average, environmental differences seem to be successfully taken into account by OD applications, and growing knowledge/experience promise to enhance this record (e.g., Golembiewski 1985).

Some Interfaces, Placid but Mostly Otherwise. The four schools or approaches do not exist in splendid isolation. Like Grodzins's marble cake, the traditions twist and swirl and blend into one another at various points even as they remain sharply distinct from one another at other points. For example, the well-known work of Perrow (1979) at times has the flavor of contingency, or Macro OB, and at other times rests firmly within the OA&T province. Four points of discussion highlight the many elements of reinforcement and conflict underlying table 7.2

—three that seem generic, and a fourth more closely associated with public management.

As for the first generic point, several of the schools or approaches derive from systems theory, or at least aspire to it. Systems theory represents a way of looking at reality that emphasizes "wholes"—their properties and interrelationships—as contrasted with specialized parts. Since our sense of any whole is continually expanding—what with anything being related to everything else—the systems view does not solve problems but provides an orientation toward progressively more comprehensive views of reality (e.g., von Bertalanffy 1968).

The systems approach variously relates to the four schools in table 7.2. Contingency theory, or Macro OB, represents the dominant management expression of the systems view (e.g., Hellriegel and Slocum 1972; Sherman 1966), which in turn contrasts most sharply with the subsystemic bias of Micro OB. The evolutionary character of the systems approach also contrasts with the self-fulfilling properties of much work in the OA&T tradition, which seeks a one-best-way. This stands in stark opposition to the contingency motto: "It all depends." OD also has been represented in systems terms (e.g., Beer and Huse 1972) but, as noted, its applications often have been limited to interaction or organizational culture, at the neglect of concern with policies/procedures and structural features.

As a second generic feature, consider the difficulty of integrating Micro OB and Macro OB. That goal seems reasonable enough, especially for those who join Staw (1984) in defining organization behavior as the "interdisciplinary field that examines the behavior of individuals within organizational settings as well as the structure and behavior of organizations themselves" (p. 628). But evidence urges that this integration will not come cheaply. As Golembiewski notes (1986):

> In effect, however, dominant micro and macro tendencies exist, and the field often functions as two separate subdisciplines or, especially in years past, as variously-hostile and armed camps. The macro-emphasis is rooted in sociology, political science, and economics, primarily; and the micro-emphasis owes most to psychology and especially social psychology. Staw observes that historically micro OB focused on applications, moreover, while macro OB has determinedly-theoretical interests. And seldom did the twain meet, although Staw observes a definite converging of contemporary interests. (P. 282)

This integrative difficulty also exists, to introduce a third feature generic to both business and public administration, because Micro OB and especially Macro OB are quite differentiated enterprises. To illustrate, at least three major OB orientations are distinguished by Bolman and Deal (1984, 2–3): (1) human resource theorists emphasize ways to develop a better fit between people's needs, skills, and values, and organizational structures, roles, and relationships; (2) political theorists see power, conflict, and the distribution of scarce resources as the central issues (e.g., Pfeffer 1981; March 1956), commonly directing attention to an organization and its environment although early versions (e.g., Dalton 1959) focused on intraorganizational dynamics; and (3) symbolic theorists focus on problems of meaning in organizations and often emphasize the limitations of our ability to create organizational cohesion through rational design (e.g., Weick 1969; March and Olsen 1976).

The fourth point directly associated with public administrationists relates to a debate over alternative action theories. As noted, OD is the most prominent available version of action research. It encompasses values, designs, or interventions for various phases of individual and organizational movement toward an ideal state and provides a technology for change, which involves changing the form of energy.

But OD does not have the stage to itself. Students of public management propose four other action theories:

(1) the New Public Administration emphasizes values like those in OD, but has evolved only a rudimentary technology for moving toward those values (e.g., Marini 1971);

(2) Democratic Administration (Ostrom 1973) proposes that smaller is better when it comes to democratic institutions (research provides variable support for this proposition, e.g., Lovrich 1985b, no doubt in part because varying an organization's size does not per se change the basic bureaucratic model of organizing), does not dwell on various developmental alternatives, and provides only a general model of change;

(3) Critical Theory (e.g., Denhardt 1981, 1984) shares values with OD, but provides a general orientation for a technology of change and only a vague sense of structural alternatives to the bureaucratic model; and

(4) other action theories (e.g., Harmon 1981) emphasize the translation for public administrationists of epistemological and methodological issues from the literature of social thought.

In effect, all five action-theory variants represent a watershed in thought about public management. They all agree on the most fundamental points. Nevertheless, the five variants prescribe—with variable clarity and completeness—alternatives that are at least palliatives of the bureaucratic model's common consequences. These prescriptions may even be the precursors of a general replacement model.

Debate and dissension concerning action theories is more characteristic than the presentation of a united front, and for some major reasons. Consider the contrasting mind-sets of Democratic Administration and OD. As Lovrich (1985a) points out, OD implies an optimistic view of people and especially their potentialities. In contrast, Democratic Administration sees people in an unredemptively pessimistic light. Moreover, many of the variants above incline more toward an action *theory* than an *action* theory.

Progress in Development

Now on to PSOBT's flip side: developmental progress viewed from two perspectives. The first is general, and the second more detailed if still harshly selective. Emphasis is then directed to an overview, and then to six significant details of progress.

Progress in Capsule Form

Not very long ago, PSOBT had low status as an area of inquiry and could not even lay claim to a literature that was substantially its own. McCurdy (1986) surveyed the entire field of public management, to illustrate. For the period before 1972, he found that public administrationists favored books by authors who had no direct connection with their area. McCurdy observed (1986, 3) that the most popular books "did not treat administration in government as intrinsically different from administration in general [and] business administration is strongly represented on [the 1972] ranking [of books]." But by 1986, the situation had changed dramatically. As McCurdy (1986) concludes: "The citing of business management and management science texts . . . drops off significantly in the new top 150 [books of 1985]. This fact reflects the refound confidence among public administrators in using their own approaches to solving problems of governmental administration" (pp. 5–6).

Perhaps most dramatically, the last few years have seen a spate of specifically tailored PSOBT textbooks (e.g., Eddy 1981; Stewart and Garson 1983; Harmon and Mayer 1986; Gortner, Mahler, and Nicholson 1987; Shafritz and Ott 1987). Earlier, teachers and students had to cope with books developed for other arenas, especially business.

A similarly optimistic conclusion also holds for the periodic literature. Payad (1986) surveyed a short list of periodicals plus other sources, which generated a 620-item bibliography on PSOBT. Payad notes, "The period of study includes publications from 1940–1984, with the bulk of the entries published within the last decade (1974–1984)" (p. viii). Note also that Payad's effort is "comprehensive, albeit selective," and the 620 items could be increased several-fold with no difficulty.

Progress in Six Significant Senses

As detailed counterpoint to the global characterization of progress, six points express specific and significant elements of progress in PSOBT. Brief introductions follow.

Two Perspectives on Achieving a Critical Mass. Only in the past decade or so have more than a few scholars been able to make a comfortable living—especially within political science or public administration—while devoting all or substantial parts of their time to PSOBT. Absent such a critical mass, two awkward outcomes dominated.

First, those trained in PS/PA with dominant PSOBT interests could remain in

PS/PA contexts and endure severe disadvantages in coming to grips with their subject matter, whose development would be stunted as a consequence. To be sure, the PSOBT literature contains its landmarks, often analytic histories by single scholars of particular agencies or programs (e.g., Selznick 1949; Kaufman 1960). But the literature particularly suffers in the development of empirical theory and goal-based empirical theories, which require the massive attention only substantial funding can provide. Garson and Overman (1981, 1982) catalog an inventory of public management research projects, and find that corpus fragmented, noncumulative, underfunded, and showing signs of chronic understaffing.

Second, individuals trained in political science or public administration but basically interested in organization behavior could migrate to a school of business or to one of the few schools of generic management. The list of migrants includes Drucker, Simon, March, this author, and others. This brain drain continues, although it has abated in recent years.

A bit of personal history may provide useful perspective. In 1958, new Ph.D. in hand, I was solemnly warned by a well-meaning elder in political science that "I should have more arrows in my academic quiver than public administration," which of course has a reach and grasp far beyond the PSOBT to which I wished to devote most of my research. In 1960, I did what for me was the reasonable thing—I secured a business school appointment. The same elder wrote me, and minced no words: "You, sir, are a TRAITOR." The capitalization is the elder's.

We can all be thankful that the times are changing. Neither of the two major alternatives personally attracts nor is well designed to induce robust activity in PSOBT.

Growing Methodological Consciousness. PSOBT has yet to have its equivalent of the Flexner Report, which by its scathing criticism helped reform practice in our medical schools. But there is a growing methodological consciousness that, among other consequences, will inhibit the past's excesses. See especially the common confusion of utopian effort with the forms of empirical inquiry, which blocked major progress in PSOBT for several decades.

The enhanced methodological consciousness concerning what constitutes acceptable empirical research has raised the stakes for both producer and consumer, and appears in many forms. Witness the recent review of public management dissertations, which concludes gravely that "few of those doctoral projects meet the criteria that conventionally define careful, systematic study in the social sciences" (McCurdy and Cleary 1984, 50). Moreover, a broader survey confirms this condition (White 1986, 225, 227). Usefully, a growing methodological scrupulousness is also manifest in a careful review of the articles in the *Public Administration Review*. That review urges increases in the funding of research and firmly recommends various sophistications—for example, emphases on longitudinal research designs as well as powerful statistical techniques, both in common use in the behavioral sciences but rare in PSOBT research (Perry and Kraemer 1986).

Burgeoning Empirical Literature. Mandating greater methodological care has not intimidated PSOBT researchers. Indeed, the recent literature contains an unparalleled increase in the number and diversity of empirical studies of two basic kinds. Thus much of the work may lead to the development of increasingly comprehensive fragments of empirical theory. Some of this research activity also leads quite self-consciously to what table 7.1 calls goal-based empirical theories, usually in that form of action theory called OD. For example, consider the recent attention to stress or burnout, whose growing empirical theory owes much to public-sector researchers (e.g., Diamond and Allcorn 1985). Our work began in the public sector (Golembiewski, Munzenrider, and Stevenson 1986) and sought to develop a valid, reliable, and convenient measuring instrument—an eight-phase model of burnout. The phases seem a useful focus for an emerging empirical theory, with the phases associated in regular and robust ways with over a hundred conventional variables tapped by both self-reports and archival data (e.g., Golembiewski, Munzenrider, and Stevenson 1986). That evolving network of empirical theory has also been recently extended into a goal-based empirical theory to reduce burnout and turnover as well as to modify worksite properties via conventional interventions guided by OD values (Golembiewski, Hilles, and Daly 1987).

No convenient approach exists to chart the range of these two basic kinds of empirical work: toward development networks of empirical theory, and toward specific goal-based empirical theories. This chapter can only sample that diversity, which includes, among numerous other empirical works,

- descriptions of the roles, behaviors, and attitudes of public managers (e.g., Rainey 1986);
- a tracing of the linkages between factors at work, self-development, and the characteristics of family life (e.g., Romzek 1985);
- efforts to distinguish variables that may differentially characterize public vs. business settings (e.g., Bozeman 1984);
- the focus on organization commitment and its correlates (e.g., Buchanan 1974, 1975);
- tests of the degree to which the intended effects of the Civil Service Reform Act of 1978 have been achieved (e.g., Ingraham and Barr 1986; Gaertner and Gaertner 1985);
- extension of the meaning and form of participation in agencies and with clients (e.g., Brudney 1985; Lundeen 1985; Miewald and Comer 1986);
- studies of various aspects of advanced training in public management, with a focus on the M.P.A. degree (e.g., McCaffery 1979; Kennedy and Walker 1981);

- reviews of the effects of various personnel and affirmative action initiatives (e.g., Sigelman, Milward, Shepard, and Dumler 1984);
- overviews of efforts to improve the quality of public work (e.g., Chisholm 1983; Morrison and Sturgess 1980; Manley and McNichols 1977);
- focus on productivity and its measurement (e.g., Hatry 1978); descriptions of cutback strategies and their consequences (e.g., Levine 1978, 1980);
- assessment of the reactions of public employees to antibureaucratic political figures (e.g., Lowery and Rusbutt 1986);
- focus on the cultures or climates of public agencies (e.g., Golembiewski and Kiepper 1976; Cronan, Jones, Shaffer, and Lovrich 1985);
- critical reviews of the adequacy of empirical research (e.g., McCurdy and Cleary 1984; Perry and Kraemer 1986; White 1986);
- assessments of managerial techniques on performance (e.g., Danziger and Kraemer 1985);
- evaluations of the effects of innovative public compensation programs (e.g., Gabris and Giles 1983; Burstein 1983);
- and efforts to assess the impact of various programs and policies—such as flexible work hours (e.g., Golembiewski 1985, 93–129; McGuire and Liro 1986), quality circles (e.g., Burstein 1983), assessment centers (e.g., Yeager 1986), agency wellness initiatives (Mirkin 1986), and employee assistance programs (e.g., Johnson 1986).

This burgeoning catalog of empirical research has been a mixed blessing. It clearly implies the sharply expanding reach and grasp of empirical theory in PSOBT, which is good; at the same time, the results of empirical inquiry have not always been flattering to the public sector. Indeed, on balance, comparisons with the business arena tend to reveal public-sector deficits and deficiencies (e.g., Rainey 1986). Thus public-employee satisfaction tends to be lower, complaints about the inadequate linkage of performance to reward are common and strident, and—perhaps most distressing—public-sector executives seem less enthusiastic about recommending that others follow in their career footsteps (Heclo 1984). To a degree, then, the growing empirical literature has played an unintended role in the public-bureaucrat bashing that is so much a part of the contemporary political scene.

Rejecting the Basic Classical Premises About Organizing. Until recently, PSOBT's view of the bureaucratic model has been curiously divided. On the one hand, a minority directed scathing criticism at the model for over fifty years. Thus Coker (1922) pointed with alarm to the methodological inelegance of the bureaucratic model, which (in present terms) sought to pass off a utopian theory as *the* empirical theory or (even worse) as the only possible goal-based empirical theory. Later, Waldo (1948) provided careful counterpoint in his demonstration of how a narrow range of values and biases influenced, if not predetermined, the bureaucratic prescriptions that were allegedly universal. Waldo implied that proponents of the bureaucratic model could not have it both ways. To a similar effect, Simon's (1946) powerful argument knocked the logical pins from beneath that model. And Golembiewski (1965) demonstrated how the bureaucratic model not only violates basic Judeo-Christian values but is often ineffective in that it induces neither high productivity nor high employee satisfaction.

On the other hand, most early students felt that the benefits of bureaucracy outweigh the costs. For some, this reflects the attractiveness of the model. To illustrate, Goodsell (1983) provides perhaps the most solid and closely reasoned defense of bureaucracy. For others, the judgment is a very close call. Waldo (1980), for example, concludes that bureaucracy is contra democratic, but unfortunately seems unavoidable.

Fashions have changed of late, in part because of the growth in empirical research. The list of those proposing that the bureaucratic model is too costly, not only in terms of effectiveness but also in terms of efficiency, is long and growing. The New Public Administration is not enamored of the bureaucratic model (e.g., Marini 1971); Ostrom's Democratic Administration sees bureaucracy as an absolute evil (1973); Denhardt's (1981, 1984) version of critical theory has a strong individualistic and subjectivistic thrust, thus being antibureaucratic; and Thayer (1973) rejects not only bureaucracy but also hierarchy and competition.

These rejections of the bureaucratic model can be a boon, but they have tended to be bane. As a boon, the rejection can facilitate getting on with the third round of mobilizing our public managerial resources (e.g., Golembiewski 1984), with the first two rounds having awkwardly settled for dealing with managerial issues as a kind of residual category, and basically by definition. In this first way of interpreting the rejection of the bureaucratic model, the problems are not so much with government employees as with the bureaucratic model applied to those employees. The problems of public governance—unresponsiveness, distance from clients, fragmentation of public services, and a proclivity to give priority to concerns internal to the bureaucracy—are in this view not a consequence of perverse and self-seeking public servants but a predictable and even reasonable set of responses to the bureaucratic structure imposed on people who have no fondness for the structure, either as employees or clients.

Hence this paradox: Many rail against our public services as an abstraction, yet most respond with basic acceptance and even warmth to the specific public employees with whom they come into contact (e.g., Katz, Gutek, Kahn, and Barton 1975).

But growing rejection of the bureaucratic model has often been more bane than boon, as when it is always tied to a low evaluation of the public service per se. In subtle ways, this awkward consequence can even be the practical effect of the entreaties of those who hold the most glowing idealizations of what public work should be like. Such enthusiasts often give little or no attention to organizational variants that will improve on the bureaucratic model. They attend even less to the development of a technology for getting from here to *their* there. The ideal, as it were, is so preoccupying as to preclude the focus on phases of development that would suggest reasonable next steps.

Integration vs. Differentiation and Emerging Alternatives. The preceding comments suggest the centrality of widely recognized alternatives to the bureaucratic model, but these were commonly absent. For example, proponents of the New Public Administration provide only a slim catalog of alternatives (e.g., Frederickson 1970); Ostrom (1973) basically proposes a down-sizing of all administrative units; Denhardt (1981, 1984) provides more of an orientation for individual choice-making than a model for collective action; and Thayer (1973) sees the organizational future in terms of ad hoc, small-group happenings. Commonly, these views are long on vision but short on how to get from our organizational today to the future.

In these terms, the bureaucratic model often won by forfeit. Indeed, why even criticize the necessary or at least unavoidable? Recently, alternatives to the bureaucratic model have appeared. A growing cadre of PSOBT observers are critical of the bureaucratic model as a set of universal principles and provide some detail about how to move toward a more efficient and effective organization future. More or less, these observers point in a common direction concerning the general character of the organization theory of the future: toward integration rather than differentiation.

This reorienting of PSOBT around integration has deep roots in the bureaucratic model and its common consequences. The classic model focuses on parts rather than the whole—on separate functions at high levels of organization, and on discrete motions or activities at workaday levels. This particularistic focus separates (even fragments) contributions to a common flow of work. Hence the bureaucratic model is oriented toward differentiation rather than integration, and that pervasive bias has increasing costs under conditions of rapid change and ever more comprehensive public services. As contingency theorists might phrase the point, the bureaucratic model is best adapted to conditions that once existed but now persist in radically altered form, if those conditions have not been fundamentally changed, on balance.

In simplified terms, the evolving integrative model will focus on permitting good things to occur far more than on inhibiting bad things. In contrast, the bureaucratic model focuses on preventing error, even as that preoccupation can become the enemy of excellence.

The focus on integration comes from diverse sources too numerous to list here. The growing emphasis on integration in PSOBT extends from at least the early 1960s (e.g., Golembiewski 1962a) to the growing chorus in the 1980s (e.g., Baber 1983; Carew, Carter, Gamache, Hardiman, Jackson, and Parisi 1977; Sayles and

Chandler 1971; Gawthrop 1984; Golembiewski 1987b; Sapolsky 1972; Rainey and Rainey 1986; Teasley and Ready 1981).

In what specific forms does the emphasis on integration become manifest? Convenient overviews exist (e.g., Golembiewski 1987b), but here the focus is on several progressive levels of organization at which the integrative spirit can exist, beginning with the simplest and proceeding to macro levels of organization: job enrichment (Locke, Sirota, and Wolfson 1976); integrator roles (Stumpf 1977); autonomous teams (e.g., Rainey and Rainey, forthcoming); cultural overlays that seek to socially counteract the fragmenting tendencies of bureaucratic structures (e.g., Golembiewski 1979a, vol. 2, 961–69), short of basic structural change; divisional vs. functional structures (e.g., Carew et al. 1977); matrix structures (e.g., McCollum 1984; Baber 1983; Teasley and Ready 1981); and various behavioral or structural interventions that help bridge the common gap between bureaucratic organizations and their clients or publics, as by participation in agency decision making (e.g., Miewald and Cormer 1986), in actual production (e.g., Brudney 1985; Lundeen 1985), and so on.

In sum, the integrative spirit is expressed in at least three specific ways: by structural variations in jobs and organizations, by behavioral technologies that seek to overcome the divisive tendencies of the bureaucratic model, or by behavioral and structural linkages between an organization and its clients or publics.

It is too early to determine whether this emphasis on integration will win the day, or in what more detailed forms it may come increasingly to influence public institutions and practices. The broad outlines of how the integrative spirit might take advantage of the common rejection of the bureaucratic model to fundamentally reform our governance structures are clear enough (e.g., Golembiewski 1984, 1987b), but such profound issues will hardly be settled by technical discussion. The bureaucratic model survived two major previous opportunities for fundamental reconsideration of the leading ideas underlying our public management concepts (Golembiewski 1984), and it may well have a third life.

One hopeful difference between today and those times may be the empirical progress in PSOBT reviewed above. Consider only the marked tendency to view as "romantics" (as by Stillman 1983) those who propose that major changes in the hegemony of the bureaucratic model in the public sector are not only desirable, but also are possible. Empirical progress in PSOBT increasingly distinguishes three kinds of romantics: (1) those who seek to provide supporting data for their view of the organization future, which in the present vocabulary would lead to the elaboration of goal-based empirical theories; (2) those whose visions are not supported by appropriate tests of their empirical consequences and hence must be considered (perhaps) attractive ideals that are either unrealizable or do not generate the expected consequences; and (3) those whose prescriptions are so framed as to inhibit testing, or even to preclude it.

This differentiation of romantics relates to two crucial levels of review of all organization theories. As always, the desirability of basic goals or values will be at issue. See, for example, Lovrich's (1985a) comparison of OD with Democratic Administration, with a focus on their respective optimistic versus pessimistic views of people. Progress in PSOBT also will permit—indeed will require—a second level of review, and one that has been uncommon. Increasingly, differentiations between sets of organizational values or goals will be data based rather than determined solely by the weight of affirmations and denials. For example, high success rates have been attributed to a large sample of OD applications in the public sector (Golembiewski 1985, 73–129), with OD being a goal-based empirical theory representing the polar opposite of the bureaucratic model. Similarly, Lovrich (1985b) reported a test of Ostrom's smaller-is-better alternative to the bureaucratic model, in which data generated mixed or negative tests of the basic model.

Improved Texts and Teaching Tools. Along with these several evidences of coming to grips with today's research, telling attention is being given to appropriately training tomorrow's public managers, as well as to orienting future researchers. One signal indication of such progress deserves re-emphasis: the recent availability of useful PSOBT texts.

Not very long ago, the public-sector cupboard of textbooks was virtually bare. Use was made of major interpretive works such as that of Simon (1947), Argyris (1969), March (1965), March and Simon (1957), Thompson (1967), Weick (1969), and others. But these are generic management efforts or determinedly focused on business and provide neither the coverage of texts nor a public-centered focus. A covey of descriptive studies fortunately was available (e.g., Selznick 1949; Kaufman 1960), and these compensated for their narrow focus by their descriptive richness. Moreover, public-sector contexts were used to illustrate the applicability of behavioral science concepts (e.g., Golembiewski 1962a), but such work was often hypothetical and focused on small units. Although not providing PSOBT texts, finally a covey of early public administrationists came close to filling the need (Simon, Smithburg, and Thompson 1950; Pfiffner and Sherwood 1960; Presthus 1965; Sherman 1966).

Times have changed decisively. Numerous major texts have appeared. General PSOBT texts include efforts by Eddy (1981), Harmon and Mayer (1986), Stewart and Garson (1983), and Gortner, Mahler, and Nicholson (1987). There are also texts and readers in specialized PSOBT areas including organization development (e.g., Zawacki and Warrick 1976; Golembiewski 1979a, 1985), behavioral descriptions of life in the organizational trenches (e.g., Chase and Reveal 1983; Heclo 1977), learning aids that direct attention to the craft and practice of public management (e.g., Berkley 1975), and descriptive/prescriptive studies of managerial coping under the duress of cutbacks and down-sizing (e.g., Levine 1978, 1980).

Summary

PSOBT is both moving and still in early process, experiencing a kind of accelerating enrichment from a limited base. Sketches of problems and progress in development establish this compound conclusion.

Problems in PSOBT development stand out in bold relief. Two basic factors inhibit coming to grips with basic issues in research and application: inadequate resources that derive from and contribute to definitions and conventions that in effect rule critical areas of inquiry as out of bounds. For an extended period, utopian theories often were confused with empirical work. Moreover, only recently has substantial effort gone into the development of goal-based empirical theories and action theories, both of which are central in the development of a comprehensive body of knowledge relevant to organizational functioning in the public sector.

Progress in PSOBT permits real optimism, nonetheless. No doubt the basic breakthrough involves the growing opinion not only of the costs of the bureaucratic model but more especially the growing conviction that viable alternatives to that model exist or can be developed.

References

Allison, Graham T. 1980. "Public and Private Management: Are They Alike in All Unimportant Aspects?" In U.S. Office of Personnel Management, *Setting the Public Management Research Agenda,* OPM Document 127-53-1. Washington, D.C.: Government Printing Office.

Argyris, Chris. 1969. *Integrating the Individual and the Organization.* New York: Wiley.

Baber, Walter F. 1983. *Organizing the Future.* University, Ala.: University of Alabama Press.

Beer, F.A. 1984. "Controlling Nuclear Weapons: The Evolution of Morality, Politics, and Science." *Journal of Applied Behavioral Science* 20:323–42.

Beer, Michael, and Edgar F. Huse. 1972. "A Systems Approach to Organization Development." *Journal of Applied Behavioral Science* 8:79–101.

Berkley, George E. 1975. *The Craft of Public Administration.* Boston: Allyn and Bacon.

Bolman, Lee, and Terrence E. Deal. 1984. *Modern Approaches to Understanding and Managing Organizations.* San Francisco: Jossey-Bass.

Bower, Joseph L. 1977. "Effective Public Management." *Harvard Business Review* 55: 132–36.

Bozeman, Barry. 1984. "Dimensions of 'Publicness': An Approach to Public Organization Theory." In *New Directions in Public Administration,* edited by Barry Bozeman and Jeffrey Straussman. Monterey, Calif.: Brooks/Cole.

Brown v. *Board of Education.* 1954. 347 U.S. 483.

Brown v. *Board of Education.* 1955. 349 U.S. 294.

Brudney, Jeffrey. 1985. "Coproduction." *Administration and Society* 17:243–56.

Buchanan, Bruce. 1974. "Government Managers, Business Executives and Organizational Commitment." *Public Administration Review* 35:339–47.

Buchanan, Bruce. 1975. "Red Tape and the Service Ethic: Some Unexpected Differences between Public and Private Managers." *Administration and Society* 6:423–38.

Burstein, Carolyn. 1983. "Designing Appropriate Control Mechanisms for Managing Performance in the Federal Sector." *Public Administration Quarterly* 7:183–98.

Cameron, Kim, and Raymond Zammuto. 1983. "Matching Managerial Strategies to Conditions of Decline." *Human Resources Management* 22:359–76.

Carew, Donald K., Sylvia I. Carter, Janice M. Gamache, Rita Hardiman, Bailey W. Jackson III, and Eunice M. Parisi. 1977. "New York State Division of Youth." *Journal of Applied Behavioral Science* 13:327–39.

Chandler, Alfred D. 1959. *Strategy and Structure*. Cambridge, Mass.: MIT Press.

Chase, Gordon, and Elizabeth C. Reveal. 1983. *How to Manage in the Public Sector*. Reading, Mass.: Addison-Wesley.

Chisholm, Rupert. 1983. "Quality of Working Life." *Public Productivity Review* 7:10–25.

Coker, Francis W. 1922. "Dogmas of Administrative Reform." *American Political Science Review* 16:399–411.

Cronan, Timothy P., Thomas W. Jones, Paul L. Shaffer, and Nicholas P. Lovrich, Jr. 1985. "Public Sector Applications of Organizational Climate Analysis." *Review of Public Personnel Administration* 6:59–68.

Dahl, Robert A. 1975. *After the Revolution?* New Haven: Yale University Press.

Dalton, Melville. 1959. *Men Who Manage*. New York: Wiley.

Danziger, J.N., and Kenneth L. Kraemer. 1985. "Computerized Data-Based Systems and Productivity among Professional Workers." *Public Administration Review* 45:196–209.

Denhardt, Robert B. 1981. *In the Shadow of Organization*. Lawrence, Kan.: Regents Press of Kansas.

Denhardt, Robert B. 1984. *Theories of Public Organization*. Monterey, Calif.: Brooks/Cole.

Diamond, M.A., and Seth Allcorn. 1985. "Psychological Responses to Stress in Complex Organizations." *Administration and Society* 17:217–39.

Drucker, Peter. 1954. *The Practice of Management*. New York: Harper & Bros.

Eddy, William B. 1981. *Public Organization Behavior and Development*. Cambridge, Mass.: Winthrop.

Emery, S.E., and Eric L. Trist. 1965. "The Causal Texture of Organization Environments." *Human Relations* 18:21–31.

Fayol, Henri. 1949. *General and Industrial Management*. London: Pitman.

Frederickson, H. George. 1970. *Recovery of Structure in Public Administration*. Washington, D.C.: Center for Governmental Studies.

Gabris, Gerald, and William Giles. 1983. "Improving Productivity and Performance Appraisal through the Use of Non-Economic Incentives." *Public Productivity Review* 7:173–89.

Gaertner, Karen N., and Gregory H. Gaertner. 1985. "Performance-Contingent Pay for Federal Managers." *Administration and Society* 17:7–20.

Garson, G. David, and E. Sam Overman. 1981. *Public Management Research Directory*. Washington, D.C.: National Association of Schools of Public Affairs and Administration.

Garson, G. David, and E. Sam Overman. 1982. *Public Management Research Directory*. Washington, D.C.: National Association of Schools of Public Affairs and Administration.

Gawthrop, Louis C. 1970. *The Administrative Process and Democratic Theory.* New York: Houghton Mifflin.

Gawthrop, Louis C. 1984. *Public Sector Management, Systems and Ethics.* Bloomington: Indiana University Press.

Golembiewski, Robert T. 1962a. *Behavior and Organization.* Chicago: Rand McNally.

Golembiewski, Robert T. 1962b. "Civil Service and Managing Work: Some Unintended Consequences." *American Political Science Review* 56:961–74.

Golembiewski, Robert T. 1972. *Renewing Organizations.* Itasca, Ill.: Peacock.

Golembiewski, Robert T. 1977. *Public Administration as a Developing Discipline.* New York: Marcel Dekker.

Golembiewski, Robert T. 1979a. *Approaches to Planned Change.* New York: Marcel Dekker.

Golembiewski, Robert T. 1979b. "The Near-Future of Graduate Public Administration Programs in the U.S." *Southern Review of Public Administration* 3:323–59.

Golembiewski, Robert T. 1982–83. "The Demotion Design." *National Productivity Review* 2:63–70.

Golembiewski, Robert T. 1984. "Organizing Public Work, Round Three: Toward a New Balance of Political Agendas and Management Perspectives." In *The Costs of Federalism,* edited by Robert T. Golembiewski and Aaron Wildavsky. New Brunswick, N.J.: Transaction.

Golembiewski, Robert T. 1985. *Humanizing Public Organizations.* Mt. Airy, Md.: Lomond Publications.

Golembiewski, Robert T. 1986a. "OD Perspectives on High Performance." *Review of Public Personnel Administration* 7:9–26.

Golembiewski, Robert T. 1986b. "Perspectives on Progress and Stuckness." In *The International Review of Industrial and Organizational Psychology,* edited by Cary L. Cooper and Ivan T. Robertson. New York: Wiley.

Golembiewski, Robert T. 1987a. "Public Sector Management Today." *Journal of Management* 13:323–38.

Golembiewski, Robert T. 1987b. "Public-Sector Organization: Why Theory and Practice Should Emphasize Purpose, and How to Do So." In *A Centennial History of the American Administrative State,* edited by Ralph Clark Chandler. New York: Macmillan.

Golembiewski, Robert T. 1988. *Men, Management, and Morality: Toward a New Organizational Ethic.* New Brunswick, N.J.: Transaction.

Golembiewski, Robert T., and William B. Eddy. 1978. *Organization Development in Public Administration.* New York: Marcel Dekker.

Golembiewski, Robert T., and Richard Hilles. 1979. *Toward the Responsive Organization.* Salt Lake City: Brighton Publishing.

Golembiewski, Robert T., Richard Hilles, and Rick Daly. 1987. "Some Effects of Multiple OD Interventions on Burnout and Worksite Features." *Journal of Applied Behavioral Science* 23:295–314.

Golembiewski, Robert T., and Alan Kiepper. 1976. "MARTA: Toward an Effective, Open Giant." *Public Administration Review* 36:46–60.

Golembiewski, Robert T., Robert Munzenrider, and Jerry S. Stevenson. 1986. *Stress in Organizations.* New York: Praeger.

Golembiewski, Robert T., Robert Munzenrider, and Jerry S. Stevenson. 1988. "Centrality of Burnout in a Federal Agency." *Review of Public Personnel Administration* 9:28–47.

Golembiewski, Robert T., Carl W. Proehl, Jr., and David Sink. 1981. "Success of OD Applications in the Public Sector." *Public Administration Review* 41:679–82.

Goodnow, Frank. 1900. *Policy and Administration.* New York: Macmillan.

Goodsell, Charles T. 1983. *The Case for Bureaucracy.* Chatham, N.J.: Chatham House.

Gortner, Harold F., Julianne Mahler, and Jeanne Bell Nicholson. 1987. *Organization Theory: A Public Perspective.* Chicago: Dorsey.

Gulick, Luther, and Lyndall Urwick, eds. 1937. *Papers on the Science of Administration.* New York: Institute of Public Administration.

Habermas, J. 1974. *Theory and Practice.* Boston: Beacon Press.

Harmon, Michael M. 1981. *Action Theory for Public Administration.* New York: Longman.

Harmon, Michael M., and Richard T. Mayer. 1986. *Organization Theory for Public Administration.* Boston: Little, Brown.

Hatry, Harry P. 1978. "The Status of Productivity Measurement in the Public Sector." *Public Administration Review* 38:28–33.

Heclo, H. 1977. *A Government of Strangers.* Washington, D.C.: Brookings Institution.

Heclo, H. 1984. "A Government of Enemies?" *Bureaucrat,* 13:12–14.

Hellriegel, Donald, and John Slocum. 1972. "Systems Concepts and Organizational Strategy." *Business Horizons* 14:71–79.

Hofstede, Gert. 1980. *Culture's Consequences.* Beverly Hills: Sage.

Ingraham, P.W., and C.R. Barr. 1986. "Models of Public Management." *Public Administration Review* 46:152–60.

Johnson, A.T. 1986. "A Comparison of Employee Assistant Programs in Corporate and Governmental Organizational Contexts." *Review of Public Personnel Administration* 6:28–42.

Katz, Daniel, Barbara A. Gutek, Robert L. Kahn, and Eugenia Barton. 1975. *Bureaucratic Encounters.* Ann Arbor: Institute for Social Research, University of Michigan.

Kaufman, Herbert. 1960. *The Forest Ranger.* Baltimore: Johns Hopkins University Press.

Kaufman, Herbert. 1969. "Administrative Decentralization and Political Power." *Public Administration Review* 39:3–15.

Kaufman, Herbert. 1981. "The Administrative Behavior of Federal Bureau Chiefs." Washington, D.C.: Brookings Institution.

Kennedy, Giles W., and A. Grayson Walker III. 1981. "Graduate Student Recruitment in American Public Administration." *Public Administration Review* 41:249–52.

Kimberly, John R., Robert H. Miles, and Associates. 1980. *The Organizational Life Cycle.* San Francisco: Jossey-Bass.

Kirkhart, Larry. 1971. "Toward a Theory of Public Administration." In *Toward a New Public Administration,* edited by Frank Marini. Scranton: Chandler.

Levine, Charles H. 1978. "Organizational Decline and Cutback Management." *Public Administration Review* 38:316–25.

Levine, Charles H., ed. 1980. *Managing Fiscal Stress.* Chatham, N.J.: Chatham House.

Locke, Edwin A., David Sirota, and Alan D. Wolfson. 1976. "An Experimental Case Study of Successes and Failures of Job Enrichment in a Government Agency." *Journal of Applied Psychology* 61:701–11.

Lovrich, Nicholas P., Jr. 1985a. "Contending Paradigms in Public Administration." *Administration and Society* 17:307–30.

Lovrich, Nicholas P., Jr. 1985b. "Scale and Performance in Governmental Operations." *Public Administration Quarterly* 9:163–95.

Lowery, David, and Caryl E. Rusbutt. 1986. "Bureaucratic Responses to Antibureaucratic Administrations." *Administration and Society* 18:45–75.

Lundeen, Richard A. 1985. "Coproduction and Communities." *Administration and Society* 16:387–402.

McCaffery, Jerry L. 1979. "Perceptions of Satisfaction-Dissatisfaction in the Internship Experience." *Public Administration Review* 39:241–44.

McCollum, James K. 1984. "The Application of Matrix Organization Concepts in Managing Pacification and Rural Development." *International Journal of Public Administration* 6:201–16.

McCurdy, Howard E. 1986. *Public Administration: A Bibliographic Guide to the Literature.* New York: Marcel Dekker.

McCurdy, Howard E., and Robert E. Cleary. 1984. "Why Can't We Resolve the Research Issue in Public Administration?" *Public Administration Review* 44:44–56.

McGuire, Jean B., and Joseph R. Liro. 1986. "Flexible Work Schedules, Work Attitudes, and Perceptions of Productivity." *Public Personnel Management* 15:65–73.

Manley, T. Robert, and Charles W. McNichols. 1977. "OD at a Major Government Research Lab." *Public Personnel Management* 6:51–60.

March, James G. 1956. "Influence Measurement in Experimental and Semi-Experimental Groups." *Sociometry* 19:260–71.

March, James G., ed. 1965. *Handbook of Organizations.* Chicago: Rand McNally.

March, James G., and Johan P. Olsen. 1976. *Ambiguity and Choice in Organizations.* Bergen, Norway: Universitetsforlaget.

March, James G., and Herbert A. Simon. 1957. *Organizations.* New York: Wiley.

Marini, Frank, ed. 1971. *Toward a New Public Administration.* Scranton: Chandler.

Miewald, Robert D., and John C. Comer. 1986. "Complaining as Participation." *Administration and Society* 17:481–99.

Miles, Robert H. 1980. *Macro Organizational Behavior.* Glenview, Ill.: Scott, Foresman.

Mirkin, Gabe. 1986. "The Personal and Professional Benefits of Wellness." *Public Management* 68:7–14.

Morrison, Peggy, and Jack Sturgess. 1980. "Evaluation of OD in a Large State Government Organization." *Group and Organization Studies* 5:48–63.

National Academy of Public Administration. 1983. *Revitalizing Federal Management: Managers and Their Overburdened Systems.* Washington, D.C.: The Academy.

Ostrom, Vincent. 1973. *The Intellectual Crisis in American Public Administration.* University, Ala.: University of Alabama Press.

Payad, Aurora T. 1986. *Organization Behavior in American Public Administration: An Annotated Bibliography.* New York: Garland.

Perkins, Dennis N.T., Vera F. Nieva, and Edward E. Lawler, III. 1983. *Managing Creation.* New York: Wiley.

Perry, James L., and Kenneth L. Kraemer. 1986. "Research Methodology in the *Public Administration Review.*" *Public Administration Review* 46:215–26.

Pfeffer, Jeffrey. 1981. *Power in Organizations.* Mansfield, Mass.: Pitman.

Pfiffner, John M., and Frank P. Sherwood. 1960. *Administrative Organization.* Englewood Cliffs, N.J.: Prentice-Hall.

Pressman, Jeffrey, and Aaron Wildavsky, 1973. *Implementation.* Berkeley: University of California Press.

Presthus, Robert V. 1965. *Behavioral Approaches to Public Administration.* University, Ala.: University of Alabama Press.

Presthus, Robert V. 1962. *The Organizational Society.* New York: Knopf.

Prewitt, K. 1984. "Field Access: A Growing Problem." *Science* 8(3):223.

Price, R.H., and T. D'Aunno. 1983. "Managing Work Force Reduction." *Human Research Management* 22:413–40.

Rainey, Glenn W., and Lawrence Wolf. 1981. "Flexi-Time: Short-Term Benefits, Long-Term . . . ?" *Public Administration Review* 41:52–63.

Rainey, Glenn W., and Hal G. Rainey. 1986. "Organizational Decentralization in the Public Sector." In *Reforming the Federal Bureaucracy,* edited by D.J. Calista. Greenwich, Conn.: JAI Press.

Rainey, Hal G. 1979. "Perceptions of Incentives in Business and Government." *Public Administration Review* 39:440–47.

Rainey, Hal G. 1983. "Public Organization Theory: The Rising Challenge." *Public Administration Review* 43:176–82.

Rainey, Hal G. 1986. "Public Management: Recent Developments and Current Prospects." Presented at the annual meeting of the American Society for Public Administration, Anaheim, California.

Rawls, John. 1971. *A Theory of Justice.* Cambridge, Mass.: Harvard University Press.

Redford, Emmette S. 1969. *Democracy in the Administrative State.* New York: Oxford University Press.

Romzek, Barbara S. 1985. "Work and Nonwork Psychological Involvements." *Administration and Society* 17:257–81.

Sapolsky, Harvey M. 1972. *POLARIS.* Cambridge, Mass.: Harvard University Press.

Sayles, Leonard R., and Margaret Chandler. 1971. *Managing Large Systems.* New York: Harper & Row.

Schein, Edgar H. 1985. *Organizational Culture and Leadership.* San Francisco: Jossey-Bass.

Scott, William A. 1964. *Values and Organizations.* Chicago: Rand McNally.

Selznick, Philip. 1949. *TVA and the Grass Roots.* New York: Harper & Row.

Shafritz, Jay M., and J. Steven Ott. 1987. *Classics of Organization Theory.* Chicago: Dorsey.

Sherman, Harvey. 1966. *It All Depends.* University, Ala.: University of Alabama Press.

Sigelman, Lee, H. Brinton Milward, J.M. Shepard, and M. Dumler. 1984. "Organizational Responses to Affirmative Action." *Administration and Society* 16:27–40.

Simon, Herbert A. 1946. "The Proverbs of Administration." *Public Administration Review* 6:53–67.

Simon, Herbert A. 1947. *Administrative Behavior.* New York: Macmillan.

Simon, Herbert A., Donald W. Smithburg, and Victor A. Thompson. 1950. *Public Administration.* New York: Knopf.

Singer, E.A., and L.M. Wooton. 1976. "The Triumph and Failure of Albert Speer's Administrative Genius." *Journal of Applied Behavioral Science* 12:79–103.

Sjoberg, G., T.R. Vaughan, and A.F. Sjoberg. 1984. "Morals and Applied Behavioral Research." *Journal of Applied Behavioral Science* 20:311–22.

Slote, Alfred. 1977. *Termination.* Indianapolis: Bobbs-Merrill.

Speer, Albert. 1970. *Inside the Third Reich.* New York: Macmillan.

Staw, B.M. 1984. "Organizational Behavior: A Review and Reformulation of the Field's Outcome Variables." *Annual Review of Psychology* 35:627–66.

Stewart, Debra W., and G. David Garson. 1983. *Organizational Behavior and Public Management.* New York: Marcel Dekker.

Stillman, Richard J., II. 1983. "The Romantic Vision in American Administrative Theory." *Dialogue* 5:2–21.

Stillman, Richard J., II. 1982. "The Changing Patterns of Public Administration Theory in America." In *Public Administration: History and Theory in Contemporary Perspective,* edited by Joseph A. Uveges. New York: Marcel Dekker.

Stumpf, Stephen A. 1977. "Using Integrators to Manage Conflict in a Research Organization." *Journal of Applied Behavioral Science* 13:507.

Susman, Gerald, and Roger D. Evered. 1978. "An Assessment of the Scientific Merits of Action Research." *Administrative Science Quarterly* 23:582–603.

Taber, Thomas D., Jeffrey T. Walsh, and Robert A. Cooke. 1979. "Developing a Community-Based Program for Reducing the Social Impact of a Plant Closing." *Journal of Applied Behavioral Science* 15:133–55.

Taylor, Frederick W. 1947. *Scientific Management.* New York: Harper & Bros.

Teasley, C., III, and R.K. Ready. 1981. "Human Service Matrix: Managerial Problems and Prospects." *Public Administration Review* 41:261–67.

Thayer, Frederick C. 1973. *An End to Hierarchy! An End to Competition!* New York: Franklin Watts.

Thompson, James D. 1967. *Organizations in Action.* New York: McGraw-Hill.

Thompson, Victor A. 1975. *Without Sympathy or Enthusiasm.* University, Ala.: University of Alabama Press.

Uveges, Joseph A., Jr. 1982. *Public Administration: History and Theory in Contemporary Perspective.* New York: Marcel Dekker.

von Bertalanffy, Ludwig. 1968. *General Systems Theory.* New York: Braziller.

Waldo, Dwight. 1948. *The Administrative State.* New York: Ronald Press.

Waldo, Dwight. 1955. *The Study of Public Administration.* New York: Doubleday.

Waldo, Dwight. 1980. *The Enterprise of Public Administration.* Novato, Calif.: Chandler and Sharp.

Walter, Gordon A. 1984. "Organization Development and Individual Rights." *Journal of Applied Behavioral Science* 20:423–40.

Weick, Karl. 1969. *The Social Psychology of Organizing.* Reading, Mass.: Addison-Wesley.

Whetten, David A. 1980. "Organizational Decline." *Academy of Management Review* 5:577–88.

White, Jay D. 1986. "Dissertations and Publications in Public Administration." *Public Administration Review* 46:227–34.

Wilson, Woodrow. 1887. "The Study of Administration." *Political Science Quarterly* 2: 197–232.

Woodward, Joan. 1958. *Management and Technology.* London: Her Majesty's Stationery Office.

Yeager, Samuel J. 1986. "Use of Assessment Centers by Metropolitan Fire Departments in North America." *Public Personnel Management* 15:57–64.

Zawacki, Robert A., and D.D. Warrick, eds. 1976. *Organization Development: Managing Change in the Public Sector.* Chicago: International Personnel Management Association.

8

Public Management: Recent Developments and Current Prospects

HAL G. RAINEY

In the past two decades, the topic of public management has come forcefully onto the agenda of those interested in governmental administration. Numerous books and articles have included the term in their titles. There have also been many management improvement initiatives at various levels of government, including efforts to implement specific procedures or technologies, and prestigious conferences and institutional reports on improving public management. Common to all these activities is the claim that the emphasis on public management is both original and highly significant for education, research, and practice in public administration and related fields.

The use of the public management rubric has increased along with a growing concern about the size, cost, and effectiveness of government. During this period, opinion polls and political elections were reflecting more and more unfavorable public opinion toward the public sector. Resentment of taxes was rife, and ballot initiatives in various states and localities aimed at reducing taxes and government spending. There was growing skepticism over the efficiency and effectiveness of large public agencies and public programs (Weiss 1980, 13–18) and a sharp intensification of the long-standing tradition of lambasting the public bureaucracy (Fiorina 1984; Goodsell 1985, 1–14; Kaufman 1981b). Political candidates at all levels frequently campaigned as aggressively against the governmental bureaucracy as against political opponents (Fiorina 1984). Governmental units and agencies increasingly faced the prospect of sharply reduced resources (Levine 1980; Rubin 1985).

The term *public management* apparently has been attractive because it implies something that is seriously needed in this context. Both the academic literature and the applied management improvement efforts have stressed the need for a vigorous public management orientation as a response to the problems noted above. These developments are therefore related to dramatic questions. Can government in the United States be well managed so that it is highly efficient and effective and widely perceived as such? Or is it destined to remain an overwhelming patchwork of officials, interest groups, programs, and policies, as some critics contend it is (Lowi 1979), unmanageable as a whole or even in parts? Since management reform efforts have often foundered (Lynn 1981; Wildavsky 1979, 205), is there no way to manage the unwieldy beast before it eats us out of house and home? Is it better to concentrate on a sustained effort to reduce government, as the Reagan administration in some ways tried to do (Rubin 1985, 1-20), or to cap public expenditures (Wildavsky 1979)?

The developments surrounding the public management topic reflect an assumption that even after attempted cuts and caps, large-scale government is here to stay, and we must seek the most effective possible administration of programs and agencies. The term *public management* has semantic origins that imply taking things in hand. It suggests a firmness and efficiency of the sort attributed in stereotype to business management. Hence much of the current fascination with the term.

Beyond that, however, the developments in public management involve many complexities and contradictions. There are wide variations in approach, involving differences over the institutional levels and locations on which the discussion should focus, and the roles and functions involved. In addition, while touted as original, the topic in a sense is not at all new (Newland 1980; White 1926; Willoughby 1927). Some of the central issues are virtually classical in the field of public administration, such as the question of how politics and administration are to be interrelated (Levine and Hansen 1985; Waldo 1984, iv). Other implications are original, such as an emphasis on the role of public managers in contemporary public policy processes and administrative systems (Lynn 1987; National Academy of Public Administration 1983) and on expanding systematic research on the topic (Garson and Overman 1981; Overman 1984).

This chapter first describes a number of these recent developments in the literature and practice of public management that illustrate the rise of this rubric and the central issues involved in its rise. It describes developments in the academic literature and disciplines that reflect a perceived insufficiency in the research, training, and practice of public management. Then a number of developments in the practice of public management are described, including governmental management improvement initiatives that reflect a similar emphasis on the need for reform and invigoration. Then, issues common to these developments are discussed in further detail, including this perception of insufficiency, the diversity of approaches to public management, the originality and adequacy of these approaches, and some of the central questions about the nature of public management that remain. Finally, prospects for further development of the topic are discussed, with a focus on four interrelated dimensions along which progress will be needed. On one dimension, concerning the clarification of distinctive roles and behaviors of public managers, a growing body of research is described. This research progress justifies guarded optimism about the value and prospects for a public management emphasis.

Developments in the Academic Literature and Academic Disciplines

A Spate of Books and Articles

Beginning in the mid-1970s and continuing to the present, two or three dozen books and many articles have appeared on management in the public sector. This burgeoning literature has reflected an increasing demand for discussion of how the topic of management applies to public administration. This demand has been based on a critique of the fields of public administration, public policy, and general management that typically includes the following assertions: The public administration literature has been information rich and skill poor, too broadly discursive and philosophical, and too preoccupied with general ethical and normative issues to provide guidelines for managers of public organizations (Allison 1980; Perry and Kraemer 1983); and the public policy literature has been too concerned with policy decisions and the broad process of policy formulation and implementation, with too little attention to the roles and practices of managers of organizational entities within those processes. Organizations have too often been treated as black boxes in the public policy literature (Beyer, Stevens, and Trice 1983).

The general management literature, in contrast, is very useful for public-sector applications but is inattentive to essential features of the governmental context of public management. These include the complex institutional and political influences, the multiplicity of authorities involved in decisions, the absence of a bottom line with the consequent ambiguity of performance criteria, and the unique ethical considerations in public management. These and many related factors must be taken into account in applying general management techniques and principles in the public sector (Rainey 1983a). In some cases, inattention to such distinctive characteristics of the public-sector context results in the failure of techniques drawn from the private sector and the disillusionment of managers who migrate from the private to the public sector and find themselves unable to operate effectively in the new circumstances.

There is a need for an improved conception of public management, and advancement in the knowledge base supporting it, because public management is a scarce commodity. It has been underemphasized in research and practice. Politically appointed officials have been relegated to a twilight zone in political analysis (Heclo 1977, 88; quoted in Lynn 1987, 5) as have other public managers (Allison 1980; Lynn 1981). Too many public managers have too little autonomy, motivation, aggressiveness, and self-conscious identification as public managers. They are too steadily abused by a variety of assailants in and out of government. Government invests too little in the development of individual managers and their careers (Malek 1974).

As mentioned previously, there are marked differences in approach to the topic, and not all contributors would join in this critique. Some authors simply announce that they will discuss the application of managerial skills and techniques in a political setting, in a way that should be useful to students preparing for such roles (e.g., Pursley and Snortland 1980). Another approach, common in management texts for both business and government or both profit and nonprofit organizations, is to treat differences among settings as relatively minor considerations in an otherwise generic process (e.g., Buchele 1977; Massie 1979; Miles 1980; Morrisey 1976; Yates 1985).

More often, however, the limits of the public administration and public policy literatures are explicitly cited (Bower and Christenson 1978; Perry and Kraemer 1983). The crucial significance of the public sector context is heavily emphasized (e.g., Allison 1980; Chase and Reveal 1983; Lynn 1981; Stewart and Garson 1983). Frequently, authors call for the development of a public management field precisely because it is underdeveloped, with consequent disadvantages for education and practice in public administration.

The Brookings Conference

These themes were reflected in a major conference at the Brookings Institution, another example of the activity related to the topic of public management. The need to improve the efficiency, effectiveness, and responsiveness of the federal government had been a central issue in Jimmy Carter's campaign for the Presidency in 1976. During the Carter administration, this issue had been translated into various efforts to improve governmental performance and management, such as the Civil Service Reform Act of 1978 (Ingraham and Ban 1984). As an outgrowth of this same theme, a conference was held at the Brookings Institution in 1979 titled "Setting Public Management Research Agendas: Integrating the Sponsor, Producer, and User" (U.S. Office of Personnel Management 1980). The conference included statements on research needs for public management by heads of the major management agencies of the federal government (i.e., Office of Personnel Management, General Services Administration, Office of Management and Budget, and Comptroller General) and by major intellectual figures in public administration and public affairs (Allison 1980; Cleveland 1980; Porter and Perry 1980; Waldo 1980).

In an introductory statement for the conference, Alan Campbell, director of the Office of Personnel Management, noted a widespread concern among both practitioners and researchers in public management with "the lack of depth of knowledge in this field" (U.S. Office of Personnel Management 1980, 7). He noted that the focal papers for the conference reinforced this view, as well as the view that much of the available knowledge was derived from research on private or business administration. A purpose for the conference, he said, was to bring together practitioners and researchers for communication over ways of filling this void and revitalizing management in the federal government.

The *Public Management Research Directory*

Also reflecting the growing interest in public management was a large-scale survey of relevant research projects by Garson and Overman (1981, 1982) that resulted in the production of a *Public Management Research Directory*. Under the auspices of the National Association of Schools of Public Affairs and Administration, they surveyed 274 programs in public administration and related disciplines to assess research projects related to public management. Their findings emphasized the need for further development of the topic.

The project was also conducted under the auspices of the Office of Personnel Management, and an advisory panel was organized from among the participants in the Brookings conference. The project was intended to increase communication among public management researchers and potential users of the research. The survey asked representatives of the programs to describe funded research projects that pertained to public management.

The project directors reported elaborate efforts to define the topic area. Many of the reported projects were not incorporated into the *Directory* because they were primarily concerned with substantive policy or program issues with no readily identifiable implications for management per se. The project directors ultimately included only projects that had relatively clear relevance for generic public management, "generic in the sense of describing a function, process or technique which could be undertaken by any major American governmental unit" (Garson and Overman 1982, 4). The project directors ultimately included as public management research projects only 262 out of a total of 798 reported by respondents. The researchers concluded that there is relatively little funded research on generic public management and that existing research is highly fragmented by location, discipline, jurisdictional focus, and other factors. Consequently, they said, there is a need for a national effort to promote development and utilization of research on the topic.

Developments Associated with the Kennedy School

Another significant development in the rise of the public management emphasis was the appearance of a number of works on the topic by authors associated with the Kennedy School at Harvard. Graham Allison's paper at the Brookings conference (Allison 1980), which has been widely cited and reprinted, firmly asserted that there are significant distinctions between public management and private business management. Allison reviewed statements by other members of the Kennedy School,

Richard Neustadt and John Dunlop, on the nature of those differences. He also cited significant shortcomings in the available research and literature and listed a number of major research needs.

Kennedy School members have also participated in developing management cases for the public sector. Bower and Christenson (1978), in a compilation of such cases, argued that the public management focus is distinct from both public policy studies and business management. Noting that business management cases were plentiful, they lamented the dearth of contemporary cases in public management, a scarcity their casebook was aimed at reducing. Cases continue to be compiled and announced in the newsletter of the Public Policy and Management Program for Case/Course Development at Boston University, and additional compilations have been published by persons with ties to the Kennedy School (Brock 1984).

A number of additional recent books and papers have made an argument similar to that of Allison. Bower's (1977) discussion of the distinctive character of public management has since been elaborated into an effort to distinguish between general conceptions of political management and technocratic management (Bower 1983). A brief text by Chase and Reveal (1983) contains Chase's lively anecdotal guidelines for handling the external environment of the public manager, developed for his courses before his tragic death. Lynn (1981), while at the Kennedy School, authored a descriptive analysis of the role of the federal executive, which also contains the theme of insufficiency and need for further development. Among other things, he reviews the recurrent efforts at management improvement in the federal government (PPBS, ZBB, Civil Service Reform) over the past several decades, noting that results have been fairly consistently disappointing. He also describes the complex constraints on the governmental executive, who is faced with difficult challenges in trying to exert some impact on the complex bureaucracy while maneuvering in a dynamic political environment that rewards style and show more readily than low-key, substantive managerial performance. Very recently, Lynn (1987) has extended this analysis with an examination of the role of the public manager in public policy formulation and implementation. Again, the picture of public management that emerges is that of an essential but scarce and imperiled commodity.

While there are points of difference among contributors, this aggregate body of work associated with the Kennedy School is probably the most significant school or shared viewpoint advancing the topic of public management. The contributors tend to focus on the role of the high-level executive, especially in the realm of strategy and policy decision making. They emphasize a generalist orientation as opposed to a concentration on administrative procedure and functional details, and they tend toward analysis and education through case description and observation. There are other approaches to public management, as described below, but this has been one of the most noteworthy and consistent recent movements in the advancement of a self-conscious conception of public management.

The Schools, the Associations, and the Journals

Related developments in the disciplines have also raised the theme of public management. The proliferation of programs in public administration and affairs, and their increasing independence as free-standing schools and departments, has obviously influenced the development of the fields of public administration and public policy. More books and articles have been demanded, and more produced. Ironically, however, the public administration field, so long derided by political scientists as intellectually impoverished because of its excessively applied and practical orientation, now apparently came under certain pressures for not being sufficiently skill oriented. Students demanded texts emphasizing managerial skills.

There was at the same time a growing recognition of the need for some degree of commonality in the curricula of M.P.A. programs, including the skills and practical knowledge they imparted. The National Association of Schools of Public Administration and Affairs (NASPAA) initiated a peer-review process in which member schools were expected to demonstrate reasonable conformity to certain curricular guidelines. These guidelines did not employ the public management rubric, but they did emphasize skills and technical knowledge, and a degree of pressure against a curriculum made up exclusively of philosophical courses or courses drawn solely from mainstream political science. The peer-review effort also reflected the perceived need to encourage uniformity as a means of making the M.P.A. as consistent and recognizable as the M.B.A., and competitive in its professional knowledge base. The issues, then, were related to those involved in the proliferation of public management materials and disciplinary activities.

In concomitant developments, the Association for Public Policy and Management (APPAM) was formed by a group of prestigious schools. The APPAM began to publish the *Journal of Public Policy and Management,* which has carried occasional articles on management. The allure of the term *management* was even stronger for public administration specialists than for public policy specialists. In the late 1970s, the *Public Management Forum* was added as a section of *Public Administration Review,* and ran regularly through the mid-1980s, carrying practitioner-oriented articles in every issue. The *Civil Service Journal* was retitled *Management* during this same period.

In the Academy of Management, the primary professional association for business professors specializing in general and behavioral management (organizational behavior, organization and management theory, strategy, ethics, and personnel), a Public Sector Division was formed in the mid-1970s and has operated ever since, but as one of the smallest divisions of the academy. Many papers presented in the other divisions of the academy are based on research in public-sector organizations, and many researchers see their work as generic to management and broadly applicable across public, private, and other kinds of organization. Many apparently feel no particular attraction to a division focusing on the public sector.

Another implication important to the prospects and progress of a public management field is less easily established but seems clear. Most management professors are in business schools and have more incentive to work with business than with government or private social service organizations. For all the discussion of the large size and power of the public sector, business is still a larger and richer sector. Business organizations have more money to spend, and more freedom and willingness to spend it on research, training, consulting, and contributions to business schools. The predominance of business in management circles is one of the important influences on the development of a public management field.

All these developments reflect the rise of an interest in public management. The activity in itself is encouraging and exciting, especially if one accepts the view that the development of a self-conscious identification with such a role is important (Allison 1980; Waldo 1980). There are complications, and the constant implication of an insufficiency raises fundamental questions about the degree to which the difficulties might arise from inevitable circumstances. Before discussing those issues, however, it is important to review some developments in the actual practice of public management.

Developments in the Practice of Public Management and Governmental Management Improvement Initiatives

No succinct description can encompass all the activity of public officials and public agencies that could be referred to as public management. The topic could expand to include all administrative activity in the various units and levels of government, and much of the related political and policy-making activity.

An ironic aspect of the literature implying the dearth of public management is that the government of the United States and the interrelated state and local governments are a monumental beehive of managerial activity. Much of it is highly skillful, sophisticated, and successful. As do many private firms, many governmental units routinely perform functions that half a century ago would have been regarded as genuinely miraculous. Certain agencies for years have had favorable reputations for their management practices (Buchele 1977; Gold 1982). Golembiewski (1985) reports extensive evidence that organization development efforts are successfully implemented in the public sector as often as in the private sector. The concept and field of city management have been elaborately developed, and now represents a relatively well professionalized occupational category, with professional standards and credentials, a professional association, a reasonable intellectual disciplinary base, and other accouterments of a fairly well advanced profession (Anderson, Newland, and Stillman 1983; White 1926). For decades, the International City Management Association has published a periodical titled *Public Management*. In various agencies at the various levels of government, and in the practice-oriented literature, one can locate numerous examples of high-quality activity on a kaleidoscopic array of topics related to public management: public-sector management assessment and development, financial management, information systems management, contract and procurement management, policy management, legislative management, and many others. Indeed, there are periodicals and professional associations for some of these topics and their practitioners.

In sum, the set of activities and topics that could be grouped under the topic of public management in practice is sprawling, diverse, and vast. The assessment of various components of it, moreover, is difficult because they are highly dynamic. They are often dependent on political developments in different jurisdictions. For example, what is the state of senior management service initiatives in various states? What will be the fate of the federal civil service reforms and the Grace Commission recommendations (Levine 1985)? To what extent are cities utilizing various management tools at any given time (Poister and McGowan 1984; Poister and Streib 1989)? What are the management initiatives of the Reagan administration, and what is their meaning (Carroll, Fritschler, and Smith 1985; Ingraham and Ban 1986; Levine 1986)?

Even recognizing all this, a number of recent developments need attention because they echo the themes identified in the literary and disciplinary developments just described. There is much public management activity, but there is widespread concern over its adequacy. There is a perceived need for improvement, for revitalization.

Management Reform Initiatives in Recent Decades
Organizational and managerial reforms are clearly nothing new in government. At the federal level, they have been recurrent during this century, as reflected in the Budget and Accounting Act of 1921, the Brownlow and Hoover commissions, and other examples (Garnett 1987; Seidman 1976). Yet, growth in government also has increased concern with managing the burgeoning structure. Managerial reform and improvement activity has increased in large part because of the growing diversity and complexity of governmental activities. One indication of this is Lynn's (1981, 74) belief that among the Presidents who have held office, Richard Nixon was probably the most supportive of management improvement efforts in the federal government.

Budgeting and Productivity Measurement Initiatives
Yet Lynn also notes that Nixon apparently did not want to spend a lot of time managing, an inclination shared by other policy makers. This orientation is actually a significant characteristic of the context of many managerial reforms in government, as Lynn (1981, 74–102) demonstrates in a review of major federal reform

initiatives in the past two decades. Common to these efforts was an apparent inclination to set in place systems that would increase efficiency, accountability, and performance through goal-oriented management. Management would thus be highly rationalized, with specific goals, and means to those goals. Goal accomplishment would be measured. Centralized, hierarchical accountability could be imposed through pressures and incentives for goal accomplishment. The Planning-Programming-Budgeting System (PPBS), Management by Objectives (MBO), Zero Based Budgeting (ZBB), and various performance and productivity improvement initiatives differed among themselves, but shared this general approach to management.

Some of these initiatives, particularly PPBS, have had beneficial impacts on certain aspects of governmental management, but none has been widely implemented in a lasting fashion. They have foundered on the difficulties involved in implementing such purportedly value-free, rationalized systems in the complex bureaucracy, where programs and their goals are often not amenable to precise specification and measurement, and where complex incentives, power relations, and value questions vastly complicate the adoption of such systems (Sherwood and Page 1976; Wildavsky 1979; Downs and Larkey 1986). The repeated efforts to adopt such reforms in the face of discouraging results reflected the widespread conviction that the federal government needs to be better managed, especially in the sense of rational hierarchical control.

Civil Service Reform and Senior Executive Service Concepts

The Civil Service Reform Act of 1978 was also based on the perception that federal management needed to be improved. Proponents of the act argued the need to tighten the requirements that federal managers take responsibility for management of their subordinates and their organizations (Lynn 1981). A number of provisions of the act were aimed at increasing incentives for performance. The act provided for the replacement of the old Civil Service Commission with the Office of Personnel Management, a step that again appears to reflect the allure of the term *management*. The act established merit pay provisions for middle-management personnel, to tighten the relation between pay and evaluations of performance. It established a Senior Executive Service to function as an elite corps of the highest career civil servants, who would have opportunities for performance bonuses. They would retain rank in person rather than position so that they could be more readily transferred among positions (Ingraham and Ban 1984).

The act was of historical significance, but the success of some aspects of it has so far been mixed at best (Ingraham and Ban 1984; Levine 1985; Rosen 1986). There have been complications in implementing the merit pay and evaluation provisions, and subsequent evaluations have indicated that managers perceive no particular improvement in the relationship between performance and pay and other incentives. Critics have argued that the act was based on a model of management too reliant on hierarchical control, on simplistic concepts of efficiency drawn from stereotypes of private-sector management, and on manipulation of extrinsic incentives such as pay (e.g., Thayer 1978). This initiative further illustrates both the broad conviction that federal management is seriously deficient and the severe difficulty of implementing rational control models for managerial enhancement.

The Senior Executive Service (SES) provisions of the act have also encountered difficulties. Hugh Heclo has reported that by 1983, 40 percent of those who had entered the SES in 1979 had left government; 22 percent were planning to leave; and 79 percent would not recommend a career in federal government to their children (Heclo 1984, quoted in Levine and Hansen 1985). These dismaying problems may result from public criticisms of the federal bureaucracy during a particularly virulent period for such attacks, and to pressures on the bureaucracy in the Reagan administration. Clearly, however, the effort to identify and dignify a set of federal executives is encountering difficulties.

Similar initiatives have been adopted in a number of states, which have set up some variant of a senior executive service. Apparently these reforms have often struggled with similar difficulties in trading off between enhancing the prestige and authority of administrative officials, on the one hand, and increasing political control by the chief executive or legislature, on the other. There have also been similar problems in implementing performance-based pay systems (Gabris 1986; Sherwood and Wechsler 1986).

The National Academy of Public Administration Report

The topic of extensive overhead controls is even more strongly emphasized in a major report on federal management by the National Academy of Public Administration (NAPA). The title *Revitalizing Federal Management: Managers and Their Overburdened Systems* carries much of the message in itself. Based on a study by a NAPA panel, the report concludes that "the role of the Federal manager is being seriously undervalued, and that the Federal management systems have become so burdensome and constraining that they reduce rather than enhance management effectiveness" (National Academy of Public Administration 1983, 1). The management of major functions such as personnel, budgeting, space allocation, travel, and procurement is centralized and tightly controlled by central overhead agencies such as the Office of Personnel Management, Office of Management and Budget, and General Services Administration. The management systems governing these functions have become highly elaborated, with complex checks, balances, and paperwork that are rigid, negative, and constraining. Ironically, this overmanagement diminishes the role of the manager. Individual managers are deprived of authority over the functions and resources essential to their performance. The circumstances tend to deprive managers of incentive, and to "choke off the kind of individual innovation and initiatives which are crucial to real management effectiveness" (p. 1).

The report argues that none of these major management systems of the federal government is in a state of crisis or near collapse but that "neglect and indifference" (p. 2) are leading to serious deterioration, and this in turn will diminish performance and professionalism in the federal government. The report goes on to make extensive recommendations for the reform of various management systems, especially in ways that would return a degree of authority and discretion to the individual manager. In sum, the report represents yet another observation of the weak role and conception of public management, but with the added ironic twist that overmanagement in the system aggravates the problem.

Developments in the Reagan Administration

Considerable activity related to management occurred in the Reagan administration. There has been a good deal of debate over its import, and it is difficult to assess conclusively, but it reveals much about the ongoing dilemmas in developing a conception of public management.

The administration, in its management philosophy, emphasized presidential control of the bureaucracy. Many high-ranking career civil servants were displaced with political appointees. Management improvement initiatives, most notably the Grace Commission report, which made 2478 recommendations for saving costs, focused on cost reduction, adoption of methods purporting to increase businesslike efficiency, productivity improvement, collection of debts, elimination of waste and fraud, reduction of government and transfer of responsibilities to the private sector, and similar priorities.

Critics argue that these actions have demoralized the career civil service (Goldenberg 1984), have increased hostility between political executives and career civil servants (Heclo 1984), have weakened the professional capacity of the career service through the emphasis on ideology and partisanship (Goldenberg 1984; Ingraham and Ban 1986; Newland 1983; Salamon and Lund 1984), have employed a narrow auditing approach to management improvement (Salamon and Lund 1984), and have raised the possibility that the bureaucracy will be transformed into a weak technocracy (Levine and Hansen 1985). Observers also note, however, that the administration placed a heavy emphasis on governmental and managerial performance, which is potentially a lasting, beneficial legacy (Carroll, Fritchsler, and Smith 1985). Lynn (1984) also points out that this administration stressed the delegation of presidential authority to subordinate executives, and this may enhance the role of public executives in the future. (See Levine and Hansen for a comprehensive review of this debate.)

On balance, there seems to be a fairly strong consensus that the Reagan administration certainly did not enhance the roles of public managers in the fashion envisaged by the NAPA report. These very recent developments serve as another illustration of the recurring points about public management: that there is a continuing conviction of insufficiency, and a need for improvement. In addition, the contrast between the orientation of the Reagan administration and the NAPA report is an example of the sharp divergences over how public management should progress in conception and practice, and thus brings the discussion to the point of assessing this array of developments in the literature and practice of public management.

Major Issues Reflected by the Developments

As mentioned, these developments in public management represent only a portion of the terrain that could be covered. Yet they are a very important set of highlights. The literature on public management and the actual practice can be very divergent. There seems little in the way of theory derived from the academic literature that currently guides the managerial reform initiatives. There are, however, certain significant characteristics that the developments in both the preceding categories have in common.

Perceived Insufficiency and Need for Development

As noted repeatedly, many of the contributions to the literature cite the lack of adequate literature, research, and casework. Similarly, many of the developments in practice, as well as the comments on it such as the NAPA report, emphasize the need for reform and complain of systemic neglect of management systems and the role of the manager.

Diversity

In both literature and practice, however, there are divergent, even profoundly conflicting approaches. This should be no surprise. An authoritative assessment of the general management field likens it to a jungle, inhabited by at least half a dozen schools that differ fundamentally in their premises (Koontz 1961). Waldo (1978) has similarly described the fragmentation in the related field of organization theory.

In the public management literature, some approaches emphasize the basic POSDCORB functions (e.g., Crane and Jones 1982; Rosenthal 1982; both reviewed in Overman 1984), sometimes heavily emphasizing control (Steiss 1982). These approaches tend toward similarity with generic management texts. In addition, as previously noted, there are innumerable treatments of the management of a blinding array of individual functions and task areas, such as information systems, personnel, grants and procurement.

In fairly sharp contrast are other approaches emphasizing the conception of a generalist public manager involved in relatively high-level decisions, dealing directly with the complex political environment. Many of these contributions are from the

Kennedy School group described earlier (Allison 1980; Bower and Christenson 1978; Chase and Reveal 1983; Lynn 1981, 1987; see also Bragaw 1980 and many readings in Perry and Kraemer 1983). It is interesting that these approaches often place a stronger emphasis on the distinctive character of public management, but much of their discussion could be characterized as high-level policy making. Relations of the public-sector context to the management of internal organizational design, control, and behavior are less clearly developed. Indeed, some of the observations are essentially assertions that certain important factors, such as personnel and organization design, are exceptionally difficult to manage in the public sector. This orientation may result from a perception that analysis of the public manager's role in public policy was the most pressing need; more attention to the relation of this role to organizational management is apparently forthcoming (Brock 1984; Lynn 1987).

Other differences in approach are similar to variations in approaches to generic management (Koontz 1961). There are sharp contrasts between treatments emphasizing human relations (Golembiewski 1985) and those emphasizing control and the operational and technical aspects of managerial functions.

These differences are in part the result of variations in purpose and focus. Generic management theory has this same character because management encompasses many levels, functions, and settings, and some fragmentation is to be expected as a result of the sheer cognitive limits and to a reasonable division of labor among scholars. Variations in approach also point out important limitations in the literature. In particular, they reflect our limited knowledge of distinctions among units and levels within organizations (top executives v. middle managers, political v. career executives, etc.) and among units and levels of government. Comparative and taxonomic studies have been insufficient (Allison 1980; Seidman 1981).

These divergences in the literature also tend to be reflected in different approaches to practice and reform. The Reagan administration emphasis on control and efficiency, for example, contrasted with the NAPA report's critique of elaborate control mechanisms and its call for the empowerment of a broad cadre of public managers at multiple levels.

Originality and Adequacy of the New Approach

Many contributors to the recent public management literature lament the limitations of the available knowledge and material. Reviews of more recent publications raise further questions about how effectively the gaps are being filled. Many of these publications contain rich descriptions of the constraints and influences of the public-sector context and/or useful discussions of management functions and tasks. The relation between the two is thinly developed, however. Some of the richest descriptions of managing the political environment are still unclear as to the implications for strategic choice, much less for internal organizational design.

170

Overman (1984) notes that a number of recent texts tend to repeat now familiar assertions about the public-sector context and then move on to loosely related discussions of operational tasks. He questions whether there is anything particularly new and different in much of this new literature.

Something Old and Something New. The marriage-of-convenience metaphor is apt. Many assertions in this new literature do not seem particularly new or original. They appear relatively familiar from the literature on bureaucratic power and discretion and other parts of the public administration and public bureaucracy literatures (Rourke 1984). In a sense, the field of public administration began with an emphasis on management. The early texts stressed many topics that recent public management advocates are citing as underdeveloped in the theory and practice of public administration. White (1926, 1927) and Willoughby (1927) emphasized the managerial role of the public administrator in internal organizational processes such as structural configuration and work design, as well as the generalist role of the public executive. They regarded business management as the appropriate guiding model for governmental administration (Waldo 1984, 38ff). While some recent public management advocates regard case studies as a major avenue toward progress (Allison 1980; Bower and Christenson 1978), the case-study approach has had a long history in public administration. The case orientation helped to bring about the current circumstances, so its potential for changing them could be debated at length. Recognizing the long tenure of these topics is important because it forces the question of what is new and valuable about the public management discussion.

Something Borrowed and Something Blue? The question of newness is important because there is a hint of futility and inevitability in critiques of current theory and practice. It is possible that we are simply borrowing the term *management* from the private sector because it implies a decisiveness and proactiveness that appear to be lacking in government, even though a conception of relatively aggressive and autonomous management may not apply in the public sector. In the political economy and cultural environment of the United States, is the public management role inexorably destined for underdevelopment and sharp limitation? The weary repetitiveness of unsuccessful managerial reform efforts in the public sector adds to the impression that such attempts are merely empty ceremony.

Public Management as Promising Direction Rather Than Panacea

Yet the developments surrounding the public management topic are more likely symbolic of inexorable forces of an opposite kind. The repeated reform efforts and the increasing discussion of public management reflect the resiliency of the belief that governmental management is important, and that government can and should be well run. Clearly some of the reform initiatives have been strongly oriented toward increasing hierarchical control and chief executive influence, in a way that has been demoralizing for career civil servants (Heclo 1984; Ingraham and Ban 1986; Rosen 1986); clearly many of the management improvement initiatives have been clumsily implemented. Still, the growing interest and activity symbolize an assumption, even by some who would overtly deny it, that large-scale government is here to stay and that managing it is crucial. The significance of the public management activity is that it involves a number of questions, both concrete and symbolic, about what it means to manage in the public sector and how it is to be done.

It is not crucial to settle on some conclusive definition of public management or establish firmly whether the public management rubric is genuinely original. Ironically, what is new about it is a renewed emphasis on long-standing issues, with an emphasis on their contemporary application. Some of the most important issues raised by the public management developments include an emphasis on self-conscious identification with a public management role, involving skills and commitments particularly suited to contemporary government. This is by no means a new issue, especially for city managers, but can use much further development for other settings and levels (Allison 1980, Ingraham and Ban 1986; Lynn 1987).

An emphasis on increasing research on and observation of the public management role and its contemporary context, with emphasis on actual behaviors and decisions, is the second important issue. Through an eclectic set of approaches, there is a trend toward sharply increasing analysis of the decisions and behaviors of public managers. This may involve updating the case approach and obtaining testimony from public executives (Allison 1980; Bower and Christenson 1978; Lynn 1987) or qualitative studies based on interviews and direct observation (Heclo 1984; Kaufman 1981a; Wechsler and Backoff 1986) or more structured survey research (Buchanan 1975; Bozeman 1987; Rainey 1983a, 1983b).

A third issue is an increasing concern with analyzing the managerial implications of contemporary developments in the executive branch, including the managerial values and philosophies inherent in executive branch policies. The literature on the Reagan administration cited earlier most clearly reflects this trend. In addition, a fourth issue is an emphasis on proactive, purposeful public management, based on the observation that many public administrators are so constrained by political influences and external controls that they become relatively passive as managers of their organizations or units. This emphasis in particular shows how the public management approach reinforces attention to certain long-standing issues, such as the relation between politics and administration

Public Management, Politics, and Administration. This classic issue of the relation between politics and administration is one of the most important raised by the public management approach, and provides an example of how the approach presses a reemphasis on important questions.

The debate over the relation between politics and administration is as old as the academic field of public administration in the United States. Yet it has never been adequately resolved (Levine and Hansen 1985; Waldo 1984, iv). An emphasis on the distinction earlier in the century has given way to the overwhelming evidence that politics and administration are not separate. Yet vestiges of the distinction remain. Governmental reformers seeking to increase chief executive influence over the bureaucracy press for a distinction because it implies limited political and policy-making authority. Administrators, on their part, sometimes cite such a distinction in defense of their domains, arguing the need for neutral competence.

More important is a need to clarify the dimensions implied by the highly general politics and administration concepts. Clearly, there can be a distinction between political criteria and technical or operational criteria in administration (Bower 1983). Yet the problem is that the two dimensions are actually intermingled in complex ways, sometimes reasonably distinct, sometimes dialectic, sometimes interactive. The public management approach underscores the question of how managerial functions are to be discharged in a political environment. Through its implications of private-sector managerial proactiveness, it forces the question of how public managers can and should gain authorization for relatively autonomous, purposeful behaviors in the political context. In some cases and at some levels, public managers act with relative autonomy from political intervention, on the basis of technical rationality. In other times and places, political interventions are dominant. In still other instances, political and administrative criteria are effectively blended (Lynn 1987; Rainey and Rainey 1986; Wechsler and Backoff 1986).

The relation of the political to the administrative is thus very complex and dynamic, but we have only begun to analyze it. We have numerous characterizations of the political and institutional context of administration and bureaucratic power in the American political system (Rourke 1984; Wamsley and Zald 1973) and a limited amount of material on the determinants of the effectiveness and influence of individual agencies and administrative officials (Lewis 1984; Rourke 1984). There have been a number of studies of governmental administrative officials over the years, mainly at the federal level, but they consistently lament our woeful lack of information about the work and behavior of such officials (Heclo 1977; Kaufman 1981a; Lynn 1987; Doig and Hargrove 1987). Much more research is needed on the commonalities and variations among officials and agencies, in different jurisdictions and levels of government and in different agencies and service areas, and at different organizational levels including political versus career service levels, especially as these variations relate to the proactive behaviors of public administrators.

In sum, the public management rubric does not represent some miraculous elixir for the field of public administration. The rise of this rubric reflects an eclectic movement toward renewed emphasis on a number of central issues in the field that are particularly important to analysis of the purposeful, effective behaviors of public administrators discharging managerial functions in a political environment. The public management approach emphasizes conceptual and observational analysis of such behaviors in relation to variations in political and administrative context. Whether the public management rubric and the topics it represents will continue to have currency and value is therefore important to the field of public administration and needs to be considered.

The Rubric Reassessed: Prospects for Public Management

The ultimate prospects for public management will depend on developments along a number of interrelated dimensions.

A Classificatory/Taxonomic Dimension

There is a need for more clarity in classifying public managers and their contexts. There will always be complications in clearly differentiating among politically elected and politically appointed administrators, career civil servants, staff professionals, nonprofit managers, and managers of public corporations. We can, however, define managerial positions with reasonable clarity (Allison 1980) and designate core categories of public managers as those in managerial-level positions in governmentally owned and funded agencies (Wamsley and Zald 1973). We have much less solid information on comparative similarities and differences by sector, type of agency, organizational level, and level of government (Abney and Lauth 1986; Allison 1980; Seidman 1981).

A Research/Theory Dimension

The research and theory underpinnings of a field of public management are clearly growing. There is a blizzard of relevant research, although much of it is diverse and fragmented, especially with regard to a general conception of public management (Garson and Overman 1981, 1982). There is a growing fund of research on that topic, however, as indicated below. There is also a good deal of relevant recent work on theories of public organization and of public administration, some of which is reviewed in Rainey (1983; see also Bozeman 1984; Denhardt 1985; Harmon and Mayer 1986).

An Institutional Dimension

Developments in the political economy and in the academic disciplines will substantially influence the prospects for a field of public management. Obviously, political and economic trends influence the quantity and the character of the demand for public management. Trends influencing the morale and strength of the public service and developments in the role of government (Newland 1987) will in turn influence demand for public management research and education. While some of these trends are currently unfavorable, the basic imperatives underlying governmental growth, which include the demands for public services in an advanced political economy, will make such trends no more irreversible than the price of oil.

As for academic disciplines and institutions, one particular problem is that the field of public administration appears to be a weak institutional base for generic public management research. The proliferation of degree programs is important to development of a public management concept, but the general commitment of the field to basic research and theory development is limited (e.g., Garson and Overman 1982; McCurdy and Cleary 1984; Perry and Kraemer 1986; White 1986). The richer, more predominant schools of business serve as a base for some relevant research but are more interested in the management of private corporations.

A Role/Behavioral Dimension

Research analyzing the actual behaviors and roles of public managers is actually developing at a reasonable pace. Table 8.1 (pages 176–79) provides a summary of selected contributions to this growing body of literature on the attitudes, behaviors, and roles of public managers. Table 8.1 shows that this work, too, is limited, diverse, and fragmented. Yet it leads toward a fairly optimistic conclusion. The work represents a growing consensus, including some of the leading figures in generic managerial and organization theory (Kurke and Aldrich 1983; Mintzberg 1972), that a reasonably distinct public management role can be distinguished within the general conception of management.

Still unclear concerning variations in unit, level, and type of agency, this body of work nevertheless provides a growing base to support the design of such comparisons. Compilations of this material (Perry and Kramer 1983) are already useful for educational purposes. Since self-conscious identification with the role of public management can be highly significant to the development of such a role (Allison 1980; Waldo 1980), this work is valuable as a contribution to that process.

In conclusion, then, there are reasons for optimism, or at least determination. If a public management emphasis contributes to our understanding of the effective blending of the political and the administrative, as it is doing at least incrementally, it will in turn be developing an important component of the governance of advanced political economies. There is also the incentive to preserve and extend something well worth defending. The excessive complaining about government and government officials in recent years has dangerously obscured the fact that this is actually a very well governed country, due in significant part to public management.

175

TABLE 8.1
Selected Contributions to the Literature on the Roles, Behaviors, and Attitudes
of Public Managers

Author, year Sample/Procedure	Findings/Conclusions

Comparative Observations by Experienced Practitioners or Consultants

Golembiewski, 1985

Observations based on personal experience and a review of research on organizational development and behavior in public organizations.	Distinctive properties of public organizations include: multiple access to external authorities, multiple interests and reward structures, and competing affiliations outside the organizational hierarchy for organizational members. These conditions result in limited delegation of authority, need for security, procedural regularity and caution, among managers a weak sense of identity as "professional managers," and general differences in organizational culture due in part to civil service rules and weak performance-reward relations.

Blumenthal, 1983

Views of experienced practitioner.	Federal executives have less control over their organizations than business executives. The organizations are more conglomerated and diverse. Congress and the press are more influential. The decision process is more cumbersome.

Dunlop, 1979

Views of experienced practitioner.	Government management involves shorter time perspectives due to political pressure and turnover of political appointees, less clarity of performance measures, more personnel constraints, more emphasis on equity, more importance of the press, Congress, and courts.

Comparisons of Judgmental or Opportunity Samples of a Variety of "Public" and "Private" Organizations

Kaufman, 1981a

Observational, descriptive study of six federal bureau chiefs.	Much of bureau chief's work is generic management: motivating, communicating, decision making. Political environment highly significant, however. Relations with Congress very important.

Kurke and Aldrich, 1983

Replication of Mintzberg study, observing four executives including a school sys-	Mintzberg's findings replicated and supported, including findings that public managers spend much more time in contact with directors and outside groups. The school administrator spent much more time in formal

Table 8.1. *Continued.*

Author, year Sample/Procedure	Findings/Conclusions
tem and a hospital executive representing public and quasi-public sectors.	activity (e.g., formal meetings), but the hospital administrator did not.
Lau, Pavett, and Newman, 1980 Compared U.S. Navy civilian executives to executives from a number of service and manufacturing firms.	Found general similarities in the work of the two types of managers, although the public managers devoted more time to "fire drills" and crisis management.
Boyatzis, 1982 Study of managerial competencies in four federal agencies and twelve Fortune 500 firms.	Private managers higher on "goal and action" competencies. This is attributed to absence of clear performance measures, such as profits and sales, in the public sector. Private managers also higher on leadership competencies of "conceptualization" and "use of oral presentations." This is attributed to more strategic decision making in the private sector and greater openness and standard procedures in the public sector.
Mintzberg, 1972 Observational study of the work of five executives from a variety of organizations, including a hospital director and a superintendent of a large school system.	The study indicated marked similarities in work roles of the five. The managers in public and "quasi-public" organizations—the school administrator and hospital administrator, respectively—spent more time in contact with directors and with external interest groups. The contacts were more structured and formalized (e.g., formal meetings) and the public administrators received more "status requests." Findings attributed to the broader public concern with the organization's activities and, particularly for the school administrator, the relation to the political system.
Rainey, 1979, 1983b Compared questionnaire responses from middle managers in four state agencies and one defense installation and four private firms.	Public managers lower on satisfaction with co-workers and promotion, relation of extrinsic rewards (pay, promotion, firing) to performance, and perceived value of monetary incentives, and slightly lower on perceived organizational formalization (rules, channels). Public managers much higher on perceived constraints on extrinsic rewards under personnel rules.

177

Table 8.1. *Continued.*

Author, year Sample/Procedure	Findings/Conclusions
	No differences on role conflict and ambiguity, task variability and analyzability, goal clarity, self-reported motivation and job involvement.
Buchanan, 1974, 1975 Compared questionnaire responses from managers in four "typical" federal agencies and four large business firms.	Public managers lower on satisfaction with work and co-workers, job involvement, organizational commitment, and perceived organizational constraints and rules. Buchanan suggested that the findings reflect weaker hierarchical authority, greater diversity of personnel, and weaker commitment expectations in public organizations. This is due to civil service rules, political interventions, diffuse goals, and complex bureaucratic procedures.
Porter and Lawler, 1968 Survey of managerial attitudes of 635 managers in four public and three private organizations.	Public managers were much less likely to feel that pay in their organizations depended on performance and that their own pay represented a reward for good performance.
Rhinehart, Barrel, DeWolfe, Griffin, and Spaner, 1969 Compared supervisory personnel in one federal agency to managers in Porter's (1962) sample from industry, with management level as a control variable.	Federal managers lower on all thirteen items in Porter satisfaction scale. Differences were statistically significant only on social and self-actualization need satisfaction for all levels. For higher levels, federal managers lower on autonomy and self-actualization.
Paine, Carroll, and Leete, 1966 Compared managers in one federal agency to managers in Porter's (1962) industry sample who were comparable in age and level.	Federal managers lower on all thirteen items in Porter need satisfaction scale, with greatest differences on job security, autonomy, and self-actualization. Authors cautioned that agency was under political pressure and concerns over job security may have had "halo effect" on other items.

Table 8.1. *Continued.*

Author, year Sample/Procedure	Findings/Conclusions

Comparisons of Samples from Analogous Organizations or Task Units in the Public and Private Sectors

Solomon and Greenberg, 1982

Compared 125 top managers in public enterprises to 125 private top managers in Israel, on nineteen climate items.	Public enterprise managers lower on perceived relations between rewards and performance. No differences on freedom, delegation, participation.

Lachman, 1985

Compared chief executives in 91 private firms and 40 public enterprises in Israel, on perceived external influences and on work satisfaction.	No differences on perceived external influences on decision processes. Public enterprise executives lower on satisfaction with extrinsic rewards (financial reward, work, social relations) and intrinsic rewards (challenge, growth, etc.), but Lachman concluded that these differences were not important.

Meyer, 1979

Qualitative and quantitative study of structural change using a national sample of state and local finance agencies.	Public bureaucracies particularly open to external pressures for changes. Their hierarchies were stable, but there were frequent changes in subunit composition. Personnel systems were increasingly formalized over time due to federal emphasis on civil service rules. External pressures for structural change were mediated by the political position and behaviors of agency leaders. Meyer concludes that public bureaucracies have no alternative to Weberian hierarchy and tend to be evaluated in terms of conformity with higher authority.

Acknowledgments

For valuable comments on earlier drafts of this paper, I wish to thank Frank P. Sherwood of Florida State University and Richard Zody of Virginia Polytechnic Institute and State University. I also wish to thank an anonymous reviewer for a detailed critique of the manuscript and many valuable comments. Charles H. Levine, of American University and the Congressional Research Service, recently deceased and lost to us as a leading scholar and beloved colleague, also provided valuable guidance and suggestions, as he always did.

References

Abney, Glenn, and Thomas Lauth. 1986. *The Politics of State and City Administration.* Albany: State University of New York Press.

Allison, Graham T. 1980. "Public and Private Management: Are They Fundamentally Alike in All Unimportant Aspects?" In U.S. Office of Personnel Management, *Setting the Public Management Research Agenda,* Document 127-53-1. Washington, D.C.: Government Printing Office.

Anderson, Wayne F., Chester A. Newland, and Richard J. Stillman. 1983. *The Effective Local Government Manager.* Washington, D.C.: International City Management Association.

Benda, Peter M., and Charles H. Levine. 1986. "The 'M' in OMB: Issues of Structure and Strategy." Presented at the annual meeting of the American Political Science Association, Washington, D.C.

Beyer, Janice M., John M. Stevens, and Harrison M. Trice. 1983. "The Implementing Organization: Exploring the Black Box in Public Policy Research." In *Organization Theory and Public Policy,* edited by Richard H. Hall and Robert E. Quinn. Beverly Hills: Sage.

Blumenthal, W.M. 1983. "Candid Reflections of a Businessman in Washington." In *Public Management: Public and Private Perspectives,* edited by J.L. Perry and K.L. Kraemer. Palo Alto, Calif.: Mayfield.

Bower, Joseph L. 1977. "Effective Public Management." *Harvard Business Review* 55: 31–40.

Bower, Joseph L. 1983. *The Two Faces of Management: An American Approach to Leadership in Business and Politics.* Boston: Houghton Mifflin.

Bower, Joseph L., and Charles J. Christenson. 1978. *Public Management: Text and Cases.* Homewood, Ill.: Irwin.

Boyatzis, Richard E. 1982. *The Competent Manager: A Model for Effective Performance.* New York: Wiley.

Bozeman, Barry. 1984. "Dimensions of 'Publicness': An Approach to Public Organization Theory." In *New Directions in Public Administration,* edited by Barry Bozeman and Jeffrey Straussman. Monterey, Calif.: Brooks/Cole.

Bozeman, Barry. 1987. *All Organizations Are Public.* San Francisco: Jossey-Bass.

Bragaw, Louis K. 1980. *Managing a Federal Agency.* Baltimore: Johns Hopkins University Press.

Brock, Jonathan. 1984. *Managing People in Public Agencies: Personnel and Labor Relations.* Boston: Little, Brown.

Buchanan, B. 1974. "Government Managers, Business Executives, and Organizational Commitment." *Public Administration Review* 35:339–47.

Buchanan, B. 1975. "Red Tape and the Service Ethic: Some Unexpected Differences between Public and Private Managers." *Administration and Society* 6:423–38.

Buchele, Robert B. 1977. *The Management of Business and Public Organizations.* New York: McGraw-Hill.

Carroll, James D., A. Lee Fritschler, and Bruce L.B. Smith. 1985. "Supply-Side Management in the Reagan Administration." *Public Administration Review* 45:805–14.

Chase, Gordon, and Elizabeth C. Reveal. 1983. *How to Manage in the Public Sector.* Reading, Mass.: Addison-Wesley.

Cleveland, Harlan. 1980. "Public Management Research: The Theory of Practice and Vice Versa." In U.S. Office of Personnel Management, *Setting the Public Management Research Agenda,* Document 127-53-1. Washington, D.C.: Government Printing Office.

Crane, Donald P., and William A. Jones. 1982. *The Public Manager's Guide.* Washington, D.C.: Bureau of National Affairs.

Denhardt, Robert. 1985. *Theories of Public Organization.* Monterey, Calif.: Brooks/Cole.

Doig, Jameson W., and Erwin C. Hargrove, eds. 1987. *Leadership and Innovation: A Biographical Perspective on Entrepreneurs in Government.* Baltimore: Johns Hopkins University Press.

Downs, George W., and Patrick D. Larkey. 1986. *The Search for Government Efficiency: From Hubris to Helplessness.* New York: Random House.

Dunlop, John T. 1979. *Public Management.* Cited in Graham T. Allison, "Public and Private Management: Are They Fundamentally Alike in All Unimportant Aspects?" In *Public Management: Public and Private Perspectives,* edited by J.L. Perry and K.L. Kraemer. 1983. Palo Alto, Calif.: Mayfield.

Eddy, William, B., ed. 1983. *Handbook of Organization Management.* New York: Marcel Dekker.

Fiorina, Morris P. 1984. "Flagellating the Federal Bureaucracy." In *The Political Economy: Readings in the Politics and Economics of American Public Economy,* edited by Thomas Ferguson and Joel Rogers. Armonk, N.Y.: M.E. Sharpe.

Gabris, Gerald T., ed. 1986. "Why Merit Pay Plans Are Not Working: A Search for Alternative Pay Plans in the Public Sector—A Symposium." *Review of Public Personnel Administration* 7:1–9.

Garnett, James L. 1987. "Operationalizing the Constitution via Administrative Reorganization: Oilcans, Trends and Proverbs." *Public Administration Review* 47:35–45.

Garson, G. David, and E. Sam Overman. 1981, 1982. *Public Management Research Directory,* vols. 1 and 2. Washington, D.C.: National Association of Schools of Public Affairs and Administration.

Gold, Kenneth A. 1982. "Managing for Success: A Comparison of the Private and Public Sectors." *Public Administration Review* 42:568–76.

Goldenberg, Edie N. 1984. "The Permanent Government in an Era of Retrenchment and Redirection." In *The Reagan Presidency and the Governing of America,* edited by L. Salamon and M.S. Lund. Washington, D.C.: Urban Institute Press.

Golembiewski, Robert. 1962. "Civil Service and Managing Work." *American Political Science Review* 66:961–73.

Golembiewski, Robert T. 1983. "Structuring the Public Organization." In *Handbook of Organization Management,* edited by William Eddy. New York: Marcel Dekker.

Golembiewski, Robert T. 1985. *Humanizing Public Organizations.* Mt. Airy, Md.: Lomond Publications.

Goodsell, Charles T. 1985. *The Case for Bureaucracy.* Chatham, N.J.: Chatham House.

Graham, Cole Blease, and Steven W. Hays. 1986. *Managing the Public Organization.* Washington, D.C.: CQ Press.

Harmon, Michael M., and Richard T. Mayer. 1986. *Organizational Theory for Public Administration*. Boston: Little, Brown.

Heclo, Hugh. 1977. *A Government of Strangers: Executive Politics in Washington*. Washington, D.C.: Brookings Institution.

Heclo, Hugh. 1984. "A Government of Enemies?" *Bureaucrat* 13:12–14.

Ingraham, Patricia W., and Carolyn R. Ban, eds. 1984. *Legislating Bureaucratic Change: The Civil Service Reform Act of 1978*. Albany: State University of New York Press.

Ingraham, Patricia W., and Carolyn R. Ban. 1986. "Models of Public Management: Are They Useful to Public Managers in the 1980s?" *Public Administration Review* 46:152–60.

Kaufman, Herbert. 1981a. *The Administrative Behavior of Federal Bureau Chiefs*. Washington, D.C.: Brookings Institution.

Kaufman, Herbert. 1981b. "Fear of Bureaucracy: A Raging Pandemic." *Public Administration Review* 41:1–9.

Koontz, Harold. 1961. "The Management Theory Jungle." *Academy of Management Journal* 4:174–88.

Kurke, L.E., and H.E. Aldrich. 1983. "Mintzberg Was Right! A Replication and Extension of *The Nature of Managerial Work*." *Management Science* 29:975–84.

Lachman, Ran. 1985. "Public and Private Sector Differences: CEOs' Perceptions of Their Role Environments." *Academy of Management Journal* 28:671–79.

Lau, Alan W., Cynthia M. Pavett, and Arthur R. Newman. 1980. "The Nature of Managerial Work: A Comparison of Public and Private Sector Jobs." *Academy of Management Proceedings* 339–43.

Levine, Charles H., ed. 1985. *The Unfinished Agenda for Civil Service Reform: Implications of the Grace Commission Report*. Washington, D.C.: Brookings Institution.

Levine, Charles H. 1986. "The Federal Government in the Year 2000: Administrative Legacies of the Reagan Years." *Public Administration Review* 46:195–207.

Lewis, Eugene. 1984. *Public Entrepreneurship*. Bloomington: Indiana University Press.

Lowi, Theodore J. 1979. *The End of Liberalism*. 2d ed. New York: Norton.

Lynn, Laurence E., Jr. 1981. *Managing the Public's Business: The Job of the Government Executive*. New York: Basic Books.

Lynn, Laurence E., Jr. 1984. "The Manager's Role in Public Management." *Bureaucrat* 13:20.

Lynn, Laurence E., Jr. 1987. *Managing Public Policy*. Boston: Little, Brown.

McCurdy, Howard E., and Robert E. Cleary. 1984. "Why Can't We Resolve the Research Issue in Public Administration?" *Public Administration Review* 44:44–56.

Malek, Frederick V. 1974. "The Development of Public Executives—Neglect and Reform." *Public Administration Review* 34:230–33.

Massie, Joseph L. 1979. *Essentials of Management*. Englewood Cliffs, N.J.: Prentice-Hall.

Meyer, M.W. 1979. *Change in Public Bureaucracies*. London: Cambridge University Press.

Miles, Robert H. 1980. *Macro-Organizational Behavior*. Glenview, Ill.: Scott, Foresman.

Mintzberg, H. 1972. *The Nature of Managerial Work*. New York: Harper & Row.

Morrisey, George L. 1976. *Management by Objectives and Results in the Public Sector*. Reading, Mass.: Addison-Wesley.

National Academy of Public Administration. 1983. *Revitalizing Federal Management: Managers and Their Overburdened Systems*. Washington, D.C.: The Academy.

Newland, Chester A. 1983. "A Midterm Appraisal—The Reagan Presidency: Limited Government and Political Administration." *Public Administration Review* 43:1–21.

Newland, Chester A. 1987. "Public Executives: Imperium Sacerdotium, Collegium? Bicentennial Leadership Challenges." *Public Administration Review* 47:45–56.

Newland, Chester A., ed. 1980. *Professional Public Executives*. Washington, D.C.: American Society for Public Administration.

Overman, E. Sam. 1984. "Public Management: What's New and Different?" *Public Administration Review* 44:275–78.

Paine, F.T., S.J. Carroll, and B.A. Leete. 1966. "Need Satisfactions of Managerial Personnel in a Government Agency." *Journal of Applied Psychology* 50:247–49.

Perry, James L., and Kenneth L. Kraemer. 1986. "Research Methodology in *Public Administration Review* 1975–1984." *Public Administration Review* 46:215–26.

Perry, James L., and Kenneth L. Kraemer, eds. 1983. *Public Management: Public and Private Perspectives*. Palo Alto, Calif.: Mayfield.

Poister, Theodore, and Robert McGowan. 1984. "The Use of Management Tools in Municipal Government: A National Survey." *Public Administration Review* 44:215–23.

Poister, Theodore, and Gregory Streib. 1989. "Management Tools in Municipal Government: Trend Over the Past Decade." *Public Administration Review* 49:240–48.

Porter, Lyman W. 1962. "Job Attitudes in Management: Perceived Deficiencies in Need Fulfillment as a Function of Job Level." *Journal of Applied Psychology* 46:375–84.

Porter, Lyman W., and Edward E. Lawler, III. 1968. *Managerial Attitudes and Performance*. Homewood, Ill.: Irwin.

Porter, Lyman W., and James L. Perry. 1980. "Motivation and Public Management: Concepts, Issues, and Research Needs." In U.S. Office of Personnel Management, *Setting the Public Management Research Agenda*, Document 127-53-1. Washington, D.C.: Government Printing Office.

Pursley, Robert D., and Neil Snortland. 1980. *Managing Government Organizations*. North Scituate, Mass.: Duxbury.

Rainey, Glenn W., and Hal G. Rainey. 1986. "Breaching the Hierarchical Imperative: Modularization of the Social Security Claims Process." In *Reforming the Federal Bureaucracy*, edited by D.J. Calista. Greenwich, Conn.: JAI Press.

Rainey, Hal G. 1979. "Perceptions of Incentives in Business and Government: Implications for Civil Service Reform." *Public Administration Review* 36:233–46.

Rainey, Hal G. 1983a. "Public Organization Theory: The Rising Challenge." *Public Administration Review* 43:176–82.

Rainey, Hal G. 1983b. "Public Agencies and Private Firms: Incentive Structures, Goals, and Individual Roles." *Administration and Society* 15:207–42.

Rhinehart, J.B., R.P. Barrel, A.S. DeWolfe, J.E. Griffin, and F.E. Spaner. 1969. "Comparative Study of Need Satisfaction in Governmental Business Hierarchies." *Journal of Applied Psychology* 53:230–35.

Rosen, Bernard. 1986. "Crises in the U.S. Civil Service." *Public Administration Review* 46:207–14.

Rosenthal, Stephen R. 1982. *Managing Government Operations*. Glenview, Ill.: Scott, Foresman.

Rourke, Francis E. 1984. *Bureaucracy, Politics, and Public Policy*. Boston: Little, Brown.

Rubin, Irene S. 1985. *Shrinking the Federal Government: The Effect of Cutbacks on Five Federal Agencies*. New York: Longman.

Salamon, Lester M., and Michael S. Lund. 1984. "Governance in the Reagan Era: An Overview." In *The Reagan Presidency and the Governing of America*, edited by L. Salamon and M.S. Lund. Washington, D.C.: Urban Institute Press.

Seidman, Harold. 1981. "A Typology of Government." In *Federal Reorganization: What Have We Learned?* edited by P. Szanton. Chatham, N.J.: Chatham House.

Sherwood, Frank P., and William J. Page. 1976. "MBO and Public Management." In *Public Management: Public and Private Perspectives,* edited by J. Perry and K. Kraemer. Palo Alto, Calif.: Mayfield.

Sherwood, Frank P., and Barton Wechsler. 1986. "The 'Hadacol' of the 1980s: Paying Senior Public Managers for Performance." *Review of Public Personnel Administration* 7:27–41.

Solomon, E., and M. Greenberg. 1982. "Organizational Climate in the Public and Private Sectors." Presented at the annual meeting of the Academy of Management, New York.

Steiss, Alan Walter. 1982. *Management Control in Government.* Lexington, Mass.: Heath.

Stewart, Debra W., and G. David Garson. 1983. *Organizational Behavior and Public Management.* New York: Marcel Dekker.

Thayer, Frederick C. 1978. "The President's Management 'Reform': Theory X Triumphant." *Public Administration Review* 38:309–14.

U.S. Office of Personnel Management. 1980. *Setting the Public Management Research Agenda: Integrating the Sponsor, Producer, and User,* Document 127-53-1. Washington, D.C.: Government Printing Office.

Waldo, Dwight. 1978. "Organization Theory: Revisiting the Elephant." *Public Administration Review* 38:589–97.

Waldo, Dwight. 1980. "Public Management Research: Perspectives of History, Political Science, and Public Administration." In U.S. Office of Personnel Management, *Setting the Public Management Research Agenda* Document 127-53-1. Washington, D.C.: Government Printing Office.

Waldo, Dwight. 1984. *The Administrative State.* 2d ed. New York: Holmes and Meier.

Wamsley, Gary L., and Mayer N. Zald. 1973. *The Political Economy of Public Organizations.* Bloomington: Indiana University Press.

Wechsler, Barton, and Robert W. Backoff. 1986. "Policy Making and Administration in State Agencies: Strategic Management Approaches." *Public Administration Review* 46: 321–27.

Weiss, Carol H. 1980. "Efforts at Bureaucratic Reform: What Have We Learned?" In *Making Bureaucracies Work,* edited by Carol H. Weiss and Allen H. Barton. Beverly Hills, Calif.: Sage.

Weinberg, Martha Wagner. 1977. *Managing the State.* Cambridge, Mass.: MIT Press.

White, Leonard D. 1926. *Introduction to the Study of Public Administration.* New York: Macmillan.

White, Leonard D. 1927. *The City Manager.* Chicago: University of Chicago Press.

Wildavsky, Aaron. 1979. *The Politics of the Budgetary Process.* Boston: Little, Brown.

Willoughby, W.F. 1927. *Principles of Public Administration.* Washington, D.C.: Brookings Institution.

Yates, Douglas. 1985. *The Politics of Management.* San Francisco: Jossey-Bass.

9

Personnel *For* and Personnel *By* Public Administrators: Bridging the Gap

Lloyd G. Nigro

Leaving aside the thorny question whether personnel administration, much less public administration, is a discipline, I have concluded that any attempt to describe the state of the discipline must be incomplete. It is simply impossible to attack such a diverse activity from all the relevant perspectives. The perspective I have chosen allows at best a partial evaluation of the current state of Public Personnel Administration. I argue that Public Personnel Administration projects two different images of the personnel function. One, the traditional personnel for managers or administrators, is alive and kicking despite a long history of attempts to replace it with Human Resources Management or personnel by managers. Human Resources Management is supposed to be the wave of the future, but it lacks well-defined implementing concepts or technologies—a problem that does not afflict personnel for managers. After describing this situation, I have proposed a way to link the two perspectives.

The reader will quickly notice two features of this chapter. First, it relies heavily on materials drawn from textbooks. In their time, textbooks communicate the state of the art to students. From a historical standpoint, they provide an excellent moving picture of the evolution of the field. Second, I have borrowed Dwight Waldo's (1955) convention of capitalizing Public Personnel Administration and Human Resources Management whenever I refer to the study of these activities or fields.

The Role of Public Personnel Administration: Personnel By *or* For *Managers?*

For over sixty years, textbook treatments of the personnel function have increasingly tended to define its role in very broad organizational terms that assign major responsibilities to general administrators, line managers, and supervisors. In the process of developing a supportive (as opposed to policing) orientation toward managerial needs, and in order to show its relevance to organizational purposes, writers on Public Personnel Administration have urged their readers to accept definitions that blur what were once rather sharply drawn boundaries between the jurisdiction and responsibilities of the personnel specialist and those of the line administrator or manager. On a conceptual level, the latest stage in this process is the Personnel as Human Resources Management approach; in practice, the 1978 U.S. Civil Service Reform Act (CSRA) is held as implementing necessary reforms designed to allow federal executives to manage their human resources more effectively.

Nevertheless, the push to redefine Public Personnel Administration along Human Resources Management lines has revealed major gaps between prescriptions (as set forth in guiding definitions and policy statements) and instruments (the operating technologies) of personnel administration that constitute the core of virtually all descriptions of the field. Survey texts, which are designed to provide their readers with a sense of the state of the discipline, reflect the difficulties associated with an effort to build solid (operational) connections between the established technologies of personnel management and the day-to-day activities of line administrators. The result is a Public Personnel Administration with a split personality. The framing definitions are now strongly organizational in perspective and managerial in orientation, but the discussions of techniques and their rationales are either so general as to be simply informative or so specific that they must be considered the province of the personnel specialist.

Similarly, under the CSRA, despite the executive-managerial thrust of the language justifying the legislation, the act does not transfer control over mainline personnel functions to federal managers on the operational level. Nor is there much evidence to suggest that managers believe they need direct control over most of the instruments of personnel administration. The overall design of merit pay and performance appraisal systems mandated by the CSRA has been mainly the responsibility of personnel offices that have worked with supervisors to implement and administer them. Those delegations of authority that have taken place under the CSRA were, for the most part, to agencies that then redelegated them to personnel specialists working in operating units (Institute for Social Research 1982, vii–viii). Evaluators report that agency personnel administrators have appreciated the added flexibility, but "most of the delegated authorities do not make any difference in agency operations and agency managers care very little where these authorities reside" (Department of Organizational Behavior 1982, 210).

Public Personnel Administration has mixed, but not fully integrated, two interpretations of personnel's place in public administration. One, originally based on the policing norms of the first civil service reform movement but now anchored in the personnel system technologies that emerged from that era, sees personnel administration as something done for those in the line. The other, stressing performance and responsiveness, assigns a leading role to public managers. In the following two sections, these interpretations are contrasted. It should be emphasized that they overlap considerably in practice, especially in areas such as performance evaluation and interviewing where line managers have traditionally played active roles.

The Personnel Administration *for* Managers Approach

In this frame of reference, contemporary Public Personnel Administration pursues three interrelated objectives: (1) the preparation of specialists in the various functional areas of personnel administration, (2) the design and implementation of personnel systems and techniques that protect merit principles and support administrative and managerial processes, and (3) the familiarization of line officials with the knowledge and skills that personnel specialists may contribute to the effort to solve a wide variety of organizational problems. These themes have been features of Public Personnel Administration over the past fifty years, and there is little reason to believe that they will not continue to be central to the field.

Closely associated with the above organizing themes are the standard concerns and related methods of public personnel administration. While it is true that these technologies have been elaborated over the years, they have not changed much as categories or standard elements of Public Personnel. For example, controlling for changes in terminology, a comparison of the responsibilities assigned to the personnel unit or office by two texts, one published in 1985 and the other in 1962, reveals a great deal of similarity. The Siegel and Myrtle text (1985) is Human Resources Management oriented, while the Stahl text (1962) is considered a prime example of the traditional approach to Public Personnel Administration (see table 9.1, page 188).

With varying degrees of specificity, all Public Personnel Administration texts discuss the purposes and methods related to this set of core activities. Some deal with them in ways intended to provide beginning students and line administrators with an appreciation of their contributions to organizational performance. Others go into far greater detail and are clearly intended for those who plan to make personnel a specialization. In both instances, however, it is in these areas where the normative and technical facets of Public Personnel are most fully developed and confidently set forth. The normative core is merit, and the need to see that it structures personnel policy and practice drives the technology of Public Personnel Administration. Stahl's characterization of merit is typical.

> In its broadest sense, a merit system in modern government means *a personnel system in which comparative merit or achievement governs each individual's selection and progress in the service and in which the conditions and rewards of performance contribute to the competency and continuity of the service.* (Stahl 1962, 28; italics in original)

187

TABLE 9.1
Comparison of Responsibilities Assigned by Two Textbooks
to Personnel Units

Siegel and Myrtle (1985)	Stahl (1962)
Compensation	Salary and wage administration
Benefits and services	
Job analysis and design	Job analysis and evaluation
Employee development	Staff training and development
Performance appraisal	Performance standards and evaluation
Personnel management systems	Policies and instructions
Recruitment; selection; equal employment opportunity	Staffing
Reassignments and promotions	
Separation	Separation
Personnel research	Personnel research
Program evaluation	
Employee-management relations	Employee relations
Employee health and safety	

Accordingly, Public Personnel Administration concentrates heavily on such matters as job evaluation and position classification, selection, placement, training, performance appraisal, wage and salary administration, the adjudication of appeals, and the administrative arrangements under which personnel systems operate. These constitute the center of gravity around which matters such as affirmative action, collective bargaining, employee rights and obligations, and productivity improvement revolve. In large governments and agencies, the central elements of personnel will usually be assigned to specialists. In Public Personnel Administration, they are all well-defined fields of applied research and evaluation. Affirmative action and collective bargaining have now achieved a similar status. For the practitioner, the technical, legal, and other knowledge required to master these areas is extensive, and some are inclined to believe that public personnel administration is nearing (if it has not already reached) the point that it deserves to be called a profession.

In the old days—back before the mid-1960s—no special preparation was really needed for a career in personnel. The procedural aspects of certification, classification, and examinations were learned on the job. Many a music, history, or English major was composing civil service examinations a few months after graduation. Validation was not a heavy concern. But a decade later validation is of paramount importance. Personnel agencies need psychologists and statisticians to write and validate examinations of all kinds. It was a similar story with labor relations. . . . Presently there is an increasing recognition that the motivational techniques of the behavioral sciences must become part of the personnelist's tool kit. . . . The 1980s will see similar searches for human resources information system specialists and productivity measurement experts.

The occupation that is public personnel administration has been inexorably growing into the professional calling of public personnel management. It is probably premature to claim professional status now, but it's coming. (Shafritz 1978, 296)

Be it an occupation or a profession, public personnel has certainly developed a series of subspecialties and techniques that, over the years, have combined to produce an organizational subsystem that must be staffed by experts if it is to meet the standards set by Public Personnel Administration. If these experts are taking on the characteristics of professionals, they may be expected to push for tighter control over standards, procedures, and qualifications. If this happens, it will likely strengthen the personnel administration *for* public managers point of view and, in turn, widen the gap between it and the personnel administration *by* managers approach.

The Personnel Administration *by* Managers Approach

This orientation, while less developed than its counterpart in a technical sense, has captured the definitions Public Personnel uses to communicate its central role or function. Since the 1930s, Public Personnel Administration has recognized (at times reluctantly) that to be effective, managers must have at least some influence on certain personnel policies and practices; however, a visibly positive connection between the personnel function and management's role emerged from Public Personnel's acceptance of the human relations approach (Nigro 1959, 30–36; Stahl 1962, 15, 197–222). Using this vehicle, Public Personnel Administration expanded its boundaries to include topics such as motivation, leadership, communication, counseling, and the psychology of training. Many aspects of applied human relations had to be attended to by those in supervisory roles and, the reasoning went, managers and administrators were therefore responsible for vital aspects of the organizational personnel function. In these areas, the prescribed role of personnel specialists is to provide information and support, but carrying out these activities must fall to the supervisor.

Once this domain claim was made, it was not difficult for Public Personnel Administration to rationalize the inclusion of a wide variety of managerial tasks. In so doing, it has taken on a distinctly managerial, as opposed to staff or regulatory, coloration. Simon, Smithburg, and Thompson (1950) noted this tendency: "In a broad sense, since all administration is concerned with people and their behavior, all administration might properly be described as personnel administration—and some specialists in personnel work would like to use this broad definition of their specialty" (p. 312). In a widely read text often used as an example of the mainline traditionalist approach to personnel administration, O. Glenn Stahl used a broad definition:

> Personnel management, like any other phase of administration, is a responsibility of line officials, of those who are accountable for the success of a public agency or program. Being such, it is necessarily interwoven at all levels of a hierarchy and in all aspects of the supervision and direction of the organization. . . . If we view the basic objective of personnel management as maintaining effective human resources and human relations in the organization, then it is largely a *manner* of management to best carry out its personnel responsibilities. The problem may also be stated as how to organize personnel administration as a "grass-roots" concept in an enterprise. (1962, 439)

It is difficult to distinguish personnel administration from public management in the following descriptions set forth in very recent texts.

> Our view of public personnel administration is strategic and managerial. We believe that public managers can ensure that their personnel practices embody much of what is known about the modern practice of human-resources management. Whether or not they do so will depend both on the extent to which personnel systems are seen as a key aspect of managerial and organizational strategy making and on the level of knowledge that managers have about modern personnel management practices. (Siegel and Myrtle 1985, ix)

> In a sense, the personnel function has no boundaries. All people who engage in management are automatically involved in the personnel process. Similarly, all other management functions are in some way dependent on the effective performance of the personnel system. (Hays and Reeves 1984, 73)

Definitions of personnel administration emphasizing a managerial orientation have been around for some time, however. In 1920, Tead and Metcalf were writing: "Personnel administration is the direction and coordination of the human relations of any organization with a view of getting the maximum necessary production with a minimum of effort and friction and with a proper regard for the general well-being of the workers" (p. 28).

It is not difficult to build a rationale for the Human Resources Management approach using the above definitions; in this sense, personnel administration by the manager is a point of view deeply rooted in Public Personnel Administration. It is a point of view that is often expressed in criticisms of the personnel specialist: "Personnel specialists and practices have continued to reflect the traditional fixation with techniques. The time has come for public personnel as a field to emphasize the management of human resources and performance over techniques development, and to broaden that orientation to include line managers" (Rabin, Teasley, Finkle, and Carter 1979, 19).

For an illustration of the personnel administration by managers perspective in practice, one need only refer to the initial enthusiasm with which advocates of the CSRA (and to a certain degree federal managers) promoted and moved to implement the performance appraisal and merit pay features of the act. For many, giving executives and managers a large measure of control over these functions was the key reform because it allowed them to administer incentives in ways designed to increase productivity and responsiveness to organizational goals. As Hays and Reeves (1984) put it:

> In addition to its traditional responsibilities for recruitment and selection, personnel management is concerned with developing, utilizing, and accommodating an organization's human resources. Implicit in this list of obligations is the view that the personnel function is responsible for motivating employees and ensuring that they make a productive contribution to the organization's mission. These tasks presuppose that personnel management is an activist, future-oriented, and organizationwide function, assumptions that are clearly incorporated in the Civil Service Reform Act of 1978. (Pp. 73–74)

Similarly, the structural reorganization of the federal personnel system and the authorization of extensive delegations was supposed to create conditions under which line administrators and supervisors could assume major roles in the personnel process, adapt practices to conditions, and effectively motivate their subordinates. Reforms along these lines were proposed on the federal level long before 1978. (It is well worth noting that 1987 marked the fiftieth anniversary of the Brownlow Committee Report.) And, on state and local levels, executive models for personnel administration have been recommended by authorities for well over thirty years. N. Joseph Cayer (1986) described the movement toward management-centered personnel administration in the following terms:

> The role of personnel offices has changed and expanded greatly in recent years. One change is that personnel is increasingly viewed as supporting all aspects of management. Public sector jurisdictions are becoming more aware of the need for making personnel part of general management and are emulating the private sector by integrating personnel into the overall management func-

tion. . . . The 1978 Civil Service Reform Act was predicated in large part on President Carter's promise to revamp management on all levels of the federal government. State and local government reforms were stimulated by similar concerns. (P. 48)

In addition to Public Personnel's affection for broadly gauged definitions, the expansion of its boundaries to include a broad range of political, social, and economic issues and problems has increased the pressure to move beyond the personnel for managers viewpoint. The role sets or networks that are seen to make up public personnel systems have expanded greatly in both scope and complexity. Along these lines, Donald Klinger identifies at least five categories of personnel-related roles that may be found in public agencies on all levels of government. These are (1) externally based consultants, (2) supervisors and line managers, (3) functional specialists or generalists employed by the organization in staff or support roles, (4) professionals housed in central personnel agencies or departments, and (5) those holding positions on regulatory commissions and merit system protection boards or appeals bodies (1980, 43–45). But this listing is far from comprehensive; most current texts proceed at least formally to enlarge the relevant boundaries of public personnel systems well beyond this largely intraorganizational focus so as to include union leaders, politically appointed executives, elected chief executives, legislators, intergovernmental actors, judges, representatives of organized interests, educators, and others in an agency's external environment (Lee 1979, 9–13).

Issues and processes such as collective bargaining, affirmative action and representative bureaucracy, and career development have been added to longstanding concerns about patronage, partisan activity, veterans' preference, and relations between career administrators and political appointees. In this regard, it is instructive to compare the contents of Public Personnel texts written at different times. The example presented in table 9.2 illustrates changes that have taken place over a quarter century.*

First, following practice, Public Personnel Administration has fragmented into a variety of relatively free-standing specialties focused on issues, types of organizations, levels of analysis, technologies, or some combination of these. Second, attempts to firmly tie personnel administration to an easily identifiable set of roles (primarily those of professionalized personnel specialists, workers in personnel offices, and members of central staff agencies) have suffered considerably.

Other recent texts add chapters on such topics as workforce planning, productivity management, management of intergovernmental personnel resources, pro-

---

* This pattern is very similar to that found in other textbooks. See, for example, Powell (1956) and Torpey (1953).

TABLE 9.2
Chapter Titles of Public Personnel Texts: 1959 and 1986

Nigro (1959)	Nigro and Nigro (1986)
What Is Public Personnel Administration?	Value Inputs and Conflicts
Organization for Personnel Administration	Organizations and the Personnel Function
Position Classification	Personnel and Organizational Performance
Compensation	The Career Concept
Recruitment and the Career Service	Collective Bargaining in Government
Selection	The Bilateral Input—The Unions
The Role of In-Service Training	Equal Employment Opportunity and Affirmative Action
The Training Program in Action	Public Personnel and Representative Bureaucracy
Service Ratings	Job Evaluation and Pay: Pressures and Conflicts
In-Service Adjustments	Selection
	Performance Appraisal and Merit Pay
Supervision	Promotions and Other Status Changes
	Training
Morale and Discipline	Grievance and Appeals
	Constitutional Rights and the Public Employee
The Future of Personnel Administration	The Future of Public Personnel Administration

fessionalism, and the constitutional issues of personnel management.* Thus, Public Personnel's inventory of concerns has grown considerably, and, in many instances, the bedrock norm of merit (as described above) is supplemented by values such as responsiveness, representativeness, equity, and organizational effectiveness.† For students of Public Personnel, the resulting complexities, instabilities, and tensions have had predictable consequences. These roles simply cannot encompass the field in practice, and the literature reflects this reality.

Personnel systems are part of the larger governmental system. A personnel system is not restricted to personnel agencies but must include the employees affected and their supervisors. Legislative bodies, chief executives, courts, and

---

* In varying detail, all Personnel texts cover these topics. See also Cooper (1983), Heclo (1977), Mosher (1968), and Thompson (1975).

† See Elliott (1985).

the general citizenry are important components. Intergovernmental relations, labor organizations, and various professional and governmental associations also are part of public personnel systems. At stake are major value issues, especially how the merit principle should be applied in personnel decisions. (Lee 1979, 13)

The contemporary scope and diversity of Public Personnel Administration diffuses pieces of the action to a large number of organizational and environmental actors and groups. In doing so, it strengthens the position of those who reason that much of the responsibility for effective personnel administration must fall to those who are, as James D. Thompson (1967) puts it, in a position to co-align people and "streams of institutional action" (p. 147).

The Uneasy Combination of Personnel For and By Public Administrators

The personnel administration *by* managers point of view is well entrenched in contemporary Public Personnel Administration. It is promoted by widely used definitions of the field that prescribe a central role for the supervisor and general administrator. Furthermore, Public Personnel now deals with issues, technologies, and processes involving large, often highly complex and dynamic, role sets that demand attention and action from managers on all organizational levels. Given these factors, it is not surprising that today's students of Public Personnel Administration are encouraged to conclude that Human Resources Management is the term that best represents and summarizes the state of the art or the leading edge of thought and (to some degree) practice. Nonetheless, the personnel administration *for* managers perspective has quietly held its own, primarily because it possesses an established set of communicable technologies, identifiable organizational roles and tasks, and a consistent normative foundation in the merit principle. The resulting tension between the two perspectives is highlighted in the following description of public personnel management:

Personnel management encompasses all activities related to people in organizations. It is the utilization of human resources to accomplish the organization's objectives as effectively and efficiently as possible.... Personnel managers must know how to recruit, select, evaluate, promote, train, discipline, and dismiss employees. They must be adept at motivating, counseling, and bargaining with workers. In addition, they are called upon to classify positions, develop compensation plans, measure productivity, and handle grievances and complaints. In short, personnel administration involves all aspects of managing the organization's human resources, and public personnel administration refers to that function in governmental entities. (Cayer 1986, 1)

This description of personnel administration is not inaccurate, but it reflects the difficulties Public Personnel Administration has encountered in its efforts to blend the *for* and *by* approaches. It reveals clearly the degree to which personnel administration as an organizational process has been extended to roles and arenas well beyond those of the personnel specialist. Equally obvious is the extent to which the core instrumentation of personnel administration remains largely in the hands of the personnel specialist. While, in a definitional and perhaps organizational sense, the Human Resources Management ball is served into the line administrator's court, sustained effectiveness often requires that it be returned to the personnel specialist because he or she understands the implementing technologies. Personnel administration *for* managers is better prepared to deliver a focused set of well-established goals, a standard package of problems, and a repertory of concepts and practices that may be applied in several (already known) ways. Personnel *by* managers is strong on rationale but weak on method. The importance of Human Resources Management to organizational performance is recognized, as are the effective administrator's potential contributions along these lines; however, how all of this is to be realized is highly uncertain.

Human Resources Management: Uncertainty Over the Roles of the Specialist and the Administrator

Personnel *for* managers is certainly open to criticisms from several vantage points. Technique may indeed overwhelm purpose, and its knowledge base and methods are demonstrably imperfect. Merit is not the only value that may legitimately be used to guide and evaluate the conduct of public personnel administration. Much of the history of Public Personnel Administration is an exercise in recognizing and grappling with these issues and problems.* However, personnel *by* managers suffers from a disability of its own: It imposes extraordinary demands on administrators while saying very little about how they should go about meeting this challenge. For example, while the image of personnel systems as lattices of many intersecting and interdependent role sets is conceptually powerful, it is not easily translated into guidelines for administrative action. J.D. Thompson (1967) noted some time ago that recognizing a problem is not the same as knowing how to solve it: "The administration of multiorganization projects and activities is the central challenge.

---

* There are many historical treatments. See, for example, Karl (1963), Van Riper (1958), White (1948, 1951, 1954).

Whether we have or will gain the knowledge about the organizations that it takes to use and control them under conditions of extreme interdependence remains to be seen" (p. 158).

The responsibilities the Human Resources Management approach assigns to managers are comprehensive, perhaps unrealistically so if it is intended that managers do more than exercise general policy control and oversight. The typical organizational response to complexity and uncertainty is to factor large problems and tasks into smaller, more manageable, ones through specialization and departmentalization. March and Simon (1958), in their discussion of the cognitive limits on rationality, explained this process in the following terms:

> An individual can attend to only a limited number of things at a time. . . . Rational behavior involves substituting for the complex reality a model of reality that is sufficiently simple to be handled by problem-solving processes.
>
> In organizations where various aspects of the whole complex problem are being handled by different individuals and different groups of individuals, a fundamental technique for simplifying the problem is to factor it into a number of nearly independent parts, so that each organizational unit handles one of these parts and can omit the others from its definition of the situation. . . . A large complex task is broken down into a sequence of smaller tasks, the conjunction of which adds up to the accomplishment of the larger. The factorization of a large task into parts can be more elaborate for an organization than for an individual, but the underlying reason is the same: the definition of the situation at any one moment must be sufficiently simple to be encompassed by a human mind. (Pp. 151–52)

March and Simon also point out that complexity increases as administrators and supervisors at successively higher levels in the organizational hierarchy are asked to deal with more and more interrelated tasks and problems. Limited human capacities, therefore, require that problems be "dealt with in grosser and more aggregative form[s]" (1958, 150). It is apparent that personnel administration *for* managers fits easily into this pattern because it offers specialized expertise in support of line managers and supervisors. It is the personnel specialist who must know how. Personnel administration *by* managers, in its most expansive form, appears to require that the manager have both the detailed knowledge and rational capabilities needed to comprehend and actively address a broad range of personnel problems and processes. In addition, it is reasonable to conclude that these human resources management activities would have to be continuously interrelated and coordinated with the many other facets of the public administrator's role.

While it may not be intended, Human Resources Management seems to be running the risk of neglecting the human limitations for which specialization and departmentalization are designed to compensate. As one moves up the hierarchy, according to March and Simon (1958), it is organizationally illogical to expect that most personnel matters will receive anything but increasingly general oversight; those that do get attention usually dealt with by applying existing routines or programs. Even new problems or situations seldom stimulate the effort needed to design new programs. "In most cases, adaptation takes place through a recombination of lower-level programs that are already in existence" (March and Simon 1958, 150). These lower-level programs are usually designed and carried out by specialists in response to higher-level needs and problems. And "the programs of members of the higher levels of the organization have as their main output the modification or initiation of programs for individuals at lower levels" (March and Simon 1958, 150). This picture of administrative or organizational behavior is at least significantly out of line with the image projected by Human Resources Management. If personnel *by* managers is to be much more than frosting on the cake of personnel *for* managers, it must be brought into closer alignment with the existing state of knowledge about how organizational work and their administrators behave.

Public Personnel Administration, therefore, would be well served by a more considered exploration of how Human Resources Management can be made real or operational from the standpoint of the line administrator and supervisor. While workshops and training programs are certainly needed and popular among line managers seeking to upgrade their personnel skills, a broader implementing strategy or technology within which such efforts might fit would be very helpful. A potentially profitable step in this direction is what might be called *strategic simplification.*

Human Resources Management and Strategic Simplification

Engaging nonspecialist administrators and supervisors as active (as opposed to largely reactive) players in the processes of personnel management will be difficult unless the logic of organizational problem solving and decision making outlined above can be accommodated. Pushing complexity up the organizational hierarchy and asking managers to create and integrate a large number of complicated problem-solving routines or programs inverts or reverses the line of attack suggested by contemporary organization theory. This theory (and a huge body of empirical research) recommends that such complicated problems or tasks as managing the human resources of a complex organization are most successfully handled by initially breaking them down into their component elements and assigning these elements to specialized units or departments. What comes back up the hierarchy should be problems related to interunit coordination (these should be kept at the lowest possible level in order to reduce the complexity faced higher up the hierarchy) and simplified routines that allow managers to exercise the kind of leverage they need to deal effectively with the problems they face.

Strategic Simplification and Position Classification

Narrowly defined routines, set forth in fine detail, are necessary and appropriate on levels of the organization where extensive specialization is possible. But personnel is one area of public administration in which there has been a pronounced inclination to impose these routines (in their fully elaborated form) on higher levels of organizational activity where they are often counterproductive. Probably the best example of this tendency is position classification. The methods and routines associated with position classification in government, because of their centrality to many other personnel technologies and merit, have reached levels of detail and complexity designed to befuddle all but those who specialize in this area. It is ironic that a process so integral to the effective functioning of American public personnel administration is so widely disliked and criticized by public administrators.

> Traditional position classification and job evaluation studies are believed by many observers to defeat productivity and managerial effectiveness. . . . Position classification studies are criticized as unreasonable constraints on top management, hurtful to employee morale, and little more than polite fictions in substance. They are viewed by many as the triumph of technique over substance. . . .
>
> Such plans are the bedrock of the merit system, and the system is under extreme attack. If job evaluation efforts are going to survive and even prosper, they must become a part of contemporary reform efforts. Rather than remain a sanctified and untouchable bastion, classification plans must incorporate job evaluation methodologies that are flexible and subject to managerial discretion. . . . (Hays and Reeves 1984, 120)

What could be added to the above is the need to develop classification procedures that managers can easily understand and routinely use. Here, the specialist may be of considerable help if a simplification rule is kept in mind. The specialist's objective should be to create conditions under which line managers can make classification decisions that are both legal and organizationally rational, and promote efforts to develop and use human resources more effectively. In other words, the system should actually allow (indeed, encourage) managers and supervisors to use job evaluation and classification as positive elements of the human resources management process, that is, the ball stays in management's court. The Naval Laboratories Demonstration Project, approved by the U.S. Office of Personnel Management (OPM) in 1980, offers an example of strategic simplification in the area of position classification.

The Naval Laboratories Demonstration Project was intended to attack a variety of personnel management problems, including the limitations of the existing federal classification system (Nigro and Clayton 1984, 153–61). In the laboratory context, the system and its associated procedures were seen by managers to be overly complex, cumbersome, and confusing. In practice, managers were heavily dependent on personnel analysts who controlled classification decisions and, therefore, the system greatly limited supervisory discretion in such matters as recruitment, pay, and performance standards. Because of the time and effort required to take classification actions, personnel specialists were often not able to provide timely support service in other areas (Nigro and Clayton 1984, 159–60). In response to these problems, laboratory managers and personnel specialists worked together to design a simplified system.

The GS-5 through GS-18 structure was replaced by five levels for professional/scientific, engineering, and administrative workers. Each level represents differing degrees of difficulty and responsibility, but broadly defined standards and benchmarks are used by managers to determine assignments to levels. In addition to the much simplified position assignment process, the expanded pay ranges created by combining GS grades allowed greater managerial discretion in pay administration (Nigro and Clayton 1984, 162). The following summarizes laboratory expectations regarding the impacts of the new classification structure:

> From the laboratories' standpoint, the new classification structure has some important benefits. It clears the way to making more competitive offers to highly qualified or scare skills candidates for jobs because managers have greater pay ranges to work with. It reduces the number of classification actions, thereby reducing the work loads of line management and personnel specialists. Highly promotable employees can advance rapidly since they are required to spend only one year in-level although the average time is longer. The pay range available to reward high performing employees is greatly extended. The system is flexible enough to allow dual career ladders where scientific and technical personnel may continue working in their disciplines rather than having to move into "management" jobs in order to increase their pay. Finally, in many cases, classification-related barriers to internal mobility are eliminated. (Nigro and Clayton 1984, 162)

Evaluation studies conducted by OPM some four years after the demonstration was implemented revealed that classification errors had been reduced about 75 percent, and supervisors were devoting significantly less time to the classification process. The time required to complete a classification action had been substantially lowered. It was also found that delays in recruitment attributable to classification procedures had been reduced. At one of the two demonstration sites, supervisors expressed the belief that their ability to influence classification decisions had been meaningfully increased. Finally, while nonsupervisory employees were no more satisfied with the new system than they were with the old one, supervisors were strongly supportive of the new classification structure and its associated procedures (Office of Personnel Management 1984, 12–15).*

Personnel offices at the demonstration laboratories were seen to be more helpful than those at the control laboratories. This finding suggests that it may be possible to operationalize Human Resources Management or personnel *by* managers in terms that recognize the technical and support functions of the personnel specialist and the imperatives of line management. As they did at the laboratories, specialists have a key role to play in the development and support of personnel instruments that managers can comprehend and use effectively. At the time of this writing, OPM was in the process of developing guidelines for an anticipated implementation of the simplified classification system in a number of agencies.

Conclusion

The themes of personnel *for* and *by* managers should be reconciled in Public Personnel Administration. A starting point is an attempt to connect what we know about the logic of organizational action with our expectations regarding relationships between personnel specialists, administrators, and supervisors. Insofar as Human Resources Management is concerned, Public Personnel must do more than set forth challenging definitions and expansive role perceptions. A strategy for implementation or action must also be provided. Strategic simplification is proposed here as one potentially useful way of building mutually reinforcing relationships between specialists and managers that may produce the kind of instrumentation that human resources management needs.

One dimension of the CSRA is the opportunity it affords personnel specialists and managers to think along lines suggested here. The act encourages innovation by establishing broad standards and objectives that permit substantial revision of existing practices and experiments such as those conducted at the Naval Laboratories. Hopefully, this opportunity will not be lost. Public Personnel Administration should take the lead by carefully reevaluating its traditional definitions as well as its inventory of concepts regarding the roles played by those in public personnel systems. A first step in this direction would be an effort to exploit the insights provided

---

* See also Coopers and Lybrand (1982) and National Academy of Public Administration (1978). I would also like to express my appreciation to OPM Research and Demonstration staff members for their very helpful comments on my description of the demonstration and its results.

by organization theory and research more fully. Public Personnel's incorporation of human relations concepts was a highly effective way to broaden the field's perspective and its relevance to managerial concerns. A contemporary challenge is to find ways in which our understanding of organizations may be used to help public administrators manage their human resources more successfully.

On 24 July 1987, Senator Ted Stevens introduced legislation entitled the "Civil Service Simplification Act of 1987." In his introductory statement, he noted that "the administration believes that the Navy experiments are a success and should now be implemented governmentwide" (*Congressional Record*—Senate 1987, S10693). The analysis accompanying the draft bill argues that the legislation would "allow for a quick implementation of a simplified position classification system, which is one of the key features of the Simplified Management System" (*Congressional Record*—Senate 1987, S10696). Senator Stevens expressed reservations about applying the Navy model to the entire federal government. He recommended continued experimentation, especially demonstrations conducted outside of DOD. At this time, there appears to be little support in the Congress for the Simplification Act or related legislation.

References

Cayer, N. Joseph. 1986. *Public Personnel Administration in the United States.* New York: St. Martin's.

Cooper, Phillip J. 1983. *Public Law and Public Administration.* Palo Alto, Calif.: Mayfield.

Coopers and Lybrand, Inc. 1982. "Evaluation of the Navy Demonstration Project for the Office of Personnel Management: Annual Report." Manuscript.

Department of Organizational Behavior. 1982. *Organizational Assessments of the Effects of Civil Service Reform—Annual Report, FY 1982.* Cleveland, Ohio: Case Western University.

Elliott, Robert H. 1985. *Public Personnel Administration: A Values Perspective.* Reston, Va.: Reston Publishing.

Hays, Steven W., and T. Zane Reeves. 1984. *Personnel Management in the Public Sector.* Boston: Allyn and Bacon.

Heclo, Hugh. 1977. *A Government of Strangers.* Washington, D.C.: Brookings Institution.

Institute for Social Research. 1982. *Organizational Assessments of the Effects of Civil Reform—Third Year Report for Fiscal Year 1982.* Ann Arbor: University of Michigan.

Karl, Barry D. 1963. *Executive Reorganization and Reform in the New Deal.* Cambridge, Mass.: Harvard University Press.

Klinger, Donald E. 1980. *Public Personnel Management: Contexts and Strategies.* Englewood Cliffs, N.J.: Prentice-Hall.

Lee, Robert D., Jr. 1979. *Public Personnel Systems.* Baltimore: University Park Press.

March, James G., and Herbert A. Simon. 1958. *Organizations.* New York: Wiley.

Mosher, Frederick C. 1968. *Democracy and the Public Service.* New York: Oxford University Press.

National Academy of Public Administration. 1978. *Revitalizing Federal Management: Managers and Their Overburdened Systems.* Washington, D.C.: The Academy.

Nigro, Felix A. 1959. *Public Personnel Administration.* New York: Holt, Rinehart and Winston.

Nigro, Felix A., and Lloyd G. Nigro. 1986. *The New Public Personnel Administration.* Itasca, Ill.: Peacock.

Nigro, Lloyd G., and Ross Clayton. 1984. "An Experiment in Federal Management: The Naval Laboratories Demonstration Project." In *Making and Managing Policy,* edited by G. Ronald Gilbert. New York: Marcel Dekker.

Office of Personnel Management Research and Demonstration Branch. 1984. *Evaluation of the Navy Personnel Management Demonstration Project: Analysis of Survey and Interview Results—1979 to 1983.* Washington, D.C.: OPM.

Powell, Norman J. 1956. *Personnel Administration in Government.* Englewood Cliffs, N.J.: Prentice-Hall.

Rabin, Jack, C.E. Teasley III, Arthur Finkle, and Luther F. Carter. 1985. *Personnel: Managing Human Resources in the Public Sector.* New York: Harcourt Brace Jovanovich.

Shafritz, Jay M., Walter L. Balk, Albert C. Hyde, and David H. Rosenbloom. 1978. *Personnel Management in Government.* New York: Marcel Dekker.

Siegel, Gilbert B., and Robert C. Myrtle. 1985. *Public Personnel Administration: Concepts and Practices.* Boston: Houghton Mifflin.

Simon, Herbert A., Donald W. Smithburg, and Victor A. Thompson. 1950. *Public Administration.* New York: Knopf.

Stahl, O. Glenn. 1962. *Public Personnel Administration.* 5th ed. New York: Harper & Row.

Tead, Ordway, and Henry C. Metcalf. 1979. *Personnel Administration* (1920), as quoted by Leonard White in *Classics of Public Personnel Policy,* edited by Frank J. Thompson. Oak Park, Ill.: Moore.

Thompson, Frank J. 1975. *Personnel Policy in the City.* Berkeley: University of California Press.

Torpey, William G. 1953. *Public Personnel Management.* New York: Van Nostrand.

Van Riper, Paul. 1958. *History of the United States Civil Service.* New York: Harper & Row.

Waldo, Dwight. 1955. *The Study of Public Administration.* New York: Random House.

White, Leonard D. 1948. *The Federalists.* New York: Macmillan.

White, Leonard D. 1951. *The Jeffersonians.* New York: Macmillan.

White, Leonard D. 1954. *The Jacksonians.* New York: Macmillan.

10

Women in Public Administration

DEBRA W. STEWART

The study of women in public administration has been guided by two questions, one normative and the other empirical. The first question asks, What variables should we manipulate to improve the status of women in public administration? The second asks, What pattern of inclusion do we actually observe over time? In response to the first question, we have relied on three theoretical frameworks, each with its own definition of the problem and associated solutions: the political, the psychological, and the sociological. In response to the second question, we have taken readings over time, examining both quantitative and qualitative aspects of involvement. This chapter describes the research in the field by reviewing responses to these normative and empirical questions and then looks forward to project the substance and process of emerging research on women in public administration.

Obstacles to Improving the Status of Women in Public Administration: Three Paradigms

The concept of paradigm helps sort the scholarly responses to the question, What variables should we manipulate to improve the status of women in public administration? A paradigm is the constellation of beliefs, values, and techniques shared by members of a scholarly community. Inquiry into improving the status of women in public administration has proceeded under three paradigms, each rooted in a different discipline, each offering distinct definitions of the problem, and each implying preferred strategies or solutions. As Thomas Kuhn notes, debates between paradigms always involve the question, "Which problem is it more significant to have solved?" (1970, 110). The political, the sociological, and the psychological approaches each provide a unique response. While each model addresses the status of women in work organizations generally, the analyses associated with these approaches provide the conceptual tools for analyzing the obstacles to women in public administration.

The Political Paradigm

The analysis of the problem from the political paradigm is rooted in the traditional concern of political science with participation in the political system. Over the years political scientists have studied the process and impact of participation, and at times have disagreed about the political system's requirements in this regard, but participation remains a central concept in political analysis. Assuming participation as a core value, political science scholarship on women as public actors falls into three categories: works that critique the way in which women's participation has historically been viewed, works on the women's movement that study how women became organized to demand more participation, and works on women in specific roles ranging from voters to elite decision makers.

By the early 1970s, feminist political scientists were dismissing the legitimacy of previous studies on women as political actors, labeling political science as one of the least responsive of the social sciences to the impact of the women's movement. Conventional political science was indicted for engaging in a paternalism that routinely drew the conclusion that women need to come up to male standards of participation and political savvy to achieve political equality, without recognizing the institutional barriers for doing so. Critics charged that the way in which political sophistication and maturity were operationalized enshrined the male model and ignored the politics of issues in the private sphere where women were more politically active (e.g., sexual relations, new forms of marriage, changes in the family structure) (Jacquette 1974). But developing simultaneously with this critique was a literature on women and politics that was self-consciously free of such faults.

One branch of the new literature recorded how women organized to make themselves heard. Some authors attempted to chronicle movement-building events from the Radical Women's Protest of the Miss America Contest in 1968 (Deckard 1979, 352) through the various twists and turns of the battle for the Equal Rights Amendment (ERA) (Boles 1976). Other scholars explored the latter linkage between the women's movement and public policy. In this vein, Jo Freeman documented the ways in which the women's movement stimulated public policy by creating publicity, by creating a climate of expectation that something would be done about problems, by creating grass roots and governmental constituencies for change, and by providing an organized clientele for enforcement officials once policy was enacted (Freeman 1975, 237). Collectively, these works mapped the infrastructure required for the full participation of women in public life.

The other branch of women and politics literature explored women's participation in political roles looking specifically at women's access to and involvement in elite roles across political systems. In Jacquette's edited collection on *Women in Politics,* Mary Lepper published one of the earliest scholarly articles on women as public administrators. Viewing female federal executives as a special case of political elites, Lepper reviewed the evolution of women's participation in the federal service and tested a series of hypotheses designed to understand the relative position of men and women in the federal service and to ascertain whether government service offers an attractive career alternative for women. In this highly quantitative study, Lepper concluded that while the total number of women at the federal executive level was small in the early 1970s, the increase over the late 1960s was significant and that a number of women in visible policy positions in the 1970s were calling for action (Lepper 1974).

Rita Mae Kelly and Mary Boutilier took a case-oriented approach in exploring the political roles of women. Classifying female political behavior in terms of the "private woman," the "public woman," and the "achieving political woman," Kelly and Boutilier describe the similarities and differences in the socialization of a sample of women in each category (1978, 7–8).

One conclusion is shared by scholars working within the political science paradigm: Women's truncated participation is the problem to be solved. Kirsten Amundsen provided one of the earliest blueprints for action: "The relationship between the sexes in America is most likely to be changed through political action. . . . It is through politics . . . that one gets the rules and regulations, the important legislation . . . that guarantees access and opportunities" (1971, 12). Prejudice, either individual or institutional, stands in the way of women's participation. We turn to the political system for solutions.

Nevertheless, policy action cannot emerge until a constituency believes that women should have the same opportunities as men, that women are denied those opportunities because of discrimination, and that government is responsible for eliminating these practices (Klein 1984, 31). In the 1970s, these factors converged to make policy change possible. As Ethel Klein describes, the women's movement was instrumental in developing and sustaining belief for this perspective (1984, 93). She claims that the actual change in women's experience through the creation of a life style centered on work rather than home contributed to a feminist consciousness that provided the constituency needed for change (Klein 1984, 93).

With the problem defined as one of discrimination, and the solutions taking the form of laws and regulations to prohibit or curb the effects of discrimination, political science scholarship increasingly paid attention to the effectiveness of alternative strategies for implementing the law (O'Sullivan and Stewart 1984; Stewart 1980). Analysis of affirmative action strategies, evaluation of affirmative action programs, and comparative studies of equal employment opportunity for women cross-nationally form a substantial body of policy literature stemming from political paradigm assumptions.*

Figure 10.1 summarizes the major categories of analysis and the principal relationships examined within the political paradigm. For each relationship identified, a scholar(s) whose work typifies research on that relationship is identified. In general, the characteristic of this approach is that it provides a very broad-sweep picture of the factors associated with women's participation in elite roles. Adhering to the political paradigm, we are invited to see that women's opportunity to participate in elite roles in public administration is facilitated by public policy enactments that are stimulated by the political pressure of a vital women's movement. Changing life styles of women and the emergence of political issues to which women laid claim nurtured the women's movement; the movement in turn continues to contribute to the issue agenda. All the categories of analysis take on meaning in relation to the workings of the political system. In contrast, other approaches are less inclined to look to the political system at all for resolution of the problem.

The Psychological Paradigm

From the perspective of the psychological paradigm, problems encountered by women in public administration, and in work organizations in general, reside in characteristics of individuals. In line with the general tendency in psychological research to concentrate on people-centered variables as determinants of behavior (Caplan and Nelson 1973), psychologists have looked for the linkage between female experiences and the development of traits that are contrary to the requirements of the managerial role (Riger and Galligan 1980).

The conventional wisdom in the pre-women's movement psychology of the 1950s and early 1960s was that, by nature and nurture, women lacked motivation to achieve in male careers. Bruno Bettelheim explained women's reticence to achieve quite simply: "We must start with the realization that, as much as women want to be good scientists and engineers, they want first and foremost to be womanly companions of men and to be mothers" (cited in Weisstein 1971). But by the late 1960s, psychologists, disturbed by the passive description of the problem, were actively probing the female psyche with the intention to change it.

Matina Horner's landmark essay on "Bright Women," published in 1969, catalyzed much research in this tradition. Horner found in her experimental work that women have a fear of success because achievement threatens their sense of

---

* Women participating as clients in the political system are not cited as directly relevant to a political paradigm that explains women's status in public administration. But women relate to political systems not simply as its agents (administrators) but also as its clients. Recent work by Barbara J. Nelson (1984) develops this perspective.

206

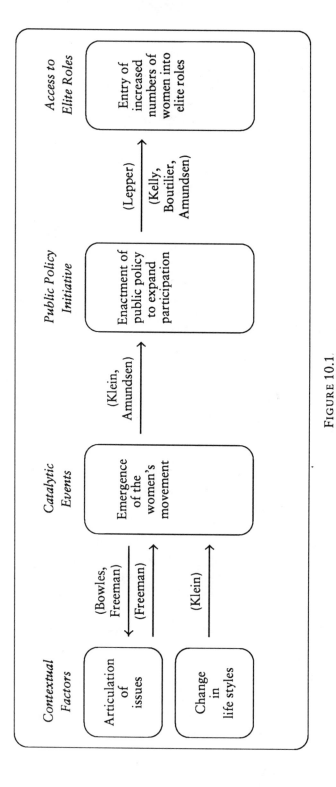

FIGURE 10.1.

The Political Paradigm: A Conceptual Framework

femininity. Women have an inner drive to avoid success given its negative consequences (Horner 1969). Similarly, Hennig and Jardim offered a women-centered, yet
more concrete, explanation of the problems women encountered in organizations.
These authors suggested that women were deficient in managerial traits, skills, and
behaviors required for success (Hennig and Jardim 1977). Like Horner, they traced
these differences to sex-role socialization in childhood and adolescence.

Whatever the source of the difference, a recurrent theme in the psychological
literature describes a male management model that men and women acknowledge
(Schein 1973, 1975) and that curbs women's options for managerial careers and
retards their progress in organizations. Compared to men, women are rated as less
desirable for management positions, are extended fewer job offers, and receive lower
salaries (Bowman, Worthy, and Greyser 1965). Traits associated with the male sex
role are perceived as required for success in management; traits associated with female sex roles are seen as incongruous with the traits of a good manager (Massengill
and DiMarco 1979; Schein 1973, 1975; Steinberg and Shapiro 1982). Further
evidence suggests that sex-role stereotypes influence perception of managerial style,
that behavior is perceived as different if coming from a male as opposed to a female
(Bartol and Butterfield 1976; Eagly and Wood 1982; Jago and Vroom 1982; Rosen
and Jerdee 1973, 1974a).

One encouraging stream of research identifies factors that moderate these
gender effects. Hennig and Jardim, for example, report a moderating effect of male
relationships. Women's deficiencies in goal setting, long-range planning, and risk
taking were less evident in women who had close relationships with their fathers and
who had close relationships and encouragement from their male bosses (Hennig and
Jardim 1977). Gomez-Mejia (1983) reports that, if given appropriate opportunities,
once in positions women may internalize the job norms and attitudes of their male
counterparts. Thus, male and female behaviors may converge over time.

Although much of the psychology literature focuses on the trait and behavior
deficiencies of women, significant attention has also been devoted to those who control the narrowing stream through which advancement in organizations occurs.
Laboratory studies show that women are less likely to be hired than men (Dipboye,
Arvey, and Terpstra 1977; Rosen and Jerdee 1973; Shaw 1972) and are less likely to
be promoted (Miner 1974; Roussell 1974). This research focuses on individuals but
shifts the target for intervention from women alone to men and women in superior
positions.

From the point of view of psychological theory, female advancement in
management is curtailed because women describe themselves, and are described by
men, as having self-concepts that make them less suitable than men for management.
Whether these self-concepts are stereotypes or whether they are grounded in behavior differences, the solution to the problem remains the same. Men and women need
to be reeducated or trained to behave in ways that enhance rather than limit

women's opportunities in public service. For women, this means developing themselves through leadership and skills training. For men, this means tilting training toward consciousness raising and toward specific strategies for enhancing female opportunity (mentoring, etc.).

But in drawing this conclusion it is important to acknowledge research that cautions against easy acceptance of the training solution. Beryl Radin's study of state and local officials found that although people who aspire to top positions in public organizations have both inside skills (interpersonal, organizational, and technical) and outside skills (political know-how and use of contacts), women managers were not aware of this model of success. Furthermore, few women were able to see a relationship between training programs and their perceived problems. In fact, Radin (1980) reports, women have only a hazy picture of the successful career pattern and really no sound description of the narrowing stream.

Figure 10.2 (page 210) summarizes the major categories of analysis and the principal relationships examined within the psychological paradigm. Again, for each relationship shown, a scholar(s) whose work typifies research on that relationship is identified. A woman's capacity for managing (traits, skills, and behaviors) is the factor that accounts for her success in management from the perspective of this paradigm. But the relationship may be mitigated by stereotypes that alter perceptions of female capabilities, by relationships with male mentors, by experience in opportunity positions, and by understanding pathways to success. Whether stereotypes will cloud the cultivation of and perception of management capabilities is related to the strength of sex-role socialization. The principal task, from a psychological viewpoint, is to refine our understanding of the personal characteristics of those who survive the narrowing process and perfect methods for cultivating those traits.

On at least one point the psychological analysis and the political analysis converge: It is the behavior of individuals that must change. From the psychological perspective, that behavioral change will emerge from new attitudes; from the political perspective, public policy will mandate it. The sociological paradigm turns the lens once more to capture a quite different perspective.

The Sociological Paradigm

From the perspective of the sociological paradigm, problems encountered by women in organizations reside neither in individual traits or states nor in the distribution of politically contrived participation, but in characteristics of the organizational situation. Sociological research is marked generally by emphasis on the nature of the organizational structures (Silverman 1971). Rosabeth Moss Kanter expressed the central theme of this analysis in an article published in 1976. "Occupations do not exist in a vacuum: they occur within institutions. Those institutions' structures —who works with whom, who dominates whom, how members of occupations come in contact with one another—are the topics of analysis and explanation . . . a

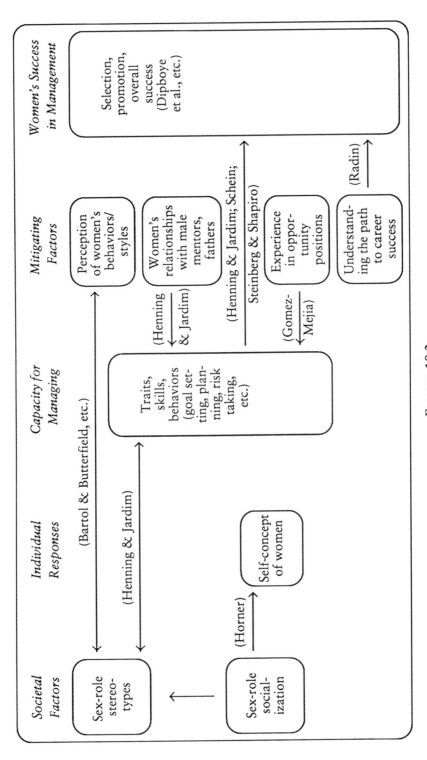

FIGURE 10.2

The Psychological Paradigm: A Conceptual Framework

number of structural and situational variables are more important determinants of organizational behavior of women (and men) than sex differences or global social roles" (Kanter 1976, 287).

In *Men and Women of the Corporation,* Kanter delineated the important variables in her organizational analysis. The distribution of opportunity, the distribution of power, and the social composition of groups are identified as the central explanatory variables. Kanter argues that certain behaviors and attitudes characterize those who are successful in organizations, and the organizational situation women are more likely to face is not conducive to the behaviors of successful people.

The distribution of opportunity refers to an employee's expectations and future prospects in a position. The structure of opportunity is shaped by promotion rates from particular jobs, the career ladder associated with a particular position, the access to organizationally recognized challenges, and the increase in skills and rewards. Women in low-opportunity positions are less motivated to achieve than their counterparts in high-opportunity slots. They tend to have lower self-esteem, seek satisfaction in activities outside work, and interrupt their careers; they tend to be peer oriented; they emphasize accommodation over achievement; they focus on extrinsic rewards and gain satisfaction more from personal relationships than through task accomplishment (Kanter 1977, 246–47). Kanter argues that blocked opportunity elicits this behavior. Since women are disproportionately represented in blocked-opportunity positions, they may appear to act in ways that are not conducive to advancement. Although this observation is true, it is true because these employees face blocked opportunity, not because they are women.

Power structure is the second variable that Kanter (1977) suggests for consideration. Power structure refers to the capacity for an employee to act efficaciously within the constraints of a wider organizational system (p. 247). Power structure varies by the amount of discretion embedded in a job, the visibility and centrality of a function, approval by higher-status people, and the mobility prospects of subordinates. People low in organizational power tend to behave in directive, authoritarian ways. Again, if women are disproportionately represented in low-power positions, they are disproportionately likely to engage in these dysfunctional behaviors—not because they are women but because they are low-power people.

The third variable is the proportion in which people are found in organizations. The suggestion is that certain dynamics prevail when tokens are present in groups, whatever the characteristic (sex, race, ethnicity, etc.) that makes a person a token in that group. People represented in low proportion in groups are likely to be scrutinized more closely, find it hard to gain credibility in high-uncertainty jobs, be excluded from informal peer networks, be stereotyped in ways that limit their effectiveness, and face more personal stress (Kanter 1977, 248–49). This affects men as well as women, Kanter argues, when they find themselves in a token situation. But since women are more likely than men to be found in token situations in contemporary management, women are the more likely victims of these experiences.

The cumulative effect of the impact of opportunity, power, and numbers is that the feedback between these structural conditions and behavior can produce upward cycles of advantage or downward cycles of disadvantage. The cycles entrap people, and those entrapped in the downward cycle are more likely to be women (Kanter 1977, 249). Since the mid-1970s, when Kanter began her social structural analysis of women in organizations, subsequent work in this paradigm has been an elaboration of her basic analysis.

One major application of the Kanter model in the public sector raises some question about its total generalizability to this setting. Markham, South, Bonjean, and Croder (1984) studied the relationship between gender and opportunity in six southwestern offices of a federal agency. Based on data drawn from personnel records and questionnaires, the authors find little support for Kanter's expectation that women would have less promotional opportunity. Although women were concentrated in occupations and career ladders at lower GS levels, the promotional opportunity within those ladders matched that available to men in male-dominated occupations. Women were as eager for promotion as men, although in reality they faced a more limited ceiling. It appeared that as long as promotional opportunity was there, whatever the limitations on the ceiling, women were not responding as Kanter would predict. Since men and women both occupy long career ladders in government, opportunity is not blocked in the same sense that Kanter describes as typical in the industrial world. They also found no support for the thesis that women represented in low proportions experience more severe organizational pressures than nontoken women (South et al. 1982).

While the jury is still out on the total applicability of Kanter's analysis to the public sector, continuing research into women and public-sector management has been profoundly shaped by this paradigm. This is especially true in the attention given to solutions that this analysis yields.

Figure 10.3 presents the major categories of analysis and the principal relationships examined within the sociological paradigm. From the sociological perspective, the problems women experience in organizations stem from the structural situations in which they find themselves. The solutions that flow from this analysis modify these structural conditions. Finding suitable male mentors is one recommended strategy (Roche 1979). Roche observes that organizational advancement for men and women often depends on the ability to find suitable male mentors throughout one's career. Other situation-centered strategies would include training managers in the uniform use of objective rating scales and specific decision rules (Norton, Gustafson, and Foster 1977; Rosen and Jerdee 1974b), changing the distribution of opportunities and power and elimination of women's token status (Kanter 1977), and reducing the salience of gender and associated stereotypes by increasing

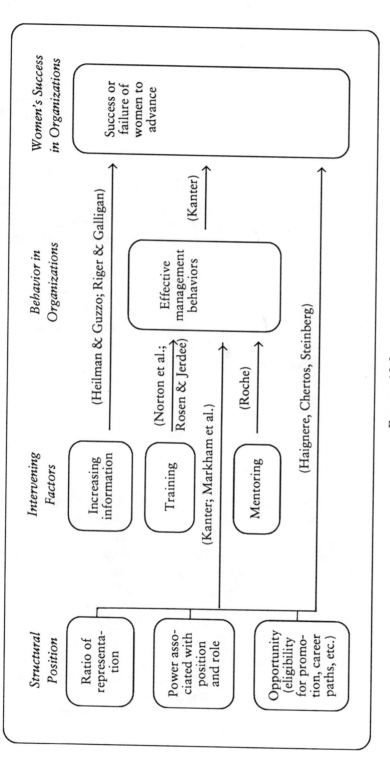

FIGURE 10.3

The Sociological Paradigm: A Conceptual Framework

the amount of information on which decisions are based (Heilman and Guzzo 1978; Renwick and Tosi 1978; Riger and Galligan 1980).

One very concrete application of this structural analysis is unfolding in New York State. There, researchers are identifying eligibility requirements for promotion that tend to constrain the opportunities for women disproportionately. Armed with this information, policy makers could explore ways to soften the hard lines between career ladders so that women will be able to make parallel moves into career ladders with higher-status top rungs. Haignere, Chertos, and Steinberg (1981) have documented the way in which the selection procedure in New York is designed to yield a pool of candidates eligible for selection to high managerial positions that are under-representative of women. This kind of careful documentation will provide the detailed information necessary to understand fully the nuances of the sociological approach to identifying and solving the problem.

Political, psychological, and sociological paradigms serve as different lenses through which the barriers to advancement of women in public administration have been examined. Increasingly, the boundaries between approaches blur in problem-solving research in public administration, as scholars bring into sharper focus the interdependencies among solutions. Public policy enactments may trigger concern with discrimination against women in public agencies, but unless that concern is channeled to alter the structure of opportunity in organizations, there may be no incentive for individual women to risk the informal sanctions levied on them as beneficiaries of special treatment. Future research in each of these traditions will increasingly look to the boundaries of each approach as old terms and concepts fall in new relationships with one another. But at this stage we can still identify three approaches that yield distinct strategies for improving the status of women in management generally.

Figure 10.4 represents the variables to be manipulated. Revealing the central strategies for improving the status of women in management generally, it serves as a blueprint for action in public administration. To make good use of this blueprint, research must build on the foundation of current knowledge about women in public-sector organizations. The second broad question raised in the introduction addresses this concern.

The Observed Pattern of Female Participation

The second question that has guided the review of research on women in public administration asks about the pattern of women's inclusion over time, both numerically and in terms of women's qualitative impact. The preponderance of work looks at the quantitative side and tracks the growth of women's representation in the public service.

214

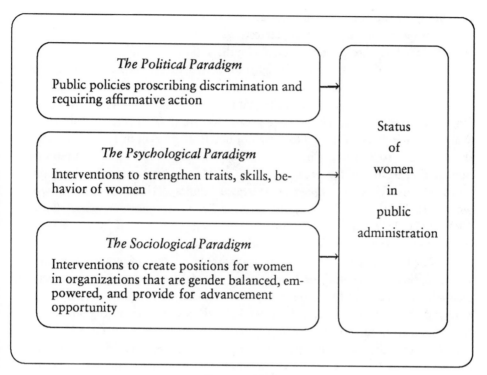

FIGURE 10.4
Central Strategies for Improving the Status
of Women in Public Administration

Quantitative Analyses

The early literature paid scant attention to the quality or quantity of women's contribution to the public service. Even as late as the early 1970s, women were nearly invisible in some leading public administration texts. The 1971 edition of Glen Stahl's *Public Personnel Administration* exemplifies this point with its one entry for women in the index, "Women employees, turnover among, 329." Paul Van Riper's (1958) work is a noteworthy exception to this pattern of neglect. His history of the U.S. Civil Service tracks the progression of women in the federal service beginning with the first federal legislation concerning "female clerks" passed in 1864, a statute that set women's pay at $600 a year, half the salary of men (Van Riper 1958, 159). Before World War I, Van Riper reports, female civil service employment ranged from 5 percent to 10 percent. Even this meager level of involvement was enabled only by a 1910 amendment to civil services rules that permitted the commission to certify women unless the appointing office specifically said that it did not want them (Van Riper 1971, 261). The first woman was appointed as bureau chief in 1912. After a study by the Women's Bureau revealed that 60 percent of the civil service examinations were closed to women, all tests were opened to both sexes in 1919. Nevertheless, the final discretion remained with the appointing officer.

The association of women's rights in the federal service with suffrage during World War I contributed to the momentum for establishing equal pay for equal work in the Classification Act in 1923 (Van Riper 1971). In the years after the war, female representation in civil service positions rose to 20 percent. During World War II, the numbers ballooned to a high of nearly 40 percent in 1944. Though their share fell back to 26 percent by 1947, still women maintained significant representation in this sector of the economy. But, as Martin Gruberg pointed out in his mid-1960s overview of *Women in American Politics*, "There are a lot of women who work for the government, but very few who do important work" (Gruberg 1968, 131). In the mid-1960s, he reported that only one of every seventy-five civilian federal executives, GS-14 level or equivalent, was a woman (Gruberg 1968).

The beginning of the systematic quantitative analysis of women in public service is marked by the work of Mary Lepper (1974). Lepper compared women and men federal executives by grade, occupational group, and rate of growth in grade. Studying the population defined by the federal executive inventory in 1972, she found women occupying less than 5 percent of any grade from GS-13 to GS-18. Women were disproportionately represented in Health, Education, and Welfare (HEW) and the Veterans Administration (VA), both agencies long on programs requiring educational backgrounds traditionally associated with women (Lepper 1974, 117). There also appeared to be little sex difference in the rate at which the percentage of occupancy of executive roles was growing from 1967 to 1971 (Lepper 1974, 115–16).

Some authors used quantitative analyses to depict the variation across agencies. Debra Stewart compared women as a percentage of the total employed by grade within selected federal agencies and concluded the opportunity picture varies considerably across agencies—a finding that lends support to the thesis that sociological factors associated with the structure of an organization might constitute the most promising factor to shape improved opportunity (Stewart 1976).

By the late 1970s, scholars were asking not merely about the percentage or proportion of women represented in government but also—apart from their representation—how women were quantifiably different from men. Naomi Lynn and Richard Vaden (1979) explored the hypothesis that executive women in the federal service had characteristics closer to their male peers than the female characteristics described in the organizational behavior literature.

Drawing on data from a larger study of career federal executives at the GS-15 to GS-18 levels, Lynn and Vaden reported that, at this high level, "too much has been made of male and female differences in the workplace" (1979, 215). These high-level women, like their male counterparts, did not seek to avoid the responsibilities of power. Like their male counterparts, they reported frustration in working with the federal bureaucracy. There was no evidence that women were more concerned with immediate relationships than men; female personal loyalty to the group was no higher than that of males; and women were less positive in evaluating their subordinates than their male counterparts. Again, counter to the stereotype, these women were more likely to have considered changing their jobs than were men—a response suggesting greater willingness to take employment risks. On rating the quality of their occupations (1–10), there was no real difference between men and women. Although women in the federal service in general had more career interruption and less experience than men, this was not true for this select sample of successful women. The picture that one gets from this study is one of amazingly modest differences between male and female executives. The main gender difference in 1978–79 was simply in the numbers in which men and women were represented —with women constituting only 2.7 percent of those in the GS-16 to GS-17 range and 3.3 percent of the GS-15s.

At state and local levels in the 1970s, the numerical pattern of female involvement mirrored the federal sector. Cayer and Sigelman studied the impact of the Equal Employment Opportunity (EEO) Act of 1972 on transforming this picture. They found that, although in terms of absolute numbers, women made marked gains in state and local governments from 1973 to 1975, they were still far below white males in median salary level and had actually lost ground to white men in this regard between 1973 and 1975 (Cayer and Sigelman 1980). Although the number of women increased in positions held in this period, they still held only 74 percent of state and local jobs that would have been their share on the basis of their proportion of the population. State and local governments in the mid-1970s revealed a continuing pattern of job stereotyping with women highly represented in traditional female occupations such as health and social work and barely visible in nontraditional jobs such as police and fire protection (Cayer and Sigelman 1980, 449). This absence of broad representation of women in upper levels of state bureaucracy was echoed by Russell Smith in his study of the demographic representation in five state bureaucracies (Smith 1980, 1).

In the 1980s, the tone of the literature that quantitatively describes women's involvement in public administration shifted. It became not only descriptive but also evaluative and even predictive. Three works produced in the 1980s illustrate this line of inquiry at the federal level.

David Rosenbloom, in a 1980 American Society for Public Administration (ASPA) conference paper that was generally critical of affirmative action, reported that it had worked to benefit women in the federal service. In the 1972–78 period, EEO was associated with increases in the employment of women as a percentage of all employees—an increase particularly pronounced in the GS-7 to GS-12 grades where female gains were close to 10 percent. According to Rosenbloom, affirmative action, with its goals and timetables is divisive, but for women it may be worth the contentiousness it has caused (Rosenbloom 1980).

Three additional works analyze federal Central Personnel File (CPF) data to determine (1) the extent to which the gap between the average female grade and the average male grade is growing, (2) the extent to which women attain positions of authority in the federal service, and (3) differences in the rates of advancement. Greg Lewis reports (1984) that while men's grades are substantially higher than women's grades (men's average grade was 10.0 in 1981 versus 6.27 for women), the grade gap between men and women has significantly narrowed, from 4.4 grades in 1966 to 3.73 grades in 1981. Neither education nor experience explains the shrinking gap. Lewis attributes women's gains to diminished discrimination but notes that, at this rate, it will take thirty-five years to eliminate the unexplained, remaining differential of 2.2 grades (Lewis 1984). In a second work, Lewis (1986b) uses the same CPF data to explore the job authority, or power, of female employees. He finds that women have less chance of obtaining supervisory authority than men. White males are significantly more likely to be supervisors or managers than are women (or others), even at the same grade level and even when they are no more educated or experienced. This quantitative analysis suggests that for women to have a policy impact proportional to their increasing numbers, they must be granted power (job authority) as well as position (status/salary). In a third study, again using CPF data, Lewis reports (1986a) that men have markedly higher early advancement rates than women, pulling ahead of comparable women (controlling for educational levels and major field of study) at the rate higher than one-tenth grade per year.

By the 1980s, scholars tracking the quantitative changes at state and local levels expressed similar concern with the implication of the numerical map that was beginning to emerge. At the macro level, Sigelman and Cayer updated their study based on EEO4 surveys and concluded that, overall, dramatic gains were registered by white females, who occupied approximately 212,000 more positions in 1980 than they had in 1973, increasing their share of state and local positions from 27.1 percent in 1973 to 31.2 percent in 1980 (Sigelman and Cayer 1983, 7). But when it came to salary, white males maintained their considerable advantage over women. In 1980, as in 1973, women were at a considerable salary disadvantage to men in the same racial/ethnic category.

The Sigelman-Cayer picture at state and local levels highlights one favorable numerical indicator. Looking only at new hires in this population, they find that "the absolute number of white female new hires exceeded the number of white male new hires, reversing the situation that prevailed in the entire state and local government workforce. More generally, in each racial/ethnic group the ratio of women to men was more favorable among new hires than among carryover employees" (Sigelman and Cayer 1983, 11). The implication for the future is increased opportunity, although it is highly dependent on growth in state and local sectors.

Focusing on a single state, researchers at the Center for Women in Government in New York probed behind the aggregate data that show women underrepresented at higher levels and overrepresented at lower levels to understand how women (and minority men) might gain access to positions of power. One of the early papers in this stream of research found that female-dominated career ladders, both professional and nonprofessional, began at lower pay grades and peaked at lower grades than career ladders dominated by men (Petersen-Hardt and Perlman 1979).

A second study, highlighted in the earlier discussion of the sociological paradigm, examined the traditional managerial promotion process and found that the major barrier to advancement of women (and minority men) is that they tend not to be employed in jobs considered appropriate training ground for a managerial promotion. Men, by contrast, were much more likely to be in positions deemed eligible bases for promotion (Haignere, Chertos, and Steinberg 1982).

The third cut at this question of obstacles to women's advancement asked how successful women were at obtaining promotion through routes other than traditional examination routes. Research found that 70 percent of promotions made in New York were made through a set of eleven possible nontraditional routes. While white men received promotion through all these routes, women advanced through only eight of the eleven, and minorities through only three of the eleven. When promoted, women were promoted primarily to positions that already had significant numbers of women in them, suggesting that promotions, when they do occur, reinforce existing job segregation. Finally, when selection for promotion is based on eligibility requirements that include experience in specific jobs, women have less access to promotional opportunities than do white men. The thrust of this study is that while the alternative route provides a kind of flexibility in promotion generally deemed good, the way it actually works in New York disproportionately benefits white men (Chertos 1984).

In summary, the earliest scholarship on the quantitative side of the ledger simply tried to document the proportions in which women were found in the administrative world. Through the 1980s the quantitative analysis has shifted from straightforward description to understanding important differences in public executive attitudes about their work and the pathways they follow to advancement. The most promising of this research builds on the theoretical work discussed earlier in trying to understand emerging empirical patterns. In particular, research activities at the Center for Women in Government and the Wellesley Center for Research on Women exemplify this thrust. Understanding the forces that drive these numbers provides the capacity to predict alternative strategies for change. But any change strategy needs to build on what we already know about women in public administration from the work discussed in this section. A partial inventory of what we now know would include the following findings.

Women are underrepresented in executive roles at all levels of government. Women are more highly represented in agencies with programs requiring educational backgrounds traditionally associated with women. Female and male federal executives report the same workplace behaviors in terms of seeking responsibilities, experiencing frustration with the bureaucracy, being concerned with immediate relationships, and reporting personal loyalty to the group. While affirmative action has been effective for women at the federal level, a significant grade gap remains and is contracting at a relatively slow rate.

In the federal sector, women have less authority than men in their jobs, even when controlling for grade. Men have markedly higher early advancement rates than women in the federal sector. At state and local levels, the absolute number of white female new hires exceeded the absolute number of white male new hires from 1973 to 1980. Occupational segregation can limit women's opportunity by offering lower pay grades and shorter career ladders in female-dominated occupations. Promotional systems that promote women primarily to positions that already have significant numbers of women in them reinforce existing job segregation. Promotional systems that establish eligibility requirements to include experience in positions where women are underrepresented indirectly frustrate women's advancement.

Qualitative Impact of Women's Involvement

Researchers ask two questions about the pattern of women's inclusion: The first, discussed above, concerns the numbers of women involved in administration at various levels, their compensation, their job power, and their career pathways. The second concerns the impact of their involvement. The earliest claim to a special impact of women in politics was made by suffrage theorists whose argument for giving women the vote was to elevate the moral tone of politics. Elizabeth Cady Stanton wrote that if women were elected to office, they would "far more effectively guard the morals of society and the sanitary conditions of the cities" (cited in Elshtain 1981, 232). While contemporary feminist writers are uncomfortable with the shift in emphasis of the feminist movement in the early 1900s from an argument from justice to an argument from expediency (Kraditor 1971), it provides an interesting starting point for this line of inquiry.

Research on whether female participation is different received renewed interest in the 1980s as a women's policy agenda became politically visible to elected and administrative public officials. Four streams of scholarship are closely related to, and provide background for, this emerging issue. Empirical studies in political science and public administration, clinical work in psychology, political philosophy, and studies in moral development converge on concern over whether women's participation in public life is qualitatively different from that of men.

Political scientists are trying to document empirically whether women as public decision makers resolve issues in unique ways. The research, which focuses principally on elected officials and for the most part looks for support of the feminist agenda as the indicator of gender-related decision making, yields mixed results. Johnson and Carroll (1978) find an "out group consciousness" reported by female officials at all levels of government, and at state and local levels they find female officials are more liberal and more feminist than their male counterparts (Johnson and Carroll 1978). Carroll thinks that the fact that these feminist leanings never emerge with female candidates may signal a closet feminist phenomenon in this group (Carroll 1979). Mueller reports that, while increasing numbers of women elected to state and local offices give low priority to issues related to the status of women, one subset of women—those with high ambition and thwarted opportunities—are feminist in the broadest sense and will support feminist policies as their numbers rise (Mueller 1982). One recently published article speaks directly to women in administrative roles and probes gender difference in the ideologies of state-level executives. Rehfuss reports, in his study of members of the California Career Executive Assignment (CEA) System, that women executives' responses to open-ended questions manifested a management ideology identical to their CEA male counterparts (Rehfuss 1986).

The theoretical work in clinical psychology tries to explain the basis for gender differences that emerge in that research setting. From a psychoanalytic tradition, Nancy Chodrow suggests that the existence of sex differences in early childhood experiences means that "girls emerge from this period with a basis for 'empathy' built into their primary definition of self in a way boys do not. Girls emerge with a stronger basis for experiencing another's needs or feelings as one's own (or of thinking that one is so experiencing another's needs and feelings)" (cited in Gilligan 1982, 8).

Viewing the issues of female involvement through the lens of Western political philosophy, Jean Elshtain concludes that women's higher ethical standards and abilities on some issues give them a moral advantage over men. She calls for a commitment to a mode of public discourse imbedded in the values of maternal thinking that would involve affirming the protection of fragile and vulnerable human existence as the basis of a mode of political discourse. "Given the concrete realities of their social life-worlds, women are uniquely placed to affirm ideals that grant inalienable dignity to human beings" (Elshtain 1981, 49). In order to flourish the "public world must nurture and sustain a set of ethical imperatives, including a commitment to preserve, protect, and defend human beings in their capacities as private persons" (Elshtain 1981, 350-351). According to Elshtain, women are uniquely qualified to make this happen.

But it is Carol Gilligan's work on levels of moral development that provides insights most applicable to the issue of women as administrative decision makers. Gilligan argues that differences in male and female personality structure produce differences in moral reasoning. Men express strong concern with rights and authority, and are more generally "comfortable with rules that abstract from the particulars of situational concerns" (Gilligan 1982; Nicholson 1983, 519). Women, by contrast, exhibit a stronger orientation toward relationships and interdependence. Their moral judgments, shaped by empathy and compassion, tend to be situationally rooted. More inclined than men to conclude "It depends," women evince contextual rather than categorical moral thinking (Nicholson 1983, 519). In Gilligan's words, men and women tend to be guided by different moral voices: "One morality is 'an ethic of care,' an ethic of responsibility relying on the concept of equity; the other is a morality of rights ... predicated on equality and centered on the understanding of fairness ... a manifestation of equal respect, balancing the claims of other and self" (Gilligan 1982, 164–65). If it is true that women engage in a relationship rather than rights grounded form of moral reasoning, one might expect this to be reflected in their actions as managers, as they give expression to relationship values in resolving ethical dilemmas in organizations.

Some research is beginning to explore this phenomenon in a public-sector setting. In a 1985 ASPA conference paper, Stewart focused on the intersection of Women and Management and the Management Ethics literature to consider, from a theoretical perspective, the relationship between gender and human responses to ethical quandaries in work organizations (Stewart 1985). She concludes that, while several factors may contribute to possible gender differences in the way in which men and women resolve ethical dilemmas in organizations, personal moral orientation is the one factor that may exhibit enduring influence. Its relative importance as a factor awaits empirical testing.

The Status of the Field: Future Trends in Research

This chapter cannot claim to be a comprehensive review of all the literature contributing to our understanding of women in public administration. Instead, it is organized around two questions that have given rise to the preponderance of work on women in public administration: What should be done to improve the status of women in public administration? And, how has women's involvement in public administration changed over time? Four models were presented in summarizing responses to the first question. Three of them depicted the main analytical categories and the relationships examined under the political, psychological, and sociological paradigms; the fourth presented the major categories of independent variables in each approach in relationship to improving the status of women in public administration. In summarizing the responses to the second question, a number of findings were reported that illustrate the main forms of current empirical knowledge about women in public administration. Projecting from the current literature, substantive research trends can be identified for the future. Here I highlight three.

First, there will be increased attention to the structural conditions of work in public-sector organizations. Laws have been enacted to curb the overt discrimination of the past. Women and their supervisors are being provided with training opportunities to help shed attitudes and behaviors that curtail female advancement. The organization itself is the next barricade. We will continue to probe how public-sector organizations structure incentives and opportunities for women to advance and succeed based on the work discussed above under the sociological paradigm.

Second, there will be heightened scholarly activity centered on the conundrum of pay equity for women in the public sector. The seemingly intractable wage gap between male and female employees at all levels of public-sector employment offers a public policy challenge to the political scientist equal in the depth and breadth of its implications to the challenge posed by the masterfully crafted civil rights policies of the 1960s and 1970s.

Third, the ultimate question whether women's involvement in public administration in any way alters "business as usual" will increasingly demand scholarly attention. As psychologists question the possibility of women decoupling the private world of relationships and the public world of administration, scholars will need to know more about the relative influences of forces that weigh for and against gender effects in administrative decision making.

In acknowledging these three emerging themes, two points stand out. First, consistent with the history of our inquiry, the questions stem from the distinct disciplines of sociology, political science, and psychology. Second, any assumption that we can pursue scholarly work strictly within the boundaries of a single discipline is naive. To conduct research on women in public administration in the future will require both deep roots in the principal discipline framing the question as well as a capacity to learn and utilize concepts and tools of related disciplines. Put simply, the requirements of doing research in our subfield are the requirements of doing public administration research more generally: solid disciplinary training coupled with a desire to work on the boundaries of that discipline.

A final comment relates to the way in which inquiry into women in public administration is likely to be organized in the future. As evidenced by the literature discussed in this state of the field review, much research has been conducted by single researchers or scholars working in teams of two or three. This is not surprising, since large-scale team research has never been as characteristic in the social sciences as it has been in the physical and natural sciences (Memory, Arnold, Stewart, and Fornes 1984). But various forces are converging to strengthen the incentive for collaborative research in a variety of disciplines, and our subfield is feeling the effects of the wind. But one very special characteristic of our subfield impels researchers to explore ways to work collaboratively in defining and investigating research problems. The number of women in top jobs in public administration in the United States and throughout the world remains small. From a research perspective, this creates problems in generalizing. The experiences of top women remain sufficiently distinctive that any study of the relatively small number of top women in any single jurisdiction would defy generalization.

The problem of small samples is not unique to studies of elites, and the solutions to this problem are clear, if not easily accomplished. Generous research funding would permit the single researcher to hire research assistants to collect data across a number of jurisdictions. Realistically, current funding levels for social science research render this possibility unlikely. Given the paucity of funding, one group of scholars has responded creatively to this challenge. Under the rubric of Women in Public Administration: Upward-Mobility and Career Advancement Project, individual researchers in fourteen countries have formulated a research team, working under the research committee on Sex Roles and Politics of the International Political Science Association. Coordinated by Jeanne-Marie Col of the United States, team members are interviewing high-level public administrators, hoping to achieve four goals: (1) to create and apply a model for cross-cultural research, (2) to examine the status of women administrators in a wide variety of countries, (3) to identify commonalities in women's experience cross-culturally, and (4) to discover strategies for enhancing women's opportunities in public-sector employment (Col 1985). In the United States, one planned spinoff of this project is a systematic, comparative empirical study of women administrators in all fifty state governments. To date, no research has been published by the international project nor the more recently launched U.S. companion project. But both projects promise to yield empirically supported theoretical models that will ultimately test the validity of the concepts, relationships, and findings discussed earlier in this chapter. The distinguishing characteristic of each project is its organizing principle. If successful, these projects will introduce a new mode of conducting research in the field of women in public administration and may move public admininistration research more generally toward collaborative endeavors.

This chapter paints a picture of women in public administration as a subfield rich in conceptual frameworks, increasingly solid in empirical data, ripe with engaging questions, and populated with scholars creative in finding ways to advance knowledge. But moving forward from here assumes reaching agreement on where we now stand. I provided the basis for a shared understanding of our foundations, and, building on those foundations, of our future research agenda.

References

Amundsen, Kirsten. 1971. *The Silenced Majority*. Englewood Cliffs, N.J.: Prentice-Hall.

Bartol, K.M., and D.A. Butterfield. 1976. "Sex Effects in Evaluating Leaders." *Journal of Applied Psychology* 61:446–54.

Boles, Janet. 1976. *The Politics of the Equal Rights Amendment.* New York: Longman.

Bowman, G.W., N.B. Worthy, and S.A. Greyser. 1965. "Are Women Executives People?" *Harvard Business Review* 43:52–67.

Caplan, N., and S.D. Nelson. 1973. "On Being Useful: The Nature and Consequence of Psychological Research on Social Problems." *American Psychologist* 28:199–211.

Carroll, Susan. 1979. "Women Candidates and Support for Women's Issues: Closet Feminists." Presented at the annual meeting of the Midwest Political Science Association, Chicago, Ill.

Cayer, N. Joseph, and Lee Sigelman. 1980. "Minorities and Women in State and Local Government: 1973–1975." *Public Administration Review* 40:443–50.

Chertos, Cynthia H. 1984. *Alternative Routes of Managerial Promotion in New York State: A Research Report.* Albany: Center for Women in Government, State University of New York.

Col, Jeanne-Marie. 1985. "Women in Public Administration and Management: Upward Mobility and Career Advancement." Research group materials.

Deckard, Barbara S. 1979. *The Women's Movement.* 2d ed. New York: Harper & Row.

Dipboye, R.L., R.D. Arvey, and D.E. Terpstra. 1977. "Sex and Physical Attractiveness of Raters and Applicants as Determinants of Resume Evaluations." *Journal of Applied Psychology* 62:288–94.

Eagly, A.H., and W. Wood. 1982. "Inferred Sex Differences in Status as a Determinant of Gender Stereotypes about Social Influence." *Journal of Personality and Social Psychology* 43:915–28.

Elshtain, Jean Bethke. 1981. *Public Man, Private Woman.* Princeton: Princeton University Press.

Freeman, Jo. 1975. *The Politics of Women's Liberation.* New York: McKay.

Gilligan, Carol. 1982. *In a Different Voice.* Cambridge, Mass.: Harvard University Press.

Gomez-Mejia, Luis R. 1983. "Sex Differences during Occupational Socialization." *Academy of Management Journal* 26:492–99.

Gruberg, Martin. 1968. *Women in American Politics.* Oshkosh, Wis.: Academia Press.

Haignere, Lois V., Cynthia H. Chertos, and Ronnie J. Steinberg. 1981. *Managerial Promotions in the Public Sector: The Impact of Eligibility Requirements on Women and Minorities.* Albany: Center for Women in Government, State University of New York.

Heilman, M.E., and R.A. Guzzo. 1978. "The Perceived Cause of Work Success as a Mediator of Sex Discrimination in Organizations." *Organizational Behavior and Human Performance* 21:346–57.

Hennig, Margaret, and Anne Jardim. 1977. *The Managerial Woman.* Garden City, N.Y.: Doubleday Anchor.

Horner, Matina. 1969. "Fail: Bright Women." *Psychology Today* 62:36–38. November.

Jacquette, Jane S., ed. 1974. *Women in Politics.* New York: Wiley.

Jago, A.G., and Victor Vroom. 1982. "Sex Differences in the Incidence and Evaluation of Participative Leader Behavior." *Journal of Applied Psychology* 67:776–83.

Johnson, Marilyn, and Susan Carroll. 1978. "Statistical Report: Profile of Women Holding Office: 1977." In *Women in Public Office: A Biographical Directory and Statistical Analysis.* Metuchen, N.J.: Scarecrow Press.

Kanter, Rosabeth Moss. 1976. "The Policy Issues: Presentation VI." *Signs: Journal of Women in Culture and Society* 1:282–91.

Kanter, Rosabeth Moss. 1977. *Men and Women of the Corporation.* New York: Basic Books.

Kelly, Rita Mae, and Mary Boutilier. 1978. *The Making of Political Women.* Chicago: Nelson-Hall.

Klein, Ethel. 1984. *Gender Politics.* Cambridge, Mass.: Harvard University Press.

Kraditor, Aileen S. 1971. *The Ideas of the Women's Suffrage Movement 1890–1920.* Garden City, N.Y.: Doubleday Anchor.

Kuhn, Thomas S. 1970. *The Structure of Scientific Revolutions.* Chicago: University of Chicago Press.

Lepper, Mary M. 1974. "A Study of Career Structures of Federal Executives: A Focus on Women." In *Women in Politics,* edited by Jane Jacquette. New York: Wiley.

Lewis, Gregory. 1984. "Men and Women in Federal Employment: Placements, Promotions, and Occupations." Doctoral dissertation, Syracuse University.

Lewis, Gregory. 1986a. "Equal Employment Opportunity and the Early Career in Federal Government." *Review of Public Personnel Administration* 6:1–18.

Lewis, Gregory. 1986b. "Race, Sex, and Supervisory Authority in Federal White-Collar Employment." *Public Administration Review* 46 (1):25–29.

Lynn, Naomi B., and Richard E. Vaden. 1979. "Towards a Non-sexist Personnel Opportunity Structure: The Federal Executive Bureaucracy." *Public Personnel Management* 3:209–15.

Markham, William T., Scott J. South, Charles M. Bonjean, and Judy Corder. 1984. *Sex and Opportunity in the Federal Bureaucracy: A Test of Kanter's Theory.* Wellesley, Mass.: Center for Research on Women, Wellesley College.

Massengill, D., and N. DiMarco. 1979. "Sex Role Stereotypes and Requisite Management Characteristics: A Current Replication." *Sex Roles* 5:561–70.

Memory, J.D., J.F. Arnold, D.W. Stewart, and R.E. Fornes. 1984. "Physics as a Team Sport." *American Journal of Physics* 53(3):270–71.

Miner, J.B. 1974. "Motivation to Manage among Women: Studies of Business Managers and Education Administrators." *Journal of Vocational Behavior* 5:197–208.

Mueller, Carol. 1982. "Feminism and the New Women in Public Office." *Women and Politics* 2:7–22.

Nelson, Barbara J. 1984. "Women's Poverty and Women's Citizenship." *Signs* 10(2): 209–31.

Nicholson. Linda J. 1983. "Women, Morality and History." *Social Research* 50(3):514–36.

Norton, S.D., D.P. Gustafson, and C.E. Foster. 1977. "Assessment for Management Potential: Scale Design and Development Training, Effects and Rater/Ratee Sex Effects." *Academy of Management Journal* 20:117–31.

O'Sullivan, Elizabethann, and Debra W. Stewart. 1984. "Evaluating Affirmative Action Programs: A Case Study." *Review of Public Personnel Administration* 4(3):71–82.

Petersen-Hardt, Sandra, and Nancy D. Perlman. 1979. *Sex Segregated Career Ladders in New York State Government.* Albany: Center for Women in Government, State University of New York.

Radin, Beryl A. 1980. "Leadership Training for Women in State and Local Government." *Public Personnel Management* 9:53–60.

Rehfuss, John A. 1986. "A Representative Bureaucracy? Women and Minority Executives in California Career Service." *Public Administration Review* 46:454–60.

Renwick, P.A., and H. Tosi. 1978. "The Effects of Sex, Marital Status, and Educational Background on Selection Decisions." *Academy of Management Journal* 21:93–103.

Riger, Stephanie, and Pat Galligan. 1980. "Women in Management: An Exploration of Competing Paradigms." *American Psychologist* 35:902–10.

Roche, G.R. 1979. "Much Ado about Mentors." *Harvard Business Review* 57:14–28.

Rosen, Ben, and T.H. Jerdee. 1973. "The Influence of Sex Role Stereotypes on Education of Male and Female Supervisory Behavior." *Journal of Applied Psychology* 57:44–48.

Rosen, Ben, and T.H. Jerdee. 1974a. "Effects of Applicants' Sex and Difficulty on Evaluations of Candidates for Managerial Positions." *Journal of Applied Psychology* 57:44–48.

Rosen, Ben, and T.H. Jerdee. 1974b. "Sex Stereotyping in the Executive Suite." *Harvard Business Review* 52:45–58.

Rosenbloom, David H. 1980. "Evaluating Affirmative Action in the Federal Service: A Comparison of Blacks and Women." Presented at the American Society for Public Administration National Conference, San Francisco.

Roussell, C. 1974. "Relationship of Sex of Department Head to Department Climate." *Administrative Science Quarterly* 19:211–20.

Schein, V.E. 1973. "The Relationship between Sex Role Stereotypes and Requisite Management Characteristics." *Journal of Applied Psychology* 57:95–100.

Schein, V.E. 1975. "Relationships between Sex Role Stereotypes and Requisite Management Characteristics among Female Managers." *Journal of Applied Psychology* 60:340–44.

Shaw, E.A. 1972. "Differential Impact of Negative Stereotyping in Employee Selection." *Personnel Psychology* 25:333–38.

Sigelman, Lee, and N. Joseph Cayer. 1983. "Minorities, Women, Public Sector Jobs: A Status Report." Presented at the annual Hendricks Symposium, University of Nebraska, Lincoln.

Silverman, David. 1971. *The Theory of Organizations.* New York: Basic Books.

Smith, Russell L. 1980. "Representative Bureaucracy: A Research Note on Demographic Representation in State Bureaucracies." *Review of Public Personnel Administration* 1:1–14.

South, Scott, Charles Bonjean, William Markham, and Judy Corder. 1982. "Social Structure and Intergroup Interaction: Men and Women of the Federal Bureaucracy." *American Sociological Review* 47:587–99.

Stahl, O. Glenn. 1971. *Public Personnel Administration.* 6th ed. New York: Harper & Row.

Steinberg, R., and S. Shapiro. 1982. "Sex Differences in Personality Traits of Female and Male Master of Business Administration Students." *Journal of Applied Psychology* 67:306–10.

Stewart, Debra W. 1976. "Women in Top Jobs: An Opportunity for Federal Leadership." *Public Administration Review* 36(4):357–64.

Stewart, Debra W. 1980. "Organizational Variables and Policy Impact." *Policy Studies Journal* 8:870–78.

Stewart, Debra W. 1985. "Gender and Management Ethics: A Preliminary Inquiry." Presented at the annual meeting of the American Society for Public Administration, Indianapolis.

Van Riper, Paul P. 1958. *History of the United States Civil Service.* Evanston, Ill.: Row, Peterson.

Weisstein, Naomi. 1971. "Psychology Constructs the Female, or the Fantasy Life of the Male Psychologist." In *Roles Women Play,* edited by M.H. Garskof. Belmont, Calif.: Brooks/Cole.

227

11

Public Budgeting in the United States: The State of the Discipline

NAOMI CAIDEN

Assessment demands perspective. How might we assess the current profusion of books and articles that constitute the discipline of public budgeting? A discipline might be evaluated according to the consistency of its premises, the existence of a solid foundation of accepted theory, or the ordering of facts on which new research might be built. But public budgeting is not easily confined within a single theory, and recent years have seen its boundaries expand even further to embrace related areas.

An alternative perspective might focus on the validity of the models employed to describe and analyze subject matter. Are they clear, consistent, and logical? Do they provide an acceptable vocabulary to enable meaningful discourse among scholars, students, and practitioners? Do they explain phenomena and portray the salient features of their environment accurately? Are they capable of predicting future developments and guiding practical courses of action and research? To answer such questions requires more searching inquiry into the multiple and often competing models and assumptions employed by analysts of public budget processes.

Yet a discipline is more than a set of models, which themselves reflect more basic preconceptions. We need to go beyond an evaluation of components to assess the vitality of the discipline as a whole. Sometimes the combined energies of those engaged in the development of a branch of knowledge produce a surge of progress; a kindling of new and exciting ideas; a continuing, critical reorientation of assumptions, concepts, and direction—as opposed to the routine regurgitation of outworn dogmas or the mindless building of fact on fact. It is legitimate to ask whether the discipline of public budgeting demonstrates the capability to develop—to grow and change. Have research and teaching shown the capacity to absorb concepts and theories from other disciplines and, reciprocally, to contribute to them? Is there a framework strong enough to structure and organize the subject matter of public budgeting yet flexible enough to admit a critical self-consciousness and self-awareness? Are the right questions being asked? Is public budgeting, in short, a dynamic, forward-looking branch of learning whose scholars and practitioners feel themselves poised at the frontiers of human discovery?

Perhaps the subject seems too mundane and familiar for such high-flown aspirations. Yet the fascination of a large number of capable scholars for the subject, the crucial relevance of financial decision making for public policy making, and the multifaceted nature of budget processes suggest that such questions are not inapposite. Moreover, in recent years the study of public budgeting has undergone significant changes that alone are worthy of critical evaluation.

Traditionally, public budgeting was studied from three different perspectives—economics, management, and political science—each posing different questions and employing different models of the budget processes. The resulting tendency to compartmentalism, as well as certain conceptual problems in the models themselves, was to some degree compensated for by the strength of the ideas and the vigor with which they were espoused and disseminated. The three strands of thought provided an acknowledged framework for scholars and, to a lesser extent, practitioners.

In recent years, changes in the environment of public budgeting have disrupted accepted modes of thought. The impact of resource constraints and uncertainties during the 1970s and 1980s has been felt in budget practice at all levels of government, forcing a corresponding realignment in its study. The sheer pace of developments has opened up new questions, linked together formerly separate areas, and provided a wealth of information about processes, policies, and outcomes (Caiden 1985).

The study of public budgeting is now characterized by a much broader scope of inquiry, abundant argument and debate, and a wide variety of models. The older frameworks coexist with newer perspectives. Public budgeting is a much more exciting field, but inevitably new developments have brought new problems. The sheer volume of the literature threatens coherence. Models overlap and compete. Confronted with complex and perplexing situations, observers often find refuge in description, avoiding theory altogether. The urgency of immediate policy or process issues drives out reflection on deeper questions regarding institutional development and appropriate forms of governmental budgeting in a period of rapid societal change.

It is virtually impossible in the span of these few pages to do justice to what is now a huge literature on public budgeting and related areas. Excellent bibliographies are available, and there is no need to duplicate them here. The approach of the chapter is therefore selective and critical rather than comprehensive or descriptive. Certain areas, such as macroeconomic policy, fiscal policy, and fund accounting, have been omitted altogether, not because they are not important, but because they are larger subjects in their own right and demand much fuller treatment. Instead, emphasis is on the development of ideas, tracing the transformation of the discipline from well-marked highways amid familiar scenery into paths and thickets along the very frontiers of inquiry.

One Discipline or Three? Economics, Management, Politics

Budgeting is in essence about resource allocation and may be viewed in almost infinite ways—there is a psychology of budgeting, a history of budgeting, an anthropology of budgeting, a mystique of budgeting. In practice, however, the study of public budgeting in the United States was dominated until recently by a triple paradigm within which economists, management experts, and political scientists each carved out their own domains. The strands of thought were divergent rather than convergent, separating rather than uniting different aspects of the subject, and emphasizing the jurisdictional property of each profession rather than common ground. There were undoubtedly areas of overlap, but they were not systematically explored. Nonetheless, the triple paradigm lent structure to the discipline and focused the efforts of scholars in definite directions.

The interest of economists in public budgets was both normative and empirical, and stemmed from their preoccupation with the workings of market economies. The normative questions go back at least to the eighteenth century when Adam Smith was concerned with setting out canons of taxation and government expenditures (Burkhead 1956, 39–42). What principles should governments follow in deciding what taxes should be employed, and what kinds of government expenditures are legitimate? Toward the end of the nineteenth century, these questions found further elaboration in the development of marginal analysis. Just as the individual was expected to maximize utility, by equalizing satisfaction from each marginal dollar spent, so the country should maximize its welfare by equalizing satisfaction for the last dollar of expenditure between public and private sectors and for different categories of public expenditure. Economists then concentrated on "the special economic attributes of public activity" (Burkhead 1956, 31), asking such questions as these: How many and what kinds of activities should government undertake? What is the optimal mix and level of governmental expenditures? (Hyman 1973, 3). How can police power be used to promote the economic objectives of society? Can government action improve upon market outcomes? (Pogue and Sgontz 1978, xvii). What ought to be the role of the public sector in influencing resource allocation in a market economy? (Boadway 1979, ix). What explains the total size of the government's budget and its apportionment among various categories of expenditure? (Wagner 1983, vii). What criteria should be applied to judge the economic efficiency of various budget policies? (Musgrave and Musgrave 1976, 4).

Economists also asked empirical questions about the effects of government budget decisions on markets: What are the effects of alternative revenues and expenditures on social objectives? (Hyman 1973, 3). How does government tax and expenditure policy affect the economy and the welfare of its citizens? (Browning and Browning 1979, 1). What are the responses of the private sector to tax and expenditure changes? (Musgrave and Musgrave 1976, 4). In short, the economic perspective was the application of welfare economics to public budgeting.

From these questions, it was but a short step to asking how collective social choices, as compared with market choices, are made. The famous question of the political scientist V. O. Key, "On what basis shall it be decided to allocate X dollars to activity A instead of activity B?" (Key 1940, 1137) and its later elaboration by Verne Lewis (Lewis 1952), gave an analytical thrust to practical debates about how public financial decision making should be organized that went back at least as far as the invention of budgeting. Nineteenth-century principles enunciated by Rene Stourm (1917) were influential in early-twentieth-century designs of executive budget processes, notably that of the U.S. budget in the 1921 Budget and Accounting Act. At the same time, experiments in using budget processes to gain greater efficiency were forerunners of later enthusiastic advocacy of budget systems incorporating analytical and managerial methods as a means of gaining greater effectiveness in public decision making. Allen Schick has traced the stages of budget reform that culminated in the adoption of Planning Programming Budget (PPB) in the federal government in his classic article "The Road to PPB" (Schick 1966, 243–58). Since then, texts have continued this normative, managerial approach, focusing on the question of how the routine processes of budgeting might be shaped to encourage more efficient and effective outcomes, primarily through the use of performance techniques, productivity measures, cost-benefit applications, and systems analysis (e.g., Babunakis 1976; Kramer 1979; Lyden and Miller 1972; Lynch 1981).

Meanwhile, the political nature of budgeting was not ignored. For economists, the major characteristic of governmental decision making was the political element, but as Jesse Burkhead (1956) put it, "Economics and politics are always separated, and very often, at least implicitly, it is assumed that economics is a rational science, but that political influences are irrational, unpredictable, and frequently evil" (p. 43). Emphasis on the executive budget from the managerial perspective also tended to downplay, if not ignore, political considerations. Moreover, the normative preoccupations of both approaches for the most part relegated actual budget processes to a kind of residual category. Although there were notable exceptions to these trends, the systematic treatment of budget processes from a political and empirical perspective was hard to find.

The appearance of Aaron Wildavsky's *The Politics of the Budgetary Process* (1964) brought the political nature of budgeting to the fore. Wildavsky was concerned with budgets as "political things," lying at "the heart of the political process" (p. 5). He believed the study of budgeting was a useful perspective from which to analyze the making of policy and asked how budgeting was actually carried out (Wildavsky 1968, 192). The short answer—incrementalism—was enormously influential in shaping debate and research in public budgeting for over a decade (see also Fenno 1966; Lindblom 1959). But Wildavsky went much further in asking theoretical questions regarding the relationship of decision rules to outcomes. Was it possible to identify budgetary models according to the elements of organization coalition, distribution of roles among the principal actors, aids to calculation, strategies responding to types of incentives, and outcomes to be expected in terms of amounts requested and received? The study of budgeting was part of a larger research agenda, which ultimately would enable prediction of consequences, the comparative analysis of governmental policy (Wildavsky 1968, 192).

It would be fair to say that none of the three disciplines really achieved its purposes for public budgeting. The economists failed to discover a practical criterion that would truly distinguish those activities appropriate to governmental decision making. Management scientists encountered repeated defeats on the battleground of budgetary reform. Political scientists never really came to grips with the sheer variety of budgetary behavior, let alone the creation of a science on which reliable predictions might be built. Yet the concepts and models that were proposed, explored, and elaborated undoubtedly lent a strength to the study of public budgeting that other areas of public administration might well have envied. That this strength carried within it the seeds of its own weakness became apparent only gradually as changing conditions revealed flawed assumptions, lack of perspective, and overconfident generalization.

Shifting Foundations: Models and Their Obsolescence

The strength and distinctiveness of the three approaches were manifest in the models they employed, which drew heavily on the mainstreams of their respective disciplines and in turn contributed to them. These models were all open to criticism but remained powerful as essential points of departure and as elements of an acceptable and readily understood vocabulary. Their influence continues today, but their intrinsic flaws have become more apparent as they have been overtaken by environmental changes.

The economists' approach rested on a model of an economy divided between private goods and public goods. The former were allocated through a market system, which, if it were working properly, tended toward efficiency through the operation of a pricing system. Efficiency was defined as a condition in which goods were produced at the lowest possible cost according to the highest preference of consumers. According to the Pareto definition, a given economic arrangement was efficient if there could be no rearrangement that would leave someone better off without worsening the position of others (see Hyman 1973, 15). Public or social goods differed from private goods because of their nonrival and/or nonexclusive nature, so they could not fulfill market criteria for efficiency: The absence of individuals' preference revelation through effective demand was a fatal flaw to the operation of a market for public goods (Musgrave and Musgrave 1976, 49–80).

The difficulties of this approach were acknowledged and ingenious solutions found. Because relatively few examples of publicly provided goods actually fitted the definition of pure public goods, the category of mixed or quasi-public goods was invented, in which publicness was assessed according to the degree of externality (positive or negative) involved, and the correct extent of public subsidy measured correspondingly (Steiner 1983, 3–41). The absence of the revealed preferences of consumers for public goods was resolved by substituting a political voting model for the market model. The difficulty of basing allocation of public goods on the sum of individual demands without regard to income differences was evaded by supplementing the criterion of efficiency with one of equity. Similarly, the benefit criterion for taxation was supplemented by ability to pay.

These resolutions enabled a variety of applications of microeconomic theory to the public sector. Public-choice theory emphasized a consumer perspective in decision making on the supply of public services (see Ostrom and Ostrom 1971; Buchanan 1972, 11–22). One notable, if arguable, application was the Tiebout (1956) theory, according to which residents acted as shoppers, choosing their residences according to their preferences for the different packages of taxes and services offered by different local jurisdictions (Tiebout 1956, 416–24; Peterkin 1981). A theory of intergovernmental grants was based on overspill of benefits or costs beyond the local area (Break 1980).

However satisfactory these theoretical excursions might be, they offered remarkably little guidance to the budgeter in the practical world. The measurement of externalities in reality was difficult if not impossible. One could not run a budget system as a kind of perpetual town meeting, quite apart from problems arising from paradoxes of voting. Even when preferences were revealed in other ways, the question of whose preferences should be taken into account was not easily resolved by theoretical criteria. The balance between allocational efficiency and distributional equity also had no self-evident, agreed-upon equation. As revenue constraints became narrower, and public activities took on the qualities of a zero-sum game, the concept of Pareto efficiency seemed less relevant, and the whole meaning of efficiency in provision of public goods grew hazier and more arguable.

To the extent that the analytical focus of the management approach incorporated the economic elements of cost-benefit analysis, it suffered from similar handicaps. But unlike the economists, its proponents could call on a specific, concrete model of the budget process. Building on the model originally conceived by

Robert Anthony (see Schick 1966), budget processes were viewed in functional terms, embracing elements of control, management, and planning. Moreover, each function found expression in specific budgetary forms, progressing historically from a simple object classification through functional and performance budgets to more sophisticated systems and program budgeting, such as PPB and zero-based budgeting (ZBB). The ultimate promise was "to recast . . . budgeting from a repetitive process for financing permanent bureaucracies into an instrument for deciding the purposes and programs of government" (Schick 1973). Budgeting was seen as a process for rational decision making.

The fates of PPB and ZBB in the federal government are by now history, and there is no need to rehash old arguments. Their central place in textbooks has yielded to other concerns. The rational decision-making model proved difficult to apply to budgeting. When the specific problems of implementation are discounted, two basic sets of obstacles had to be confronted. The first was the question whether budget format is in fact relevant to actual budgetary decision making. Does any formal system actually determine the nature of the decisions made, or is the budget driven by entirely different variables such as custom and inertia, irreducible complexity, or simple power relationships? Unless, as Allen Schick (1966) suggested, behavior followed form, we might as well forget the whole exercise. A second problem lay in the nature of rational decision making. A conventional view of the budget process as a neutral set of procedures producing rational solutions ignored the rationality of political processes concerned with resolving conflicts within an acceptable time frame, and the problematic and political nature of budgetary decision making (Wildavsky 1966). To the extent that the budget process was an instrument for deciding the purposes and programs of government, any model would have to take into account its relationship with the political system and the causes and consequences of political behavior.

A political model of the budget process as incremental behavior was satisfying for a number of reasons. The view of the budget as a base to which increments were added each year seemed, to many with practical experience of budgeting, an intuitively accurate portrayal. In addition, it fitted in with a growing literature of disenchantment with a normative model of rational decision making and its replacement with such concepts as muddling through or satisficing (Braybrooke and Lindblom 1963; Lindblom 1959, 79–88; Simon 1945). The budget process of Congress in the late 1950s and early 1960s also seemed to accord well with an incrementalist framework of mutual stable expectations within which participants carried out strategies and tactics to achieve their purposes. Incrementalism appeared as an integral element in the political pluralist world of group bargaining and adjustment. It was a flexible and functional mechanism for conflict resolution, an acceptable means for handling the burdens of calculation and complexity, and the keystone of a politics of accommodation (see Parker 1985). This useful model captivated an entire generation of budget scholars, who spent much ink and paper attempting to detect and verify incremental spending patterns in a variety of contexts.

The attack was probably inevitable (Witte 1984, 3–23). Criticisms concentrated on the definition of an increment, the empirical question whether budgetary outcomes were actually incremental and whether the behavior of budgetary participants followed incremental patterns. How large was an increment, or was it defined not by size but by regularity? Was research at one level of analysis, such as the agency, confirmed or disproved by data relating to lower administrative levels or different components of budgetary allocations? (Dempster and Wildavsky 1979; Goodin and Waldner 1979; LeLoup 1978) Could a single theory encompass all varieties of budgetary behavior or, in stretching to encompass more and more phenomena, was it drained of meaning? Was incrementalism as a normative concept a front for a conservative ideology and a spurious determinism?

Argument and counterargument were finally overwhelmed by changes in the budgetary scene in the 1970s and early 1980s: the disappearance of the so-called fiscal dividend, the entrenchment of automatic spending mechanisms in the federal budget, and transformations in budget processes in response to cutback policies. Perhaps incrementalism should be thought of as a descriptive model of budgeting in a particular time and place rather than a universal explanation of budgetary behavior.

Academic disciplines rarely scrape the past clean. The economic, management, and political models discussed here have by no means disappeared. Despite their flaws and changing circumstances, they are still employed, but their current significance lies in a residue of patterns of thought and influence on a far more varied and fragmented panorama, dominated by different (though no less problematic) models. The effects of resource constraint at all levels of U.S. government have provided a fertile field for scholars, who have found it necessary to employ other, more integrated models.

Models of Budgetary Capacity and Incapacity: Budgeting in the Federal Government

Dramatic developments in the federal budget over the past decade have provided an irresistible attraction for scholarly and not-so-scholarly attention. Since the passage of the Congressional Budget Act in 1974, there has been a veritable flood of argument, polemic, controversy and explanation regarding its causes, consequences, strengths and weaknesses. Much of the literature is descriptive and explanatory, rehearsing familiar facts at greater and greater elaboration. The preponderance relates to the congressional budget process, with somewhat less attention to the executive process. The sheer weight and detail of microscopic investigation of an unfolding history tends to conceal theoretical concerns: Enormous effort has been necessary to clarify what has happened and what is happening in a highly complex arena (Ippolito 1981; LeLoup 1980; Schick 1980a, 1983a; Wander, Hebert, and Copeland 1984). Recent scholarship has contributed considerable information to our understanding of such budget components as credit programs; tax expenditures (Ippolito 1984; King 1984; Rivlin and Hartman 1984); authorizations, appropriations, and outlays (Fisher 1983; Kamlet and Mowery 1983; LeLoup 1984; Mowery and Kamlet 1984; Shuman 1984); institutional relationships between President and Congress (Kamlet and Mowery 1985; Schick 1983a); committees and subcommittees of Congress, and congressional leadership and members of both houses of Congress (Cohen 1980); budget policies related to presidential initiatives, the workings of the economy, and macroeconomic theory (Kamlet and Mowery 1984; Mills and Palmer 1984); and budget execution (Draper and Pitsvada 1981; Pitsvada 1983). Examination of the record has yielded many more clues to the questions, How does the budget process work and in what ways has it changed?

It would be misleading, however, to give an impression of consensus. Agreement certainly exists on the general outline of the elements of change in recent years. There have been changes in Congress associated with party decline and relaxation of older constraining rules and norms. There have been changes in the congressional budget process related to the 1974 act attempting greater integration and providing more information. There have been changes in the composition of the federal budget, including a larger uncontrollable element, greater recourse to off-budget measures, differing relationships between authorizations and appropriations, growing externalization of federal expenditures, and entrenchment of structural deficits. There have been changes in political and ideological orientation, initially increasing domestic expenditures at the expense of defense and, later, reversing the trend through imposition of cutbacks. All these changes are not in doubt, but their causes, interrelationships, and significance are open to argument.

It is understandable that there should be confusion, and it is unlikely that it may be easily, let alone definitively, resolved. But beneath the clutter of argument and counterargument and beneath the welter of facts and figures, twin undercurrents of ideas arising from different sources may be detected. Sometimes blending but generally distinct, they are related to different ideas of the budget process, budgetary effectiveness, and the nature of budgetary reform. These general groupings of ideas might be labeled respectively models of budgetary capacity and incapacity.

According to the model of budgetary incapacity, problems of the federal budget process stem from fundamental features of the contemporary political environment, which are in turn related to specific behavioral characteristics. The model has a number of different facets, which may be reduced to five major components.

First, there is a difference between actions and their sum. To quote Wildavsky, "The sum of our actions over time is not necessarily subject to the same considerations as our particular acts at particular times. We can (and do) want this or that expenditure now, and yet we object to the total amount of spending to which our actions have contributed" (Wildavsky 1980, 2). When the tally is made, the rational individual decision becomes the irrational collective decision. It is the exact opposite of the "invisible hand," where if everyone looked after his or her own business, the correct result would ensue. Where once incrementalism as the expression of political pluralism was lauded as a system ensuring that everything would work out just right, it now seems that the connection has been broken, and even that everything might work out all wrong.

Second, a fundamental problem of democratic political decision making is an intrinsic bias that ends by subverting the general interest. Whereas benefits are concentrated to accrue to particular interest groups, costs are diffused over the whole population, so benefits are easily perceived as outweighing costs. While benefits are obvious, costs are easily concealed. Similarly, while representatives look after the interests of their districts, no one speaks for the common interest. This bias of the political system results in a reciprocal upward bias in government expenditures.

Third, there is a general ideological predisposition against the growth of government expenditures vis-à-vis the private sector. Increased government activities are associated with loss of personal freedom, growth of individual dependency, reduction of variety and innovation, system unreliability, and unproductive use of societal resources. Moreover, evidence is adduced that contemporary public sentiment is overwhelmingly in favor of contraction of government at all levels.

Fourth, it is suggested that current politics in the United States, like that of other industrialized nations, has reached a point of immobilism where changes are impossible because of the stranglehold large distributive interest groups and powerful vested interests have on policy-making channels. The resulting political gridlock in the face of constrained resources portends irreversible stagnation (Olson 1983).

Fifth, the development of federal budgetary decision making has been characterized by a decline in formal and informal institutional norms that previously acted as restraints on spending growth, enforced a division of labor among participants (Kamlet and Mowery 1985), disciplined individual members of Congress, and promoted the interests of the whole over the parts. There has been a progressive deterioration of the fiscal constitution.

The recent history of the federal budget process is one of a system that cannot adjust itself and so is locked into an upward spiral of expenditures that it is powerless to reverse. The Congressional Budget Act failed because it did not restrain expenditures (Fisher 1985). One conclusion that might be drawn is that only extrapolitical action, such as a constitutional amendment to enforce expenditure limitations, can provide a remedy. The theory of budgetary incapacity is then a theory of political incapacity.

The theory of budget capacity confronts the same facts but interprets them differently. The budget is seen as a mechanism to resolve conflicts and achieve consensus on a set of revenue and expenditure policies. By definition, it faces two ways, simultaneously attracting and rationing claims. The budget process therefore reflects shifting relationships among participants. It represents a constant battle between pressures toward legislative fragmentation, on the one hand, and budgetary integration, on the other. The balance at any one time is achieved through formal rules and informal norms of behavior enabling consensus. This balance may favor either values of representation, encouraging claims on the budget, or values of integration, favoring leadership, cohesion, coordination and streamlined decision making (Schick 1980a, 7).

Budget processes, then, are the product of political preferences and may be framed to accomplish whatever purposes are desired at any time. To quote Allen Schick,

> A budget process can generate pressure for higher expenditures or provide a mechanism for restraining the growth of government.... As political conditions change, so, too, will the results produced by the budget process. The balance between the claiming and rationing functions of budgeting will vary, therefore, from year to year. (1980a, 570)

In this sense, the budget process, as such, is neutral toward outcomes. Political preferences shape its institutions and procedures, but these have no particular legitimacy beyond the particular agreements, compromises, and power-sharing arrangements of any one time. If current processes give rise to undesired outcomes, the fault lies in politics, not process.

A budget process is therefore adaptive, and an explanation for the past decade of turbulence may be found in efforts to respond to changes in political and social climate (Schick 1983c). During the two decades after World War II, Congress became a distributive institution, a role facilitated by a growing economy. Gradually its processes adjusted to distributing a fiscal dividend, benefits financed by economic growth. But, paradoxically, just as Congress had institutionalized this role, economic conditions changed. Congress was called on to take up a different stance, one of redistribution, where policies have to be financed through tax increases, other social costs, or transfer of funds among public programs. Just as there was a lag in adjustment to a distributive role, so there is a lag in adapting institutions and procedures to the tasks of redistribution.

Many of the shortcomings of current processes—difficulties in meeting deadlines, heightened level of conflict, repetitive processes, and so on—may be attributed to this lag in adjustment. At the same time, many adaptations have taken place, such as a longer time perspective, a more focused process, stronger congressional leadership, more sources of information, the reconciliation procedure, and the development of a credit budget (Caiden 1983a; Caiden 1983b). Their emergence denotes the vitality of the budget process and its potential to reflect political and social values.

The models of budget capacity and incapacity have much in common. Both find much in present processes to criticize. Both regard institutions and frameworks as reflecting political conditions and influencing political outcomes. But at this point, they part company. The model of budgetary incapacity evinces mistrust of the political system and sees salvation as extrapolitical. The model of budget capacity sees adaptation and reform occurring only through the political system. Budgetary incapacity theorists argue from axiom, the irrationality of the system as opposed to its parts. Theorists of budget capacity center their arguments on observed workings of institutions that in some way reflect popular will. For one, explanation is found in the immutable logic of human nature; for the other, in changing historical conditions. Budget incapacity takes as its substantive criterion a firm ideological position in favor of conservatism, reduction of government spending, and balanced budgets. Budget capacity refuses to adopt a substantive criterion at all, leaving this to political choice at any given time. Reviewing the same phenomena, one side draws a conclusion of breakdown and incapacity, while the other finds evidence of adaptation and renewed capacity (Caiden 1982).

The lines of course are not neatly drawn. Positions are complicated by attitudes toward the 1974 Congressional Budget Act and its accomplishments or lack of them, applause or distaste for the policies and tactics of the Reagan administration, and the uncertainty of present directions. In any event, there is much pragmatic work that traces the shifting executive-legislative balance, evaluates the performance of different institutions, analyzes outcomes, and describes developments. The problem does not lie in lack of information.

Variations on an Obbligato Theme:
Models of Fiscal Stress and Cutback Budgeting

It is virtually impossible to describe the current literature on budgeting at state and local government levels in the United States today without reference to the issue of fiscal stress and its response in cutback budgeting. The definition, causes, and dynamics of constraint in revenues and expenditures form an indispensable accompaniment, an obbligato theme, to any discussion of public budgeting, permeating every subject to such a degree as to become an integral part of the tune.

The fiscal stress of local governments in the late 1970s and 1980s is a direct descendant of the fiscal crisis of the cities that dominated the literature of local public finance for some time previously. But it differs in two important respects. First, the fiscal crisis of the cities referred to identifiable jurisdictions, specifically the northeastern large cities whose poverty translated into local budgets as high service expenditures and constrained revenue bases. Such cities might be pinpointed or targeted through the applications of a formula composed of socioeconomic variables that yielded an index of distress and a list of the most distressed cities. The fiscal stress of the 1980s is conceived as a much more widespread phenomenon, affecting virtually every local jurisdiction and defined in more general and more complex terms.

Second, the fiscal crisis of the cities was seen as capable of solution through the intergovernmental system. The federal government could redistribute resources to effect more equitable geographical balance, compensate localities for the impacts of national trends and other externalities beyond their control, and create a new intergovernmental balance in which the federal government did what it did best (i.e., raise money), and local governments did what they did best (i.e., spend it). The practical reflections of this model might be found in attempts toward a national urban policy in the mid-1970s, the enactment of general revenue sharing, and the federal bailout of New York City. In contrast, one of the major features of contemporary characterizations of fiscal stress is the declining role played by the federal government, whose previous efforts at crisis resolution are now seen as at best papering over the cracks and at worst fostering a dangerous dependency on, or even addiction to, federal aid (Burchell 1984). Contemporary fiscal stress apparently demands not an external savior but an internal revolution in budgeting, revenue raising, the organization of public services, and the scale and scope of government.

If fiscal stress is to be the primary organizing concept for discussion of local government budgeting, it requires careful definition, but no single acceptable formulation seems to have emerged. Irene Rubin has written, "There are nearly as many definitions as authors, and, not surprisingly, there is little consensus on how wide-spread fiscal stress is" (Rubin 1982, p. 5). The number of urban hardship indices has proliferated, but their very abundance emphasizes the difficulty of establishing definitive characteristics (Aronson 1980; Burchell and Listoken 1980; Groves, Godsey, and Shulman 1981; Kamer 1983; Ross and Greenfield 1980, 89–112). More general definitions differ considerably. For example, Stanley's summary of trouble is a picture of imminent collapse: "a city government fiscal situation so unfavorable as to impair borrowing ability, require reduction of municipal services, pose a threat to public health and safety, and thus [not surprisingly!] diminish the quality and satisfaction of urban life" (Stanley 1980, 95). In Levine's definition, a fiscal stress situation seems to have been reached long before this, in the development of a "gap between the needs and expectations for government services and benefits and the inability of the economy to generate enough growth to expand or sustain programs without putting unacceptable demands on tax payers' take-home pay" (Levine 1980a, 4). One difficulty with both definitions is the ability to recognize an actual situation of fiscal stress, short of positive catastrophe; there are too many qualitative judgments to be made about needs, expectations, economic capacity, and acceptable tax burdens. As Allen Schick has commented, budgetary scarcity is "a matter of attitude and circumstance," and perception rather than reality determines the budget condition (Schick 1980b, 116). Like obscenity, we find it difficult to come up with an exact definition, but we know it when we see it. Nevertheless, a growing fiscal indicators movement has provided practical help to jurisdictions attempting to monitor their financial condition.

One of the main problems is that the definitions are necessarily colored by their purposes: to elicit aid from another level of government, to give warning of imminent financial difficulties, or to provide some foundation on which remedial action may be based. Definitions therefore tend to go beyond immediate questions of budget balance and to reflect their authors' views of the longer-term situation, in other words, the deeper causes of present predicaments.

Irene Rubin has admirably summarized no less than nine different models of the causes of fiscal stress in local government, and most discussions compose a variety of permutations of the elements of her typology (Rubin 1982, 6–8). Briefly, there are three main models, each of which may be broken down into three submodels. First is an immigration model according to which fiscal stress is blamed on demographic movements increasing demand for service expenditures and reducing revenue bases. Second is a bureaucratic growth model, in which oversupply of government services results from an absence of constraints on demands for services by self-interested groups, bureaucratic aggrandizement, and high-service maintenance resulting from entitlements. The third model is one of political vulnerability, which may be traced to a collapse of voter coalitions, structural weaknesses in the form of government, and the operation of interest groups.

These are often combined into composite models that endeavor to put forward explanations and diagnoses of fiscal stress. For example, Pascal hypothesizes a waning of the real estate boom affected property-tax income; consumer conservation actions affected revenues from utility taxes; voters were unlikely to approve tax overrides or new bonding proposals; and cities were afraid to raise taxes and drive away business. When federal aid to cities declined at the end of the 1970s, the revenue position became critical (Pascal, Menchik, De Tray, Fernandez, Caggiano, Neels, and Stucker 1985). Burchell's analysis concentrates on the dislocations caused by the decline of the "intergovernmental city," a prototype of the 1970s, an older, economically declining industrial city characterized by high levels of federal and state revenue transfer. Losses of industry, population, retail trade, housing stock, economic base, and revenue-producing capacity, combined with escalating demands for public services, have produced overwhelming pressures of municipal fiscal stress. The underlying cause is private disinvestment, which stems from global forces beyond the control of decision makers (Burchell 1985, 3). Pfiffner (1983) sees the critical problem as inflexible budgets at all levels of government; for Sbragia (1983), the precipitating force is increasing dependence on intergovernmental aid; to Stanley (1980), fiscal stress stems from economic stagnation, inflation, recession, and poor fiscal management.

Such explanations are characteristic of a large body of literature and provide a point of departure for further research describing reactions to fiscal stress. This general literature of cutback budgeting covers four main areas. The first attempts to make sense of what has actually happened by tracing budget cuts and their impacts. The second describes pragmatic policy responses of local governments and often incorporates normative proposals. The third analyzes structural changes in methods of budgeting related to the political environment, and the fourth examines how organizations respond to the necessity for cutbacks.

One indicator of the problem of coming to grips with the current situation is the extraordinary difficulty in trying to find out what has been and is happening. Works whose figures typically run anywhere from three to five years behind publication seem out of date almost as soon as they appear. The conventions of official published statistics may make them almost useless for analytical purposes (Bahl, Jump, and Schroeder 1978, 3–5). The complexity of the intergovernmental system with its large number of units and types of authorities, highly differentiated and fragmented systems of grants, and idiosyncratic relationships precludes simple models and makes generalizations dangerous. Notable among those who have attempted empirical evidence of the effects of cuts are John Ellwood and Richard Nathan and their associates at Princeton (Ellwood 1982). Their work is a sober antidote to facile theorizing on inadequate data. For example, Nathan throws considerable doubt on the dependency theory as far as federal grants are concerned (Nathan and Doolittle 1982, 203). But it is worth noting that work of this kind took several years, large numbers of people, and considerable resources to complete. It is so highly detailed and complex that it is difficult to draw conclusions from it.

Other changes are easier to document and discuss. Observers have noted growing diversification of revenue sources, particularly greater emphasis on user fees (Downing 1984; Mushkin and Vehorn 1980; Straussman 1981). There is a renewed interest in productivity measures (Fosler 1980; Hatry 1980; Hayward 1980; Washnis 1980) and contracting-out of services (Fisk, Kresling, and Muller 1978; Florestano and Gordon 1985; Savas 1985). Local governments have stepped up efforts to promote economic development, entering into various kinds of public-private partnerships as entrepreneurs (Clarke and Rich 1985; Peterson 1981). The budget literature has expanded into the areas of fiscal impact analysis, risk analysis, cash-flow management, long-term bond finance, cost management, and strategic planning. The old days, when you budgeted by the seat of your pants, are apparently over; from now on, professional public managers, no less than their private counterparts, will be equipped to run efficient organizations in a close relationship with the private sector. Or will they? Once again, prescriptions may have outgrown validation. Even more important, there is relatively little discussion of how the new decision rules are affecting the traditional role of local governments.

Yet there is no question that in many places the terms of discourse have undergone transformation. A case in point is New York City, where the disaster of 1975 resulted in radical changes in the whole political environment of budgeting. Horton and Brecher (1985) have shown that far from being in the grip of uncontrollable expenditures, the city was able to make deliberate policy choices that broke with past patterns. Robert Bailey (1984) has documented the political realignment that took place, the strategies and effects of new institutions, and the new emphasis on a side view of budgeting in which traditional policy debates are overlaid or crisscrossed by such concerns as labor costs, debt service, capital maintenance, and productivity (p. 48). There seems to have been few attempts to undertake similar analyses in less dramatic circumstances, although Peterson and Wong's (1985) differentiated models of intergovernmental relations and economic development strategies and Clark and Ferguson's (1983) work on political cultures would seem to hold implications for the budget process and the relationships that underlie it.

Meanwhile, of course, what everyone really wants to know is what to do now, and theory has done its best to replace incrementalism with decrementalism, or since decrementalism does not work (Behn 1985, 155–77), with cutback budgeting. Conventional budget systems are likely to be inadequate for the tasks of accomplishing organizational decline, "since the cushion of spare resources necessary for coping with uncertainty, risking innovation, and rewarding loyalty and cooperation" (Levine 1980b, 13) is by definition absent. Instead, the organization faces paradoxes at every step so that strategic planning is necessary to overcome them (Levine 1980b). Specific responses will depend on such factors as the severity of stress, the size and power of the unit affected, the power and alignment of interest groups, and the power of political leaders (Levine 1980a, 6–7). Wolman (1980) has suggested that responses of organizations to fiscal stress follow a cycle that starts with attempts to buy time and ends with resignation in the cutting of spending and services. Levine and others have hypothesized a developmental five-stage model but were unable to validate it completely (Levine, Rubin, and Wolohojian 1981). Similarly, Rubin found that earlier models in which initial confusion following a drop in resources was replaced by improved management were not necessarily valid. Instead, efforts to cut back might become self-defeating in an environment of uncertainty where decisions had to be constantly made and remade and information became distorted. In organizations with weak authority structures without budget flexibility, attempts to control budgets and limit expenditures might be less effective than allowing greater discretion within reduced resource levels (Rubin 1980, 175).

Models are tools for analysis. They abstract from complexity and direct attention to critical variables and dynamics. Empirical models are useful to the extent that they accurately portray the germane features of a situation; normative ones, to the degree that they are capable of changing and improving it. The models of fiscal stress and cutback management purport to do both. To what degree are they successful?

These models contrast with earlier models of public budgeting in important respects. They combine economics, politics, and management in a composite that relates definitions, causes, consequences, and prescriptions. They are not neutral but favor, whether by choice or necessity, organizational decline and reductions in public expenditures. They are strongly related to their environment and assume that different kinds of budgeting are appropriate for different contexts.

The models' limitations lie in their scope and utility. It is unclear to which jurisdictions the empirical models apply. Whereas the model of the depressed northeastern or midwestern city is well developed and falls easily into the category of fiscal distress, its applicability to other areas is less clear. There is no well-accepted typology that separates out the different situations, no model of different degrees of fiscal stress, no demarcated relationships between specific causes of financial problems and policy advocacy. In other words, the models may be overgeneralized, subsume too much under all-embracing headings, and fail to distinguish meaningful patterns within the complexities that confront us.

Overgeneralization affects utility as well as description. How do we know which policies are appropriate if we do not know whether we fall within the given category? But the normative question goes beyond this. Unlike the earlier models of fiscal crisis, which offered solutions in the form of restructuring of the federal system or a national urban policy, these models offer no solutions at all. Cutback budgeting is both means and end, process and policy. The very neatness and self-containment of the models—definition, causes, consequences—implies its dependence on broader assumptions regarding the role of government and the nature of economy and society. But these assumptions are rarely made explicit, and there is a danger that in rushing to implement some of the attractive proposals of cutback budgeting, practitioners and researchers alike may forget the larger context.

The Great Globe Itself: Epilogue and Prologue

The field of public budgeting is now characterized by increased scope, complexity, and dynamism. Researchers are called on to conceptualize and integrate a vastly expanded area, trace seemingly infinite relationships, and second-guess situations where the unexpected has become normal. The newer models are interdisciplinary, combining elements of economics, management, and politics. They endeavor to capture all the wide variety of dynamic elements in the budget system, including budgetary politics, revenue raising, service delivery, fiscal and debt policy, intergovernmental relations, and budget implementation. Practitioners have found themselves closely involved in issues of economic development and change, relationships with the private sector, entrepreneurship, and forecasting.

The study of public budgeting has met the challenge; an enormous amount of detailed empirical work is now available. Academic texts have expanded their definition of the subject to include a wide variety of related topics. Articles on all aspects of public budgeting, domestic and foreign, have been encouraged by the founding of the journal, *Public Budgeting and Finance* (sponsored by the Section on Budgeting and Financial Management of the American Society for Public Administration and the American Association of Budget and Program Analysis). There is no lack of primary or secondary sources on federal budget history, current developments, or statistical analyses, to say nothing of a large polemical literature. The subject is no longer the preserve of a few scholars with knowledge of specific techniques or skills. There is open season on budgeting, and everyone, it seems, is armed for pursuit.

It is not surprising that the discipline as a whole appears fragmented. The newer models have not supplanted the earlier ones, and the older disciplines continue to exert considerable influence. Contemporary models, whatever their individual strength, are difficult to integrate. Apart from the single theme of resource constraint, for example, there is a glaring discontinuity between the study of the federal government and state and local governments; the models, terms of discourse, questions asked, and researchers themselves are quite distinct. Public budgeting is undoubtedly a discipline in the dictionary definition of the term as "a branch of knowledge or learning" (Webster 1977, 520). Researchers have also generated an interesting variety of questions and models. But if the study of public budgeting is to be more than a collection of disparate concerns, it requires stronger themes, and theories that act not only to unify them but also to reveal the philosophical assumptions underlying empirical description and normative proposals.

The quest for "a theory of the economics and politics of state finance" (McDonald and Ward 1984, 13) is not a new one and may be traced back at least as far as Joseph Schumpeter's "The Crisis of the Tax State," written in 1954. Such a theory would presumably account for revenues, and expenditures beyond immediate events and actors, and would have some potential for predicting the future. It seems unlikely that such a theory will emerge. Simple unicausal explanations are inadequate to grapple with the highly complex variables and relationships that constitute the budget nexus, and fail to account for changes or trace their future direction (see, for example, the discussion of structural functionalism in urban fiscal history in McDonald and Ward 1984, 20–22). Where attempts are made to build in more variables, analysis easily reverts to description, and everything explains everything. Seen from a systems perspective, budget theory may easily dissolve into a general theory of society. Moreover, insofar as budgeting stands for politics, budget theory incorporates standards of value that have not been universally agreed on.

If comprehensive theory is a mirage, are there other theoretical frameworks influencing contemporary research and practice? If we leave aside Marxism, Keynesianism, or supply-side economics, there are a number of candidates. Public-choice theory is often accepted as an explicit or implicit normative guide to budgetary decision making. Researchers into the dynamics of public expenditures have suggested past and future directions of development in public finance. Comparative analysis has attempted to provide a common vocabulary to discuss different budgetary phenomena. All these lines of inquiry share a high degree of generality. Their focus lies beyond the borders of the United States to embrace the great globe itself.

Public-choice theorists take the tools and methods of economic theory and apply them to the government sector as "the economic theory of politics" (Buchanan 1972, 13). They see individuals as ranking bundles of public goods in the same way as they do private goods. Collective choice is the aggregation of all the individual choices, and government is simply the set of processes that enables ensuing collective action to take place (Buchanan and Tullock 1962, 13). Because in making collective choices individuals act indirectly, with costs and benefits not directly related, it is important to set out the rules or constitution according to which these decisions will be made (Buchanan and Wagner 1977, 5). The normative standard for assessing these rules is unanimity, and the higher the cost imposed on the individual, the greater the need for unanimity. Emphasis is on the element of choice, with the citizen in the role of consumer.

The influence of these ideas on the field of public budgeting has already been marked. Public-choice theory provides a clearly demarcated theoretical reference point and philosophical criterion against which both budget processes and policies may be set. On an empirical level, it relates "the behavior of persons in their various capacities . . . to the composition of outcomes that we observe or might observe" (Buchanan 1972, 13). On a normative level, public choice sets up standards for design of systems of fiscal decision making, legitimizing decentralization and the decoupling of service provision and service delivery (Beam, Conland, and Walker 1983, 259–60; Ostrom and Ostrom 1971). It also grounds fiscal decision making in individual assessment of costs and benefits and democratic participation in decisions.

Public-choice theory has been criticized for abstractness, difficulties in application, and oversimplified assumptions regarding the nature of both private and public decision making (Dunleavy 1985, 299–328). In promoting individual choice as the normative foundation for collectively financed action, public-choice theorists expressly exclude any other notion of the public interest. Essentially, individual demands, whether for private or collective goods, take precedence over public needs where these are unperceived or unvalued by the majority. Emphasis on unanimity in cohesive local communities risks neglect of obligations to the wider community and denial of its impacts. The paradox that needs for public action are greatest in areas where resources are least available to meet them is ignored. The equating of legitimate public provision with majority preference entirely involves the relegation of many activities with significant externalities to the status of minority interests and private funding. This construction not only reopens the free-rider problem (dealt with in traditional public finance texts through compulsory payments), but also raises the possibility that the underfunding of these activities, through underestimation of benefits not captured in effective demand, may result in economic inefficiency. On a practical level, application of public-choice theory may contribute to environmental degradation and social disintegration.

A second area of theoretical interest is exploration of the comparative dynamics of public-sector expenditures. The United States is only one country in which both popular and academic opinion evinces disturbance regarding the size, direction, and financing of government spending. The focus of research has been on the discovery of explanations for expenditure growth. There are excellent summaries of the research on government growth (Larkey, Stolp, and Winer 1981; Tarschys 1975; Wildavsky 1985b), as well as several studies dealing specifically with the United States (Borcherding 1977; Lewis-Beck and Rice 1985; Lowery and Berry 1983; Thomas 1980). The search for explanatory variables has not been particularly successful, however, and there is little consensus on the specific reasons for differential rates of expenditure growth. Wilensky (1975) has suggested that an aging population has been a major contributing factor, while Peltzman (1980) singles out an equalizing tendency as an explanation, but it is difficult to account for all cases.

A related area of research is concerned with the common fiscal problems of contemporary industrialized economies. The work of Ysander and Robinson (1982), Tarschys (1983), Rose (1985), and Peters (1985), for example, has concentrated on the similar difficulties of many countries in financing welfare state expenditures in conditions of slow economic growth. Analyses of comparative public finance and budgeting summarize changes in policies and processes, search for common developments, and establish concepts of budget capacity to serve as guides to future directions (Organisation for Economic Cooperation and Development 1987; Schick 1986, 1988a).

It seems likely that as the problems of public finance in Western industrialized countries converge, comparative analysis will become more influential as a source of concepts, predictions, and prescriptions in the United States. Nevertheless, the current literature would require considerable strengthening. It is difficult to produce accurate comparative studies of developments in public budgets, given their complexity, and such studies sometimes tend to be polemics in support of preconceived assumptions about excessive government expenditures. The transferability of institutions and proposals is often problematical, given differences in political and cultural contexts. The majority of research relates to national governments, neglecting regional and local issues. Nevertheless, the growth of interest in comparative developments is significant, and, it is to be hoped, will generate practical benefits.

Meanwhile, a true theory of comparative budgeting is lacking. Is it possible to relate particular types of budgeting to specific kinds of conditions? Three problems are involved in undertaking this kind of exercise. First, it is necessary to define a realistic typology of budget forms into which actual budget systems will fit. Second, some means of categorizing environments must be devised. Third, it is necessary to relate the former to the latter, preferably with some explanation of why the relationship exists and how it might change over time. If the effort were successful, it might provide a useful vocabulary with which to describe budgeting and its setting, an organizing structure for discussion, and a means of predicting how budget systems are likely to behave in given circumstances. Attempts at this kind of systematic comparative theorizing have been relatively few. Naomi Caiden (1978) has set out a typology of historical budget patterns related to degree of revenue mobilization, accountability, and control. Jeffrey Straussman (1979) has posited a typology of budget environments and examined their implications for reform. Aaron Wildavsky has applied the model of scarcity and uncertainty originally developed by Caiden and Wildavsky to conceptualize budget practices in poor countries to broader circumstances (Caiden and Wildavsky 1974; Wildavsky 1975). He has also attempted to relate characteristics of budgeting to political regimes, the outcomes reflecting the relative dominance of the respective cultures of sects, markets, and hierarchies (Wildavsky 1985a). Allen Schick (1980b) has used a differentiated model of poverty as explaining four different forms of budgeting. In a further effort to construct generic empirical theory, Schick (1985) has identified the basic elements of budgeting, claiming and allocating resources, as analogous to supply and demand in market allocation. None of these attempts at comparative method has found any great popularity as a basis for analysis or description, however, partly because the categories employed are too broad, and policy and institutional prescriptions are not easily derived from them.

But if the study of public budgeting in the United States is to survive and thrive, there is probably a need for a broad framework of theory. The older models of budgeting, while still available and relevant, are no longer adequate to the task as the subject has developed beyond them to become broader in scope and more interdisciplinary in nature. In the process, the discipline runs the risk of increasing fragmentation and loss of cohesion, until the study of budgeting itself as a definable entity may disappear altogether, remaining only as a subset of other fields.

It is unlikely that a single theory of budgeting will emerge; the subject is many-faceted and may legitimately be viewed from a multitude of standpoints. What, then, might budgeting theories be expected to do? At a minimum the following functions might be suggested:

> *Definition:* What are the components and boundaries of a budget system? On what should we focus?

Description: How are the budget systems of the United States located in a historical and comparative context? What vocabulary should we use to describe and analyze them?

Explanation: What is the relationship between institutions and outcomes? How may budget institutions be designed to achieve given results?

Prediction: How do budget processes change over time? What are the driving forces, mechanisms, and directions of change?

Evaluation: How is budgetary effectiveness to be defined and evaluated? What constitutes improvement?

There are probably a number of answers to each of these questions, differing according to the viewpoints of observers and their situations. What is important is that they should be asked, and continuing efforts be made to conceptualize and reconceptualize the discipline in a self-conscious kind of way.

In 1961, Aaron Wildavsky wrote "there is virtually nothing of substance about how or why budgetary decisions are actually made" (p. 30). Since then, the field of budgeting has become a much more lively place, and we know a good deal more about all kinds of different aspects of the subject. Yet, as far as the actual process of making decisions about resource allocation is concerned, there is still much to be discovered. It is unlikely that researchers will run out of material for some time to come.

References

Aronson, J. Richard. 1980. *Municipal Fiscal Indicators.* Washington, D.C.: Department of Housing and Urban Development.

Babunakis, Michael. 1976. *Budgets: An Analytical and Procedural Handbook for Government and Non-Profit Organizations.* Westport, Conn.: Greenwood Press.

Bahl, Roy, Bernard Jump, and Larry Schroeder. 1978. "The Outlook for City Fiscal Performance in Declining Regions." In *The Fiscal Outlook for Cities,* edited by Roy Bahl. Syracuse: Syracuse University Press.

Bailey, Robert W. 1984. *The Crisis Regime: The MAC, the EFCB, and the Political Impact of the New York City Financial Crisis.* Albany, N.Y.: State University of New York Press.

Beam, David R., Timothy J. Conlan, and David B. Walker. 1983. "Federalism: The Challenge of Conflicting Theories and Contemporary Practices." In *Political Science: The State of the Discipline,* edited by Ada Finifter. Washington, D.C.: American Political Science Association.

Behn, Robert D. 1985. "Cutback Budgeting." *Journal of Policy Analysis and Management* 4(2):155–77.

Boadway, Robin. 1979. *Public Sector Economics.* Cambridge, Mass.: Winthrop.

Borcherding, Thomas E. 1977. *Budgets and Bureaucrats: The Sources of Government Growth.* Durham: Duke University Press.

Braybrooke, David, and Charles Lindblom. 1963. *A Strategy of Decision.* New York: Free Press.

Break, George. 1980. *Financing Government in a Federal System.* Washington, D.C.: Brookings Institution.

Brecher, Charles, and Raymond D. Horton. 1985. "Retrenchment and Recovery: American Cities and the New York Experience." *Public Administration Review* 45(2):267–74.

Browning, Edgar, and Jacqueline Browning. 1979. *Public Finance and the Price System.* New York: Macmillan.

Buchanan, James M. 1972. "Politics without Romance: A Sketch of Positive Public Choice Theory and Its Normative Implications." In *The Theory of Public Choice,* vol. 2, edited by James Buchanan and R.D. Tollison. Ann Arbor: University of Michigan Press.

Buchanan, James M., and Gordon Tullock. 1962. *The Calculus of Consent.* Ann Arbor: University of Michigan Press.

Buchanan, James M., and Richard E. Wagner. 1977. *Democracy in Deficit: The Political Legacy of Lord Keynes.* New York: Academic Press.

Burchell, Robert W. 1984. *The New Reality of Municipal Finance: The Rise and Fall of the Intergovernmental City.* New Brunswick, N.J.: Transaction.

Burchell, Robert W., and David Listoken. 1980. "Measuring Urban Distress: A Summary of the Major Urban Hardship Indices and Resource Allocation System." In *Cities Under Stress: The Fiscal Crisis of Urban America,* edited by Robert W. Burchell and David Listoken. New Brunswick, N.J.: Center for Urban Policy Research.

Burkhead, Jesse. 1956. *Government Budgeting.* New York: Wiley.

Caiden, Naomi. 1978. "Patterns of Budgeting." *Public Administration Review* 38(6): 539–44.

Caiden, Naomi. 1982. "The Myth of the Annual Budget." *Public Administration Review* 42(6):516–23.

Caiden, Naomi. 1983a. "Guidelines to Federal Budget Reform." *Public Budgeting and Finance* 3(4):4–22.

Caiden, Naomi. 1983b. "The Politics of Subtraction." In *Making Economic Policy in Congress,* edited by Allen Schick. Washington, D.C.: American Enterprise Institute.

Caiden, Naomi. 1985. "The Boundaries of Public Budgeting: Issues for Education in Tumultuous Times." *Public Administration Review* 45(4):495–502.

Caiden, Naomi, and Aaron Wildavsky. 1974. *Planning and Budgeting in Poor Countries.* New York: Wiley.

Clark, Terry, and Lorna Crowley Ferguson. 1983. *City Money: Political Processes, Fiscal Strain and Retrenchment.* New York: Columbia University Press.

Clarke, Susan E., and Michael J. Rich. 1985. "Making Money Work: The New Urban Policy Arena." In *Research in Urban Policy,* vol. 1, *Coping with Urban Austerity,* edited by Terry Nichols Clark. Greenwich, Conn.: JAI Press.

Cohen, Richard. 1980. *Congressional Leadership: Seeking a New Role.* Beverly Hills: Sage.

Dempster, M.A.H., and Aaron Wildavsky. 1979. "On Change: Or There Is No Magic Size for an Increment." *Political Studies* 27(3):371–89.

Downing, Paul B. 1984. "User Charges and Service Fees." In *Crisis and Constraint in Municipal Finance,* edited by James H. Carr. New Brunswick, N.J.: Center for Urban Policy Research.

Draper, Frank D., and Bernard T. Pitsvada. 1981. "Limitations in Federal Budget Execution." *Government Accountants Journal* 30(3):15–25.

Dunleavy, Patrick. 1985. "Bureaucrats, Budgets and the Growth of the State: Reconstructing an Instrumental Model." *British Journal of Political Science* 15(3):299–328.

Ellwood, John W., ed. 1982. *Reductions in U.S. Domestic Spending: How They Affect State and Local Governments*. New Brunswick, N.J.: Transaction.

Fenno, Richard. 1966. *The Power of the Purse*. Boston: Little, Brown.

Fisher, Louis. 1983. "Annual Authorizations: Durable Roadblocks to Biennial Budgeting." *Public Budgeting and Finance* 3(1):23–40.

Fisher, Louis. 1985. "Ten Years of the Budget Act: Still Searching for Controls." *Public Budgeting and Finance* 5(3):3–28.

Fisk, Donald, Herbert Kresling, and Thomas Muller. 1978. *Private Provision of Public Services*. Washington, D.C.: Urban Institute.

Florestano, Patricia, and Stephen B. Gordon. 1985. "A Survey of City and County Use of Private Contracting." In *Crisis and Constraint in Municipal Finance,* edited by James H. Carr. New Brunswick, N.J.: Center for Urban Policy Research.

Fosler, R. Scott. 1980. "Local Government Productivity: Political and Administrative Potential." In *Fiscal Stress and Public Policy,* edited by Charles Levine and Irene Rubin. Beverly Hills: Sage.

Goodin, Robert, and Ilmar Waldner. 1979. "Thinking Big, Thinking Small, and Not Thinking at All." *Public Policy* 27(1):1–24.

Groves, Sanford M., W. Maureen Godsey, and Martha A. Shulman. 1981. "Financial Indicators for Local Government." *Public Budgeting and Finance* 1(2):5–20.

Hatry, Harry. 1980. "Current State of the Art of State and Local Government Productivity Improvement and Potential Federal Roles." In *Managing Fiscal Stress,* edited by Charles Levine. Chatham, N.J.: Chatham House.

Hayward, Nancy. 1980. "The Productivity Challenge." In *Managing Fiscal Stress,* edited by Charles Levine. Chatham, N.J.: Chatham House.

Hyman, David. 1973. *The Economics of Governmental Activity*. New York: Holt.

Ippolito, Dennis S. 1981. *Congressional Spending*. Ithaca: Cornell University Press.

Ippolito, Dennis S. 1984. *Hidden Spending: The Politics of Federal Credit Programs*. Chapel Hill: University of North Carolina Press.

Kamer, Pearl M. 1983. *Crisis in Urban Public Finance: A Case Study of Thirty-Eight Cities*. New York: Praeger.

Kamlet, Mark S., and David C. Mowery. 1983. "Budgetary Side Payments and Government Growth: 1953–1968." *American Journal of Political Science* 17(4):637–64.

Kamlet, Mark S., and David C. Mowery. 1984. "A Comparative Analysis of Congressional and Executive Budgetary Priorities." Presented at the annual meeting of the American Political Science Association, Washington, D.C.

Kamlet, Mark S., and David C. Mowery. 1985. "The First Decade of the Congressional Budget Act: Legislative Imitation and Adaptation in Budgeting." *Policy Sciences* 18(4):313–34.

Key, V.O., Jr. 1940. "The Lack of a Budgetary Theory." *American Political Science Review* 34:1137–40.

King, Ronald F. 1984. "Tax Expenditures and Systematic Public Policy." *Public Budgeting and Finance* 4(1):14–30.

Kramer, Fred, ed. 1979. *Contemporary Approaches to Public Budgeting*. Cambridge, Mass.: Winthrop.

Larkey, Patrick D., Chandler Stolp, and Mark Winer. 1981. "Theorizing about the Growth of Government: A Research Assessment." *Journal of Public Policy* 1(2):157–220.

LeLoup, Lance. 1978. "The Myth of Incrementalism: Analytical Choices in Budgetary Theory." *Polity* 10:488– 509.

LeLoup, Lance. 1980. *The Fiscal Congress.* Westport, Conn.: Greenwood Press.

LeLoup, Lance, ed. 1984. "Appropriations Politics in Congress: The House Appropriations Committee and the Executive Agencies." *Public Budgeting and Finance* 4(4):78–97.

Levine, Charles. 1980a. "The New Crisis in the Public Sector." In *Managing Fiscal Stress: The Crisis in the Public Sector,* edited by Charles Levine. Chatham, N.J.: Chatham House.

Levine, Charles. 1980b. "Organizational Decline and Cutback Management." In *Managing Fiscal Stress,* edited by Charles Levine. Chatham, N.J.: Chatham House.

Levine, Charles, Irene S. Rubin, and George G. Wolohojian. 1981. *The Politics of Retrenchment.* Beverly Hills: Sage.

Lewis, Verne. 1952. "Toward a Theory of Budgeting." *Public Administration Review* 12(1):43–54.

Lewis-Beck, Michael S., and Tom W. Rice. 1985. "Government Growth in the United States." *Journal of Politics* 47(1):2–30.

Lindblom, Charles. 1959. "The Science of Muddling Through." *Public Administration Review* 19:79–88.

Lineberry, Robert L., and Robert E. Welch, Jr. 1974. "Who Gets What: Measuring the Distribution of Public Services." *Social Science Quarterly* 54 (4):700–712.

Lowery, David, and William D. Berry. 1983. "Growth of Government in the United States: An Empirical Assessment of Competing Explanations." *American Journal of Political Science* 21:665–94.

Lyden, Fremont J., and Ernest G. Miller, eds. 1972. *Planning, Programming, Budgeting.* Chicago: Markham.

Lynch, Thomas, ed. 1981. *Contemporary Public Budgeting.* New Brunswick, N.J.: Transaction.

McDonald, Terrence J., and Sally K. Ward. 1984. "Introduction." In *The Politics of Urban Fiscal Policy,* edited by Terrence J. McDonald and Sally K. Ward. Beverly Hills: Sage.

Mills, Geoffrey, and John L. Palmer, eds. 1984. *Federal Budget Policy in the 1980s.* Washington, D.C.: Urban Institute Press.

Mowery, David C., and Mark S. Kamlet. 1984. "Games Presidents Do and Do Not Play: Presidential Circumvention of the Executive Branch Budget Process." *Policy Sciences* 16:303– 27.

Musgrave, Richard A., and Peggy B. Musgrave. 1976. *Public Finance in Theory and Practice.* 2d ed. New York: McGraw-Hill.

Mushkin, Selma, and Charles Vehorn. 1980. "User Fees and Charges." In *Managing Fiscal Stress,* edited by Charles Levine. Chatham, N.J.: Chatham House.

Nathan, Richard P., and Fred C. Doolittle. 1983. *The Consequences of Cuts: The Effects of the Reagan Domestic Program on State and Local Governments.* Princeton: Princeton Urban and Regional Research Center.

Olson, Mancur. 1983. *The Rise and Decline of Nations: Economic Growth, Stagflation and Social Rigidities.* New Haven: Yale University Press.

Organisation for Economic Cooperation and Development. 1985. *The Role of the Public Sector: Causes and Consequences of the Growth of Government.* OECD Economic Studies, No. 4.

Organisation for Economic Cooperation and Development. 1987. *The Control and Management of Public Expenditure.* Paris: OECD.

Ostrom, Elinor, and Vincent Ostrom. 1971. "Public Choice: A Different Approach to the Study of Public Administration." *Public Administration Review* 31:302–16.

Ostrom, Elinor, and Vincent Ostrom. 1980. "Public Economy Organization and Service Delivery." In *Financing the Metropolis,* edited by Kent Mathewson and William B. Neenan. New York: Praeger.

Parker, Glenn R., ed. 1985. *Studies of Congress.* Washington, D.C.: CQ Press.

Pascal, Anthony, Mark David Menchik, Dennis De Tray, Judith Fernandez, Michael Caggiano, Kevin Neels, and James Stucker. 1985. "Financing Local Government in Tough Times: A Summary of Research Findings and a Proposal for Reform." In *Research in Urban Policy,* vol. 1, *Coping with Urban Austerity,* edited by Terry Nichols Clark. Greenwich, Conn.: JAI Press.

Peltzman, Sam. 1980. "The Growth of Government." *Journal of Law and Economics* 23(2):209–88.

Peterkin Symposium on Local Provision of Public Services. 1981. *The Tiebout Model After Twenty-Five Years.* Houston: Rice University.

Peters, B. Guy. 1985. "The Limits of the Welfare State." In *Political Economy in Western Democracies,* edited by Norman J. Vig and Steven E. Schier. New York: Holmes and Meier.

Peterson, Paul. 1981. *City Limits.* Chicago: University of Chicago Press.

Peterson, Paul, and Kenneth K. Wong. 1985. "Toward a Differentiated Theory of Federalism: Education and Housing Policy in the 1980s." In *Research in Urban Policy,* vol. 1, *Coping with Urban Austerity,* edited by Terry Nichols Clark. Greenwich, Conn.: JAI Press.

Pfiffner, James P. 1983. "Inflexible Budgets, Fiscal Stress, and the Tax Revolt." In *The Municipal Money Chase,* edited by Alberta M. Sbragia. Boulder, Colo.: Westview Press.

Pitsvada, Bernard T. 1983. "Flexibility in Federal Budget Execution." *Public Budgeting and Finance* 3(2):83–101.

Pogue, Thomas, and L.G. Sgontz. 1978. *Government and Economic Choice: An Introduction to Public Finance.* Boston: Houghton Mifflin.

Rivlin, Alice M., and Robert W. Hartman. 1984. "Control of Federal Credit." In *Reconstructing the Federal Budget: A Trillion Dollar Quandary,* edited by Albert T. Sommers. New York: Praeger.

Rose, Richard. 1985. "Maximizing Tax Revenue While Minimizing Political Costs." *Journal of Public Policy* 5:289–320.

Ross, John P., and James Greenfield. 1980. "Measuring the Health of Cities." In *Fiscal Stress and Public Policy,* edited by Charles Levine and Irene Rubin. Beverly Hills: Sage.

Rubin, Irene. 1980. "Retrenchment and Flexibility in Public Organizations." In *Fiscal Stress and Public Policy,* edited by Charles Levine and Irene Rubin. Beverly Hills: Sage.

Rubin, Irene. 1982. *Running in the Red: The Political Dynamics of Urban Fiscal Stress.* Albany: State University of New York Press.

Savas, E.S. 1985. "Alternative Institutional Models for the Delivery of Public Services." In *Crisis and Constraint in Municipal Finance,* edited by James H. Carr. New Brunswick, N.J.: Center for Urban Policy Research.

Sbragia, Alberta M. 1983. "The 1970s: A Decade of Change in Local Government Finance." In *The Municipal Money Chase,* edited by Alberta Sbragia. Boulder, Colo.: Westview Press.

Schick, Allen. 1966. "The Road to PPB: The Stages of Budget Reform." *Public Administration Review* 26:243–58.

Schick, Allen. 1973. "A Death in the Bureaucracy: The Demise of Federal PPB." *Public Administration Review* 33(1):146–56.

Schick, Allen. 1980a. *Congress and Money: Budgeting, Spending, and Taxing.* Washington, D.C.: Urban Institute.

Schick, Allen. 1980b. "Budgetary Adaptations to Resource Scarcity." In *Fiscal Stress and Public Policy,* edited by Charles H. Levine and Irene Rubin. Beverly Hills: Sage.

Schick, Allen. 1983a. "Politics Through Law: Congressional Limitations on Executive Discretion." In *Both Ends of the Avenue: The Presidency, the Executive Branch and Congress in the 1980s,* edited by Anthony King. Washington, D.C.: American Enterprise Institute.

Schick, Allen, ed. 1983b. *Making Economic Policy in Congress.* Washington, D.C.: American Enterprise Institute.

Schick, Allen. 1983c. "The Distributive Congress." In *Making Economic Policy in Congress,* edited by Allen Schick. Washington, D.C.: American Enterprise Institute.

Schick, Allen. 1986. "Macrobudgetary Adaptations to Fiscal Stress in Industrialized Democracies." *Public Administration Review* 46:124–34.

Schick, Allen. 1988a. "Microbudgetary Adaptations to Fiscal Stress in Industrialized Democracies." 48:523–33.

Schick, Allen. 1988b. "An Inquiry into the Possibility of a Budgetary Theory." In *New Directions in Budget Theory,* edited by Irene Rubin. Albany: State University of New York Press.

Schumpeter, Joseph. 1954. "The Crisis of the Tax State." *International Economics Papers* 4:5–38.

Shuman, Howard E. 1984. *Politics and the Budget: The Struggle between the President and the Congress.* Englewood Cliffs, N.J.: Prentice-Hall.

Simon, Herbert. 1945. *Administrative Behavior.* New York: Free Press.

Stanley, David. 1980. "Cities in Trouble." In *Managing Fiscal Stress,* edited by Charles Levine. Chatham, N.J.: Chatham House.

Steiner, Peter. 1983. "The Public Sector and the Public Interest." In *Public Expenditure and Policy Analysis,* edited by Robert H. Havemann and Julius Margolis. Boston: Houghton Mifflin.

Stourm, Rene. 1917. *The Budget.* New York: Appleton.

Straussman, Jeffrey. 1979. "A Typology of Budgetary Environments: Notes on the Prospects for Reform." *Administration and Society* 11(2):216–26.

Straussman, Jeffrey. 1981. "More Bang for the Buck? Or How Local Governments Can Rediscover the Potentialities (and Pitfalls) of the Market." *Public Administration Review* 41:150–57.

Tarschys, Daniel. 1975. "The Growth of Public Expenditures: Nine Modes of Explanation." *Scandinavian Political Studies* 10:9–31.

Tarschys, Daniel. 1983. "The Scissors Crisis in Public Finance." *Policy Science* 15:205–24.

Thomas, John C. 1980. "The Growth of American Public Expenditures: Recent Trends and Their Implications." *Public Administration Review* 40(2):160–65.

Tiebout, Charles M. 1956. "A Pure Theory of Local Expenditures." *Journal of Political Economy* 64:416–24.

Wagner, Richard. 1983. *Public Finance: Revenues and Expenditures in a Democratic Society.* Boston: Little, Brown.

Wander, W. Thomas, F. Ted Hebert, and Gary W. Copeland. 1984. *Congressional Budgeting: Politics, Process and Power.* Baltimore, Md.: Johns Hopkins University Press.

Washnis, George, ed. 1980. *Productivity Improvement Handbook for State and Local Government.* New York: Wiley.

Wildavsky, Aaron. 1961. "Political Implications of Budgetary Reform." *Public Administration Review* 21:183–90.

Wildavsky, Aaron. 1964. *The Politics of the Budgetary Process.* Boston: Little, Brown.

Wildavsky, Aaron. 1966. "The Political Economy of Efficiency: Cost Benefit Analysis, Systems Analysis, and Program Budgeting." *Public Administration Review* 26: 292–310.

Wildavsky, Aaron. 1968. "Budgeting as a Political Process." In *International Encyclopedia of the Social Sciences,* vol. 2. New York: Free Press.

Wildavsky, Aaron. 1975. *Budgeting: A Comparative Theory of Budgetary Processes.* Boston: Little, Brown.

Wildavsky, Aaron. 1980. *How to Limit Government Spending.* Berkeley: University of California Press.

Wildavsky, Aaron. 1985a. "Budgets as Social Orders." In *Research in Urban Policy,* vol. 1: *Coping with Urban Austerity,* edited by Terry Nichols Clark. Greenwich, Conn.: JAI Press.

Wildavsky, Aaron. 1985b. "The Logic of Public Sector Growth." In *State and Market,* edited by Jan-Erik Lane. Beverly Hills: Sage.

Wilensky, Harold. 1975. *The Welfare State and Equality: Structural and Ideological Roots of Public Expenditures.* Berkeley: University of California Press.

Witte, John F. 1984. *The Politics and Development of the Federal Income Tax.* Madison: University of Wisconsin Press.

Wolman, Harold. 1980. "Local Government Strategies to Cope with Fiscal Pressure." In *Fiscal Stress and Public Policy,* edited by Charles Levine and Irene Rubin. Beverly Hills: Sage.

Ysander, Bengt-Christer, and Ann Robinson. 1982. "The Inflexibility of Contemporary Budgets." *Public Budgeting and Finance* 2:7–20.

12

Public Law and Public Administration: The State of the Union

PHILLIP J. COOPER

Members of the public administration community recall Woodrow Wilson and "The Study of Administration," which marks the founding of the discipline (1941). Yet few of those commemorating the occasion remember that Wilson saw himself as a professor of public law (Link 1968–69, 6:412). Fewer still are aware that he defined public administration as a subfield of public law (Link 1968–69, 7:114–15 and 6:483–85) and that his goal was to found a school of public law with public administration as a major unit within that institution (Link 1968–69, 5:729–30). The place of law in public administration has changed dramatically since those days. Dwight Waldo (1968b), concerned by the virtual absence of administrative law in the field, warned that the obvious antilaw bias in public administration was "dangerously obsolete and self-defeating" (pp. 14–15). Later still, as the centennial of the field approached, there has been a resurgence of interest in law in the discipline, both as a focus within the scholarly community and among practitioners at all levels of government.

Any study of the state of administrative law as a subfield of public administration must contemplate the rocky history of the subject as a fundamental influence. This chapter considers the rise, fall, and resurgence of law in public administration. It surveys the practical forces that seem to drive contemporary interest in the subject and the focal points of recent scholarly attention. It concludes with an assessment of some of the gaps in recent scholarship and suggestions for the future.

Law in the Emerging Discipline

In the years between Wilson's seminal article and the publication of the early public administration texts by Leonard D. White (1955) and William F. Willoughby

(1927), the role of law in the field began to shift. Early scholars considered it central to administration and used a broad definition of administrative law, but forces were developing that brought about a subtle transition.

Leading figures in the developing field of public administration, including Frank Goodnow at Columbia, Woodrow Wilson at Johns Hopkins, Bryn Mawr, and Princeton, and Ernst Freund at the University of Chicago, were themselves legally trained and taught public administration as public law. Wilson considered Goodnow's 1893 volume titled *Comparative Administrative Law: An Analysis of the Administrative Systems, National and Local, of the United States* the "only systematic work in English devoted distinctly to Administration as a separate discipline" and used it extensively in his early lectures and courses (Link 1968–69, 7:120). For Goodnow and Wilson, administrative law was an extremely broad subject, covering much of what we now refer to as the discipline of public administration. Writing in 1935, Haines and Dimock observed:

> [I]t is not too much to state that the general content of Goodnow's course on administrative law did not differ substantially from the usual substance of a course on public administration today. The principal differences in scope and emphasis today are that legal materials are not utilized to any great extent and that modern public administration emphasizes much more finance and non-legal techniques. (Pp. xi–xii)

Wilson declared that administrative law was "[t]he sum of legal rules obtaining in a State in respect of the public administration" (Link 1968–69, 7:143).

Both Goodnow and Wilson rejected the then prevalent overemphasis within political science on constitutional law, defined largely in terms of formal structural factors such as separation of powers. Those issues were necessary but not sufficient areas of scholarly inquiry if we were to learn how, as Wilson put it, "to run a constitution" (Wilson 1941, 481). For both, administration was a combination of techniques of governance, law, and issues of power and discretion. Simplistic analyses passed on with little reexamination, suggesting that Wilson and Goodnow were committed to a vigorous politics/administration dichotomy, do not withstand close scrutiny (see Cooper 1984a). Certainly Goodnow's administrative law writings and Wilson's lecture notes do not sustain that position. As Paul Appleby (1949) contended, "Recognizing these constitutional and historical facts and something of the actualities of practice, Goodnow's early discussion drew a line less abrupt between policy and administration than some who later quoted him seemed to know" (p. 16).

The first casebook in the field was authored by Ernst Freund, earning him the title in some quarters of father of administrative law. Freund received his legal training on the Continent, took his political science graduate work at Columbia, and played a key role in the developing public administration group at Chicago. Like Goodnow and Wilson, he approached administrative law broadly (Kraines 1974). His principal work (largely ignored for the past four decades), *Administrative Powers Over Persons and Property* (Freund 1928), is no narrow treatment of legal remedies for administrative abuses but a treatise on the subject of administrative power. Freund was concerned with the question of administrative discretion, the capacity that permitted administrators to be flexible enough to do justice in individual cases but that, taken to an extreme, would embody "the principle of unfreedom" (Freund 1928, 97).

On the other hand, Freund, along with a few others, altered the perspective of legal writers on administrative law in a subtle but significant way. Elihu Root anticipated Freund, Dickinson, Felix Frankfurter, and others when he observed that

> there is one special field of law development of which has manifestly become inevitable. We are entering upon the creation of a body of administrative law quite different in its machinery, its remedies, and its necessary safeguards from the old methods of regulation by specific statutes enforced by the courts. There will be no withdrawal from these experiments. We shall go on; we shall expand them, whether we approve theoretically or not, because such agencies furnish protection to rights and obstacles to wrongdoing which under our new social and industrial conditions cannot be practically accomplished by the old and simple procedure of legislatures and courts in the last generation. . . . If we are to continue a government of limited powers these agencies must themselves be regulated. . . . A system of administrative law must be developed, and that with us is still in its infancy, crude and imperfect. (1916, 534–35)

Whereas Goodnow and Wilson viewed administration from the inside out, Freund took more of an external perspective, writing from the vantage point of a lawyer with a client who faced action by an agency. That approach was even more pronounced in John Dickinson's *Administrative Justice and the Supremacy of Law in the United States* (1927) and in the writings of legal critics of the growing New Deal administration some years later. Dickinson saw law not as an instrument for governing but as a device for protecting citizens against government. "In Anglo-American jurisprudence, government and law have always in a sense stood opposed to one another; the law has been rather something to give the citizen a check on government than an instrument to give the government control over the citizen" (Dickinson 1927, 32).

Dickinson attacked the very legitimacy of administration. Unlike many critics of the New Deal, he did not challenge public administration on grounds of constitutional separation of powers, but as violative of the basic concept of the rule of law.* He charged that any system that would be acceptable within a regime truly governed by the supremacy of law must involve a logically coherent system of rules developed by some orderly process, adequate due process protections where agencies made important adjudicative decisions determining the legal rights or status of a citizen before the agency, and access to a court for appellate review of administrative decisions as a means of integrating administrative rulings with the larger corpus of the law.

The growth of administration during the New Deal prompted many critics in the legal community to move toward reform of the law to provide at least minimally adequate safeguards against abuses of power. (The ABA formed a committee to suggest reforms. See Caldwell 1933, 197.) Other, more vehement criticisms, insisting that separation of powers barred the exercise of broad delegated authority by non-elected administrators, fell by the wayside. But there were also defenders of public administration in the late 1930s and early 1940s who rejected the charge that the growing federal agencies represented a headless fourth branch of government (see, e.g., Brownlow Commission 1937).

Those defenses included three extremely important works in administrative law by James Landis (1938), Walter Gellhorn (1941), and Jerome Frank (1942). All three argued that the rise of agencies with substantial rulemaking and adjudicative authority was a practical necessity and not based on some ideological predisposition to remove power from the people and their elected representatives. Instead, the agencies remedied defects or gaps in the governing structure that the legislature and the President could not accommodate. While these commentators agreed that a more adequate body of administrative law was necessary, they warned against the development of overly rigid rules that would prevent administrators from retaining the discretion necessary to apply their expertise and experience to the problems that administrative agencies had been created to address. Frank, who had served both in administrative posts and as a judge of the U.S. Circuit Court of Appeals for the Second Circuit, rejected the proposition that administrators were somehow suspect or less capable than judges of reaching fair and equitable decisions. Like others of the period, Landis and Gellhorn accepted the need to improve administrative rulemaking procedures, ensure adequate due process safeguards, and make available appropriate judicial review.

The Administrative Procedure Act (APA), adopted in 1946, was the result of the reform efforts, particularly the work of the Attorney General's Committee on Administrative Procedure (5 U.S.C. §553 et seq.). The committee's report is another of the generally forgotten but truly significant documents in the history of adminis-

---

* Kenneth Culp Davis argued that some of the critics were their own worst enemies, failing to obtain some of their reform objectives because they insisted upon an unworkable "extravagant version of the rule of law" (1969, 28).

trative law (U.S. Senate 1941). The act was structured along the lines of the three core problems rulemaking procedures, adjudicative hearings, and judicial review. Also of importance were Federal Register Act provisions ensuring adequate publication of government decisions and other portions of the APA providing protection against interference with the independence of hearing examiners, later called administrative law judges. The APA was not a constitution of administrative law. It was a collection of procedural reforms intended both to provide practical solutions to existing administrative problems and to meet the minimum standards necessary to bolster the legitimacy of the administrative system. It is this legitimacy-enhancing feature of administrative law that has been ignored by practitioners and some judges in the years since. From the enactment of the APA on, however, lawyers viewed administrative law narrowly as administrative procedure. By this point, the legal community had substantially separated itself from the discipline of public administration.

The Decline of Administrative Law

The scholars shaping the field of public administration reciprocated the lawyers' antipathy, rejecting administrative law as insignificant to the discipline. Not long thereafter, political science and public administration faced a schism, some features of which healed, although tensions remained severe. That left administrative law almost exclusively in the hands of lawyers. Their domination of the field had important effects on its development. Moreover, these tensions between legally trained professionals and administrators continued to grow. Manifestations of principles undergirding both professions exacerbated the tensions between administrators and lawyers.

Reading Law Out of the Discipline

Although it was a serious mistake for public administrationists to reject administrative law and lawyers, scholars and practitioners of the emerging discipline did have legitimate grounds for complaint against the legal community. The large numbers of lawyers entering responsible positions in government (bypassing career civil servants, particularly during the New Deal), the lack of concern by lawyers about important management questions, and the constant reminder from courts that administrators' actions were to be limited and reexamined by others not familiar with the substantive policies agencies were called on to administer all contributed to the growing rift between the two groups.

Quite apart from these day-to-day frustrations, there were important and growing scholarly divisions. The progressive reformers of the early twentieth century stressed the removal of patronage politics from administration, while the growing scientific management movement in the private sector contributed the overriding dedication to efficiency as the preeminent goal. Scientific administration advocates insisted that generic principles of management could be applied to all organizations, public or private. The *Papers on the Science of Administration* provided the scripture for public administration as scientific management (Gulick and Urwick 1937). (For a solid history of the field from this point through the 1960s, see Waldo 1968a.) The actual formal declaration of a movement by the discipline away from law and toward management came in the first widely recognized introductory public administration text. Leonard White (1955) wrote that "the study of administration should start from the base of management rather than the foundation of law" (p. xvi).

The scientific management advocates of the 1920s and 1930s were themselves challenged in the 1940s. Simon's criticisms and his own *Administrative Behavior* (1957) gave rise to the administrative science movement in postwar public administration scholarship (Simon 1946, 1957). He charged that the POSDCORB and principles advocates (Gulick and Urwick 1937) had engaged in far too little research and too much armchair philosophizing. Simon argued for a more rigorous inquiry into the behavior of people within agencies and of the organizations themselves. The administrative science movement that emerged from his efforts did not address the significance of law to administration. The other critical approach, symbolized by Waldo's *Administrative State* (1948), produced what came to be known as the public administration and democracy literature. Waldo challenged the scientific management advocates on their efforts to press a strong politics/administration dichotomy and insisted that core concepts such as efficiency could not be seriously addressed apart from their important political implications. Much of the public administration and democracy work that followed from that critique was concerned with the significance of critical political theory concepts central to public administration, not particularly with legal issues or practice (Waldo 1952).

As Simon pressed his public administration as administrative science paradigm, an important methodological discussion emerged that had implications for the status of administrative law (or the lack of it) in the field. The critical issues emerged in a debate between Robert Dahl and Herbert Simon in 1947 in the pages of the *Public Administration Review*. The rise of the behavioral movement in the postwar years meant a commitment to seek scientific status, an effort to increase rigorous research techniques, and a move toward an empirical emphasis in social sciences. Simon and Dahl had no quarrel over the latter two requirements, but they differed on whether, given its nature, public administration could aspire to the status of a scientific discipline. Dahl's "The Science of Administration: Three Problems" (1947) argued that public administration could not achieve that status because of its purpose and its research focus. It was about practice and not theory, concerned with normative questions about policy and its administration. Simon answered that it was indeed possible to "create a pure science of human behavior in organizations—and, in particular, governmental organizations—who are dissatisfied with the traditional, formalistic, and legalistic administrative theory, and who propose to raise a more solid theory on the foundation of social psychology" (Simon 1947, 202). If Simon's model were to dominate and support a science of administration, there seemed little place for public law.

Even within the public law subfield of political science, key methodological issues shaped the developing patterns of scholarship such that administrative law would not find a home there either. Three forces were at work in the area. (On the development of public law as a subfield of political science, see Baum 1983; Murphy and Tanenhaus 1972; C. Herman Pritchett 1968.) First, scholars of public law in the 1950s and later felt the need to establish the legitimacy of their own claim to academic status. That meant, on the one hand, an effort to differentiate the goals of political science public law scholars from those pursued by lawyers and, on the other, a desire to present evidence of sufficient rigor, defined in the terms of postwar behavioral tenets. The first issue was no real problem, since lawyers tended to take a somewhat narrower instrumental approach to law and because political science scholars were interested in the politics of the judicial process, a subject rarely addressed in polite company by attorneys.

The second concern was more complex. At a minimum, the commands for political science *qua* science required that research should be explanatory and predictive and not normative or principally descriptive. Moreover, the subject to be studied was behavior, not the substance of rules and the institutions that generated them. The study of the substance of law or normative discussions of appropriate directions in legal development that had for so long dominated political science was fast on the wane.

The third element in the changing approach to the field involved the jurisprudential base for much public law scholarship. The neorealist school of legal philosophy, which was very important during the 1930s, seriously challenged the claim that the substance of law was of primary importance. Legal decisions were neither unerring discoveries by judges of absolute principles of law nor conclusions based solely on logic and clear evidence. They were decisions made by people in politically powerful positions. To understand the decisions, one must understand the people who made them and the processes within which they were developed.

Jack W. Peltason, one of the leading scholars of the period, summarized the trend in public law research: "The concern is with process rather than product. The orientation is Bentleyan, behavioristic, actional and nonmotivational" (Peltason 1958, 1). Even the term *public law* was abandoned by many, in favor of judicial process and behavior. Administrative law simply did not fit the literature of the field as it was then developing. (There were a few rare exceptions such as Martin Shapiro's *The Supreme Court and Administrative Agencies* 1968.)

The Problem of Lawyer Domination

With both public administration and political science rejecting administrative law, the subject was left to the lawyers. That produced several significant consequences, not only for what was studied but also for how it was examined. Within the legal community, the study of administrative law largely became the examination of the Administrative Procedure Act (APA) and the various judicial opinions interpreting it. Kenneth Culp Davis, a staff member during the Attorney General's Committee on Administrative Procedure study, produced the first administrative law treatise in 1951. It was in large part a commentary on the APA. He expanded that work over the years, producing the better-known multivolume edition of the treatise in 1958.

Although lawyers disagreed about the precise nature of the field, there was general agreement that it should be defined in narrow terms, an approach that excluded issues of importance to administrators. Whereas earlier scholars such as Wilson and Goodnow had urged a broad definition, distinguished law professors called for a narrower conception. Bernard Schwartz's (1976) efforts at definition typify the lawyers' approach. After noting that the broad definitions had included "not only administrative powers, their exercise, and remedies but also such subjects as the various forms of administrative agencies; the exercise of and limitations upon regulatory power; the law of the civil service; the acquisition and management of governmental property; public works; and administrative obligations" (p. 2), Schwartz declared:

> To the American lawyer, these are matters for public administration, not administrative law; they are primarily the concern of the political scientist. In this country, administrative law is not regarded as the law relating to public administration, the way commercial law is the law relating to commerce, or land law the law relating to land. (1976, 2)

In particular, the narrow definition was limited to procedures appropriate for setting limits on agency action that affected someone outside of government, the external versus internal dichotomy. Such an approach excluded intergovernmental conflicts and a host of other intragovernmental problems. The narrow interpretation rejected the substantive actions by agencies and considered only procedure, which prompted Martin Shapiro (1968) to conclude that many of the most important problems were left in "some sort of nonlegal limbo" (p. 106). The narrow approach was limited to situations where the actions of agencies could be classified as quasi-legislative or quasi-judicial. Unfortunately, any number of problems in administration do not fit neatly into either category. (See, e.g., *United States* v. *Florida East Coast Railroad,* 1973; *United States* v. *Allegheny-Ludlum Steel Corp.,* 1972; and *Citizens to Preserve Overton Park* v. *Volpe,* 1971.) Moreover, lawyers tended to react to important controversies as though they were merely two-party adversary proceedings, ignoring the importance of interest-group litigation and questions concerning the public interest quite apart from the particular parties in a case. Little attention was devoted to the management significance of administrative law issues. Finally, the work done by lawyers was generally published in law reviews rather than journals that scholars and practitioners of administration were likely to read.

The Administrator/Lawyer Tension: The Problem of Administrative Discretion

There was another dimension to conflict between lawyers, judges, and public administrators, a tension between the values and premises underlying their approaches to administrative law questions. From White's early public administration text on, a set of administrative imperatives emerged, including efficiency, expertise, and flexibility. Legally trained professionals, in contrast, have tended to emphasize due process, equal protection, and substantial justice. Given their premises, public administrationists have often seen law as a constraint on their managerial flexibility, inhibiting their ability to utilize their expertise to accomplish agency goals in an efficient manner. That proposition, however, mistakenly assumes an absolute positive correlation between administrative discretion and efficiency. (I have treated this issue at greater length in Cooper 1983, 217–29.) Such a management-against-law notion ignores the important role played by administrative law in providing support for the legitimacy of public administration, as well as the more instrumental advantages to be gained by developing some administrative law instruments like rulemaking and due process as tools for effective management.

As fewer public administration scholars and practitioners were exposed to administrative law courses and materials in professional training, the level of misunderstanding and distance between legal professionals and administrationists grew. For some, the fear of lawsuits became very nearly a paralyzing anxiety. Each piece of litigation, whether successful or not, seemingly prompted institutional changes aimed at preventing legal action. The assumption seemed to be that the interactions between courts and agencies were unnatural and that litigation was not a normal part of the policy process.

Some lawyers and judges did little to help matters, taking a win-at-any-cost notion and failing to provide administrators with useful guidance on how to integrate important legal considerations with managerial techniques (Davis 1969, 160). The law-against-administration tendency can be traced at least as far back as John Dickinson. Just as unbridled discretion is no guarantee of maximum efficiency, so extreme restrictions on discretion cannot guarantee fair and just administrative decisions. One can hardly be fair to a person with an administrative problem if one lacks the ability to make exceptions where warranted (Wright 1972, 576). Nevertheless, this general orientation has predisposed some judges and lawyers to be suspicious of administrative actions purportedly justified on grounds of efficiency, flexibility, and expertise. For others, the complexity of administrative problems has made it difficult to establish and maintain an appropriate judicial role. The question of how much deference is due experienced and expert administrators in cases where judges are responsible for ensuring that agencies act within their proper range of authority, obey APA procedural strictures, and do not act arbitrarily or capriciously is constantly in need of new responses.

In sum, by the late 1960s the problems of disunion between law and administration had manifested themselves in several respects. The approach taken to the field, with rare exception, was the lawyers' approach, which tended to be narrow and procedural. Few universities taught the subject as a required part of their public administration programs, and when it was taught, it was generally left to the lawyers and not those who were principally trained and produced scholarship in public law and public administration. The literature of public administration virtually ignored the subject. Graziano and Rehfuss (1974) found in a study of *Public Administration Review* articles from 1949 to 1969 that administrative law accounted for 1 percent of the articles and that administrative responsibility, a category that includes some law related material, represented another 4 percent (p. 269). Fortunately, things were about to change.

Resurgence

John Rohr (1986) has recently distinguished between public administration foundings in fact and foundings in word or theory. His use of founding is drawn from writings in political theory that stress the importance of the creation of governments and the premises upon which they are established for their operation and consequences. He argues that the events are important, but so are the writings that provide the intellectual support for the actions. Those intellectual foundings may precede, be coterminous with, or postdate the founding in fact. Similarly, administrative law has experienced a resurgence in public administration both in fact and in word during the 1970s and 1980s. The scholarship that has emerged clusters in several specific areas. It is useful to consider briefly each of these factors in the reinvigoration of law in the field, since they have shaped both what we have addressed in, and omitted from, recent literature.

Reemergence in Fact

Several forces that were developing during the 1950s and 1960s gave rise to renewed attention to administrative law. First, there was a growing recognition of the need for reform. Those who believed that passage of the APA resolved the complexities of administrative law had been shown to be mistaken by decades of practice. Many agencies were slow to implement the act, and then did only what was absolutely necessary to accommodate its strictures. Inadequate attention was given to integrating the concepts behind the law into agency decision making. The first Hoover Commission observed: "Administrative justice today unfortunately is not characterized by economy, simplicity, and dispatch" (Commission on Organization 1949, 436).

The Task Force on Legal Services and Procedure of the second Hoover Commission (1955) issued an extensive critique, finding that the APA had not been implemented in some areas, due process protections such as adequate notice and prompt opportunity for a hearing were frequently not available in adjudicatory decisions, and agencies were refusing to make rules stating their guidelines but were announcing policy through adjudication (even though they were not bound by the rule of *stare decisis* that made common-law development possible in the judicial setting). The task force admonished agencies to issue their policies and standards as rules through the process set forth in the APA, not only to clarify the policy, allowing for better implementation and eliciting increased compliance, but also to remove the impression that agencies were making up the rules as they went along. It called for voluntary action by administrators, but also insisted on more and better judicial review to ensure agency action.

James Landis, the former defender of the administrative state, reported to President-elect John F. Kennedy that administrative justice was characterized by neither efficiency nor fundamental fairness (U.S. Senate 1960). Judge Henry J. Friendly issued his influential *The Federal Administrative Agencies: The Need for a Better Definition of Standards* (1962), calling, as had other reformers before him, for more rulemaking and less ad hoc policy development by all agencies. Following a similar general trend, Kenneth Culp Davis issued his *Discretionary Justice* (1969), urging that the only way to preserve essential administrative discretion and simultaneously protect the values of fairness and equality was for administrators to structure their own discretion through voluntary rulemaking. If they were not prepared to act on their own initiative, then judges ought to compel them to do so. Peter Woll (1963) warned that adjudicatory processes had become so costly and difficult that people affected by such rulings were more or less forced to resolve their cases by informal and sometimes inadequate procedures whether they really wanted to or not (p. 61). There was little disagreement among those contemplating the subject that administrative law required serious attention if it was to accomplish even the instrumental purposes it was expected to serve.

In addition to specific calls for reform, administrative law was also changing in character because of growing challenges of scope and scale. The postwar period brought increasing demands for service delivery across a wide range of fields from housing to job programs. The administrative world of 1970 was very different from that of 1946. There were more programs affecting more people in more serious ways than before. The pure size of government was an issue. The contemporary administrative environment concerned more social service issues than mainline regulatory problems involving the classic independent regulatory commissions. At the same time that challenges to the administrative state were developing, there were more demands for all levels of government to respond to such problems as civil rights enforcement, education for handicapped children, occupational safety and health, automobile safety, the energy crisis, air and water pollution, nuclear power regulation, consumer protection, and toxic chemical disposal. These programs were often intergovernmentally complex, with options accorded to states and localities to participate in the development of standards and administration along with the federal agencies created to take primary responsibility for the new policies.

There was not merely a multiplicity of new laws but a change in the nature of statutes. Earlier criticisms of broad delegations of authority to agencies with little more than an admonition by Congress to carry out the public interest were answered with more specific statutes. The contemporary statutes still delegated responsibility for the resolution of major problems and afforded substantial amounts of discretionary authority, but there were frequently more detailed substantive and procedural requirements than before, including mandatory announcement of regulations by expanded techniques known as hybrid rulemaking, increased citizen participation obligations, and more specific due process rules where agencies adjudicated disputes. Toward the mid-1970s, the new statutes increasingly included legislative veto provisions permitting legislative review of agency rulemaking. (Congress continued to place legislative veto provisions in new statutes even after the Supreme Court and lower courts had found them unconstitutional. See *Consumer Energy Council* v. *Federal Energy Regulatory Commission* 1982; *INS* v. *Chadha* 1983.) Another more or less standard feature of recent statutes is the sunset provision requiring reauthorization of programs or agency authority, usually in five to seven years from original enactment.

Along with these additions to substantive statutes, Congress also responded to challenges to administrative law with a variety of amendments to the APA and other independent but comprehensive mandates. The section of the APA that had consisted of Federal Register Act requirements for publication of policy by the White House and agencies was transformed into a far more complex fair-information practices section with the adoption and expansion of the Freedom of Information Act [P.L. 89-554, 80 Stat. 378, as amended, 5 U.S.C. §552 (1976)], the passage of the Right to Privacy Act [P.L. 93-579, 88 Stat. 1896, 5 U.S.C. §552a (1976)], the Government in the Sunshine Act [P.L. 94-409, 90 Stat. 1241, 5 U.S.C. §552b (1976)], and the Federal Advisory Committee Act [P.L. 92-463, 86 Stat. 770, 5 U.S.C. App. 2 (1976)]. The Paperwork Reduction Act [P.L. 96-511, 94 Stat. 2812, 20 U.S.C. §§1221–3, 44 U.S.C. §§2904, 2905, 3501 et seq. (1982)] required assessment of the burdens in sheer documentation needed to support agency pronouncements. The Regulatory Flexibility Act [P.L. 96-354, 94 Stat. 1164, 5 U.S.C. §601 et seq. (1982)] obligated agencies to perform hybrid rulemaking and make impact assessments where rules would have substantial effects on small business, small units of government, and not-for-profit organizations.

The calls for improvements in agency rulemaking and demands for less deference and more effective judicial review of agency policy making produced important changes during the 1970s. Specifically, courts insisted on a meaningful application of APA notice and participation requirements in rulemaking and demanded preparation of rulemaking records adequate to permit full judicial review and congressional oversight (see *Environmental Defense Fund* v. *Ruckelshaus* 1971; *Natural Resources Defense Council* v. *Nuclear Regulatory Commission* 1976. See also Fuchs 1977; Williams 1975.) This judicially mandated hybrid process—so named because it was more complex than simple notice and comment procedures and less structured than formal procedures requiring formal adjudicative-type hearings—met with stern admonitions from the Supreme Court to avoid judicial Monday morning quarterbacking (*Vermont Yankee Nuclear Power Corp.* v. *Natural Resources Defense Council* 1978). By the late 1970s, however, Presidents had begun to require hybrid rulemaking by executive order (Executive Order 12044, 1978). President Reagan took things well beyond Carter's requirements, delegating major authority to the Office of Management and Budget to play a central role in executive branch rulemaking (Executive Order 12291, 1981; Executive Order 12498, 1985). Congressional statutes creating or reauthorizing independent regulatory agency authority imposed hybrid rulemaking requirements where the President had no authority to do so. The same executive and legislative initiatives also required regulatory analyses calling for impact assessment and cost-benefit calculations of proposed agency rules.

The other factors that gave renewed impetus to administrative law were the growing significance of constitutional issues and the increase in tort actions against officials and units of government. Because of the problems in agency adjudications encountered in the postwar period and given the expanding scope, scale, and significance of administrative activities, there were pressures for enhanced due process protections. While the Warren Court majority was ideologically sympathetic to such demands, it is clear that the so-called due process revolution was not simply an ideological crusade by liberal judges. (For a detailed discussion see Cooper 1983, chapter 6.) In addition to civil rights and civil liberties questions, the courts were facing interesting and complex constitutional issues involving legislative-executive relations, such as those presented by the legislative veto cases.

Another development of the early 1970s was a series of Supreme Court rulings affording greater opportunity for suits for money damages against individual officers, their superiors, and local government units for violation of constitutional and statutory rights. Most of those suits against state and local officials were brought under 42 U.S.C. §1983, the Civil Rights Act of 1871. On the other hand, the Court fashioned relatively broad immunities against such suits. The Supreme Court also concluded that local government units, as municipal corporations, were subject to liability under the 1871 act and did not enjoy immunity from liability (*Monell* v. *Department of Social Services* 1978; *Owen* v. *City of Independence* 1980). Though the Supreme Court action has been seen as a dramatic expansion of opportunities to sue local government, the fact is that most suits were brought under state law, and all but a few of the states relaxed immunity statutes during the same period. The Court also held, however, that suits could be brought against some federal officials directly as constitutional torts (*Bivens* v. *Six Unknown Named Agents of Federal Bureau of Narcotics* 1971). Suddenly, administrators who had ignored legal issues for years developed a driving interest in the subject.

By the time scholars and practitioners began to give renewed attention to public law issues in public administration, things were beginning to change. Some public administrationists felt as though they were under siege, with courts seemingly attacking them from all sides in an ever-expanding intervention in the administrative process. While the perception had some grains of truth in it, the situation was not nearly that bleak. One reason why so many administrators responded this way was their lack of information and training in the field, ranging from a gap in substantive knowledge of administrative law to an inability to use the most basic legal reference sources. Another was that there was so much change in such a brief period that it was impossible to keep pace with the demands of developments in the legislature, the chief executive's office, and the courts. Yet another factor was the increasing political and popular rhetoric against the administrative state, particularly in the post-Watergate period.

In truth, many judges, including a majority of the Supreme Court, were moving to limit what was perceived as excessive intrusion into the administrator's domain. During the last half of the 1970s and into the 1980s, the Supreme Court issued rulings limiting standing to sue, warning against judicially imposed procedural requirements for rulemaking not mandated by statute, admonishing judges to consider costs and administrative burdens in determining the nature and quantity of process due someone with a decision before an agency, insisting on deference to management considerations in personnel issues, charging federal courts to limit the use of injunctions to intervene in administrative practices, and expanding the immunities available against tort suits. (These developments are summarized in Cooper 1985.) In fact, one could argue that the Court has gone further than it should have in the direction of deference, if we recall that the purpose of administrative law is not merely an instrumental effort to provide minimum standards of administrative responsibility. It also plays an intrinsic role in assisting in the legitimation of administrative power within the American constitutional system.

Reemergence in Scholarship

The renewed interest in administrative law developed among scholars in the 1970s and has increased since then, although it has a long way to grow before the treatment of the subject in the literature can be said to reflect its true importance in public administration.

The promise of more interesting and fruitful scholarship first emerged in the work of lawyers and a few political scientists. (The political scientists included Shapiro 1968; Woll 1963; Lorch 1969). Kenneth Culp Davis's highly regarded *Discretionary Justice* (1969) was the culmination of a running debate Davis had waged with Raoul Berger during the 1960s over the problems of judicial review and administrative discretion. (See Berger 1965, 1966a, 1966b, 1967, 1969; Davis 1965, 1966a, 1966b, 1967). Davis's volume in turn brought Louis Jaffe (1969) and J. Skelly Wright (1972) into the discussion, creating a body of work that still reflected a relatively narrow conception of administrative law but suggested that developing problems and issues of the field would require a wider approach. Other authors responded with attempts at broader conceptualizations and proposals for change. Richard Stewart (1975), and Glenn Robinson, Ernest Gellhorn, and Harold Bruff (1980) were leading examples. The Administrative Conference of the United States began to support and encourage research, though by relatively few people and on a limited scale. By the late 1970s, law school texts began to reflect a concern with a wider range of law and administration issues (see Gellhorn, Byse, and Strauss 1979; Robinson, Gellhorn, and Bruff 1980).

Within the public administration community there was a growing awareness that a number of scholars around the country intended to reassert the importance of law in the discipline. ASPA programs in the late 1970s and after featured at least some panels on broadly defined law and administration. Regional ASPA programs followed suit. A general network of those active in the field developed around the *Public Law and Public Administration* newsletter. Also during the 1970s, scholars and practitioners called on departments of public administration to reintegrate courses on law for administrators into their curriculum. That effort has met with varying degrees of success, producing courses often entitled administrative law, the legal environment of public administration, public law and public administration, constitutional principles for public administrators, and the like. A host of texts followed, with several issued within months of one another (for a review of the batch of texts, see Dolan 1984).

Despite the fact that there was progress, the literature of public administration still provided relatively few articles in the subfield. Where Graziano and Rehfuss (1974) found that 1 percent of *Public Administration Review* articles (a total of ten) between 1945 and 1969 were administrative law pieces, Bowman and Hajjar (1978) determined that 1.7 percent (or seven administrative law manuscripts) were published in that journal between 1970 and 1976 (p. 160). Overall, the Bowman and

Hajjar study calculated that 2.4 percent of the articles published in seven public administration journals during the 1970–76 period were administrative law pieces. *Administration & Society* and the *Midwest Review of Public Administration* had none, while *Administrative Science Quarterly* had only three and the *Bureaucrat* but one. The editors of *Administration & Society* were so concerned about this lacuna that in their May 1981 issue they announced a call for law-related manuscripts (Editorial Note 1981, 3). Since then, *Administration & Society* has produced a half dozen pieces in the general field of law and administration. The *Public Administration Review* has published more law-related manuscripts since 1976 than it had in its entire prior history. Even so, that amounted to fewer than twenty-five in nearly a decade. The trend has clearly been in the right direction and has been further supported by the activities surrounding the bicentennial of the Constitution. Moreover, the *Public Administration Review* published an entire special issue on "Law and Public Affairs" (Wise and O'Brien 1985). The *Public Administration Quarterly* also ran a symposium on administrative law in 1982 (Cooper 1982a).

The Focal Points of Renewed Attention
In part because relatively few scholars have been at work in the law and administration area and because of difficulties in finding outlets for publication, much of the work that has been done during the past fifteen years clusters around particular concepts, issues, or themes. They include problems of legitimacy, issues of responsibility, development of instruments of governance, issues of rights against government, the counterpoint of individual rights versus majoritarian policy making, and a category that might be called actors, institutions, and policies. The summary that follows deliberately focuses on material published in public administration journals and books rather than in law reviews.

Issues of power, authority, and legitimacy have received renewed attention. Concern with constitutional topics and wider questions of the legitimacy of administrative power has been long overdue. These issues were very much a part of the literature of administrative law in the early days of the field. The discussion of the compatibility of important authority to determine legal rights and status with a constitution of limited and divided powers, however, was and is incomplete. We do not have an adequate constitutional theory of the administrative state. The Administrative Procedure Act compromise of regular policy making by orderly promulgation of rules, minimal due process protection in adjudications, and the availability of judicial review is an important element in the argument for the legitimacy of administrative power, but it is not a constitution of administrative law.

The post-Watergate efforts by Congress to recapture power it had seemingly lost to the executive branch was one impetus for the reinvigoration of debate over these issues. Analyses of the legislative veto by Robert Gilmour (1982) and Barbara Hinkson Craig (1983) provide examples of attempts to understand this tension (see

Gilmour and Craig 1984). The discussion of interbranch relations is not solely about conflicts, however, but also concerns formal and informal means by which power-sharing arrangements have been developed. Louis Fisher (1981, 1985) has produced several major works attempting to explain this "politics of shared power" (see also Rosenbloom 1983). The Gilmour and Craig pieces contributed here as well. Another factor was the importance of litigation raising constitutional rights and liberties issues (see Rosenbloom 1971; Cooper 1982b, 1983). The attack on the bureaucracy of the late 1970s that continues to date was yet a third and very significant influence.

John Rohr has played a particularly important role in this constitutional defense of public administration. Rohr and his colleagues at Virginia Polytechnic Institute (VPI) prepared a paper known informally as the "Blacksburg Manifesto," arguing for the legitimacy of the administrative state on both constitutional and competency grounds (Goodsell, Rohr, Wamsley, White, and Wolff 1983). The Blacksburg document has prompted widespread discussion of constitutional issues at regional and national ASPA meetings since it was originally read in 1983. More recently, Rohr (1986) has produced a volume entitled *To Run a Constitution,* taking a substantial next step toward a constitutional theory of administrative authority, arguing that the framing of the Constitution contemplated, indeed required, an energetic public administration.

Another of Rohr's works, *Ethics for Bureaucrats* (1978), has played an important role in the cluster of work that has emerged in the general area of administrative responsibility. Although the responsibility literature has traditionally distinguished between external and internal mechanisms of responsibility, Rohr's work attempts to connect both approaches by grounding administrative ethics in regime rules that he finds explicit or implicit in the Constitution.

Others have added to the body of work on external checks, including the literature on the legislative veto and Office of Management and Budget (OMB) review of agency rulemaking (see Ball 1984; Gilmour 1983). Traditional judicial mechanisms of ensuring administrative responsibility have included judicial review, injunctive orders requiring remedies for maladministration, and criminal liability. Judicial review was the staple of the subfield from the 1930s on. Indeed, if there was a core of the administrative law literature during the 1960s, it was the scope of judicial review of agency decisions. Those commentaries continued into the 1970s in response to the development of hybrid rulemaking. The issues that have arisen surrounding the use of remedial decrees in a variety of policy areas have become sufficiently important to constitute a new branch of the law and administration literature, about which more is said below. The matter of criminal liability for malfeasance has not been a popular subject for public law scholars, perhaps because it is fortunately an infrequent phenomenon. Issues of tort judgments seeking to recompense individual victims for abuses of rights by administrators have, however, been quite important.

Indeed, a collection of work has been published on issues of rights against government concerning disputes brought by government employees and cases prosecuted by private citizens against individual officers and government units. This second class of suits has spawned much of the literature on sovereign and official immunity. These works range from the history and origins of the concepts to analyses of Supreme Court rulings of the past decade to calls for changes in the money-damages approach to maladministration (Cooper 1984b; Groszych and Madden 1981; Grumet 1982; Rosenbloom 1980; Wise 1985). The work done on litigation of rights claims by employees, exemplified by Rosenbloom's *Federal Service and the Constitution* (1971), in contrast, focuses less on remedies than on substantive issues regarding due process in adverse personnel actions, First Amendment claims of freedom of speech, Hatch Act disputes, patronage challenges, and charges of interference with freedom of association (see also Hayford 1985; Martin 1973; Masters and Breiman 1985; Meier 1981). It is unclear what the future of this body of work will be given the Supreme Court's efforts in recent years to draw back from what had been a trend toward increased public employee procedural and substantive rights, coupled with a general decline in the influence of public sector labor unions.

One of the more interesting areas of scholarship during the resurgence of public law in public administration has centered on the counterpoint of individual rights and majoritarian policy. This conflict has manifested itself in debates over court-ordered remedies in school desegregation, prison conditions, right to treatment in mental hospitals, housing desegregation, and police abuse cases. These issues present situations in which individuals and groups demand that the courts force government to act where the political majority would rather not respond. This literature falls into three general categories. First, and most common, is the normative work challenging judicially ordered remedies on grounds that they involve the courts in situations beyond their institutional competence or place judges in inappropriate roles (Cramton 1976; Horowitz 1977). Second, is a body of analytic work that attempts to understand the interactions of judges and administrators in such settings (Cooper 1988; Gilmour 1982; Yarbrough 1981, 1985). The third set, which overlaps with the second in several respects, concerns the impact of judicial orders on administrative agencies (Harriman and Straussman 1983; Johnson 1979). The analytic literature has been far more useful than the normative, though even this material tends to view the judicial/ administrative relationship almost exclusively from the administrator's viewpoint rather than attempt to determine the problems facing the judge in such cases.

A small but extremely interesting body of material on the budgetary implications of judicial involvement in administration has emerged. The work of George Hale (1979) and Linda Harriman and Jeffrey Straussman (1983) has been particularly useful. The literature of law and administration has often suffered from a lack of law and management balance. The critical fiscal issues have received the least attention of any of the important administrative questions that arise in cases involving remedial decrees.

Woodrow Wilson urged the study of the process of administration in a period when most political scientists studied structural and institutional issues in constitutional law. We have moved to the other extreme. The narrow procedural approach to administrative law has meant very little attention to the key actors, institutions, and policies involved in administrative law disputes. There has been some reinvigoration of institutional interest. Louis Fisher's work on congressional-executive relations played an important role in keeping institutional questions before the field (1981, 1985). Several specific substantive issues have drawn attention, although it has been sporadic and ad hoc. Affirmative action, information policy (including both privacy and freedom of information questions), and the Ethics in Government Act are examples (See Nigro 1974. This symposium is human resources rather than public law oriented. See also Relyea 1979; Walter 1981.) The Social Security Administration, particularly the disability program, has provided grist for studies of law and policy and for consideration of a key actor, the administrative law judge (Cofer 1986; Marquardt and Wheat 1978; Mashaw 1983; Mashaw, Goetz, Goodman, Schwartz, Verkuil, and Carrow 1978). There has been a body of material developing within political science on the role of lawyers as actors in the political process. There is also some work in this area in public administration literature, but not much (Plumber 1981; Wollan 1978).

Finally, recent publications feature a number of pieces on instruments of governance. The Administrative Procedure Act, and the narrow approach to administrative law predicated on it, assumes three basic instruments of administration: rules, orders, and licenses. But the growth and changes in administration since 1946 have meant that the tools of government are and must be more complex and varied. For example, a literature has emerged focusing on new developments in rulemaking, particularly presidential and congressional devices for rulemaking review and requirements for regulatory analyses and judgments about their impact (Ball 1984; Craig 1983; Gilmour 1982; Gilmour and Craig 1984; Kent 1982; Schmandt 1985; Viscusi 1985). Moreover, other instruments of importance have been addressed by those interested in law and administration, including contracts (Cooper 1980; Florestano and Gordon 1980; Hunt 1984, 1985), government corporations (Moe 1979), sunset provisions (Adams and Sherman 1978), the ombudsman (Danet 1978; Dimock 1983), and executive orders (Cooper 1986). Even so, we have generally given far more attention to the processes of administration than to the instruments or tools we actually use to promulgate and implement policy.

The Future

Although the resurgence of law in public administration has produced a variety of interesting approaches to the relationship of law, management, and politics, much remains to be done. There are several particularly significant shortcomings in the literature today and a number of important questions that should be addressed in the future. Both the problems and the opportunities can be conceptualized as macro-level, mid-range, and micro-level issues.

Some Problems Before Us

A central macro-level problem in our existing literature is the relative lack of material on the constitutional nature and foundation of public administration, as well as the role of law in administrative theory. These are broad issues, not questions of specific assertions of constitutional rights and limits, but problems of the legitimacy of administrative power and its role in the constitutional scheme. Rohr's work (1986) has taken us a good deal further than we were a decade ago, but other contributions are needed as well. In order to make progress in this area, we must rediscover some of the classic literature of the field, ranging from founding documents to the pre-New Deal works of Goodnow (1905), Freund (1928), and Dickinson (1927) to the pre-APA defenses by Landis (1938), Gellhorn (1941), and Frank (1942). A comprehension of this material is certainly not sufficient, but is at least a necessary condition for further efforts toward a constitutional theory of the administration state. Consideration of the separation of powers is clearly an important feature in that discussion, but, as the critics of the legal literature of the 1920s and 1930s observed, that is but one element of the essential inquiry. Similarly, treatments of administrative procedure often do not comprehend the role the APA and comparable state statutes play in legitimation or their relationship to constitutional issues of administrative law. Rulemaking and adjudication requirements respond both to issues of responsibility and to legitimacy.

Related to this broad problem is the relative absence of discussions of the rule of law in American public administration. The phrase "a government of laws and not men" is not a mere platitude. It has a long philosophical and jurisprudential history. Neither that phrase nor "the rule of law" is mentioned in the Constitution. In the current period of attacks on administrative rulemaking, it is all the more important to confront such fundamental questions if we are to deal with issues of administrative authority. Finally, Wilson, Goodnow, and Freund were particularly concerned with the theoretical as well as the practical question of the relationship of law, policy, and management. This important but complex relationship is not adequately addressed in contemporary literature.

An examination of administrative law material during the recent reemergence of the subfield suggests two mid-level weaknesses. The first is a tendency toward an adversary characterization of the relationship between law and administration.

There is a strong sense of hostility about law and courts with such references as "intervention" and "the imperial judiciary" common to the genre. The suggestion is that law and courts play no legitimate role in administration but are somehow recently engrafted burdens on the already heavy baggage to be carried by administrators. That hostility is counterproductive. Law is an essential and normal part of policy making. As Wilson and his contemporaries insisted, public administration is a law-based endeavor. The fact that it is also management grounded does not eliminate its legal character. Instead of the position that public administration should begin from the basis of law and not management, White (1955) should have contended that both management and law are essential. Indeed, prefaces to later editions of his public administration text indicate that he had second thoughts about his initial declaration (see White 1955, viii–ix). In order to ameliorate some of the hostility, it is important for work on law and administration to explain and synthesize the actions of courts and judges as well as to criticize them. In particular, we need more work that seeks to understand the differing problems facing judges and administrators in any given policy area. That undertaking will require that we deal with judges at all levels, not merely the U.S. Supreme Court.

Another problem is the lack of diversity in methodologies. While traditional case-law analysis is central to administrative law research, our literature should be more eclectic than it has been to date. We need empirical work as well as opinion analysis and philosophical inquiry. It is interesting, but perhaps not comforting, to observe that the only recent symposium on empirical methods in administrative law appeared not in a public administration journal but in the *Administrative Law Review*. There is progress in this area, but more diversity is needed.

At the micro level, a number of specific areas are in need of more attention. The literature does not address the full range of features in the relationships between judges and administrators. Treatments limited to standard judicial review of agency rulemaking and adjudication, proceeding from the requirements of the Administrative Procedure Act, are inadequate to comprehend the full dimensions of the judges' situation and the nature of their interactions with administrators. Another gap in our scholarship is a lack of attention to agency adjudication. Most of what has been written concerns the Social Security disability program or broad issues of constitutional due process. A substantial portion of the material published on administrative law judges in agency adjudications is directed to the disability program as well (see, e.g., Cofer 1985; Mashaw 1983; Mashaw et al. 1978). Although there are many times more adjudicative decisions made than rules promulgated, the literature focuses primarily on rulemaking. More generally, while the study of administrative procedure is extremely important, it is insufficient for a full picture of law and administration. And although substantive policy issues are coming to play a more substantial role in the literature, a lack of attention to institutions remains. Thus, for example, there is very little in the literature concerning the role of the Department of

Justice and state attorneys general. Another need is for more attention to administrative law in the states. To be of greatest value, of course, studies on administrative law in particular states should be prepared in ways that will be useful to scholars and practitioners in other states. Finally, although contributions have been made in the area of judicial administration in public administration journals (see Cannon 1973; Fetter and Stott 1980; Flango 1975), much more needs to be done.

Important Issues for Tomorrow

An examination of these gaps in our present literature, supplemented by a concern with breaking issues in the field, suggests several areas that require attention in the future. At the macro level, these include further scholarship on the constitutional legitimacy of administration, attention to the overlap of law and ethics, explorations of administrative jurisprudence, and studies aimed at a better understanding of the relationship of procedure and substance.

One important mid-range topic worthy of further effort is consideration of law and administration in an environment of scientific and technological complexity. The questions in need of study concern the problems posed for legal decision makers who must face cases emerging from the public bureaucracy that present difficult issues in which members of the scientific community disagree about key issues or those in which technical and political rationality are in conflict. Another significant field of inquiry centers on the relationship of formal and alternative dispute resolution techniques. Federal and state courts around the nation are experimenting with alternative dispute resolution, yet, apart from work on ombudsmen, the public administration literature has given little or no attention to the subject.

Whatever the subject matter that we select for study, we need to avoid the problem that has plagued public law scholarship within political science. For more than two decades, there has been a gulf between judicial process and behavior scholars and students of traditional public law and law and policy. What we need is both continuing attention to case law and more general studies using other methodologies that address all levels of courts.

Other needs include better understanding of the role of judicial and legal impact upon administrative strategies and tactics. The concern here is not so much with compliance, although further efforts are needed there as well, but with forward-looking opportunistic surveillance and for developing tactics to meet the challenge of problemistic search. Public administrationists continue to be surprised by legal developments that should have been anticipated. Given their predictability, the likely outcomes should have been contemplated in the planning and conduct of administrative activities. For example, great surprise was expressed when the U.S. Supreme Court struck down the limitations on federally mandated labor standards at the local government level in *Garcia* v. *San Antonio Mass Transit Authority* (1985). One need not have been a sophisticated legal analyst to have recognized that the probability was extremely high of a reversal of the *National League of Cities* v. *Usery* (1976) case that had established the limits on federal regulation in the first place. Similarly, in many cases involving prison or mental health conditions, administrators knew, or should have known, of the likelihood that they would lose a suit. Yet there is little in the literature that suggests how such knowledge should be used. In particular, we need more attention than we have had to date to the relationship of legal activity to budgeting.

Our literature should invite better understanding of the interaction of actors, institutions, and policies in addition to our concern with process. It should reflect a greater appreciation of the uses of instruments of governance and of the relationship of statute to management and law. We need to pay attention to the significance of administrative law for organization theory. Finally, we have concentrated in the past on administrative excesses, the arrogation of power, but there are increasingly important questions concerning the failure to exercise authority that agencies do possess that merit scholarly consideration.

Conclusions

Administrative law has experienced a dramatic transition in the years since public administration first developed. That history explains much of why our literature contains both its present strengths and weaknesses. Law has moved from the core of the public administration to virtual rejection by the field. It has come back again to a more significant role after direct pressure by the legal environment made it impossible for administrators to ignore the subject any longer, and because it became increasingly clear that public law concepts are central to fundamental public administration problems ranging from legitimacy to responsibility to the nature and limits of administrative discretion. The public administration literature has not yet come to reflect fully that importance, although there is a significant trend in the right direction.

The literature that has emerged during the resurgence of the field addresses a variety of important and interesting concepts. Yet significant gaps remain to beckon future scholars, not merely at the traditional levels of administrative law analysis but across the range of problems presented by the study of administration. The trend in the direction of reinvigoration and an expanded scope of administrative law within public administration is a wholly fitting tribute to the centennial of the discipline.

References

Adams, Bruce, and Betsy Sherman. 1978. "Sunset Implementation: A Positive Partnership to Make Government Work." *Public Administration Review* 38:78–81.

Appleby, Paul. 1949. *Policy and Administration.* University, Ala.: University of Alabama Press.

Ball, Howard. 1984. *Controlling Regulatory Sprawl.* Westport, Conn.: Greenwood Press.

Baum, Lawrence. 1983. "Judicial Politics: Still a Distinctive Field." In *Political Science: The State of the Discipline,* edited by Ada W. Finifter. Washington, D.C.: American Political Science Association.

Berger, Raoul. 1965. "Administrative Arbitrariness and Judicial Review." *Columbia Law Review* 65:55–95.

Berger, Raoul. 1966a. "Rejoinder." *University of Pennsylvania Law Review* 114:816–22.

Berger, Raoul. 1966b. "Administrative Arbitrariness—A Reply to Professor Davis." *University of Pennsylvania Law Review* 114:783–95.

Berger, Raoul. 1967. "Sequel." *Minnesota Law Review* 51:601–41.

Berger, Raoul. 1969. "Synthesis." *Yale Law Journal* 78:965–1006.

Bivens v. *Six Unknown Named Agents of Federal Bureau of Narcotics.* 1971. 403 U.S. 388.

Bowman, James S., and Sami G. Hajjar. 1978. "The Literature of American Public Administration: Its Contents and Contributors." *Public Administration Review* 38:156–65.

Caldwell, Louis G. 1933. "Remarks to the ABA Convention." *Reports of the ABA* 58:197–203.

Cannon, Mark W. 1973. "Can the Federal Judiciary Be an Innovative System?" *Public Administration Review* 33:74–79.

Citizens to Preserve Overton Park v. *Volpe.* 1971. 401 U.S. 402.

Cofer, Donna Price. 1985. *Judges, Bureaucrats, and the Question of Independence: A Study of the Social Security Administrative Hearing Process.* Westport, Conn.: Greenwood Press.

Cofer, Donna Price. 1986. "The Question of Independence Continues: Administrative Law Judges within the Social Security Administration." *Judicature* 69:228– 35.

Commission on Organization of the Executive Branch of Government. 1949. *The Hoover Commission Report on the Organization of the Executive Branch of Government.* New York: McGraw-Hill.

Consumer Energy Council v. *Federal Energy Regulatory Commission.* 1982. 673 F.2d 425. D.C. Cir.

Cooper, Phillip J. 1980. "Government Contracts in Public Administration: The Role and Environment of the Contracting Officer." *Public Administration Review* 40:459–68.

Cooper, Phillip J., ed. 1982a. "Public Administration and Public Law in the Burger Court Years." *Southern Review of Public Administration* 6:5–110.

Cooper, Phillip J. 1982b. "Due Process and the Burger Court." *Southern Review of Public Administration* 6:65–98.

Cooper, Phillip J. 1983. *Public Law and Public Administration.* Palo Alto, Calif.: Mayfield.

Cooper, Phillip J. 1984a. "The Wilsonian Dichotomy in Administrative Law." In *Politics and Administration: Woodrow Wilson and American Public Administration,* edited by Jack Rabin and James Bowman. New York: Marcel Dekker.

Cooper, Phillip J. 1984b. "The Supreme Court on Governmental Liability: The Nature and Origins of Sovereign and Official Immunity." *Administration and Society* 16:259–88.

Cooper, Phillip J. 1985. "Conflict or Constructive Tension: The Changing Relationship of Judges and Administrators." *Public Administration Review* 45:643–52.

Cooper, Phillip J. 1986. "By Order of the President: Administration by Executive Order and Proclamation." *Administration and Society* 18:233–62.

Cooper, Phillip J. 1987. *Hard Judicial Choices: Federal District Judges and State and Local Officials.* New York: Oxford University Press.

Cramton, Roger C. 1976. "Judicial Law Making and Administration." *Public Administration Review* 36:550–56.

Craig, Barbara Hinkson. 1983. *Legislature Veto.* Boulder, Colo.: Westview Press.

Dahl, Robert. 1947. "The Science of Administration: Three Problems." *Public Administration Review* 7:1–11.

Danet, Brenda. 1978. "Toward a Method to Evaluate the Ombudsman Role." *Administration and Society* 10:335–70.

Davis, Kenneth Culp. 1965. *Administrative Law Treatise,* 1965 Supplement. St. Paul, Minn.: West.

Davis, Kenneth Culp. 1966a. "A Final Word." *University of Pennsylvania Law Review* 114: 814–15.

Davis, Kenneth Culp. 1966b. "Postscript." *University of Pennsylvania Law Review* 114: 823–26.

Davis, Kenneth Culp. 1967. "Not Always." *Minnesota Law Review* 51:601–41.

Davis, Kenneth Culp. 1969. *Discretionary Justice: A Preliminary Inquiry.* Baton Rouge: Louisiana State University Press.

Dickinson, John. 1927. *Administrative Justice and the Supremacy of Law in the United States.* New York: Russell and Russell.

Dimock, Marshall. 1983. "The Ombudsman and Public Administration." *Public Administration Review* 43:467–70.

Dolan, Michael W. 1984. "Administrative Law and Public Administration." *Public Administration Review* 44:86–89.

Editorial Note. 1981. *Administration and Society* 13:3–4.

Environmental Defense Fund v. *Ruckelshaus.* 1971. 439 F.2d 584. D.C. Cir.

Executive Order 12044. 1978. 43 Fed. Regis. 12661.

Executive Order 12291. 1981. 46 Fed. Regis. 13193.

Executive Order 12498. 1985. 50 Fed. Regis. 1036.

Fetter, Theodore J., and E. Keith Stott, Jr. 1980. "Court Administration in Rural Areas." *Public Administration Review* 40:34–39.

Fisher, Louis. 1981. *The Politics of Shared Power.* Washington, D.C.: CQ Press.

Fisher. Louis. 1985. *Constitutional Conflicts Between Congress and the President.* Princeton, N.J.: Princeton University Press.

Flango, Victor Eugene. 1975. "Court Administration and Judicial Modernization." *Public Administration Review* 35:619–24.

Florestano, Patricia, and Stephen B. Gordon. 1980. "Public vs. Private: Small Government Contracting with the Private Sector." *Public Administration Review* 40:29–33.

Frank, Jerome. 1942. *If Men Were Angels: Some Aspects of Government in a Democracy.* New York: Harper & Brothers.

Freund, Ernst. 1928. *Administrative Powers Over Persons and Property.* Chicago: University of Chicago Press.

Friendly, Henry J. 1962. *The Federal Administrative Agencies.* Cambridge, Mass.: Harvard University Press.

Fuchs, Ralph F. 1977. "Development and Diversification in Administrative Rule Making." *Northwestern University Law Review* 77:83–119.

Garcia v. *San Antonio Mass Transit Authority.* 1985. 469 U.S. 528.

Gellhorn, Ernest, and Glen O. Robinson. 1975. "Perspectives on Administrative Law." *Columbia Law Review* 75:771–99.

Gellhorn, Walter. 1941. *Federal Administrative Proceedings.* Baltimore: Johns Hopkins University Press.

Gellhorn, Walter, Clark Byse, and Peter L. Strauss. 1979. *Administrative Law: Cases and Comments.* 7th ed. Mineola, N.Y.: Foundation Press.

Gilmour, Robert S. 1982a. "Agency Administration by Judiciary." *Southern Review of Public Administration* 6:26–42.

Gilmour, Robert S. 1982b. "The Congressional Veto: Shifting the Balance of Administrative Control." *Journal of Policy Analysis and Management* 2:13–25.

Gilmour, Robert S. 1983. "Presidential Clearance of Regulations." Presented at the annual meeting of the American Society for Public Administration, New York.

Gilmour, Robert S., and Barbara Hinckson Craig. 1984. "After the Congressional Veto." *Journal of Policy Analysis and Management* 3:373–92.

Goodnow, Frank. 1905. *The Principles of Administrative Law in the United States.* New York: Putnam.

Goodsell, Charles T., John A. Rohr, Gary L. Wamsley, Orion F. White, and James E. Wolff. 1983. "The Public Administration and the Governance Process: Refocusing the American Dialogue." Presented at the annual meeting of the American Society for Public Administration, New York.

Graziano, Joseph, and John Rehfuss. 1974. "Twenty-Five Years of PAR Research: A Study of Professional Change." *Public Administration Review* 34:268–73.

Groszych, Walter S., Jr., and Thomas W. Madden. 1981. "Managing without Immunity: The Challenge for State and Local Government Officials in 1980." *Public Administration Review* 41:249–52.

Grumet, Barbara S. 1982. "Who Is 'Due' Process?" *Public Administration Review* 42:321–26.

Gulick, Luther, and Lyndall Urwick, eds. 1937. *Papers on the Science of Administration.* New York: Institute of Public Administration.

Haines, Charles Grove, and Marshall E. Dimock, eds. 1935. *Essays on the Law and Practice of Governmental Administration.* Baltimore: Johns Hopkins University Press.

Hale, George E. 1979. "Federal Courts and the State Budgetary Process." *Administration and Society* 11:357–68.

Harriman, Linda, and Jeffrey Straussman. 1983. "Do Judges Determine Budget Decisions? Federal Court Decisions in Prison Reform and State Spending for Corrections." *Public Administration Review* 43:343–51.

Hayford, Stephen L. 1985. "First Amendment Rights of Government Employees: A Primer for Public Officials." *Public Administration Review* 45:241–48.

Horowitz, Donald L. 1977. "The Courts as Guardians of the Public Interest." *Public Administration Review* 37:148–54.

Hunt, Raymond G. 1984. "Cross Purposes in the Federal Contract Procurement System: Military R & D and Beyond." *Public Administration Review* 44:247–56.

Hunt, Raymond G. 1985. "Award Fee Contracting as a J-Model Alternative to Revitalize Federal Program Management." *Public Administration Review* 45:586–92.

Immigration and Naturalization Service v. *Chadha*. 1983. 462 U.S. 919.

Jaffe, Louis. 1969. Book Review. *Villanova Law Review* 14:773–78.

Johnson, Charles A. 1979. "Judicial Decisions and Organizational Change." *Administration and Society* 11:27–51.

Kent, William F. 1982. "The Politics of Administrative Rulemaking." *Public Administration Review* 42:420–26.

Kraines, Oscar. 1974. *The World and Ideas of Ernst Freund: The Search for General Principles of Legislation and Administrative Law*. University, Ala.: University of Alabama.

Landis, James M. 1938. *The Administrative Process*. New Haven: Yale University Press.

Link, Arthur, ed. 1968–69. *The Papers of Woodrow Wilson*. Princeton: Princeton University Press.

Lorch, Robert S. 1969. *Democratic Process and Administrative Law*. Detroit: Wayne State University Press.

Marquardt, Ronald G., and Edward Wheat. 1978. "Hidden Allocators: Administrative Law Judges and the Paradox of Power." Presented at the annual meeting of the Southern Political Science Association, Atlanta, Ga.

Martin, Philip L. 1973. "The Hatch Act in Court: Some Recent Developments." *Public Administration Review* 33:443–48.

Mashaw, Jerry L. 1983. *Bureaucratic Justice*. New Haven: Yale University Press.

Mashaw, Jerry L., Charles J. Goetz, Frank I. Goodman, Warren F. Schwartz, Paul R. Verkuil, and Melton M. Carrow. 1978. *Social Security Hearings and Appeals: A Study of the Social Security Hearing System*. Lexington, Mass.: D.C. Heath.

Masters, Marick F., and Leonard Breiman. 1985. "The Hatch Act and the Political Activities of Federal Employee Unions: A Need for Policy Reform." *Public Administration Review* 45:518–26.

Meier, Kenneth J. 1981. "Ode to Patronage: A Critical Analysis of Two Recent Supreme Court Decisions." *Public Administration Review* 41:558–63.

Moe, Ron. 1979. "Government Corporations and Erosion of Accountability: The Case of the Proposed Energy Security Corporation." *Public Administration Review* 39: 566–71.

Monell v. *Department of Social Services*. 1978. 436 U.S. 658.

Murphy, Walter F., and Joseph Tanenhaus. 1972. *The Study of Public Law*. New York: Random House.

National League of Cities v. *Usery*. 1976. 426 U.S. 833.

Natural Resources Defense Council v. *Nuclear Regulatory Commission*. 1976. 547 F.2d 633. D.C. Cir.

Nigro, Lloyd, ed. 1974. "Mini-Symposium on Affirmative Action." *Public Administration Review* 34:234–46.

Owen v. *City of Independence*. 1980. 445 U.S. 622.

Peltason, Jack W. 1958. *Federal Courts in the Political Process*. Garden City, N.Y.: Doubleday.

Plumber, John D. 1981. "Lawyers as Bureaucrats: The Impact of Legal Training in the Higher Civil Service." *Public Administration Review* 41:220–28.

Pritchett, C. Herman. 1968. "Public Law and Judicial Behavior." *Journal of Politics* 30:480–509.

Relyea, Harold, ed. 1979. "The Freedom of Information Act a Decade Later." *Public Administration Review* 39:310–32.

Robinson, Glenn O., Ernest Gellhorn, and Harold H. Bruff. 1980. *The Administrative Process*. 2d ed. St. Paul, Minn.: West.

Rohr, John. 1978. *Ethics for Bureaucrats.* New York: Marcel Dekker.

Rohr, John. 1986. *To Run a Constitution.* Lawrence, Kan.: University Press of Kansas.

Root, Elihu. 1916. "Public Service at the Bar." In *Elihu Root: Addresses on Government and Citizenship,* edited by Robert Bacon and James Scott. Cambridge, Mass.: Harvard University Press.

Rosenbloom, David. 1971. *Federal Service and the Constitution.* Ithaca, N.Y.: Cornell University Press.

Rosenbloom, David. 1980. "Public Administrators' Official Immunities and the Supreme Court: Developments during the 1970s." *Public Administration Review* 40:166–73.

Rosenbloom, David. 1983. "Public Administration Theory and the Separation of Powers." *Public Administration Review* 43:219–26.

Schmandt, Jurgen. 1985. "Managing Comprehensive Rule Making: EPA's Plan for Integrated Environmental Management." *Public Administration Review* 45:309–18.

Schwartz, Bernard. 1976. *Administrative Law.* Boston: Little, Brown.

Shapiro, Martin. 1968. *The Supreme Court and Administrative Agencies.* New York: Free Press.

Simon, Herbert. 1946. "The Proverbs of Administration." *Public Administration Review* 6:53–67.

Simon, Herbert. 1947. "A Comment on the 'Science of Public Administration.'" *Public Administration Review* 7:200–203.

Simon, Herbert. 1957. *Administrative Behavior.* 2d ed. New York: Free Press.

Stewart, Richard B. 1975. "The Reformation of American Administrative Law." *Harvard Law Review* 88:1667–1813.

Task Force on Legal Services and Procedure. 1955. *Report on Legal Services and Procedure for the Commission on Organization of the Executive Branch.* House Doc. No. 128, 84th Cong., 1st sess.

United States v. *Florida East Coast Railroad.* 1973. 410 U.S. 224.

United States v. *Allegheny-Ludlum Steel Corp.* 1972. 406 U.S. 742.

U.S. Senate. 1941. *Report of the Attorney General's Committee on Administrative Procedure in Government Agencies.* Sen. Doc. No. 8, 77th Cong., 1st sess.

U.S. Senate. 1960. *Report of Regulatory Agencies to the President-Elect.* 86th Cong., 2d sess.

Vermont Yankee Nuclear Power Corp. v. *Natural Resources Defense Council.* 1978. 435 U.S. 519.

Viscusi, W. Kip. 1985. "Presidential Oversight: Controlling the Regulators." *Journal of Policy Analysis and Management* 2:157–73.

Waldo, Dwight. 1948. *The Administrative State.* New York: Ronald Press.

Waldo, Dwight. 1952. "Development of the Theory of Democratic Administration." *American Political Science Review* 46:81–103.

Waldo, Dwight. 1968a. "Public Administration." *Journal of Politics* 30:443–79.

Waldo, Dwight. 1968b. "Scope of the Theory of Public Administration." In *Theory and Practice of Public Administration: Scope, Objectives and Methods,* edited by James C. Charlesworth. Monograph. Annals of the American Academy of Political and Social Science.

Walter, J. Jackson. 1981. "The Ethics in Government Act: Conflict of Interest Laws and Presidential Recruiting." *Public Administration Review* 41:659–65.

White, Leonard D. 1955. *Introduction to the Study of Public Administration.* 4th ed. New York: Macmillan.

Williams, Stephen. 1975. " 'Hybrid Rulemaking' under the Administrative Procedure Act." *University of Chicago Law Review* 42:401–56.

Willoughby, William F. 1927. *Principles of Public Administration*. Baltimore: Johns Hopkins University Press.

Wilson, Woodrow. 1941. "The Study of Administration." *Political Science Quarterly* 56: 481–506.

Wise, Charles R. 1985. "Suits Against Federal Employees for Constitutional Violations: A Search for Reasonableness." *Public Administration Review* 45:845–56.

Wise, Charles, and David M. O'Brien, eds. 1985. "Law and Public Affairs." *Public Administration Review* 45:641–804.

Woll, Peter. 1963. *Administrative Law: The Informal Process*. Berkeley: University of California Press.

Wollan, Laurin A., Jr. 1978. "Lawyers in Government the Most Serviceable Instruments of Authority." *Public Administration Review* 38:105–11.

Wright, J. Skelly. 1972. "Beyond Discretionary Justice." *Yale Law Journal* 81:575–97.

Yarbrough, Tinsley E. 1981. *Judge Frank Johnson and Human Rights in Alabama*. University, Ala.: University of Alabama.

Yarbrough, Tinsley E. 1985. "The Political World of Federal Judges as Managers." *Public Administration Review* 45:660–66.

PART THREE

Intergovernmental and Comparative

13

Intergovernmental Management: The State of the Discipline

VINCENT L. MARANDO AND PATRICIA S. FLORESTANO

Purpose of the Study

Intergovernmental management is an emerging topic of inquiry within the discipline of public administration. Our interest is to identify what contemporary public administration has to offer management within an intergovernmental system. We take the perspective that Intergovernmental Management (IGM) is related to the character of our federal system and the complex phenomena of Intergovernmental Relations (IGR), yet IGM has its own characteristics revolving around the issue of problem solving within a complex, multijurisdictional environment. Thus a discussion of federalism and IGR provides the necessary context for understanding Intergovernmental Management. Interest among scholars of public administration in identifying Intergovernmental Management as a distinct focus of analysis has only recently emerged in the literature. As a functional concept, IGM is still in embryonic form, and its value to scholars and practitioners is as yet uncertain. Given IGM's nascent state, drawing distinct boundaries around IGM behavior, particularly separating it from intergovernmental relations, is not only tenuous but also subjective. The burden of our literature assessment will be to argue that IGM is sufficiently different to warrant separate attention within the discipline of public administration.

We reason that IGM is sufficiently focused and distinct from intergovernmental relations for two reasons. First, the management aspect of intergovernmental relations is stressed in recognizing overtly that management blends and melds politics and administration. Managers in an intergovernmental system do affect policy significantly. Various aspects of management, such as the problems to be solved, the resources available, and professional training, have a very direct impact on both the policy and administration processes and outcomes. For example, how managers are trained makes a difference in problem definition and policy administration. In the increasingly complex integration of jurisdictional systems, management provides a bridge between politics and administration, and between generally stated policies and specific problems that differ by locational circumstances. This political and administrative bridging process is a primary function of management that implies the relevance of related issues. These issues include (1) a problem-solving orientation that provides the context for defining and distinguishing IGM from management generally and IGR specifically, (2) the necessity of considering the mix between normative and empirical approaches to problem resolution, (3) the extent to which the policy administrative systems require alteration or reformation, and (4) the mix between analysis and evaluation.

Second, IGM implies a broader scope for analysis than an exclusive focus on constituent governmental units, agencies, and personnel of the federal system. IGM involves interorganizational networking between the private and public sectors as well as within the public sector. Thus, our perspective of IGM encourages a broader interdisciplinary approach to problem solving than is assumed by exclusively examining relationships among governmental units.

The term *intergovernmental* implies several issues that we also included in an IGM perspective: (1) a multijurisdictional decision-making context, (2) the various mixes between central and constituent authorities, (3) interpersonal and organizational networking, and (4) the reliance on governmental and nongovernmental approaches to problem resolution. Given intergovernmental as a common core, the value in delineating IGM from IGR is the former's potential for a more penetrating and accurate analysis of the American political system. The vital policy and administration roles assumed by public managers are not sufficiently captured by the concept of intergovernmental relations. The role of managers, particularly how they function to mesh the political and administrative process and how they attempt to expand their "policy space," escapes intergovernmental analysis (Agranoff 1985). The dynamics and subtleties of how management functions to solve problems, given legal and resource constraints, does not receive much attention in most contemporary IGR literature. We highlight the value and potential of IGM by drawing some distinctions between it and IGR. Selected differences in character or emphasis between the two concepts are compared in table 13.1.

Furthermore, IGM is a process by which cooperating and conflicting personnel (elected officials, politically appointed and career) mesh activities designed for a specific goal. As Robert Agranoff points out, IGM is specifically focused on the "how to manage" dimension of intergovernmental relations. The complexity of the intergovernmental system has led managers to look for ways to expand their residual decision-making authority after legal and other external proposed program demands have been met (Agranoff 1985, 192, 193). It is also a system of interjurisdictional management, both public and private, in which power and authority are fragmented. Thus to manage requires that consent, authority, and power are aggregated from across units and directed toward problem solving.

Given such a broad and defined perspective on IGM, our assessment ex-

TABLE 13.1
Selected Differences Between Intergovernmental Management (IGM)
and Intergovernmental Relations (IGR)

IGM	IGR
Problem oriented	Process oriented
Programmatic/pragmatic	Theoretical/historical
Professional	Disciplinary
Evaluation	Analysis
Operational level	Policy level
Prescriptive	Descriptive
Tactical	Strategic
Governmental reform	Governmental organization/relationships

amines concepts derived from both the disciplines of public administration and political science. Although political science may have spawned public administration, it is recognized that both disciplines have roots that go back many years and share many conceptual paradigms and intellectual issues of inquiry. This close association between the two disciplines is manifested by each discipline claiming the same phenomena—intergovernmental relations—as a legitimate subject of inquiry. While we have chosen in this chapter to emphasize the management aspect of intergovernmental activities, we fully recognize the significance, if not overriding importance, of politics in the management process. In essence, IGM as a focus of inquiry is intermeshed in the well-recognized perspective that politics and administration blur together to fashion public policy (Appleby 1949).

An essay commissioned by the American Political Science Association reviewed the literature on federalism and intergovernmental relations, stressing their political aspects and arguing that the system is overloaded and in decay (Beam, Conlan, and Walker 1982.) Although we have reservations concerning their conclusions on overload and decay, we have chosen not to re-explore this intellectual debate. Instead, we are interested in how the management function is assessed in intergovernmental studies. By taking this approach and assuming that political issues provide the context, we seek to identify and highlight the study of management within an intergovernmental environment.

Because the concept of IGM is in its nascent stage and has not been consistently defined, there is no consensus as to whether IGM is sufficiently important and distinct to warrant attention separate from IGR. In fact, issues of boundaries and interpretation among such concepts as federalism, IGR, and IGM remain subjects of debate among many of the authors cited in this chapter. Nevertheless, those who are contributing to the task of defining IGM do so because the study of management in the intergovernmental system needs reconceptualization and redefinition. The constant adjustments needed to work out problems and get things done are intermeshed in many daily activities of complexity and subtlety. There is a growing recognition that developing a concept of IGM would be of value to public managers and scholars alike. Public officials are looking for political and administrative solutions to problems, while scholars are seeking to advance the state of knowledge of the role of management in the public sector. Thus both groups are interested in how the system is managed and how management can be made better. We start our discussion of IGM by focusing on the politics/administration issue.

Management: The Linking of Politics and Administration

Central to the IGM concept is the role of management in relation to the politics and administration dichotomy. This issue has been raised in the literature of public administration and political science at least since Woodrow Wilson's often cited classic, "The Study of Administration" (1887). Attributed to Wilson is a position in which politics and administration could be neatly separated; by contrast, Appleby (1949) contended that public administration is policy making. In a recent inquiry, Wright (1986) argued that Wilson's views on the subject of politics and administration were only preliminary and contained many qualifiers. To varying degrees, all students of public administration, including Woodrow Wilson, have recognized the difficulty of specifying precisely the dimensions of the dichotomy. The development of the literature on intergovernmental relations has further complicated the specification of the nature of a dichotomy between politics and administration within a single unit of government. It is even more difficult to separate them in a contemporary public sector that is highly intergovernmental in its approach to problem solving. To the extent that clear conceptual boundaries around politics and administration are approached in an empirical fashion, the dichotomy remains difficult, although not impossible, to investigate.

In a recent article, James Svara (1985) examined the politics/administration dichotomy for council-manager cities. He concluded that there are several models of politics and administration relevant to understanding the extent and type of involvement of policy makers (council persons), elected officials, and administrators (city managers). Svara demonstrated that the politics/administration dichotomy is viewed by public officials (elected and appointed) as having separation at the extremes of a continuum that runs from mission (political) at one end to administration at the other end—and both are identifiable. The mission phase of government, the setting of fundamental goals, is the most political and therefore the primary responsibility of elected officials, whereas the administration of government is the least political and most technical and therefore the primary responsibility of administrators. For a preponderance of governmental activities, public officials (elected and appointed) perceive and act as if there were relatively clear separation at the extremes of the continuum between the political and administrative functions. For example, administrators do not see their tasks generally as including electoral campaigning, and elected officials do not involve themselves generally in the daily operations of administering programs. Svara's work offers an empirical basis for making distinctions between politics and administration and for bridging the two with management activities. The role of managers in bridging politics and administration is to make policy; in fact, elected officials expect no less as long as the politics is agency policy, not electoral or legislative politics. As some recent research indicates, agency administration may be where the most profound policies are often made (Williams 1982).

The empirical and normative aspects of the politics/administration dichotomy take a different tone within the intergovernmental context. The notion that states and localities administer federal policies has not only been considered suspect; it is also not reflective of the American system (Grodzins 1962; Pressman and Wildavsky 1973). During the administration phase of federal programs, states and localities make policies or sufficiently alter policy to make it different from what was originated. If administrators make policy in the process of carrying out federal programs, can it be said that they are only administering? The answer seems to be that they are managing. This definition of management differents from administration; management, including politics, is the bridge between politics and administration.

The bridging function of management is most vital in the broad middle area of the continuum where politics and administration are blurred into an inseparable mix. The intergovernmental dimension of the management scope broadens this perspective to include intergovernment and public/private components, as contrasted to exclusive focus on intragovernment components. If this interpretation of intergovernmental is not sufficiently different from intragovernment's analysis, it certainly adds complexity to public-sector management. It is often the federal government's reliance on states and localities, as well as private agencies, to administer programs that raises the management issue. Brian W. Rapp and Frank M. Patitucci (1977) offered the perspective that management is the function that ties policy to administration. They argued that the management process links the political and the administrative processes. By focusing on performance, the management process integrates public policy with administrative results, bringing political science and public administration together in the study of public management (Rapp and Patitucci 1977). Management is thus part politics and part administration. Given the nature of the American system of governance, this melding function translates into IGM by necessity. Those individuals at state or local levels responsible for implementing higher-level governmental programs are involved in IGM. Similarly, individuals at the national level alter, abolish, or create new policies with regard to management realities at state and local levels.

A recent International City Management Association (ICMA) publication with reference to local managers takes the perspective that actions by other governments—in Washington, in the state capitol, and in nearby localities —influence the conduct of daily business and require the manager to assume a role in intergovernmental relations (Anderson, Newland, and Stillman 1984). The division of labor between an elected official and an appointed manager tends to follow the policy and administration line, but less so in intergovernmental programs than with programs exclusively encompassed within a single government. The increasing intergovernmental nature of program funding and mandates requires more reliance on managing than administering.

Whether the issue of separating politics from administration can ever be satisfactorily resolved is of less concern than attempting to define and analyze a manager's bridging function. This perspective assumes that the intergovernmental system is a mix of policy and authority that functions in a hierarchical top-down fashion. A more contemporary view posits that policy and administration are intertwined in multiple directions and managers are involved in policy formation at all levels of the public sector. Thus a functioning concept of management as a bridging process is necessary even though an explicit theory setting forth IGM is still in a relatively nascent stage of development.

Federalism, IGR, and IGM

Although federalism represents an American contribution to the science of government, there exists considerable debate as to what constitutes a theory of federalism (Beam, Conlan, and Walker 1983). Rather than get into this debate, we discuss management within the American federal system, which is characterized by divided control and shared powers. For our discussion, we concur with Daniel J. Elazar (1981) that federalism is a generic term for what may be referred to as self-rule/shared-rule relationships, while intergovernmental relations has to do with particular ways and means of operationalizing a federal system of government. IGM has characteristics, however, that extend beyond the confines of federalism and are applicable also to unitary forms of government. In addition, IGM encompasses interactions between and among public- and private-sector organizations. IGM focuses on administering programs and achieving results at the operational level and carries a normative as well as an empirical dimension of inquiry into political/administrative study. Much of the contemporary study of IGM is concerned with normative issues, either recognized or implicit, about the nature of complex governmental structures, interpersonal relationships, and political/ administrative processes.

Theories and frameworks for understanding the American federal system presented by various authors have implications for IGM. (See Anton 1985; Beer

1974; Diamond 1966; Elazar 1962, 1974; Landau 1973; Ostrom 1971; Wildavsky 1980; Wright 1982.) Their foci for understanding federalism's implications for management include such issues as the extent of centralization/decentralization of authority among units, the extent of conflict and cooperation among governments, the relationship between values of professionalism and citizen needs, the extent of unity and diversity among the constituent federal components on varying issues, the impact of federalism on problem solving, and whether the extent of growing national influence and control represents decay of the system itself. Obviously, all are important issues in federalism, but managers must function within a complex decentralized system of shared power without constantly seeking to answer the fundamental questions of federalism. In their daily activities, does it matter to managers how the immediate demands on them relate to the fundamental federal issues?

Some authors have argued that our federal system, becoming overloaded with demands, is centralizing power and authority at the national level and that the federal system is decaying (Beam, Conlan, and Walker 1982). Thomas J. Anton (1985), in a careful and penetrating assessment of intergovernmental change, challenged and clarified several normative assumptions concerning decay of the system. He argued persuasively that if there is a problem of intergovernmental change, then it is primarily an intellectual problem. Neither do we know enough about patterns of interaction over time to sustain empirical theories of change nor do we possess conceptual frameworks adequate to the task based on the data we have. Change in the intergovernmental system is the normal state and does not necessarily represent decay or crisis. We assume that Anton also means that change in the system additionally affects the role of managers. Without an empirically tested conceptual framework, the study of managerialism in an intergovernmental system is an abnormally difficult task. The study of IGM can be subjected to the same conclusion that Anton makes concerning the study of American federalism: "We need to develop analytic concepts capable of organizing the wealth of information into general statements regarding system structure and change. If we can do so, politics as well as scholarship may be enhanced" (Anton 1985, 52).

Those aspects of federalism that speak to management in the intergovernmental system continue to be assessed from multiple theoretical frameworks that are as varied as the writers who express their concerns. We examine the selected issue of politics/administration in an intergovernmental context from a very different perspective than did John Kirlin (1984) in his essay "A Political Perspective." Kirlin observed that many researchers and writers have removed politics from their study of government and overemphasized the administrative aspects of service delivery, at the same time that they neglected or minimized the political dimensions of governmental performance. He said that definitions of governmental performance should be replaced, or at least complemented, by analysis focusing on the capacity of the political system. Limiting analysis to service provisions within jurisdictions has limited relevance and provides ineffective (sometimes even dysfunctional) counsel to policy makers (Kirlin 1984, 186). Kirlin's position concerning the importance of politics in understanding the delivery of services or policy implementation is difficult to refute. Nevertheless, a political perspective is not sufficient for understanding intergovernmentally related service-delivery issues. In contrast, we note that the management process in the federal system also influences the capacity of government to deliver services or programs. Neither politics nor management can be minimized by researchers in their effort to understand governmental performance and capacity.

A symposium presented in *Publius* (Elazar 1981b) provided several penetrating essays on the relationship between federalism and IGM. The theme of the symposium was the issue and implications of whether a hierarchical interventionist management system was developing in the American federal system—a development identified by the shorthand term *prefectorial federalism*—and, if so, what are the consequences? The question of the emergence of a prefectorial system touches the core of the relationship between federalism and IGM. The prefectorial system implies a centralized authority and hierarchical arrangement for the allocation of power and resources throughout the governance system. Under a prefect system, states and localities would be managed by the national government, and the term *management* would parallel very closely the common understanding for *administration,* rather than be equated with a bridging of politics and administration.

The extent to which the American federal system has adopted the characteristics of the prefect system is open to disagreement and debate. Robert C. Fried (1981) argued that, if the prefect system was emerging in American public administration, it would mean that we were adopting the administrative pattern of many other advanced industrial states. In those countries, the central government is collective and impersonal, but in every locality it has a personal representative, the prefect, who speaks for all members of the government. He argued that it is just the opposite in the United States, wherein our national government is personified pragmatically in the President but has no local personification in the various regions, states, and localities.

Daniel J. Elazar, in the opening essay of the same symposium (1981b), discussed the profound significance to the American federal system if a prefectorial administration were to develop here. Because such a system reflects centralizing tendencies, the major decisions would be made by the national government and transmitted to the states and localities. A central implication of a prefectorial system is a hierarchical structure in which the national government is at the top and the states and localities—in the middle and bottom respectively—are not full or equal partners in the federal system; instead, they are managed by the national government. Elazar further argued that the commitment of managerialism—cum prefect—to the hierarchical form of organization finds expression in the terminological emphasis on the levels of government, a key feature of managerialism. Under such conditions, the political system is conceptualized as a classic bureaucratic model with a top level (federal), a middle level (state), and a bottom level (local). The most articulate expression of managerialism as embodied in administrative hierarchy can be found in the writings of Max Weber (Gerth, Mills, and Weber 1974) and Frank Goodnow (1900). The acceptance and advocacy of an administrative hierarchy can still be found in some contemporary descriptions of the American System (Clayton, Conklin, and Shapek 1975).

Yet, is the prefect, a hierarchical administrative system, consistent with American federalism? Obviously not! Elazar argued that hierarchical administrative structures have been failures more often than successes. In effect, hierarchical administration is incompatible with a federalism that is conceptualized as a matrix of decision making among constitutionally established components or de facto units (local governments). The decision matrix includes the federal government, the states, the localities, and all their constituent components. Power, authority, and capacity to administer programs exist across all units, to be tied together in a functioning system by IGM. Federalism was not designed by the framers of the Constitution as a hierarchical system of government, nor has it evolved into a hierarchical form. Thus, how can a hierarchical system of national administration function within a federal system where politics and administration are mixed with and among interacting constitutionally or legitimately established units? Elazar added further that in a system of interlocking arenas (which is what exists in the United States, despite all the talk about levels), there is no top from which orders are given. Instead, coordination and continuous adjustments for melding politics and administrative activities are participated in by all units that are trying to solve problems.

Vincent Ostrom (1973) has argued persuasively that the issue of whether the American federal system is a hierarchical or a decentralized policy system represents an intellectual crisis because the perception of management depends on the conceptualization of how the federal system is organized. The federal system is a hierarchical system neither in theory nor in practice; yet much public administration and organizational theory depicts federalism as hierarchical in nature, with authority flowing downward from the national government. If, as Ostrom contends, the federal system is a compound republic, then policy-making authority and related management capabilities exist within and among all the government units (Ostrom 1971).

The concept of IGM is shaped quite dramatically by how the American federal system is defined, given the debate concerning the prefect. To the extent that it can be documented that the federal system is in effect a matrix of decision-making nodes and not a superior (national)-subordinate (state, local) situation, a concept and supporting theory of IGM is needed to describe and explain how the blending of politics and administration is applied among governmental units to problem solving. Notions of administrative hierarchy, although difficult to dispel, have never provided accurate assessments of how American federalism functions and are inappropriate for explaining how problems are defined and managed. Over the past few decades, several scholars have contributed to our understanding of policy-making management-administration within a federal system conceptualized as a matrix-oriented, redundant, and compound republic. Notable among these are Martin Landau (1973), Vincent Ostrom (1971), Samuel Beer (1978), and Daniel Elazar (1981a, 1981b). From different theoretical perspectives, each of them challenged the notion of hierarchical administrative systems that lean heavily on classical managerial ideologies implying that state and localities are predominantly administrating federal policies. Hierarchical models of administration in the American federal system—more descriptive of what may occur within, rather than among, organizations—misrepresent the relationship between politics and administration. Thus there is a recognition that a conceptualization of IGM is needed to explain how the system operates. IGM may be the most recent stage in expanding the conceptualization of IGR (Wright 1986).

Intergovernmental Management (IGM)

Stephen L. Schechter (1981) attributed the ambiguities involved in defining IGM, in part, to the chameleon-like qualities of the verb *to manage,* which seem to depend in turn on the subject to be managed. A commonly accepted definition may not be necessary for exhibiting the value of IGM to scholars and practitioners of public administration. Sufficient discussion has set a context for debate, and a common core of concepts is associated with IGM so that it is possible to allude to the essence of the term, even though its boundaries may not be specified with clarity. Many scholars use varying working definitions that contribute to our understanding of politics and management within an intergovernmental system.

Robert Agranoff and Valerie A. Lindsay (1983) discussed IGM's differences from intergovernmental relations. They argued that IGM is the portion of IGR that emphasizes the goal-achievement component of these relationships, inasmuch as management is a process by which cooperating officials direct their actions toward some goal. Although policy making and implementation behavior are operative in IGM, they said that IGM's primary emphasis is on the process by which specified objectives are met. Further, Agranoff and Lindsay placed politics within a management context rather than as its antecedent. They took this perspective when they stated:

> Successful intergovernmental management involves emphasis on developing a solution to the problem at hand while recognizing the importance of the substantive, jurisdictional, and political issues. IGM involves focusing on intergov-

ernmental tasks while recognizing the importance of and operating within the structural-legal, political, and technical context of IGR. Most officials implicitly recognize this pattern as they search for ways to seek adjustments in federal and state programs. (1983, 228)

The observations of these authors are particularly pertinent because they are based on empirical analysis of intergovernmental bodies in six metropolitan areas. Their study represents one of the very few that specifically examined IGM as a process by focusing on operations-based, multijurisdictional problem solving. Thus their perspective of IGM is both normative (successful problem solving) and analytical (identifiable patterns of public officials' behavior).

An obvious connection exists between IGR and IGM, but there is a subtle distinction that revolves around the all-inclusiveness of IGR and the apparently more circumscribed focus of IGM on management processes. Myrna P. Mandell (1979) was among the first to draw this distinction when she stated:

Whereas intergovernmental relations identifies who the actors are in the system and how they relate, intergovernmental management provides the tool needed to understand how and why these levels interrelate the way they do and how we can cope in the system. It is an action-oriented process that allows administrators at all levels the wherewithal to do something constructive. . . . It allows a perspective that looks at networking and communications as positive ways to make things work in the intergovernmental system. The term intergovernmental management connotes action, problem solving, and reform of the intergovernmental relations "system" to make it more "manageable." (Pp. 2, 6)

A study of federal grants management that attributed similar characteristics to IGM observed that an explosion of political demands on federal categorical grants necessitated improvements in their management (Advisory Commission on Intergovernmental Relations 1977). The ACIR report examined organizational and procedural issues involved in the management of categorical grants, leaving the broader political context basically intact and beyond the scope of the study. ACIR was wrestling with a dilemma facing those who argue that a distinct IGM concept exists: that management can be improved without changing the fundamental features of the American political system. Acceptance of this assumption distinguishes those scholars who say that IGM is conceptually distinct from IGR and those who see management as a part of, and responsive to, the politics of federalism. Allen Schick (1975) argued that the primary reforms involved in better federal program management are essentially political issues and that the role of Congress is central to any truly significant management reform of the federal categorical aid system. From this perspective, the mismanagement of federal programs reflects congressional action or inaction on the issue of comprehensive federal grant reform. In Schick's view, management flows from politics; it is not a process that can be significantly reformed independent of political action.

To what extent can IGM stand as a meaningful concept if it ignores or minimizes the political aspects of management? If politics rather than management is the key function influencing IGR, then politics will always be the more important of the two processes. Yet elected officials may be restricted (by the civil service merit system, for example) in their efforts to get involved in management, or management can be sufficiently isolated from politics as a distinct process. The 1977 ACIR report subscribed to the approach that politics and management can be separated, at least analytically if not in practice. ACIR took a middle-range perspective on grant reform by implying that while politics is a given, management improvements can be made within existing political parameters (ACIR 1977). By focusing on IGM, ACIR stressed the potential for establishing a managerially oriented approach to problem solving in the American federal system. This reform-oriented approach, which stresses good government, has various consequences for the nature of the system itself. The proactive perspective of management implied by IGM is not neutral in its impact on various constituencies and the functioning of the political system itself. Also, decisions by professional managers do not always take into full account the constitutional basis for the government within which management functions. Arguing strongly that there may well be political danger in Intergovernmental Management, Schechter (1981) questioned whether IGM is compatible with the U.S. Constitution. His concern was that by concentrating solely on reform of the system to achieve better management, the basic principles underlying the Constitution may be sacrificed in the interest of problem solving. A problem-solving IGM approach that blends politics and administration may be so inclusive that purely political issues no longer can be identified.

George J. Gordon (1979) extended the argument that IGM and federalism may not only be incompatible but that IGM may spell the end of federalism. In his view, the developments of the past two decades reflect the implicit belief that politics is failing but that we can manage our way out of our problems. Gordon concluded his assessment of IGM's impact on the federal system by saying that federalism will survive because it can adapt by incorporating increased professional management into the overall political system. He was hopeful that federalism would survive the increasing influence of managers, although no evidence was presented to warrant his optimism.

Obviously, we need better management as well as better politics in order to resolve problems: IGM's focus is on the particular balance between the two. A strongly normative term that is not scientifically neutral, IGM raises issues of better government (for whom?), problem solving (which?), action (by whom?), as well as a host of issues difficult to conceptualize, let alone verify. For these reasons, the formulation of a description of IGM separate from IGR is worth the attention of public administration scholars and practitioners. Recognizing the normative implications of IGM may prove useful empirically in describing the functions and processes of complex governmental organizations. IGM is a bold step toward recasting the politics/administration issue within the context of contemporary assessments of the American federal system (Anton 1985; Elazar 1981b; Ostrom 1971; Wright 1986). Old as well as new questions are opened up for discussion, with more sophisticated understanding of human and organizational behavior. Must all involved parties have a visible stake in the outcome for IGM to be successful? How much inequality in the authority, status, and resources among intergovernmental actors can be assumed in the IGM process? To what extent do different problem areas require variation in IGM approaches? Our assessment is that the effort to separate and define IGM is not yet theoretically neat, but the beginnings of a more powerful analytic perspective are emerging.

Toward a Theory of IGM

The distinguishing feature of IGM is that it *emphasizes* the management processes. We stress the perspective of emphasis because our interpretation indicates that, conceptually, IGM is the process that allows the system to function on a daily basis. We approach the task of laying a theoretical foundation for IGM by suggesting some of the characteristics that distinguish it from IGR.

Deil Wright (1983), in one of several seminal works, indicated that the understanding of IGM as a distinct subject for analysis is in its embryonic form. He presented a useful historical discussion of the evolving usage of IGM as a separate subject of analysis from IGR. Discussing both within the overall context of federalism, he said that federalism has been under study for over two hundred years, IGR roughly since the Great Depression, and IGM for only a decade. While IGR is a pivotal concept reflecting the interests of both political science and public administration, IGM has a decidedly public administration flavor in its linkage of strategy and operations within the politics of governance. To highlight this distinction, Philip M. Burgess (1975) subdivided the term management into three separate functions: policy management, program management, and resource management.

Thus policy management is viewed as a process that involves the *strategic functions* of guidance and leadership with respect to a jurisdictional or territorial arena. The exercise of strategic management functions is also considered to include the capacity to relate these functions to other participants or entities whose policies affect the performance of these functions. (Burgess 1975, 707)

These are precisely the goal-setting functions that Svara references as a mission (political) function. Policy management as defined by Burgess also fits our definition of IGM as including both politics (policy) and administration (implementation).

Burgess (1975) further elaborated the linkage characteristics of IGM with the concept of program management, which, he said, "is used to refer to the public management capacity to perform the administrative functions and tactical requirements of executing policy by undertaking programs, activities, or services" (p. 707). As opposed to the exclusively political processes that set general courses of governmental action, IGM melds political/administrative activities that emphasize the strategic aspects of governmental functions.

The development of the IGM concept has a decidedly professional tone, as opposed to a disciplinary orientation. In a workshop titled "The Intergovernmental Challenge," Donald C. Stone (1983) examined the meaning of management in an intergovernmental system. Such a meaning, he argued, would be more valuable from an operational than a theoretical, descriptive, or historical perspective. The concept of IGM is valuable for its utility in helping policy makers understand how governmental capacity is related to the implementation of policies and programs. From Stone's perspective, no matter how theoretically meritorious, policy is of no practical value unless it can be implemented. Thus the existing dialogue on formulating a theory of IGM is not only in an embryonic stage but the dialogue is also beset with conflicting questions that engross scholars in attempting to distill an intellectually utilitarian concept. For example, where does politics stop and administration begin? How much influence does the federal government have over states and localities? What role do managers have in defining public problems? Through the review of a wide selection of literature, we have taken a step toward developing a theory of IGM that describes and explains how the intergovernmental system is managed.

Although some scholars recognize IGM as a worthy subject of study, there does not seem to be a consensus about what is to be included in its theoretical framework. As is the case in new lines of inquiry, the creation of a field of study will evolve with the development of consensus among scholars. This may be achieved, if at all, later in the intellectual process of formulating an IGM theory. In the development of IGM as an analytical concept, however, Wright (1983) and Agranoff and Lindsay (1983) have identified some of the special qualities of IGM: a problem-solving focus, a useful and coping approach, and networking and communication. We continue this chapter by building on their views in order to discuss the following selected conceptual characteristics of IGM: organizational interaction and networking, professionalism, pragmatic problem solving, and goal/ results orientation.

Organizational Interaction and Networking

A growing body of literature on IGM stresses the importance of organizational interaction within an intergovernmental system. Pattakos and Palmer (1983) indicated that management capacity among government organizations took on new life under Reagan's brand of federalism and that the capacity of any government includes an intergovernmental dimension. Few governmental organizations, they said, can have the capacity to solve the problems confronting them without the assistance or support of other governments; for example, the federal government may or may not have the fiscal resources or the administrative personnel to implement programs. Whereas a local government may understand the nature of the problem, it may not have the necessary resources to fund a solution of the problem. At one time or another, various governments may have to rely on others and/or the private sector for assistance in addressing problems.

Agranoff and Lindsay's study of IGM (1983) observed that "the most central IGM task issue is that administration is ordinarily set by joint actions by separate organizations" (pp. 234–35). With reference to central IGM task issues, the authors concluded that IGM more commonly involves a complex execution of decisions by mutual carrying out of agreements through the two or more independent units that have participated in the problem solution. The authors suggested that IGM is entwined with such organizationally relevant issues as capacity building, task focus, and problem solving. To understand the functioning of the system, there is need for IGM theory that focuses on interorganizational management processes and components.

IGM implies more than governments interacting exclusively with one another in resolving public problems because many public problems are beyond governments' ability to define clearly, let alone manage. Complex interaction and networking have developed not only among governments but also within the public and private sectors. Lester M. Salamon (1982) introduced the term "third-party government" to describe an imaginative new mode of government operation that has developed in this country, for which our existing theories and even our available political lexicon have failed to prepare us. He said that the concepts of federalism and IGR are not sufficiently inclusive to explain how governments function in an environment where diverse interests are represented with different degrees of effectiveness at different levels of government, and in a way that is consistent with a strong national norm favoring local control. An IGM perspective is consistent with what is described by Salamon. It is a conceptualization of how to resolve problems among the constituent governments in the federal system which recognizes at the same time the vast complexity and interdependence between the public and private sectors. Thus intergovernmental networking is to be studied among governmental units and between governmental units (including subunits) and private sector organizations. Although related to IGR, IGM is a more inclusive and a more comprehensive con-

301

cept that encompasses the wide array of networking necessary for resolving public problems.

Professionalism

Professionalism influences the division of power among the levels of government. Professionalism and technocracy are key elements being exhibited at all levels of governments, which diminish the differences among governments in problem solving. Samuel Beer (1978) made an eloquent argument in favor of the centralizing trend of increased networking among professionals at all levels of government. Increased reliance on professional skills, he said, would result in a growth in power and influence of technically and professionally trained persons in government.

Beer's perspective on the expanding influence of professionals raises a question central to understanding IGM: What is the role of the manager in relation to the citizen? The role of the citizen is not emphasized in IGM literature because the management of the federal system is primarily left to the public officials and professional managers. Much of IGM is concerned with sophisticated functional policy areas where professionals from different levels or units of government have more in common and share policy/management more than do nonprofessionals at the same level or within the same unit of government (Wright 1982). Thus IGM is the process by which functionally differentiated professionals network to solve problems. In technical policy making, the pressures and proposals arise within government and its associated circles of professional and technically trained cadres (Beer 1982). IGM is the process that links professional bureaucrats in problem-solving networks. The issue of how the manager is responsible for defining or interpreting citizens' needs and demands is not yet addressed by IGM. From this perspective, IGM is significantly different from the related concepts of federalism and IGR.

Pragmatic Problem Solving

IGM has a pragmatic orientation, as opposed to a theoretical or legal orientation: Problem solving is at the core of IGM. Agranoff and Lindsay (1983) said that "successful intergovernmental management involves emphasis on developing a solution to the problem at hand, while recognizing the importance of the substantive, jurisdictional, and political issues" (p. 228). IGM offers an orientation for examining the political system from the results perspective rather than the means perspective. To the extent that administrative processes are examined and judged valuable, it is based on their effectiveness at problem solving. Certainly it is not hard to see this theme in IGM literature.

Much of the work published by government agencies and research associations is prescriptive in that it cites the management problems and suggests the various cures. An excellent example is the report issued by the Executive Office (1975) titled *Strengthening Public Management in the Intergovernmental System*. At the end of the same year, a special issue of *Public Administration Review* included the Executive Summary of the report, in addition to other papers from members and staff. Focused on the need for coordination in management, both publications recommended solving the coordination problem at the delivery points.

James Sundquist with David W. Davis (1969) recognized this central emphasis of IGM on problem solving when he argued that selected states should be rewarded with increased authority over federal projects based on their management capacity. Sundquist acknowledged that states with higher levels of management competency than others could not legally be granted additional authority by the federal government. But he argued that if management capacity exists and its enhancement is in conflict with the legal system, then the law should be altered. The identification and management of problems provides the context for understanding and reforming the IGR system. Although few writers are explicit about the exact management of the problem solutions, it is assumed that practitioners will implicitly recognize how the IGR system can be used to address problems. Presumably this determination will be made on the basis of good management tenets from public administration.

We include in the IGM problem-solving literature research that stresses coordination, accountability, and capacity building. In any analysis of IGM, coordination usually has been discussed by deploring the lack thereof. Thomas Anton (1984) said, however, that the absence of visible attempts to coordinate does not mean an absence of coordination. He pointed to works by Warren, Rose, and Bergunder (1974) and Sonenblum, Kirlin, and Ries (1977) as evidence that conflicts among metropolitan urban governments are the exception rather than the rule, that each government has a turf that is respected by others, and that tacit coordination among governments is shown by their refusal to invade another's turf except under extreme conditions. Anton (1985) found that visible coordination is seldom necessary; he said, indeed, that "visible conflicts over jurisdictional space are a sign that existing coordination has broken down" (p. 81). A great deal of coordination and interpersonnel networking does take place invisibly as a matter of normal routines in the management process.

Yin, Bateman, Marks, and Quick (1979), in studying federal aid to urban economic development, also found little visible coordination at the local level. What he and his colleagues did observe was coordination across time rather than across units. In other words, to keep a project in operation usually necessitated the ability to maintain support over a span of time. Catherine Lovell (1979), commenting on the state of intergovernmental relations, observed that coordination is an unresolved problem badly needing a response. She said that it is necessary to modify our traditional views of what constitutes coordination and "search for new instruments which will serve as bulwarks to diversity" (p. 12). The problem with coordination, she said, is that, for many people, it still connotes a central decision maker, to whom all other decision makers adapt. In reality, coordination must often be achieved by mutual adjustment through bargaining, information sharing, and other linking relationships, without a central decision maker coordinating.

Much of the problem-solving work on IGM also focuses either directly or indirectly on the question of accountability. It is generally agreed that the notion of accountability means that the public should be able to control the policies and behaviors of public organizations and to hold them answerable for what they do. Agreement on how to operationalize this concept is more elusive. While the literature in this area generally deals with accountability as one of a number of concerns, Lovell (1979) said directly that we need new theories of accountability and new mechanisms for achieving it, and that such mechanisms should be appropriate to multiorganizational policy making and implementation processes. Together with the traditional concept of formal, hierarchical accountability, she said that we need to consider Mosher's (1980) concept of "subjective accountability," which relies on individual responsibility together with experience, values, and professional relationships. While this form of accountability is focused on professional norms rather than public control, it would likely enhance subjective responsibility in the complex arena of IGM.

The 1977 ACIR study, covering two decades of IGM issues, suggested strategies for middle-range reform, especially in the area of the competence and capacity of recipient management. Feller (1975) examined capacity building in the special *PAR* issue on management assistance, and capacity building has continued to be a frequent subject of IGM literature (Brown 1980; Gargan and Moore 1984; Honadle 1981a, 1981b; Honadle and Howitt 1985; Lenz 1980).

In sum, this subset of the IGM literature focuses on ways to solve problems and get results. Support is given to the importance of accountability and coordination, and of basing state authority on management capacity. Agranoff and Lindsay (1983), Honadle (1985), Lovell (1979), Sundquist and Davis (1969), Yin et al. (1979), and others pragmatically discuss their overriding concern about the achievement of specific desired ends.

Goal/Results Orientation

The results/goal-oriented body of the IGM literature is exemplified, we believe, by studies on evaluation, implementation, monitoring, and retrenchment in the intergovernmental setting. Evaluation requires some goal or standard against which success is judged. Myrna Mandell (1979) said that being able to cope with the system is a necessary standard and that administrators at all levels of government need tools to cope with and make sense of the system. She pointed out quite dramatically the normative nature of IGM.

Harry H. Jones recognized the close yet underdeveloped link between IGM and evaluation. Writing in 1975, he stated:

Presently, there is no well-defined program of independent intergovernmental roles regarding evaluation or policy management, let alone their joint application.... It is clear, however, that intergovernmental rules for evaluation pertinent to policy management are yet to be defined and effective assistance mechanisms are yet to be constructed. (P. 739)

His observations remain an accurate assessment of IGM today. In the same piece, Jones presented factors to be considered for the development of intergovernmental support systems for evaluating policy management. Included in his discussion on development is the observation that since policy is oriented to the future and to societal values, its management simply adds a measure of concreteness to that orientation, and that the technical evaluation approach should be formative and impact oriented rather than program oriented. This concern for impact orientation, referred to as problem resolution, continues to be a central feature that distinguishes IGM from IGR.

Although no formal boundaries exist between implementation and monitoring research, they are closely related and often mutually inclusive. We examine them separately in order to note their relationship to IGM. Much of the literature on implementation is IGM literature by a different name. Van Horn and Van Meter (1976) proposed that the central focus of intergovernmental relations research be the process of policy implementation. They said that the study of policy implementation attempts to describe and explain the process by which policies are transformed into public services and program objectives are or are not realized. Although it is customary to date policy implementation studies from the well-known Pressman and Wildavsky book (1973), important early research that laid the groundwork for the Pressman and Wildavsky research includes studies by Kaufman (1960) of the U.S. Forest Service, Bailey and Mosher (1968) of the Elementary and Secondary Education Act of 1965, and Derthick (1970) of federal grants-in-aid programs and (1972) of the Johnson administration's efforts to create communities on federally owned land in metropolitan areas. The Pressman and Wildavsky (1974) study portrayed the complexity of implementing Economic Development Administration programs in Oakland, California. Since the publication of the Pressman and Wildavsky book, public policy implementation studies have multiplied, and a new field of study has been identified. Examples include Radin (1977), who studied HEW implementation of school desegregation policy, and Tropman (1977), who examined the implementation processes of separate social security programs in the same federal department. Marshall (1975) studied the history of federal poverty and welfare policy, and Frieden and Kaplan (1975) studied urban policy making. The implication of this research for IGM is that implementation strategy, whatever the strategy, is always more complicated and difficult than it was thought to be, but especially so in an intergovernmental setting. Another finding that bears directly on IGM is the need for more flexibility and variation in national policy so that intergovernmental managers can respond to local differences.

Some IGM research adheres to a particular methodology referred to as monitoring. The monitoring approach to IGM evaluation is based on the field network evaluation process, in which a central staff develops a research framework utilized by designated field associates in selected sites across the country. In their jurisdictions, the field associates observe and report on the operation of the particular intergovernmental program under study. Based on the associates' reports, the central staff produces a final research study (Dommel and Hall 1984; Hall and MacManus 1982; and Nathan 1982). Over a ten-year period, field network evaluations examined the impacts of various major federal domestic programs on state and local governments.

Comprehensive studies of general revenue sharing were directed by the University of Michigan, which surveyed 817 local units (Juster 1977) and studied five cities in detail (Anton, Larkey, and Linton 1975; Larkey 1975, 1979), and by the Brookings Institution, which directed field studies in 57 local jurisdictions (Nathan, Manuel, Calkins, and Associates 1975; Nathan, Adams, and Associates 1977). Among other findings, these studies showed that the uses of federal revenue sharing monies were predominantly determined by local conditions and priorities. Once again, the implication for IGM is the attempt of these studies to learn what were the actual results of the programs and differences in management at federal, state, and local levels.

Other monitoring implementation studies were done on the Elementary and Secondary Education Act, ESEA (Porter, Warner, and Porter 1973), the public service employment portion of the Comprehensive Employment Training Act, CETA (Nathan, Cook, Rawlins, and Associates 1979; Cook, Adams, Rawlins, and Associates 1985), and the Community Development Block Grant Program, CDBG (Nathan et al. 1977; Dommel, Nathan, Liebschutz, Wrightson, and Associates 1978). These studies also found that whatever the federal constraints, the uses of federal funds were largely determined by local priorities. Brookings directed studies of federal grants in twelve cities including Houston (MacManus 1979), Phoenix (Hall 1979), and St. Louis (Schmandt, Wendell, and Tomey 1979). Nathan (1983; Nathan and Doolittle 1984) focused on the effects on state and local governments of the domestic policy changes of the Reagan administration's first term. While the earlier field network studies analyzed specific programs in IGM, this work used the methodology to look across a variety of intergovernmental programs delivering a number of services. It evaluated the effect of the major cuts resulting from the 1981 Reconciliation Act on a sample of fourteen states and on selected jurisdictions within each state (Nathan, Doolittle, and Associates 1983; Hall 1985). Monitoring research has thus aggregated large masses of data to evaluate important questions in IGM, but especially to concentrate on the evaluation of results.

While it is obvious that program evaluation studies are closely related to monitoring research, we think that there are some subtle differences between the two procedures. Monitoring studies usually have had as their focus the implementation at the local level of federal programs and policy, and occasionally those of the states. Program evaluations have been focused more often on the delivery of a specific service or the working of a selected unit, agency, or government organization regardless of level. An important example of program evaluation is the series of major studies directed by Elinor Ostrom on the delivery of law enforcement services and the operation of police agencies across the country (Ostrom, Parks, and Whittaker 1978). She and her colleagues empirically analyzed the consequences of alternative institutional designs for the delivery of police services.

Analysts of program effectiveness often make their judgments by comparing articulated program goals with reported actual activities. Anton (1984) criticized the lack of sufficiently long time periods used in some program evaluations. For example, he cited Martin Anderson's (1964) well-known criticism of federal urban renewal, which was followed by research (Sanders 1979) that refuted many of Anderson's observations. Kirlin (1984) said that judgments of governmental performance should not be based solely on evaluations of service delivery. In his view, evaluations of the performance of intergovernmental policy implementation within various service areas does not yield sufficient information by and of itself to evaluate the IGM system. Overall, evaluation research in IGM literature displays an attention to quality of management not emphasized in most of the politically oriented intergovernmental relations studies. To talk about the quality of management and the way to manage things better, we have to include evaluation and its standards.

The research on retrenchment in the public sector and its impact on IGM is also included within the achievement/results oriented literature of IGM. The passage of California's Proposition 13 and similar state and local tax expenditure limits, together with the erosion of the local economic base in many areas, erratic national economic performance, and the election of a conservative President, focused the attention of scholars and public officials on the concept of retrenchment and its potential impact on the intergovernmental system. Did these events signal major changes in IGM or only an end to expanding government budgets and activities? If the size and scope of government were reduced, what would be the size, impact, and permanence of this reduction? Although numerous studies have been available since the mid-1970s on the subject of urban fiscal strain (Rose and Peters 1978; Shefter 1977; Stanley 1976), the retrenchment literature clearly began with the publication in 1978 of Charles Levine's "Organizational Decline and Cutback Management." The article and accompanying symposium assembled the available knowledge about retrenchment in public-sector organizations. Because of the pressure of the events noted, Levine led a new round of research on the process of retrenchment and its impacts on IGM. Together with his colleagues Irene S. Rubin and George G.

Wolohojian, Levine authored an impressive share of existing studies (Levine 1979, 1981; Levine, Rubin, and Wolohojian 1981; Rubin 1985) about organizational decline and cutback within the intergovernmental system, strategies for retrenchment, and the costs and benefits associated with these choices.

In summary, a major portion of the IGM literature is oriented toward goals and results on an operational level. In order to control programs and look at the end results of their work, managers in an intergovernmental setting must resolve the issues of evaluation and evaluation standards. Because they must understand implementation pragmatically, monitoring has an important role in IGM. Finally, because of its obvious impacts on the end results of IGM, managers need to understand and be aware of retrenchment in governmental programs.

Conclusion

In this chapter we have explored the subject of IGM. More directly, we have sought to discover if there is a focus on IGM that is discrete from general management and intergovernmental relations. We believe that while the effort is not yet theoretically neat, IGM is an emerging conceptualization that recasts a portion of IGR in a different direction. IGM provides the rudiments of a more powerful analytic perspective for understanding how problems are worked out and daily adjustments are made in getting things done. Its components are a problem-solving focus and interorganizational networking toward a results-based orientation.

Thus, we say that IGM is evolving into a separate and identifiable body of literature, albeit in an embryonic stage. It is difficult to articulate its present scope because there are as yet no accepted standards for that scope. We cannot say with precision what its clear boundaries are or what it should or should not include. We also cannot yet say for sure that there are big holes in the literature, that certain things are falling between the cracks, or that important aspects are missing. Several characteristics of IGM are fairly clear, however, and present guideposts about what is included now and what will probably be on the future research agenda.

In research that we have identified and included as part of the growing body of IGM literature, the focus is on making things work more than on academic or theoretical questions concerning the role and responsibilities of government. The articles, studies, and reports designed to improve the system have a strong practitioner orientation. Thus IGM literature has two readerships: the traditional academic, and the practicing public manager.

It is a problem that this research recommends making changes that may or may not work; in the future it will be necessary to test and verify these recommendations. Even though this literature endorses change before research and analysis, it may be very helpful to practicing managers because it provides them with guidelines on functioning within the intergovernmental system. Disturbing as it may be to some academics, managers do not always need tightly constructed and elegant theories that have been subjected to empirical testing.

Existing literature provides a great deal of understanding on how management functions within an intergovernmental system, and the effect of the research is becoming more penetrating as issues are debated, clarified, and tested. Although in its embryonic form, IGM is evolving in a way that may present federalism and intergovernmental relations in a different light. Behind the IGM literature lurks the suggestion of an ethic of good government, but this reformist aspect is aimed at improving the process and the results, not at changing the structure. The politics/ administration issue is raised in a sophisticated way that offers observers more insight about how the IGM system actually "works," rather than idealized models of how it should work. Issues such as problem solving, evaluation of programs and management efforts, monitoring of policies into programs, and assessment of results are all part of this developing focus on IGM. The interest in results and getting things done somewhat blurs the usual distinctions between managers and elected officials. While the emphasis is on good management, it is unclear who is the target of making things better: citizens, other bureaucrats, or perhaps politicians.

We are well aware that while we say IGM literature is separate and distinct, the full case must still be made. The various research, trends, and themes we have identified need amplification and further conceptualization. When he shifts his attention from intergovernmental relations to IGM, Wright (1986) presents a historical perspective and offers a rationale as to why the study of IGM is worthwhile. We are perhaps at the stage for IGM to conceptualize ideas that need synthesizing and testing.

In a final thought, we wonder if much of public administration is not now intergovernmental. Is IGM another way of talking about a new public administration because such management is now part of all governmental activities? The identification of IGM as a distinct body of research could be a major refocusing in confronting the modern problems of managing the contemporary American federal system, but it will take many years to sort out and verify. The effort should be both refreshing and worthwhile. And all the while, public officials and their constituencies will gain as academics labor at the effort.

References

Advisory Commission on Intergovernmental Relations. 1977. *Improving Federal Grants Management* A-53. Washington, D.C.: The Commission.

Advisory Commission on Intergovernmental Relations. 1980. *The Federal Role in the Federal System,* A-77. Washington, D.C.: Government Printing Office.

Agranoff, Robert J. 1985. *Intergovernmental Management: Human Services Problem-Solving in Six Metropolitan Areas.* Albany: State University of New York.

Agranoff, Robert, and Valerie A. Lindsay. 1983. "Intergovernmental Management: Perspectives from Human Services Problem Solving at the Local Level." *Public Administration Review* 43(3):227–37.

Agranoff, Robert, and Alex N. Pattakos. 1984. "Intergovernmental Management: Federal Changes, State Responses and New State Initiatives." *Publius* 14:49–84.

American Society for Public Administration Task Force on Intergovernmental Management. 1979. *Strengthening Intergovernmental Management: An Agenda for Reform.* Washington, D.C.: The Task Force.

Anderson, Martin. 1964. *The Federal Bulldozer.* Cambridge, Mass.: MIT Press.

Anderson, Wayne F., Chester A. Newland, and Richard V. Stillman II. 1984. *The Effective Local Manager.* Washington, D.C.: International City Management Association.

Anton, Thomas J. 1984. "Intergovernmental Change in the U.S.: An Assessment of the Literature." In *Public Sector Performance: A Conceptual Turning Point,* edited by Trudi C. Miller. Baltimore: Johns Hopkins University Press.

Anton, Thomas J. 1985. "Decay and Reconstruction in the Study of American Intergovernmental Relations." *Publius* 15(1):65–97.

Anton, Thomas J., Patrick D. Larkey, and Toni R. Linton. 1975. *Understanding the Fiscal Impact of General Revenue Sharing.* Ann Arbor: University of Michigan Press.

Appleby, Paul. 1949. *Policy and Administration.* University, Ala.: University of Alabama Press.

Bailey, Stephen K., and Edith Mosher. 1968. *ESEA: The Office of Education Administers a Law.* Syracuse, N.Y.: Syracuse University.

Beam, David R., Timothy J. Conlan, and David B. Walker. 1982. "Government in Three Dimensions: Implications of a Changing Federalism for Political Science." Presented at the annual meeting of the American Political Science Association, Denver.

Beam, David, and Margaret Wrightson. 1983. "Federalism: The Challenge of Conflicting Theories and Contemporary Practice." In *Political Science: The State of the Discipline,* edited by Ada W. Finifter. Washington, D.C.: American Political Science Association.

Bebout, John F. 1982. "Space, Time, and Jurisdiction and the New Federalism." *National Civic Review* 71:526–35.

Beckman, Norman. 1981. "Intergovernmental Relations: The Future Is Now." *Public Administration Review* 41(6):693–701.

Beer, Samuel H. 1974. "The Modernization of American Federalism." In *The Federal Policy,* edited by Daniel J. Elazar. New Brunswick, N.J.: Transaction.

Beer, Samuel H. 1978. "Federalism, Nationalism and Democracy in America." *American Political Science Review* 72:9–21.

Beer, Samuel H. 1982. "Federalism: Lessons of the Past, Choices for the Future." In *Federalism: Making the System Work,* edited by Center for National Policy. Washington, D.C.: Center for National Policy.

Bish, Robert L. 1978. "Intergovernmental Relations in the United States: Some Concepts and Implications from a Public Choice Perspective." In *Interorganizational Policy Making: Limits to Coordination and Central Control,* edited by Kenneth Hanf and Fritz Sharpf. Beverly Hills: Sage.

Bombardier, Gary. 1975. "The Managerial Function of OMB: Intergovernmental Relations as a Test Case." *Public Policy* 23:317–54.

310

Brown, Anthony. 1980. "Technical Assistance to Rural Communities: Stop Gap or Capacity Building?" *Public Administration Review* 40(1):18–23.

Brown, L. David. 1983. *Managing Conflict at Organizational Interfaces.* Reading, Mass.: Addison-Wesley.

Buntz, C. Gregory, and Beryl A. Radin. 1983. "Managing Intergovernmental Conflict: The Case of Human Service." *Public Administration Review* 43(1):403–10.

Burgess, Philip M. 1975. "Capacity Building and the Elements of Public Management." *Public Administration Review* 35:707.

Clayton, Ross, Patrick Conklin, Raymond Shapek. eds. 1975. "Policy Management Assistance—A Developing Dialogue." *Public Administration Review* 35.

Coleman, William G. 1981. "An Overview of the American Federal System: Entering an Era of Constraint." Presented to the Governors Roundtable of the Lincoln Institute of Land Policy, Boston.

Commission on Intergovernmental Relations. 1955. *A Report to the President for Transmission to the Congress.* Washington, D.C.: Government Printing Office.

Congressional Quarterly. 1985. *American Intergovernmental Relations.* Washington, D.C.: CQ Press.

Conlan, T.J. 1984. "Federalism and Competing Values in the Reagan Administration." Presented at the annual meeting of the American Political Science Association, Washington, D.C.

Cook, Robert F., Charles F. Adams, Jr., V. Lane Rawlins, and Associates. 1985. "Public Service Employment: The Experience of a Decade." Kalamazoo, Mich.: W.E. Upjohn Institute.

Derthick, Martha. 1970. *The Influence of Federal Grants: Public Assistance in Massachusetts.* Cambridge, Mass.: Harvard University Press.

Derthick, Martha. 1972. *New Towns In-Town.* Washington, D.C.: Urban Institute.

Diamond, Martin. 1966. *The Democratic Republic: An Introduction to American National Government.* Chicago, Ill.: Rand McNally.

Dommel, Paul R., and John Stuart Hall. 1984. "Field Network Research in Policy Evaluation." *Policy Studies Review* 4:49–59.

Dommel, Paul R., Richard P. Nathan, Sara Liebschutz, Margaret Wrightson, and Associates. 1978. *Decentralizing Community Development.* Washington, D.C.: Government Printing Office.

Eddy, William. 1983. *Handbook of Organizational Management.* New York: Marcel Dekker.

Edner, Sheldon M. 1976. "Intergovernmental Policy Development: The Importance of Problem Definition." In *Public Policy Making in the Federal System,* edited by Charles Jones and Robert Thomas. Beverly Hills: Sage.

Edner, Sheldon M. 1977. "The Blind Men and the Elephant: How Do Intergovernmental Actors Compensate for Their Handicap or Is There a Cure for Hereditary Blindness?" Presented at the annual meeting of the American Political Science Association, Washington, D.C.

Elazar, Daniel J. 1962. *The American Partnership: Intergovernmental Cooperation in the Nineteenth Century.* Chicago: University of Chicago Press.

Elazar, Daniel J. 1974. "First Principles." In *The Federal Policy,* edited by Daniel J. Elazar. New Brunswick, N.J.: Transaction.

Elazar, Daniel J. 1981a. "The Evolving Federal System." In *The Power to Govern,* edited by Richard M. Pious. New York: Academy of Political Science.

Elazar, Daniel J. 1981b. "Is Federalism Compatible with Prefectorial Administration?" Symposium, American Federalism and Prefectorial Administration. *Publius* 11(2): 3–22.

Ellwood, John Williams, ed. 1982. *Reductions in U.S. Domestic Spending, How They Affect the State and Local Governments*. New Brunswick, N.J.: Transaction.

Elmore, Richard F. 1978. "Organizational Models of Social Program Implementation." *Public Policy* 26(2):185–228.

Executive Office of the President. 1975. *Strengthening Public Management in the Intergovernmental System: A Report Prepared for the Office of Management and Budget by the Study Committee on Policy Management Assistance*. Washington, D.C.: Government Printing Office.

Feller, Irwin. 1975. "Issues in the Design of Federal Programs to Improve the Policy Management Capabilities of State Legislatures." *Public Administration Review* 35:780–85.

Freilich, Robert H., David S. Frye, and Dianne T. Carpenter. 1983. "The New Federalism—American Urban Policy in the 1980s: Trends and Directions in Urban, State, and Local Government Law." *Urban Lawyer* 15:159–230.

Fried, Robert C. 1981. "Prefectorialism in America." *Publius* 11(2):23–29.

Frieden, Bernard, and Marshall Kaplan. 1975. *The Politics of Neglect: Urban Aid from Model Cities to Revenue Sharing*. Cambridge, Mass.: MIT Press.

Gage, Robert W. 1984. "Federal Regional Councils: Networking Organizations for Policy Management in the Intergovernmental System." *Public Administration Review* 41(2):134–44.

Gargan, John J., and Carl M. Moore. 1984. "Enhancing Local Government Capacity in Budget Decision Making: The Use of Group Process Techniques." *Public Administration Review* 41(6):504–11.

Gerth, H.H., and C. Wright Mills. 1974. *From Max Weber: Essays in Sociology*. New York: Oxford University Press.

Gold, Steven. 1983. "States Treat Localities Well Despite Financial Problems." *State Legislatures* 9:24–28.

Goodnow, Frank J. 1900. *Politics and Administration*. New York: Macmillan.

Gordon, George J. 1979. "Will Intergovernmental Management Be the End of American Federalism?" Presented at the annual meeting of the American Society for Public Administration. Baltimore.

Graves, W. Brooke, ed. 1940. "Intergovernmental Relations in the U.S." *Annals of the American Academy of Political and Social Science* 207.

Graves, W. Brooke. 1964. *American Intergovernmental Relations: Their Origins, History, Development and Current Status*. New York: Scribners.

Gregg, Phillip. 1974. "Units and Levels of Analysis: A Problem of Policy Analysis in Federal Systems." *Publius* 4(4):59–86.

Grodzins, Morton. 1962. *The American System: A New View of Intergovernmental Cooperation in the Nineteenth Century*. Chicago: University of Chicago Press.

Hall, George E., and Marian L. Palley. 1981. *The Politics of Federal Grants*. Washington, D.C.: CQ Press.

Hall, John Stuart. 1979. *The Impact of Federal Aid on the City of Phoenix*. A case study for the Brookings Institution Federal Politics in Big Cities Project presented to the U.S. Department of Labor.

Hall, John Stuart. 1985. "Local Implementation of National Domestic Policy in the 1980s: The Bottom Line." Presented at the annual meeting of the American Political Science

Association, New Orleans.

Hall, John Stuart, and Susan A. MacManus. 1982. "Tracking Decisions and Consequences: The Field Network Evaluation Approach." In *Studying Implementation: Methodological and Administrative Issues,* edited by Walter Williams. Chatham, N.J.: Chatham House.

Hawkins, Robert B., Jr. 1983. *American Federalism: A New Partnership for the Republic.* San Francisco: Institute of Contemporary Studies.

Hero, Rodney. 1983. "Perspectives on American Federalism." *Social Science Journal* 20: 59–74.

Honadle, Beth Walter. 1981a. "A Capacity-Building Framework: A Search for Concept and Purpose." *Public Administration Review* 41(5):575–80.

Honadle, Beth Walter. 1981b. *Capacity-Building (Management Improvement) in Local Governments: An Annotated Bibliography* RDRR-28. Washington, D.C.: U.S. Department of Agriculture, Economic, and Statistical Services.

Honadle, Beth Walter, and Arnold Howitt, eds. 1985. *Perspectives on Management Capacity Building.* Albany: State University of New York Press.

Howitt, Arnold M. 1984. *Managing Federalism. Studies in Intergovernmental Relations.* Washington, D.C.: CQ Press.

James, Judson L. 1979. "Intergovernmental Administration in a Period of Fiscal Constraint and Productivity Demands." Presented at the annual meeting of the American Political Science Association, Washington, D.C.

Jones, Charles O., and Robert D. Thomas, eds. 1976. *Public Policy Making in a Federal System.* Beverly Hills: Sage.

Jones, Harry H. 1975. "Evaluation Bases and Management." *Public Administration Review* 35:737–42.

Juster, F. Thomas. 1977. *The Economic and Political Impact of Government Revenue Sharing.* Ann Arbor: Survey Research Center, Institute for Social Research, University of Michigan.

Kane, Thomas J., Jr. 1984. "City Managers View Intergovernmental Relations." *Publius* 14:121–33.

Kaufman, Herbert. 1960. *The Forest Ranger.* Baltimore: The Johns Hopkins University Press.

Key, V.O., Jr. 1937. *The Administration of Federal Grants to States.* Chicago: Public Administration Service.

Kirlin, John J. 1984. "A Political Perspective." In *Public Sector Performance: A Conceptual Turning Point,* edited by Trudi C. Miller. Baltimore: The Johns Hopkins Press.

Klinger, Donald E., Sandra Lehnen, and Philip Schervish. 1984. "Intergovernmental Fiscal Trends Affect Urban Human Service Delivery." *National Civic Review* 73:283–91.

Kouka, D. 1984. "Significant State Actions Affecting Local Governments." *The Municipal Yearbook.* Washington, D.C.: International City Management Association.

Landau, Martin. 1973. "Federalism, Redundancy and System Reliability." *Publius* 3:173–96.

Larkey, Patrick Daniel. 1975. "Political Budgeting: A Framework for an Institutional Analysis of Swedish National Accounts. Scandinavian Political Evaluation: The Impact of General Revenue Sharing on Municipal Fiscal Behavior." Doctoral dissertation, University of Michigan.

Larkey, Patrick Daniel. 1979. *Evaluating Public Programs: The Impact of General Revenue Sharing on Municipal Government.* Princeton: Princeton University Press.

313

Leach, Richard H., ed. 1979. "Intergovernmental Relations—A Symposium." *Southern Review of Public Administration* 3(1).

Lenz, R.T. 1980. "Strategic Capability: A Concept and Framework for Analysis." *Academy of Management Review* 5(2):225–34.

Levine, Charles H. 1978. "Organizational Decline and Cutback Management." *Public Administration Review* 38(4):316–25.

Levine, Charles H. 1979. "More on Cutback Management." *Public Administration Review* 39(3):179–83.

Levine, Charles H. 1981. "Cutting Back the Public Sector: The Hidden Hazards of Retrenchment." Presented at third Inaugural Lecture, University of Kansas, Lawrence, Kansas.

Levine, Charles H., and Paul L. Posner. 1979. "The Centralizing Effects of Austerity on the Intergovernmental System." Presented at the annual meeting of the American Political Science Association, Washington, D.C.

Levine, Charles H., Irene S. Rubin, and George G. Wolohojian. 1981. *The Politics of Retrenchment: How Local Governments Manage Fiscal Stress.* Beverly Hills: Sage Publications.

Lovell, Catherine H. 1979. "Where We Are in IGR and Some of the Implications." *Southern Review of Public Administration* 3(1):6–20.

MacManus, Susan A. 1979. *Federal Aid to Houston.* Washington, D.C.: Brookings Institution.

Mandell, Myrna P. 1979. "Intergovernmental Management: Letters to the Editor." *Public Administration Times* 2:2,6.

Marando, Vincent L. 1981. "States, Cities, and the Reagan New Federalism." Presented at the 1981 meeting of the American Society for Public Administration, Detroit.

Marshall, Dale R. 1975. "Implementation of Federal Poverty and Welfare Policy: A Review." In *Analyzing Poverty Policy,* edited by Dorothy James. Lexington, Mass.: Lexington Books.

Massie, Joseph L. 1979. *Essentials of Management.* 3d ed. Englewood Cliffs, N.J.: Prentice-Hall.

Mikulecky, Thomas J. 1980. "Intergovernmental Relations Strategies for the Local Manager." *Public Administration Review* 40(4):379–81.

Mosher, Frederick C. 1980. "The Changing Responsibilities and Tactics of the Federal Government." *Public Administration Review* 40(6):541–47.

Nathan, Richard P. 1977. *Block Grants for Community Development.* Washington, D.C.: Brookings Institution, contracted by the U.S. Department of Housing and Urban Development.

Nathan, Richard P. 1982. "A Methodology for Field Network Evaluation Studies." In *Studying Implementation: Methodological and Administrative Issues,* edited by Walter Williams. Chatham, N.J.: Chatham House.

Nathan, Richard P. 1983. "State and Local Governments under Federal Grants: Toward a Predictive Theory." *Political Science Quarterly* 98:47–57.

Nathan, Richard P., Charles Adams, and Associates. 1977. *Revenue Sharing: The Second Round.* Washington, D.C.: Brookings Institution.

Nathan, Richard P., Robert F. Cook, V. Lane Rawlins, and Associates. 1979. *Public Service Employment: A Field Evaluation.* Washington, D.C.: Brookings Institution.

Nathan, Richard P., and Fred Doolittle. 1984. " The Untold Story of Reagan's New Federalism." *The Public Interest* 77:96–105.

Nathan, Richard P., Fred C. Doolittle, and Associates. 1983. *The Consequences of Cuts: The Effects of the Reagan Domestic Program on State and Local Governments.* Princeton: Princeton Urban and Regional Research Center.

Nathan, Richard P., Allen D. Manuel, Susannah E. Calkins, et al. 1975. *Monitoring Revenue Sharing.* Washington, D.C.: Brookings Institution.

Oates, Wallace. 1977. *The Political Economy of Fiscal Federalism.* Lexington, Mass.: Heath.

Ostrom, Elinor, Roger Parks, and Gordon Whittaker. 1978. *Patterns of Metropolitan Policing.* Cambridge, Mass.: Ballinger.

Ostrom, Vincent. 1971. *The Political Theory of a Compound Republic: A Reconstruction of the Logical Foundations of American Democracy as Presented in the Federalist Papers.* Blacksburg, Va.: Center for Public Choice, Virginia Polytechnic Institute.

Ostrom, Vincent. 1973. *The Intellectual Crisis in Public Administration.* Rev. ed. University, Ala.: University of Alabama Press.

Pattakos, Alex N., and Kenneth T. Palmer. 1983. "State/Local Relations under Reagan's New Federalism: An Intergovernmental Perspective." Prepared for delivery at the annual meeting of the American Political Science Association, Chicago.

Porter, David O., David C. Warner, and Teddie M. Porter. 1973. *The Politics of Budgeting Federal Aid: Resource Mobilization by Local School Districts.* Beverly Hills: Sage.

Pressman, Jeffrey, and Aaron Wildavsky. 1973. *Implementation.* Berkeley: University of California Press.

Radin, Beryl A. 1977. *Implementation, Change, the Federal Bureaucracy: School Desegregation Policy in HEW 1964–68.* New York: Teachers College Press.

Rapp, Brian W., and Frank M. Patitucci. 1977. *Managing Local Government for Improved Performance: A Practical Approach.* Boulder, Colo.: Westview Press.

Rose, Richard, and Guy Peters. 1978. *Can Governments Go Bankrupt?* New York: Basic Books.

Rosenbaum, Allan. 1978. "Federal Programs and State Governments: On Understanding Why Forty Years of Federal Efforts Haven't Fundamentally Altered Economic Inequality in American Society." Presented at the annual meeting of the American Political Science Association, New York.

Rosenthal, Stephen R. 1984. "New Directions for Evaluating Intergovernmental Programs." *Public Administration Review* 41(6):469–76.

Rothenberg, Irene Fraser. 1984. "Out with the Old, In with the New: The New Federalism, Intergovernmental Coordination and Executive Order 1237." *Publius* 14:31–47.

Rubin, Irene S. 1985. *Running in the Red: The Political Dynamics of Urban Fiscal Stress.* Albany: State University of New York Press.

Salamon, Lester M. 1982. "Federalism and Third-Party Government: The Challenge to Public Management." In *Federalism: Making the System Work.* Washington, D.C.: Center for National Policy.

Sanders, Heywood T. 1979. "Urban Renewal and the Revitalized City: A Reconsideration of Recent History." Manuscript.

Schechter, Stephen L. 1981. "On the Compatibility of Federalism and Intergovernmental Management." *Publius* 11(2):127–41.

Schick, Allen. 1975. "The Intergovernmental Thicket: The Questions Still Are Better Than the Answers." *Public Administration Review* 35:717–72.

Schmandt, Henry J., George Wendell, and E. Allan Tomey. 1979. "The Impact of Federal Aid on the City of St. Louis": A Case Study for the Brookings Institution Federal Politics in Big Cities Project. Prepared under the direction of Richard P. Nathan and

Shannon, John. 1985. "Interstate Competition for Industry." Presented at the annual meeting of the American Political Science Association, New Orleans.

Shapek, Raymond A. 1981. *Evolution and Development of the Grant-in-Aid System.* Charlottesville, Va.: Community Collaborators.

Shefter, Martin. 1977. "New York City's Fiscal Crisis: The Politics of Inflation and Retrenchment." *Public Interest,* Summer, 98–127.

Sonenblum, Sidney, John J. Kirlin, and John C. Ries. 1977. *How Cities Provide Services: An Evaluation of Alternative Delivery Structure.* Cambridge, Mass.: Ballinger.

Stanley, David T. 1976. *Cities in Trouble.* Columbus, Ohio: Academy for Contemporary Problems.

Stone, Donald C. 1983. "Strategies and Methods for Improving Organizations, Administrative Systems, and Management." National Institute of Public Affairs Seminar/ Workshop, The Intergovernmental Challenge, Leesburg, Virginia, 4–7 December, Section N.

Sundquist, James, and David W. Davis. 1969. *Making Federalism Work: A Study of Program Coordination at the Community Level.* Washington, D.C.: Brookings Institution.

Svara, James H. 1985. "Dichotomy and Duality: Reconceptualizing the Relationship between Policy and Administration in Council-Manager Cities." *Public Administration Review* 45(1):221–32.

Talley, Bruce B. 1980. "Intergovernmental Cooperation." In *Productivity Improvement Handbook for State and Local Government,* edited by George J. Washinis. New York: Wiley.

Thompson, Frank J., and Michael J. Scicchitano. 1983. "State Implementation of Federal Regulatory Policy: The Case of Occupational Safety and Health." Presented at the annual meeting of the Southern Political Science Association, Birmingham.

Tropman, John E. 1977. "American Welfare Strategies: Three Programs under the Social Security Act." *Policy Sciences* 8(1):33–48.

U.S. Accounting Office. 1984. *States Use Several Strategies to Cope with Funding Reductions under Social Services Block Grant: A Report to the Congress by the Comptroller General of the United States.* Washington, D.C.: Government Accounting Office.

U.S. Congressional Budget Office. 1983. *The Federal Government in a Federal System: Current Intergovernmental Programs and Options for Change.* Washington, D.C.: Government Printing Office.

U.S. Congress, House Committee on the Budget, Task Force on Federalism/State-Local Relations. 1983. *New Federalism from the Local Perspective.* Washington, D.C.: Government Printing Office.

U.S. Office of Management and Budget. 1980. "Managing Federal Assistance in the 1980's. Working Papers." Washington, D.C.: Government Printing Office.

Van Horn, Carl E., and Donald S. Van Meter. 1976. "The Implementation of Intergovernmental Policy." In *Public Policy Making in a Federal System,* edited by Charles Jones and Robert Thomas. Beverly Hills: Sage.

Van Riper, Paul P. 1983. "The American Administrative State: Wilson and the Founders—An Unorthodox View." *Public Administration Review* 43(6):477–90.

Walker, David B. 1981a. "Intergovernmental Relations and Dysfunctional Federalism." *National Civic Review,* February, 68–82.

Walker, David B. 1981b. *Toward a Functioning Federalism.* Cambridge, Mass.: Winthrop.

Warren, Roland L., Stephen M. Rose, and Ann F. Bergunder. 1974. *The Structure of Urban Reform.* Lexington, Mass.: Heath.

Wildavsky, Aaron. 1980. "The 1980s: Monopoly or Competition." *Intergovernmental Perspective* 6(3):15–18.

Williams, Walter. 1982. *Studying Implementation.* Chatham, N.J.: Chatham House.

Wilson, Woodrow. 1887. "The Study of Administration." *Political Science Quarterly* 2: 197–222.

Wilson, Woodrow. 1986. "Management." In *A Centennial History of the American Administrative State,* edited by Ralph Clark Chandler. New York: Macmillan.

Wright, Deil S. 1975. "Intergovernmental Relations and Policy Choice." *Publius* 5(4):1–24.

Wright, Deil S. 1980. "Intergovernmental Games: An Approach to Understanding Intergovernmental Relations." *Southern Review of Public Administration* 3(4):383–403.

Wright, Deil S. 1982a. "New Federalism: Recent Varieties of an Older Species." Draft of an article for the *American Review of Public Administration.*

Wright, Deil S. 1982b. *Understanding Intergovernmental Relations.* 2d ed. Monterey, Calif.: Brooks/Cole.

Wright, Deil S. 1983. "Managing the Intergovernmental Scene: The Changing Dramas of Federalism, Intergovernmental Relations, and Intergovernmental Management." In *Handbook of Organizational Management,* edited by William B. Eddy. New York: Marcel Dekker.

Wright, Deil S. 1984. *Federalism and Intergovernmental Relations.* Washington, D.C.: American Society for Public Administration.

Wright, Deil S. 1986. "A Century of the Intergovernmental Administrative State: From Woodrow Wilson's Federalism to Intergovernmental Management." In *A Centennial History of the American Administrative State,* edited by Ralph Clark Chandler. New York: Macmillan.

Yin, Robert K., Peter K. Bateman, Ellen L. Marks, and Suzanne K. Quick. 1979. *Changing Urban Bureaucracies: How New Practices Become Routinized.* Lexington, Mass.: Lexington Books.

Zeitz, G. 1975. "Interorganizational Relationships and Social Structure: A Critique of Some Aspects of the Literature." In *Interorganization Theory,* edited by A.R. Neghandhi. Kent, Ohio: Kent State University Press.

Zimmerman, Joseph F. 1979. "Partial Federal Preemption and Changing Intergovernmental Relations." Presented at the annual meeting of the American Political Science Association, Washington, D.C.

14

Comparative Public Administration:
The Search for Theories

ROBERT C. FRIED

If we had a universal theory of comparative public administration, it might look like this: We would have before us a scheme for classifying the administrative systems of the 150 countries in the world; there would, one hopes, be fewer than 150 categories into which to classify those systems; the criteria for classification would be easy to use; and we would all agree on the results of the classification. Once we had placed each national administrative system into its category, our theory would tell us a vast amount about that system. Members of each category would have so many characteristics in common that, knowing a system's class, we would effortlessly and accurately predict a large number of structural and behavioral characteristics.

Our theory, if we had one, would of course be more than a taxonomy; it would also tell us why systems resemble one another, why they differ, and what consequences ensue from these similarities and differences.

We would know, moreover, how and when our system types arose, and how their stages of development, decay, and demise arranged themselves. From this we could deduce the secrets of change—the means of hastening or altering the bureaucratic fate of nations.

Our theory, if we had one, would be based on empirical facts: Key variables would be quantifiable and quantified; classification would be based on empirical indicators; interrelationships among the variables, both currently and across time, would be measured in probabilistic, recursive multiple-regression formulas.

Our theory would also (since we're dreaming) be value neutral: Our variables, concepts, methods of analysis, standards of evidence, reading of history, etc., would be 99 and 44/100 percent scientifically pure.

There was a moment, after World War II, when the creation of such a science of comparative administration seemed a possibility. A critical mass of scholars assembled under the auspices of the American Society for Public Administration

(ASPA) and the American Political Science Association (APSA)—the two relevant national professional associations (those, in fact, sponsoring this volume)—in the form of the Comparative Administration Group, CAG (Arora 1972; Heady 1978; Loveman 1976; Riggs 1976; Savage 1976; Siffin 1976). CAG had the intellectual and financial resources, and the moral enthusiasm, to match the ambitiousness of its goal, the creation of a genuinely universal comparative theory of public administration.

The members of CAG in 1960 did not start, needless to say, from a tabula rasa. Administrative theory had long been a part of the commerce among the Western nations, indeed an integral part of their emergence and development. Innovations in administrative theory—notions regarding the way in which the executive branch of government should be structured, empowered, and limited—were a basic ingredient in the constitutional evolution of Western nations from at least the eighteenth century. Nations, then as now, innovated administratively in ways that were studied, copied, or rejected by their actual or would-be peers.

Revolutionaries and reformers in the eighteenth and nineteenth centuries looked across boundaries (and across history) for institutions to copy or reject. Some of this (unpatented) institutional knowledge was formulated by academic writers, particularly in the field of comparative administrative law (e.g., Goodnow, 1893; Orlando 1900–1910). Comparativists first formally exchanged ideas in International Congresses of the Administrative Sciences held in 1910, 1923, and 1927. The International Institute of Administrative Sciences began publication of its Review in 1928, and in 1930 it sponsored publication of *The Civil Service in the Modern State,* edited by Leonard D. White, with documents on bureaucracy in fourteen countries (White 1930).

Undoubtedly the most important comparative research was carried out between 1895 and 1920, not by comparative law professors or participants in international congresses, but by a sociologist, Max Weber (Bendix 1962; Gerth and Mills 1946; Weber 1947). Weber lifted the level of analysis to a height of sophistication, and with a breadth of scope seldom attained since. Weber developed the core concept of the field—*bureaucracy*—as part of a comparative typology of the forms of domination (*Herrschaft*): tradition, charisma, and legal-rationality. Each form of domination or authority had its matching type of administrative staff (*Verwaltungs-stab*—Weber 1976, 551–79). Bureaucracy was the form of administrative staff associated with legal-rational authority. The bureaucratic "ideal type"—marked by hierarchy, specialized and delimited responsibilities, achievement-based recruitment and promotion, rules, and rationality (behavior dominated by organization goals) —became the dominant topic in the analysis of public (and private) organizations in the "modern" state.

Weber's works, sponsored by eminent American sociologists, became available in translation to American scholars in 1946. Reception of Weber's works was

319

facilitated at this point by the presence in the United States of scholars with close ties to Europe. In fact, during the 1930s major comparative studies had been made by European-trained scholars (Finer 1961 [1932]; Friedrich 1950 [1937]). The central role that bureaucracies played in modern government was stressed in all these studies. Friedrich called bureaucracy "the core of modern government" (Friedrich 1950, 37).

The chances for a universal theory of comparative public administration now seemed favorable. The center of comparative study shifted to the United States, which was becoming the world's center for academic research, particularly in the social sciences. American academicians were well financed, cosmopolitan in interests, rigorously trained, unafraid of fieldwork, and optimistic about research possibilities.

Interest in comparative administration was formalized and institutionalized by the formation of the Comparative Administration Group (CAG). CAG had the minds, the finances, and the will to create a universal theory. It had an interest in the whole world, including and especially the Third World. It had in Fred Riggs a leader with great intellectual powers, a strong interest in the Third World as well as experience in American public administration, and an awareness of major concepts in economics and sociology. In the early 1960s, Riggs published major theoretical works, formulating ideal-typical models of bureaucracy—a set of models more adapted to the study of existing systems in various parts of the world than the Weberian ideal types (Riggs 1961, 1962, 1963, 1964; see also Riggs 1966, 1971, 1973).

Riggs's major effort was devoted to the understanding of non-Western countries. (It was assumed by him and by most others at the time that the Western experience had been fully analyzed and digested.) Riggs developed the theory of Prismatic Society—the ideal type of a Third World country evolving and/or developing from traditionality to modernity. Prismatic societies had neither the undifferentiated ("fused") institutions of traditional societies nor the (supposedly) fully differentiated institutions of modern society: Their institutions were legal-rational in form (in manifest function), but traditional in fact (in latent function).

Weber's key concepts had been hierarchy, specialization, impersonality, rules, rationality, predictability, and office. Riggs's key concepts—formalism, heterogeneity, and overlapping—alerted the researcher that Weberian bureaucracy might not be entirely predictive of behavior in most Third World countries. (Riggs did not deal with the possibilities of using Weber's traditional and charismatic authority and administration in Third World contexts.)

An even more important concept for Riggs was the ecology of administration. Here he joined the camp in the academic analysis of government bureaucracy that stressed the importance of social forces in shaping bureaucratic behavior and conditioning performance. Implicitly, Riggs was combatting the technocratic camp that stressed the acultural (or supracultural) imperatives of administrative organization and behavior. These camps derived from reactions to the asserted dichotomy between politics and administration, reactions to the traditions of scientific management, and reactions to the notion that there is one best way of scientifically organizing any government enterprise anywhere. Adaptation to sociocultural expectations and traditions as a means to achieving greater efficiency was rationality to one camp, irrationality to the other.

Riggsian theory was sensitive to the context of administration. It was behavioral theory, oriented not to the elaboration and imposition of organizational behavior codes (such as the doctrines of the other camp might appear to be when benignly viewed) but to actual behaviors and the "hidden rationality" of discrepancies in Weberian formalism (Hirschmann 1963).

The ambition of Riggs, and of CAG, was to develop a science of comparative administration, an empirically derived set of generalizations about administration. Cross-sectional variance was to be explained largely in developmental terms: All systems were moving toward the same Weberian destination; some systems were farther along than others. Systems could be expected to evolve in correlation with their ecologies.

Much, therefore, augured favorably for the development of a scientific comparative theory. Scholarly interest had expanded from America and Europe to Latin America, Africa, Asia, and the Middle East. Concepts were being developed that attempted to set Western and non-Western administration into a common framework (the developmental framework), and scholars were empirically oriented, interested in measuring discrepancies from form and ideal type. There was strong support for the endeavor from eminent members of the academic community, from universities, from foundations, from international organizations, and even from some of the governments under study. The study of comparative administration was being promoted by an enormous growth of American interest in other countries (the end of isolationism), by the revitalization of domestic studies of American public administration that occurred with the participation of American scholars in wartime and postwar administration, and by the explosion in the study of comparative politics.

In fact, from 1955 to 1965, under all these favorable stimuli, comparative public administration flourished—in books and monographs, conferences, new university courses, university FTE allocations, field trips, consultancies, and government and foundation grants.

Yet, at the end of this period and in subsequent years, little progress was made toward the creation of a universal scientific theory of comparative public administration. CAG was disbanded in 1965. Postmortem inquests on the field were, somewhat belatedly, held in 1976. What had happened?

321

Why Universal Theory Remains Elusive

The failure to produce a science of comparative public administration can be ascribed to two sets of factors, one relating to the nature of the subject matter and the other relating to the nature of the knowledge industry concerned with that subject matter.

An Elusive Prey

National administrative systems are more difficult to study than other political institutions (e.g., parties, mass publics, legislatures, and courts), particularly when studied in terms of performance. The outputs of other political institutions are more readily available, and in quantitative form (e.g., votes, decisions, seats). The outputs of administrative systems are incredibly diverse, subject to no single form of output measurement. Electoral outcomes, legislative outcomes, judicial outcomes, even military outcomes are more easily tallied and related to inputs than are the multi-form outcomes of administrative processes. Administrative systems are everywhere composed of many kinds of agencies, doing many kinds of things. (Studying systems of interest groups poses much the same problem.)

The boundaries of administrative systems are difficult to establish. Administrative systems consist of agencies specialized by function, agencies at different levels of government, and agencies with differing formal-legal attachments to the regular governmental machinery. Insofar as comparative public administration is the comparative study of policy implementation, delimiting the sets of actors involved in each country becomes extremely difficult. All kinds of actors not belonging to the regular public administrative machinery are involved in implementation, including courts, mass publics, mass media, local governments, and private economic organizations. The myriad actors involved in operating world markets can be seen as part of the administrative process, since governments use markets to implement public policies. The marble-cake metaphor—so apt for describing American federalism—is becoming as apt for describing the demarcation between public and private, and between national and international actors in comparative public administration.

Moreover, since implementation networks vary by function, variance within countries may easily be as great as between countries. Bureaucracies within the United States, Yates has noted, vary in at least eleven ways—task, problem, natural history, constituency, hierarchy, technology, expertise, SOPs, openness, centralization, and dominance (Yates 1982). How ironic, therefore, when one uses, as one must, the term "the bureaucracy" when referring to this congeries!

Adding to the problem of complexity is the problem of change. Administrative arrangements are constantly changing. How could anyone or even any international organization keep up with the changes in 150 countries, even if they tried?

If the subject matter to be studied combines diversity with complexity, change with formalism—all to be understood only within total ecological contexts—then it qualifies as difficult.

Countries vary in the degree of their participation in the researchable world. Some countries, most notably the Soviet Union, deliberately exclude themselves from this world; international data on socioeconomic indicators (demography, health, housing, etc.), while including statistics from many other communist nations, regularly omit such data for the USSR. One of the major problems with comparative public administration is that it *is* (in aspiration at least) comparative. If bureaucracies (Western and non-Western) were Weberian in their rationality and *glasnost*, they would see comparison as fruitful for self-evaluation and improvement. Few bureaucracies, however (Western or non-Western), see comparison as nonthreatening. Many are therefore tempted to manipulate or shred data about their performance. Bureaucrats everywhere protect careers, privacy, and even agency missions by data manipulation. Since in most cases bureaucracies monopolize information about their performance (or structure, manpower, finances, or operations), it should come as no surprise that it is difficult for outsiders to obtain genuinely useful structural or performance data instead of multicolored pamphlets.

Another major problem with comparative public administration is that it has been (at least in intent) behavioral. Behavioral research, seeking to penetrate the normal bureaucratic camouflage of legal-rationality, is as threatening as comparative research. Even in advanced countries, bureaucrats trained in legal or technical disciplines find the questions of behavioral researchers (What really happens? How do you make decisions?) puzzling at best, intrusive at worst. Efforts to get at bureaucratic politics can meet with a wall of uncomprehending resistance; the politics vs. administration dichotomy is as useful in fending off researchers as in fending off politicians.

The nonparticipation of many countries or agencies in the researchable world is involuntary. They are simply not equipped to provide the data. Accurate data on performance are relatively recent in the agencies of even the most advanced countries—countries that only in the 1970s installed automatic data-processing equipment to monitor internal operations. In the formally centralized police system of France, for example, reliable data on the performance of police districts became available to the Ministry of the Interior in Paris only in the 1970s.

Had the CAG attempted in the 1950s and 1960s to mount a survey of world bureaucracies in order to test some of its hypotheses about the factors conditioning bureaucratic behavior and the ability of bureaucracies to condition their environment, much of the data would have been unavailable, even if every country had been open and researchable. The crucial data involved relationships between bureaucracies and environments that were largely new. The interactions were just taking place; it was far too soon for anyone to be able to delineate the patterns. Thus, much of the CAG production in the 1960s was literally a priori theorizing and speculation based on extrapolating often idealized experiences in the West. In the 1980s, the data exist on bureaucratic-environment interactions—data that simply did not exist in the CAG era.

In the days of CAG, there was little agreement on what kind of variance anyone could or should measure and explain. Neither Weber nor Riggs provided an overwhelmingly cogent paradigm to guide the data collectors. CAG papers and monographs display a dazzling variety of approaches, foci, methods, and orientations. There was no party line as to what the correct basic assumptions or the orthodox paradigm had to be.

A final obstacle to a science of comparative administration stems from the absence of an international party line, which would suppress alternative conceptions and expressions of world social reality. All central and sometimes even some peripheral capitalist societies allow public expression of divergent theories. If some dogmatic authority should gain control over the world and impose uniform concepts, definitions, methods, and assumptions, then a universal social science might, in some sense, become achievable. Until such time, writers in social science journals (in the core capitalist societies at least) will continue to compete actively in presenting alternative theories of administrative and social reality, based on radically different readings of history—past, current, and future.

Supply and Demand

In the absence of a party line defining reality, the task of acknowledging and understanding diversity in the public administration of 150 nation-states is a massive one, requiring the efforts of thousands, not the dozens or hundreds who were involved in CAG activities. It requires the efforts, moreover, of experts in dozens of fields —history, sociology, politics, public administration, economics, law, urban planning, public health, etc. What professional group, worthy of the name, has no contribution to make? As the scope of public administration expands, so does the scope of expert talents required to analyze its development. Comprehensive cross-national research requires the efforts of specialists in every geographic area of the populated world: How else can one conduct behavioral, nonformalistic research into the bureaucracies and ecologies of every country in the world?

Clearly, the supply of talent for universal comparative work has been limited. Most experts have preferred to cultivate gardens, not entire fields. Many public administration experts, moreover, have assumed (in contrast to Riggs) that ecology is not that important, that correct managerial techniques have been discovered (mostly, hitherto, in the United States, perhaps now in Japan) and need merely to be introduced in every country so as to secure economical and efficient administration. Rather than wait for comprehensive, time-consuming ecological research, it would surely be better to copy the leaders and get right down to the job (cf. Esman 1980; Stokes 1980).

Demand factors have also been at work. Governments, foundations, and international funding agencies have been much less interested in sponsoring the creation of universal theory than in action-oriented efforts that focus on a segment of the world's bureaucracies—those of the Third World—and promise practical payoffs. European and American public administration is supposedly well-known, déjà vu. Bureaucracy in the new nations is unknown—more appealing, certainly more politically impelling to study (someone might understand bureaucratic behavior in the Third World before we do). What government agencies and foundations wanted came to be called *development administration* and what they wanted was supplied. As a result, development administration research has almost driven out comparative research.

More recently, the threat to comparative research has escalated. Now international funding agencies, such as the World Bank, have concluded that the public sector in the Third World has largely failed and that reliance should henceforth be placed on elements outside the government bureaucracy: local communities and private entrepreneurs. Privatization in the Third World—diminishing the role of foreign aid bureaucracies and domestic government bureaucracies—threatens to convert the study of comparative development administration into the study of comparative administrative history.

For all these reasons, the development of a comprehensive science of public administration has been difficult. Instead of a mighty hierarchical, specialized frontal attack on the secrets of the world's bureaucracies, academics have preferred to imitate non-Weberian organizations—simplifying, examining conspicuous alternatives, focusing sequentially on narrow problems, and rejecting a synoptic approach in favor of incremental analysis.

Tributary Streams

The lack of a Grand Theory—empirical, comprehensive, and behavioral—does not mean that comparative public administration scholars have been inactive or that interest in understanding comparative bureaucracy has flagged. The CPA movement has continued to move along many divergent streams, each examining and attempting to explain a particular kind of bureaucratic variance. These variances include bureaucratic wealth, bureaucratic power, bureaucratic scope, and bureaucratic functions (policy). I shall deal with only the first three; function or policy as a variable affecting and affected by the role of bureaucratic agencies has been treated in Hancock (1983), and I have expressed my own reading of some of the literature in Fried (1975).

Bureaucratic Wealth

The variances among European and North American administrative systems studied before World War II—though they included extremes in human rights among the democracies, the fascist dictatorships, and Stalinist Russia—were nevertheless variances among relatively advanced, industrial nations. (The differences in human rights were all the more shocking in that they involved "advanced" countries.) The variances that comparativists sought to understand and explain after World War II expanded to cover not only human rights but the total spectrum of societal differences in all parts of the world.

It was reasonable for development administration to drive out comparative administration as a priority concern, since the task of understanding what came to be known as the Third World required (and still requires) any talents available. Not only were the places exotic to Western officials and academics, but many of them had rather suddenly become nation-states. Much of our understanding of the advanced world depends on our knowledge of fixed historical routines (institutions). When nations are new, there are no national standard operating procedures for comparativists to study.

Some Third World nations, to be sure, are relatively old nation-states. Latin American states, for example, have had more than a century of national independence. Decolonization in North and South America occurred a century before decolonization in Asia, Africa, and the Middle East. This means that the Third World is not a very homogeneous grouping of countries. Not surprisingly, the reception of Riggs's theory of Prismatic Society—derived from the study of Thailand, Korea, the Philippines, and Taiwan—received mixed reactions in Africa (Kasfir 1969). Given the diversity of the Third World, ethnocentrism is inevitable—not Western ethnocentrism, nor chauvinistic ethnocentrism, but ethnocentrism based on the constant need to extrapolate from the experience of only a sample of countries.

The Third World may be a heterogeneous grouping, but contrast between its center of gravity and that of the advanced world is ever more enormous. Most of our ability to predict performance differences derives from one predictor variable: per capita gross domestic product (GDP). Despite (probably growing) differentiation within and among Third World nations, the contrast on the one hand between First World (advanced democratic countries) and Second World (rather advanced communist countries)—now grouped as "North"—and on the other hand all the other countries—now grouped as "South"—remains fundamental. North-South differences, differences measurable in money—the measure of access to many things —predict more powerfully than power, property, or due process the performance variance among the world's bureaucracies.

Some bureaucracies in the world are rich, some are poor; most populate the middle strata of an international class structure. Many (though by no means all) of the dimensions of the quality of life—health, safety, nutrition, education, transportation, housing, civic amenities—are measured, monitored and to a great extent co-produced by public bureaucracies (i.e., produced through the collaboration of public and private actors). What these bureaucracies can achieve at their best depends heavily on their budgets and the budgets of the people they serve.

Wealthy bureaucracies can recruit highly trained people and acquire and use the latest and most effective technologies; they can meet a wide range of client expectations; they can maintain what they construct; they can sacrifice some effectiveness in the interests of due process; they can buy a large share of attention from their employees and discourage illicit sources of employee income. Only the wealthier countries—the fifth of mankind that lives in the advanced democracies—can afford many such bureaucracies, although some countries starve certain bureaucracies in order to make others (e.g., the army and the police) wealthy.

The contrast between rich and poor bureaucracies is illustrated in table 14.1. Wealthy bureaucracies tend to be produced by, and to produce, wealthy societies. (Their wealth, of course, is relative to the costs of their tasks and might therefore be measured in per capita Swiss francs of overhead.) After World War II, the Western nations, with their wealthy public bureaucracies, sought through "development administration" to transmit some of the secrets of their wealth to the public bureaucracies of the less wealthy countries. These poorer areas, it was thought, would develop economically (by developing industrial and commercial bureaucracies), politically (by developing political bureaucracies), and administratively (by converting poor bureaucracies into rich bureaucracies). Paradoxically, economic, political, and administrative bureaucracies (concentrations of power) would be necessary to democratize economics, politics, and society and thus diffuse access to modern values.

In the 1950s and 1960s, when the less developed nation-states were being established and when the richer nations established programs to accelerate the modernization process, modernization was widely considered to be not only desirable but inevitable (Esman 1980). In the ensuing generation, modernization has in fact occurred, but neither at the rate nor in the clearly defined fashion anticipated. More often than not, experience since the 1950s and 1960s has provided ambiguous lessons. Time, and the people of the world, have made no social science more certain except in more certain indeterminacy. Few linearities have survived, except in the form of simplistic ideology.

We know now that modernization (say, economic growth for its own sake) may or may not be desired (Iran shows that modernization can be successfully resisted not only by traditional elites but by happily traditionalistic masses willing to kill and to die for noneconomic ideals [Arjomand 1986]); may or (more likely) may not produce equality; may or may not be a self-sustaining process (Huntington 1968a); may or may not be successfully induced from exogenous forces by the simple transfer or attempted transfer of exotic social technologies; may or may not

TABLE 14.1
The Contrast between Rich and Poor Bureaucracies

Rich Bureaucracies	Poor Bureaucracies
Rational	Irrational, nonrational
Hierarchically disciplined	Ill disciplined/fanatically disciplined
Expensively trained and specialized	Less skilled and specialized
Rational division of labor	Irrational division of labor
Efficient, productive	Inefficient, unproductive
Full-time	Moonlighting
Staff shortage	Overstaffed
Merit recruitment and promotion	Clientelistic, welfare recruitment
Legalistic, rational rules	Formalistic, arbitrary decision making, red tape ridden
Rich in equipment, advanced in technology	Poor in equipment and technology
Rational slack (reserves)	Waste
Planning oriented	Disorganized
Honest, well-paid	Corrupt, ill paid
Feedback oriented	No feedback
Part of large public sector ("big governments")	Part of small public sector

involve or require in the late twentieth century the processes, policies, and phases that produced modernization in Europe and America in the eighteenth and nineteenth centuries; may or may not depend on Weberian rationalization, as "hidden rationalities" may justify the use of different techniques in different cultures to achieve similar goals; may or may not require Weberian-style bureaucracy even in Third World settings (cf. Hirschman's contrast between "wide-latitude" and "narrow-latitude" tasks, 1983); and may or may not be helped by public bureaucracies, which can be instruments of reform or repression, of order or disorder, of stability or (usually through their collapse) revolution or at least elite circulation, of strength or weakness vis-à-vis international traders, creditors, and investors, and facilitators or not of economic enterprise. Modernization may or may not be promoted by the corruption of public bureaucracies; corruption may facilitate economic growth and the development of public support (Abueva 1966; LaPalombara 1974; Riggs 1963), or it may impede development by raising the costs of doing business, alienating some parts of the public, or violating the norms of "modern" administration (see Ben-Dor 1974; Braibanti 1962; Carino 1975; Ekpo 1979; Johnston 1986).

Modernization may or may not be promoted by bureaucratic power over the government and government power over the country; Riggs's assertion that performance is inverse to bureaucratic control is supported by the correlation between economic growth and democracy, but it is countered by the economic success of authoritarian regimes. Modernization may or may not be promoted by military takeovers (see below) or by contact between a given developing area and the institutions of the advanced world (e.g., aid agencies, multinationals). Such contacts can create and maintain dependency, exacerbate inequalities, encourage brain drains, enhance repression, and be underdeveloping; or they can provide transfers of capital and of scientific, technological, and organizational knowledge, and provide pressure for liberalization (respect for human rights) that stimulates development (Streeten 1984; Shepherd and Nanda 1985).

Finally, modernization may or may not be promoted by democracy or dictatorship: Adopting or imposing either form (or any given mixed form) of political regime provides no guarantee or even probability of success in achieving modernization, whether measured in wealth, enlightenment, health, or whatever. For those interested in modernization, social science has not made the choice of regime obvious.

Ironically, however the above issues were settled in each Third World country, most developing nations outpaced the advanced nations in rate of economic growth during the three decades from 1950 to 1980. They grew faster than the advanced nations at the same level of development, and they grew faster than they had ever previously grown (Krasner 1984). In spite of this undoubted absolute development, the gap in relative development between wealthier and poorer bureaucracies increased, and per capita growth masked persisting unequal, and even worsening, distributions of the benefits of growth.

The development administration approach to comparative public administration tends to validate a Manichean view of administrative systems—all wonderful in the North, all despicable in the South (or vice versa). It tends to miss the hidden rationalities in Third World administration—the means of being effective and respectful of human dignity in different cultures. It tends to downplay the effectiveness and humanity of prebureaucratic, informal social means of controlling behavior and solving problems (e.g., crime control in Japan). It exaggerates the irrelevance of Third World studies to the understanding of the advanced world (Streeten 1984) and downplays the potentialities for irrational-bureaucratic performance in the advanced world. It produces the same unrealistic view of government bureaucracy performance in the Third World as its objective correlative—the often idealized, just as often demonized, performance of advanced world bureaucracies.

The virtues (as the vices) of bureaucratic wealth can easily be exaggerated. There are societal conditions, such as urban safety, that even rich bureaucracies, with private aid, produce less well than individuals, families, and neighborhoods with bureaucratic backup. Prebureaucratic institutions can work quite well, better than bureaucracies, just as poorer bureaucracies can outperform richer ones. The workings of bureaucratic wealth and income can be affected by variables such as bureaucratic morale, ideology, and idealism—ideals that enable poorer bureaucracies to become richer or defeat richer bureaucracies in conflict and competition (e.g., Vietnam 1965–70). This may be a way of saying that bureaucratic wealth (just as

329

bureaucratic status, bureaucratic power, bureaucratic knowledge or expertise, bureaucratic age, and bureaucratic size) can in the stream of situations become ill adapted. It can lead to overconfidence and the underestimation of environmental challenge (Proverbs 16:18).

The indeterminacies regarding development that I have recorded may be taken as demonstrating the failure of today's minds to replace the linear certainties of a generation ago with new and improved linear certainties. They may also be taken as demonstrating our acknowledgment of multiple teleologies and multivariation, the order in the chaos, the possibilities of choice. To our dismay or amusement, the people of the world seem to be eluding our categories (and those of even our most illustrious predecessors).

Bureaucratic Power

An ever-current theme in comparative bureaucratic studies is the question of bureaucratic power. Two dimensions of bureaucratic power (not always carefully distinguished or easily distinguishable) have been studied: variance in bureaucratic control over state policy, and variance in bureaucratic control over society.

Control over state policy. The variance in bureaucratic control over state policy is illustrated in table 14.2. Locating a national set of bureaucracies on the scale of power is not, ideologically at least, difficult. Woodrow Wilson, developing the ideology for civil service, argued that bureaucracies would have no power, only administrative burdens. Marx and Engels, developing the ideology for communist parties, argued that bureaucracies were under all conditions dominated by the property-owning class, and thus had power under no political or economic system.

Bureaucratic power, as a researchable variable rather than an ideological constant, is unusually difficult to measure. Electoral and legislative forces can be vectored; presidential batting averages can be calculated; yet the power of bureaucratic agencies remains elusive. Bureaucrats do not run slates; nor do they form distinctive legislative parties so that we can test their comparative power (they have historically managed elections for others). The best measure devised so far to compare bureaucratic power is the ratio between budgetary requests and appropriations. This measure is possible only in those countries (probably N = the United States) that have an adversarial budgetary process. And it compares mostly the power of bureaucrats (and their allies) versus like coalitions.

Only the power of military bureaucracies has been scaled with any degree of precision because the military are less subtle and discreet than their civilian colleagues in masking their power. Civil bureaucracies have rarely monopolized government power (e.g., coups by the police) to the exclusion of influence from outside social elites. Military bureaucracies have been much more politically aggressive and successful at conquering state power and establishing bureaucratic dictatorship.

TABLE 14.2
Comparative Bureaucratic Power over State Policy

Null power	Weak political interest group	Strong political interest group	Bureaucratic dictatorship
	Dominated by	*Power shared with*	
	Rulers	Rulers	
	Party elites	Party elites	
	Military elites	Military elites	
	Foreign elites	Foreign elites	
	Social elites	Social elites	
	Publics	Publics	
Wilson (1887); Marx (1848)	China under Mao USA under Jackson	USA USSR	Military dictatorships Colonial governments
Few policy areas in any government	Some policy areas in many governments	Some policy areas in many governments	Few policy areas in any governnment

There is an important strand of comparative bureaucratic studies dealing with the origins, characteristics, and performances of military dictatorships (Finer 1976). Most studies focus on the role of the military in the Third World—where the military have been politically most active. In most advanced democracies and communist countries, the military have shared power with other elites. Their power in the Third World has been more variable, ranging from zero (Costa Rica) to total control.

In the early 1960s, military control was thought to be a positive force for modernization. The military were, through functional determinism, thought to be a force for rationalism. (Maybe not entirely legal-rationalism: Could an ill-disciplined, nonspecialized, charismatic army survive, much less win, in the 1960s?) Military men, it was thought, were necessarily modernizers, uniquely well organized, and disciplined, prestigious sources of national leadership (Halpern 1963; Johnson 1962; Pauker 1959; Pye 1962; Shils 1962). A counterliterature saw in the military a regressive force (Bienen 1968; Liewen 1961; Nordlinger 1970, 1977).

Subsequent actual empirical study of the military in power as compared with civilians in power seems to show that military regimes share few characteristics; they vary about as much among themselves as do civilian regimes. Knowing whether a military or a civilian regime is in power is not predictive of policy or administration. There is no correlation even between military domination and military appropriations; the military do not uniformly act as rent-seeking Praetorians (Feit 1968; McKinlay and Cohan 1975; Van Doorn 1968, 1969).

With regard to the power position of civil bureaucracies, the facts are less certain. The extreme positions (null and total power) seem to be rare in both life and literature. Total bureaucratic power (the meaning, after all, of "bureaucracy") seems uncommon, although many colonial and rightist authoritarian regimes (e.g., those of Petain, Franco, Salazar, and their Third World epigones) may approximate this category. Typically in such regimes power is shared with a charismatic (well-known, maybe even popular) leader, and with social elites and the military. The top category—bureaucratic monopoly of state power—may also be occupied by regimes that are dominated by what some neo-Marxists see as an all-powerful state bourgeoisie.

Category 1 situations (null bureaucratic power), since they usually involve the dissolution of the state (as in Lebanon), are rare, not so much because of the inherent strength of the modern state as because of the strength of the international system, which, populated by so many weak states, normally props up even the most hopeless member of the club (Jackson and Rosberg 1982).

In most polities, bureaucracies compete for power as political interest groups, albeit interest groups with more than the usual obligation to speak for the public interest. To apply the interest-group concept to state bureaucracies seems suitable on a variety of grounds. Bureaucratic interest groups make up a useful level of abstraction between the bureaucracy and the action of recognizable individual bureaucrats. Miles's Law ("where one stands depends upon where one sits"), from which there seems to be no major dissent, asserts that individual bureaucratic behavior is for the most part predictable on the basis of group membership (Allison 1971). Differentiated functions correlate with differentiated interests, missions, ideologies, amounts of power, and autonomy; differentiated functions usually entail also differential meanings for different social groups (differential representation roles). Then, too, there is the tendency, noted by Selznick, for bureaucrats to subvert formal goals in favor of professional or self-interest goals (Selznick 1949). Finally, we may note the congruence between the interest-group concept of bureaucracy and the right-wing view of bureaucracies as inherently self-aggrandizing (Niskanen 1971; but cf. Dunleavy 1986).

Bureaucratic power tends (not by accident) to be colinear, even multicolinear—embedded in highly correlated relationships that make it difficult to isolate the bureaucratic component. Thus bureaucracies often act in alliance with social classes, interest groups, legislative factions, attentive publics, co-producing publics, ideological blocs, and political executives.

The concept of state bureaucracies as interest groups competes with but does not displace the normative and descriptive view of them as superordinate mediators among interests or as collectively constituting a rent-seeking state bourgeoisie.

There is a rich literature dealing with the ability of bureaucracies to compete with other political formations for shares of state power. Weber predicted increasing success for bureaucracies or their leaders in getting shares of state power, together with party leaders (Weber 1947, 1976). More recent studies (Aberbach et al. 1981;

Aberbach and Rockman 1983; Dogan 1975; Rose 1987) find this conjugation of bureaucrats and politicians running the state in most advanced democracies, though as a result of different historical developments. In Japan and Italy, bureaucratic rule has been traditional, and the modern democratic state results from the willingness of bureaucrats to share power with politicians. In Britain and the United States, rule by politicians is traditional, and modern democracy results from the willingness of politicians to share power with bureaucrats (Aberbach et al. 1981).

The leading political science typologies of bureaucracy posit neither bureaucratic nullity nor bureaucratic domination, but rather bureaucratic sharing in power, as junior or senior partner.

Fainsod, in 1963, proposed a five-fold typology: (1) representative bureaucracy, (2) party-state bureaucracy, (3) military-dominated bureaucracy, (4) ruler-dominated bureaucracy, and (5) ruling bureaucracy. He did not attempt to place the world's bureaucracies within his categories. Heady, in one of the few comparative administration textbooks, classifies bureaucracies first by economics—developed vs. developing—then by politics—bureaucratic-prominent political regimes vs. party-prominent regimes (polyarchal, semicompetitive dominant-party, mobilizational dominant-party, communist systems).

The assumption of this schema is that the most variance in bureaucratic power is predicted by GNP; additional variance is then explained by the nature of the political system. The exact kind of variance to be explained by this economics-plus-politics formula is not clear. It requires the student of comparative bureaucracy to know a country's per capita GNP (easy) and then to know its political-regime type (not always so easy). The implication is, however, that within the constraints of economic development (or development however defined), the comparative bureaucracy student must depend on the student of comparative politics to set out some generally acceptable classification scheme of political regimes in order to explain more of the variance. Unfortunately, the study of total political systems is no more advanced than the study of bureaucratic components of those systems. Classifications are idiosyncratic and outdated by this morning's newspaper.

There is an international competition among the world's bureaucracies—governmental, semigovernmental, private—for support. One tends to support the efforts of bureaucracies flying one's own flag (but not all of them). People tend to be selective in their support for and trust in bureaucracies—as voters, consumers, opinion expressers, insurgents. It is difficult, therefore, to identify the consequences of variations in bureaucratic power in any value-free way. Representative bureaucracy is a reality.

Control over society. Less attention has been paid in the literature to the variance in the power that state bureaucracies exert over and draw from society. Wealthy bureaucracies and/or bureaucracies with great control over policy are not necessarily bureaucracies that secure effective implementation of state policy. Relevant here may be the current distinction between "weak" and "strong" states. Weak states (in at least one acceptation of the term) may be those unable to collect taxes, enforce law and order, control borders, and in general assert and maintain statehood.

Even when states are strong enough to maintain sovereignty, their bureaucracies mobilize varying degrees of consent, trust, and support from the population. Cultural variables seem important in explaining the differential capability of government bureaucracies, at similar levels of modernization, in securing citizen support and cooperation in the implementation of government programs (Almond and Verba 1963; Peters 1978; Pye and Verba 1965; Wildavsky 1986).

Studies of bureaucratic power tend to have two limitations: They tend to use reputational methods for identifying power patterns, and they tend to see power in Weberian terms, as *Herrschaft* (domination) rather than in terms of collective empowerment (public-private partnership).

The Scope of Bureaucracy

Even bureaucracies that are effective in enlisting consent, support, trust, and even partnership from those whom they serve and regulate seem to have fallen under the same cloud of suspicion and doubt that afflicts less legitimate bureaucracies. In the antigovernment climate of the 1980s, divorce between government and society came into fashion. As part of what may be a pendulum process, there seemed to be a shifting of responsibility toward self, family, friendship networks, patron-client networks, tribes, ascriptive associations, voluntary groups, and self-help groups, and away from bureaucratized forms of cooperation (e.g., organized interest groups, labor unions, political parties, international organizations, and governments).

The variances. Two variances are interesting here: how the scope of government has changed over time, and how varied the current results of this change are. Ideology apart, neither variance is easy to plot, for governments are often hesitant to accomplish their purposes directly through state bureaucracies, and nongovernmental actors are equally reluctant to acknowledge, or even to be aware of, their role as government policy implementors. The traditional line between the private sector and the public sector that is supposed to aid the comparativist scholar at this point has been badly smudged. Public policy is implemented through a dazzling variety of forms. An important, though not much studied, subvariance is thus the scope and variety of institutions and techniques used to implement public policy (Ashford 1978).

Governments, indeed, have become increasingly sophisticated in camouflaging their means of policy implementation, the realms over which they have acquired control, and the extent of their extractions from society. (The beneficiaries of government largesse, the silent partners, have become no less artful and discreet.) The classic illustration is the invention of the income tax and social security tax based on withholding: Not only does this diminish taxpayer resistance, it also keeps tax administration small while mobilizing hundreds of thousands of ostensibly private institutions as part of the tax-raising machinery of the state. Organizations survive by never disclosing the true rules of their allocations; glasnost (freedom of information, etc.) is always strategic.

Still, the variance in the scope of bureaucratic functions is one of the more measurable aspects of bureaucracy available for international comparison. Given the fuzzy boundaries of the public sector, it cannot be precisely surveyed; but we have some useful parameters, such as (1) the percentage of national GDP collected and spent by government, (2) the percentage of various economic sectors in government ownership, (3) the absolute size of government finances at any time compared to their size in previous periods, (4) the government share in investment, and (5) the government share in employment.

It may become more difficult to trace the boundaries of the public sector as societies become more advanced. Riggs postulated "diffraction" as the core characteristic of modern society; but, if anything, the "fused" blurring of boundaries more than keeps pace with the division of labor and specialization in advanced developing societies. Government and society do not become more differentiated but less so, as compared, say, to the same societies in the eighteenth or nineteenth century. Governments in modern societies are expected to do many of the things that families and neighbors used to do, or at least to supplement them.

There are curiously few studies of public-sector size in Third World countries. This is partly because, in many of them, the statistics are lacking or unreliable. Often there is no accurate count of public employees, or even of the population. We know, in any event, that there is major variation among the world's countries in the size of the public sector, however it is measured, and that there is a variance in all countries over time. We also know that, seemingly with no regard to these variances, there has been a widespread feeling in most societies that the public sector, no matter how measured or how modest in size, has become too large.

Causes of variance. Why the variance in public-sector size, cross-sectionally or over time? The growth in, and consequent size of, the public sector can be caused by a variety of factors, pathological or therapeutic, including rent-seeking predatory bureaucracies; regime socialism; government takeover of bankrupt private firms; political development (growth in collective efforts); military-industrial complex exploitation; development of the repressive apparatus; the electoral strategies of democratically elected politicians; the programmatic commitments of electorally successful social democratic parties (Cameron 1978); availability of funds and man-power; the politicization of patron-client networks; legislative hypertrophy; provision of merit goods; deficiencies in the private labor market; nationalization of solvent corporations; population growth; Wagner's Law; efforts to save or legitimize capitalism, to be democratically responsive, or to promote balanced economic development.

Richard Rose, a close student of the growth and decline of "big government," disaggregates the variable government into organizations, programs, employment, laws, and revenues. He finds no simple law to explain the size or growth of the public sector; the latter reflect "the interactions of conscious choices, unanticipated events, and long-term political, social, and economic processes" (Rose 1984, 31–32). Variables that he examines as possible sources of government growth include economic growth; consumer demand; buoyant revenues; buoyant costs; demographic change; changes in social structure and political values; changes in politician, bureaucrat, interest-group, and party wants; and inertial commitments (Rose 1984, chap. 2).

Rose's analysis deals only with advanced industrial democracies. There seem to be no worldwide examinations of public-sector growth. We do know that ideology/property-system is not crucial in predicting the size of the public sector. Pryor, in 1968, compared 1962 data for seven market economies and seven centrally planned (communist) economies, and found the same range in the ratio of government expenditures to gross national product, 17 to 33 percent (Pryor 1968; see also Bahry 1980). Many right-wing regimes expand the public sector. Most Italian nationalization was carried out by Mussolini, most French nationalization by deGaulle. In the Dominican Republic under Trujillo, 65 to 85 percent of the economy was under the control of the government.

Factors inhibiting the growth of bureaucracy have been less rigorously studied. Most theories of bureaucratic growth, quite naturally as theories of growth, posit indefinite capacities for expansion (e.g., Niskanen 1971; but cf. Meyer et al. 1985). Growth of government employment, finance, and regulation in the twentieth century induced a certain metaphysical pathos, a certain Weberian feeling of inevitable bureaucratization (Gouldner 1955). Yet in the 1970s a threshold of bureaucratic development was reached in many countries and debureaucratization became not only theoretically conceivable but central to many political agendas.

The disappearance of large private industrial bureaucracies in the private sector, especially in advanced industrial economies (and their reappearance in Third World newly industrializing economies) is taken for granted, given the logic of free trade, the disparity in international wage scales, and the law of supply and demand. Somehow, public bureaucracies are assumed to be free from similar hazards, since they are normally not subject to market shifts.

Bureaucratic vulnerability to decline as well as growth is more explicable when evolutionary concepts are applied. Evolutionary hypotheses prepare us better to expect thresholds in bureaucratic (and any other kind of) development.

The variables associated with the overall size of the bureaucratic structure have not been systematically examined, partly since debureaucratization is such a recent and theoretically (ideologically?) unexpected development. It has been suggested that many of the processes thought to expand bureaucracy (e.g., majority voting, fiscal illusion [hidden costs], monopolistic bureaucratic drives, redistributive policies, and Keynesian cyclical compensation policy) can all be bidirectional. It may be just as easy for antispending coalitions to form, for politicians to seek reelection by cutting taxes, for governments to prefer visible and direct taxes, for Keynesian governments to raise taxes rather than increase public employment, for bureaucratic executives to achieve promotion by cutting costs, and for the group of losers under redistribution to outweigh the winners.

Consequences. The consequences of variations in the scope of the public sector have not been studied extensively, thus giving almost completely free rein to the political debate. Abstract believers in less government have been pitted against abstract believers in more government; those who feel represented by certain bureaucracies have been pitted against those who feel represented by other bureaucracies.

The negative effects of too much government in general (rather than too much of the wrong kind and too little of the right kind) are alleged to be undue encouragement of leisure (sloth), the underground economy, and other nontaxed activities; overtaxation; diminished economic growth, together with rising inflation and unemployment (cf. Cameron 1978); government rent seeking and exploitation of society; too much redistribution; alternatively, too little effective redistribution; alternatively, socialism for the rich (i.e., redistribution to the wrong people); overregulation of the market; and insufficient use of more efficient market mechanisms.

The public sector may also be reduced because of policy failure. In mixed economies, policy failures are often attributed to institutional arrangements; the failure of policy is blamed not on policy itself but on its institutional sponsors. Policy failure leads to institutional readjustment, sometimes within government (e.g., centralization vs decentralization) and sometimes between government and the private sector. Disenchantment with the public sector in the 1970s and 1980s seems to reflect not only tax concerns but also the desire to give the other sector a try, given the failure of the public sector either to govern the economy or to shape character.

Ironically, the correlation between scope and performance is problematical. Grossly richer (more costly) bureaucracies outperform poorer (less costly) bureaucracies. But spending can translate into many nonservice channels: waste, inflation, corruption, shorter working hours, prestige equipment. Leaner bureaucracies may deliver better than fatter bureaucracies.

337

Future Directions

I have been able, in this brief chapter, to touch on only a few themes. There is a vast literature that no one in this hyperspecialized world can follow or appreciate. I have stressed the value of one kind of comparative study, the multivariate cross-national study based on a large number of cases. The great bulk of "comparative" studies —studies that deal with small numbers of cases—contribute to the understanding of particular cases perhaps as much as the "genuinely" (large N of cases) comparative studies.

Increasingly, the environment for meaningful multivariate multinational research is favorable. The world may be becoming more, rather than less, researchable; as bureaucracies become less defensive or more subjected to *glasnost*, international organizations refine their surveying methods and achieve more reliable and comprehensive response rates.

As the world's states become more interdependent politically, economically, militarily, and ecologically, it makes less and less sense to expect domestic variables by themselves to determine bureaucratic performance. Nations differ in their *autarky*, their self-determination. Increasingly, the size, power, and effectiveness of their public and private bureaucracies are internationally determined (Cameron 1978). This is true not only of "weak states" (Jackson and Rosberg 1982) but of the strong states of the First World. International dependency may be a secular trend or a wave of an autarky-interdependency cycle; observers in the next century will have a better view. In the short term, it behooves the student of comparative administration to examine interactive effects in the performance of states.

Another neglected dimension in comparative administrative studies is what has come to be known as human rights. The stress in international comparisons has been on economic growth and other dimensions of political economy. More or less left out have been correlations with the development of human rights, except when these have been conceived as socioeconomic rights (Shepherd and Nanda 1985). What are the variances over time in due process (e.g., the systematic nonuse of torture) in the countries of the world? Is due process positively correlated with the indicators of economic and political development? Unfortunately, due process has seldom been studied in a multivariate cross-national fashion, such methods being even more alien to students of public law than to students of public administration.

Co-production may be another target of opportunity for comparativists. Stress on the split between the public vs. private sectors should not lead us to neglect the public-private partnerships that are important in all systems. Cooperation between bureaucracies and volunteers/communities/clients/citizens are crucial in many areas of public administration, from policing to education, tax administration to health. Almond and Verba in *The Civic Culture* attempted to get at comparative political-administrative cultures, but this was many years ago. The comparative interaction between organizational cultures (conceivably more and more internation-alized) and environmental cultures badly needs reexamining (Wildavsky 1986).

The Third World experience also needs to be reexamined. Many early studies had little experience to analyze and data from the 1950s and 1960s only. There should be greater exchange between specialists in the Third World and specialists in the advanced world. The experiences of the newly industrializing countries may help to bridge the conceptual barriers between these two specialized concerns.

All of these themes are involved in what has become the most exciting prospect for comparativists: the study of de-bureaucratization—of *perestroika*—in Eastern Europe. The international interdependency of bureaucracies (even and espe-cially "totalitarian" bureaucracies); the universalizing of demands for human rights; the crucial role of publics in resisting or promoting bureaucratic reform; the chancy nature of status as a member of the First, Second or Third Worlds—all of these themes present students and practitioners of comparative public administration with unexpected challenges to understanding, unexpected opportunities for research and conceptual development, unexpected excitement.

References

Aberbach, Joel D., Robert D. Putnam, and Bert A. Rockman. 1981. *Bureaucrats and Politicians in Western Democracies*. Cambridge, Mass.: Harvard University Press.

Aberbach, Joel D., and Bert A. Rockman. 1983. "Comparative Administration: Methods, Muddles, and Models." *Administration and Society* 18:473–506.

Abueva, J.V. 1966. "The Contribution of Nepotism, Spoils, and Graft to Political Devel-opment." *East-West Center Review* 3:45–54.

Adamolekun, Ladipo. 1983. *Public Administration: A Nigerian and Comparative Per-spective*. London: Longman.

Allison, Graham T. 1971. *Essence of Decision*. Boston: Little, Brown.

Almond, Gabriel A., and Sidney Verba. 1963. *The Civic Culture*. Princeton: Princeton Uni-versity Press.

Ames, Barry. 1977. "The Politics of Public Spending in Latin America." *American Journal of Political Science* 21:149–76.

Arjomand, Said Amir. 1986. "Iran's Islamic Revolution in Comparative Perspective." *World Politics* 38:383–414.

Arora, Ramesh K. 1972. *Comparative Public Administration: An Ecological Perspective*. New Delhi: Associated Publishing House.

Ashford, Douglas. 1978. *Comparing Public Policies: New Concepts and Methods*. Beverly Hills: Sage.

Bahry, Donna. 1980. "Measuring Communist Priorities: Budgets, Investments, and the Problem of Equivalence." *Comparative Political Studies* 13:267–92.

Barker, Ernest. 1944. *The Development of Public Services in Western Europe*. London: Oxford University Press.

Bendix, Reinhard. 1962. *Max Weber: An Intellectual Portrait*. New York: Doubleday.

Ben-Dor, Gabriel. 1974. "Corruption, Institutionalization, and Political Development: The Revisionist Theses Revisited." *Comparative Political Studies* 7:63–83.

Bienen, Henry, ed. 1968. *The Military Intervenes: Case Studies of Political Development.* New York: Russell Sage Foundation.

Bienen, Henry, ed. 1971. *The Military and Modernization.* Chicago: University of Chicago Press.

Braibanti, Ralph. 1962. "Reflections on Bureaucratic Corruption." *Public Administration* (London) 40:357–72.

Bunce, Valerie. 1980. "Measuring Communist Priorities: A Reply to Bahry." *Comparative Political Studies* 13:293–98.

Caiden, Gerald. 1969. *Administrative Reform.* Chicago: Aldine.

Caiden, Naomi, and Aaron Wildavsky. 1974. *Planning and Budgeting in Poor Countries.* New York: Wiley.

Cameron, David. 1978. "The Expansion of the Public Economy: A Comparative Analysis." *American Political Science Review* 72:1243–61.

Carino, Ledivina V. 1975. "Bureaucratic Norms, Corruption, and Development." *Philippine Journal of Public Administration* 19:278–92.

Deva, Satya. 1979. "Western Conceptualization of Administrative Development: A Critique and an Alternative." *International Review of Administrative Sciences* 45:59–63.

Diamant, Alfred. 1962. "The Bureaucratic Model: Max Weber Rejected, Rediscovered, Reformed." In *Papers in Comparative Public Administration,* edited by Ferrel Heady and Sybil Stokes. Ann Arbor: Institute of Public Administration, University of Michigan.

Diamant, Alfred. 1966. "European Models of Bureaucracy and Development." *International Review of Administrative Sciences* 32:309–20.

Diamant, Alfred. 1973. "Bureaucracy and Administration in Western Europe: A Case of Not-So-Benign Neglect." *Policy Studies Journal* 1:133–38.

Dogan, Mattei. 1975. "The Political Power of the Mandarins: Introduction." In *The Mandarins of Western Europe: The Political Role of Top Civil Servants.* New York: Wiley.

Donnelly, Jack. 1984. "Human Rights and Development: Complementary or Competing Concerns?" *World Politics* 36:255–84.

Dunleavy, Patrick. 1986. "Explaining the Privatization Boom: Public Choice versus Radical Approaches." *Public Administration* (London) 64:13–34.

Ekpo, Monday U. 1979. *Bureaucratic Corruption in Sub-Saharan Africa: Toward a Search for Causes and Consequences.* Washington, D.C.: University Press of America.

Esman, Milton J. 1967. "The Ecological Style in Comparative Administration." *Public Administration Review* 27:271–78.

Esman, Milton J. 1980. "Development Assistance in Public Administration: Requiem or Renewal." *Public Administration Review* 40:426–31.

Fainsod, Merle. 1963. "Bureaucracy and Modernization: The Russian and Soviet Case." In *Bureaucracy and Political Development,* edited by Joseph LaPalombara. Princeton: Princeton University Press.

Feit, Edward. 1968. "Military Coups and Political Development: Some Lessons from Ghana and Nigeria." *World Politics* 20:179–93.

Finer, Herman. 1961. *The Theory and Practice of Modern Government.* London: Methuen.

Finer, Samuel E. 1976. *The Man on Horseback: The Role of the Military in Politics.* Harmondsworth, England: Penguin.

Fried, Robert C. 1975. "Comparative Urban Policy and Performance." In *The Handbook of Political Science,* vol. 6, edited by Fred I. Greenstein and Nelson W. Polsby. Reading, Mass.: Addison-Wesley.

Friedrich, Carl. 1950. *Constitutional Government and Democracy.* Boston: Ginn.

Gerth, H.H., and C. Wright Mills. 1946. *From Max Weber: Essays in Sociology.* New York: Oxford University Press.

Goodnow, Frank J. 1893. *Comparative Administrative Law: An Analysis of the Administrative Systems, National and Local, of the United States, England, France, and Germany.* New York: Putnam.

Goodsell, Charles T. 1976. "The Empirical Test of 'Legalism' in Administration." *Journal of Developing Areas* 10:485–94.

Gouldner, Alvin W. 1955. "Metaphysical Pathos and the Theory of Bureaucracy." *American Political Science Review* 49:496–507.

Halpern, M. 1963. *The Politics of Social Change.* Princeton: Princeton University Press.

Hancock, M. Donald. 1983. "Comparative Public Policy: An Assessment." In *Political Science: The State of the Discipline,* edited by Ada W. Finifter. Washington, D.C.: American Political Science Association.

Heady, Ferrel. 1978. "Comparative Public Administration: A Sojourner's Outlook." *Public Administration Review* 38:358–66.

Heady, Ferrel. 1979. *Public Administration: A Comparative Perspective.* 2d ed. revised. New York: Marcel Dekker.

Heady, Ferrel, and Sybil L. Stokes, eds. 1962. *Papers in Comparative Public Administration.* Ann Arbor: Institute of Public Administration, University of Michigan.

Heaphey, James. 1968. "Comparative Public Administration: Big Science Model for the Future." *Public Administration Review* 28:242–49.

Heaphey, James. 1969. "The Philosophical Assumptions of Inquiry in Comparative Administration: Some Introductory Comments." *Journal of Comparative Administration* 1:133–39.

Henderson, Keith. 1969. "Comparative Public Administration: The Identity Crisis." *Journal of Comparative Administration* 1:65–85.

Hirschman, Albert O. 1963. *Journeys Toward Progress: Studies of Economic Policy-Making in Latin America.* New York: Norton.

Hirschman, Albert O. 1983. "A Dissenter's Confession: 'The Strategy of Economic Development' Revisited." In *Pioneers in Development,* edited by Gerald M. Meier and Dudley Seers. New York: Oxford University Press.

Hough, Jerry F. 1973. "The Bureaucratic Model and the Nature of the Soviet System." *Journal of Comparative Administration* 5:134–68.

Huddleston, Mark W. 1984. *Comparative Public Administration: An Annotated Bibliography.* New York: Garland.

Huntington, Samuel P. 1968a. "Political Development and Political Decay." *World Politics* 17:386–430.

Huntington, Samuel P. 1968b. *Political Order in Changing Societies.* New Haven: Yale University Press.

Ilchman, Warren. 1971. *Comparative Public Administration and "Conventional Wisdom."* Beverly Hills: Sage.

Islam, Nasir, and Georges M. Henault. 1979. "From GNP to Basic Needs: A Critical Review of Development Administration." *International Review of Administrative Sciences* 36:253–67.

Jackson, Robert H. 1966. "An Analysis of the Comparative Public Administration Movement." *Canadian Public Administration* 9:108—30.

Jackson, Robert H., and Carl G. Rosberg. 1982. "Why African Weak States Persist: The Empirical and the Juridical in Statehood." *World Politics* 34:1–24.

Janowitz, Morris. 1964. *The Military in the Development of New Nations.* Chicago: University of Chicago Press.

Johnson, J.J., ed. 1962. *The Role of the Military in Underdeveloped Countries.* Princeton: Princeton University Press.

Johnston, Michael. 1986. "The Political Consequences of Corruption: A Reassessment." *Comparative Politics* 19:459–77.

Jones, Garth N. 1976. "Frontiersmen in Search for the 'Lost Horizon': The State of Development Administration in the 60's." *Public Administration Review* 36:99–109.

Jreisat, Jamil E. 1975. "Synthesis and Relevance in Comparative Public Administration." *Public Administration Review* 35:663–71.

Jun, Jong S. 1976. "Renewing the Study of Comparative Administration: Some Reflections on the Current Possibilities." *Public Administration Review* 36:641–47.

Kasfir, Nelson. 1969. "Prismatic Theory and African Administration." *World Politics* 21:295–314.

Krasner, Stephen D. 1984. "A Reply." *Review of International Studies* 10:85–88.

LaPalombara, Joseph, ed. 1963. *Bureaucracy and Political Development.* Princeton: Princeton University Press.

LaPalombara, Joseph. 1974. *Politics within Nations.* Englewood Cliffs, N.J.: Prentice-Hall.

Liewen, E. 1961. *Arms and Politics in Latin America.* New York: Praeger.

Lindblom, Charles E. 1959. "The Science of Muddling Through." *Public Administration Review* 19:79–88.

Loveman, Brian. 1976. "The Comparative Administration Group, Development Administration, and Antidevelopment." *Public Administration Review* 36:616–21.

McKinlay, R.D., and A.S. Cohan. 1975. "Comparative Analysis of the Political and Economic Performance of Military and Civilian Regimes." *Comparative Politics* 8:1–30.

Meyer, Marshall W., William Stephenson, and Stephen Webster. 1985. *Limits to Bureaucratic Growth.* Berlin: Walter de Gruyter.

Milne, R.S. 1962. "Comparisons and Models in Public Administration." *Political Studies* 10:1–14.

Milne, R.S. 1970. "Mechanistic and Organic Models of Public Administration in Developing Countries." *Administrative Science Quarterly* 15:411–26.

Milne, R.S. 1973. "Bureaucracy and Development Administration." *Public Administration* 51:411–26.

Murray, David J. 1983. "The World Bank's Perspective on How to Improve Administration." *Public Administration and Development* 3:291–97.

Niskanen, William A., Jr. 1971. *Bureaucracy and Representative Government.* Chicago: Aldine.

Nordlinger, Eric A. 1970. "Soldiers in Mufti: Impact of Military Rule upon Social and Economic Change in Non-Western Societies." *American Political Science Review* 64:1131–48.

Nordlinger, Eric A. 1977. *Soldiers in Politics: Military Coups and Governments.* Englewood Cliffs, N.J.: Prentice-Hall.

Odetola, Olatunde. 1982. *Military Regimes and Development: A Comparative Analysis in African Societies.* London: Allen and Unwin.

Orlando, Vittorio E., ed. 1897–1935. *Primo trattato completo di diritto amministrativo italiano.* 18 vols. Milan: Societa Editrice Libraria.

Page, Edward C. 1985. *Political Authority and Bureaucratic Power: A Comparative Perspective.* Brighton, England: Wheatsheaf.

Pauker, Guy. 1959. "South-East Asia as a Problem Area in the Next Decade." *World Politics* 11:325–45.

Peters, B. Guy. 1978. *The Politics of Bureaucracy: A Comparative Perspective.* New York: Longman.

Pryor, Frederic L. 1968. *Public Expenditures in Communist and Capitalist Nations.* London: Allen and Unwin.

Pye, Lucian W. 1962. *Politics, Personality, and Nation Building: Burma's Search for Identity.* New Haven: Yale University Press.

Pye, Lucian W., and Sidney Verba. 1965. *Political Culture and Political Development.* Princeton: Princeton University Press.

Raphaeli, Nimrod. 1967. *Readings in Comparative Public Administration.* Boston: Allyn and Bacon.

Riggs, Fred W. 1961. *The Ecology of Public Administration.* Bombay: Asia Publishing House.

Riggs, Fred W. 1962. "An Ecological Approach: The 'Sala' Model." In *Papers in Comparative Public Administration,* edited by Ferrel Heady and Sybil Stokes. Ann Arbor: Institute of Public Administration, University of Michigan.

Riggs, Fred W. 1963. "Bureaucrats and Political Development: A Paradoxical View." In *Bureaucracy and Political Development,* edited by Joseph LaPalombara. Princeton: Princeton University Press.

Riggs, Fred W. 1964. *Administration in Developing Countries: The Theory of Prismatic Society.* Boston: Houghton Mifflin.

Riggs, Fred W. 1966. *Thailand: The Modernization of a Bureaucratic Polity.* Honolulu: East-West Center Press.

Riggs, Fred W. 1969. "Bureaucratic Politics in Comparative Perspective." *Journal of Comparative Administration* 1:5–38.

Riggs, Fred W., ed. 1971. *Frontiers of Development Administration.* Durham: Duke University Press.

Riggs, Fred W. 1973. *Prismatic Society Revisited.* Morristown, N.J.: General Learning Press.

Riggs, Fred W. 1975. "Organizational Structures and Contexts." *Administration and Society* 7:150–90.

Riggs, Fred W. 1976. "The Group and the Movement: Notes on Comparative and Development Administration." *Public Administration Review* 36:648–54.

Rose, Richard. 1984. *Understanding Big Government: A Programme Approach.* London: Sage.

Rose, Richard. 1987. "Steering the Ship of State: One Tiller but Two Pairs of Hands." *British Journal of Political Science* 17:409–32.

Savage, Peter. 1968. "Comparative Administration: An Assertion of Themes." *Comparative Political Studies* 1:171–74.

Savage, Peter. 1976. "Optimism and Pessimism in Comparative Administration." *Public Administration Review* 36:415–23.

Schaffer, Bernard B. 1971. "Comparisons, Administration and Development." *Political Studies* 19:327–37.

Seitz, John L. 1980. "The Failure of U.S. Technical Assistance in Public Administration: The Iranian Case." *Public Administration Review* 40:407–12.

Selznick, Philip. 1949. *TVA and the Grass Roots.* Berkeley: University of California Press.

Shepherd, George W., Jr., and Ved P. Nanda, eds. 1985. *Human Rights and Third World Development.* Westport, Conn.: Greenwood Press.

Shils, Edward A. 1962. *Political Development in the New States*. The Hague: Mouton.

Siffin, William J. 1976. "Two Decades of Public Administration in Developing Countries." *Public Administration Review* 36:61–71.

Sigelman, Lee. 1972. "Do Modern Bureaucracies Dominate Underdeveloped Polities? A Test of the Imbalance Thesis." *American Political Science Review* 66:525–28.

Sigelman, Lee. 1974. "Bureaucratic Development and Dominance: A New Test of the Imbalance Thesis." *Western Political Quarterly* 27:308–13.

Sigelman, Lee. 1976. "In Search of Comparative Administration." *Public Administration Review* 36:621–25.

Skilling, H. Gordon. 1982. "Development or Retrogression?" *Studies in Comparative Communism* 15:125–30.

Springer, J. Fred. 1977. "Observation and Theory in Development Administration." *Administration and Society* 9:13–44.

Stokes, Donald E. 1980. "The Environment of Administration: Insights from Our International Experience." In *Critical Cornerstones in Public Administration*, edited by Philip Schorr. Boston: Oelgeschlager, Gunn, and Hain.

Streeten, Paul P. 1984. "Development Dichotomies." In *Pioneers in Development*, edited by Gerald M. Meier and Dudley Seers. New York: Oxford University Press.

Suleiman, Ezra. 1974. *Politics, Power and Bureaucracy in France*. Princeton: Princeton University Press.

Suleiman, Ezra. 1984. *Bureaucrats and Policy Making: A Comparative Overview*. London: Holmes and Meier.

Van Doorn, Jacques. 1968. *Armed Forces and Society: Sociological Essays*. The Hague: Mouton.

Van Doorn, Jacques, ed. 1969. *Military Profession and Military Regimes*. The Hague: Mouton.

Van Nieuwenhujze, C.A.O. 1973–1974. "Public Administration, Comparative Administration, Development Administration: Concepts and Theory in Their Struggle for Relevance." *Development and Change* 5:1–18.

Weber, Max. 1947. *The Theory of Economic and Social Organization*, translated by A.M. Henderson and Talcott Parsons. New York: Oxford University Press.

Weber, Max. 1976. *Wirtschaft und Gesellschaft: Grundriß der verstehenden Soziologie*, edited by Johannes Winckelmann. 5th ed. revised. Tübingen, Germany: Mohr.

Whitaker, Gordon P. 1980. "Coproduction: Citizen Participation in Service Delivery." *Public Administration Review* 40:240–46.

White, Leonard, ed. 1930. *The Civil Service in the Modern State*. Chicago: University of Chicago Press.

White, Leonard, Charles Bland, Walter Sharp, and Fritz Morstein Marx. 1935. *Civil Service Abroad*. New York: McGraw-Hill.

Wildavsky, Aaron. 1975. *Budgeting: A Comparative Theory of Budgeting Processes*. Boston: Little, Brown.

Wildavsky, Aaron. 1986. "Constructing Preferences by Constructing Institutions: A Cultural Theory of Preference Formation." *American Political Science Review* 81:3–22.

Yates, Douglas. 1982. *Bureaucratic Democracy: The Search for Democracy and Efficiency in American Government*. Cambridge, Mass.: Harvard University Press.

PART FOUR

Methodology

15

Research Methodology in Public Administration: Issues and Patterns

JAMES L. PERRY AND
KENNETH L. KRAEMER

Public administration was in an early stage of development when Luther Gulick (1937) called for a science of administration. His exhortation became a source of heated and continuing controversy (Dahl 1947; Simon 1947) that centered on positivist versus alternative views of appropriate research methodology. That debate, which continues today, has derailed public administration from attention to the real issue. That issue is not positivist versus other research methods, but the quality, continuity, and usefulness of research, whatever the methods. Traditional social science methods are valuable as a means of advancing the field. Indeed, the most valued research in the field comes from the social sciences and is based in its methods. Alternative methods may be equally valuable, although we do not espouse them. The test of methodology is whether it produces useful knowledge over time. Therefore, the current status of public administration research methodology is assessed, and changes for its future development are suggested.

Our assessment was conducted by examining research articles in *Public Administration Review* (*PAR*) and *Administration and Society* (*A&S*) published from 1975 through 1984. We conclude that public administration research is primarily applied rather than basic, lacks cumulativeness, and lacks the institutional supports required to change either of the first two conditions. Therefore, we concentrate our suggestions on institutional supports while giving attention to fostering basic research and cumulativeness of research.

As Lynton Caldwell (1968) noted in an earlier essay on methodology in public administration: "Method is not solely, or even most importantly, a matter of technique. It is first and foremost a way of thinking" (pp. 219–20). In search of a working understanding of methodology, we rely on Kaplan's discussion of this concept in *The Conduct of Inquiry* (1964). He distinguishes several senses of methodology: *techniques,* the specific procedures used in a given science; *honorifics,* a ritual invocation attesting to concern with meeting standards of scientific acceptability; and *epistemology*, involving the most basic philosophical questions about the pursuit of truth. The first and third of these senses have the greatest bearing on this inquiry.

In addition, our primary concern is methodology used in academic research; that is, the conscious effort to advance knowledge about public administration. Thus, methods generally used in the social sciences are included, whether qualitative or quantitative in nature. We excluded methodologies for administrative research, such as program evaluation, client surveys, and productivity measurement. These methods focus on generating knowledge about the problems of particular organizations or programs, and are excluded from the scope of this study. They are oriented to the practice of administration rather than the study of administration.

As the foregoing suggests, methodology and research are closly linked. Methodology exists to guide the conduct of research; methodology is reflected in research. As a practical matter, therefore, our assessment of methodology is necessarily an assessment of public administration research.

Historical Issues in Public Administration Research Methodology

Public administration research methodology has been assessed infrequently, but five themes consistently emerge from the literature: (1) The eclectic nature of public administration makes it difficult to identify methodologies that define or are associated exclusively with the field; (2) research reflects too little interdisciplinary communication; (3) public administration research has not been cumulative; (4) the bridge between research and practice is an important consideration in the selection of research methodology; and (5) institutional support for research is inadequate for remedying knowledge deficiencies in public administration.

Public Administration: Academic Discipline or Profession?

The question "Is there a discipline of public administration?" has occupied a good deal of attention in the history of public administration thought (see, among others, Dahl 1947; Honey 1957; Mosher 1956). The practical import of this question is twofold. First, identification of the "stuff" of the field, as Dwight Waldo has often termed it, would help identify the phenomena and problems requiring investigation by its practitioners and, in turn, may help them to design appropriate methods for inquiry. Second, locating public administration in the larger constellation of social and natural sciences would have a direct bearing on identifying acceptable, common, or perhaps even paradigmatic research methodologies.

Writing in 1957, John Honey concluded that "a common pool of understanding was lacking with regard to (*a*) what public administration is and whether it is a separate field or discipline from other social sciences, and (*b*) the nature of research that has meaning for public administration" (p. 238). In the intervening years, the intellectual core has sometimes been the topic of intense debate, and assertions about an identity crisis have been common (Marini 1971), but public administration seems to have arrived at an operative, if not a consensual, solution to the field question. Among the components of this operative solution are that public administration is centrally concerned with the operation and social role of public enterprises and therefore is a practical or professional field; while the scope of public administration practice is broad, the study of public administration is rooted in the social sciences and therefore in the methods of social science; and the problems associated with administering public enterprises demand research of both an applied and basic orientation.

From a research methodology perspective, this solution describes a field characterized by methodological diversity and a mixture of basic and applied research. This state of affairs is a wholly predictable outgrowth of directions identified by Dahl (1947) and Simon (1947) forty years ago (see also Waldo 1984). At mid-century, the controversy about excluding normative considerations from public administration was perhaps the dominant concern of the field. Dahl (1947) considered it perhaps the greatest stumbling block to creating a science of public administration. Simon (1947) argued that Dahl's concern was misplaced, contending it was the result of seeing the problem as characteristic of social versus natural science. He asserted that normative considerations are characteristic of applied as distinguished from basic science because the applied scientist's role involves reaching decisions grounded only partially in scientific knowledge. In Simon's terms, public administration has evolved as a basic and an applied science, the former concerned with establishing empirical propositions independent of the value system of the inquirer and the latter devoted to assisting with application of the empirical propositions for a specified set of values.

Interdisciplinary Communication

The breadth of public administration and its methodological diversity create unusual problems in spanning several boundaries—to academic disciplines, to others within public administration, and to the real world. When Mosher (1956) wrote about these problems in the 1950s, he lamented the absence of systematic ways for those in public administration to keep abreast of relevant developments in other fields and the ignorance about research from public administration within other fields.

Both the stock of knowledge and its rate of growth have increased significantly in the past thirty years, so it would hardly be persuasive to argue that the cause of this problem has abated. Nevertheless, the boundary-spanning problem has been partially resolved by the evolution of new organizational arrangements among and within academic disciplines. One of the trends identified by Mosher in 1956, that the other social sciences are converging with public administration with respect to interests and purposes, is partially responsible for generating these changes.

Among the manifestations of these new organizational arrangements are the creation of groups within or spinoffs from traditional academic disciplines, such as political science and economics, with central interests in public issues. Examples include the sections on Public Administration and Public Policy within the American Political Science Association. These groups have generated theory relevant to public administration and have provided opportunities for public administration scholars to keep abreast of developments in the traditional disciplines.

A new generation of interdisciplinary organizations has also sprung up to accommodate heightened interest in public problems. The Public Choice Society and the Association for Public Policy Analysis and Management (APPAM) are prime examples of this new generation of organizations. Still another development has been the evolution of public-sector groups within a wide range of professional organizations, such as the College of Public Programs in the Operations Research Society of America—The Institute of Management Science (ORSA-TIMS) and the Public Sector Division of the Academy of Management.

These changes in the organization of academic and professional interests have not been an unqualified blessing; nor have they eliminated all boundary-spanning problems. Scholars interested in public administration are now confronted with an overload problem of a new sort: how to select from among all the organizational options available for their professional development.

Perhaps a potentially more serious consequence of the multiplication of locations for public administration activity is the decline of agreement among scholars and practitioners about the basic terms of their field (Garson and Overman 1983). The community of scholars that existed in public administration until the 1960s have been supplanted by minicommunities. Although some public administration scholars view this as desireable because it improves the manageability of developments within accepted specialties (Golembiewski, Welsh, and Crotty 1969), other scholars are concerned because it portends that the values used to assess the worth of new knowledge are no longer widely shared (Newland 1984).

Cumulation of Knowledge

While interdisciplinary communication problems have perhaps diminished as new communities of scholars have organized to address new issues, another integrative problem has increased in importance: the cumulativeness of relevant knowledge. This criticism has been raised several times in the past (Kronenberg 1971; Mosher 1956). It is important to point out that the process of knowledge accumulation is not linear; the acquisition of new understanding is more probably a step function or an upward-sloping cyclical function. Our diagnosis of this problem is not predicated

350

on the current level of achievement, but on processes and efforts to systematize empirical theory about public administration.

Impediments to cumulation arise from many sources, including disagreements among competing scholarly interests, changing public problems, and lack of a fixed-core content for the field. The vast scope of the field is a bar to any rapid accumulation of knowledge given the limited human and institutional resources focused on investigating relevant phenomena. The lack of cumulative knowledge also may result from some specific problems associated with incentives for research or investigator preferences for certain research methodologies. Whatever the causes, inadequacies of methodology for cumulating knowledge are reflected in certain characteristics of public administration research. For example, meta-analysis, the critical review and reanalysis of prior research and a popular method for synthesizing research in other fields, is little used in public administration. It is also our belief that a preponderance of public administration research focuses on early stages of theory development (i.e., problem delineation and variable identification), with only minimal attention to more advanced research reflecting the maturation of prevailing theories.

Bridging Theory and Practice

The need for utilitarian research within public administration was recognized in the earliest days of the field. The bureaus of municipal research, credited by Mosher (1956) as a parent of public administration, practiced strictly applied research. This tradition survives today in a wide array of governmental research bureaus and institutes. The practical orientation of these bureaus frequently drives out investments in basic research. Historical tradition, expectations of core funders, and bureau staff tend to work for applied research and against the advancement of basic public administration research. Thus academic public administration is simultaneously provided with and robbed of the means for advancement of knowledge by some of its own institutionalized values.

The perpetuation of the theory-practice distinction is primarily attributable to the limited scientific authority of public administration theory—and not to the value of theory se. Public administration would benefit from strong basic and applied research institutes, responsible to their constituencies, but free to pursue their separate objectives.

Institutional Support

Previous reviews of public administration research have found considerable fault with the adequacy of institutionalized support. Publication outlets (Mosher 1956) and funded support (Garson and Overman 1983; Honey 1957) were among the areas most heavily faulted. The availability of financial support continues to be a problem, but, as suggested above, academic public administration's own values also fail to support research adequately.

Indeed, public administration does not lack historical models, publication outlets, or governmental support for basic research. The Committee on Public Administration of the Social Science Research Council was a major force in the publication, support, and sponsorship of research from 1935 until 1945. The problem of publication outlets has abated significantly. At least a dozen journals, many of them founded since 1970, now complement *Public Administration Review* (Morgan, Meier, Kearney, Hays, and Birch 1981; Vocino and Elliott 1984). And governmental support for basic research in public administration has been steady, with occasional exhibitions of largess such as the National Science Foundation's Research Applied to National Needs (RANN) Program and the Office of Personnel Management's Organizational Assessments of the Civil Service Reform Act (CSRA) of 1978.

While increases in the level of these institutional supports could make a difference for public administration research, they are not enough by themselves. What public administration lacks, in addition, and what is a central problem for advancing research, are values supportive of basic research. The low priority given to research is reflected in faculty recruitment and promotion, training of new Ph.D.s, and program goals and design. Universities are producing an abundance of nonresearch Ph.D.s and a dearth of research-oriented Ph.D.s in public administration (McCurdy and Cleary 1984).

University support for research does not automatically accompany support for teaching programs. Moreover, public administration programs tend to be viewed by university administrators as service rather than academic components (Dunn, Gibson, and Whorton 1985). Thus, when research bureaus are provided to support public administration programs, they tend to be viewed as service extensions of the university and oriented toward applied research and technical assistance rather than toward basic research.

Recent Critiques of Public Administration Research

Recent assessments of public administration research methodology reflect concern with two primary issues. The first is the degree to which research is adding to a verifiable knowledge base. The second issue is epistemological, involving the kinds of research questions that we can pierce with our methodologies, and whether our methodologies produce usable knowledge.

Several recent studies have looked at different bodies of research in public administration from the standpoint of their contributions to knowledge. Garson and Overman (1983) reviewed public management research, a subset of public administration research, for the years 1981–82. They concluded that the research was fragmented, noncumulative, and underfunded. A more recent study by McCurdy and Cleary (1984) analyzed abstracts from public administration doctoral dissertations published in *Dissertation Abstracts International* for 1981. They found that the vast majority of dissertations neither dealt with significant issues nor were conducted in a way that would produce findings in which one could have much confidence. They concluded that the lack of methodological progress, as evidenced by the low quality of dissertations, results from inadequate standards among leading public administration programs as well as the nature of the field itself. Jay White's (1986a) replication of McCurdy and Cleary's study found that dissertation research is not published and therefore not communicated beyond the dissertation committee. Whatever reasons explain the lack of publication (e.g., poor quality, lack of interest in publishing the dissertation), White concluded that dissertation research does not appear to be a major source of knowledge in the field.

The second issue, which is epistemological, has been addressed by a number of public administration theorists, most notably Catron and Harmon (1981), Denhardt (1984), Hummel (1977), and White (1986b). White argues that most critiques of public administration research have been grounded in positivist models, indicative of the natural and mainstream social sciences. He argues, however, that public administration research has not been viewed in the light of two other modes of research: interpretive and critical. He suggests that growth of public administration knowledge be interpreted in the light of all three modes of research.

Following White, we believe that methodological diversity in public administration is both appropriate and acceptable. Nevertheless, debates among the advocates of alternative modes are no substitute for research on substantive theoretical issues. The ultimate test of the value of these modes is whether they contribute to the development of a stock of knowledge and illuminate understanding of the field.

Contemporary Research Methodology

Methods and Data

Research articles published in *Public Administration Review* (*PAR*) and *Administration and Society* (*A&S*) from 1975 through 1984 were chosen as the population for assessing contemporary research methodology within public administration. *PAR* is the journal of the American Society for Public Administration (ASPA), a professional society whose mission is "to advance the science, processes, and art of public administration." It has a dual set of objectives aimed simultaneously at communicating with practitioners and advancing the science of the field. *A&S* is an unaffiliated journal published by Sage Publications. Its editorial policy "seeks to further the understanding of public and human service organizations, their administrative processes, and their effect on society."

In addition to considerations of manageability and convenience, several factors led us to choose research published in these two journals. First, *PAR* and *A&S* are among the premier journals in the field and, therefore, should be representative of current research methodology in the field. Second, research articles in these journals are peer reviewed to assure that they meet broad professional standards.

Symposia articles, professional stream essays, review essays, and special issues were excluded from the domain of *PAR* articles analyzed. Included in the analysis were 289 *PAR* and 194 *A&S* articles.

Analytic Categories

Each article was coded on eleven variables, about half reflecting purely descriptive information and the others requiring some interpretation of the contents of the article. The complete variable code book is presented in the Appendix. Seven variables provided primarily descriptive information, some of it purely for identification purposes, about each of the cases: year of publication, volume, issue number, author(s), author's organization, general subject area, sources of research support.

Four other categories were used to record information about the methodology used in the study. *Research Stage* is a taxonomic variable derived from earlier work by Gordon, MacEachron, and Fisher (1974). It represents the stage of social science research, reflecting the purpose for which the study was conducted. These research stages and purposes are summarized in table 15.1 (page 355). *Research Methodology* was adapted from an earlier taxonomy by Caldwell (1968). The categories of this taxonomic variable reflect general methods of inquiry used in the social sciences. *Methods of Empirical Analysis* was based on Gordon, MacEachron, and Fisher (1974), Rogers and Agarwala-Rogers (1976), and Vogel and Wetherbe (1984). This variable applied only to studies that used empirical observation. The categories of this variable range from case study to controlled field experiments. Each category of the taxonomy represents increasing internal validity (Campbell and Stanley 1963). *Focus* is a dichotomous variable that distinguishes whether the study was oriented toward theory building or problem resolution.

Research Results

Descriptive Characteristics of Public Administration Research. Figures 15.1 through 15.6 present research by primary subject matter, focus, source of research support, stage, general methodology, and methods of empirical analysis. These data are useful for two purposes: (1) characterizing public administration research in general and (2) identifying journal-specific variations. Our primary interest is with the former of these purposes.

The distribution of research by primary subject matter, reported in figure 15.1 (page 356), confirms the broad distribution of research in the field. Although the subject matters addressed in *PAR* are more evenly distributed than those in *A&S*, the journals share the four most frequent subject matters: administrative the-

TABLE 15.1
Classification of Research Strategies

Research state	Research purpose
1. Problem delineation	To define what we are looking for, and the extent to which it constitutes a social problem
2. Variable identification	To identify variables that might be linked to the problem, and to describe possible relationships among these variables
3. Determination of relationships among the variables	To determine the clusters of relevant variables required for prediction, and to analyze their patterns of relationships
4. Establishment of causality among the variables	To determine which factors are critical in promoting or inhibiting the problem
5. Manipulation of causal variables for policy formation purposes	To determine the correspondence between a theoretical problem solution and the manipulable factors
6. Experimental evaluation of alternative policies and programs	To assess the expected, as well as the unanticipated, consequences of various programs and policies before and after they are applied on a large scale, and to determine the effectiveness of such programs in overall problem solution

ory, public management, public policy, and planning. Of these areas, *PAR* articles emphasize public policy significantly more frequently, and *A&S* articles focus on administrative theory relatively more intensively. Comparison of subject matters also indicates administrative functions (e.g., personnel, budgeting) are addressed much more frequently in *PAR* articles than *A&S* articles. Figure 15.2 (page 357) also shows that a majority of articles published in both *PAR* and *A&S* emphasize problem solving over theory development. Despite these similarities, the profiles for two journals also differ in one significant respect. *PAR* articles are predominantly problem oriented, whereas *A&S* publishes about equal numbers of theory and problem-focused articles.

The low levels of support for public administration research are apparent from figure 15.3 (page 358). Overall, 80 percent of the articles did not identify any sources of institutional support. The most important sponsorship category for articles published in both journals was "other," which primarily consisted of research funds provided to faculty by their universities. The National Science Foundation supported the largest amount of published research, but it was identified in relatively few *PAR* or *A&S* articles (5.5 percent and 6.7 percent, respectively).

Most articles reported the results of research at an early stage of development, as reflected in figure 15.4 (page 359). Over 60 percent of the articles in each journal dealt with either problem delineation or variable identification, the two

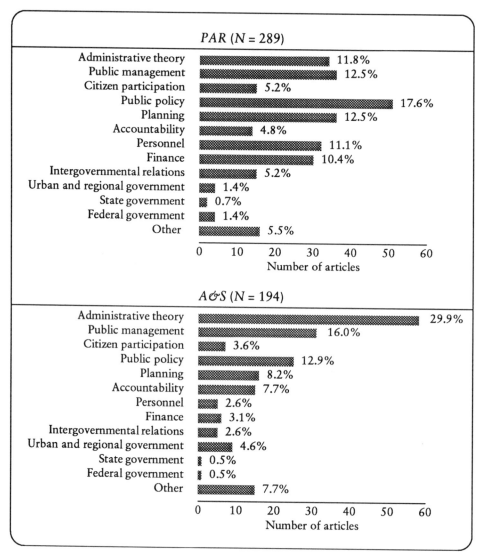

FIGURE 15.1
Distribution of Articles by Primary Subject Matter

lowest stages in the taxonomy. *A&S* published a moderately higher proportion of articles addressing determination of relationships among variables than did *PAR*. But only about 5 percent of articles published in both journals reported research that had been conducted at one of the three most advanced stages.

Figure 15.5 (page 360) indicates that the general research methodologies in

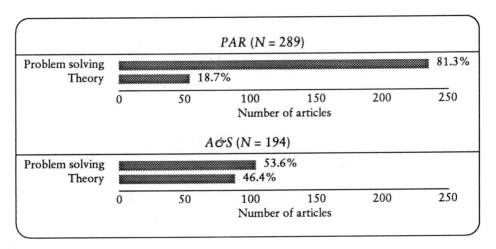

FIGURE 15.2
Relative Frequency of Theory vs. Problem-solving Orientation

PAR and *A&S* clustered in three categories: logical argumentation, legal briefs, and empirical analysis. Methodologies often associated with interpretive or critical theory, that is, historical or descriptive approaches (White 1986b), were infrequently represented. Mathematical models or comprehensive literature reviews were used in very small proportions, less than 3 percent of *PAR* articles and less than 8 percent of *A&S* articles. About half of all articles (52.2 percent for *PAR* and 49.5 percent for *A&S*) employed some type of empirical analysis. Figure 15.6 (page 361) indicates, however, that most empirical research consisted of either case studies or cross-sectional analysis. Very little empirical analysis involved field experiments, structural equations, or longitudinal studies.

Changes in Research Methodology over Time. As a means for identifying changes in public administration research methodology, the data were categorized into two five-year periods 1975–79 and 1980–84. The *A&S* distribution of research by primary subject topic was quite stable during these two periods, but there were significant shifts in the subject areas covered in *PAR* (table 15.2, page 362). Administrative theory, citizen participation, planning, and personnel all declined in significance as a proportion of total research. Finance, intergovernmental relations, and public policy increased significantly as focal areas for research. Few differences for the two periods were found for research sponsorship or research stage. In contrast, general methodologies changed significantly, with much greater emphasis on empirical analysis in both the *PAR* and *A&S* samples from 1980 to 1984 (table 15.3, page 363). The increased use of empirical analysis was distributed among three methods: case studies, cross-sectional analysis, and longitudinal analysis.

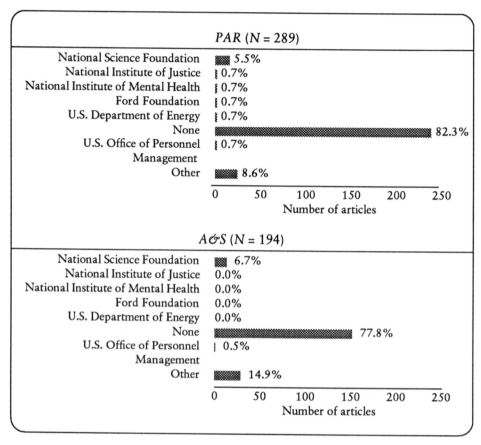

FIGURE 15.3
Sources of Research Support

Discussion

The analysis identified several differences between *PAR* and *A&S*. Among the differences were the distributions of subject matter and the greater emphasis of *A&S* on theory development. The editorial goals and objectives of the journals obviously influenced these variables. The similarities in results far outweigh journal idio-syncracies, however. Moreover, replication and extension of our analysis by Stallings and Ferris (1988), covering forty years of *Public Administration Review*, produced similar results. Given the consistency of findings over time and across journals, three general evaluative statements about public administration research can be drawn.

First, public administration research is primarily applied rather than basic. Nearly three-fourths of the articles dealt with either problem delineation or variable

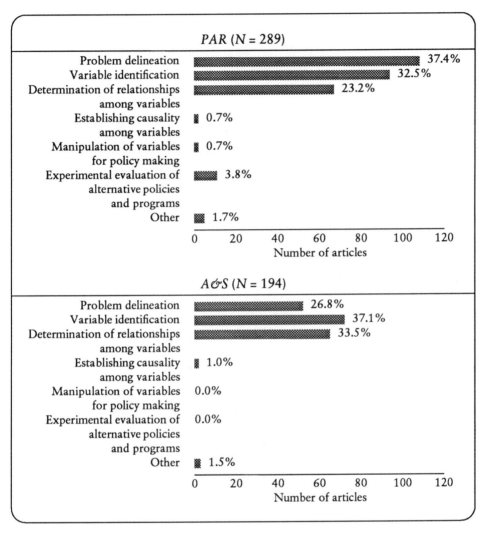

FIGURE 15.4
Distribution of Articles by Research Stage

identification; less than one-fourth dealt with theoretical relationships among variables. Moreover, the research lacks detachment from immediate and instrumental concerns. Most of the articles reporting empirical research were of either the casestudy or cross-sectional-survey variety; few articles involved field experiments, structural equations, or longitudinal studies. Finally, the underlying purposes of conducting research tend to be problem oriented, which limits development and testing of empirical theory. Problem-oriented research tends to reduce the chances

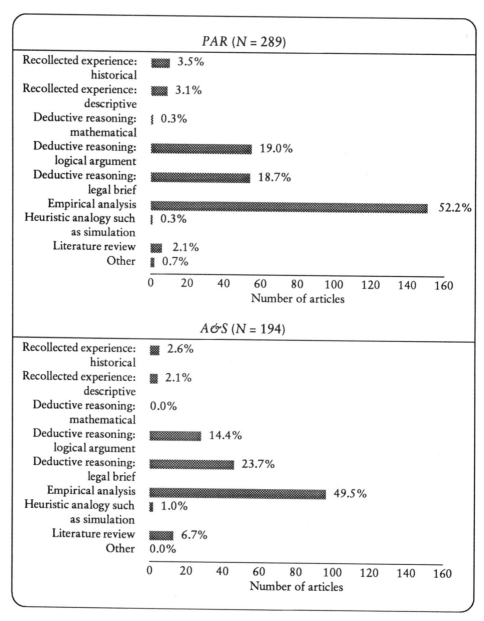

FIGURE 15.5
Distribution of Articles by General Research Approach

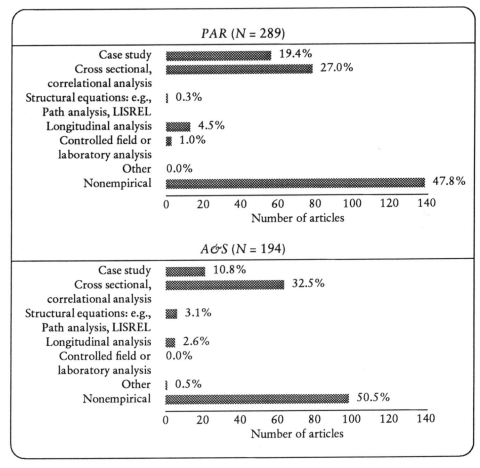

FIGURE 15.6
Distribution of Articles by Methods of Empirical Analysis

that propositions about the field will be adequate statements of explanation and will be linked together in a system of explanation (Kronenberg 1971, 193).

Second, public administration research lacks cumulativeness. Both the methodology and the stage reflected in public administration literature indicate that research is not cumulative. Less than 4 percent of the articles in *PAR* and *A&S* combined were literature reviews of empirical research, a methodology indicative of a general concern with cumulation. Moreover, our personal reading indicates that much of the literature provided only citation reference to previous research and did not seriously engage the linkages between the current article and prior or contemporary research.

TABLE 15.2
Comparison of 1975–79 and 1980–84 Distribution
of Articles by Primary Subject Area

	PAR (N = 289)					
	1975–79		1980–84		Total	
Subject matter	N	%	N	%	N	%
Administrative theory	18	16.1	16	9.1	34	11.8
Public management	13	11.6	23	13.1	36	12.5
Citizen participation	9	8.0	6	3.4	15	5.2
Public policy making	9	8.0	42	24.0	51	17.6
Planning	20	17.9	16	9.1	36	12.5
Accountability	4	3.6	10	5.7	14	4.8
Personnel	15	13.4	17	9.7	32	11.1
Finance	6	5.4	24	13.7	30	10.4
Intergovernmental relations	4	3.6	11	6.3	15	5.2
Urban and regional government	1	0.9	3	1.7	4	1.4
State government	1	0.9	1	0.6	2	0.7
Federal government	4	3.6	0	0.0	4	1.4
Other	8	7.1	8	3.4	16	5.5
Total	112	100.1	177	99.8	289	100.1

	A&S (N = 194)					
	1975–79		1980–84		Total	
Subject matter	N	%	N	%	N	%
Administrative theory	27	28.1	31	31.6	58	29.9
Public management	18	18.8	13	13.3	31	16.0
Citizen participation	3	3.1	4	4.1	7	3.6
Public policy making	8	8.3	17	17.3	25	12.9
Planning	11	11.5	5	5.1	16	8.2
Accountability	6	6.2	9	9.2	15	7.7
Personnel	0	0.0	5	5.1	5	2.6
Finance	5	5.2	1	1.0	6	3.1
Intergovernmental relations	1	1.0	4	4.1	5	2.6
Urban and regional government	6	6.2	3	3.1	9	4.6
State government	0	0.0	1	1.0	1	0.5
Federal government	1	1.0	0	0.0	1	0.5
Other	10	10.4	5	5.1	15	7.7
Total	96	100	98	100	194	100

Note: Percentages may not sum to 100 due to rounding.

TABLE 15.3
Comparison of 1975–79 and 1980–84 Distribution
of Articles by Methods of Empirical Analysis

PAR (N = 289)

Method of empirical analysis	1975–79 N	1975–79 %	1980–84 N	1980–84 %	Total N	Total %
Case study	16	14.3	40	22.6	56	19.4
Cross sectional, correlational analysis	29	25.9	49	27.7	78	27
Structural equations: e.g., path analysis, LISREL	0	0.0	1	0.6	1	0.3
Longitudinal analysis	1	0.9	12	6.8	13	4.5
Controlled field or laboratory analysis	2	1.8	1	0.6	3	1
Nonempirical	64	57.1	74	41.8	138	47.8
Other	0	0.0	0	0.0	0	0
Totals	112	100.0	177	100.1	289	100

A&S (N = 194)

Method of empirical analysis	1975–79 N	1975–79 %	1980–84 N	1980–84 %	Total N	Total %
Case study	7	7.3	14	14.3	21	10.8
Cross sectional, correlational analysis	27	28.1	36	36.7	63	32.5
Structural equations: e.g., path analysis, LISREL	4	4.2	2	2.0	6	3.1
Longitudinal analysis	1	1.0	4	4.1	5	2.6
Controlled field or laboratory analysis	0	0.0	0	0.0	0	0
Nonempirical	57	59.4	41	41.8	98	50.5
Other	0	0.0	1	1.0	1	0.5
Totals	96	100.0	98	99.9	194	100

Note: Percentages may not sum to 100 due to rounding.

Third, public administration research lacks adequate institutional support such as university and extramural funding, organized research institutes, collaborative groups and external rewards. The primary indicator of support for research was financial. Eighty percent of the articles failed to identify any sources of financial or other institutional support. This omission is not caused by poor reporting, journal policy, or faculty ingratitude. Instead, it is indicative of the low level of such support.

To compare the level of support for public administration research with another professional field, we analyzed reported support from articles published in the Academy of Management's two publications, the *Review* and *Journal,* for calendar year 1984. From a total of 105 articles, 40 percent acknowledged some kind of support, 22 percent reported receiving extramural support and another 18 percent received assistance from their university. This is twice the proportion of articles in *PAR* and *A&S.*

Thus, given the assessments above, we conclude that there is a notable convergence between the past and the present. Public administration research continues to be eclectic, noncumulative, skewed toward problem solving, and poorly supported. Public administration research methodology has not matured to a point where it is capable of sustaining the knowledge creation needs of the field. We find ourselves in basic agreement with Fritz Mosher (1956) who, over thirty years ago in a review of research methodology in public administration, concluded:

> The field has not channeled its research efforts; its scope of interest seem unlimited; it has not developed a rigorous methodology; it has been pretty blase about definitions; it has not agreed on any paradigms or theorems or theoretical systems; it has not settled on any stylized jargon or symbols; with a very few experimental exceptions, the field has not been modeled or mathematized into an "adminimetrics." (P. 176)

In order to advance the status of research methodology in public administration, we believe three general changes are necessary: (1) focus on core phenomena, (2) institutionalize research, and (3) improve specific methodologies.

Focus on Core Phenomena in Public Administration

As noted above, public administration is a remarkably diffuse field encompassing contributions from many disciplines. It is also a relatively small field, in terms of scholars pursuing its study, when compared with similar fields such as business administration. Public administration, therefore, needs to focus the scope of its scholarship if progress is to be made in understanding phenomena within its general domain. Golembiewski (1977) has suggested guidelines for achieving this goal. Among the guidelines is a "next bite" approach, that is, avoiding development of comprehensive theories and focusing instead on smaller pieces of appropriate reality. In addition to this strategy, two sets of core phenomena could provide a sharper focus for research within the field.

The Study of Characteristics and Processes That Differentiate Public Administration from Other Administration. This could be attacked as both an issue of political theory and as an empirical issue. A political theory approach would concentrate, as suggested by Woodrow Wilson (1887, 197), on those public purposes that define public administration. Empirical research should be grounded in the premise that public administration is a subset of two generic social processes: administration and governance (Willbern 1968).

Political-administrative System Interface. The second anchor we propose for a redefined public administration core is the study of phenomena at the interface of the political-administrative system. Among the phenomena that would be the object of research given this definition of legitimate concerns are responsiveness or non-responsiveness to the political system; legitimacy of the administrative system in carrying out its politically mandated functions; legislative oversight of administrative agencies; representativeness of administrative agencies; and administrative reform (e.g., civil service reform for increasing the responsiveness of administrators to both the executive and the public).

Institutionalize Research
It is apparent that public administration research is very much a product of institutionalized norms and incentives. Substantial advancements in research methodology will occur only if new norms and incentives are legitimated. These changes would need to include the following.

Upgrade the Importance of Research in Faculty Roles. At the micro level, considerable progress can be made by better developing the capacity and incentives for public administration faculty to do high caliber research. Where the capacity does not exist, we suggest bringing in first-rate scholars from other disciplines. For existing faculty, vehicles such as the Interuniversity Consortium on Political and Social Research (ICPSR) summer program could be used to upgrade faculty research skills. Faculty incentives can be influenced by institutionalizing research as a promotion and merit criterion. The faculty tenure and promotion policies of individual universities could be significantly reinforced by the National Association of Schools of Public Affairs and Administration's (NASPAA) adoption of standards that defined research as a faculty responsibility and required that public administration faculty be substantially engaged in teaching, service, and research. A recent study by Joseph A. Uveges, Jr., (1985) indicated that NASPAA standards have had a modest impact on M.P.A. curricula and program autonomy. Thus there is some evidence that the leverage of NASPAA standards might contribute to institutionalizing research.

Improve the Quality of Ph.D. Programs. A change related to upgrading faculty research roles involves increased emphasis on research-oriented Ph.D. programs. Public administration continues to debate the issue of whether the Ph.D. should be conferred exclusively for research competence or whether a doctorate for practitioners is not equally appropriate (Birkhead and Netzer, 1982). The M.P.A. should be the terminal professional degree, and doctoral study should be devoted to developing a candidate's research competence. Schools that offer the Ph.D. or D.P.A. (Doctor of Public Administration) should provide intensive training in research and adequate numbers of research-oriented faculty to sustain the programs.

Develop Research Unit–Public Administration Program Ties. An expanded emphasis on the value of research would be greatly facilitated by stronger ties between formal research units and public administration programs. Universities considering creation of public administration programs should give serious consideration to funding research units at high levels relative to the instructional programs, for example, one-half the program resources.

Increase Funding for Public Administration Research. Without financial resources, adequate research cannot occur. This is an issue that needs to be resolved collectively by the profession and leading public administrators. The National Academy for Public Administration might initiate a dialogue with Congress about the needs for, and benefits from, research on public administration. Given the scale of our modern administrative state and its centrality in our society, Congress might consider creation of a National Institute along the lines of the National Institutes of Health. Within the current fiscal climate, such proposals would appear to be inopportune, but the scale of problems of modern public administration could easily justify a moderate amount of earmarked funds likely to repay the initial investment in a few short years.

Specific Methodological Improvements
In addition to changing incentives and norms, there is need for specific improvements in research methods used by public administration scholars.

More Extensive Use of Meta-analysis. One of the most important of these changes involves steps to increase the cumulation of research. Kronenberg's (1971) earlier call for a public administration proposition inventory was one means for dealing with this problem, but it has not been implemented in the fifteen years since it was suggested, probably because it was dependent on a large-scale, collaborative effort. An alternative means for increasing cumulativeness of research is wider use of meta-analysis. Meta-analysis refers to the set of methods used to establish facts by cumulating results across studies. These methods include literature reviews (Salipante, Notz, and Bigelow 1982), counting statistically significant findings, and averaging results across studies (Hunter, Schmidt, and Jackson 1982). Also, the empirical analysis indicated that literature reviews were used infrequently and few studies advanced to mature stages of social science research. Both of these findings suggest the need for more attention to meta-analysis. An ancillary benefit of greater use of meta-analysis is that it can also be valuable for integrating results across different academic fields, a particularly important objective for an interdisciplinary enterprise such as public administration.

Case Study Methodology. Case studies have been stereotyped as a method of last resort, exploratory, and an attractive nuisance (Miles 1979; Yin 1981a). Given these critical views about case-study methodology, it would be appropriate to call for a significant reduction in the use of case studies in public administration research. Nevertheless, case studies will continue to be a popular method given the subject matter of the field and therefore a more realistic strategy is to focus on their improvement. Furthermore, abandonment of case studies fails to consider a revisionist view about their value that has developed in the past decade (Yin 1981b; Yin and Heald 1975). Recent refinements in the conduct of case studies have increased their potential validity (McClintock, Brannon, and Maynard-Moody 1979; Yin and Heald 1975). Considering their widespread use in the field, public administration scholars might undertake further refinements in case-study methods as a means for enhancing public administration research and contributing generally to development of social science methods.

Qualitative Methodologies. Another specific area for improvement is the use of qualitative methodologies within public administration. A grasp of qualitative methodologies is becoming increasingly important as interpretation and rhetoric regain prominence and respectability in the social sciences (Winkler, 1985). The empirical analysis confirmed public administration's already strong preference for qualitative research, an albeit diminishing one, but also questioned the adequacy of researchers' grasp of the tools and craft associated with qualitative methodology. There has been a small explosion of materials in recent years about qualitative research (Van Maanen 1979), and public administration scholars need to become both more proficient practitioners of this craft and contributors to the advancement of these methods.

Advanced Quantitative Methodologies. The call for better qualitative methodology is not a slap at its opposite number—more appropriately its complement—quantitative methodology. Although the empirical analysis indicated a significant increase in the amount of quantitative research in public administration, the techniques used were primarily confined to simple correlation and linear regression analysis. This represents an advance in the field's application of quantitative techniques, but public administration still lags behind other social sciences in the ap-

367

plication of advanced statistical techniques. Thus public administration scholars need to make more substantial use of causal analysis, structural equation models, and longitudinal statistical methods, and to develop working competence with new statistical methodologies sooner after they become available to social scientists than they do currently.

Two examples of advanced statistical techniques that would significantly enhance opportunities to investigate research questions characteristic of the field are Box-Jenkins time-series models and covariance structural modeling. Box-Jenkins is a technique for modeling changes in a time series of data to test the effects of specified interventions. Although it has not yet been applied widely, it has already been used to study such issues as the policy implications of economic change (Catalano, Dooley, and Jackson 1985) and the effects of the CSRA merit pay intervention on organizational performance (Pearce, Stevenson, and Perry 1985).

Covariance structural modeling, commonly known as LISREL (Joreskog and Sorbom 1981), is a causal data analysis technique that is much more powerful than path analysis, which became popular in the 1960s. LISREL permits simultaneous estimation of the relationship between observed measures of latent independent and dependent variables. LISREL has begun to appear with increasing frequency in sociology and management journals for research problems involving social and individual behavior.

Some attention needs to be given not only to specific techniques that might be integrated into the field but also to how those techniques are acquired by students and current scholars. An earlier study (Gazell 1973) of empirical research in public administration and political science found a high degree of methodological stability over time. Scholars kept using familiar, traditional approaches instead of learning new methods. Thus the field needs to develop support systems, for example, research workshops and doctoral consortia at professional conferences, to facilitate learning. Such support systems are equally applicable and necessary for public administration scholars interested in positive, interpretive, or critical research modes to develop and stay abreast of appropriate research methodologies. Clearly, such steps are only a partial answer. But they are necessary not only for moving the field to the forefront but also for improving the state of research practice.

Conclusion

Even if all the suggestions outlined above could be implemented instantly, it would take several years before their consequences would be noticeable. Although some of our suggestions require collective or institutional action, many can be implemented by individual scholars in the routine practice of their craft. For example, individual scholars can stay with research issues over the long term, improve the methodologies associated with case studies, and increase the application of more advanced statistical methodologies appropriate to the problems of public administration. The acceptance of these suggestions by the public administration community could serve to advance both the science and the art of public administration.

Appendix: Codebook for Analysis of Articles

VARIABLE 1: Year (1975–84)
VARIABLE 2: Volume (35–44)
VARIABLE 3: Number (1–6)
VARIABLE 4: Title
VARIABLE 5: Author(s)
VARIABLE 6: Institutional Affiliation(s)
VARIABLE 7: Topic

    1. Administrative theory/bureaucracy/organizational theory
    2. Managerial roles/public management
    3. Citizen participation/representation
    4. Public policy making/policy analysis/policy evaluation
    5. Planning/administrative systems
    6. Accountability/responsiveness/public interest values
    7. Personnel
    8. Other
    9. Budgeting/finance
    10. Intergovernmental relations
    11. Urban and regional government
    12. State government
    13. Federal government

VARIABLE 8: Source of Research Support

    1. National Science Foundation
    2. Office of Naval Research
    3. National Institute of Justice
    4. National Institute of Mental Health
    5. Ford Foundation
    6. U.S. Department of Energy
    7. None indicated
    8. Other
    9. U.S. Office of Personnel Management

VARIABLE 9: Research Stage/Purpose

    1. Problem delineation

2. Variable identification
3. Determination of relationships among variables
4. Establishing causality among variables
5. Manipulation of variables for policy making
6. Evaluation of alternative policies and programs
7. Other

VARIABLE 10: Research Methodology

1. Recollected experience: anthropology
2. Recollected experience: historical
3. Recollected experience: descriptive
4. Deductive reasoning: mathematical
5. Deductive reasoning: logical argument
6. Deductive reasoning: legal brief
7. Empirical analysis (inductive inference)
8. Other
9. Heuristic analogy (e.g., simulation)
10. Literature review

VARIABLE 11: Method of empirical analysis

1. Case study
2. Cross-sectional, correlational analysis
3. Structural equations (e.g., path analysis, LISREL)
4. Longitudinal analysis
5. Controlled field or laboratory analysis
6. Not applicable
7. Other

VARIABLE 12: Focus

1. Theory building (theoretical)
2. Problem resolution (practical)

References

Birkhead, Guthrie S., and Dick Netzer. 1982. "Doctorate in Public Affairs and Administration." Mimeographed.

Caldwell, Lynton K. 1968. "Methodology in the Theory of Public Administration." In *Theory and Practice of Public Administration: Scope, Objectives, and Methods*, edited by James C. Charlesworth. Philadelphia: American Academy of Political and Social Sciences.

Campbell, Donald T., and Julian C. Stanley. 1963. *Experimental and Quasi-Experimental Designs for Research*. Chicago: Rand McNally.

Catalano, Ralph A., David Dooley, and Robert L. Jackson. 1985. "Economic Antecedents of Help Seeking: A Reformulation of the Time-Series Tests." *Journal of Health and*

Social Behavior 26:141–52.

Catron, Bayard, and Michael Harmon. 1981. "Action Theory in Practice: Toward Theory without Conspiracy." *Public Administration Review* 42:535–41.

Dahl, Robert A. 1947. "The Science of Public Administration: Three Problems." *Public Administration Review* 7:1–11.

Denhardt, Robert B. 1984. *Theories of Public Organization*. Monterey, Calif.: Brooks/Cole.

Dunn, Delmer D., Frank K. Gibson, and Joseph Whorton, Jr. 1985. "University Commitment to Public Service for State and Local Governments." *Public Administration Review* 45:503–9.

Garson, G. David, and E. Sam Overman. 1983. *Public Management Research in the United States*. New York: Praeger.

Gazell, James A. 1973. "Empirical Research in American Public Administration and Political Science: Is the Estranged Relative Outstripping the Rest of Its Former Household?" *Midwest Review of Public Administration* 7:229–44.

Golembiewski, Robert T. 1977. *Public Administration as a Developing Discipline,* pt. 2. New York: Marcel Dekker.

Golembiewski, Robert T., William A. Welsh, and William J. Crotty. 1969. *A Methodological Primer for Political Scientists*. Chicago: Rand McNally.

Gordon, Gerald, Ann E. MacEachron, and G. Lawrence Fisher. 1974. "A Contingency Model for the Design of Problem-Solving Research Programs: A Perspective on Diffusion Research." *Health and Society* 52:185–222.

Gulick, Luther. 1937. "Science, Values, and Public Administration." In *Papers on the Science of Administration,* edited by Luther Gulick and Lyndall Urwick. New York: Institute of Public Administration.

Honey, John C. 1957. "Research in Public Administration: A Further Note." *Public Administration Review* 17:238–43.

Hummel, Ralph. 1977. *The Bureaucratic Experience*. New York: St. Martin's Press.

Hunter, John E., Frank L. Schmidt, and Gregg B. Jackson. 1982. *Meta-analysis: Cumulating Research Findings Across Studies*. Beverly Hills: Sage.

Joreskog, K.G., and D. Sorbom. 1981. *LISREL V: User's Guide*. Chicago: National Educational Resources.

Kaplan, Abraham. 1964. *The Conduct of Inquiry*. San Francisco: Chandler.

Kronenberg, Philip S. 1971. "The Scientific and Moral Authority of Empirical Theory of Public Administration." In *Toward a New Public Administration: The Minnowbrook Perspective,* edited by Frank Marini. Scranton, Pa.: Chandler.

McClintock, Charles C., Diane Brannon, and Steven Maynard-Moody. 1979. "Applying the Logic of Sample Surveys to Qualitative Case Studies: The Case Cluster Method." *Administrative Science Quarterly* 24:612–29.

McCurdy, Howard E., and Robert Cleary. 1984. "Why Can't We Resolve the Research Issue in Public Administration?" *Public Administration Review* 44:49–55.

Marini, Frank, ed. 1971. *Toward a New Public Administration: The Minnowbrook Perspective*. Scranton, Pa.: Chandler.

Miles, Matthew B. 1979. "Qualitative Data as an Attractive Nuisance." *Administrative Science Quarterly* 24:590–601.

Morgan, David R., Kenneth J. Meier, Richard C. Kearney, Steven W. Hays, and Harold B. Birch. 1981. "Reputation and Productivity among U.S. Public Administration and Public Affairs Programs" *Public Administration Review* 41:666–73.

Mosher, Frederick C. 1956. "Research in Public Administration: Some Notes and Suggestions." *Public Administration Review* 16:169–78.

Newland, Chester. 1984. *Public Administration and Community: Realism in the Practice of Ideals.* McLean, Va.: Public Administration Service.

Pearce, Jone L., William B. Stevenson, and James L. Perry. 1985. "Managerial Compensation Based on Organizational Performance: A Time-Series Analysis of the Impact of Merit Pay." *Academy of Management Journal* 28:261–78.

Rogers, Everett M., and Rekha Agarwala-Rogers. 1976. *Communication in Organizations.* New York: Free Press.

Salipante, Paul, William Notz, and John Bigelow. 1982. "A Matrix Approach to Literature Reviews." *Research in Organizational Behavior* 4:321–48.

Simon, Herbert A. 1947. "A Comment on the Science of Public Administration." *Public Administration Review* 7:200–203.

Stallings, Robert A., and James M. Ferris. 1988. "Public Administration Research: Work in *PAR*, 1940–1984." *Public Administration Review* 48:580–87.

Uveges, Joseph A., Jr. 1985. "Identifying the Impacts of NASPAA's MPA Standards and Peer Review Process on Education for the Public Service: 1975–1985." Presented at the Southeast Regional Meeting of the American Society for Public Administration, Charleston, S.C.

Van Maanen, John, ed. 1979. "Symposium on Qualitative Methodology." *Administrative Science Quarterly* 24:519–671.

Vocino, Thomas, and Robert H. Elliott. 1984. "Research Note: Public Administration Journal Prestige: A Time-Series Analysis." *Administrative Science Quarterly* 29:43–51.

Vogel, Douglas R., and James C. Wetherbe. 1984. "MIS Research: A Profile of Leading Journals and Universities." *Data Base* 16:3–14.

Waldo, Dwight. 1984. *The Administrative State.* 2d ed. New York: Holmes and Meier.

White, Jay D. 1986a. "Dissertations and Publications in Public Administration." *Public Administration Review* 46:227–34.

White, Jay D. 1986b. "On the Growth of Knowledge in Public Administration." *Public Administration Review* 45:15–24.

Willbern, York. 1968. "Comment on Caldwell's Paper." In *Theory and Practice of Public Administration: Scope, Objectives, and Methods,* edited by James C. Charlesworth. Philadelphia: American Academy of Political Science.

Wilson, Woodrow. 1887. "The Study of Administration." *Political Science Quarterly* 2: 197–222.

Winkler, Karen J. 1985. "Questioning the Science in Social Science, Scholars Signal a 'Turn to Interpretation.'" *Chronicle of Higher Education* 5–6.

Yin, Robert K. 1981a. "The Case Study as a Serious Research Strategy." *Knowledge* 3: 97–114.

Yin, Robert K. 1981b. "The Case Study Crisis: Some Answers." *Administrative Science Quarterly,* 26:58–65.

Yin, Robert K., and Karen A. Heald. 1975. "Using the Case Survey Method to Analyze Policy Studies." *Administrative Science Quarterly* 20:371–81.

16

Formal Models of Bureaucracy:
A Review

JONATHAN BENDOR

Formal analysis is fairly new in public administration, and there is some skepticism in the field about the intellectual advantages of mathematical methods. This is quite appropriate. As with any new tool, there is a faddishness associated with these methods, and a corresponding danger of goal displacement. A formal model of bureaucracy should be a tool for extending and deepening our knowledge about public organizations. If the underlying ideas are silly, translating them into mathematics will do little good, but if they are promising, deductive reasoning can help us explore their potential: If one believes A is a general property of bureaucracies, it would be throwing away information not to work out A's logical implications. This analysis can also increase the falsifiability of our ideas: If A implies B, but empirically we discover not-B, the truth status of A is brought into question. Or it may turn out, as Kenneth Arrow discovered about democratic principles, that our informal ideas are logically inconsistent: We thought properties C and D either describe existing institutions or could describe potential ones, but recasting the ideas into mathematical form reveals this is impossible. Finally, some problems are just too hard to tackle without the aid of formal tools. It is hard to imagine, for example, that Robert Axelrod (1984) would have discovered the robustness of the simple strategy of tit-for-tat in the two-person prisoner's dilemma without the help of a computer (to put tit-for-tat against many opponents in thousands of rounds of play) and of mathematics (to prove some generic properties of tit-for-tat).

Thus, the advantages of formal reasoning are numerous and genuine. They will endure after the initial burst of enthusiasm for mathematical models has passed, and even after some realistic disillusionment has taken hold.

This chapter is a selective review of recent work on formal models of bureaucracy. Comprehensive coverage has been sacrificed in order to examine selected pieces more intensely than otherwise would have been possible. The first section studies William Niskanen's theory of bureaucracy and its descendants. The second

373

covers principal-agent models. Section 3 focuses on the design of hierarchical institutions. Section 4 examines models based on ideas of bounded rationality.

The Niskanen Tradition

William Niskanen's *Bureaucracy and Representative Government* (1971), an analysis of the bureaucratic causes of governmental growth, was the forerunner of numerous formal models of bureaus. Even today it is probably the single most cited study, and it deserves close attention.

The basic model is designed to examine the budgetary relations between a legislature and an agency. The legislators have a demand for the bureau's output; the more expensive the output, the less they want. The agency is assumed to have one goal—pursuing ever larger budgets. The relationship is an exchange: The legislature funds the bureau, and in return the agency promises to deliver a specified amount of services. Two assumptions are particularly important in giving the agency the upper hand in the deal. First, it is assumed that the bureau knows the legislature's demand for its services—the maximum the legislature is willing to pay for any amount of output. Second, the agency is not required to reveal a complete cost schedule (i.e., cost as a function of quantity); instead, it can make all-or-nothing offers to the politicians. The only constraint placed on the bureau is that it must deliver the quantity of output it has promised; accordingly, the budget must cover the output's total costs.

These assumptions imply that the agency can offer the legislature a price-output combination that the politicians barely prefer to zero output and budget. In effect, the agency engages in perfect price discrimination: At every point along the demand curve, it charges the maximum price the legislature is willing to pay. Consequently, the bureau's budget is too large, and the politicians realize no gains from the exchange. Assuming that legislative demand represents voters' preferences, bureaucratic output is also excessive. For the socially optimal amount, the cost of the last unit of output just equals its benefit. The bureau, however, will produce past the point where marginal cost equals marginal value. As long as the legislature is willing to pay anything for additional output, the agency will provide it. Thus it produces up to the point where the legislature no longer values its services at all, that is, where the marginal value of output is zero.

It may be that costs rise so steeply that the bureau cannot cover the costs of producing output for which the legislature's marginal value is zero. If so, this solution is infeasible. Instead, the bureau chief will offer to produce the maximum feasible quantity, where costs are just covered by the budget. (Niskanen calls this second solution the budget- or cost-constrained solution; the first solution is named the demand-constrained result.) As before, for every unit of output the agency charges the maximum price the legislature is willing to pay, hence again the budget is too large, and the legislature does not gain from the exchange. Most important, once again output exceeds the socially optimal amount.

Because some scholars may find Niskanen's demand-supply language unfamiliar, it may be worthwhile to recast his ideas in more familiar terms. Following Romer and Rosenthal (1978), we focus on the logic of a budgetary process marked by agenda control. In their reformulation, the median legislator (M in figure 16.1) has a particular budget that she prefers to all others. Using the standard terminology of spatial models, call this her ideal point. Her preferences are symmetric about this point: Her utility would fall at the same rate if anything higher or lower is appropriated. The bureaucrat wants as large a budget as possible, but he must obtain approval of the median politician. Fortunately, he enjoys the power to manipulate the set of alternatives from which the politician will choose. (In legislatures this is equivalent to a committee offering a bill under a closed rule—the bill cannot be amended on the floor.)

Because the politician dislikes underspending and overspending equally, she is willing, given a choice between no appropriation and one nearly twice as big as her ideal, to settle for the latter, as figure 16.1 indicates. Romer and Rosenthal emphasize that this result is driven by the level of the no agreement appropriation,

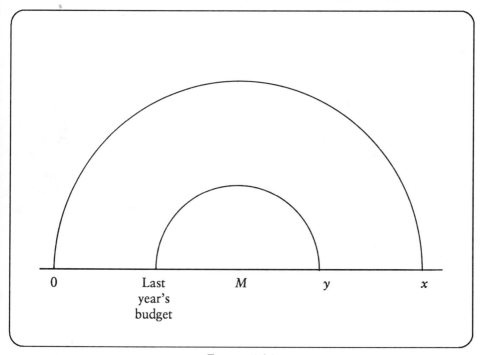

FIGURE 16.1

namely, zero. Should the budget revert to a higher level when the decision makers fail to agree, say the previous year's appropriation (as it might under a continuing resolution), then the agenda setter cannot induce the politician to agree to x; instead, he must settle for y.

The logic of this agenda-setting model is clear; what is problematic is its empirical interpretation. As Miller and Moe (1983) have argued, assuming that bureaus have this kind of power is implausible.* Certainly bureaucrats manipulate the choice sets of their political superiors, but their kind of agenda control derives from expertise: for example, an armed services bureaucrat forwards biased evaluations of proposed weapons systems to the secretary of defense. Thus, this second kind of agenda control is based on asymmetric information, whereas the Niskanen/Romer and Rosenthal kind derives from differential authority, which can occur despite complete information about the set of feasible options and their effects.

The difference between authority-based and information-based agenda control is clear in Romer and Rosenthal's paper (see also Altfeld and Miller 1984). This distinction is less clear in Niskanen's work because there are inconsistencies between his formal model and the accompanying informal text. As noted, the model assumes authority-based agenda control; in the text he recognizes that bureaucratic influence may depend on superior information.

Why the inconsistency? The explanation is simple: When Niskanen was working on his book in the late 1960s and early 1970s, the technology for modeling games with incomplete and asymmetric information did not exist. Accordingly, he could not translate his informal insights into a formal model. This is not the first or the last time that a scholar, knowing more about a subject than he can formally represent, introduced a slip 'twixt the lip and the cup.

Later on, in *Bureaucracy and Representative Government,* Niskanen (1971) does try to bolster his formal model by introducing a legislative committee that really wields authority-based agenda control over the rest of the legislature. This is certainly more reasonable; indeed, such models have received considerable attention from formally inclined students of legislatures in recent years (e.g., Denzau and Mackay 1983; Shepsle and Weingast 1984). Niskanen argues that the self-selection pattern of gaining seats on committees in Congress implies that committee members usually have a high demand for an agency's services. Thus the committee will pose the same take-it-or-leave-it choice to the rest of the legislature as the agency would, and the basic model's results go through unchanged (p. 148).

This justification of the basic model encounters two problems. The first is empirical: Appropriation committees in Congress rarely send their bills out under a

---

* Romer and Rosenthal's interpretation is that the agenda setter is an elected official—specifically, a school board member—and that the final decision makers are voters. This is an empirically reasonable application of the agenda model.

closed rule. The second is theoretical: Niskanen's argument presumes that high-demand committees and budget-seeking agencies will collude against the rest of the legislature, but the basis for that collusion and how it is carried out are left opaque. If in the reformulation the only source of influence were authority-based agenda control, collusion would be unnecessary—the committee would not need the agency. In this case, the basic bureaucratic model turns out to have been superfluous; the heart of the process is committee-floor interactions, and overly large budgets are unrelated to bureaucratic supply.

If the agency continues to have influence, presumably it does so because of superior information (Niskanen 1971, 148), for in the reformulation the agency no longer has authority-based agenda control. In this case, collusion is necessary but problematic: Would the agency want to use this expertise to manipulate the committee? Although it is conventional wisdom that budget-seeking bureaus and high-demand committees are allies—these are two of the supports of subgovernments or iron triangles—allies need not have identical preferences (Mackay and Weaver 1979). By definition, such a committee is oriented toward output; the agency, toward funding. This difference might matter; the committee wants the agency to operate at full efficiency to produce maximum output per dollar, just as a monopolist owner of a private firm wants the firm to operate at maximum technical efficiency. The agency, however, will prefer to function inefficiently if doing so would increase its budget (Munger 1984).

Because of the foregoing problems, modeling in this field has moved toward explicitly endowing the bureau with information-based agenda control. No one now assumes that agencies have authority-based agenda control. An important contribution here was by Miller and Moe (1983). Their fundamental point is that Congress can choose to organize the budgetary process in different ways. Thus, unlike Niskanen's model, which specifies only a single procedure, Miller and Moe compare two sequences. In one specification, the legislature reveals its demand for the agency's services; in the other, it conceals it. In both sequences, Miller and Moe reject the idea that a bureau has authority to set agendas; instead, the agency's influence in the model—not just in the informal story—derives from its superior information about costs. The agency must announce a per unit price schedule; it is forbidden to present take-it-or-leave-it offers. Miller and Moe show that even if the legislature reveals its demand, it always obtains higher net benefits than it does in Niskanen's model. Because the two models are comparable in almost all other respects—linear demand, quadratic costs, and so forth—it is clear that the key difference is dropping authority-based agenda control. Even facing extremely asymmetric information—the bureau knows the true demand function, whereas the legislature relies on the bureau chief's claim concerning cost—the politicians experience net gains. The reason is illustrated in figure 16.2. With the legislature committed to paying a constant amount, p, for each unit of output, the bureau cannot

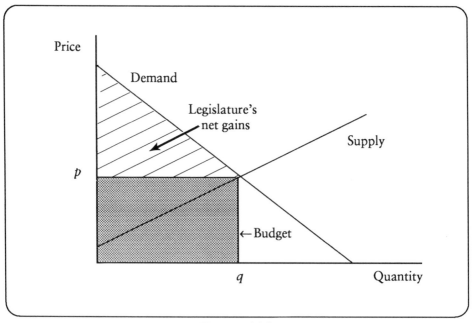

FIGURE 16.2

price discriminate (announce a supply curve that reproduces the demand curve). Instead, the agency must settle for a budget that is the constant price multiplied by quantity; the shaded rectangle in figure 16.2. Because the median legislator's value of the service is represented by the demand curve, this legislator's net benefits equal the area under the curve minus the budget—the shaded triangle in figure 16.2. Thus "we can now see that these rules of thumb [i.e., assuming constant unit costs] are *rational* in these kinds of budgetary games, regarding their consequences for both the committee and society as a whole. . . . Perhaps surprisingly, then, a legislative rule of thumb adopted entirely in ignorance and not designed to discover true bureaucratic costs is in fact well suited to the pursuit of legislative and social ends" (Miller and Moe 1983, 319–20, emphasis in the original). The advantage of using such a crude heuristic is indeed surprising. The conventional wisdom is that using rules of thumb generate inferior outcomes, yet Miller and Moe show that remaining committed to the belief that costs increase linearly in output prevents the bureau from manipulating the legislature at will. In some strategic circumstances it may pay to be simple-minded.*

---

* For a similar argument concerning how the simple decision rules of voters may make them less vulnerable to strategic manipulation by politicians, see Ferejohn (forthcoming).

The final major point of the Miller and Moe article is that exploiting asymmetric information is a game two can play. Although bureaucrats know more about supply than politicians do, the latter know more about demand. Therefore Miller and Moe conjecture (p. 321) that the more Congress keeps administrators in the dark about its own preferences, the more the bureaucrats will toe the line and tell the truth. Hence, in their second model, Miller and Moe examine demand-concealing oversight. They conclude that in this circumstance the bureau chief will reveal his true average cost curve (p. 305). Their basic idea that legislators can use their own private information about demand to control bureaucrats is undoubtedly sound; their specific argument, however, is incomplete. In their model, the bureau chief is indifferent to risk: Because he is trying to maximize budgets, he does not care whether he receives budget X for sure or gambles getting 80 percent of X versus 120 percent of X with equal likelihood. Moreover, the bureaucrat's beliefs about demand are not represented in the model. Therefore, it is puzzling why concealing demand would affect his behavior.

Bendor, Taylor, and van Gaalen (1985) explore the Miller and Moe thesis regarding two-sided asymmetric information by filling in the gaps about risk aversion and beliefs. They show that if the bureau chief is made less certain about legislative demand, he communicates more accurate cost information—if he is risk averse. If he is risk neutral, the legislature cannot affect his strategic behavior by concealing its own preferences.

Bendor, Taylor, and van Gaalen (1987b) subsequently show that the above result is not highly general, however. Politicians will not invariably receive better information from bureaucrats (even risk-averse ones) if they obscure their demand for bureaucratic services in an indiscriminate manner. The result in the 1985 paper is valid only for bureaucrats with a certain kind of risk-averse utility function; positing risk aversion by itself is insufficient to generate the expected conclusion.

This negative result indicates that the role of information asymmetry in hierarchical relations is more subtle than it first appears. On reflection, why would we expect that concealing legislative demand would invariably result in greater control over bureaus? If a bureau chief is risk averse, making his budget less certain, no matter what he does, will of course make him worse off. But that is not the desired effect. What is wanted is to lower the utility of deception, not to lower his utility regardless of how he behaves. Accordingly, in their second paper, Bendor, Taylor, and van Gaalen show that if "the legislature controls the degree of uncertainty in anticipation of the bureau's strategy (i.e., if it increases the uncertainty when the bureau chief requests a big budget but not if he requests a small one), then the bureaucratic response is always the intended one: The bureau is less likely to make inaccurate claims about its program's costs or benefits" (1987b, 23). The essence of this strategy is to reward a risk-averse bureaucrat with a predictable budget if he reveals accurate cost-benefit information and to punish deception, if it is discovered by monitoring, by making his appropriation uncertain.

Once it is recognized that the budgetary process can be reorganized, that it is in large measure a decision variable of the legislature, we see that Niskanen's model is really a *partial equilibrium* theory: The politicians are represented as a passive mechanism—a demand function—rather than as strategic actors in their own right. The bureaucrat takes the demand function as a constraint, optimizing within it. The field exhibits a growing consensus that it is more reasonable to portray all the central decision makers as active, if not fully strategic. Thus a model's predictions must be full equilibrium outcomes; loosely speaking, what happens when everyone is making their best move.

Comments on the Niskanen Tradition

It has been almost twenty years since the publication of *Bureaucracy and Representative Government*. What can be said about the line of research triggered by this work? First, although it is unclear whether our knowledge has cumulated in any simple sense, the techniques of formal modeling have certainly aided systematic inquiry. For example, because Niskanen laid bare his agenda-control assumptions in generating his oversupply result, later researchers could modify this model by dropping this postulate while retaining other features of the model. In addition, a kind of theoretical sensitivity testing became possible as researchers discovered that certain results depended on rather specific assumptions. Thus the process of theoretical trial and error became more rapid as the community of scholars discovered which assumptions were crucial for various conclusions.

Of course, trial and error means discarding some ideas as well as retaining others, and currently it is safe to say that there has been more of the former than the latter. In particular, the old consensus that bureaucratic organization per se leads to oversupply has broken down—among others, see Miller and Moe (1983), Conybeare (1984), and Bendor, Taylor, and van Gaalen (1985). Nevertheless, negative knowledge is knowledge; it is informative to find out that a proposition is less well grounded than one had believed. On the positive side, the field has moved decisively toward models of information-based agenda control, leaving authority-based models to students of legislatures. This kind of progress is probably more difficult in nonmathematical areas of public administration, where it is harder for scholars to modify predecessors' theories because key assumptions have not been explicitly specified.

Second, the growing consensus to model asymmetric information as the foundation of bureaucratic influence will not be paralleled by a convergence on how to represent this asymmetry. Instead, we will see a proliferation of specialized models with different assumptions about what bureaucrats know that politicians do not (the set of feasible alternatives, the costs and benefits of a known set of alternatives, and so forth). Even within a class of models focusing on, for example, cost uncertainty, the analyses will differ on the precise specification of uncertainty. (Do politicians have unbiased beliefs? Are their beliefs approximated by a normal distribution, a uniform, or any continuous distribution?) We should be prepared for a bewildering thicket of results; it may be a while before general patterns emerge.*

Third, the Niskanen tradition has stayed within a dyadic framework: A bureau and a political superior confront each other. The superior is often labeled a legislature, but the potential multiplicity of decision makers is usually suppressed by taking the median legislator as decisive. This is done to keep the models tractable; as Terry Moe has forcefully argued (1984, 1987), the cost is substantially lessened realism. Conflict among politicians, between and within branches, is a central fact of life for most agencies. Moreover, there are new theoretical arguments (Hammond, Hill, and Miller 1986; Hill 1985), to be examined shortly, showing that crunching legislative politics down to a single dimension dramatically reduces bureaucratic discretion. Therefore, the as-if assumption of a single political superior has serious substantive implications.

Fourth, modelers in this tradition assume a restricted set of bureaucratic objectives. Simple budget maximization has been the modal assumption. There are a few departures from this, such as discretionary budget maximization (Niskanen 1975), but these have been of modest proportions. The idea that administrators may have policy preferences is left to modelers working in the spatial tradition (Calvert, McCubbins, and Weingast 1986; Hill 1985) and to models of search (Bendor, Taylor, and van Gaalen 1987a) that do not fit easily into the traditional supply and demand framework.

Fifth, virtually none of the models in this tradition say anything about implementation. They are basically theories of exchange: The bureau promises to generate a certain quantity of output in return for a budget. How revenues are transformed into programs is rarely analyzed. (Indeed, here the field has experienced some retrogression, for Niskanen devoted a chapter to issues of production.) Implementation questions are finessed by positing that the agency knows that the political superior can perfectly and costlessly observe final output, so it will do whatever it must to generate that amount.

This is an awkward patch job for two reasons. First, as a generation of policy analysts has learned to its sorrow, measuring bureaucratic output is difficult. Output indicators are always imperfect; collecting them is always costly. Ironically, Niskanen acknowledged that the observable output assumption was problematic:

---

* Establishing general patterns will require that scholars in the field acquire greater mathematical sophistication. For example, to show that a bureau is advantaged whenever its political superior becomes less certain about program implementation requires more high-powered mathematics if the superior's beliefs are represented by any continuous distribution than if they are uniformly distributed.

Bureaucrats and their sponsors do not, in fact, talk much about output—in terms of military capability, the value of educational services, the number and condition of the poor, etc. Most of the review process consists of a discussion of the relation between budgets and activity levels, such as the number of infantry divisions, the number of students served, the number of poor served by a program, etc. The relation between activity level and output is usually left obscure and is sometimes consciously obscured. (1971, 26–27)

Second, even granting the assumption does not resolve all implementation issues, for the output constraint yields determinate predictions about bureaucratic behavior only when it is binding. That is, only when producing the promised quantity means that the bureau must use the minimum-cost technology and allocate the entire budget to production. These conditions need not be satisfied. Consider the simple example of linear demand and constant marginal costs (figure 16.3). If the legislature uses a Miller and Moe rule-of-thumb and stipulates that the budget equals $p \cdot q$, then the budget-maximizing price is the one that makes the percentage change in quantity demanded equal to the percentage change in price. Thus, if the true cost function is below p^*, as it is in figure 16.3, the administrator will want to overstate his costs while promising to deliver q^*, which is feasible. Since the bureau can actually produce at cost c, what does the model predict the bureau will do with the extra funds? No answer is forthcoming because the model has made no claims about bureaucratic preferences for the use of appropriations (preferences for perquisites, desires to appease powerful producer groups by using inefficient technologies, and so forth). Thus, whenever the output constraint is not binding, one needs a model similar to managerial theories of the firm, specifying bureaucratic preferences for resource allocation. Budget maximization does not suffice.

Criticizing a formal model for overly simple assumptions is easy; constructing a superior alternative is another matter. Progress in this field often moves like an amoeba; moving forward in one direction (replacing an implausible assumption by a more plausible one) is matched by greater simplification in another. The reason, as usual, is analytical tractability.

One could loosen this constraint by realizing the models as simulations, letting the computer crank out the solutions instead of deriving them analytically. A thorough evaluation of simulation models is beyond the scope of this chapter. Briefly, however, it should be noted that simulation is a well established method in behavioral and organizational decision theory (Cohen 1981, 1984; Cohen, March, and Olsen 1972; Crecine 1969; Cyert and March 1963; Levinthal and March 1981). And concerning the specific problems noted above—dyadic analysis, simplified bureaucratic objectives, and neglect of implementation—some recent work (Bendor and Moe 1985, 1986) indicates that computer models can make progress on all these fronts simultaneously.

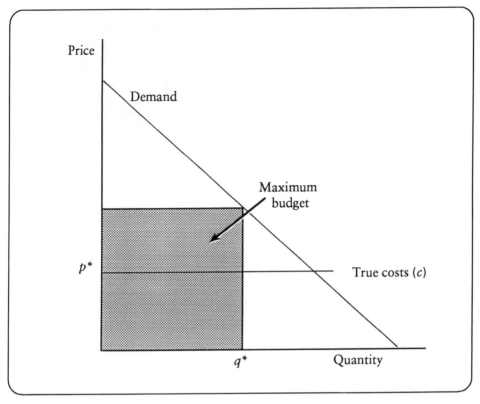

FIGURE 16.3

Political Control and Principal-Agent Models

Empirical students of bureaucracy have long observed that career officials have programmatic preferences and that agencies, particularly those dominated by a single profession, tend to develop a sense of mission, an orientation toward a particular means as well as ends (Halperin 1974). This mission orientation promotes biased advocacy. As Huntington noted, "The sensitivity of military groups to new program needs depends largely upon service doctrine and service interests. The Air Force was active in pushing strategic deterrence and the Army in innovating European defense since each program was closely related to existing service doctrine. All the services were hesitant in pushing continental defense and limited war, however, which were alien to existing service doctrine" (1961, 288). Because "alleged 'options' are often advocacy in more sophisticated guise, one real choice and two or three straw men" (Destler 1974, 135), students of public administration warned other political scientists not to overemphasize the final policy choices made by political appointees or elected politicians. Instead, scholars should spend more time examining how alternatives are rigged by bureaucrats.

More recently, however, public-choice theorists have pushed the idea of examining stretches of a decision-making sequence one step further. Why stop with the alternative-generating and advice-giving stages? Why not go back further and examine the reward structures established before bureaucratic maneuvering? The basic idea here is that politicians can anticipate the manipulation that Huntington and others have described—they are not so naive as to believe they are being advised by disinterested experts—and they will take steps to reassert control over their more informed subordinates. The analytical point is similar to the criticism directed against Niskanen's basic model: Any theory that represents politicians as the passive targets of agenda manipulation is a partial equilibrium model. Surely the politicians could do better by recognizing the inherent dangers of asymmetric information and taking countermeasures.

This argument undoubtedly has empirical merit. Experienced politicians are suspicious of advice from careerists whom they believe have markedly different policy preferences (Aberbach and Rockman 1976). But these claims of public-choice theorists have been driven as much by the internal logic of equilibrium analysis (why would politicians let themselves be manipulated?) as by evidence. Adding to this momentum, over the last dozen years economists have devoted considerable attention to analyzing problems of control inside firms, problems bearing a strong family resemblance to those described by public administrationists. Using the classical rational-choice assumptions in new ways, they have created a class of models known as principal-agent analysis. Ross (1973) is usually cited as the seminal work. See Baiman (1982), Arrow (1985), and Levinthal (1988) for surveys, and Moe (1984) for a clear, nontechnical introduction.

Principal-agent models have two essential components: asymmetric information and conflict of interest. The agent knows something the principal does not, and there is a danger that the agent will exploit this edge strategically. A key question is whether the principal can devise incentives that will induce the agent to act in the principal's interests.

A simple example may clarify the approach. The board of directors of a large firm must decide on a compensation scheme for the head of one of its divisions. The division's profits are a function of the manager's actions (effort) and local variations in the division's operating environment (morale of workers, performance of suppliers, and so forth). Let profit = actions + θ, where θ is a normally distributed random variable representing the local context. The board knows the general form of the profits equation, and it will observe the division's profits, but it cannot observe the manager's day-to-day actions or the local context. (Since it observes profits, if it could also observe the value of θ, it could infer what the manager did, making the control problem trivial.) The board is risk neutral and seeks to maximize the expected net profits of the division: gross profits minus the manager's compensation. Two variables affect the manager's utility: effort, which he dislikes, and money. He is risk neutral in effort, risk averse in money. His utility is additive.

What kind of contract should the board offer? Because the board knows the production function, it can calculate the optimal action the manager should take. Thus it would like to write a contract stipulating that the manager perform that action. But this contract could not be verified, since the board can neither observe the manager nor perfectly infer his action based on the observed outcome. (Low profits could be due to unlucky local context.) And the manager, of course, cannot be trusted to report accurately what he did. Therefore, the contract can be based only on what will be commonly known, the division's profits.

Consider two schemes. In scheme 1, the board gives the manager a percentage of the division's profits. (As in most principal-agent models, it is assumed that the principal, the board, can pre-commit to a compensation scheme.) This gives the manager an incentive to work hard: He knows that doing so increases the division's expected profits, hence his share. There is a problem, however: This plan makes the manager's income depend on the division's profits, which, due to the unpredictability of θ, is a random variable. Thus the manager's income is itself a random variable. This would not matter were he indifferent to risk; indeed, if that were so, the control problem could be completely eliminated by a contract that gave the stockholders a fixed, lump sum payment every year and the manager the randomly fluctuating remainder. (Such schemes have existed between tenant farmers and landowners.) This arrangement, in effect, internalizes the agency relation, guaranteeing that the manager will act optimally.

It is more empirically plausible, however, to assume that agents are risk averse in income. (A quick check: The reader might ask herself whether she would prefer her current salary with certainty or a fair gamble of double or nothing.) A risk-averse manager prefers that the firm pay him a fixed salary instead of the expected commission of scheme 1. Indeed, he would take somewhat less than the expected commission to make his income certain. The board, being risk neutral, would happily pay the manager that fixed salary, for doing so would increase its expected profits. Therefore, both parties prefer scheme 2—a fixed salary—to scheme 1; hence, the latter is pareto-inefficient. But if the manager is paid a fixed salary, his compensation is not contingent at all on the outcome, so scheme 2 provides no effort incentives. Consequently, in this setting it is impossible to implement a pareto-efficient contract. Pareto-efficient contracts require all risk to be borne by the risk-neutral party, which destroys effort incentives. The problem—headquarters' inability to observe the manager's actions—creates inefficient arrangements.*

Public administrationists may shrug at this analysis. It is, after all, a toy problem. The production function is absurdly simple, and both principal and agent know exactly what it is. Both know the distribution of the disturbance term, θ. The principal knows the agent's utility function. All this poorly approximates real political-control problems. Note, however, that even in this toy world the principal and the agent are unable to implement a pareto-efficient contract. The real lesson is to show that even if one assumes the principal knows more than most real-world principals know, control problems emerge nonetheless.

Ironically, whereas economists often use principal-agent models to explore potential control problems, it appears that political scientists often refer to such models to exorcise them and the specter of bureaucratic influence. I cannot document this claim—it is based on comments in conference panels—but my impression is that some scholars believe that these models show that the problem of controlling bureaucrats can be solved by sophisticated politicians, who have only to design appropriate incentives. I believe that this seriously underestimates the empirical difficulties, and wastes principal-agent analysis. It is trivial to show that given enough information about subordinates and sufficiently powerful instruments, politicians can induce bureaucrats to act as they want; it is much more interesting to show how control inefficiencies can emerge despite a principal knowing a great deal.

Currently, it is fair to say that in political science principal-agent models are more talked about than written down. Because these models will become increasingly popular in the formal branches of public administration, specifying their minimal components may be a useful aid to consumers. In the basic principal-agent model, both parties must be active optimizers; representing either as a passive mechanism makes it impossible to depict the essence of the problem—how the agent could strategically exploit asymmetric information and how the boss controls this. There must be some conflict of interest. The boss must suffer from some informational handicap: In some models, he cannot observe the agent's action (often called *moral hazard* or *hidden action* problems); in others, the agent has information about

---

* One might conjecture that, over time, the board will infer the manager's actions from the outcomes in an increasingly precise manner, especially if θ is independently and identically distributed over time. This information should allow more efficient arrangements to be supported as Nash equilibria. Radner (1985) shows that for an infinitely repeated game, this conjecture is true in the sense that the less the players discount the future, the closer they can approach a fully efficient contract. In addition to the value of repeated play, the literature has explored two other methods for ameliorating control problems: monitoring—obtaining some (possibly imperfect) indicators of the agent's behavior—and comparing the performance of agents to each other. See Levinthal (1988) for a review of all three.

himself or the task environment that the superior lacks (*adverse selection* or *hidden information* models). Aside from this asymmetry, in the stripped-down models the two actors have homogeneous beliefs. Thus, in the preceding example of the decentralized firm, the board and the manager both knew (or believed) that profits = effort + a disturbance, both knew the distribution of the random variable and the range of values that effort could take on, and both observe the outcome (the amount of profit realized). This implies that in the basic models, the principal already knows what action she would like the agent to take; the problem is in inducing it.* Further, in hidden-action models, it is typically assumed that she knows the agent's utility function, enabling her to predict how the agent would respond to any incentive scheme she may contemplate. Her decision problem is to devise an incentive scheme that maximizes her expected utility—knowing in advance that after the scheme is announced, the agent will act in his own self-interest. The contract must be self-enforcing vis-à-vis the agent: he will only carry out actions that maximize his own expected utility, in the light of the incentives. The principal, however, can pre-commit to what she has promised the agent.† The contract must satisfy a participation constraint: It must yield the agent at least as much expected utility as he can obtain at his next-best opportunity outside the organization in question. Finally, the set of feasible contracts must be specified. (For example, must the agent's wages be positive, or can the principal extract a fine—negative wages—should the outcome fall below a predetermined level?)

If these properties are not specified, mathematically or in words, a reader may be unable to ascertain whether a particular formulation is a genuine principal-agent model. It may instead be an exercise in relabeling, in which hierarchical superiors are called principals and subordinates, agents. Nonmathematically inclined public administrationists have good reason to be suspicious of such exercises, for they may have little content that is genuinely novel.

Alternatively, a formulation may be a genuine agency analysis, but the imprecise specification makes it difficult for readers to figure out how results are derived. It is especially important to state what incentives are feasible, for this assumption strongly influences the agent's optimal behavior. To see this we reconsider the example of the decentralized firm. Assume that the manager's effort can range between

---

* Because in the simple moral hazard framework the principal can, in principle, solve the technical optimization problem just as well as the agent can, these models do not capture the phenomenon of asymmetric expertise in the ordinary sense of the word.

† If she could not make legally binding promises, the model would become a prisoner's dilemma: Both sides are better off if they cooperate (establish a relationship) than if they both defect, but each party is tempted to double cross the other. In the basic one-period model, there would be as usual only one solution: Since the agent believes that the boss would defect by not paying him, he would not work.

zero and 100 and the disturbance term is uniformly distributed between −1 and 1. Contracts with arbitrarily large penalties are legal. The principal, knowing that profits = effort + θ, commits herself to the following deal: As long as profits are at least 99, she will pay the manager a fixed salary of k. (Knowing the agent's preferences and the participation constraint, she has computed k so that the agent's utility of $u(k) - u$ (maximum effort) barely induces him to join the firm.) If profits fall below 99, the principal will extract an exceedingly large fine from the agent. Note the combined effect of unbounded penalties and a bounded disturbance. Because the principal knows that θ cannot fall below −1, if she observes a profit of 98 she can flawlessly infer that the agent could not have been exerting maximal effort. Since the agent knows this too, he can guarantee that he will not have to pay the fine by pegging his effort at 100. In this informational setting a negative wage is a threat that will never be used; the availability, however, of arbitrarily large penalties enables the principal to arrange a deal that is just as efficient as the one she would establish were she to observe the agent's actions directly. If such penalties were legally or financially impossible, or if there were a significant possibility of an inferential error (the boss mistakenly believing that the agent shirked) or of the boss's double-crossing the agent, this arrangement would not work. (The economist James Mirrlees has shown that even if the disturbance can take on any value, e.g., the normal, this scheme can get arbitrarily close to how well a fully informed superior would do, as long as arbitrarily large penalties are allowed.)

Several pieces in the literature on political control have some, but not all, of the above components of principal-agent models. In particular, it is common for one of the two parties to be represented as a mechanism rather than as a decision maker. In Bendor, Taylor, and van Gaalen (1985), for example, their first model treats the legislature as a demand function plus an exogenously fixed monitoring and penalty system; the bureaucracy is the more active decision maker in that its strategy is endogenously determined. On the other side, Fiorina's models of delegation (1982, 1986) treat the bureaucracy as an exogenously fixed, though noisy, machine that transforms legislative intent into a distribution of outcomes; legislators are the active decision makers. This pattern results from an interaction between academic specialization and the constraints of formal modeling. Most people working on models of political control specialize in either the bureaucracy or the legislature. Like most specialists, they focus on what they know best—their particular institution. In the craft of formal modeling, this means making the better-known institution the active (choosing) figure against the passive ground of its environment, represented as a mechanism or constraint. Such decision-theoretic models are easier to construct than the game-theoretic ones of principal-agent analysis.

I do not mean that decision-theoretic models are useless. On the contrary, these models can yield significant insights. For example, in an analysis of advice giving, Calvert (1985) has proven an interesting result: Under some circumstances, a superior will prefer to listen to the suggestions of more-biased subordinates rather than those of less-biased ones. (The reason: When a subordinate known to be biased against a choice alternative recommends it nonetheless, the odds are good that the option is worthwhile. Thus his advice may contain much information or surprise value, and is potentially valuable.) Though the subordinates in this model are not active decision makers—they are probabilistic black boxes that emit pro or con signals—Calvert's basic result may have implications for how principals select agents, and it may stand up in a fully strategic model.

Recently there have been some attempts by political scientists to construct genuinely bilateral principal-agent models. In Bendor, Taylor, and van Gaalen (1987a), the superior's problem arises from a classical division of labor: The subordinate, who has expertise but no formal authority, designs the set of alternatives; the politician, who has authority but little expertise, makes the final choice. The bureaucrat has programmatic preferences and wants to rig the superior's agenda to boost the odds that his preferred program will be selected. He does so by allocating more design time to his preferred program. The search for policy alternatives, long considered by behavioral theorists as central to any nonroutine choice process (March and Simon 1958), constitutes agenda manipulation.*

The politician, anticipating the manipulation, controls it in two distinctly different ways. In model 1, the politician cannot pre-commit to anything; instead, she threatens to reject the bureaucrat's options if other policy experts are likely to generate better alternatives. This threat must be credible: It must be in the superior's interest to carry it out should the bureaucrat design unacceptable alternatives. In model 2, she can pre-commit to an incentive scheme, a budgetary schedule that rewards the bureaucrat for designing proposals that benefit the superior. Thus, whereas the second model is a principal-agent analysis, the first model—lacking the necessary property of pre-commitment—is not.

This distinction is not a mere technicality; it is substantively important. In model 1, the superior is sometimes unable to prevent her agenda from being completely rigged, and only under the most fortuitous circumstances does the agency carry out search as a fully informed superior would want. In model 2, once the superior pre-commits to an appropriately conceived budgetary scheme, the bureaucrat plans in an unbiased manner. And the models' results differ in more subtle ways. The technique of comparative statistics (changing a parameter's value and comparing the new equilibrium to the old equilibrium) show that when the budgetary in-

---

* Search models traditionally have been associated with behavioral theories (Nelson and Winter 1982; Simon 1957). Though most rational-choice models assume that the set of alternatives is exogenously fixed (e.g., in most spatial models of legislatures, proposals—mere points in a policy space—need not be designed), this is not a logical necessity. Optimal-search models have been studied in economics for quite some time.

centives are in place, changes in the larger environment (such as the quality of options offered by competing specialists) affect the superior's well-being in intuitively expected ways. In model 1, however, these changes can, via the agency's mediating influence, have perverse effects. Thus, model 1 directs our attention to bureaucracy's role in policy formation, whereas model 2 implies we can ignore it. (Indeed, model 2 specifies sufficient conditions for treating the executive branch as a unitary rational actor, in Graham Allison's sense of the phrase.)

The application of principal-agent models to the political control of bureaucracy is in its infancy. Because it builds on the empirically relevant properties of hierarchy (the principal can, within limits, fix the agent's payoff schedule), asymmetric information, and conflicting objectives, and because of its extensive development in the study of the internal organization of the firm, it will be used increasingly by formal modelers of bureaucracy. A few cautions are therefore in order.

The first criticism is the least important. In most of these models, the agent's action is interpreted as effort, which he dislikes. Mechanical transfers of this choice variable to public administration may be inappropriate, particularly if one is studying interactions between politicians and senior administrators. Richard Nixon did not worry that bureaucrats in Health, Education, and Welfare (HEW) were sleeping instead of working; political and programmatic subversion was on his mind.

In part this is a matter of interpretation. The mathematical formalism of principal-agent models typically states only that the agent's choice variable is a real number that varies continuously between an upper and lower bound, and that his utility decreases monotonically as this variable increases. Effort is a natural interpretation, but it is not the only one. The problem is a bit deeper, however: The formal assumptions may not be the most appropriate representation of politician-bureaucrat relations. In cases of policy conflicts, it is more natural to represent the bureaucrat's choice variable as influencing policy implementation—perhaps picking a point in a policy space, subject to constraints established by his political superiors (Calvert, McCubbins, and Weingast, 1986; Hammond, Hill, and Miller 1986; Hill 1985). In a spatial setting, it is also natural to depict the bureaucrat's utility as being a single-peaked function, with its maximum being his ideal policy. Thus, utility need not decrease steadily in his choice variable. But this does not pose an insuperable barrier to using principal-agent models. Because the essential ingredients of conflicting interests (different ideal points) and asymmetric information (implementation may be hard to observe) are often present, a control problem may still exist: Some of the politicians want the administrator to implement a policy more to their liking than his. At this point, the standard apparatus of agency theory can be brought to bear on the problem: What incentives can the principal(s) deploy to induce the agent to implement the desired policy, how can the principal(s) select, from the set of possible agents, the one that minimizes control problems, and so forth.

Therefore, the original Taylorite interpretation of principal-agent models does not seriously constrain their use in public administration.

The second issue concerns the assumption that the principal can pre-commit to an incentive scheme. The agent, knowing this, can choose without fear that the boss will renege on the deal. This assumption is a good first approximation for firms creating contracts in the shadow of the law. The matter becomes more delicate when the referent is government. Careful attention must be paid to the incentives; if, for example, the agent is to be rewarded by a policy concession, is it plausible to assume that politicians can bind themselves to complex policy decisions? If not, a principal-agent approach is inappropriate; instead, one should construct a model in which the decision makers behave opportunistically, making their best moves at every choice point. But if the reward is a budget, pre-commitment is more plausible. (The President, for example, can at least affirm budgetary figures in a public document.)

In general, the literature has dichotomized the possibility of pre-commitment: Either the principal has unlimited commitment ability or none at all. Neither of these may be a good approximation of governmental control problems. For example, politicians may be able to commit to an appropriation for a single year but not beyond that, or certain policies may be easier to commit to than others. In neither case is commitment an all-or-nothing matter. There has been some progress on developing models of intermediate commitment. In Radner's (1985) repeated-play model, the principal can guarantee a compensation scheme only for a single period. Melumad and Mookherjee (1989) explore the intriguing idea that a principal can augment his commitment abilities by delegating authority to an agent; their work may shed some light on the strategic implications of a partially independent civil service.

Third, almost all these models assume a single principal. This may be a reasonable approximation if one is trying to get some insight into relations well inside a bureaucracy, where one might plausibly assume that the hierarchical pressures on a subordinate are channeled through his immediate superior. Senior bureaucrats, however, often respond to a diverse set of political superiors who may disagree among themselves about the direction the agent should take. We look at models with multiple political superiors next.

Fourth, though principal-agent theory has received little systematic empirical scrutiny, even a casual comparison of its predictions with data indicate problems. Kenneth Arrow has commented in a recent survey, "The theory tends to lead to very complex fee functions. It turns out to be difficult to establish even what would appear to be common-sense properties of monotonicity and the like. We do not find such complex relations in reality. Principal-agent theory gives a good reason for the existence of sharecrop contracts, but it is a very poor guide to their actual terms" (1985, 48). Bengt Holmstrom, a pioneer in this field, notes that results are often very sensitive to a model's assumptions; even the third moment of the disturbance term can matter (1986). Arrow suggests that it is costly to specify complex relations, thus creating a pressure for simple contracts. And the results' hypersensitivity to the fine structure of the assumptions results from the use of classical rationality postulates: Because principal and agent have unlimited powers of computation, they are sensitive to the smallest of changes. It is possible to introduce a cost of writing (and enforcing) contracts into these models; modifying the rationality postulates is a more fundamental change.

Political Control and Multiple Superiors

Most of the preceding works have relied on informational asymmetries as the driving force in causing agency problems. In a stimulating paper, Jeffrey Hill (1985) has shown that bureaucratic discretion—hence control problems—can appear even when information is complete. Problems can arise solely from the legislature's difficulties in reaching stable collective choices. His analysis has been extended by Hammond, Hill, and Miller (1986); the following discussion focuses on the more recent paper.

A simple diagram will help us understand their argument. Figure 16.4 depicts a policy choice facing a legislature. The policy is described by two dimensions, x and y. Each legislator has an ideal policy, points 1, 2, and 3 in the figure. Following the standard Downsian framework, the further away an alternative is from a legislator's ideal, the less she likes it.

Now suppose this mini legislature chooses point r as the policy to be implemented by the agency. (The location of this alternative is immaterial.) The bureau chief, however, has policy preferences of his own: His ideal alternative is point B. The question posed by Hammond, Hill, and Miller is, Can the bureau chief get away with implementing a policy closer to the one he most prefers? The answer is yes, even though the legislature can observe his actions. Consider point i. Because it is closer to the ideal points of legislators 1 and 2, they prefer it to the bill they helped pass.* Therefore, they will not raise an outcry or conduct oversight hearings when the bureau chief implements policy i. The chief, of course, also prefers the new policy. What he has done is to construct an *implementation coalition* that differs from the legislative coalition, a phenomenon observed by many students of American politics. His discretion derives not from defying legislative intent but from the opportunity to construct new majorities. It is interesting to note that senior bureaucrats in the United States see their roles as having a greater political content than do their European counterparts (Aberbach, Putnam, and Rockman 1981). This role orientation is consistent with experiences of creating implementation coalitions.

---

* For simplicity Hammond, Hill, and Miller assume that the legislators weight the two dimensions equally, so the indifference curves are circles.

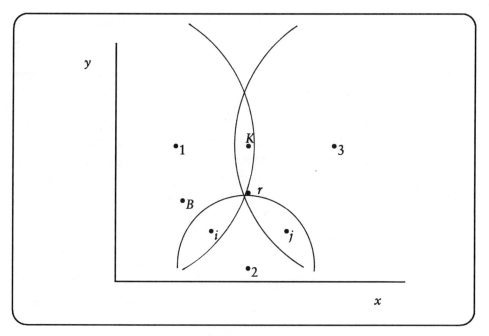

FIGURE 16.4

Figure 16.4 illustrates a possibility; it does not establish a general result. Is this possibility an artifact of the example? As Hammond, Hill, and Miller emphasize, the example is not at all peculiar. Social-choice theorists have established that in moderately complex political situations—those in which policies must be described by at least two dimensions—it will almost always be the case that every alternative is vulnerable under majority rule (McKelvey 1976). Refer back to figure 16.4. Even though point *r* is centrally located, we saw that legislators 1 and 2 prefer point *i*. Similarly, legislators 2 and 3 prefer alternative *j*; 1 and 3 prefer *K*. Thus, latent in the situation are multiple winning coalitions, which the administrator exploits.

The authors show that if the President knows the legislators' ideal points, he can craftily appoint a bureau chief who thereafter, for his own policy reasons, creates an implementation coalition that the chief executive prefers to the legislative coalition. The legislature has the authority to veto an appointment; it will approve the nominee if a majority prefers what he will implement to the status quo. (As usual in the multidimensional setting, such a majority almost always exists.) Thus their spatial model shows how top administrative personnel selections fit into the presidential-congressional game.

These papers, by showing how bureaucrats can influence policy outcomes by colluding with previously latent legislative majorities, are an important contribution to our understanding of political control. The following points remain to be addressed.

First, scholars will disagree over how much influence each side of Pennsylvania Avenue has over appointments. Nevertheless, it is unlikely that any legislature would tolerate an appointee whose ideal policy was outside the legislators' pareto region (the area bounded by the ideal points of the most extreme legislators). Yet, in the authors' diagrammatic examples, the official's ideal is outside this region. Because the administrator will implement a point as close as possible to his ideal point, a policy outlier moves the final outcome farther from the legislative point than would a moderate official. These examples convey an impression of greater administrative influence than is empirically plausible.

Second, the very property of majority rule—the lack of an invulnerable policy—that provides an opening for bureaucratic discretion also makes the authors' predictions less than crystal clear. The model has two stages, concluding with implementation. It appears to yield a determinate prediction: Among all alternatives a majority prefers to the legislative outcome, the bureaucrat implements the policy closest to his ideal. But in the real world policy making never stops, so whatever the administrator implemented this year could be modified the next. And because the property of latent multiple-winning coalitions still holds, legislators who dislike the implementation will be able to find a majority that prefers some new alternative to the one implemented by the agency. Neither paper addresses this issue of equilibrium outcomes (although see Hammond and Miller 1987) or, failing a completely stable outcome, what a statistical distribution of outcomes may look like.

Moreover, since policy making repeats itself over time, politicians may recognize a long-run value in not allowing legislative coalitions to be overturned during implementation, despite a majority's short-run temptation to do so. Hence, one may be able to demonstrate, in the context of a noncooperative game, that it will be an equilibrium strategy for each legislator to support the winning legislative coalition by agreeing to punish the administrator for deviating from legislative intent. (Because typically there are many equilibria in repeated games, however, it should also be possible to show that there are equilibria in which some legislators collude with the agency.)

Third, the results require that the politicians cannot bind themselves to inferior decisions: if the bureau chief implements the bill in a way that makes legislators 1 and 2 better off, they will accept what he has done. (The absence of precommitment means, strictly speaking, that these are not principal-agent models.) This is a substantively important and possibly controversial assumption. On the one hand, the bureau chief's implementation does make the new majority better off, making it easier for these legislators to explain their behavior back home. On the other hand, a bill passed by both chambers and signed by the President has the force of law, so one may contend that the courts will punish administrative deviations from statutory mandate. If the legislators knew in advance that such legal enforcement were guaranteed, in effect they would be pre-committed to the policy. An empirically reasonable position is that it is easier for politicians to pre-commit in certain policy arenas than in others (e.g., the Reagan administration discovered that the courts would enforce legislatively established criteria for disability payments) and that the model applies only when pre-commitment is unavailable. The size of the model's domain is, of course, an empirical question.

Fourth, these papers are interesting partly because they demonstrate that agency problems can occur for a quintessentially political reason—the existence of multiple winning coalitions—and despite complete information. Nevertheless, there is something unsettling about the verbal story that accompanies the model. With an unambiguous statute, the administrator is going against the manifest will of Congress, and with complete information, he is doing so in the full light of day. This is hard to swallow. The authors do present a variant, similar to Hill's original model, that relaxes the complete-information assumption. Following developments in the economic analysis of contracts, they argue that bills will rarely specify all politically relevant contingencies; it is either infeasible (not all contingencies can be foreseen) or too costly to do so. Their model represents this by allowing the legislature to vote on one dimension; the second dimension is left unspecified (see figure 16.5). Since the statute is silent regarding y, the bureau chief has formal discretion to pick any point on x_m. Presumably he will implement the incompletely specified legislation to be closest to his own preferred policy, point V in figure 16.5.

So far, so good. But the authors then argue that the administrator can do still better. Once the legislature recognizes the new dimension, new latent majorities appear. For example, legislators 1 and 2 prefer W to V. (In one dimension, representative 2, as the median voter, could do no better than to support the line x_m.) Therefore, the administrator can get legislators 1 and 2 to go along with an implementation of W. But this raises the same disquieting issue of administrative disregard of legislative intent. Although the bill did not specify everything, it did specify the line x_m. By implementing W, the bureau chief would be flaunting the aspect of the bill that was unambiguous. And again, he would be doing so openly. It seems that the model, ingenious as it is, needs a dose of incomplete information to make it more plausible.

Oversight, Political Control, and Equilibrium Analysis

Although the formal tools of principal-agent theory have diffused slowly into public administration, some of the ideas have penetrated more quickly. In particular, the concept of equilibrium analysis has influenced how we might think about the political control of bureaucracy, as well as how we should interpret evidence about oversight and control.

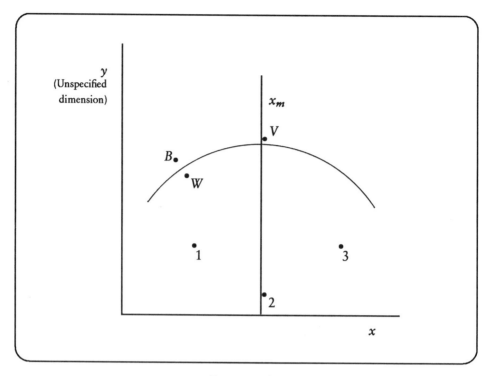

FIGURE 16.5

Several empirically oriented scholars have observed that legislators do not seem to spend much time overseeing agencies or attempting to influence policy implementation (see Wilson 1980 on regulatory agencies; more generally, see Ogul 1976). These conclusions are plausible enough: Little observed oversight activity suggests little influence.

Yet consider the following sketch of a model of monitoring (McCubbins and Schwartz 1984; Weingast 1984). An administrator either follows legislative intent or implements a program more to his own liking. If he does the former he gets a utility of x. If he does the latter—and his deviation is undiscovered by the legislature—he gets y, which exceeds x. With probability p, however, an interest group or some other affected party (not necessarily the politicians) will discover that he has not carried out legislative intent. If this fire alarm is activated, the legislature ensures that he follows their instructions, and imposes a sanction (such as embarrassing publicity or budget cuts) at a cost s to the administrator.

The bureaucrat, therefore, faces a choice of acting as the perfect agent and getting a sure payoff of x or deviating and getting an expected payoff of $(1 - p)y + p(x - s)$. If $x > (1 - p)y + p(x - s)$, and the bureaucrat perceives this accurately, no alarms go off and the administrator is never grilled on Capitol Hill. Yet by hypothesis we know that this is not because Congress is uninfluential. On the contrary, its sanctions are such an effective deterrent that administrative compliance is assured. Thus, though the model is simple, it reveals an essential point about behavior in equilibrium. As Weingast has stressed, *"The smooth operation of these institutional arrangements (i.e., agency policy equilibrium) involves little direct participation by Congress.* The more effective this system, the less direct and visible the role of Congress in agency decisions" (1984, 157, emphasis in the original). Indeed, the hypotheses that Congress is in complete control and that it exerts no influence are observationally equivalent; both predict that scholars will find no legislative oversight.

The analysis also shows that the arrangement can guarantee administrative compliance even if the underlying chance of detection, p, is small. The value of p denotes the intensity of monitoring. Clearly p could be small—monitoring is casual —yet $x > (1 - p)y + p(x - s)$, if the sanction s is severe enough. (This is essentially an application of Mirrlees's principal-agent theorem.)

Such ideas, enlightening as they are about the logical implications of equilibrium analysis, do not demonstrate that Congress controls the bureaucracy. It is important for scholars not to be swept away by purely mathematical arguments, such as, for any strictly positive p, no matter how small, there exists an s sufficiently large so that $x > (1 - p)y + p(x - s)$. The statement is valid; its empirical implications, however, are less certain, and are limited in several ways. Most obviously, constitutional prohibitions against cruel and unusual punishments limit the magnitude of feasible sanctions in the United States.

There is a more subtle issue. Earlier I stressed that if the sanctions are sufficiently big, they will never be used—in equilibrium, and if the administrator perceives the monitoring and sanction system accurately. Both provisos are important. Suppose the bureaucrat underestimates the sanctions, and believing that s and p are small enough so that $x < (1 - p)y + p(x - s)$, he deviates.

At this point, there are two possibilities: Either he is detected or not. If he is not, what should an outside observer infer about bureaucratic compliance with legislative intent? It is unclear. A Weingastian analysis, buttressed by an accurate assessment of the sanctions, would imply that the bureaucrat would comply (in equilibrium), which is consistent with the fact that no alarm has sounded. But, as stipulated, the bureaucrat has deviated. Now we can probe more deeply into the meaning of equilibrium analysis. The administrator has not complied with legislative intent because he underestimated the penalty for doing so. Eventually his implementation path will be discovered, and he will be sanctioned. Learning what the true penalties are, he will no longer deviate. Thus a complete equilibrium analysis means that not only must an agent's actions be optimal, given his beliefs; in addition his beliefs must be an accurate, or at least unbiased, description of his environment. If his beliefs were biased, he would be making systematic errors. But because systematic errors are correctable, in equilibrium he cannot have biased beliefs. This is a version of the rational expectations hypothesis.

The recent emphasis of equilibrium analysis on actors' beliefs is in some ways a salutary development. In most important organizational situations, payoffs are not common knowledge, so the development of models that can accommodate this fact is potentially significant to students of public administration. In addition, the theorists' insistence that beliefs must be part of equilibrium analysis is a check against some poor methodological practices. Specifically, it is all too easy to defend the rationality postulate from empirical criticism if beliefs are excluded from the analysis. It is virtually guaranteed that any behavior can be rationalized as optimal behavior in the light of some set of beliefs. (I have heard there is an unpublished theorem that proves this.) It has long been known that the rationality postulate is irrefutable unless specific claims are made about the utility function that is being maximized. In a game of incomplete information, however, specifying the content of a utility function does not guarantee falsifiability; beliefs must be specified as well.

The extension of equilibrium analysis to encompass beliefs has a certain logical momentum behind it. It is, however, a purely conceptual analysis of what equilibrium analysis means; it has no empirical content. The statements that our hypothetical administrator will not in equilibrium deviate when $x > (1 - p)y + p(x - s)$, and that with those payoffs no oversight hearings will be observed in equilibrium precisely because the bureaucrat is complying, are not empirical claims about what any particular official is doing. A key empirical question, perhaps the key question, is to establish whether the situation is, in fact, in equilibrium. It is certainly possible that much high-level administrative behavior reflects inaccurate perceptions of one kind or another; hence the behavior is out of equilibrium. Thus the empirical domain of equilibrium analysis may be limited. This does not mean that analysis or even prediction is impossible. It certainly makes both tasks more difficult, however, for they would require empirical work on systematic biases in belief formation and theories of adaptive (disequilibrium) behavior.

One reason why equilibrium analysis in games with incomplete information may have a limited empirical scope is that it is often difficult for decision makers to formulate accurate beliefs. Forming unbiased perceptions of complex issues is not an incidental task, to be completed quickly before the main job of choosing an optimal strategy; it is a major part of the job. Indeed, I have the uncomfortable feeling that what the game theorists have given with one hand—the greater empirical relevance of games with incomplete information—they have taken away with the other—the requirement that decision makers act as perfect Bayesians, fully equipped with Ph.D.s in statistics. The as-if assumption becomes ever more heroic, a polite way of saying increasingly implausible.

The Design of Hierarchical Institutions

Students of bureaucracy have long suspected that citizens want public organizations to satisfy contradictory criteria. For example, in his cogent essay Herbert Kaufman (1956) argued that Americans have been torn between the values of representativeness, competence, and executive leadership. Recently, these arguments have been recast in a formal framework (Hammond and Miller 1985; Thomas and Hammond 1989). These authors have used the axiomatic approach of social-choice theory by specifying intuitively reasonable criteria that any bureaucratic organization should satisfy and then investigating whether the set of criteria is internally consistent. If a set is inconsistent, the authors have established an impossibility result: One cannot design an institution with the desired qualities. Note how such a result deepens the insights of Kaufman, Simon (1946), and others: It is not merely difficult to design such an organization, it is impossible in principle. If we think about institutional design as a search over a set of alternatives, we see that an impossibility result says that if our stopping rule has the form, "terminate the search once we have discovered an organizational form with properties *a, b, c*," the search will never end. This is useful information, for it tells us that our aspirations are unrealistic.

To see what is involved, consider one of these impossibility results covered by Hammond and Miller (1985). Four design criteria are examined: decentralization, universal domain, the pareto property, and acyclicity. *Decentralization* means that the organization delegates authority concerning nonoverlapping sets of alternatives to different experts. *Universal domain* mandates flexibility; the choice process must work on any possible combination of experts' preference orderings over the alternatives at hand. The *pareto criterion* means that if every bureaucrat prefers *x* to *y*, the organization itself must rank *x* over *y*. *Acyclicity* means that if, at the end of a choice process, the conclusion is that *x* is better than *y* and *y* is better than *z*, then *x* must be rated at least as well as *z*. With some reinterpretation of terms, it can be shown that this case is covered by a result of the social-choice theorist Amartya Sen: No institution can satisfy all criteria.

Hammond and Miller (1985) present four other impossibility theorems. All the results have several principles of administration in common. First, each posits some kind of decentralization as a design criterion. The nature of the decentralization varies: Authority may be distributed horizontally or vertically; jurisdictions may be overlapping or nonoverlapping. The decentralization may even be conditional: Theorem 3 examines a management-by-exception rule (if all subordinates agree on a ranking of options, that fixes the organization's ranking; if not, their superior decides).

Second, each theorem presumes that flexibility is desirable: The universal domain criterion is stipulated as an organizing criterion. Finally, each requires that individual rankings must aggregate to an acyclic organizational ranking. Thus "the proofs of Theorems 1–5 have a key feature: in each case, universal domain allows us to construct a set of preferences which, when aggregated via [the posited structure of authority], violates acyclicity" (Hammond and Miller 1985, 22). As they point out, "At root, decentralization . . . cause(s) trouble because it creates *multiple points of decision-making authority*" (p. 22, emphasis in the original). And because violations appear in the context of several rather different authority structures, it seems there is a deep inconsistency between the general idea of decentralization and other important principles of organizational design.

The theorems are valid, but what is their relevance to bureaucracies? Several objections may be made. The first is that the theorems' appropriate empirical domain includes voters and legislators, who are indeed trying to aggregate individual preferences into a collective choice. It is not sensible to stretch the results to cover bureaucrats; they are not free actors, and bureaucracies as institutions are not established to aggregate individual preferences over alternatives. Judgments, yes; opinions, yes; preferences, no.

But this objection underestimates the generality of Sen's theorem and the other impossibility results. A theorem, like any purely mathematical object, is uninterpreted, referring only to sets, elements of sets, relations (such as orderings) between those elements, and so forth. Thus xPy could be interpreted specifically as "x is preferred to y," but all that the abstract theorem claims is that a relation of ordering obtains between x and y. In some sense, x outranks y; what that sense is depends on the specific application of the theorem. Regarding bureaucracies (and juries and advisory committees), it is indeed more sensible to interpret the ordering as one of judgments—bureaucrat 1 believes that x is a superior alternative to y in terms of some organizational criterion, whereas bureaucrat 2 believes the opposite. This interpretation of institutions aggregating judgments rather than preferences is perfectly appropriate for this theorem, and for social-choice results in general (Sen 1977). Therefore, although Hammond and Miller mainly refer to preferences, in what follows I shall interpret the orderings as judgments.

The second objection concerns the significance of the results. The punch of an impossibility theorem depends on the plausibility of the principles; the less stringent they are, the more surprising the result. In the five results reported by Hammond and Miller, most of the design criteria seem sensible enough, with one exception: universal domain. This is a demanding condition because it requires that an organization's decision process work on any configuration of judgments of individual officials. (Universal domain is also assumed in the most celebrated of all impossibility results, Arrow's theorem on democratic procedures.) This limitless flexibility is tantamount to demanding a kind of perfection, so perhaps it is unsurprising that no institution can pass the test.

Hammond and his colleagues have several replies to this objection. First, we do not yet know how bizarre sets of individual orderings must be in order to create intransitive institutional orderings. Some scholars initially thought Arrow's result was only a mathematical curiosity, and that preference combinations creating majority rule intransitivity were empirically odd. We now know, thanks to a decade of hard work by high powered theorists, that—outside the simple world of unidimensional policy spaces—just the opposite is true: Preference configurations yielding coherent majoritarian choices are extremely special. It is therefore possible that rather tame judgment profiles in the bureaucratic setting will also yield intransitive institutional orderings.

Second, Hammond (1984, 1985) has investigated, via Monte Carlo simulation, the odds that a problematic profile of individual judgments—one necessitating the violation of a principle—will appear in an agency. Although such simulations cannot be completely conclusive, it seems that the more officials whose opinions matter, and the greater the number of alternatives, the greater the probability that the institution's judgment ordering will be intransitive. It should be noted that in these simulations all individual orderings were equally likely, an extreme form of the universal domain property. Empirically, bureaucrats in an agency probably exhibit more homogeneous beliefs due to self-selection and socialization. Judgmental homogeneity within an agency may be purchased at the price of heterogeneity among agencies (Hammond and Miller 1985, 17), however, so the problems may be displaced rather than solved.

A third objection is that the theory's empirical predictions are incorrect: Agencies do not cycle endlessly over different alternatives. This objection rests on the incorrect perception that Hammond and Miller are making unconditional empirical claims about the frequency of indecisive institutional behavior. Their social-choice theorems, however, are not directly about choices; they are about the relation between individual and collective orderings of alternatives. To see the difference, let us consider an example from Hammond (1985, 5) that illustrates another impossibility result. The rules defining the institution are simple. Some decisions are delegated to small groups of subordinates who have expertise. If a group can agree, the matter is settled for the organization; if not, a common superior makes the choice. In this example, subordinates 1 and 2 agree that x is superior to y; since they have jurisdiction over these options, the ranking xP_oy (x is organizationally preferred to y) is established. Subordinates 3 and 4 do not agree about the relative merits of y and z, so their superior imposes the ordering yP_oz. Finally, because the pair (x, z) was not delegated, the boss has jurisdiction and imposes zP_ox. All together we have $xP_oyP_ozP_ox$: The organization's judgment ordering is cyclic.

But we must be careful to understand precisely what is being stated. The institution's underlying ordering of alternatives is cyclic; we have not predicted that its choice behavior will be cyclic or unstable. Indeed, the relevant impossibility theorem, derived by Thomas and Hammond, makes no direct prediction about the choice behavior of a bureaucracy. Instead, it states one of several principles must give in a situation like this. Empirically, of course, the organization may exhibit decisive behavior: The boss, confronted with the orderings xP_oy and yP_oz, but believing that z is better than x, simply imposes his own views and picks z. This decisiveness does not constitute a counterexample to the Thomas and Hammond result, for the latter did not predict unstable choice behavior. The latent intransitivity of the institution's judgment ordering has not disappeared; it has been evaded by hierarchical fiat.

Concerning empirical theory, we are interested in predicting choices, not latent orderings. An empiricist might say, if the outcome is stable and predictable, who cares if there are latent inconsistencies?* And I think it is fair to say that some of the shock value of the Hammond, Miller, and Thomas work rests on their apparent claim that even hierarchies are vulnerable to choice instability. Such predictions surprise us, for the common supposition is that hierarchy almost by definition guarantees decisiveness; after all, with a single chief executive, the buck stops here.

Some of the authors' own language promotes this misinterpretation: "Even with a 'boss' who steps in and makes the decisions when the subordinates are in disagreement, organizational preference cycles can still occur" (Hammond 1985, 2). A more careful reading shows that behavioral instability—agencies indecisively cycling over alternatives—is not an implication of the theorems. I would recommend that formal theorists avoid the term *cycles* if they are referring to preference or judgment orderings. In ordinary language, the word connotes choice instability over time.

Although the impossibility results do not make unconditional predictions about choice behavior, they do have empirical content. Since they demonstrate that no agency can simultaneously satisfy principles *a*, *b*, and *c*, it immediately follows that if a particular bureaucracy has implemented the first two principles, it is not implementing the third. As Hammond and Miller (1985) emphasize, different bureaucracies will exhibit different types of pathologies, that is, violations of different criteria. For example, if agencies make decisive choices, is it because a combination of personnel selection and organizational socialization create sufficiently homogeneous beliefs so that troublesome judgment profiles do not appear (a violation of universal domain)? Or is it due to organizational procedures, such as a bureau chief imposing a choice in the face of underlying judgmental confusion (a violation of decentralization)?

Perhaps surprisingly, then, this most abstract type of theorizing relates directly to much more empirical ways of studying agencies: to social psychological studies of organizational socialization, to behavioral analyses of standard operating procedures, and to sociological studies of the internal authority structure of bureaucracies.

---

* There are problems with focusing on orderings even for a normative theory of bureaucracy. Sen (1977) has suggested that requiring institutions to produce a complete ordering of alternatives is a bit of a luxury; all we need is that they make choices.

Something along these lines occurred in the study of legislatures. Initially, empirical scholars believed that the McKelvey and Cohen results (on the nonexistence of majority-rule winners) implied a simple unconditional claim that legislative choices are unstable. This was a misinterpretation. These results state that if a certain bare-bones majoritarian procedure is followed, any alternative can almost always be defeated. If A, then B. We do not observe such massive instability: not-B, therefore not-A. Hence these theorems, combined with the empirical observation that legislative choice is relatively stable, have triggered a search for procedures (such as rules about agenda formation) and institutional arrangements (such as committees) that create stability where instability would have otherwise reigned—in Shepsle's (1979) apt phrase, a structure-induced equilibrium.

Just as social-choice theory promoted the new institutionalism in the study of legislatures and emphasized the significance of institutional properties in determining policy choices, so it may for the study of bureaucracy. We may look forward to a rapprochement between formal modelers who understand the importance of fine-grained descriptions of bureaucratic procedures and empiricists who understand the theoretical significance of the procedures and structures they have described. For a stimulating example of this integration of the theoretical and the empirical, see Hammond (1986). This essay also provides a nontechnical introduction to social choice theories of bureaucracy.

Models of Bounded Rationality

The preceding models have differed on many counts, but one property they share: Decision makers are assumed to be perfectly rational. Rational-choice models are spreading throughout political science generally, but there is a special irony associated with their diffusion into public administration; two of the giants of our field, Herbert Simon and James March, have been the main pioneers of models of bounded rationality.

There have been numerous attempts to reconcile the two families of theories, mostly along the line that taking costs of information gathering into account makes apparent differences vanish. Simon, however, would have none of this bland ecumenism, arguing that if a decision maker tries to incorporate costs of information gathering, he is merely adding one more layer of complexity to his decision-making task. Suppose, for example, that an administrator is searching for a choice alternative. Because he hears about alternatives sequentially, there may be a benefit to postponing his selection—something better may turn up. On the other hand, the program constituents are impatient, so, *ceteris paribus*, the administrator prefers to implement sooner rather than later. At this point a modeler can proceed in either of two directions. One could posit that the official satisfices; that is, he has an aspiration level that divides options into acceptable and unacceptable ones. Alternatively, one can assume that the administration uses an optimal acceptance rule. What are the differences? At first glance, there are none. Both decision rules partition the set of all feasible options into two subsets, at least in simple environments.* The rational-choice approach presumes that the decision maker behaves as if he knows the probability distribution of future alternatives, discounts them appropriately, and sets his acceptance level to equate the expected marginal benefits of receiving one more alternative with the expected marginal costs. (A Bayesian might posit that the official does not know the true distribution and has only a subjective distribution in his head. This assumption is more plausible, but it leaves unanswered the question of mental calculations and raises the new issue of belief revision.)

Simon was well aware of this interpretation of the search problem. In the appendix to "A Behavioral Model of Rational Choice" (1957), he formalized an optimal search model using as an example a person trying to decide when to accept an offer on his house. Noting the probabilistic information presumed by the rational-choice approach, he said,

> Now the seller who does not have this information, and who will be satisfied with a more bumbling kind of rationality, will make approximations to avoid using the information he doesn't have. First, he will probably limit the planning horizon by assuming a price at which he can certainly sell and will be willing to sell in the nth time period. Second, he will set his initial acceptance price quite high, watch the distribution of offers he receives, and gradually and approximately adjust his acceptance price downward or upward until he receives an offer he accepts—without ever making probability calculations. (Pp. 259–60)

The two approaches differ significantly. They use different assumptions about information available to decision makers, how this information is used, or both. I believe it would be a major methodological error—a self-inflicted wound—to rob ourselves of theoretical pluralism by ignoring these differences. Indeed, at a time when cognitive psychology has experienced an intellectual renaissance, when experimentalists are examining ever more carefully whether human beings follow the axioms of rational choice, it would be ironic for political scientists to believe that theories of rational choice and theories of limited rationality are equivalent.

Probably more models of boundedly rational choice have been realized as

---

* If the alternatives are not independent, it may be suboptimal to use the simple rule of accepting alternatives above a certain quality and rejecting those below that level. For an example of less intuitive acceptance policy in a more complex environment, see Bendor, Taylor, and van Gaalen (1987a), property 2f.

computer programs than as purely mathematical theories whose solutions are worked out by hand. There are several reasons for this. First, there is a natural correspondence between substance and method; a wide variety of adaptive strategies can be easily represented by programming languages. Second, behavioral theorists tend to incorporate more organizational and political complexity in their theories, which renders mathematical models intractable. The following models are, therefore, a sample of the smaller wing of behavioral theory. The sample focuses on three areas that scholars in this tradition have worked on: the effects of experientially driven behavior, models of budgeting, and the role of cognitive heuristics.

Backward-Looking Behavior
Rational-choice models assume that decision makers are relentlessly forward looking.* In contrast, behavioral theorists emphasize that decision makers are often heavily influenced by experience, by what they have learned.† Does this assumption matter? Two examples show that it can.

First, suppose an administrator has two options, a and b. Neither one is sure to work or doomed to fail; this much he knows. Objectively, the probability that a succeeds is p, the chance that b works is q. We will suppose $p > q$. (They need not sum to one.) These probabilities are constant and independent over time. The decision maker starts off with an initial propensity to try a in the first period,

$$p_1(a),$$

and a similar propensity to try b,

$$p_1(b) = 1 - p_1(a).$$

Over time, he adapts via a simple learning rule: If in period i he tried a and it worked, then his propensity to try a again is strengthened:

$$p_{i+1}(a) = p_i(a) + \alpha(1 - p_i(a)).$$

---

* This assumption produces the bizarre prediction that if it is common knowledge that both players are game theoretically rational, they will not cooperate in any round of a prisoner's dilemma that is repeated a known number of times—no matter how long. In general, this assumption makes game theorists agonize over what could happen at the very end of a game. As usual, there is a good idea here—things can fall apart when a relationship is ending—but to assume that people work out their entire strategies by first figuring out what they should do in the last period and then work backward to the present seems a bit farfetched for long-term matches.

† Again, the differences are real, though incomplete. Dynamic models of rational choice do incorporate learning; the difference is that these models assume decision makers act as perfect Bayesian statisticians in updating their beliefs.

The parameter α, which represents the rate of learning, is between zero and 1. If a failed, the administrator's propensity to try it is weakened:

$$p_{i+1}(a) = \beta p_i(a)$$

with β also between zero and 1. The equations for alternative b have the same form.

What will the administrator do over the long haul? This is a simple Bush-Mosteller model of learning, and its properties are well known. A decision maker who learns in this manner will tend, in the long run, to use a over half the time

$$\frac{1-q}{(1-p)+(1-q)}$$

and b the remainder. But this is suboptimal. An expected utility maximizer will, once she or he becomes subjectively certain that $p > q$, use a always. Perhaps surprisingly, even in this simple environment adaptive behavior need not converge to the optimal strategy.

One might object by pointing out that this is an artificial environment. Rarely do decision makers face a choice situation in which the probabilities of success are stationary. If they change, it will generally not be optimal to stick to one alternative because it may pay to experiment. The point is well taken. Specifying optimal behavior in a changing environment is much more difficult, however, and it is not at all clear that adaptive strategies converge to the optimal one in this context either.

For some enlightening extensions of simple learning theory, see Cross (1983). His examples are of economic behavior, but anyone interested in adaptive models will benefit from reading the book.

Second, interorganizational cooperation sometimes has the structure of a prisoner's dilemma: Two section chiefs may be better off helping each other than not, but each may prefer to receive aid and not to endure the cost of giving any. If the situation is repeated over time, Axelrod (1984) has shown that the simple and behaviorally plausible strategy of tit-for-tat (TFT)—cooperate in the first period and thereafter do what your partner did in the previous round—is very robust, doing well in a diverse set of strategic environments. If the players do not discount the future too much, TFT is in Nash equilibrium with itself: One cannot do better than to play TFT against someone else who is also playing TFT. Note that TFT, like the basic form of reciprocity, is a backward-looking strategy.

Suppose, however, that payoffs are a function of the player's moves plus an exogenous disturbance and that the players observe only their own payoffs, being unable to discriminate between the action of their partner and the disturbance. How does TFT perform in this environment? It can be shown (Bendor 1987) that simple backward-looking strategies do not do well in noisy environments; by failing to discriminate between intended and unintended effects, two players using TFT cannot sustain high levels of cooperation. Indeed, it can be shown that in a wide class of stochastic environments, TFT is no longer in Nash equilibrium with itself. A perfectly rational player, looking forward rather than backward, may try to test the hypothesis that his partner is playing TFT; if the hypothesis continued to be confirmed, and the rational player valued the future sufficiently, he would ignore idiosyncratic fluctuations, maintaining a steady level of cooperation.

Thus, in both a decision context (games against nature) and a strategic setting, experientially driven behavior can be observationally distinguished from future-oriented behavior.

Padgett's Model of Budgeting

The study of budgeting in public organizations has long been the province of behaviorally inclined researchers. Wildavsky's pioneering work in 1964 (3d ed. 1979) drew explicitly on the concept of bounded rationality; interestingly enough, Simon's own thoughts on cognitive limits were partly inspired by some practical problems of resource allocation in several municipal agencies that he encountered in his student days. For the most sustained effort to construct a nonoptimizing model of budgetary behavior, however, we must turn to the work of John Padgett (1980, 1981).

Padgett's work is impressive. Unlike the foregoing simple adaptive models that depict only one organizational level, Padgett's model grapples with the hierarchical nature of budgeting (Crecine 1970). He demonstrates how fiscal and political constraints from the presidential level (ceilings on departmental totals) can be filtered through the standard operating procedures of the Office of Management and Budget (OMB)—cutting alternative amounts from different programs—and through the attention-focusing patterns of OMB and the departments. Before Padgett, scholars used simulations to analyze how environmental pressures were transmitted by organizational routines (Crecine 1969). To do this in a closed-form mathematical model, one yielding testable predictions about the predicted distribution of budget changes, was quite an achievement.

How executive branch officials search for and test alternatives is one key aspect of the model. This feature is the most purely bureaucratic component of the model and is central to most of the important results. To understand what Padgett has accomplished we must set his work in historical perspective. The standard search metaphor in budgeting had been incrementalism, which clearly derived its justification from bounded rationality: "Incrementalism and other such devices to simplify and speed decisions are inevitable responses to the extra-ordinary complexity of resource allocation in governments of any size" (Wildavsky 1979, 216). But searching in the neighborhood of last year's appropriation is only one way of cutting the decision tree down to size. As both Lindblom (1959) and Wildavsky recognized, there are other rules-of-thumb or heuristics for narrowing search. Clearly, if bounded rationality means anything, it must imply that search is limited;

it does not, however, imply that search is always local (incremental).* Nevertheless, partly because dollars provide a natural metric for measuring the geometry of search and partly because political and fiscal constraints typically do mandate small changes, budgetary scholars have concentrated upon the specific heuristic of incrementalism. Accordingly, when Davis, Dempster, and Wildavsky (1974) developed their quantitative models, they represented the then Bureau of the Budget's spring ceiling for a program as a simple linear function of the previous year's obligational authority (x), plus a normally distributed disturbance:

$$Y_{i+1} = \alpha \cdot x_i + \varepsilon_{i+1}$$

In this model, incrementalism means that α is close to 1 and that the variance of ε is not too big. This kind of equation is fine for regression analysis, but it is only a rough approximation of the verbal descriptions of Wildavsky and others. Indeed, this specification left the modelers open to the criticism that they viewed budgeting as a mechanical process; the OMB plugs in an α for each program, there is an idiosyncratic pulling and hauling summarized by ε, and that's that.

In this context—a widespread acceptance of verbal descriptions of budgeting informed by ideas of bounded rationality combined with dissatisfaction with their mathematical translation—Padgett's model (1981) is an attempt to close the gap between the verbal and mathematical representations.

In this model, the search of OMB examiners is guided by an overall departmental constraint, B, fixed by their superiors. Program submissions at this stage total A, so the examiners must find $\Gamma = A - B$ worth of cuts. In every round there is a fixed probability, θ_i, that an examiner's attention will focus on program i. This attention probability can vary across the n programs; of course

$$\sum_{i=1}^{n} \theta_i = 1.$$

Given that an examiner has focused on the ith program, he generates a limited number of salient cut alternatives, anchoring or starting his search at zero cut. (It is assumed that the magnitude of the cut alternatives is distributed exponentially; the parameters of the exponential vary across programs.) The examiner's task is completed when all the cuts he recommends sum to or exceed Γ. Because his attention across programs is governed by a probabilistic process and because he generates alternatives probabilistically, the number of cutting rounds needed to reach the target Γ is a random variable as well.

---

* For example, George Marshall's problem after Pearl Harbor was to decide which integer multiple of the War Department's 1941 appropriation he should request. He probably did not think of many alternatives; however, of those he considered, it is unlikely any were in the neighborhood of the status quo.

Note that though the behavior is goal directed, no optimization is posited. The examiner's conduct is well within the limits of rationality as we understand them. Two central premises of bounded rationality are explicitly represented by the mathematical model: Only a limited number of alternatives will be generated, and a simple test will be applied (have I reached Γ?) to end the search. These simple, plausible postulates suffice to yield testable predictions about resource allocation. My only serious reservation about the model pertains to the assumption that the cut alternatives are generated exponentially. As Padgett notes, this is equivalent to positing that the chance a decision maker will perceive a salient alternative within a given dollar interval d is proportional to the size of that interval, or just λd with $\lambda >$ zero. The location of the interval is immaterial. To see concretely what this means, consider the problem of a department secretary trying to decide how much to add to a program. (Since budgets cannot be negative, it is harder to think through the implications of the exponential assumption for cuts.) The exponential hypothesis implies that if the secretary has not perceived a salient alternative in the [0–10 percent] range, then the distribution of salient alternatives in the [10–20 percent] range will be exactly the same, and similarly for [20–30 percent] and so on. (This is the memorylessness property of the exponential.) This seems implausible, for one would expect perceptions of budget increases to become coarser—bigger jumps between alternatives—the farther one moves from the status quo. (The exponential assumption did, however, receive some empirical support [Padgett 1980, 369].)

This is only one objection, and clearly Padgett's work goes a long way toward an adequate mathematical representation of microsearch processes in budgeting.

March and March's Model of Performance Sampling

In terms of the cognitive capabilities attributed to decision makers, the simple models of adaptation and reciprocity described earlier are almost at the opposite spectrum compared to rational-choice models. These simple behavioral models depict decision makers as adaptive machines responding to reinforcement; if something works, one is more inclined to try it again. Obviously this underestimates the cognitive complexity of human beings. As Michael Cohen once remarked to me, in order to construct tractable mathematical models, it seems that scholars postulate either that decision makers are virtually mindless or have perfect minds. And it is true that the hard middle ground where modelers assume that people are boundedly rational, yet can form complex beliefs and strategies, has been dominated by simulation studies (see especially Cohen 1981, 1984; Taylor 1986).

Empirically, this middle ground is home to cognitive psychologists who have uncovered an interesting variety of heuristics that can produce biased judgments and choices. A sensible strategy for organization theorists is to focus on heuristics that have strong experimental support and are substantively important in bureaucratic decision making. For an unusual effort to analyze the organizational effect of a particular bias—overdependence on small samples—let us consider March and March's (1978) model of performance sampling in educational institutions.

Their basic model is composed of several intuitively plausible components. The performance of school administrators is observed episodically by their superiors. Performance may be either a success or a failure.*After a small number of observations, the organization will make a personnel decision based on the observed proportion of successes. An administrator who has achieved above a cutoff of, for example, 0.80 will be promoted; one who falls below a lower cutoff will be fired. The remainder will be retained, their performance will continue to be sampled, and they may be promoted or fired later on in their careers. Thus the model joins the sampling of a stochastic performance process to a pair of aspiration levels. Unlike Simon's (1957) original binary concept of satisficing, in this model the two cutoffs partition performance into three values—unsatisfactory, satisfactory, and superior.

The model has two kinds of implications. The macroimplication, primarily of interest to students of internal labor markets, is that this simple performance-sampling process generates a widely observed distribution of decision times; for a population of officials, the promotion and demotion rates rise at the beginning of appointments and then fall. The microimplication is that overconfidence in small samples "can yield subjectively compelling impressions of causal determinacy" (March and March 1978, 450). (Though March and March do not derive this result formally, it can be easily demonstrated.) Two examples are particularly worth noting:

> *Hero effect.* Within a group of managers of varying abilities, the faster the rate of promotion, the less likely it is to be justified. Performance records are produced by a combination of underlying ability and sampling variation. Managers who have good records are more likely to have high ability than managers who have poor records, but the reliability of the differentiation is small when records are short.
>
> *Disappointment effect.* On the average, new managers will be a disappointment. The performance records by which managers are evaluated are subject to sampling error. Since a manager is promoted to a new job on the basis of a good previous record, the proportion of promoted managers whose past records are better than their abilities will be greater than the proportion whose past records are poorer. As a result, on the average, managers will do less well in their new jobs than they did in their old ones, and observers will

---

* March and March consider the cases of heterogeneous administrators whose abilities remain constant (some are more able than others, but everyone has a fixed probability of success), of homogeneous administrators who learn over time, and of homogeneous administrators whose probability of success is constant.

come to believe that higher level jobs are more difficult than lower level ones, even if they are not. (P. 451)

These effects will appear even when, as in this model, the observations of performance are flawless.

One of the most robust findings of cognitive psychology is that most people are rather poor intuitive statisticians. We see patterns even when evidence is generated by a random process; we place excessive confidence in small samples, particularly when the evidence is concrete and vivid; perhaps most important, we underestimate the effects of sampling bias (Nisbett and Ross 1980, 260). The March and March model (1978) is an important first step in extending this psychological finding to an organizational setting. The decision makers in their world form more complex beliefs about their environments than do the rather primitive actors in the models of adaptation and reciprocity described in the first part of this section. They are not perfect, however. This seems to be a plausible middle range.

Concluding Remarks

Substance and method, assumptions and formalism, are intertwined in the study of bureaucracy. Take a random sample of political scientists and ask them what they think are the properties of formal models of bureaus. I wager that one would hear two answers: (1) mathematical models and (2) rational-choice assumptions. As we have seen, many prominent examples fit this description. Yet this is an overly narrow interpretation of the formal study of bureaucracy. The one key property, the only key property, is that an analysis be deductive, that one can show that certain conclusions must follow from specified assumptions. If the analysis in question has this property, it is a formal model of bureaucracy, even if the assumptions state that a decision maker acts suboptimally.

This point is elementary; it is also fundamental. I think that our imaginary sample of political scientists would reveal that a premature consensus is forming about the nature of formal models of bureaus. An indicator of this is that some scholars now ask, "What do bureaucrats maximize?" (budgets? utility?), without asking the logically prior question, "Do bureaucrats maximize anything in complex choice situations?" It is as if they think the latter question has already been raised and answered—and answered affirmatively.

This is ironic. It is ironic because Herbert Simon, who pioneered the idea of bounded rationality, has won a Nobel Prize in Economics, the home of deductive theorizing. Simon has shown that it is possible to construct formal models of organizations based on the assumption that individual decision makers have limited computational ability. This line of work has been carried on by James March, Michael

Cohen, Roy Radner, John Padgett, Serge Taylor, Robert Axelrod, and Sidney Winter, among others. Individually and collectively, their work constitutes an existence proof that one can analyze deductively with nonmaximizing assumptions.

It is impossible here to examine thoroughly the relative merits of rational-choice theories and behavioral theories. Suffice it to say that I believe that neither approach dominates the other in the sense of being better across all the important criteria that social scientists use to evaluate theories. There are tradeoffs. Consider just two criteria: the fruitfulness of the theory in helping us look at familiar phenomena in new ways, and the consistency of the theory with established knowledge in related fields.

Rational-actor models have been quite fruitful. For example, by connecting spatial theories of majority-rule voting to the classical question of bureaucratic discretion, Hill (1985) has shown how crafty administrators can influence policy outcomes—not by defying the (one and only) legislative majority but by helping to form a new winning coalition. This is an important insight about the problem of the political control of bureaucracy in democracies.

On the second criterion, consistency with knowledge in the related field of cognitive psychology, behavioral theories score better than rational-actor models. There is little doubt that rational-actor theories, whether game theoretic or expected utility maximization, are less consistent with psychologists' understanding of how we think and choose than are behavioral theories. This relative ranking should matter to us. Presumably the reason for assuming perfect rationality is that it allows us to focus our attention on the strategic logic of relations among decision makers rather than focus on the internal intricacies of individual choice. Because this methodological choice reflects the bounded rationality of scientists, behavioral theorists should sympathize with the position. Nevertheless, the simplification is costly. Physicists use ideal gas laws, but they recognize the price they are paying. So should we.

Because no one approach dominates the formal study of bureaus, we should maintain a theoretical pluralism. I am concerned that this pluralism is threatened by a premature consensus on rational-choice assumptions, a consensus that is self-fulfilling. If most formal modelers use rational-choice models, when these models run into empirical difficulties, scholars will tend to patch up the models with ad hoc assumptions rather than move into the uncharted territory of adaptive models. Empirical difficulties will be swept aside as irritating anomalies. Familiar cries will go up: "Optimization models are the only game in town," "You can't beat something with nothing" (i.e., empirical criticism cannot dethrone a theory if no replacement is available); and most important, "We don't know how to construct nonoptimization models." Since the mathematics appropriate for adaptive models are not the same as the mathematics relevant for optimization models, if the field does not invest in behavioral theories now, the odds are good that we will suffer from collective amnesia, forgetting the relevant techniques. And having forgotten how to use screwdrivers, modelers will continue hammering.

This self-fulfilling prophecy will be reinforced by self-selection into the subfield of formal models of bureaus. If Ph.D. students perceive that doing this work requires using theories built on rational-choice foundations, those unwilling to make the necessary tradeoffs will not enter the subfield. Instead, they will do field research or quantitative empirical work that lacks an explicit theoretical base. The result of this self-selection could be two different communities of scholars, sealed off from one another by the reinforcing cleavages of different techniques of inquiry and different substantive assumptions.

To prevent this and to maintain the existing pluralism, we need to expand the mathematical tool kit of students who want to work on formal models of bureaus. This is where the interaction between substance and method is crucial. Requiring a background only of calculus will produce a pool of graduate students predisposed to rational-choice models. Although Newton did not invent the differential calculus to solve utility maximization problems, it is a natural method for that class of problems. Hence, the hammer syndrome would prevail. With only one tool in his kit, a student will be driven by what the formalism is preadapted for.

What, then, in addition to calculus? I would name two major techniques: (1) probability theory and the allied study of stochastic processes, and (2) computer simulation. Students with a background in probability theory will see, for example, that one can represent the behavior of a bureau searching for a new policy by the sample path of a suitably defined stochastic process, and that the probability of coming up with a satisfactory alternative is the probability that the path enters a specified region of the search space. Similarly, a student with a background in simulation will see that a wide variety of adaptive decision-making strategies can be realized in computer programs. Indeed, as Simon, March, and Cohen have emphasized, computer programs are as natural a formalism for representing rule-governed strategies as calculus is for optimal ones. Students with a background in these techniques, as well as in calculus, will let the problem and their substantive theoretical hunches guide the choice of formalism, rather than let the formalism dictate the content of assumptions.

There would be a second benefit. There are significant complementarities among these techniques. For example, in initially representing the rich complexity of a decision process, a researcher may find simulation most useful. Once he understands the process's central features, he may wish to show that the results hold under more general assumptions than the simulation used. An excellent example of this complementarity is Axelrod's (1984) work on the prisoner's dilemma. Without his simulation tournament, discovering the power of the tit-for-tat strategy would have been much more difficult. But because simulations have to run with specified strategies, this method could not prove that TFT is collectively stable against the invasion of any arbitrary strategy. Therefore, to prove that TFT is collectively stable and under what conditions, Axelrod used purely deductive analysis.

A more general example of complementarity is to examine whether an adaptive process, represented by a simulation or a stochastic process, converges to the equilibrium result of an optimizing model. We would all feel more comfortable in using neoclassical models if we show that a realistic process of learning leads decision makers to optimal alternatives, and does so in real time. Whether or not we get this mental comfort, we will learn a good deal by understanding when convergence does occur and when it does not. I believe this kind of knowledge alone is important enough to warrant maintaining a pluralism of theory and technique in the formal study of bureaus. After all, what does not diverge cannot converge.

It is well to recognize, however, that important disagreements in the field crosscut the arguments over microassumptions. Most prominently, there is a running debate over the extent of bureaucratic influence in national politics. There are those who assert that agencies greatly influence policy outcomes (James Q. Wilson and William Niskanen form an otherwise odd pair), those who assert that Congress subtly controls the bureaucracy (Barry Weingast), and those who have a more pluralist view of institutional influence (Terry Moe). This argument correlates poorly with the rational-choice–behavioral debate: Niskanen, Weingast, and Moe have all constructed rational-choice models, but they have different views on bureaucratic power. This is fortunate because cross-cutting cleavages promote constructive dialogue; reinforcing cleavages foster dogmas. In any event, most students of public administration are probably more interested in macroquestions of influence and power than in the microfoundations of individual choice.

References

Aberbach, Joel, Robert Putnam, and Bert A. Rockman. 1981. *Bureaucrats and Politicians in Western Democracies.* Cambridge, Mass.: Harvard University Press.

Aberbach, Joel, and Bert A. Rockman. 1976. "Clashing Beliefs within the Executive Branch: The Nixon Administration Bureaucracy." *American Political Science Review* 70: 456–68.

Altfeld, Michael, and Gary Miller. 1984. "Sources of Bureaucratic Influence: Expertise and Agenda Control." *Journal of Conflict Resolution* 28:701–30.

Arrow, Kenneth. 1985. "The Economics of Agency." In *Principals and Agents,* edited by John Pratt and Richard Zeckhauser. Boston: Harvard Business School Press.

Axelrod, Robert. 1984. *The Evolution of Cooperation.* New York: Basic Books.

Baiman, Stanley. 1982. "Agency Research in Managerial Accounting." *Journal of Accounting Literature* 1:154–213.

Bendor, Jonathan. 1987. "In Good Times and Bad: Reciprocity in an Uncertain World." *American Journal of Political Science* 31:531–58.

Bendor, Jonathan, and Terry Moe. 1985. "An Adaptive Model of Bureaucratic Politics." *American Political Science Review* 79:755–74.

Bendor, Jonathan, and Terry Moe. 1986. "Agenda Control, Committee Capture, and the Dynamics of Institutional Politics." *American Political Science Review* 80: 1187–1207.

Bendor, Jonathan, Serge Taylor, and Roland van Gaalen. 1985. "Bureaucratic Expertise versus Legislative Authority: A Model of Deception and Monitoring in Budgeting." *American Political Science Review* 79:1041–60.

Bendor, Jonathan, Serge Taylor, and Roland van Gaalen. 1987a. "Stacking the Deck: Bureaucratic Missions and the Search for Alternatives." *American Political Science Review* 81:873–96.

Bendor, Jonathan, Serge Taylor, and Roland van Gaalen. 1987b. "Politicians, Bureaucrats, and Asymmetric Information." *American Journal of Political Science* 31:796–828.

Calvert, Randall. 1985. "The Value of Biased Information: A Rational Choice Model of Political Advice." *Journal of Politics* 47:530–55.

Calvert, Randall, Matthew McCubbins, and Barry Weingast. 1986. "Bureaucratic Discretion or Political Control: Process Versus Equilibrium Analysis." Presented at the annual meeting of the American Political Science Association, Washington, D.C.

Cohen, Michael. 1981. "The Power of Parallel Thinking." *Journal of Economic Behavior and Organization* 2:285–306.

Cohen, Michael. 1984. "Conflict and Complexity: Goal Diversity and Organizational Search Effectiveness." *American Political Science Review* 78:435–51.

Cohen, Michael, James March, and Johan P. Olsen. 1972. "A Garbage Can Model of Organizational Choice." *Administrative Science Quarterly* 17:1–25.

Conybeare, John. 1984. "Bureaucracy, Monopoly, and Competition: A Critical Analysis of the Budget-Maximizing Model of Bureaucracy." *American Journal of Political Science* 28:479–502.

Crecine, John. 1969. *Governmental Problem-Solving.* Chicago: Rand McNally.

Crecine, John. 1970. *Defense Budgeting: Organizational Adaptation to External Constraints.* Memorandum RM-6121-PR. Santa Monica: Rand.

Cross, John. 1983. *A Theory of Adaptive Economic Behavior.* New York: Cambridge University Press.

Cyert, Richard, and James March. 1963. *A Behavioral Theory of the Firm.* Englewood Cliffs, N.J.: Prentice-Hall.

Davis, Otto, M.A.H. Dempster, and Aaron Wildavsky. 1974. "Toward a Predictive Theory of Government Expenditures: U.S. Domestic Appropriations." *British Journal of Political Science* 4:1–34.

Denzau, Arthur, and Robert Mackay. 1983. "Gatekeeping and Monopoly Power of Committees: An Analysis of Sincere and Sophisticated Behavior." *American Journal of Political Science* 27:740–61.

Destler, I.M. 1974. *Presidents, Bureaucrats, and Foreign Policy.* Princeton, N.J.: Princeton University Press.

Ferejohn, John. Forthcoming. "Introduction." In *Information and Democracy,* edited by John Ferejohn and James Kuklinski. Champaign: University of Illinois Press.

Fiorina, Morris. 1982. "Legislative Choice of Regulatory Forms: Legal Process or Administrative Process?" *Public Choice* 39:33–66.

Fiorina, Morris. 1986. "Legislative Uncertainty, Legislative Control, and the Delegation of Legislative Power." *Journal of Law, Economics, and Organization* 2:33–50.

Halperin, Morton. 1974. *Bureaucratic Politics and Foreign Policy*. Washington, D.C.: Brookings Institution.

Hammond, Thomas. 1984. "The Probability of an Organizational Preference Cycle." Presented at the annual meeting of the American Political Science Association, Washington, D.C.

Hammond, Thomas. 1985. "Instability in Hierarchical Decision Making: A Probabilistic Analysis." Presented at the annual meeting of the American Political Science Association, New Orleans, La.

Hammond, Thomas. 1986. "Agenda Control, Organizational Structure, and Bureaucratic Politics." *American Journal of Political Science* 30:379–420.

Hammond, Thomas, Jeffrey Hill, and Gary Miller. 1986. "Presidential Appointment of Bureau Chiefs and the 'Congressional Control of Administration' Hypothesis." Presented at the annual meeting of the American Political Science Association, Washington, D.C.

Hammond, Thomas, and Gary Miller. 1985. "A Social Choice Perspective on Authority and Expertise in Bureaucracy." *American Journal of Political Science* 29:1–28.

Hammond, Thomas, and Gary Miller. 1987. "The Core of the Constitution." *American Political Science Review* 81:1155–74.

Hill, Jeffrey. 1985. "Why So Much Stability? The Role of Agency Determined Stability." *Public Choice* 46:275–87.

Holmstrom, Bengt. 1986. "Economic Theories of Organization." Lecture given at the Graduate School of Business, Stanford University.

Huntington, Samuel. 1961. *The Common Defense*. New York: Columbia University Press.

Kaufman, Herbert. 1956. "Emerging Conflicts in the Doctrines of Public Administration." *American Political Science Review* 50:1057–73.

Levinthal, Daniel. 1988. "A Survey of Agency Models of Organizations." *Journal of Economic Behavior and Organization* 9:153–85.

Levinthal, Daniel, and James G. March. 1981. "A Model of Adaptive Organizational Search." *Journal of Economic Behavior and Organization* 2:307–33.

Lindblom, Charles. 1959. "The Science of 'Muddling Through.'" *Public Administration Review* 19:79–88.

McCubbins, Matthew, and Thomas Schwartz. 1984. "Congressional Oversight Overlooked: Police Patrols versus Fire Alarms." *American Journal of Political Science* 28:165–79.

Mackay, Robert, and Carolyn Weaver. 1979. "On the Mutuality of Interests between Bureaus and High Demand Committees: A Perverse Result." *Public Choice* 34:481–91.

McKelvey, Richard. 1976. "Intransitivities in Multidimensional Voting Models and Some Implications for Agenda Control." *Journal of Economic Theory* 12:472–82.

March, James C., and James G. March. 1978. "Performance Sampling in Social Matches." *Administrative Science Quarterly* 23:434–53.

March, James G., and Herbert A. Simon. 1958. *Organizations*. New York: Wiley.

Melumad, Nahum, and Dilip Mookherjee. 1989. "Delegation as Commitment: The Case of Income Tax Audits." *Rand Journal of Economics* 20:139–63.

Miller, Gary, and Terry Moe. 1983. "Bureaucrats, Legislators, and the Size of Government." *American Political Science Review* 77:297–322.

Moe, Terry. 1984. "The New Economics of Organization." *American Journal of Political Science* 28:739–77.

Moe, Terry. 1987. "An Assessment of the Positive Theory of 'Congressional Dominance.'" *Legislative Studies Quarterly* 12:475–520.

Munger, Michael. 1984. "On the Mutuality of Interests Between Bureaus and High Demand Review Committees." *Public Choice* 43:211–15.

Nelson, Richard, and Sidney Winter. 1981. *An Evolutionary Theory of Economic Change.* Cambridge, Mass.: Harvard University Press.

Nisbett, Richard, and Lee Ross. 1980. *Human Inference: Strategies and Shortcomings of Social Judgment.* Englewood Cliffs, N.J.: Prentice-Hall.

Niskanen, William A., Jr. 1971. *Bureaucracy and Representative Government.* New York: Aldine-Atherton.

Niskanen, William A., Jr. 1975. "Bureaucrats and Politicians." *Journal of Law and Economics* 18:617–44.

Ogul, Morris. 1976. *Congress Oversees the Bureaucracy.* Pittsburgh: University of Pittsburgh Press.

Padgett, John. 1980. "Bounded Rationality in Budgetary Research." *American Political Science Review* 74:354–72.

Padgett, John. 1981. "Hierarchy and Ecological Control in Federal Budgetary Decision Making." *American Journal of Sociology* 87:75–129.

Radner, Roy. 1985. "Repeated Principal-Agent Games with Discounting." *Econometrica* 53:1173–98.

Romer, Thomas, and Howard Rosenthal. 1978. "Political Resource Allocation, Controlled Agendas, and the Status Quo." *Public Choice* 33:27–43.

Ross, Stephen. 1973. "The Economic Theory of Agency: The Principal's Problem." *American Economic Review* 63:134–39.

Sen, Amartya. 1977. "Social Choice Theory: A Re-examination." *Econometrica* 45:53–89.

Shepsle, Kenneth. 1979. "Institutional Arrangements and Equilibrium in Multidimensional Voting Models." *American Journal of Political Science* 23:27–59.

Shepsle, Kenneth, and Barry Weingast. 1984. "Uncovered Sets and Sophisticated Voting Outcomes with Implications for Agenda Institutions." *American Journal of Political Science* 28:49–74.

Simon, Herbert A. 1946. "The Proverbs of Administration." *Public Administration Review* 6:53–67.

Simon, Herbert A. 1957. *Models of Man: Social and Rational.* New York: Wiley.

Taylor, Serge. 1986. "Organizational Learning." Manuscript, Graduate School of Business, Stanford University.

Thomas, Paul, and Thomas Hammond. 1989. "The Impossibility of a Neutral Hierarchy." *Journal of Law, Economics, and Organizations* 5:155–84.

Weingast, Barry. 1984. "The Congressional-Bureaucratic System: A Principal-Agent Perspective (with Applications to the SEC)." *Public Choice* 44:147–91.

Wildavsky, Aaron. 1979. *The Politics of the Budgetary Process.* 3d ed. Boston: Little, Brown.

Wilson, James Q. 1980. "The Politics of Regulation." In *The Politics of Regulation,* edited by James Q. Wilson. New York: Basic Books.

PART FIVE

Public Policy

17

Conflicting Evaluations of Policy Studies

Stuart S. Nagel

The purpose of this chapter is to assess the evaluations that have been made of the field of public policy studies. This chapter is especially concerned with the observation that most of the evaluations are conflicting in the sense that public policy studies is criticized for having too much of a certain characteristic and for having too little of the same characteristic.

Those conflicting characteristics include being (1) a temporary fad or stale material, (2) too practical or too theoretical, (3) too multidisciplinary or too narrowly focused on political science, (4) too quantitative or too subjective, (5) underutilized or overutilized, and (6) too liberal or too conservative.

On each of these dimensions, this chapter takes the position that public policy studies is a combination of diverse ideas that enable the field to deal better with the systematic evaluation of alternative public policies. In that sense, the field is based on both long-term philosophical principles and new analytic methods/substantive problems, theory and practice, political science and multiple disciplines, inherent subjectivity and potential objectivity, occasional utilization and frequent nonutilization necessary to generate the important successes, and liberal and conservative uses.*

Policy Studies as a Temporary Fad or Stale Material

The Long-Term Philosophical Concern for Policy Studies
One can define philosophy as the study of ultimate truth, beauty, and goodness. Truth generally refers to observable reality as manifested in natural and social science. Beauty refers to the subjectively, sensually desirable qualities of visual art,

---

* For further details concerning the nature of public policy studies, see Dror (1971), Lasswell (1971), Nagel (1980b, 1983, 1984a). For materials specifically dealing with conflicting evaluations of policy studies, see Nagel (1984a, 33–36).

music, literature, and nature. Goodness refers to what individuals, groups, and societies should do when interacting because it is somehow inherently right or because doing so leads to higher goals.

Philosophy has existed since human beings were intelligent enough to question what is truth, beauty, and goodness. At an early stage in that kind of thinking, humans were probably concerned with such truths as what would be the effect of adopting a rule concerning such matters as the division of labor within early human groups. Early examples of group policies might include a collective decision that men should hunt and fish, and women should take care of children. Adopting such a policy was based on the implicit perception that doing so would be more efficient in terms of group benefits minus costs. Such an implicit perception was not arrived at through statistical analysis, but through impressionistic experience. Nevertheless, it was a form of policy-relevant truth finding. It was also a form of ethics or social philosophy as to what ought to be, although not based on operations research, management science, or decision analysis.

Thus, human beings have been conducting policy analysis ever since they have existed. They have been recording policy analysis ever since there were written languages. One can find implicit policy analysis in the legal rules of the Babylonians, the ancient Hebrews, and the Egyptians, as well as in written and unwritten legal systems of ancient groups in Asia, Latin America, and Africa. Among the first philosophical books in ancient Greece, one can find a concern for political principles, such as how governments should be structured. Plato's *Republic* and Aristotle's *Ethics* represent a concern for evaluating public policy, even if they did not use the same kinds of analyses that are used by contemporary policy analysts.

The roots of public policy evaluation thus go back to prehistoric and ancient times. The more philosophical examples have survived partly because of their concern for a high level of generality. The examples that would qualify as current events analysis have generally been lost in antiquity, but are referred to by ancient historians. Policy evaluation in medieval times was not as lively as in ancient Greece or Rome. In the Middle Ages there was more of a tendency to accept governmental matters as given, not to be questioned. One is more likely to find vigorous policy analysis when there is encouragement of free thinking and constructive political opposition, scholarly inquiry as to the causes and effects of natural and social phenomena, and encouragement of new ways of improving the quality of life through collective action.

The Renaissance brought a flood of evaluative political thinking in the form of such political philosophers as Machiavelli, Hobbes, Locke, Montesquieu, Rousseau, and Hegel, who laid the philosophical foundations for the modern state. They were followed by utilitarians like Adam Smith, Jeremy Bentham, John Stuart Mill, and more recently, John Dewey, who explicitly talked in terms of adopting public policies that would maximize benefits minus costs.

As of the nineteenth century, policy evaluation became more class oriented. One set of policy evaluators was especially favorable toward policies oriented toward the working class and equalitarianism, such as Karl Marx, Leon Trotsky, Nikolai Lenin, Harold Laski, and contemporary ideologists for socialist political parties. A second set of policy evaluators was especially favorable toward policies oriented toward capitalism and elitist elements, such as Nietzsche, Pareto, Hitler, and contemporary ideologists for conservative political parties. One should, however, make a distinction between philosophies of democratic and dictatorial socialism and capitalism.

Also, political science began during the late nineteenth century. The origin was in universities where legal, philosophical, and societal scholars proceeded systematically to explain the causes and effects of variations in governmental structures and policies. As a division of labor developed among societal scholars, the economists emphasized such policy problems as unemployment, inflation, labor relations, and business organization. Sociologists emphasized policy problems such as crime, the family, suicide, alcoholism, racism, and social services. Political scientists emphasized policy problems dealing with international war, freedom of speech, safeguards for the innocent in criminal procedure, electoral procedures, public finance, government efficiency, and so on.

By the twentieth century, the American Political Science Association (APSA) had been formed. Its better-known presidents and activists include many political scientists deeply concerned with evaluating governmental institutions and policies, such as Woodrow Wilson, Charles Merriam, Harold Lasswell, William Willoughby, Arthur Bentley, Stephen Bailey, and V.O. Key. One might particularly mention Charles Merriam for his active role in seeking to offer systematic policy prescriptions for running the city of Chicago during the 1920s and the New Deal in the 1930s. On a more theoretical level, one might consider Harold Lasswell to be the founder of systematic policy science partly by virtue of his editing *The Policy Sciences* (1951). He is also considered by many to have been the most influential modern political scientist by virtue of his important role in developing behavioral research within political science, as well as the policy-science orientation.

Thus it is difficult to accuse policy studies of being only a temporary fad. On the contrary, it has been around since the dawn of humankind, and probably always will be. That does not mean that policy studies is guilty of being an unchanging, stale presence. The newness of policy studies is the subject to which we now turn as the other side of this dimension of conflicting evaluations.*

---

* For further details on the long-term philosophical concern for policy studies, see such classic histories of political thought as Sabine (1950) and Wanlass (1953). See also such histories of political science as Somit and Tanenhaus (1967) and Seidelman and Harpham (1985).

The Newness of Contemporary Policy Studies

Policy evaluation has increased substantially over the past ten years in social science programs and government agencies. Indicators of that growth include new organizations, schools, journals, curricula, government and academic job openings, books and book series, conferences, articles, scholarly papers, reports, courses, legislative provisions, and evaluative government agencies.

The general growth, which began about 1970, has been stimulated by three sets of factors. The pushing factors or social forces include the intense concern as of 1970 for policy problems related to civil rights, poverty, Vietnam, women's liberation, and environmental protection. In the 1980s, the issues shifted to an increased concern for inflation, unemployment, federal spending, Central America, the Middle East, and international trade, but still with considerable intensity. In order to be able to convert those pushing factors into meaningful policy analysis products, the social sciences developed better methods, interdisciplinary relations, data banks, and data processing equipment, all of which has occurred over the past twenty years. Policy analysis has also been stimulated by the increased attractiveness of government as a source of research funding and job opportunities, as well as the government's increased concern for getting more output from reduced tax dollars.

Policy analysis has four key elements, all of which have been undergoing change over the past ten years: (1) the goals with which policy analysis is concerned, (2) the means for achieving those goals, (3) the methods for determining the effects of alternative means on goal achievement, and (4) the policy analysis profession that is applying those methods in relating means to goals.

Newness that relates to goals or values. Policy analysts have traditionally taken policies as givens; they then attempt to determine their effects, especially their effects on the intended goals. There is, however, a trend toward taking goals as givens and then attempting to determine what policies will maximize or optimize them. The effects or impact approach is associated more often with the sociology and psychology, whereas the goals or optimizing approach is associated more often with economics and operations research. The crime-reduction field provides a good example of both approaches. Impact research on crime reduction includes studies of the effects of the use of halfway houses for released convicts, diversion from traditional criminal procedure in prosecuting arrested persons, and policewomen in making arrests. While those research projects may produce interesting and possible useful results, they tend to be rather piecemeal approaches to the problem of crime reduction. In contrast, if one begins with the goal of crime reduction, one may be stimulated to think of policies that might otherwise be missed, since they have not been adopted or tested for impact. General categories include decreasing the benefits of crime, increasing the costs of crime, decreasing the probability that the benefits will be obtained, and increasing the probability that the costs will be imposed. One could then proceed to more specific potential policies, although conservative think-ers are likely to emphasize policies different from those stressed by liberal thinkers. For example, when increasing the costs of crime, conservatives are likely to empha-size longer prison sentences, and liberals are likely to emphasize opportunity costs in the sense of losing opportunities to become a professional person, a corporate exec-utive, and so on if one is caught.

Policy analysts are becoming more sensitive to social values with more ques-tioning of goals when evaluating alternative policies. A number of research and training programs across the country now emphasize the analysis of goals, rather than, or in addition to, the achievement of goals, such as the programs at Notre Dame, Maryland, Georgetown, Duke, Delaware, and the Hastings Institute. Goals can be analyzed through survey research to determine to what extent they are sup-ported, relational analysis to determine how achieving them would affect higher values, or philosophical analysis to determine how they fit into more general philo-sophical systems. Political scientists are increasingly questioning the sufficiency of the traditional economic goals of the three *E*s of effectiveness, efficiency, and equity in policy analysis. Some political scientists advocate the need for more sensitivity to the three *P*s of public participation, predictability, and procedural fairness.

Newness that relates to means or policies for achieving goals. Policy evalua-tion is showing increasing sophistication in considering political and administrative feasibility. In the past, policy analysis has often resulted in recommendations that did not adequately consider the likelihood of the recommendations being adopted by political decision makers, or what might happen in implementing or administer-ing the policy recommendations. The concern for political and administrative feasibility reflects the increasing role of political science and public administration in policy analysis. In the early 1970s, policy analysts tended to recommend a system of pollution taxes to provide business firms with an incentive to reduce their pollution. Such a system is too politically infeasible in view of the business opposition it generates, as compared to a system of subsidies and regulation. In the early 1970s, policy analysts recommended homeownership programs for the poor. Those pro-grams were administratively infeasible in view of the abuses to which they were sub-jected by the real estate industry. An administratively feasible program would have involved government employees serving as brokers to the poor, as is done in the scandal-free Legal Services Program, as compared to the scandal-ridden Medicare/Medicaid program.

Policy evaluation is becoming increasingly interdisciplinary, drawing on a variety of disciplinary sources for ideas as to means or policies for achieving given goals. Relevant disciplines include economics, political science, sociology, and psy-chology among basic disciplines, and include business administration, planning, pub-lic administration, law, social work, and education among applied disciplines. A good example of the need for a more interdisciplinary perspective on policy problems might be the negative-income-tax experiment conducted around 1970 in New Jersey. The experiment was dominated by economists and psychologists concerned mainly with the relation between dollars given to welfare recipients and their ambition to get jobs. Within the allowable range of the alternative dollar amounts, very little difference in getting jobs was observed. If political scientists and public administrators had been involved in the experiment, they would have probably recommended determining the relation between alternative delivery systems and ambition. Perhaps recipients under either highly oppressive or permissive delivery systems would show substantially less ambition than those operating under a middling system.

Newness that relates to methods for testing relations. Policy evaluation has been building on business analysis, but it is developing its own methodology. Policy analysis builds on the basic business principle of maximizing income minus costs. There are, however, at least four areas in which policy analysts are increasingly recognizing the need for developing their own methods. The first area is measuring benefits, since they are so often nonmonetary and highly subjective in public-sector analysis. An example might be evaluating how well private law firms are doing, as contrasted to government-run legal services agencies. The second is taking equity matters into consideration. An example might be the need to provide minimum allocations to all states based on population in the law enforcement assistance program. Private business firms can allocate resources to sales forces across the states in terms of efficiency, without needing to include any state. The third is working with negative detriments such as crime, pollution, and disease. For example, it is quite difficult to analyze whether a city with 100 crimes and $50 in anticrime expenditures is more or less efficient than a city with 200 crimes and $25 in anticrime expenditures. There is no meaningful way to divide crimes by dollars to obtain the equivalent of a benefit/cost ratio. The fourth area deals with problems of administrative psychology, which are especially prevalent in the labor-intensive public sector. For example, one government agency may be inefficient but show big improvement, and a second agency may be efficient but show little improvement. If one allows economic analysis, one might allocate all of an incremental budget to the improving agency, since it has the higher slope or marginal rate of return, but that could be demoralizing to the efficient agency.

Policy evaluation is developing increased precision in its methods, but at the same time there is increasing recognition that simple methods may be all that is necessary for many policy problems. This is especially so since the typical policy problem asks which policy is best, not how much better it is than the second-best policy, and not how all the policies compare with one another on an interval scale or even a rank-order scale. One can often obtain many policy analysis insights simply by listing the feasible alternatives along the top of a sheet of paper and the generally agreed-upon goals along the side. One can then insert pluses and minuses along each row to indicate which policies do relatively well and not so well on each goal. From that matrix, one can often conclude which policy or combination of policies is best for achieving a given set of goals with or without different weights for the goals.

Policy evaluation is becoming increasingly proactive or preadoption, rather than reactive or postadoption. Too often, the effects of an adopted policy cannot be meaningfully determined because of the lack of availability of a meaningful control or experimental group, or the lack of availability of before-or-after data. Waiting for policies to be adopted before they are evaluated may also lead to harm being done before the unsatisfactory policies can be changed. It can also lead to inertia and vested interests that resist needed changes. As a result, there is an increasing trend toward using preadoption projections or deductive modeling, rather than just post-adoption before-and-after analysis. A good illustration of predictive modeling involves attempting to determine the effects on conviction rates of changing from twelve-person juries to six-person juries. Comparing across states is meaningless in view of how the states differ in terms of laws, procedures, and people. Comparing over time also does not work, since the cases brought to trial differ when a state switches from twelve-person juries to six-person juries. Showing a videotape of a typical criminal trial to a random set of twelve-person and six-person juries tends to result in 100 percent convictions with both sets of juries because a typical criminal case results in conviction. One can, however, deduce the effects of changing jury sizes from knowing how twelve-person juries and jurors behave. The U.S. Supreme Court used such a deductive modeling approach in the late 1970s but relied on more traditional, less meaningful social science research in the early 1970s.

Newness that relates to the public policy profession. There is substantial growth occurring in policy evaluation training programs, research institutes, funding sources, publishing outlets, scholarly associations, government agencies, and other public affairs institutions. In addition to such growth, there is a filtering and merging process whereby diverse kinds of institutions are coming together. In the realm of training, the policy analysis programs are showing more interest in public administration, and vice versa. Among research institutes, there is an increasing attempt on the part of university institutes to show more responsibility for meeting specifications. Nonuniversity institutes are also seeking to improve their creativity partly by drawing more on university people. Publishing outlets and associations are also merging and reorganizing, as are government agencies that deal with policy analysis.

Systematic policy evaluation is becoming increasingly used in government at the federal, state, and local levels and in the executive, legislative, and judicial branches. That utilization reflects an increased sensitivity among policy analysts to dealing with actual data, not just abstractions. At the same time, policy analysis is developing broad principles that cut across specific subject matters. The main way in which policy analysis ideas get used is through the training of people in government who come in contact with policy analysis methods in graduate and undergraduate courses. The simpler versions of such methods soon may even be taught in high school social science classes. Systematic policy evaluation is also more often referred to in congressional hearings, administrative agency reports, and Supreme Court opinions. Routine governmental decisions, however, are not so likely to be influenced directly by such methods. In addition to the use of policy analysis ideas, there is also a preference toward government applicants who have analytic skills along with substantive skills, and a trend toward providing analytic training in government programs.

Because of causal forces, policy evaluation is likely to continue to grow or at least to stabilize at a high level of academic and governmental activity. Those causal forces include public concern for public policy problems, improved ability of social science to deal with policy problems, and the relative attractiveness of government as a social science employer and research sponsor, including increased government concern for trying to stretch its scarce resources. In general, policy analysis research seems to be thriving as a subdiscipline of various social sciences, as a discipline in itself, and as an interdiscipline drawing on people, courses, and ideas from other disciplines. In view of its growth and vitality, this is indeed an exciting time to be in the field of policy analysis.*

Policy Studies as Too Practical or Too Theoretical

The Theoretical Nature of Policy Studies

Five meta-problems. On a high level of generality, there are at least five meta-problems that cut across all the methodological and substantive problems in policy studies. Those meta-problems include (1) Which decision makers will decide among the alternative ways of dealing with the substantive and methodological problems? (2) How will one obtain values to use as criteria and perceptions of relations between alternatives and criteria? (3) What goals are worth achieving and what is their relative importance? (4) What are the alternatives on a high level of generality? and (5) What is good policy analysis?

As for the nature of the relevant decision makers, the answer depends on the

---

* On the newness of policy studies, see Nagel (1984b). Also see books cited in note 1. For an emphasis on the newness of the methodology, see Nagel (1980a). For an emphasis on the newness of the substance, see Nagel (1975a).

subject matter. The Supreme Court is an authority, for example, on what goals are legitimate in satisfying the right-to-counsel clause of the Sixth Amendment to the Constitution. The Court has said that saving money is not an appropriate goal but that saving innocent persons from being convicted is. If, however, the issue is not whether right to counsel should be provided but how it should be provided, then saving money is an appropriate goal. For this issue, the goals of a county board would be relevant because it generally appropriates money to pay court-appointed lawyers to represent the poor. Such goals might include satisfying the local bar while minimizing expenditures. The board might therefore decide on a salaried public defender system, rather than on a less expensive but less politically feasible assigned-counsel system or a less legally feasible volunteer system. For other policy problems, the key authorities or decision makers might be legislative opinion, public opinion, the head of an administrative agency, or the like.

As for how one determines values and relations, the answer refers to four sources, which are not mutually exclusive: (1) authority, or consulting one or more persons, books, articles, or other sources considered reliable; (2) statistical or observable analysis, or analyzing specific instances in order to generalize about what the goals, policies, or relations might be; (3) deduction, or drawing a conclusion from premises established from authority, observation, and/or intuition; and (4) sensitivity analysis, or guessing the goals, policies, or relations and then determining what effect, if any, the guessed values have on the final decision regarding which policy is best.

As for what goals are worth achieving and their relative importance on a high level of generality, we are talking about effectiveness, efficiency, and equity. *Effectiveness* refers to the benefits achieved from alternative public policies. *Efficiency* refers to keeping costs down in achieving benefits, as measured by benefits minus costs or benefits divided by costs. *Equity* refers to providing a minimum level of benefits or a maximum level of costs across persons, groups, or places. Those are the three *Es* generally associated with economics. There are also the three *Ps* as high-level goals, generally associated with political science, including public participation, predictability, and procedural due process. *Public participation* refers to decision making by the target group, the general public, relevant interest groups, or other decision makers whose involvement appeals to our desires to use democratic procedures for achieving given goals. *Predictability* refers to decision making by way of following objective criteria in making decisions so that a similar decision would be arrived at by others following the same criteria. *Procedural due process,* or procedural fairness, means those who have been unfairly treated are entitled to have notice of what they have done wrong, the right to present evidence, the right to confront their accusers, a decision maker who is not also an accuser, and an opportunity for at least one appeal.

As for the policy alternatives on a high level of generality, they especially relate to using positive and negative incentives, decreasing discretionary abuses while preserving flexibility, balancing public- and private-sector implementation, and structuring government for greater goal achievement. *Incentives* refer to increasing the benefits of doing right, decreasing the costs of doing right, decreasing the benefits of doing wrong, increasing the costs of doing wrong, increasing the probability of the benefits and costs occurring, and decreasing situations where one has to decide between doing right or doing wrong. *Discretionary abuses* can be decreased by lessening discretion, by channeling discretion through incentives, and by controlling it through checks and balances. *Economic structure issues* relate to socialism versus capitalism, with the traditional emphasis of socialism on government ownership and equal income and the more contemporary emphasis of socialism on worker-consumer control and equal opportunity. Government structural issues relate to central systems, especially government-electorate relations regarding universal adult voting rights and rights of those holding minority viewpoints to try to convert the majority.

As for what constitutes good policy analysis, the key criteria relate to validity, importance, usefulness, originality, and feasibility.

Elements of good policy analysis. Validity, in general, refers to being accurate. In the context of policy evaluation, validity refers to the internal consistency of logically drawing a conclusion that follows from the goals, policies, and relations; the external consistency with empirical reality in describing the relations between the alternative policies and the goals; the policies being considered encompass the total set of feasible alternatives (feasibility in this context refers to being capable of being adopted and implemented by the relevant policy makers and policy appliers); and the listed goals include all the major goals and only the goals of the relevant policy makers in this context.

The concept of *importance* can be defined in two ways. First, does the research deal with issues on which there are big societal benefits and/or big societal costs being analyzed? For example, research on avoiding nuclear war is more important than research on whether the city of Champaign should have a strong mayor form of government or a city manager. Second, does the research deal with a subject matter or a set of causal hypotheses that potentially have broad explanatory power? This is theoretical importance, as contrasted to policy importance.

Usefulness at its lowest level involves doing policy research that is not referred to by the people who make policy in the subject-matter area. At the next level is research referred to by policy makers orally or in a citation, even if the research cited is not on the winning side. At a higher level is research that reinforces preconceived decisions. Policy researchers should be pleased if their research accelerates a worthwhile decision that otherwise might be delayed. At the highest level is the rare case of policy research that converts decision makers from being negative to being sensitive, or vice versa, on an issue.

Originality refers to the extent to which policy research differs from previous research, although even highly original research builds and synthesizes prior research. *Feasibility* is an additional criterion for judging proposed policy research, as contrasted to completed policy research. Feasibility is concerned with how easily research can be implemented given the limited time, expertise, interest, funds, and other resources of the researcher.*

The Practical Nature of Policy Studies

The most practical activity that policy studies can probably engage in is the improvement of societal productivity. Productivity improvement at the societal level can be defined as increasing societal benefits minus societal costs. In that context, policy studies refers to a set of skills associated with deciding which of various alternative public policies will maximize or increase benefits minus costs in achieving a given set of goals. Policy evaluation is especially capable of furthering productivity improvement by emphasizing management science methods as applied on a societal or public policy level. Those methods tend to fall into five basic categories covering benefit-cost analysis, decision theory, optimum-level analysis, allocation theory, and time-optimization models.

Benefit-cost analysis (optimum choice among discrete alternatives without probabilities). Discrete alternatives in this context mean alternatives where each one is a lump-sum project. A government agency can meaningfully adopt only one unit of such a project, not multiple units and no factions of units. Under those circumstances, an agency that is interested in maximizing the good it does should spend its whole budget, or as much as possible, as long as diminishing absolute returns do not set in. It should spend its budget for each of its alternative projects in the order of their benefit/cost ratios. This situation can be illustrated in choosing the optimum combination of a set of dam-building projects.

Decision theory (optimum choice with contingent probabilities). Contingent probabilities in this context means probabilities that events will occur that influence the benefits and/or costs that alternative projects or decisions produce. Under those circumstances, if the probability of the contingent event occurring is greater than the benefit/cost ratio or greater than the ratio of the Type 1 error costs to the sum of the error costs, then the project ought to be adopted; otherwise, it ought to be rejected.

---

* On the theoretical aspects of policy studies, see Frohock (1979), Goodin (1982), Diesing (1982), Gregg (1976), and Nagel (1984c).

This situation can be illustrated by the problem of deciding whether or not to gather expensive data, and the problem of how to classify persons for special treatment.

Optimum-level analysis (finding an optimum policy where doing too much or too little is undesirable). These situations involve policies that produce benefits at first, but then the benefits reach a peak continuum where the benefits are maximized. These situations may also involve policies that reduce the costs at first, but then the costs reach a bottom and start to rise. The object, then, is to find the point on a policy continuum where the costs are minimized. That situation can be illustrated by the problem of deciding the optimum percentage of defendants to hold in jail prior to trial, the optimum level of pollution, or the optimum speed limit on interstate highways.

Allocation theory (optimum-mix analysis). The object is generally to allocate one's scarce resources across activities or places in such a way as to use all the available budget while equalizing the marginal rates of return of the activities or places so that nothing is to be gained by switching from one activity or place to another. That kind of allocation recognizes that a good activity or place should not be given too much. After a while, the diminishing marginal rate of return becomes smaller than what can be gained by shifting a dollar or unit of effort to another normally less productive activity or places. This situation can be illustrated by allocating the resources of the Legal Services Corporation between routine case handling and law reform activities, or allocating the resources of the Law Enforcement Assistance Administration across a set of cities.

Time-optimization models (decision-making systems designed to minimize time consumption). Time-optimization models often involve variations on optimum choice, risk, level, or mix analysis but apply to situations in which the goal is to minimize time. Some time-optimization models are peculiar to a temporal subject matter such as queuing theory for predicting and reducing waiting time and backlogs from information concerning arrival and service rates, optimum sequencing for determining the order in which matters should be processed so as to minimize the average waiting time, and critical path analysis for determining what paths from start to finish are especially worth concentrating on with regard to delay reduction efforts.

In general, policy evaluation based on management science methods seems capable of improving decision-making processes. Decisions are then more likely to be arrived at that will maximize or at least increase societal benefits minus costs. Those decision-making methods may be even more important than worker motivation or technological innovation in productivity improvement. Hard work means little if the wrong products are being produced in terms of societal benefits and costs. Similarly, the right policies are needed to maximize technological innovation, which is not so likely to occur without an appropriate public policy environment. *

Policy Studies as Too Multidisciplinary or Too Narrowly Focused on Political Science

The Important Political Science Component in Policy Studies

One can show the relevance of all fields of political science to all public policy problems. As a concrete example, we can use public policy toward the elderly. Political science can be defined as the study of the structures, processes, and policies of the entities people establish in order to make collective decisions for a society or a community as a whole. Government structures refer to the entities that establish or apply rules of legislatures, public administrators, and courts. All three branches of government, however, tend to engage in all three kinds of activities. The processes are the activities themselves, and the policies are the rules or decisions that result from the activities.

The fields of political science can be organized in terms of governmental institutions, levels of government, and general matters. Fields emphasizing certain governmental institutions include public law (courts), public administration (executive agencies), the legislative process (legislatures), and political dynamics (voters, interest groups, and parties). Fields emphasizing levels of government include state and local governments, American national government, comparative government, and international relations. The more general fields include political theory and political science methodology.

Governmental and political institutions. The public law field within political science includes civil liberties and the judicial process. Civil liberties refer to First Amendment freedoms, safeguards for the innocent in legal proceedings, and equal protection under the law. All three subfields affect the elderly and aging policy. Freedom of speech is especially important because without freedom to communicate that the rights of elderly people are being violated, then those rights become substantially less meaningful. Freedom of speech guarantees that the elderly can petition the government for a redress of grievances, can assemble to hear people with relevant ideas, and can communicate via print and electronic media. Even those constitutional rights are not very meaningful unless they are exercised. How they are exercised by the elderly is part of the political science field of political dynamics.

---

* On the practical nature of policy studies, see Frohock (1979), Goodin (1982), Diesing (1982), Gregg (1976), and Nagel (1984c).

Safeguards for the innocent include elementary due process regarding a denial of Social Security benefits or other governmental benefits that are important to the elderly. Elementary due process includes the right to know the charges, to present one's own witness, to cross-examine opposition witnesses, to have a neutral decision maker who is not responsible for bringing the complaint, and the right to bring an attorney, although not necessarily to have the government provide one. Equal protection means that the government cannot arbitrarily categorize people for the purpose of receiving benefits that are important to the elderly. For example, it would be unconstitutional to categorize people by race for the purpose of providing public housing for the elderly. It is also unconstitutional to provide more Social Security benefits to females than males on the grounds that males can more easily find jobs. It is, however, not unconstitutional to provide higher benefits to the elderly than to mothers of dependent children on the theory that those mothers can more easily find jobs than the elderly can.

Political scientists who study the judicial process, like political scientists in general, are sometimes concerned with the role of older people in the political process, rather than the impact of the process on older people. Studies of how older judges or jurors differ from younger judges or jurors would be included in this contest. The consensus is that older decision makers are more conservative, but not because they have grown more conservative with time. On the contrary, older judges and older people in general are usually more liberal after age seventy than the same people were before age thirty because they have become more liberal as society becomes more liberal on issues that relate to equalitarianism and the more positive role of the government in the economy. Older judges are more conservative than younger judges because the older judges were socialized at an earlier period in time when nondiscrimination and governmental planning were not well-accepted ideas. A related policy issue has been the matter of compulsory retirement of judges after a certain age. That issue was particularly controversial during the 1930s on the Supreme Court, although it was raised in terms of adding additional judges for every judge who continued to serve beyond age seventy.

The public administration field within political science very much affects the elderly by virtue of the increased contact that elderly people have with government bureaucrats. The principles developed in public administration for efficiently administering government programs apply to such programs for the elderly as Social Security, Medicare, and other social services. Public administration tends to emphasize government activities that relate to structural organization, general management, financing, personnel, public relations, and administrative control. Structural organization includes the study of the effects of having a separate Department of Health and Human Services, which is the most important federal department concerned with the problems of the elderly. It includes the Administration on Aging, which administers a variety of service programs, the Social Security Administration, which administers the old-age and survivors insurance program, and the Health Care Financing Administration, which administers the Medicare program for providing health benefits to the elderly. Establishing specialized agencies for dealing with the special problems of the elderly is likely to result in those problems receiving more consideration. In the context of the elderly, general management refers to operating a government agency so as to get the most output for the least money. Personnel management affects the elderly by determining the quality of the people who administer the programs, but it can do so more directly by way of affirmative action programs to hire the elderly and retirement incentives/requirements for retiring them from public employment. Government bureaucrats are becoming increasingly sensitive to public relations with the elderly as they become better organized. Administrative control refers partly to judicial and legislative review, which are subjects covered in other political science fields.

The legislative process field of political science is particularly concerned with the workings of legislative committees, since they tend to be responsible for most of the decisions reached in legislative bodies. Within both the U.S. Senate and the House of Representatives, there are committees on aging. On all legislative committees, elderly legislators tend to be especially important because the seniority system is the prevailing method for choosing committee chairpersons. Thus the values of the elderly may receive an extra boost in the legislative process. Legislators are particularly sensitive to getting reelected, which means a concern for groups that are large in number and likely to vote. The elderly are a large group, and growing larger as longevity increases. They are also more likely to vote than any other age group, especially relatively new voters. That may give the elderly an advantage out of proportion to their numbers. They also think more in terms of a feeling of common interest, which younger voters do not do, given their greater diversity of interests.

The legislative process field is closely related to the political dynamics field, which emphasizes political parties, interest groups, public opinion, and voting behavior. The voting behavior of the elderly and their opinions on international relations and moral or civil liberties issues tend to be more conservative than younger voters'. On economic issues, however, the elderly tend to favor some tax-supported public services and government regulation of the economy to fight inflation and unemployment. Their mild economic liberalism stems from their own often precarious economic status; they do not consider themselves as likely to become rich as do younger but equally poor voters. The pocketbook liberalism of the elderly especially extends to Social Security benefits, as contrasted to Federal Aid to Education or Aid to Families with Dependent Children (AFDC). The social conservatism and limited economic liberalism of the elderly tend to align them with the Republican party. That alignment, however, depends partly on the age cohort they are in. For example, elderly people who came of voting age during the Great Depression years are more likely to be Democrats than elderly people who came of voting age during the prosperous 1920s. One of the best-known contemporary interest or organized pressure groups representing the elderly is the Gray Panthers, which was founded in the early 1970s by Maggie Kuhn as an aggressive organization designed to rock boats, not chairs, on behalf of the elderly. Its activities include picketing in the style of a civil rights group of the 1960s as well as more conventional letter writing and visits to congressmen. The Gray Panthers seem to have some lasting significance given their broad interests and their many younger members, unlike transitory pro-elderly pressure groups such as the Townsend movement of the 1930s.

Levels of government. The state and local government field of political science is primarily concerned with policy problems that relate to housing, transportation, poverty, crime, education, and environmental protection. Most of those fields have an important counterpart that relates to the elderly. In the matter of housing, there are now special housing projects for the elderly. That is not considered illegal segregation, since the elderly have legitimate interests in common that make it meaningful to provide them with special physical, recreational, and other facilities. Governmental housing for the elderly, though, cannot be legally segregated by race. In the matter of transportation, city governments commonly provide special rates to the elderly to ride on municipally owned transportation. On poverty, state/local governments tend to deal with the aged poor through the public aid system, which provides aid to the aged. The system, however, provides more dignity to aged recipients than the AFDC program does, since caseworkers are voluntary, not compulsory. What may be needed is a more vigorous attempt to provide job opportunities for the elderly. That would require federal help, especially in the form of making the economy more prosperous, which is beyond the control of state and local governments. In the matter of crime, the elderly present special problems, given their vulnerability to being robbery victims. They tend to avoid situations, though, where they are subject to being robbed. As a result they have relatively low robbery victimization rates, but they and society have high anxieties about their being victimized.

The field of American national government tends to be particularly concerned with federalism, separation of powers, judicial review, the two-party system, and universal adult suffrage combined with relative freedom for unpopular viewpoints to be heard. The last point is more a matter of political dynamics and civil liberties. Each of the other four points also influences aging policy in America. Federalism tends to decentralize American domestic policy. As a result, governmental services received by the elderly tend to come from state/local governments and are unequal across states and cities. Funding tends to come from the federal government, but with minimum strings attached. Those service programs will be even more decentralized and probably more unequal as a result of the state block-grant programs toward which the Reagan administration moved. American separation of powers between the President and Congress manifests itself in an uncoordinated program for dealing with the elderly. President Reagan indicated a desire to raise the Social Security retirement age and eliminate the minimum Social Security payment. Those suggestions were opposed by the Democratic-controlled House of Representatives and to a considerable extent by the Republican-controlled Senate. As a result, solutions to the crisis in funding Social Security have been as deadlocked as solutions have been to the energy crisis.

Judicial review has not held back the Social Security system as it did other economic reforms. The United States was about the last industrialized country to adopt a social security insurance system because Congress had not provided for one. When Congress did so in 1938, the Supreme Court upheld the legislation, although in a divided decision. A few years before, the Supreme Court might have declared the legislation unconstitutional as an undue interference in Tenth Amendment states' rights and lacking constitutional authorization. The two-party system was relevant to the timing of the Social Security system—Republicans opposed the system when they were in power in the 1920s, and Democrats favored the system when they came to power in the 1930s. The system acquired Republican respectability when Eisenhower expanded the system in 1952, rather than contract it, as had been threatened. Now both parties tend to compete with one another as to who can run the system more efficiently.

Political scientists concerned with comparative government frequently used social insurance as an example for cross-national analysis. That is so in the standard comparative public policy textbooks authored by Heidenheimer, Heclo, and Adams (1983), Siegel and Weinberg (1977), and Groth (1971). A good example of such a political science treatment is Howard Leichter (1979). He analyzes Germany as a pioneer in national health care, Great Britain as an example of health care in a modern welfare state, the Soviet Union as illustrating health care in a communist state, and Japan as an example of health care in an Asian nation. Since the elderly disproportionately need health care, that analysis is especially relevant to cross-national aging policy. As with most comparative government studies, the emphasis is on industrialized countries in Europe, with a key purpose being to explain why the United States is different and to suggest procedures from which the United States might benefit. Many of the differences are attributed to the private-sector emphasis in America, which is likely to cause private insurance carriers to play a more prominent role in social insurance programs that are established than they would in other countries. One can, however, obtain even better predictability with regard to aging policy from knowing that a country is an affluent industrial country than from knowing that it is a socialist or capitalist country. Thus, both the Soviet Union and the United States provide more economic benefits to the aged than developing countries do, regardless of whether they are socialist or capitalist.

The international relations field in political science may not be as relevant to aging policy or the politics of the elderly as are other fields of political science. Nevertheless, important concerns for the well-being of the elderly are expressed in some of the specialized agencies of the United Nations. The International Labor Organization is concerned with the problem of labor retirement and providing adequately for it, although it is more concerned with the problems of unionization and working conditions. The World Health Organization is concerned with the health problems of the elderly, although it is more concerned with using its scarce resources to innoculate younger people against diseases. Political scientists who study foreign policy making sometimes express opinions on the influence of having elderly foreign policy makers. Their opinions are sometimes conflicting and not subjected to any systematic qualitative analysis. For example, elderly chief executives may be especially cautious and less adventuresome, and therefore easier to deal with in foreign affairs. On the other hand, perhaps elderly chief executives are less sensitive to the loss of youthful lives and thus more difficult to deal with in foreign affairs. The truth of the matter may be that being elderly in this context is almost totally irrelevant. The stubbornness of a chief executive is a function of his or her long-term personality, which is heavily influenced by environmental conditions, not age.

General fields of political science. Political philosophy generally deals with what causes broad political phenomena and what constitutes good government. In the realm of aging policy, the causal analysis tends to be better handled by comparative government. There are, however, important controversial issues in aging policy with which normative political philosophy might be and is concerned. A key issue is how societal resources should be allocated between the old and the young. That issue can be raised in the policy context of how much burden should be placed on the young to support pension programs for the elderly, as contrasted to encouraging the elderly to work more and/or live on less. The allocation issue is more dramatically illustrated in discussing the ethical values involved in deciding whether terminally ill old people should receive life-prolonging health care. That becomes a governmental problem when the government is providing most of the health-care financing in a society. Political philosophy also concerns itself with problems of intergenerational equity in which the government reaches decisions to conserve natural resources for the next generation or to consume them now. Those who advocate consuming now may be disproportionately elderly, who may have less concern for the earthly future. Thus, intergenerational equity problems may be partly elderly versus young problems. Classical political philosophers have seldom said anything explicitly with regard to allocating values between the elderly and the young. However, many of them, including Aristotle, Aquinas, Locke, Bentham, and Marx, have discussed general matters of allocation equity that would be applicable.

Political science methodology can be classified in various ways. One classification particularly relevant to policy analysis is in terms of methods involved in establishing causal relations and methods involved in choosing among alternative policies. Causal or relational methods tend to be cross-sectional (i.e., across persons, places, or things) or over time (i.e., where the units of analysis are time points for a given person, place, or thing). Until recently, political science emphasized cross-sectional analysis. That approach may be particularly inapplicable in analyzing the political effects of aging. For example, if we compare older bureaucrats with younger bureaucrats, then we are likely to find the older bureaucrats are more conservative on due process. If, however, we can obtain decisional data for those older bureaucrats over the past thirty years, we would probably find that they have become more liberal over time, but not as liberal as younger bureaucrats. It is interesting to note that if one desires to reduce such conservatism, one might advocate compulsory retirement at a relatively early age, regardless of whether the cause of increased conservatism among older decision makers is the aging process or the time period when one acquires one's basic values.

As for evaluation or optimizing methods, they can also be classified in various ways. One classification is in terms of methods that involve choosing among policies that have no inherent order and methods that involve policies that can be inherently arranged along a continuum. An example of the first type of problem is choosing among Medicare, socialized medicine, and charity clinics for providing medical services to indigent elderly. Those three policies have no inherent order. Choosing among them might involve estimating the benefits from each program in terms of patients serviced and the total cost for each program to the government or society. The best program might be the one that scores the highest on benefits minus costs, after one gives a monetary value to patients serviced. No program, though, could qualify as *best* unless it meets a minimum constraint on patients' services and stays within a maximum constraint on total costs. An example of the second type of problem is trying to decide the optimum retirement age for a set of government employees. Age categories have inherent order and can be arranged along a continuum from low to high. The higher the retirement age is, the greater the lost productivity for those employees. That upwardly sloping curve can probably be determined by correlating age with worker performance. The lower the retirement age is, however, the greater the total pension costs that the government will have to pay. Those costs can be determined by accounting calculations. The optimum retirement age is the age where the sum of the monetarist lost-productivity costs plus the pension costs are minimized. In other words, the optimum age is where the total curve bottoms out. One should, however, note that such an economic optimum may not be politically, legally, or administratively feasible if Congress cannot adopt that compulsory retirement age because of political pressures from civil servants, if the Supreme Court says the cutoff age as applied to that group is an arbitrary classification of people, or if the agency finds it administratively demoralizing to retire people at so early an age or to require them to continue working until so late an age. On matters of political, legal, and administrative feasibility, political scientists generally tend to be more competent than on the application of economics-related methods.

From this analysis, one can readily conclude that all fields of political science are relevant to understanding public policy toward the elderly. Some of the underlying themes that especially distinguish a political science orientation from those of other social sciences and the natural sciences include a concern for political feasibility, which involves making policy recommendations that are likely to be adopted or at least evaluating what the adoption likelihood is; administrative feasibility, with regard to policies being able to be administered without scandal or chaos; goal values such as public participation, predictability, and procedural due process, which economists and other policy analysts sometimes slight; and a concern for the relevance to policy problems on international relations, civil liberties, and reform of governmental institutions.*

Inherently Multidisciplinary Nature of Policy Studies

Policy studies or policy analysis can be broadly defined as the study of the nature, causes, and effects of alternative public policies. All fields of scientific knowledge, but especially the social sciences, are relevant to such a study.

Sociology, for example, has developed a substantial amount of factual knowledge and theory in broad fields such as social control, socialization, and social change that can be helpful in understanding the effects of alternative policies and the behavior of policy makers and appliers. Sociology is also especially concerned with why certain societal practices are considered social problems and how society seeks to cope with them. In addition, sociology has also attempted to cover (more so than other social sciences) the specific policy problems of race relations, family problems, and criminology.

Of all the social sciences, the field of economics has clearly developed the most sophisticated mathematical models for synthesizing normative and empirical premises in order to deduce means-ends policy recommendations. These mathematical models relate to the optimum allocation of scarce resources, the optimum level at which to pursue a given policy where doing too much or too little is undesirable, and the optimum strategy to follow when the net benefits are dependent on the occurrence of a contingent event. Economic reasoning, which assumes people attempt to maximize their perceived benefits minus costs, can often lead to deductive models that enable one to predict the effects of some policies before they are adopted. The work of institutional economists has been especially relevant to providing discussions of the role of economic class structures, ownership systems, and technology in determining policy choices. Economists have also concerned themselves, more so

---

* On the political science component in policy studies, see Spadaro, Dye, Golembiewski, Stedman, and Zeigler (1975), Ranney (1968), and Sharkansky (1970).

than other social scientists, with the specific policy problems of union-management relations, consumer problems, unemployment, and inflation.

Psychology is the social science that has probably done more to develop techniques of statistical inference, cross-tabulation, survey research, and multivariate analysis, especially with regard to imprecise variables. Unlike econometricians, psychologists do not deal with monetarily measurable variables. In recent years, psychologists have been particularly active in applying variations on their experimental methodologies to evaluating the effects of alternative public policies. They have thereby given birth to the field of evaluation research and the methodology of quasi experimentation. That methodology compares places having one policy with places having another policy where policy adoption is not randomized. Psychology also provides an important focus on the dynamics of individual or small-group behavior (as contrasted to sociological institutions), especially with regard to attitudes, perceptions, and motivations. Psychology also has special relevance to social problems dealing with alcoholism, suicide, drug addiction, and related mental health problems.

Anthropology, geography, and history provide a broader perspective over space and time than the other social sciences. That kind of cross-cultural and historical perspective can help to make policy analysis less culture bound and less time bound. The theoretical and practical findings of policy studies thereby become more broadly meaningful when dealing with the causes and effects of alternative public policies. Anthropology also has a special relevance to policy problems that affect present or former preliterate people. Geographers are becoming increasingly concerned with the optimum location of various facilities or districts. Historians, by extrapolating trends or analogizing to the past, can add a futuristic element to policy studies.

Without philosophy, especially normative social philosophy, policy studies might tend to lack direction with regard to what they are seeking to achieve. One of the major criticisms of quantitative policy analysis is that it is too capable of being used to maximize socially undesirable, as well as socially desirable goals. Philosophy, in spite of its contemporary positivistic emphasis, is still the leading discipline for discussing what is socially desirable on a high level of abstraction. Philosophy also provides a high level of abstraction with regard to discussing ultimate causes as to why societies make certain basic policy choices. In addition to its normative and causal components, philosophy provides the most developed principles of logical and semantic analysis on which the more narrow social sciences can build.

Without quantitative and computer science tools that are ultimately associated with mathematics, policy studies might tend to overemphasize evaluative gut reactions, armchair speculation, and isolated historical anecdotes. Mathematics provides the basis for both an empirical statistical approach to policy studies and a deductive, syllogistic approach. Through the mathematics of algebra and calculus, syllogistic premises can have greater precision than is provided by the dichotomous reasoning normally associated with symbolic logic. Physical and biological sciences provide models to emulate in the development of mathematically scientific laws, provided one always considers the differences in the behavioral instability of people as compared to physical or biological objects. Natural science is also substantively relevant to specific policy problems such as environmental protection, energy development, and population control.

The field of law has important social science elements when it involves studying why the law is what it is or the effects of alternative laws, as contrasted to studying what the law is and how to use it as a lawyer. As a social science, the legal field is close to the heart of policy studies because virtually all policy problems are capable of at least attempted resolution by legislatures, courts, or lawmaking administrative agencies. Legal literature can be helpful in generating policy hypotheses, providing large quantities of data, especially with regard to policy decisions, and providing a better understanding of the societal rules that relate to the problems of such institutions as the family, the economy, and the criminal justice system.

Since policy studies particularly refers to the study of the causes and effects of governmental policy, one would expect political science to be especially relevant, even though political scientists may be dependent on other social sciences for some methodological tools and substantive knowledge. Political scientists have traditionally devoted much of their intellectual resources to analyzing how governmental policy gets made and administered, with special emphasis on the role of interest groups and, more recently, individual decision makers. Political scientists are now turning more toward the analysis of specific policy-problem areas (like welfare and taxation) rather than more abstract studies of the policy-making process. Along with this concern for specific policy problems, political scientists have shown increasing concern for the impact of various policies, such as those in the civil liberties field. The subject matter of political science has made the discipline especially relevant to policy problems related to the reform of elections, legislatures, courts, administrative agencies, reform of other governmental institutions, and problems of international relations and foreign policy.

From this collection of social sciences, one can readily perceive that the study of governmental policy problems is clearly an interdisciplinary activity, since many disciplines have something to contribute. For any social scientist, it would be too much to acquire expertise in all the perspectives relevant to public policy study. Indeed, it would simply be unrealistic to expect every policy analyst to become an expert in all the subfields within his or her own social science or discipline. Nevertheless, there probably is a consensus that if one is interested in developing competence in policy studies work, he or she should be familiar in a general way with the potential contributions and drawbacks of various social sciences. Such familiarity will at least enable one to know when to call on a fellow social scientist or a treatise in another social science, the way a lay person has a general idea of the meaning of what the doctor or lawyer says.

Many examples could be given of policy analysis projects that could have substantially benefited from using social and other scientists from a greater variety of disciplines. For example, the economists who conducted the negative-income-tax experiments (which emphasized the relation between dollars granted and ambition to work) might have benefited from political science input. Such input could have caused the experimenters to broaden the scope of the experiments to include an analysis of the effects on ambition of alternative delivery systems, such as having or not having a compulsory caseworker. Similarly, economists who advocate a pollution tax to protect the environment often fail to consider the great difficulties involved in passing such legislation over the opposition of affected business groups. In studying the effects of switching from twelve-person juries to six-person juries, one might gain insights from knowing the social psychology of group decision making, the mathematics of probability, and the legal requirements for convictions. What may be needed are more interdisciplinary research teams and more interaction among policy-oriented people from different disciplines in interdisciplinary conferences, symposia, associations, journals, teaching programs, and other activities.*

Policy Studies as Too Quantitative or Too Subjective

The Inherent Subjectivity of Policy Studies
One particularly interesting set of issues worth discussing with the problems of optimizing in public policy analysis relates to the role of values in policy analysis. The most basic issue is being value free in conducting research. By definition, policy analysis at least partly involves seeking to achieve or maximize given values or social goals rather than ignore them. Policy analysts, like other researchers, should, however, be value free in the sense of not allowing their values to influence how they record or present information. In fact, the concern for objectivity and replicability in policy analysis research should probably manifest itself in taking extra precautions to keep the bias of researchers from influencing their results. This is so because stronger feelings generally exist about policy problems, as contrasted to research problems that lack policy implications. These precautions can include drawing on multiple sources and individuals for cross-checking information, making available raw data sets for secondary analysis, and making assumptions more explicit.

---

* On the multidisciplinary component in policy studies, see McCall and Weber (1984), MacRae and Wilde (1976), and Nagel (1975b).

Many policy analysis problems involve taking goals as givens and determining what policies will maximize those goals. The goals, however, may be only intermediate values directed toward achieving other, more general values. For example, a policy analysis problem might involve determining how to reduce the pretrial jail population (Y). Proposals might relate to methods for increasing pretrial release (X_1) and reducing delay from arrest to disposition (X_2). There might, however, be some policy makers who think the pretrial jail population should be increased (rather than reduced) as a means for punishing arrested defendants who might otherwise escape punishment through plea bargaining or lack of admissible evidence. A second-stage policy analysis could deal with the effect of the pretrial jail experience on reducing crime rates (Z), which can be taken as a higher-level goal. To make policy analysis more manageable between X and Y, one may merely refer to the possibility of doing further research on the relation between Y and Z without actually undertaking it.

Like any research tool (including a calculator or a typewriter), policy analysis can be used for good or evil purposes. A computerized analysis of the effects of alternative legislature redistricting patterns, for example, can be used to facilitate a kind of proportional representation whereby the percentage of districts dominated by Democrats roughly approximates the percentage of Democrats in the state. On the other hand, the same redistricting programs can be used to minimize black representation in a state legislature. Quantitative policy analysis, however, is less likely to be used for purposes that are unconstitutional or for which there is a negative consensus because policy analysis tends to make more explicit the values, assumptions, input data, and other parameters used in arriving at the decisions than does the more traditional decision making. In the computer redistricting example, one can check the programs and the input data to see what was the basis for the redistricting outputs.

Sometimes people involved in policy analysis may be asked to maximize what they consider to be socially undesirable goals. This brings out the need for professional ethics. Policy analysts need to choose carefully for whom they work, to try to improve the caliber of those people if they can, to call illegal matters to the attention of appropriate authorities, and to look elsewhere if they are dissatisfied with the goals of their government agency or employer. Normally, in a democratic society, elected officials and their political appointees try to achieve goals that will make them popular and will be in conformity with the law. Therefore, a policy analyst's desire to work legally and in the public interest is not so likely to conflict with his or her employer.

Value decisions are particularly relevant to policy analysis in the sense that optimizing solutions are much influenced by the values plugged into the analysis. In the redistricting example, the optimum plan is likely to depend on whether the goal is merely to provide an equal population across the districts or as well to provide such things as proportionality of party representation and competitiveness within districts. Similarly, what constitutes an optimum jury size depends partly on how many guilty people we are willing to acquit in order to save one innocent person from conviction. A tradeoff higher than ten to one may be irrelevant if the maximum reasonable jury size is twelve persons. As another example, the optimum mix of funds in the Legal Services Corporation between law reform and routine case handling may depend on who is evaluating the legal services agencies that constitute the data on which the analysis is based. Lawyer evaluators may tend to give higher ratings to agencies involved in more difficult appellate court precedent-setting cases, but representatives of the poor may give higher ratings to agencies involved in easier but more immediate family, housing, and consumer negotiations. Policy analysts should be particularly concerned with presenting sensitivity analyses in their projects whereby they demonstrate how the optimum would vary when one makes changes in the values being maximized.*

The Potential Objectivity of Policy Studies

In order for policy evaluation to be reasonably objective, it is necessary to have a set of widely accepted procedures for dealing with frequently occurring analytic problems. Perhaps the most frequently occurring problems in policy evaluation are how to deal with multiple goals measured on multiple dimensions, information that is missing or imprecise, multiple alternatives that are too many to determine the effects of all of them, multiple and possibly conflicting constraints, and the need for simplicity in spite of all that multiplicity.

To facilitate dealing with the problem of multiple goals, one can determine their relative importance by noting which goal is the least important and then note how many more times as important each other goal is as compared to the base goal. Those relative weights can then be multiplied by the raw scores of each policy on each goal. A more comfortable alternative involves first converting the raw scores into part/whole percentages by dividing each raw score by the sum of the raw scores on each goal. That creates a set of dimensionless numbers for dealing better with the problem of adding apples and oranges.

To facilitate dealing with the problem of multiple missing information, select software that can compute what-if analysis. Goals and alternatives can then be changed so that one can quickly see the effects of the changes on the bottom line of what alternative to adopt. If the weight of a goal or the score of a policy/goal relation is unknown, choose software that can process threshold analysis, whereby the threshold value of the weight of each goal or relation score is determined. The bottom-line conclusion of what alternative to adopt depends on whether one is

---

* On the role of values in policy studies, see Dunn (1983), Fischer (1980), Regan and Van DeVeer (1982), and Fleishman and Payne (1980).

above or below a threshold value on a weight or relation. It is easier to determine whether one is above or below a threshold value than it is to determine the exact value of a weight or relation. If multiple weights or relations are unknown, adopt software that can conduct indifference-curve analysis. The computer screen then shows a curve or set of curves above which one alternative is better and below which another alternative is better. It is easier to determine whether a combination of unknowns is above or below such a curve than it is to determine the exact values of the weights and relations.

One may need to deal with the problem of deciding among an infinite number of alternatives on a continuum. To do so, divide the continuum into intervals or categories, with the end intervals being under and over a certain number if necessary. One may need to deal with the problem of deciding among an infinite number of alternative ways of allocating scarce resources to various objects. To do so, give relative scores to the allocation objects and then use those relative scores as allocation percentages.

To facilitate dealing with minimum or maximum constraints on the alternatives or goals, follow the above principles for optimizing without considering the constraints. Then observe whether any of the constraints are unsatisfied and make adjustments to satisfy them. If some of the constraints are conflicting, then prioritize them so as to satisfy the more important ones fully or partially.

To facilitate simplicity in drawing and presenting conclusions, use a policies/ goals (PG) table. The policy alternatives are shown on the rows, and the goals/ criteria are shown on the columns. Go down one goal-column at a time to relate each of the policies to each goal. Use words or symbols rather than numbers if necessary to express the relation. Then later, convert the words or symbols into numbers. After recording each relation, go across each policy row to make an overall statement about each policy. Conclude by noting which policy or combination of policies is best in the light of goals and relations. This kind of PG analysis can be aided by a microcomputer where the screen provides prompting and shows how the results change as a result of changing the goals, their weights, the policies, their constraints, the relations, and their measurement.*

Policy Studies as Underutilized or Overutilized

One can easily criticize policy analysis as being underutilized by emphasizing the many examples of policy analysis that have not been used in any way by policy

---

* On the objectivity of policy analysis, especially in the context of procedure for dealing with methodological problems, see Quade (1982), Pitz and McKillip (1984), Thompson (1980), and Nagel (1986).

446

makers. It is more difficult to criticize policy analysis as overutilized, but Laurence Tribe argues that policy analysis has that potential by causing policy makers to think such analysis is more meaningful than it really is. The truth of the matter seems to be that policy analysis is sometimes utilized and sometimes not. The more interesting question is, What factors explain why some policy analysis examples are more utilized than others? Also, how can those factors be used to increase the utilization of good policy analysis, as previously defined?

There are about a dozen factors relevant to facilitating the utilization (by legislative, judicial, and administrative policy makers) of policy evaluations based largely on operations research and management science. In this context, policy evaluation refers to analyzing the effects of alternative public policies in order to determine which one or combination will optimize or improve benefits or costs in achieving given goals under various constraints, conditions, and relations. Utilization refers to being useful or influential in the decision making of governmental policy makers from any branch or level of government.

Many articles on research utilization state or imply that the keys to utilization are doing valid research and communicating it well. More relevant may be factors that relate to opposition and support, intended goals, achieved effects, and the nature of decision makers. Those factors are more substantive than methodological. They also relate more to political science (especially in emphasizing the opposition-support factors) and more to economics (especially in emphasizing the benefits and costs of implementing the research findings). The policy evaluation related to management science and operations research (MS/OR) is more likely to be used when it is valid and communicated well, there is low opposition and possibly high support, the communication is to the appropriate government decision makers, it is oriented toward the intended goals, and it produces more benefits than costs in the eyes of the decision makers.

Low Opposition and High Support

A set of factors that are especially important to the utilization of MS/OR-related research in public policy making are factors that relate to who is opposed and who is supportive of the research findings. Most likely to be used is research that has bipartisan support—research findings that appeal to both liberals and conservatives, and to both Democrats and Republicans. A good example is the research that recommends determinate sentencing of convicted defendants to provide for relatively fixed, rather than discretionary, sentencing. Liberals tend to like those research results because they perceive fixed sentencing as decreasing discriminatory practices. Conservatives tend to like those research results because they perceive discretionary sentencing as resulting in overly lenient sentences.

The fact that research findings are more likely to be utilized if they appeal to bipartisan ideologies should not cause MS/OR researchers to change their findings to other than what the data show. It should likewise not cause researchers to avoid controversial topics that are apt to result in findings that will antagonize one ideological side or another. The bipartisan support factor should, however, influence MS/OR researchers to test policy alternatives that are compromises between purer, but less politically feasible, alternatives that they might otherwise emphasize. A good example is the research on providing legal services for the poor. Research findings that have advocated relying on volunteer attorneys or reimbursed attorneys from the private sector are attacked by liberals because they believe such systems are unlikely to provide attorneys who are visible, specialized, aggressive, and broad thinking enough to represent the interests of the poor. Research findings that have advocated relying on full-time government-salaried attorneys are attacked by conservatives as socialistic and overly disruptive. Recent research that has been much more acceptable has dealt with a compromise system involving full-time salaried attorneys who, as one of their main functions, coordinate the work of volunteer private attorneys and provide them with training so that they can be more effective.

Merely having some good support for one's findings may not be enough to result in the findings being utilized by the relevant decision makers. This is true no matter how valid the research is, and how well it is communicated, if there is opposition from a counterbalancing interest group. A good example is the extensive research showing the desirability of graduated pollution taxes for internalizing the external damage done by polluters in order to provide them with an incentive to reduce their pollution and in order to provide a fund for clean-up, research, compensation, and other antipollution activities. The recommendations of that research have not been adopted because the advantage of such legislation is its overwhelming disadvantage. Threatening to put the burden of paying pollution costs on polluters causes them to muster their strength through numerous trade associations that are strong enough collectively to block any legislation. Even some environmentalists oppose pollution taxes. They do so on the grounds that waiving them is like paying rewards for complying with pollution laws, and people should not be given rewards for doing what they are obligated to do anyway.

On the other hand, merely having no strong opposition to one's findings may not be enough to cause the findings to be utilized if there is no substantial interest group support. A good example is the research on the effects of excluding illegally seized evidence from criminal cases. It shows that excluding such evidence does not greatly deter wrongful police behavior, but may result in a guilty defendant's going free. That research often advocates a system of police suspensions and dismissals as a more effective approach to deterring the police from illegally seizing evidence without affecting the defendant's conviction. That research has been endorsed by the chief justice of the U.S. Supreme Court. No legislature has adopted those ideas, however, largely because there is no substantial interest group supporting such a legislative policy.

Appropriate Government Decision Makers

In evaluating alternative public policies for achieving given goals, one should consider the substantive jurisdiction of the decision makers who are to use the evaluation. Stories are often told about MS/OR researchers who performed evaluations without an adequate awareness of the constitutional constraints under which various governmental decision makers operate. One such story relates to a prestigious firm in the Washington, D.C. area that received a contract to find ways of reducing delay in the criminal justice system of Washington, D.C. After spending considerable time and money performing a variety of queuing, critical path, dynamic programming, and other analyses, the firm concluded that a key means for reducing delay was to get rid of the grand jury indictment stage, since it was such a bad bottleneck. Their report showed no awareness that the judicial administrators had no jurisdiction over the grand jury: It is a requirement of the Fifth Amendment to the Constitution.

In evaluating alternative public policies, one should also consider that different governmental decision makers operate according to different procedures and structures that may influence whether they react favorably to an evaluation. For example, evaluations that conclude in favor of expanded free speech, safeguards for the innocent, or equal protection along racial lines are more likely to be favorably received in federal courts than in state courts in the same geographical location. This is so mainly because federal judges are appointed for life, whereas state judges are generally elected for limited terms. Therefore, federal judges tend to be more immune from majoritarian pressures than state judges and thus more receptive to minority rights. Testimony in a legislative hearing where witnesses are given considerable leeway may also be quite different from testimony in a judicial hearing subject to cross-examination by the other side. The ability to work within those contexts may be as important as the ability to conduct valid research.

Orientation toward Intended Goals

A policy evaluation is not so likely to be used if its goals, criteria, or objective functions are not considered acceptable by the decision makers who decide among the alternative policies and must justify their decisions. A good example might be the controversy over whether judges should be elected or appointed and whether they should serve for short or long terms. The acceptable societal goal in that situation is supposed to be maximizing the competence of the judges chosen by the alternative selection methods. Thus an evaluation designed to show how elected judges differ from appointed judges on liberalism-conservatism in economic decisions or civil liberties decisions might be interesting to a legislative judiciary committee. The committee is likely, however, to reject using the evaluation explicitly, since ideological results are not considered an acceptable societal goal in choosing among alternative methods of judicial selection. That was a reason for rejecting the political science evaluation of alternative selection proposals by the Illinois House Judiciary Committee in 1979.

An evaluation may not be used even if it does use acceptable societal goals, where those goals conflict with the group or individual goals of the responsible decision makers. Alternative legislative redistricting evaluations provide a good example of that. Many of these evaluations involve MS/OR models that relate by analogy to warehousing, transportation, combinatorial models, or integer programming. They generally concentrate on meeting the constitutional constraint that no district should deviate in population from the average district by more than a few percentage points. They may, however, fail to show an awareness of the effects of alternative redistricting plans on how many districts will be dominated by Democrats or Republicans or how many districts will be dominated by blacks, Hispanics, white, or other ethnic groups. They may also fail to show an awareness of the impact of alternative redistricting plans on political incumbents. That lack of concern may make the redistricting report substantially less likely to be used than one that shows such a concern and particularly one that attempts to reconcile possibly conflicting societal, group, and individual goals.

An evaluation can be valid and be sensitive to acceptable societal goals as well as expressed group and individual goals and yet still not be utilized. This is so when the expressed goals are mainly for public consumption and the decision makers really want to know the effects of the policies on unexpressed goals. An example is the Federal Paperwork Commission in the early 1970s. Research suggestions for reducing government paperwork were more likely to be favorably received if they would also reduce government regulation of business. On the other hand, research advocating eliminating itemized income tax deductions that would reduce a lot of paperwork was not as likely to be favorably received because that would mean that those who avoid taxes through itemized deductions would pay more taxes. Another example is the 1983 White House Conference on Productivity. The expressed concern for increased productivity may cover unexpressed goals to decrease rules that relate to employment, discrimination, environmental protection, and consumer protection. Thus, research advocating increased productivity through a more centralized industrial policy comparable to the Japanese Ministry of International Trade and Industry is not likely to be favorably received.

Achievement of Favorable Effects

A fourth set of principles relates to the effects the findings of the evaluations are likely to have, as contrasted to the goals or criteria with which the evaluation is concerned. Recommended policies are much more likely to be adopted if they produce desired effects with no offsetting adverse side effects. A good example of how adverse side effects can destroy potential research utilization is in the area of developing more meaningful jury instructions. Research studies show that in order for jurors to be likely to apply a threshold probability of guilt at about the .90 level, they have to be given instructions as to what "beyond a reasonable doubt" means, preferably in quantitative terms. Otherwise, they tend to vote to convict if the evidence favors the prosecution, regardless of how small the margin might be. Judges, however, are reluctant to give such quantitative instructions, partly because of the adverse side effects of increasing the difficulty of obtaining convictions of guilty defendants. The relevant evaluations are thus not used in spite of their possible validity and concern for important societal goals.

One especially important effect that facilitates policy research utilization is for the policy research to reinforce previously made decisions. This does not mean the research has been wasted, since that reinforcement could provide the push that results in adopting a policy that is highly desirable. A good example of an evaluation that was successfully utilized possibly because of its reinforcing quality is the evaluation made of the effects of alternative jury sizes on conviction rates. The study in question tended to show that an optimum jury size would be between twelve and six if one wanted to minimize the sum of the weighted errors of convicting innocent defendants and not convicting guilty defendants (Nagel 1981). That study was given special emphasis by the Supreme Court, possibly because it reinforced the idea that allowing juries to be smaller than twelve was acceptable, and because it reinforced the feeling that there was a bottom limit of about six, below which a jury would in effect cease to be a jury for constitutional purposes.

A policy evaluation is more likely to be adopted if it shows how prior results can be achieved with less time or money, or how one can get more benefits for the same time or money. A policy evaluation is less likely to be adopted if it shows how a substantial amount of money could be saved but at reduced benefits, and how more benefits can be obtained but with a greater expenditure. Those four possibilities are arranged roughly in the order of their general acceptability. Delay reduction in the courts represents a good example of the kind of policy evaluation that tends to be utilized when it shows ways of saving time without increasing costs. Examples relate to new ways of docketing cases so as to minimize conflicting appointments of trial lawyers, which would otherwise result in more requests for postponements. More systematic case docketing can also make better use of available judicial and jury time. The same computer systems used for docketing and other courthouse governmental recordkeeping can also be used to flag cases that would otherwise exceed the speedy trial constraints. Flow-chart analysis can reveal bottlenecks that may need more personnel, more diversion of cases, or more accelerated processing. Those are examples of where the incremental benefits in terms of time saved are greater than the incremental costs of the docketing, recordkeeping, and analysis. Effects or evaluations that involve reduced benefits (although with reduced costs) or that involve increased costs (although with increased benefits) are likely to be more controversial and less likely to be adopted.

The ideas presented can be summarized in terms of the twelve factors, rather than the five groups of factors. In those terms, an MS/OR-related policy evaluation is more likely to be used when it is in a favorable position with regard to (1) bipartisan support; (2) sensitivity to compromise; (3) no overwhelming opposition; (4) some interest-group support; (5) sensitivity to jurisdictional matters; (6) sensitivity to alternative government procedures; (7) acceptable societal goals; (8) congruence between societal, group, and individual goals; (9) sensitivity to the real goals of the decision makers; (10) no offsetting side effects; (11) reinforcement of previously made decisions; and (12) the achievement of prior results with less time or money.

The overall theme cutting across those factors is that validity and proper communication are important in research utilization, but one must also consider political and economic factors in order to explain why some MS/OR research is utilized or utilized more frequently than other research. The political factors emphasize opposition and support, and the economic factors emphasize the benefits and costs of implementing the research findings. The primary obligation of a policy researcher is to conduct valid research rather than research that is utilized. Greater sensitivity to the factors that facilitate research utilization can, however, be helpful in suggesting legitimate ways to increase the probability that valid research will be utilized. This is especially true of such factors as considering compromise alternatives, jurisdictional matters, government procedures, and making more explicit the relations between alternative recommendations and the salient benefits and costs to the decision makers.*

Policy Studies as Too Conservative or Too Liberal

Some policy analysis studies arrive at conservative conclusions that favor relatively well-off groups in a society. Other studies arrive at liberal conclusions that favor relatively deprived groups. Some conservative studies arrive at their conclusions because they start with conservative goals or the researcher perceives relations between alternatives and goals that favor conservative alternatives. Similarly, some liberal studies arrive at their conclusions because they start with liberal goals or the researcher perceives relations between alternatives and goals that favor liberal alternatives.

The kind of studies that are most likely to generate objections from liberals

---

* On the subject of policy research utilization, see Weiss and Bucuvalas (1980), Weiss (1977), Lindblom and Cohen (1979), and Glaser, Abelson, and Garrison (1983).

may be studies relevant to environmental protection, occupational health/safety, and antidiscrimination, which argue that the high monetary costs are not justified by the nonmonetary benefits. Those studies place a relatively high value on the cost of pollution equipment, safety devices, and affirmatively seeking minority employees, and a relatively low value on clean air/water, worker health/safety, or equal opportunity.

The studies that are most likely to generate objections from conservatives may be studies designed to decrease pollution, on-the-job injuries, and discrimination. They may also be studies seeking neutral goals such as reduced inflation, unemployment, or crime, but they conclude that the way to do it is through the public sector rather than the private sector. Such conclusions may reflect different weights assigned to the same individual goals, or they may reflect different perceptions of what happens when one relies on public versus private means for dealing with social problems.

The important point is that there is nothing inherently liberal or conservative in systematic policy analysis. The methods can be used for maximizing liberal or conservative goals. They can and are used by socialistic or capitalistic governments. Conservatives tend to like such methods because it sounds businesslike to talk in terms of benefits minus costs analogous to income minus expenses. Conservatives also like policy analysis because of its stress on feasibility and the use of market analogies regarding incentives. Liberals tend to like such methods because they sound like national economic planning, urban-regional planning, or at least positive governmental thinking. Liberals or reformers also like policy analysis because analysts get a lot of credit if they succeed in pushing big changes. Thus analysis tends to encourage change. Liberals may also like policy analysis because it appeals to their cognitive planning modes rather than the decentralized, individualistic modes of practical policy makers. Perhaps the even more important point is that any ideological orientation is likely to be more effective and efficient in achieving its goals if it uses systematic public policy analysis for choosing among alternative public policies. *

---

* For an example of a liberal policy evaluation of American political institutions and policies, see Greenberg (1977). For an example of a conservative evaluation, see Saeger (1982). Other examples of policy analysis from a liberal perspective can be found in the book catalogs of the Institute for Policy Studies, Washington, D.C., and examples from a conservative perspective in the book catalogs of the Cato Institute, Washington, D.C. Slightly to the right of center is the American Enterprise Institute for Public Policy Research, Washington, D.C., and slightly to the left of center is the Brookings Institution, Washington, D.C. These research institutes illustrate how systematic policy analysis covers the range of the liberal-to-conservative ideological spectrum.

Policy Studies and Public Administration

Perhaps the most important way in which public administration relates to policy studies is by encouraging more sensitivity to the importance of considering how alternative policy proposals are likely to be implemented and administered. No matter how desirable a proposal is in various ways, it is likely to be unacceptable if it is administratively unfeasible or undesirable.

The Need for Satisfying Administrative Feasibility

A good example comes from the field of housing policy. Economists in the late 1960s often recommended government programs designed to convert poor people from tenants into homeowners. In theory, the idea sounds fine. By becoming homeowners, poor people would have a greater stake in their dwelling units and thereby take better care of them. They would be especially unlikely to burn them down, as they were sometimes doing during the 1960s. By becoming homeowners, poor people might acquire a more positive self-image and a more favorable attitude toward society, thereby becoming better citizens in ways other than just taking better care of their homes.

Partly in reliance on that kind of economic analysis, the Nixon administration pushed a homeownership program for the poor that involved government-guaranteed mortgages with low payments per month, comparable to what the Federal Housing Authority had for years been providing for middle-class people. The program turned out to be a dismal failure. Homes were sold to poor people at inflated assessments, often as a result of sellers bribing government assessors to exaggerate the value of the homes in order to increase the government guarantee. Homes were also sold to poor people without adequately informing them of expensive maintenance costs and defects in the plumbing, heating, or electrical systems. As a result, maintenance and repair costs were often too high for them to handle. They used the mortgage payments for repairs, thereby incurring foreclosures. Some of those foreclosed houses exchanged hands more times than a repossessed car. The program was wracked with the same kind of supplier fraud as the suppliers for the Medicaid and Medicare programs—doctors, dentists, pharmacists, optometrists, nursing-home owners, and others overcharging for services rendered and not rendered.

What may have been needed in designing the program was more concern for the effects of alternative administrative systems. Perhaps a big mistake of the Nixon homeownership program was that it involved government funding through the private sector's real estate system. An alternative way of administering or delivering the program would be for salaried government employees to sell to the poor homes that the government had previously obtained through tax foreclosures, government purchases, or government construction. Salaried government employees selling government-owned housing to the poor would have no incentive to inflate the assessed valuation of the property, or to withhold information on likely maintenance or repair costs.

An analogous government program is the Legal Services Corporation, which consists of salaried government attorneys providing legal services to the poor. No attorney from the Legal Services Corporation or its predecessor, the Office of Economic Opportunity's Legal Services Agency, has been involved in any scandal related to overcharging the poor for actual or fictitious services. Such a system would be administratively feasible for selling houses or supplying medical services. The system might, however, not be politically feasible for medical services, given the fear of the American Medical Association that such a system would lead to socialized medicine for the total population. Because there is no likelihood that the government is going to go into the real estate business for the total population, having salaried government home finders for the poor might be politically feasible.

The Need to Consider Alternative Delivery Systems

The negative-income-tax experiments represent a related example where economic modeling may have missed some important insights by not adequately considering alternative administrative systems. More specifically, over $10 million was spent in New Jersey to test such relations as the effects of being given alternative amounts of money on getting jobs. Families were randomly assigned to various income-receiving groups. One group may have received enough money to satisfy only about 33 percent of minimum needs, as under the Mississippi welfare system; a second group may have received income at the 66 percent level, which corresponds roughly to the Texas welfare system; and a third group may have received income at the 100 percent level, as provided by most northeastern states. Conservatives hypothesize that as welfare payments go up, ambition to get a job goes down, because the welfare recipient has less need for a job. Liberals hypothesize that as low welfare payments go up, ambition to get a job may also go up, because the welfare recipient may have his appetite whetted and his expectations raised. The true relations might involve employment going up to a point and then going down. The expensive experiment, however, shows a nearly flat relation between getting jobs and welfare payments within the monetary range of the experiment.

Perhaps a much steeper relation might have been observed if the families had been randomly assigned to alternative delivery systems as well as, or instead of, alternative welfare amounts. The basic alternative delivery systems consist of the compulsory caseworker, as exists under the present aid to dependent children system, or the check in the mail associated with the negative income tax system that seeks to minimize administrative interference in the lives of the poor. Maybe the compulsory caseworker stimulates getting jobs by informing the welfare recipient about their availability or by harassing the welfare recipient into taking a job on his or her own. On the other hand, maybe the compulsory caseworker lowers the self-esteem of the welfare recipient and makes him more dependent than he would be in the absence of a caseworker. Unfortunately, that kind of alternative administrative hypothesis was never tested, possibly because of a lack of participation by public administrators in the negative income tax experiments.

The Need to Be Aware of Literature That Bridges Both Fields

Many books bridge both policy studies and public administration. One example is Rhodes, *Public Administration and Policy Analysis* (1979). It probably represents the best book-length treatment of the subject, although much of what is included is particularly applicable to Great Britain where the author teaches at the University of Essex. The book contains six chapters. After a brief introductory chapter indicating what the subsequent chapters will deal with, the author discusses "The Scope of American Public Administration in the 1970s," emphasizing the role of organizational behavior, political theory, and political economy. Chapter 3 deals with "The Search for Policy Analysis," including varieties of policy analysis, the role of social scientists in policy making, and such theories of decision making as rational versus incremental. Under varieties of policy analysis, the author refers to policy studies as a type of policy analysis that emphasizes policy content, as contrasted to varieties that emphasize evaluative methodology. To some extent, that distinction reflects the association of the term "policy studies" with political science and the term "policy analysis" more with economics, although they are often used interchangeably.

Chapter 4 discusses "Teaching Public Administration and Policy Analysis in America" with an emphasis on programs associated with the National Association of Schools of Public Affairs and Administration including Syracuse, Michigan, Berkeley, and Stanford. Chapter 5 does the same for Britain, using the University of Birmingham as an illustrative example. The final chapter lists key conclusions such as the multidisciplinary nature of public administration; policy analysis as prescriptive rather than descriptive public administration; the diversity of public administration programs, especially the extent to which they train generalists versus specialists; the growth of public administration policy analysis in both Britain and the United States; and the desirability of encouraging diverse approaches to public administration and policy analysis.

Other books that deal with relations between public administration and policy studies tend to be of three types, all less general than the Rhodes book. One type might be called the hortatory book, since it represents a call to public administrators to show more concern for the prescriptive orientation of policy analysis. There are good chapters of that nature in Robert Golembiewski (1977) and H. George Frederickson and Charles Wise (1977). A second type attempts to describe the extent to which evaluation and optimizing models are used by public administrators and is well represented by Arnold J. Meltsner (1976) and Michael J. White,

Michael Radnor, and David Tanski (1975). A third type is the undergraduate or graduate public administration textbook that shows an above-average interest in management science, program evaluation, and related prescriptive methods, such as Nicholas L. Henry (1975) or Barry Bozeman (1979).

One might also note the recent special issues of the *Policy Studies Journal, Policy Studies Review,* and books in the Policy Studies Organization (PSO) book series, which contain symposia on cross-cutting subjects. These include David H. Rosenbloom (1985), Gerald Caiden and Heinrich Siedentopf (1982), George Edwards (1984), and Edwin Benton and David R. Morgan (1986).

Other Relations between Policy Studies and Public Administration

The field of public administration has long been concerned with the means of administering policies more effectively in order to achieve given goals. Public administrators have also shown interest in developing government structures that can produce a greater degree of goal achievement. The budgeting field within public administration has become particularly important as it focuses on ways of explaining and evaluating alternative allocation decisions. Contemporary public administration discusses the improvement of public administration, transcending obvious clichés about the need for hiring more competent people and spending money more efficiently. It has also moved beyond the institutional description of hiring rules and budgeting procedures to place greater emphasis on the psychology of organizational behavior and on allocations that reflect a combination of incrementalism, functionalism, and management science. On a more general level, public administration may be especially useful in clarifying alternative administrative arrangements for implementing government policies.

One might also note that the way in which the field of policy studies is subdivided is virtually the same as the way in which the field of public administration is subdivided. The subdivisions of policy studies can be observed by noting the table of contents of the *Encyclopedia of Policy Studies* (Nagel 1983). The subdivisions of public administration can be observed by noting the sections into which the American Society for Public Administration is subdivided. Both fields have general cross-cutting subfields that relate to research methodology, decision analysis, intergovernmental relations, and cross-national comparisons. The substantive or line fields within public administration correspond closely to the specific policy problems with which policy studies people are concerned, including criminal justice, national security, civil rights, labor relations, business regulation, environmental protection, and human services.

Conclusions

Sometimes a politician will emphasize that he or she is attacked by both left-wing and right-wing groups, and therefore he must be doing something correct. This implies that being attacked on both sides of an issue indicates one is taking a moderate or reasonable position.

An attack from both sides of an ideological, methodological, or other spectrum, however, may be worse than being attacked by only one side. It may indicate one is too moderate, indecisive, or mugwumpish; so far to the left, the right, or otherwise off the relevant spectrum that one is disliked by both the normal left and right; or so bizarre in what one is advocating that everyone agrees it is wrong, such as giving driver licenses to salamanders.

The ideal position to be in is not to be attacked by everybody but to be praised by everybody, if the choices are between universal attack and universal praise. It might be even better to be attacked by those who are wrong, and praised by those who are right. There may be considerable disagreement, though, as to who is wrong and who is right.

This chapter has perhaps overemphasized conflicting negative evaluations of policy studies. The other side of that analysis is to emphasize the conflicting positive evaluations of policy studies. One can note, for example, that the policy studies field is simultaneously praised for being a new perspective on political and social phenomena and at the same time preserving substantive and methodological principles that have been developed over many years; both highly practical in being relevant to increased societal productivity and at the same time concerned with high-level issues in political theory, social philosophy, and the philosophy of science; an interdisciplinary perspective across all fields of knowledge and at the same time emphasizing the importance of political science in policy formation, implementation, and evaluation; a scientific field with a methodological tool kit from statistical analysis, optimizing research, mathematical modeling, and psychological decision analysis and at the same time concerned with highly normative questions as to the good society, ultimate values, and the good polity; increasingly utilized at the national, state, and local levels, as well as in administrative agencies, legislatures, and courts, and at the same time being subjected to sophisticated skepticism on the part of street-wise policy makers; and used by liberals as a form of economic planning and at the same time used by conservatives as a form of bringing good business sense to government.

One can conclude from this analysis that the field of policy studies scores well on a loft of dimensions. It has a long-term philosophical foundation, originality, a theoretical side, a practical side, an important political science component that involves all fields of political science, a multidisciplinary component that involves all fields of knowledge, especially the social sciences, a qualitative value-oriented side, a quantitative, reasonably objective way of dealing with analytic problems, an ability to get utilized when deserved in the light of democratic processes, nonutilization when deserved in the light of those same democratic processes, value to conservative policy makers, and value to liberal policy makers.

A key problem in policy analysis is not that it is going to be rejected. Instead, policy analysis could become overaccepted so that there is not sufficient questioning of its procedures and assumptions, as well as its substance. Also, it could become so much a part of political and social science that it loses its separate existence. That, too, would be unfortunate, since the methods and substance of policy analysis are partly distinct from, as well as the same as, those of other fields of political and social science. The optimizing methodology as applied to the public sector may be the most distinct aspect of policy analysis deserving of separate treatment.

In the 1985 presidential address to the International Political Science Association (ISPA), Klaus von Beyme commented that the development of policy analysis may be the most important development within political science during the twenty years since IPSA was formed. That is indeed high praise for a field that has developed so rapidly. The field may now be plateauing out on a high level of importance and activity.

There have been some struggles for recognition as a field in teaching curricula, scholarly journals, convention programs, book publishing, grants, research centers, associations, and other indicators of scholarly activity. Those struggles have been largely successful.

Perhaps we can consider 1985 as a year of graduation or commencement in the sense of policy studies now having truly arrived, as reflected in the IPSA presidential address. After having achieved that respectability, it is time now, as we move into the 1990s, to move on to further developing more applications of political and social science to important policy problems.

References

Benton, Edwin, and David R. Morgan, eds. 1986. *Intergovernmental Relations and Public Policy.* Westport, Conn.: Greenwood Press.

Bozeman, Barry. 1979. *Public Management and Policy Analysis.* New York: St. Martin's Press.

Caiden, Gerald, and Heinrich Siedentopf, eds. 1982. *Strategies for Administrative Reform.* Lexington, Mass.: Lexington Books.

Diesing, Paul. 1982. *Science and Ideology in the Policy Sciences.* Chicago: Aldine.

Dror, Yehezkel. 1971. *Design for Policy Sciences.* New York: Elsevier.

Dunn, William, ed. 1983. *Values, Ethics and the Practice of Policy Analysis.* Lexington, Mass.: Lexington.

Edwards, George, ed. 1984. *Public Policy Implementation.* Greenwich, Conn.: JAI Press.

Fischer, Frank. 1980. *Politics, Values, and Public Policy: The Problem of Methodology.* Denver, Colo.: Westview.

Fleishman, Joel, and Bruce Payne. 1980. *Ethical Dilemmas and the Education of Policy Makers.* Hastings-on-Hudson, N.Y.: Hastings Center.

Frederickson, H. George, and Charles Wise, eds. 1977. *Public Administration and Public Policy.* Lexington, Mass.: Lexington Books.

Frohock, Fred. 1979. *Public Policy: Scope and Logic.* Englewood Cliffs, N.J.: Prentice-Hall.

Glaser, Edward, Harold Abelson, and Kathalee Garrison. 1983. *Putting Knowledge to Use: Facilitating the Diffusion of Knowledge and Implementation of Planned Change.* San Francisco: Jossey-Bass.

Golembiewski, Robert. 1977. *Public Administration as a Developing Discipline.* New York: Marcel Dekker.

Goodin, Robert. 1982. *Political Theory and Public Policy.* Chicago: University of Chicago Press.

Greenberg, Edward. 1977. *The American Political System: A Radical Approach.* Boston: Winthrop.

Gregg, Phillip, ed. 1976. *Problems of Theory in Policy Analysis.* Lexington, Mass.: Lexington.

Groth, Alexander. 1971. *Comparative Politics: A Distributive Approach.* New York: Macmillan.

Heidenheimer, Arnold J., Hugh Heclo, and Carolyn Teich Adams. 1983. *Comparative Public Policy: The Politics of Social Choice in Europe and America.* 2d ed. New York: St. Martin's Press.

Henry, Nicholas L. 1975. *Public Administration and Public Affairs.* Englewood Cliffs, N.J.: Prentice-Hall.

Holzer, Marc, and Stuart Nagel, eds. 1984. *Productivity and Public Policy.* Beverly Hills: Sage.

Lasswell, Harold. 1971. *A Preview of Policy Sciences.* New York: Elsevier.

Lasswell, Harold, and Daniel Lerner, eds. 1951. *The Policy Sciences.* Stanford: Stanford University Press.

Leichter, Howard. 1979. *A Comparative Approach to Policy Analysis: Health Care Policy in Four Nations.* New York: Cambridge University Press.

Lindblom, Charles, and David Cohen. 1979. *Usable Knowledge: Social Science and Social Problem Solving.* New Haven: Yale University Press.

MacRae, Duncan, Jr., and James Wilde. 1976. *The Social Function of Social Science.* New Haven: Yale University Press.

McCall, George, and George Weber, eds. 1984. *Social Science and Public Policy: The Roles of Academic Disciplines in Policy Analysis.* New York: Associated Faculty Press.

McKenna, Christopher. 1980. *Quantitative Methods for Public Decision Making.* New York: McGraw-Hill.

Meltsner, Arnold J. 1976. *Policy Analysis in the Bureaucracy.* Berkeley: University of California Press.

Nagel, Stuart, ed. 1975a. *Policy Studies in America and Elsewhere.* Lexington, Mass.: Lexington.

Nagel, Stuart. 1975b. *Policy Studies and the Social Sciences.* Lexington, Mass.: Lexington.

Nagel, Stuart, ed. 1980a. *Improving Policy Analysis.* Beverly Hills: Sage.

Nagel, Stuart, ed. 1980b. *The Policy Studies Handbook.* Lexington, Mass.: Lexington.

Nagel, Stuart. 1982. *Policy Evaluation: Making Optimum Decisions.* New York: Praeger.

Nagel, Stuart. 1983. *Encyclopedia of Policy Studies.* New York: Marcel Dekker.

Nagel, Stuart, ed. 1984a. *Basic Literature in Policy Studies: A Comprehensive Bibliography.* Greenwich, Conn.: JAI Press.

Nagel, Stuart. 1984b. *Contemporary Public Policy Analysis.* University, Ala.: University of Alabama.

Nagel, Stuart. 1984c. *Public Policy: Goals, Means, and Methods.* New York: St. Martin's Press.

Nagel, Stuart. 1989. *Evaluation Analysis with Microcomputers.* Greenwich, Conn: JAI Press.

Pitz, Gordon, and Jack McKillip. 1980. *Decision Analysis for Program Evaluation.* Beverly Hills: Sage.

Quade, E.S. 1982. *Analysis for Public Decisions.* 2d ed. New York: Elsevier.

Ranney, Austin, ed. 1968. *Political Science and Public Policy.* Chicago: Markham.

Regan, Tom, and Donald Van DeVeer, eds. 1982. *And Justice for All: New Introductory Essays in Ethics and Public Policy.* Totowa, N.J.: Rowman and Littlefield.

Rhodes, R. 1979. *Public Administration and Policy Analysis.* London: Saxon House.

Rosenbloom, David H., ed. 1985. *Public Personnel Policy: The Politics of Civil Service.* New York: Associated Faculty Press.

Sabine, George. 1950. *A History of Political Theory.* New York: Holt.

Saeger, Richard. 1982. *American Government and Politics: A Neoconservative Approach.* Glenview, Ill.: Scott, Foresman.

Seidelman, Raymond, and Edward Harpham. 1985. *Disenchanted Realists: Political Science and the American Crisis.* Albany: State University of New York Press.

Sharkansky, Ira, ed. 1970. *Policy Analysis in Political Science.* Chicago: Markham.

Siegel, Richard L., and Leonard B. Weinberg. 1977. *Comparing Public Policies: United States, Soviet Union, and Europe.* Homewood, Ill.: Dorsey Press.

Somit, Albert, and Joseph Tanenhaus. 1967. *The Development of American Political Science.* Boston: Allyn and Bacon.

Spadaro, Robert, Thomas Dye, Robert Golembiewski, Murray Stedman, and Harmon Ziegler. 1975. *The Policy Vacuum: Toward a More Professional Political Science.* Lexington, Mass.: Lexington Books.

Thompson, Mark. 1980. *Benefit-Cost Analysis for Program Evaluation.* Beverly Hills: Sage.

Wanlass, Lawrence. 1953. *Gentell's History of Political Thought.* New York: Appleton-Century-Crofts.

Weiss, Carol H., ed. 1977. *Using Social Research in Public Policy Making.* Lexington, Mass.: Lexington-Heath.

Weiss, Carol H., and Michael Bucuvalas. 1980. *Social Science Research and Decision Making.* New York: Columbia University Press.

White, Michael J., Michael Radnor, and David Tanski, eds. 1975. *Management and Policy Science in American Government.* Lexington, Mass.: Lexington Books.

Wilde, James. 1979. *Policy Analysis for Public Decisions.* Duxbury, Mass.: Duxbury Press.

461

18

Implementation: A Review and Suggested Framework

HELEN INGRAM

Since 1973 when Pressman and Wildavsky christened an infant area of study *implementation,* prodigious growth and development has occurred (Pressman and Wildavsky 1973, 1979, 1984). The gap in political scientists' understanding of public policy, which Erwin C. Hargrove once called the "missing link," has now become crowded with journal articles, books, and texts.* The popularity of implementation studies has succeeded in drawing public policy scholars from what was once almost an exclusive attention to the politics of making laws to consider what happens once laws are passed. Further, the political scientists who study implementation have been led to a renewed appreciation of the intellectual heritage of the study of public administration. To administer and to implement have a great deal of similarity, and while implementation scholars tend to emphasize policy rather than organization, as do public administration scholars, every implementation study leans heavily upon classic and contemporary public administration insights (Hargrove 1980, 3; Sabatier and Mazmanian 1983, 143).

Even though the bibliographic population explosion of implementation studies has done a great deal to heighten appreciation for the policy implications of administration, the field of implementation has not yet achieved conceptual clarity. Implementation scholars exhibit wide differences on a number of crucial issues. Implementation scholars themselves have been critical of a dearth of theory (Hargrove 1980) and empirical verification (Goggin 1986). Even so, implementation scholarship is showing signs of increasing maturity. Some convergence of opinion on conceptual issues is emerging (Sabatier 1986). Further, along with the welter of atheoretical case studies about which some have complained (Hargrove 1980, 2; Ingram 1987), the implementation literature is coming to include explanatory and predictive theory. The purpose of this chapter is twofold: (1) to review the terms of

---

* A good overview is provided in Sabatier and Mazmanian (1983).

controversy within implementation literature; and (2) to develop a flexible framework for identifying the most critical variables affecting implementation of particular kinds of policies and the appropriate criteria to evaluate each kind of policy.

Conceptual Issues in Implementation Literature

Identifying and Evaluating Implementation

A concern with implementation emerged as an outgrowth of the renewed interest in the substance of policy among postbehavioral era political scientists (Ripley 1985, 16). Two volumes edited by eminent scholars Austin Ranney (1968) and Ira Sharkansky (1970) signaled that it had become legitimate for political scientists to relate policy content to characteristics of the policy-making process. The essays in these two early volumes treated policy content in terms of statutory language and putative results, not as it emerged through action by government. However, interest in policy content led scholars to question why numbers of Great Society programs passed by Congress were not, when administered, achieving expected outcomes. Pressman and Wildavsky (1973, 1979, 1984) hoped to improve governmental performance through implementation studies. "By concentrating on the implementation of programs, as well as their initiation, we should be able to increase the probability that policy promises will be realized" (1984, 6).

It is ironic that implementation studies have exemplified their own lesson: Vague and contradictory policies are hard to implement. Implementation is in many ways a slippery subject (Majone and Wildavsky 1979, 164). Differences among implementation scholars have sometimes been grouped into "top-down" or "bottom-up" approaches (Sabatier 1986), but in reality disagreements have a variety of dimensions. Where implementation starts or ends is not even settled. While implementation is commonly referred to as a stage, boundaries are not clear. Authors vary in their selection of critical factors affecting implementation. Criteria for evaluating implementation success are conflicting. Moreover, the simplest, most straightforward path for implementation studies has proven to be misleading.

Where Implementation Begins

A number of implementation scholars make a conceptual distinction between policy formulation and policy implementation, which for them means carrying out a prior decision (Sabatier 1986, 31; Sabatier and Mazmanian 1983, 145). Chronologically, implementation is thought to occur "after the adoption of a policy and before the routinization of operations, activities, and tasks that are governed by the policy" (Schneider 1982, 716). It appeals to democratic instincts to mark the start of implementation following the completion of policy making. Separating policy from administration and the function of legislative bodies and administrative agencies are deeply entrenched American values related to popular accountability and limiting bureaucratic discretion (Sabatier 1986, 31). Moreover, treating policy goals or intent as given provides implementation scholars with a clear benchmark from which to measure extent of achievement (Sabatier and Mazmanian 1983, 147).

Despite the instinctive appeal and operational convenience of beginning implementation studies with a statute that establishes policy, serious issues have been raised by critics of this approach. Implementation scholars, they argue, should begin by focusing on what realistically influences action. To start out with policy handed to implementors through a statute distorts reality.

Statutes are often so vague, general, and contradictory that they provide very sketchy implementation discretion. Moreover, policy statements may be poorly related to policy action. Michael Lipsky (1978), among others, has called into question whether the stated objectives of policy can be taken as authoritative. Rather than begin the analysis with the policy or statute, it would be far better, he suggests, to observe the behavior of policy deliverers as the primary actors and proceed to analyze the structural and personal factors that influence behavior. Berman and McLaughlin (1978) give far more credit to localized, grass-roots influences than to policy direction from statutes in explaining the implementation of educational innovations.

Policy continually evolves instead of being initially established and thereafter perhaps reformulated. Angela Browne and Aaron Wildavsky (1984, 208) view implementation as a process of mutual adaptation in which policies and programs adapt to their environment and each alter the other. Instead of the "forward mapping" framework suggested by beginning with a statement of congressional intent and mapping out compliance with the original mandate, Richard Elmore (1982, 19) has suggested that "backward mapping" will provide a more realistic understanding of implementation. This approach begins with the implementor closest to the problem and traces backward the influences on action.

Implementation scholars should select their starting point with a view to serving the ultimate goal of improving policy. Walter Williams (1982) writes, "At basic issue is the extent to which implementation studies can yield 'pertinent, sound, timely' information to aid those who formulate and execute policies" (p. 1). A concept of implementation that separates policy formulation from implementation cannot help policy because its objectives have become its preconditions. Instead of ending up with more effective implementation, it is apparently deemed necessary to begin with it by specifying what sort of statute must come first (Browne and Wildavsky 1984, 231).

Effective implementation is said to be partially preordained by the strength of the statute, including clear delineation and ranking of unambiguous objectives. Yet it may not be helpful for implementation scholars to ground their hopes on something rare (Mazmanian and Sabatier 1983, 22). Political scientists have long observed Congress's propensity to enact vague and internally contradictory legislation. By avoiding explicit policy objectives and delegating the hard choices to federal bureaucracies, members of Congress derive more broad-based support and have more leeway in blaming federal agencies for failure in achieving policy intent. Prescribing clear legislation as a cure for implementation problems may be begging the question. Fully resolving disagreements early in the legislative process, so that clear statutory guidelines will follow, is not possible most of the time (Rein and Rabinovitz 1978, 324). If Congress were restricted to legislating only in areas in which it could speak clearly, the legislative agenda would be very short. Further, much of the learning and accomplishments that accompany implementation of unclear statutes would be foregone (Van Horn 1979, 161).

Where Implementation Ends

Some implementation scholars favor cutting short analysis before the end results occur. Van Horn (1979, 9–10) argues that implementation analysis should be concerned only with measuring the extent to which the policy outputs of implementing agencies conform to various objectives rather than with the policy's ultimate impact on target groups. Schneider (1982) sees implementation as a phase in the life cycle of policy and envisions its ending when new policies have become routine procedure. Yet, as Mazmanian and Sabatier (1983, 148) point out, terminating implementation studies prior to policy effects excludes some of the most interesting aspects of implementation analysis: the adequacy of underlying causal theory and the degree of target groups' compliance. Further, such truncated analysis leaves open the not very useful possibility of good implementation and bad results—or doing the inappropriate thing very effectively.

Critical Determinants of Implementation

Among the most important contributions of the implementation literature has been to heighten sensitivity to the numbers of factors that may adversely affect implementation. Pressman and Wildavsky expressed their concern in 1973:

> People now appear to think that implementation should be easy; they are, therefore, upset when expected events do not occur or turn out badly. We would consider our effort a success if more people began with the understanding that implementation, under the best of circumstances is exceedingly difficult. They would, therefore, be pleasantly surprised when a few good things really happen. (P. xiii)

Once scholarly investigation began to illuminate one after another the critical factors affecting implementation, an impressive list emerged.

Early on, the adequacy of the causal theory embodied in law was identified as important. Laws implicitly embody causal theories which predict how target groups will react given certain incentives. They also make suppositions about how physical and economic systems operate. False notions of causal relationships assumed to exist in law may exacerbate implementation problems (Pressman and Wildavsky 1984, 147). There may, for example, be no threshold of air pollution levels below which human health is unaffected, while the ambient standards built into the Clean Air Act of 1970 suppose such standards exist. In such cases, physical reality affects implementation as much as legal mandates.

Many discoveries of factors affecting implementation were not really new but reformulations of public administration insights concerning bureaucratic behavior and relationships in the federal system. The principal distinguishing feature of implementation analysis was the overarching concern with policy consequences rather than structures or processes. For instance, Pressman and Wildavsky (1984, 147) observed the same loosely coupled interagency system that public administration scholars had long studied, but teased from their analysis policy-oriented conclusions. Multiplicity of decision points, they said, introduces overwhelming complexity of joint action, which stifles policy intent. Directness and simplicity were identified as keys to implementation.

Van Meter and Van Horn (1975, 447) went beyond the usual structural metaphors that have dominated federalism research to uncover the policy relationships. Rather than paint pictures of marble cakes or picket fences, these authors concentrated on interorganizational communications and enforcement activities related to policy. Along with unclear and vague policies, Van Horn concluded in 1979 (p. 163), the fundamental autonomy that state and local governments enjoy in the federal system is the principal explanation for the minimal impact of public laws and federal implementing agencies. Characteristics of implementing agencies, predispositions of implementors, and resources, among other things, were identified as critical.

Like Van Meter and Van Horn, Milbrey McLaughlin (1976) identified the implementors closest to the action and their immediate environment as crucial. "The amount of interest, commitment, and support evidenced by the principal actors had a major influence on the prospects for success" (pp. 167–80). The context in which these implementors operated emerged as very important in the Rand study on educational innovations from which McLaughlin drew her conclusions. It characterized organizational features of schools and districts and determined that these contextual variables were related to how effectively innovations were implemented. Further, implementation strategies and fixed organizational elements appeared to be interactive (Berman 1980, 213). The presence of an implementation entrepreneur can make a crucial difference in local situations. Levin and Ferman (1985) stress that leadership can be the significant political hidden hand that guides disorganized and disparate interests to converge in support of implementing policy.

External monitoring of the implementation process was a crucial variable uncovered by Eugene Bardach (1977, 268–83) in *The Implementation Game*. What he terms "a fixer," an important legislator or executive official who controls resources to monitor closely and to intervene almost continually, can greatly facilitate action. Browning, Marshall, and Tabb (1984, 237) reinforce the importance of the time dimension so that evolutionary adaptations, which occur as various levels of government contend in the intergovernmental system, are not overlooked.

As implementation studies have multiplied, the list of variables affecting them have gotten longer. The most comprehensive treatment of factors can be found in the work of Mazmanian and Sabatier (1983, 22). They identify seventeen independent variables summarized under three headings: tractability of the problem, the ability of the statute to structure implementation, and the nonstatutory variables. In their quest to consider everything, the list Mazmanian and Sabatier provide loses parsimony and becomes too cumbersome to use as a framework of analysis. It is not possible to predict which variables are likely to be most important under what circumstances (see criticism in Browne and Wildavsky 1984, 229; Hargrove 1980, 2; Wagner 1986, 12). Having achieved a completeness that will be difficult to match, subsequent implementation scholars are finding diminishing returns in adding further to the list of factors. Instead, the challenge has clearly become to develop theories or causal patterns associated with implementation outcomes and to test these theories empirically (Goggin 1986).

Considerable theoretical headway has been provided by scholars who have built on Lowi's (1964, 1972) policy typology. The argument made by researchers, including Ripley and Franklin (1986), Hargrove (1980), and Meier (1987), is that the pattern of benefits and costs conferred by the policy largely determines the relationships that emerge in implementation and whether implementation will succeed. Implementation varies according to policy type. Table 18.1 portrays the essentials of the argument.

From the perspective of explaining the implementation difficulties likely to be encountered in different policy areas, policy typology-based studies are extremely helpful. But they offer less aid than one would wish in guiding implementation toward evolution and improvement. If implementation studies are to make policy better, they need to suggest which tools or mechanisms may work in areas where risk of failure is moderate to high.

Criteria for Evaluation

The most simple criterion, and that most often employed in implementation literature, is whether statutorily prescribed goals are met (Mazmanian and Sabatier 1983; Van Horn 1979). Nevertheless, when the process of implementation must account for the vague, inconsistent, and contradictory character of legislation, it cannot be straightforward. As Majone and Wildavsky (1984) remark, "A faithful

TABLE 18.1

Relationships among Actors and Success in Implementation by Policy Type

Policy Type	Nature of Relationship among Actors	Relative Difficulty of Successful Implementation	Process Critical to Successful Implementation
Distributive[a]	Federal bureaucracy (central and regional) mainly concerned with smoothness of process and absence of complaints. Central federal bureaucracy is close to national groups representing beneficiaries. Federal field, state, and local bureaucracies close to local groups representing beneficiaries. General level of conflict: low.	Low	System management and operating routines to deliver the goods.
Competitive regulatory[b]	Federal bureaucracy mainly concerned with smoothness of process and absence of complaints. Central federal bureaucracy maintains formal distance from competing interests; may work closely, informally. General level of conflict: low with short higher bursts.	Moderate	Operating routines to make decisions and review performance.
Protective regulatory[c]	Federal bureaucracy mainly concerned with smoothness of process and absence of complaints. Central federal bureaucracy in adversary relationship with restricted clients and friendly relationship with beneficiaries, or vice versa. General level of conflict: moderate with some sustained higher bursts.	Moderate	Involvement of federal implementors to enforce restrictions.

Table 18.1. *Continued.*

Policy Type	Nature of Relationship among Actors	Relative Difficulty of Successful Implementation	Process Critical to Successful Implementation
Redistributive[d]	Federal bureaucracy (central and regional) mainly concerned with smoothness of process and absence of complaints; may promote some evaluative efforts on both process and impact. Central federal bureaucracy has distant, impersonal relationship with beneficiaries and restricted clients. State and local bureaucracies have close relationships with beneficiaries —sometimes friendly, sometimes hostile. General level of conflict: moderate to high.	High	Bargaining relationships between bureaucrats and beneficiaries.

SOURCE: Ripley and Franklin, 1986.
a. Distributes benefits that aid interests.
b. Regulates competition to ensure service or public good.
c. Imposes costs on private action to protect public.
d. Reallocates values from one broad class to another.

translation of an ill-formed policy idea or theory would bring into being all the inconsistencies, inadequacies and/or unfortunate consequences inherent in the pristine conception. A faithless interpretation would straighten out all the logical defects and/or alter elements so the consequences were more desirable than the original plan" (p. 178).

Evaluating results solely in terms of explicit statutory goals leads to partial and/or incorrect conclusions. It is possible for policies to achieve their goals yet, because they also foster other activities, result in problems more grave than those solved. Legislation often creates undesired expectations for services and activities that many times evidence themselves in ways that are irrelevant or counterproductive (Dexter 1981, 417). Sometimes there may be hidden goals that are intended though not explicit. Legislation may have latent and unspecified functions that may be fulfilled through implementation, even though manifest goals are unattained (Jennings 1980).

Ann Schneider (1982, 726–29) suggests relative criteria by asking "good as compared to what?" She suggests several possibilities. One possibility is to compare the level of performance of an agency under a new policy with operations under old policy. Or, performance of agencies under one policy can be juxtaposed to performance of the same kind of agency under a different policy. Alternatively, rather than be preoccupied with standards, the focus can be on improvement.

Good implementation occurs when the implementation process introduces improvement. Measuring improvement and progress introduces policy evaluation into implementation studies. Implementation provides the experience that evaluators evaluate, and, in turn, implementors are the market for evaluation (Browne and Wildavsky 1984, 184–205). Implementation and evaluation taken together prescribe a process of evolution.

A Flexible Framework for Implementation Studies

Much of the implementation literature, as the foregoing review suggests, constitutes a rebuttal of straightforward, unidimensional approaches to implementation.* Instead, researchers are coming to recognize that implementation experience varies and that approaches adopted by the analyst must be tailored to particular circumstances. The challenge presented to implementors depends very much on the problems passed along to them by policy formulators. Success in implementation must be evaluated within the context of particular problems, and critical factors affecting implementation will vary with what is being attempted. Implementation studies would profit

---

* Simplified approaches to implementation have been called variously programmed, systems, or top-down models.

from a broad, flexible framework that synthesizes and orders the insights of the large implementation literature.

Broad Scope

The analysis of implementation needs to be broad enough to include policy formulation and impacts in order to be realistic and useful. Policy formulation, implementation, and outcome need to be seen as a seamless web rather than distinct stages affected by separate variables. Therefore, it makes sense to begin implementation studies, as do Nakamura and Smallwood (1980), by considering the challenge presented to formulators.

Policies as they are formulated are fairly accurate mirrors of the kinds of costs they impose on policy makers. Salisbury and Heinz (1970, 47) explored the relation of policy to the decision-making costs imposed on legislators (see also Nakamura and Smallwood 1980; Rein and Rabinovitz 1978). They separated costs into two basic types: negotiation costs and information costs. *Negotiation costs* are the costs of coming to agreement, including the costs of discovering the distribution of value preferences among others and expanding the necessary effort to construct a position on which parties can agree. Negotiation costs are low when it is clear what interests are at stake and there is a consensus among interests or a predominance of support in favor of particular policy aims. *Information costs* are costs related to obtaining information about the operative causal connections between governmental actions and policy impacts and linkages among involved agencies. Information costs are low when it is clear that certain governmental actions will have predictable results with no or few unintended or unpredicted consequences. Even when such relationships are not known, information costs are low when Congress has a high level of confidence in the administrative agency's will and capacity to discover necessary information to implement policy. Table 18.2 displays the kinds of statutes that are likely to result from different distributions of decision-making costs.

As Kathryn Wagner (1986) has intelligently suggested, straightforward, routine implementation of a statute can be expected only when there are clear goals that give administrative agencies guidance in implementation and at the same time the statute embodies sufficient procedural flexibility to allow the agency to set its own timetable for specific action. Yet table 18.2 indicates such statutes are likely to emerge only when the costs of negotiating agreement are low and there is a great deal of information available about how specific goals may be accomplished (Type 1). If costs of negotiation remain low, that is, there is a great deal of congressional support for accomplishing a goal but little information and much uncertainty about how the issue can successfully be handled, Congress is likely to pass agency- and technology-forcing legislation, such as it has in the environmental field. While Congress may have to leave a certain amount of discretion to the agency in terms of defining standards, leeway is closely circumscribed by specific timetables and dead-

TABLE 18.2
Decision-Making Costs and Structure of Statutes

	Negotiation Costs	
	Low	High
Information costs		
Low	Type 1: clear goals; procedural flexibility	Type 2: open-ended goals; procedural flexibility
High	Type 3: clear goals; procedural specificity	Type 4: open-ended goals; procedural specificity

Note: This table combines concepts drawn from Salisbury and Heinz (1970) and Wagner (1986).

lines with little procedural flexibility (Type 3). Even though it is not known through what specific technology environmental quality goals can be met, Congress deliberately sets aims beyond what is known to be achievable to force technical developments. Like a college instructor knows what should be taught but is insecure about the students' commitment or the appropriate pedagogy, Congress is giving bureaucracy lots of "exams" through procedural specificity to check its progress.

The sort of statute likely to be enacted by Congress changes substantially when negotiation costs are high. If it is difficult to reach agreement on policy goals, Congress is likely to opt for being vague and general and to pass the job of forging the agreement on to bureaucracy. Salisbury and Heinz (1970) have called this a structural decision, which simply sets up authority structures or rules to guide future negotiations. Examples of such structural decisions can be found in standard regulatory legislation such as that prescribing securities exchanges and in many of the Great Society programs, including Head Start and Job Corps.

The bureaucracies granted authority by structural decisions may be given wide or narrow latitude depending on the nature of available information about the issue. When Congress is neither insecure about how the issue can be dealt with and the consequences nor distrusts the expertise of the implementing agency, it will give agencies broad discretion (Type 2). Congress, for instance, has been happy to let the Federal Reserve Board exercise broad autonomy in setting objectives and means. In other cases, Congress may be nervous about the uncertain impact of actions on constituencies and lack confidence in the expertise of the implementing agency. Consequently, the agency is given little flexibility in terms of specific actions (Type 4).

Timetables, particular distributions of resources, and procedures for decisions and redress can be made specific. The Food and Drug Administration and the Occupational Safety and Health Administration provide examples. A number of program grant-in-aid policies also fit Type 4. While pursuing vague and general congressional goals, implementing agencies have become hedged with numbers of specific requirements and burdened by detailed reporting rules.

Appropriate Approaches and Criteria

The appropriate criterion for evaluating performance is policy evolution and improvement. As Wildavsky (1979) has noted, policy problems are seldom solved, they are only worked on. Further, attempts at solving one problem often sows the seeds of other problems because of negative and sometimes hidden consequences of actions. The most direct course for solving problems is seldom chosen because of lack of agreement, inadequate capability, or concern for damaging side effects. The policy search must not be for some idealized best solution but for one that is doable and agreeable. Evolution and improvement mean that, over time, the search becomes less difficult. Therefore, the test of implementation success is less whether specific problem-related objectives are achieved than whether the resulting problems are preferable to the initial problems.

Congressional passage of a statute needs to be seen as a benchmark from which to measure, not the achievement of the embodied objectives, but progress toward doable and agreeable policy. Statutes are predispositions that signal, not just what implementors must do, but, more important, what additional information gathering or consent building is needed to reach a condition where problems are preferable (i.e. more tractable) than those that preceded them.

Depending on which tasks are presented to implementors by virtue of the structure of the statute, the implementation process is likely to follow different approaches or models. Further, different criteria for evaluation need to be applied with reference to the tasks implicit in statutory structure. Table 18.3 displays the analytical models and criteria associated with each statutory type in table 18.2. Row 1 suggests that for the idealized statute that builds in many of the preconditions for successful policy implementation, it is reasonable to employ a command-control or forward mapping framework for analyzing implementation and to match achievements with statutory goals as criteria for success.

Row 2 presents the sharply different statutory situation where goals are vague and implementors are given flexibility. Under this situation, as Lipsky (1978) suggests, the statute will be all but irrelevant and implementation analysis must focus on factors proximate to the implementor. Backward mapping becomes an appropriate analytical strategy. Since policy accomplishment depends very much on the synergism that occurs at the local level, it is appropriate to evaluate implementation in terms of creativity and entrepreneurship.

TABLE 18.3
Appropriate Approaches and Evaluative Criteria for
Types of Statutory Structures

Statute type	Approach	Criteria
Type 1	Command-control; programmed	Achievement of goals
Type 2	Street level; adaptive	Creativity and bureaucratic entrepreneurship
Type 3	Oversight and reformulation	Policy learning
Type 4	Bargaining	Agreement and support

Row 3 presents a statutory situation with which scholars of environmental policy are familiar. Implementors are presented with ambitious goals and specific targets and deadlines. Policy formulation and implementation become intermingled stages with continued legislative involvement in agency activities. The test to be applied to this situation is the extent of policy learning. Implementation can be viewed as successful if the policy generates a great deal more information about the problem, operative cause and effective relationships, and more security about administrative capability.

Row 4 presents the challenge to implementors of forging agreement that did not exist in policy formulation, hence the vague policy goals. Implementors also have the burden of dispelling the lack of information and uncertainty about consequences that led formulators to impose procedural constraints. Some regulatory and grant-in-aid programs have vague goals but specific reporting, monitoring, and auditing requirements. A bargaining model of implementation is likely to be most appropriate here with negotiation occurring among interests involved in implementation (Ingram 1977). Bargaining results in formulating goals to attract wide support. Specific procedures generate information about efficiency, fairness, and equity of agency action and its impacts. Since the policy problem is lack of agreement, certainty, and security, implementation can be regarded as productive if it results in higher levels of consensus on policy.

In summary, much of the controversy over where implementation begins and ends, what framework to apply, and how to measure success can be handled in two ways. First, a broad perspective should be taken on implementation, incorporating both policy formulation and policy results. Second, frameworks and evaluative criteria need to be responsive to the kind of implementation problem presented by the nature of the statute or policy being implemented. Analysts must adjust their tools to the analytical problem.

Variable Determinants of Implementation

The difficulty with the work of many implementation scholars attempting to identify the critical determinants of implementation has been either the listing is too inclusive and lacks parsimony or the factors identified are peculiar to the case under study. The flexible framework offered here suggests that the implementation analyst must choose factors strategically, expecting crucial conditions for implementation to vary. The implementation breakdown that occurs is likely to be associated with what is being attempted in policy (Nakamura and Smallwood 1980, 114). Depending on the characteristics of the policy being implemented, two basic kinds of problems may emerge.* First, the implementing agency may not have the will, competence, skill, and resources to perform implementation. Second, the implementing agency must succeed at constituency politics. It must avoid being dominated or captured by a single clientele group that gains a monopoly over the benefits being provided and avoids any costs the agency may have to impose (Chubb 1985, 290). It must also avoid sharp divisions among constituencies that produce deadlocks. Challenges related to administrative capability or clientele relations and the strategies agencies employ to cope with them are intertwined in ongoing administration. Agencies that have internal strength and resources can also deal with external pressures from clientele. At the same time, the structure of particular policies call on agencies to employ either negotiating strategies or bureaucratic expertise. Table 18.4 (page 476) indicates how the problems or clusters of critical variables are associated with statutory structures set out in table 18.2.

Table 18.4 suggests that where an agency has clear goals and procedural flexibility, neither administrative nor clientele problems will predominate, and neither is expected to overwhelm the agency. Barring changes in the more general policy environment, implementation problems should not be serious (Type 1). When the agency is placed under procedural specificity, however, severe administrative problems are introduced into implementation. Pressure is placed on bureaucracy to discover means to meet tight deadlines or develop intelligence that can be used in policy modification (Type 3). Where the goals of an agency are unclear, the agency is orphaned to fend for itself among contending interests. Under such circumstances, the central implementation problem will be to formulate a strategy to prevent domination or capture (Type 4). Where the statutory structure provides open-ended goals and procedural specificity, both administrative and clientele problems are likely to be severe and will need to be dealt with together (Type 2). Critical to implementation will be creative entrepreneurship by bureaucratic leaders.

---

* There is an obvious similarity between these two problem types and the rational/bureaucratic imperative and the consensual imperative as discussed in Rein and Rabinovitz (1978).

TABLE 18.4
Association of Types of Statutory Structures with Key Clusters of
Variables Affecting Implementation

	Administrative Capability	
	Less important	Critical
Clientele relationships		
Less important	Type 1	Type 3
Critical	Type 4	Type 2

Conclusion

The ferment and excitement of a field of research is probably better measured by disorder and lack of conceptual clarity than order and agreement on theoretical constructs. Judged by these criteria, the field of implementation is exhilarating indeed. Implementation scholars have disagreed among themselves on a wide variety of fundamentals: when the implementation stage begins and ends; whether the appropriate perspective for implementation research is statutory authorization or deliverers' actions; how to measure good implementation; and what are the crucial factors affecting implementation. This chapter has reviewed these controversies and taken a position on how they should be resolved.

Table 18.5 summarizes a flexible framework for analyzing implementation and is offered as a response to the controversies and criticisms in the implementation literature. The framework is broad, comprehending the nature of the decision costs faced by policy formulators and the consequent policy challenges presented to implementors through signals in statutory structure. The flexible framework offered in table 18.5 skirts the controversies in the literature between top-down, bottom-up, programmed, adaptive, and other approaches to implementation by arguing that patterns of implementation will vary with the implementation challenge presented by the statutory structure. The implementation phase should contribute toward policy improvement or the evolution toward more tractable problems for which there are more doable and agreeable responses. Since the sort of accomplishments necessary for evolution change according to the implementation model and structure of the statute, the criteria for evaluating implementation need to vary also.

There is a good deal of controversy in the implementation literature over which factors are most important in determining implementation success or failure. The flexible framework presented here anticipates that different determinants or clusters of variables associated with administrative competence or responsiveness to

TABLE 18.5

Summary Table: Flexible Framework for Analyzing Implementation

Nature of Decision Costs	Structure of Statute	Appropriate Approach	Criteria for Evaluation	Critical Variables Affecting Implementation
Low negotiation costs / low information costs	Clear goals; procedural flexibility	Command-control; programmed	Achievement of goals	Changes in external circumstances or policy environment
High negotiation costs / low information costs	Open-ended goals; procedural flexibility	Adaptive; backward mapping	Grass-roots creativity; modifying proximate policy behavior	Bureaucratic entrepreneurship; "fixers" and "double agents"
Low negotiation costs / high information costs	Clear goals; procedural specificity	Oversight; policy reformulation	Policy learning	Administrative capability
High negotiation costs / high information costs	Open-ended goals; procedural specificity	Bargaining	Broad agreement and support; avoidance of agency capture	Clientele relationships

clientele will take on critical status depending on the nature of the challenge presented to implementors.

Implementation is likely to evolve over time as certain tasks of consensus building or information gathering are accomplished and others emerge. Therefore, the flexible framework for analyzing implementation is dynamic. When decision costs embodied in policy are altered, the expected patterns of implementation also change. The analytical approaches and evaluative criteria implementation analysts employ must be modified to fit the evolving circumstances. It is possible, for instance, that successful implementation of a statute that at first fits the last row of table 18.5 may later move toward the implementation circumstances portrayed in the second-to-the-last row. Analysts in such circumstances must shift their attention from bargaining among interests with conflicting goals to the administrative capability of agencies in gathering information and engendering confidence.

In closing, some overall assessment of the contribution to understanding made by the virtual outpouring of implementation among accomplishments has been the linkage that implementation studies have provided between the fields of political science and public administration. Implementation research has been the conduit through which much of the subject matter of public administration, in a new, policy-oriented formulation, has been reintroduced into political science. Without question, before the 1970s, political scientists had concentrated too exclusively on policy formulation and therefore missed much political and policy significance (Dexter 1981, 420).

Implementation studies have also improved the appreciation for the factors which lead to policy success and failure. Early implementation studies were overly preoccupied with policy failure and were unduly pessimistic about the chances that any policies would be implemented successfully. As the field has matured, however, the notion that policies are preordained to failure has faded (Goggin 1986, 328). It has come to be recognized that policy problems evolve rather than are solved.

Implementation studies have sensitized their readers to the burdens policies place on the operation and maintenance of the political system. The load has come to be understood not simply in terms of financial, personpower, and other resources. Policies also challenge the capability of the system to supply creative leadership and forge convergence of interests. It would be reactionary to suggest that only easily implementable policies should be pursued. It would be foolish to pursue policies without sensitivity to the demands they place on governmental capacity to implement.

References

Bardach, Eugene. 1977. *The Implementation Game: What Happens When a Bill Becomes a Law.* Cambridge, Mass.: MIT Press.

Berman, Paul. 1980. "Thinking About Programmed and Adaptive Implementation: Matching Strategies to Situations." In *Why Policies Succeed or Fail,* edited by Helen M. Ingram and Dean E. Mann. Beverly Hills: Sage.

Berman, Paul, and Milbrey McLaughlin. 1978. "Implementation of Educational Innovation." *Educational Forum* 40:345–70.

Browne, Angela, and Aaron Wildavsky. 1984. "Implementation as Mutual Adaptation." In *Implementation,* edited by Jeffrey L. Pressman and Aaron Wildavsky. Berkeley: University of California Press.

Browning, Rufus, Dale Rogers Marshall, and David Tabb. 1984. *Protest Is Not Enough.* Berkeley: University of California Press.

Chubb, John E. 1985. "Excessive Regulation: The Case of Federal Aid to Education." *Political Science Quarterly* 11:287–311.

Dexter, Lewis Anthony. 1981. "Undesigned Consequences of Purposive Legislative Action: Alternatives to Implementation." *Journal of Public Policy* 1:413–31.

Elmore, Richard F. 1982. "Backward Mapping: Implementation Research and Policy Decisions." In *Studying Implementation,* edited by Walter Williams. Chatham, N.J.: Chatham House.

Goggin, Malcolm L. 1986. "The 'Too Few Cases/Too Many Variables' Problem in Implementation Research." *Western Political Quarterly* 39:328–47.

Hargrove, Erwin C. 1980. *The Search for Implementation Theory.* Nashville: Vanderbilt University Institute for Policy Studies.

Ingram, Helen M. 1977. "Policy Implementation through Bargaining: The Case of Federal Grants-in-Aid." *Public Policy* 25:499–526.

Ingram, Helen M. 1987. "Review of *The Political Hand: Policy Implementation and Youth Employment Program.*" *American Political Science Review* 81:640–41.

Jennings, Edward T. 1980. "Urban Riots and Welfare Policy: A Test of the Piven-Cloward Theory." In *Why Policies Succeed or Fail,* edited by Helen M. Ingram and Dean E. Mann. Beverly Hills: Sage.

Levin, Martin A., and Barbara Ferman. 1985. *The Political Hand: Policy Implementation and Youth Employment Programs.* New York: Pergamon.

Lipsky, Michael. 1978. "Standing the Study of Public Policy Implementation on Its Head." In *American Politics and Public Policy,* edited by Walter Dean Burnham and Martha Weinberg. Cambridge, Mass.: MIT Press.

Lowi, Theodore J. 1964. "American Business, Public Policy, Case Studies, and Political Theory." *World Politics* 16:677–715.

Lowi, Theodore J. 1972. "Four Systems of Policy Choice." *Public Administration Review* 32:298–310.

McLaughlin, Milbrey. 1976. "Implementation as Mutual Adaptation." In *Social Programs in Implementation,* edited by Walter Williams and Richard Elmore. New York: Academic Press.

Majone, Giandomenico, and Aaron Wildavsky. 1979. "Implementation as Evolution." In *Implementation,* edited by Jeffrey L. Pressman and Aaron Wildavsky. 2d ed. Berkeley: University of California Press.

Mazmanian, Daniel A., and Paul Sabatier. 1983. *Implementation and Public Policy.* Glenview, Ill.: Scott, Foresman.

Meier, Kenneth J. 1987. *Politics and Bureaucracy.* 2d ed. Monterey, Calif.: Brooks/Cole.

Nakamura, Robert T., and Frank Smallwood. 1980. *The Politics of Policy Implementation.* New York: St. Martin's Press.

Pressman, Jeffrey L., and Aaron Wildavsky. 1973. *Implementation.* Berkeley: University of California Press.

Pressman, Jeffrey L., and Aaron Wildavsky. 1979. *Implementation.* 2d ed. Berkeley: University of California Press.

Pressman, Jeffrey L., and Aaron Wildavsky. 1984. *Implementation.* 3d ed. Berkeley: University of California Press.

Ranney, Austin. 1968. *Political Science and Public Policy.* Chicago: Markham.

Rein, Martin, and Francine F. Rabinovitz. 1978. "Implementation: A Theoretical Perspective." In *American Politics and Public Policy,* edited by Walter Dean Burnham and Martha Weinberg. Cambridge, Mass.: MIT Press.

Ripley, Randall B. 1985. *Policy Analysis in Political Science.* Chicago: Nelson Hall.

Ripley, Randall B., and Grace A. Franklin. 1986. *Policy Implementation and Bureaucracy.* 2d ed. Chicago: Dorsey Press.

Sabatier, Paul A. 1986. "Top-Down and Bottom-Up Approaches to Implementation Research." *Journal of Public Policy* 6:21–48.

Sabatier, Paul A., and Daniel A. Mazmanian. 1983. "Policy Implementation." In *Encyclopedia of Policy Studies,* edited by Stuart S. Nagel. New York: Marcel Dekker.

Salisbury, Robert, and John Heinz. 1970. "A Theory of Policy Analysis and Some Preliminary Applications." In *Policy Analysis in Political Science,* edited by Ira Sharkansky. Chicago: Markham.

Schneider, Ann. 1982. "Studying Policy Implementation: A Conceptual Framework." *Evaluation Review* 6:715–30.

Sharkansky, Ira, ed. 1970. *Policy Analysis in Political Science.* Chicago: Markham.

Van Horn, Carl E. 1979. *Implementation in the Federal System.* Lexington, Mass.: Lexington Books.

Van Meter, Donald S., and Carl E. Van Horn. 1975. "The Policy Implementation Process: A Conceptual Framework." *Administration and Society* 6:445–88.

Wagner, Kathryn D. 1986. "Implementation Gap: Congress, EPA, and the Development of Environmental Policies." Presented at the annual meeting of the American Political Science Association, Washington, D.C.

Wildavsky, Aaron. 1979. *Speaking Truth to Power.* Boston: Little, Brown.

Williams, Walter. 1982. *Studying Implementation.* Chatham, N.J.: Chatham House.

PART SIX

Looking to the Future

19

The End of an Alliance: Public Administration in the Eighties

HERBERT KAUFMAN

In a rare moment of prescience thirty years ago, I suggested that the doctrines of public administration as they had been formulated up to that time were likely to undergo significant change because they had been formulated when those who took part in the shaping of our governmental machinery were concerned primarily with building a professional bureaucracy, whereas the next generation of governmental designers would be in turmoil over how to control it (Kaufman 1956). The proposition has held up pretty well, and the effects on public administration are increasingly apparent.

Underlying the prediction was the argument that the design of our government was strongly influenced by the quest for three values in the conduct of the public business: representativeness, politically neutral competence, and executive leadership. Although all three values are always pursued in the ordering of our government, one or another has usually been emphasized more heavily than the others in different periods, with the result that different institutions have been strengthened at different times. Thus, in reaction against the English monarch and his royal governors in the colonies, representativeness was given precedence, and legislatures and the parties were ascendant in the early history of the Republic. The abuses attending this state of affairs sparked measures to insulate governmental administration from political influences in order to achieve expertise and political neutrality in the conduct of the public business; whence came civil service reform, the short ballot, and the assignment of authority to independent, nonelected boards and commissions (and, later, government corporations). These arrangements, added to the effects of the earlier stress on representativeness, produced a high degree of fragmentation in governmental administration, which in turn engendered efforts to equip chief executives to coordinate the far-flung and diverse administrative operations of the expanding public sector. The executive budget, enlargement of executive staffs, executive reorganization powers, and the grouping of bureaus in superdepartments responsible to chief executives followed.

This portrait, of course, is neater than reality. It is a schematic diagram, not an actual blueprint. Thus, for example, representativeness benefited not only legislatures and parties; it also generated what may be termed special-interest administrative agencies—such as the Departments of Agriculture, Commerce, Labor, Housing and Urban Development, Education, and Health and Human Services—for groups in American society realized that administrative institutions are as important to them as elected officials and electoral organizations are. Similarly, weakening the grip of partisan politics on administration not only enhanced the political neutrality and the ability of public agencies; it also helped chief executives by providing a workforce not beholden principally to party officers rather than to the official nominally in charge of their appointments. And, to cite a third instance, increasing the capacity of chief executives to lead the administrative machinery of government brought into the open policy choices and bargains that had previously been made in obscurity, and thus buttressed the process of representation.

Still, the general pattern seemed to hold in 1956. Even though pursuit of each value had spillover effects, the major consequences of each value are still discernible and help explain the development of our institutions and our administrative doctrines. As the late Wallace Sayre used to say, the benefits of governmental reform are usually immediate and the costs are usually cumulative. When the costs mount, we start looking for new reforms.

The doctrines of public administration in the 1930s and 1940s subscribed simultaneously to two of the values and two sets of reforms. They embraced the goal of neutral competence by advocating extension of the merit system upward, outward, and downward, as the President's Committee on Administrative Management (the "Brownlow Committee") phrased it (1937, 7). But they also esteemed executive leadership and endorsed new budgetary, reorganization, and other powers for executives. The Brownlow Committee went even further, proposing presidential authority over personnel management that the President then lacked and recommending that the administrative duties of the independent regulatory commissions, which the committee described as a headless fourth branch of government, be removed from those bodies and lodged in executive departments (1937, 39-42).

A disinterested observer might have wondered about the apparent contradictions in these recommendations. Is it really feasible to enlarge the chief executive's authority over the administrative apparatus of government and still insulate that apparatus from political influence? Chief executives, after all, are by no means politically neutral. How can anyone embrace the notion of keeping the administrative establishment out of politics and at the same time placing it unambiguously within the executive's jurisdiction?

This seemed possible at that time because those who wanted to advance bureaucratic professionalism and those seeking to build executive leadership happened to have common interests at the moment. This was true at all levels of government, to some extent, but particularly so at the federal level, and public administration doctrines were then, as now, especially influenced by federal experience. To be specific, the rapid expansion of the workforce under the New Deal, and the administrative problems accompanying this sudden growth, lent support to the argument that recruitment of untrained personnel through political channels could not meet the requirements of modern government. The need for training and ability was never more apparent. Moreover, the new civil servants were the spearheads of social innovation and therefore enjoyed considerable public approval. In addition, many were gifted people who would not have entered government service but for the depression, which buttressed the case for broad delegations of power to them. The New Deal was thus a boon for the advocates of neutral competence. And since the new bureaucrats themselves had incentives both to support the President and to protect their discretion and job security, they found the ideas of executive leadership and neutral competence easily reconcilable.

At the same time, supporters of the President could endorse steps toward neutral competence because a professionalized civil service would not be dependent on, and therefore owe its allegiance to, local political satraps. Moreover, many of the New Deal agencies had been staffed with Democratic stalwarts, and the prospect of blanketing them into tenured status through extension of the merit system had its political attractions. Furthermore, of neutral competence, were New Dealers backing the President for ideological reasons. Consequently, a curious and somewhat implausible alliance was formed, and its strategic considerations, sometimes disguised as scientific principles, were stamped on the discipline of public administration.

The strains in the alliance were already perceptible in 1956. President Eisenhower, who had taken office after twenty years of Democratic control of the White House, was confronted by an executive branch run by officers and employees long associated with his political adversaries. He moved promptly to take control by increasing the number of posts not subject to formal civil service procedures so that he could appoint people of acceptable ideological persuasion. His action met with outcries of concern from the defenders of neutral competence (Emmerich and Belsley 1954, 1, 3–4). They had some grounds for fearing that the merit system was under attack. Republican party leaders, long excluded from federal patronage, were pressing for the rewards of victory. But that is another story. My point is that the early experience of the new conservative President was the first indication that the fortuitous coalition of the neutral competence school and the executive leadership school might come apart.

The rift has widened and deepened steadily. It was not merely partisan in origin; even under President Johnson's Great Society administration, the antipoverty programs were entrusted to the new Office of Economic Opportunity. Ranking presidential advisory staff members felt that giving the money for the new programs to the existing agencies would not produce any innovation (Levitan 1969). The old bureaucracies were not deemed capable of changing their ways, let alone inventing new approaches. The permanent government, as it came to be called, was not admired more by Democrats than Republicans, or more by liberals than conservatives.

But the tensions did grow sharper in the Nixon administration. The President and his staff regarded the bureaucracy with suspicion and even hostility. They enlarged the Executive Office staff—calling it a counter-bureaucracy—and impounded funds and tried to reorganize the executive branch, all with the end of increasing their control of the administrative agencies (Nathan 1983). A House investigating committee even charged violations of civil service laws in that campaign (U.S. Congress, House Committee 1976). Some Nixon aides invoked the arguments of the Brownlow Committee to support their actions on behalf of presidential leadership. But they did not mention the committee's enthusiasm for the merit system. The two values had ceased to coincide.

The split grew wider and deeper under President Reagan. His administration should be called more antigovernment (except, perhaps, for the military) than antibureaucracy, but the impact of its policies—deregulation, transfer of functions to the states, reduced budgets, and contraction or elimination of programs—on the morale of broad segments of the civilian workforce has apparently been negative (Nathan 1983). And if any sense of bureaucratic partnership in governance survived these broad programmatic developments, the breaking of the air controllers' strike must have laid it to rest. When more than 11,000 air traffic controllers went on strike in 1981, the Reagan administration fired them for violating the law against strikes by federal employees, stripped their union of collective bargaining rights, and hired replacements. More than five years elapsed before a new union was formed and recognized, and its leaders were careful to proclaim, "Confrontation politics have no place on our agenda" (Witkin 1986; Molotsky 1987). In addition the Executive Office, building on a practice begun in the Carter administration, instituted more rigorous and sweeping controls on proposed agency regulations than had ever been employed before, while using presidential appointing power adroitly to ensure unity of outlook and adherence to presidential policies throughout the upper reaches of the governmental establishment. New political appointees were encouraged to use their powers energetically to overcome bureaucrats' pursuit of their own concepts of program goals (Nathan 1983). Nobody is likely now to cheer both the President and the bureaucracy as many did during the New Deal; the partisans of one are not well disposed toward the other. The situation has reached the point where one must choose between the two institutions. The alliance has disappeared.

Conceivably, it may reappear in time. Some observers think President Reagan was so successful in imprinting his policy preferences on the bureaucracies that they will bear his stamp for many years to come. While he or others of his persuasion (such as President Bush) are in office, the coalition of executive leadership advocates and neutral competence proponents may therefore form anew. But when a President of a different philosophy comes to power and confronts the Reagan-fashioned bureaucracies, tensions are likely to surface again. The honeymoon period of harmony and consensus that obtained during the New Deal and influenced the doctrines of academic public administration seems improbable in the future, except perhaps for the most fleeting intervals. Public administration will now have to deal with a wholly different set of conditions.

One response will be that just as the public service improved because of the fairly successful struggle against political interference by legislators and party officials, so it would now benefit from protection against presidential intervention. That is, politics is politics, and taking administration out of politics means taking it out of presidential politics as well as out of legislative and party politics. This goal could be accomplished in part by reducing the powers of the President and his political appointees (1) to block, suspend, alter, or rescind bureau regulations; (2) to appoint, assign, transfer, promote, discipline, and remove personnel; (3) to exercise control over the details of bureau budgets; (4) to supervise bureau relations with Congress; (5) to issue commands to bureaus; and (6) by restrictions on executive controls. The goal could be furthered also by preserving the status of the independent regulatory commissions, by reinforcing the tenure of civil servants and bringing more top positions within civil service requirements, and by vesting in these officers most agency authority over policy, organization, and procedure. Such measures, added to the present limitations on control of bureaucrats by elected officers and the courts, and to the existing civil service protections surrounding public servants, would constitute a significant weakening of the capacity of the traditional branches of government to influence what the agencies do from day to day. In other words, the discretion, autonomy, and freedom of action of bureaucracies would be broadened by a wide margin.

Not all bureaucracies would welcome steps of this kind; they would not want to be exposed to the intense political heat that would then be focused on them. But many would be pleased. In their experience, political intrusion into their affairs is usually intended to do special, often questionable, favors for political constituents or other special interests. It is generally motivated by short-run political opportunities rather than the long-run effects of the favor on the mission of the agency, on the well-being of the program, and on other clients. It is frequently arranged privately, even clandestinely. It is often based on little or no information, or even on misinformation, especially in technical and complex fields. Under the circumstances, bureaucrats with long service and expertise, who have learned all the implications and repercussions of their actions, should be expected to contend that they are far better qualified than any outsiders, even elected ones, to administer the programs within their purview. In addition, they can justifiably claim to impart an element of policy stability to their programs, which might otherwise change direction so often and so swiftly, following every slight change in the electoral fortunes and the attitudes of politicians, that the public would never be able to plan or invest or keep track of its rights and duties under the law. The bureaucrats would contend that they do not seek or want a totally free hand to do anything they wish; the other organs of government are amply equipped to contain them without getting involved in individual cases or minute details and without casually overriding carefully considered agency judgments. They simply want, the bureaucrats would say, to be accepted as equal partners with the three traditional branches in the process of governing, and to be accorded recognition as at least equally virtuous, legitimate, democratic members of the political structure. We can all understand why many bureaucrats would see themselves in this light and advance this view.

But what of the academic students of public administration? Will they opt to back governmental bureaucracies in this new environment, or will they, after so many years of describing the public chief executive as the legitimate and appropriate manager and head of the administrative establishment (a proposition, by the way, that legislative bodies never accepted in practice), find it intellectually impossible now to characterize the chief executive as an equal co-worker with agency staffs and the higher civil service? Will they insist that chief executives stand at the apex of an administrative pyramid and therefore have the obligation and the right to command the agencies as subordinate officers, or will they hold that the agencies are answerable to the people just as elected officers are, and therefore can legitimately treat with elected executives and legislators as constitutional coordinates?

To those reared in the tradition that officers and employees appointed to positions in governmental agencies are subordinates of the elected stratum of government and are legally and morally obligated to obey the directives of that stratum to the best of their ability, even when they disagree with the policies they are ordered to carry out, the contention that they are constitutional co-equals sounds strange and somewhat menacing. Yet the end of the alliance between the adherents of neutral competence and the believers in executive leadership does lead a few students of public administration to adopt this view.

The alternatives of which I speak are moral injunctions, not empirical descriptions. We all know that bureaucracies possess significant power to determine the content of governmental policies. We all know that their political resources are substantial—information, constituency support, decision-making authority, access to the communication media, control of the speed and distribution of services, connections with key political officers and staffs, and so on—and that they therefore are already independent participants and bargainers in the process of governing. The facts are not at issue. What is at issue are the legitimating myths of our system —myths in the anthropological sense of unifying belief systems subscribed to by most of the members of a society that limit and channel the behavior of all the members and particularly the behavior of those in formal positions of authority and leadership. Invariably, these myths work imperfectly. Without them, however, social groupings soon disintegrate because there are no generally accepted distinctions between legitimate and illegitimate authority; they are essential to social order. Much of political philosophy is a search for myths that will win a large measure of assent, and a remarkable variety of myths have proven effective in different places and at different times. One of the axioms of modern Western-style democracies is that the authority of officials springs from the will of the people expressed through elections. Every appointed officer holds office and acquires legitimate authority ultimately by action of elected officials; that is true even of members of the Supreme Court. To be sure, we have conferred on the federal judiciary special sources of autonomy granted no other officials in our polity. But the judges are probably protected as much by our belief that they should be immune from ordinary political pressures and manipulations as by the procedural shields devised for them. In the case of our public bureaucracies, though we have provided them with some procedural shields, we have never adopted the myth that they, like the judges, are coordinate with the elected officials who gave them office. That is why the contention that they are equals of the elected officials is so startling to those who have hitherto thought of them as loyally subordinating themselves to their political superiors. If the new view prevails, it would greatly enhance bureaucratic power vis-à-vis other political actors.

That some of the literature of public administration tacitly harbored such an assumption—that is, an assumption that bureaucrats are and ought to be constitutionally coordinate with elected officials—was pointed out nearly four decades ago by Dwight Waldo (1948). In *The Administrative State*, he noted in the literature the implication that administrative technicians should be of the ruling class, a premise he thought rested on exceedingly weak foundations. "All the conflicts and inconsistencies in the public administration movement meet at this point," he added with characteristic foresight (Waldo 1948, 160–61). Several years later, in a 1952 essay titled "Bureaucracy and Constitutionalism," Norton Long provided a spirited explicit defense of bureaucratic equality, closing with the dictum, "The theory of our constitution needs to recognize and understand the working and the potential of our great fourth branch of government [the bureaucracy], taking a rightful place beside President, Congress, and Courts" (p. 818). But Long directed his remarks exclusively at the doctrine of legislative supremacy and based his argument on the contention that the federal bureaucracy as a whole is more representative than Congress and therefore has as good or better claim to speak for the people; on these grounds, he concluded that it should not be considered, treated, or act as, a subordinate institution—"a gun for hire by any party" (Long 1952, 818). On the question of its relationship to the President, he said nothing. One may infer either that he did not at the time apply his logic to the chief executive, perhaps still cleaving to a belief in the validity of executive leadership, or that he considered it obvious that what he said fit the President as well as Congress; the article itself is ambiguous. Nonetheless, it is an early assertion of the constitutional justification for bureaucratic independence.

The Blacksburg Manifesto issued by five noteworthy public administration scholars in 1984 and 1986 contains no ambiguities:

> The popular will does not reside solely in elected officials but in a constitutional order that envisions a remarkable variety of legitimate titles to participate in governance. The Public Administration, created by statutes based on this constitutional order, holds one of these titles. Its role, therefore, is not to cower before a sovereign legislative assembly or a sovereign elected executive. Our tradition and our constitution know no such sovereign. Rather the task of The Public Administration is to share in governing wisely and well the *constitutional order* that the framers of the Constitution intended as an expression of the will of the people who alone are sovereign. (Wamsley, Goodsell, Rohr, White, and Wolf 1984, 13)

Clearly, the executive leadership assumption that the administrative edifice of government should be looked at as a hierarchy under the stewardship of the chief executive cuts no ice with this group. For them, the separation of the two schools of thought in the old coalition is complete. They go with the bureaucracies.

Most members of the public administration community will doubtless part company with this extraordinary zeal. Even most of those who decide to stick with the bureaucracies will be content to espouse the traditional impediments to political intervention in administration without claiming a constitutional basis for bureaucratic autonomy. But many will go with the chief executive rather than the bureaucracies. For them, executive leadership will retain its value precisely because bureaucracies are already so independent that our governmental administrative organization is fragmented and dispersed. If fragmentation could occur while there was a broad consensus that agencies belong under the command of the chief executive, what, they will ask, would happen if this conceptual restraint were removed?

It is not only the pro-executive camp that will be aroused by the demands, strategies, and occasionally extravagant assertions of the pro-bureaucratic camp; the admirers of legislatures will also be drawn into the fray. Historically, chief executives and legislatures have jousted with each other over which of them owns the bureaucracies. In many ways, the bureaucracies have benefited from this rivalry by playing the two elected branches one against the other. If one stands in the way of what they want, they invoke the assistance of the other. In my opinion, they tend to be more responsive to Congress than to the President because Congress can do more to and for them most of the time, and because members of Congress and their staffs maintain steadier contact with the agencies under their jurisdiction (Kaufman 1981, 164–66). But even Congress is uneasy about the growth of bureaucratic power, and those who claim that the bureaucracies are as representative of the popular will as are elected officials—if not more so!—simply reinforce and intensify congressional fears. Accordingly, it is conceivable that the officials of both elected branches may start to lower the level of competition between their branches and join hands to contain the perceived threat to their preeminence as representatives of the people. Since the Constitution virtually builds into the government a contest between the two branches, such collaboration would be a monumental modification of the way our system works. On the other hand, if we were to get a substantial increase in bureaucratic autonomy based on a presumed constitutional equality of the bureaucracy with the President and Congress, it is as least plausible that we would get a legislative-executive entente in response.

In that event, the stage would be set for a new battle over the extent to which bureaucrats should be—and, indeed, have been—insulated from the influence of elected officials. From time to time in the past, occasional commentators have complained that these protections have already been carried too far and should be rolled back (Lemann 1977; Peters 1976). They believe it is at this time too difficult for newly elected political leaders to make the government respond to their directives. Imagine, then, what they will say about proposals to raise the ramparts shielding bureaucrats still higher and about the contention that doctrine up to now has overstated the constitutional obligation of professional civil servants to be obedient. A coalition of elected officers and their supporters will not only resist this movement; they will answer with efforts of their own to reduce the bases of administrative independence. The efforts will be particularly energetic whenever the winds of political change blow strong, whether from the right or left.

If this struggle materializes as I have postulated, the outcome is uncertain. On the one hand, the bureaucracies and their allies have a great many impressive resources. There are 16 million public employees (U.S. Bureau of the Census 1985). They are well organized, politically active, politically sophisticated, and well financed. Public-service unions are now a major part of the labor movement. A whole industry has grown up to prepare applicants for civil service tests, and there is not much doubt which side it will take. And, above all, civil service has become a kind of sacred symbol; no public official wants to be identified as an opponent of the merit system or to take a position that permits him or her to be characterized as a friend of the spoils system. In any event, civil service laws and procedures notwithstanding, one can make the case that administrative agencies have been responsive to elected leaders. So the attempts to reduce the familiar sources of bureaucratic autonomy will have the heavy sledding.

On the other hand, civil servants are not a unified bloc. They are an immensely varied collection of occupations, ranging from highly trained professionals and technicians to relatively unskilled labor. They comprise a diversity of income levels and social statuses. They contend with one another for shares of governmental income. They are not all of the same political persuasion. Their interests are not identical. They do not speak with a single voice; numerous public-service unions compete for membership. Furthermore, civil servants are often the scapegoats for governmental shortcomings and program failures not of their making, convenient victims on whom unwise policy makers can blame their own follies; bureaucracy in the abstract is therefore a frequent target of hostility and derision despite the popularity of the merit system idea. Bureaucracies consequently enter the fray under significant handicaps.

So the battle could go either way. If a single party with a coherent program sweeps both houses of Congress and the presidency, and if the new incumbents then conclude that their endeavors to put their program into action have been frustrated by the bureaucracies, they might manage to undo some of the protections attained by the civil service. But if scandals involving high political officials are unearthed, demands for further insulation of bureaucracies from politics are likely to enjoy a sympathetic reception. If the courts are staffed by judges inclined to reexamine the constitutional basis of power delegated to bureaucracies, bureaucracies may find their authority curtailed. But if the courts are disposed to throw constitutional protections around appointed administrative officeholders, as the Supreme Court did in *Elrod* v. *Burns* (427 U.S. 347, 1976), the position of the bureaucracies may be strengthened. The outcome of the struggle is by no means foreordained.

But one thing is certain: If this outline of the future resembles even vaguely the actual course of events, the cleavages in the public administration community, dimly perceived in 1956, should soon appear sharply and unmistakably. Some academics will praise the heroic and virtuous civil servants who refuse to bow to the evil demands of wicked elected politicians, and will strive to reinforce and encourage such fortitude. Others will lament the decline in discipline, hierarchical loyalty, and respect for leadership evinced by such attitudes and actions, and will deplore the potential disintegration of government these trends allegedly entail. Some will disparage electoral and legislative processes as methods of reflecting the popular will, extolling administrative procedures for personnel selection and management, rule-making, and policy making generally. Others will rediscover the admirable qualities of political leaders whose hold on office depends on their ability to win electoral support, and will decry the arrogance of tenured bureaucrats several steps removed from such uncertainty. Some will take up their pens against the unsavoriness of many politicians, others will sound the alarm about bureaucratic overzealousness and the managerial revolution. Students of public administration and practitioners, too, who once thought they all shared the same values, will discover that they were only temporarily in harmony.

In 1956, I speculated that the ideational split would be accompanied by an organizational split. "One may . . . hazard the guess," I wrote, "that the American Society for Public Administration will remain firmly in the hands of the neutral competence group while the executive leadership school in public administration looks more and more to the American Political Science Association as its forum" (Kaufman 1956, 1073). I am not aware of any studies that would tell us whether any such tendency has revealed itself at this point; one cannot be sure from casual observation. But if it has not yet done so, I still believe it will because of the dynamics of the situation. My argument here—that champions of the elected chief executive and students of parties, elections, and the legislative process in political science will probably join forces—is a refinement of my original stand. But the thrust of my hypothesis is essentially unchanged and still seems valid to me: The adherents of the competing values are likely to identify with different organizations.

The actual division will not be a neat, clean split. Some members of the professional public administration community will remain committed to executive leadership doctrines, while many political scientists will subscribe to the campaign for increased bureaucratic independence. But the practitioner-oriented American Society for Public Administration, the schools of public administration and public policy studies, the institutions that train people for administrative posts in substantive fields such as health and hospital and school administration, the unions and professional associations of government officers and employees, the management consultants, and the National Academy of Public Administration will line up for the most part on one side; academic observers and analysts of American government processes will incline largely the other way.

No doubt a sizable fraction of both groups will continue to seek a middle ground that reconciles the divergent positions. They will find this much harder to do than it was before the alliance that prevailed a generation ago broke apart. The positions are logically and tactically incompatible as things now stand.

People of equal goodwill, high principles, and intellectual stature will turn up in all the camps. Philosophical differences will engender clashing perceptions of the facts and opposing interpretations of the Constitution. Policy differences will produce switches from one camp to another, depending on which organ of government happens to further particular policies in any given period. No single, unambiguous overarching principle will resolve these controversies by winning overwhelming endorsement as the incontrovertible truth. Instead, a continuously evolving modus vivendi will permit us to live with the differences. At least I hope so, for differences there will surely be.

Tomorrow's students of public administration, wherever they study, will thus encounter a field more divided than their predecessors did. I think they will find the ferment interesting, but they should be aware of the famous Chinese curse, "May you live in interesting times." Those are times of challenge and trial. They are also stimulating, exhilarating, and often productive. In all this upheaval, my analysis may be invalidated. If it is not, I will be most gratified. But I will find the effort rewarding if all it does is contribute a little constructive bit to the discussion on which our profession has embarked.

Acknowledgments

This chapter is a slightly revised version of the John M. Gaus Lecture delivered at the annual meeting of the American Political Science Association on 29 August 1986. I should like here to acknowledge my debt, and express my gratitude, to John Uhr for the ideas and information he contributed to the lecture, and to Robert A. Katzmann for his helpful comments on the first draft of the manuscript.

References

Emmerich, Herbert, and Lyle G. Belsley. 1954. "The Federal Career Service—What Next?" *Public Administration Review* 14:1–12.

Kaufman, Herbert. 1956. "Emerging Conflicts in the Doctrines of Public Administration." *American Political Science Review* 50:1057–73.

Kaufman, Herbert. 1981. *The Administrative Behavior of Federal Bureau Chiefs*. Washington, D.C.: Brookings Institution.

Lemann, Nicholas. December, 1977. "The Case for Political Patronage." *Washington Monthly* 9:8–17.

Levitan, Sar A. 1969. *The Great Society's Poor Law: A New Approach to Poverty*. Baltimore: Johns Hopkins University Press.

Long, Norton E. 1952. "Bureaucracy and Constitutionalism." *American Political Science Review* 46:808–18.

Molotsky, Irvin. 1987. "Air Controllers Vote New Union." *New York Times*, 12 June.

Nathan, Richard. 1983. *The Administrative Presidency*. New York: Wiley.

Peters, Charles. September, 1976. "A Kind Word for the Spoils System." *Washington Monthly* 8:26–30.

The President's Committee on Administrative Management. 1937. *Report with Special Studies*. Washington, D.C.: Government Printing Office.

U.S. Bureau of the Census. 1985. *Statistical Abstract of the United States: 1986*. Washington, D.C.: Government Printing Office.

U.S. Congress, House Committee on Post Office and Civil Service. 1976. *Final Report on Violations and Abuses of Merit Principles in Federal Employment, Together with Minority Views*. 94th Cong., 2d sess. Washington, D.C.: Government Printing Office.

Waldo, Dwight. 1948. *The Administrative State*. New York: Ronald Press.

Wamsley, Gary L., Charles T. Goodsell, John A. Rohr, Orion F. White, and James F. Wolf. 1984. "The Public Administration and the Governance Process: Refocusing the American Dialogue." *Dialogue: The Public Administration Theory Network* 6(2).

Witkin, Richard. 1986. "Air Controllers Plan a New Union." *New York Times*, 24 September.

20

Emerging Issues in Public Administration

Charles T. Goodsell

My task is staggering: to identify emerging trends in the overall field of public administration, itself an "emerging superdiscipline," as John Rouse (1982) has aptly termed it.

To make this task manageable, I have taken two decisions. First, the word *emerging* is interpreted as referring to an issue that is on the way to trend status but not quite there. Issues that have already emerged—and are still very hot (e.g., cutback management, pay comparability)—are left to other authors of this book to examine. I shall review issues that are currently in the process of emerging, or that ought to be emerging. These would be candidates for future trend status, so to speak.

Second, I am being shamelessly subjective in selecting candidates for future trend status. A Naisbitt-like content analysis of the latest faddish ideas appearing in recent periodicals does not underlie this chapter (Naisbitt 1982). Instead, five issue areas have been picked for discussion that reflect my own orientation to the field. They are proposed as lines of inquiry in which the field could profitably invest substantial work in the decades to come. In making this selection I have deliberately avoided futuristic-sounding choices that are "far out" for attention-grabbing reasons, concentrating instead on notions that have clear ties to current research and close association with norms already embedded in the field.

Administrative Ethnography

The first of the five issue areas concerns organizational culture. This topic has already emerged in the field of business management and is now doing so in the study of public management. For several years, certain management scholars have been fascinated with the shared values, habits, folklore, symbols, and rituals of business

495

corporations. In effect, this interest has required such researchers to become amateur anthropologists, writing thumbnail ethnographies of the firms under scrutiny (Deal and Kennedy 1982; Kilmann, Saxon, and Serpa 1985; Sathe 1985; Schein 1985).

This new ethnographic interest has enlivened business management research, known for its often plodding character. Concern and curiosity have been aroused about what exists beyond the corporation's formal organization chart and official goals of production and profitability. The presumption of the research is that corporate life is characterized by extrarationality as well as rationality, and by pattern initiation at the level of rank-and-file workers as well as top management. The ultimate objective of this study seems, however, frankly instrumentalist: how to help the manager (especially the incoming manager) fit into and then shape the corporation's unique culture.

It is not as if organizational culture in government bureaucracies has never been investigated. Herbert Kaufman's classic on the Forest Service possesses elements of this orientation (Kaufman 1960). Harold Seidman's discussion of culture and personality within the federal establishment is also germane (1980, chap. 6). Nachmias and Rosenbloom (1978) have characterized the distinctive (and fascinating) culture of an entire national bureaucracy, that of Israel. Maynard-Moody, Stull, and Mitchell have dissected the subcultures of reorganization in a Kansas department (1986).

What is now needed is a more systematic research on the cultures of public bureaucracy. Less I be misunderstood, I do not mean by *systematic* an organized program of research that adheres faithfully to a single paradigm or methodology and thereupon accumulates scientific knowledge. My proposal is more open-ended, calling for increased work on the cultures of administration in a number of ways simultaneously. The research can be carried out with positivist, interpretist, or radical humanist ontological perspectives. It can employ ideational or adaptationist concepts of culture. Methodologies can be qualitative or quantitative, using interviews, observation, or participation. My own view is that any of a variety of research approaches are capable of contributing insights on this matter; the task is not to agree on the single rigorous research design that will then supposedly yield validated findings but to commit ourselves to basic exploration, using middle-range theories and multiple methodologies.

My personal preferences are for fairly tangible indicators of organizational attitudes and behaviors and an explicitly comparative approach. Patterns of speech, written language, internal governance, dress and deportment, and internal interaction should be examined. Studies can be made of architectural settings, office accouterment, and personal life styles. Other topics of research can be organizational stories, ceremonial rites of passage, logos and nomenclatures, and models of heroes and villains. While preliminary hypotheses and hunches will by necessity govern how we study these matters, it is important always to expect the unexpected and accept the discovered cultures on their own terms. Uniqueness and diversity must characterize such ethnography, not elegant typologies and proven hypotheses. Comparisons between carefully selected bureaucracies will help, by providing contrasts that highlight features that will otherwise be hidden from view. Admittedly, the consequence of such cultural study will not be ethnoscience, but a process of lively and diverse inquiry that will generate fresh insights, informed speculation, and reasoned interpretation (see Goodsell 1981).

The fascinating possibilities that could be uncovered by such research can be imagined by such questions as: What are the cultural differences between, say, bureaucracies that serve the poor (welfare departments) and those that serve the middle class (Social Security offices)? Do diplomats have a negotiating culture and military planners a confrontational one? Are consumer-protection agencies liberal and utility regulators conservative? Are staff planning units big spenders and budget offices tightwads? How do soldier policemen compare to clubhouse firemen? Do city managers in small towns operate in a peacetime atmosphere and their big-city counterparts in a wartime climate? The hypothetical cultural contrasts to be explored, discarded, and uncovered are endless.

The objects of such administrative ethnography would be two. First, as students of public administration, we will come to understand in richer detail than before the descriptive variety of administrative life. Like business management, public administration has traditionally been preoccupied by formal structures, not informal realities. Also, it has had a holistic bias, expressed by such notions as the civil service, integrated management, and the executive branch. We need constantly to disaggregate these artificially compounded ideas that are popular in our field and then describe faithfully the differentiations that are found.

Second, this emerging research could lay the basis for a deeper sense of identity and self-awareness on the part of members of bureaucracies. As its culture becomes more visible, participants in the single organization can begin to see themselves more clearly, as can a crowd seated in a rounded amphitheater as compared to the flat floor of, say, a hotel ballroom. This cultural awareness can lead to deeper bonds, more pride, and greater morale. Individuals are no longer mere bureaucrats, but members of a unique cultural entity whose content is clearly seen.

Administrative Biography

The second proposed research direction for the field is to write on the lives of people. In other words, more biography as well as more ethnography is needed in public administration. Just as we must know and appreciate organizational cultures more fully, we must become better acquainted with the field's past leaders and noteworthy personalities.

497

Once again, our business colleagues seem to be ahead of us. An established tradition in the subfield of business history is the preparation of biographies of great entrepreneurs. Books abound on leading historical figures like Henry Ford, Thomas Edison, Eli Whitney, E.I. DuPont, John D. Rockefeller, and Andrew Carnegie. Also, a tendency to glorify corporate chief executive officers has created a proliferation of profiles of individual businessmen. Business best-sellers such as *In Search of Excellence* stress the importance of the executive's personality and charisma (Peters and Waterman 1982).

In public administration, we do not seem to give as much credence to the individual life story. Our historical materials tend to direct attention to such classic writings as Wilson's essay and great documents such as the Brownlow report. Another tendency in administrative history is to stress eras, as in the Leonard White volumes, or civilizations, as in E.N. Gladden's work (1972). Individual founders, entrepreneurs, pioneers, administrators, and intellectuals of the field do not emerge as flesh-and-blood men and women but as figures immersed in events and historical periods. Exceptions can be found to this tendency, for example, Robert Caro's (1975) *The Power Broker,* Eugene Lewis's (1980) *Public Entrepreneurship,* and Doig and Hargrove's (1987) *Leadership and Innovation,* but they are rare.

At least three reasons for writing added administrative biography can be advanced. First, it is an effective way of teaching the history of the field and the history of public agencies. Forgotten incidents and arcane details become vivid when narrated from a human perspective. The unfolding of an individual life is a convenient temporal framework for coverage of a given chronological timeline of events. Because of the great impact certain individuals have had on our public institutions, biography can become a key to unraveling causality. One does not have to insist on a great-man theory to agree that the history of the Forest Service cannot be understood without studying the life of Gifford Pinchot. Similarly, the FBI cannot be understood without J. Edgar Hoover, the TVA without David Lilienthal, NASA without James Webb, and the modern Pentagon without Robert McNamara. And as for the field as a whole, a superb book that simply must be written will relate the history of American public administration itself through the life of Luther Gulick.

The second reason for biography is its capacity to convey values. When administrative norms are presented as ethical codes or legal precepts, they are disembodied from life. While case studies, such as those developed by the Inter-University Case Program, place normative dilemmas in concrete situations, they are rarely compelling as conveyors of values; the human actors themselves are usually not center stage, hence the reader finds it difficult to relate to the dilemmas personally. In biography, however, we have the opportunity to identify in an immediate, human way with others' ethical struggles. To illustrate, Kenneth Lasson's (1978) book on six frustrated federal officials gives us a more vivid picture of civil service morale problems than all of the Office of Personnel Management's Federal Employee

Attitude Surveys combined. Similar biographical sketches could be done for whistleblowers, striking schoolteachers, politicized bureau chiefs, and bribe-tempted police officers. Exposure to such material will impart to civil servants far more ethical consciousness than the code of ethics hung on an office wall.

A third reason is suggested by a comment of Dwight Waldo's, offered during an interview conducted by Brack Brown and Richard Stillman (1985): "Where I think we fall down badly is in failing to provide what I will boldly call an inspirational component in our training programs. What I have in mind, for example, are biographies and essays in which public service careers are portrayed honestly but favorably" (p. 463).

Indeed, inspiration can be the clinching reason to make the writing of administrative biography an emerging trend in the field. Biography does not merely teach history or convey values, but can instill a sense of dedication and commitment. It can help provide young men and women headed for the public service with the motivational grounding that substitutes for the almighty dollar, the incentive that prevails elsewhere in the employment world. Extended portrayals of great administrators such as William Jump, Rexford Tugwell, George Marshall, Frances Perkins, and William Ruckelshaus are capable of demonstrating the driving power of a sense of mission apart from naked greed or mere thirst for power. Moreover, such biography can put to practical work David Hart's (1985) splendid idea of utilizing the search for fame as an appropriate motivating force for serving the public good.

At the same time, hagiographic glorification of our discipline's great figures is not desirable. In fact, it would detract from the capacity of biography to show that administration involves compromise and requires dirty hands as well as holiness and halos. A model here could be Lytton Strachey's (1918) *Eminent Victorians,* whose sympathetic but myth-destroying biographic sketches of nineteenth-century figures such as Florence Nightingale (herself a great administrator) created role models for the literate young of the World War I era. Indeed, recent articles in the pages of *Public Administration Review* on Paul Hoffman, Paul Appleby, Eleanor Roosevelt, and Charles Beard seem to point us pretty squarely in this direction (Burke 1984; Cleveland 1982; Goodsell 1986).

The Analysis of Analysis

The third issue area that should emerge relates to the technology of administration. In the past, public administration has generally been a rather unreflective consumer of technology. This tendency has many roots, including the central place of the efficiency criterion in our constellation of values, the presence of inexorable political demands to cut costs, and a sense of defensiveness and insecurity that makes the field gimmick prone. Public administration as a fraternity always seems to fear being behind the times—hence becoming an easy prey for aggressive hucksters of the latest technological hardware and management acronyms.

I propose that we move from being unthinking enthusiasts of new technology, bedazzled by the substantive features of the technology itself, to more sober, self-conscious acquirers and users of new products and services. To accomplish this end, we must study more adequately the extended implications of present and contemplated administrative technology. This study would cover the technology's long-term consequences, its actual (rather than imagined) deployment, and peculiarities of the process of technological change itself, as experienced within the specific context of political administration.

By technology, I do not refer alone to pieces of machinery or physical methods of production but as well to their surrounding social and organizational aspects—what is sometimes called the "sociotechnical system." In public administration, we honor several such systems: financial management systems, management information systems, systems of office automation, and systems of organizational development intervention, to name a few.

Let me elaborate on my proposal for reflective inquiry by reference to the technology of policy analysis. We may not always think of policy analysis as a technology, yet one could argue that its combined elements of quantification, modeling, prescription, and evaluation constitute the most enduring and significant sociotechnology to enter public administration in half a century. Policy analysis, as a field and movement, has gone a long way toward reshaping the basic character of the discipline. Moreover, its influence shows no sign of receding. Without making any judgments on the issue, it is time we conduct a concerted study of the uses, impacts, and processes of policy analysis as it is actually employed in concrete organizations. We need analysis of analysis, so to speak: a deployment of the very modeling, prescriptive, and evaluative techniques contained in this technology to examine the technology itself.

Some such work has already been done. We are seeing increasing numbers of studies that examine and reflect on whether analysis is in fact a problem-solving process, as it purports to be. Also under study is the influence of analysts in policy making, and the culture of analyst shops in government (Hansen 1983; Jenkins-Smith and Weimer 1985; Springer 1985; Wildavsky 1979).

A constructive way in which to extend and amplify this reflection is to employ the thought categories of technology studies. Such studies are usually directed to substantive problems such as hazardous waste and biotechnology, but they can be used to scan wider issue areas. Three concepts seem particularly promising.

First, the process of technological diffusion in policy analysis should be empirically studied. Although we know that every respectable administrative agency possesses a unit for policy development, program planning, or program evaluation, we do not know exactly what they really do. At the operations level, we have not closely analyzed the reports and memoranda to come from these shops or the actual activities of analysts (exceptions are Doty 1983; Meltsner 1976). At the decision level, we have not determined the extent to which—or under what circumstances—analytical output is taken seriously, used to justify prior decisions, or employed as a symbol of rationality. As J.D. Eveland (1983) has pointed out, technological adoption typically depends on local conditions, that is, the social details of the micro environment, not the fact that it is being dispersed generally in the society.

Second, the concept of technological assessment is helpful. Although when first introduced, the scope of this term was confined mainly to mathematical risk analysis or systems forecasting, it now incorporates speculation on long-term, unintended, or delayed social, environmental, and political consequences (Lawless 1977; O'Brien and Marchand 1982; Otway and von Winterfeldt 1982). In policy analysis, we simply do not know enough about the long-term consequences of decision analysis or program evaluation. As specific examples, we do not know enough about what impact statements do to the speed of the decision process, what the process of data collection does to goal structures, and what cost-benefit analysis does to valuation of organizational ends.

Finally, the concept of technological fit can be applied. Many argue that new technologies are not equally desirable in all settings and that at times appropriate (sometimes described as soft) technologies rather than state-of-the-art should be adopted. Although microcomputers give even the smallest and most unsophisticated organization great information-processing capacity, the efforts required to gather large volumes of information to take advantage of this capacity may not always be desirable. Stuart Nagel (1982) has provided a service to policy analysis by pointing out that simple, back-of-the-envelope analytical techniques are sometimes best.

A Global Perspective

As a fourth candidate for an emerging issue in public administration, a more global perspective for the field is needed. In some respects, the discipline of public administration as we know it today has its origins in America. A sizable proportion of the world's teachers, books, and scholars associated with the field as strictly defined is American. Moreover, ethnocentrism continues to pervade much of our thinking, our research, and our conference panels. We need to escape the Americanization of public administration; also, we need to transcend national boundaries generally in administrative studies.

Let me suggest, then, two separate foci for achieving a more global perspective. One is to decolonize the present subfield of comparative administration. It is colonialist in its thinking, empirically and conceptually. Comparative administration as a field of research is not so much comparative as it is the study of public adminis-

501

tration in foreign countries. Moreover, at least half of this study has been centered on a handful of countries, namely Britain, France, and Germany, and to a lesser extent Japan and the USSR. The remaining 170-odd nations of the world have individually received relatively scant attention; they are, in fact, usually grouped into gross categories derived from degrees of modernization or democratic rule. We simply must break out of this habit of uneven depth of treatment and escape a "leading models" syndrome. While granted that some national administrative systems have been more influential worldwide than others (mainly because of historical colonialism), it is high time to learn more details and seek deeper understanding of those that are only superficially known. After that is done, we can perhaps recategorize systems by less ethnocentric variables, such as country size, character of legislative-executive interaction, administrative style, language or religious diversity, economic system, or resource base.

Comparative administration is also ethnocentric with respect to its leading theoretical constructs. It can be argued that the Weberian model, perennially a favorite framework for comparative analysis, possesses a highly Western bias. Ideas such as modernization or development invariably imply progress toward Western ideals. Then, too, instrumentalist notions of administration that stress efficiency, effectiveness, and political neutrality are closely associated with the Anglo-American idea of a politics-administration dichotomy. Public administration can (and does) serve noninstrumental functions in many countries, such as making the power of the state concrete and expressing the regime's values toward certain groups. Also, of course, bureaucracy can operate as an employment agency of last resort or as a means of mobilizing political power, functions that should not be sneered at simply because they do not fit capitalist or democratic ways of thinking. Finally, organizing concepts commonly employed to diagnose the problems of Third World bureaucracies, such as corruption, formalism, and imbalance, imply better-worse scales of value on which the bureaucracies of rich and pluralistic politics are assumed to occupy the good end of the continuum, leaving all the rest strung out toward the bad end. These frameworks for thinking are ethnocentric, despite the comparative empirical incidence of such phenomena.

A second way to achieve a more global perspective for the field of public administration is to conduct more research than is currently being done on internation public policy. I am not referring here to international public policy, a term best reserved for the actions of international bodies. Nor am I referring to comparative public policy studies, an area preoccupied with the variety of national policies.

Instead, such a focus would be directed at the growing interdependency of national governmental policy actions. Others have already pointed out this need. Fred Riggs (1976) contends that the requirement for a generalized or global framework for thinking about problems will inevitably lead to a pan-world recasting of the field, with American aspects of public administration being reduced to the status of a subfield (p. 652). Lynton Caldwell (1984) has called attention to the highly interdependent nature of land-use policy and the resultant rise of attempts to coordinate and control interventions across national boundaries; siltation of rivers in one country destroys hydrogeneration in another, for example, and intercontinental wind carriage of soil dust sets off desertization thousands of miles away. Harlan Cleveland (1985) argues that the enormous wealth, mobility, and diffusion of information in a world equipped with computers and united by satellite communications is causing the nation-state to leak out of its confines in three directions at once: to international coordination at the top; to multinational corporations at the sides; and to citizen participation at the bottom.

To illustrate some of the forces at work in this globalist trend, satellite remote sensing and aerial photography have led to revolutionary opportunities for world weather forecasting and natural resource discovery. Planetary population growth and varied levels of industrialization compel individual nations to join forces in such areas as immigration, hunger, fisheries, and acid rain. The eruption of international terrorist activity throughout the world requires the closest coordination on matters of air piracy, airport security, and the movements of suspects. In space, as we begin to exploit and colonize rather than just explore, governments will need integrated programs of space tracking, rescue, and the removal of debris. In short, as the globe shrinks and as national policies increasingly interconnect, policy research must transcend the nation state.

Two models are available for such a global policy perspective. One is strategic military and security policy. Another is the worldwide focus of international business and finance. Both models employ a global perspective to scan the environment, develop strategies, and pursue concrete objectives. Both do so by amalgamating vast informational and intellectual resources and then applying those resources in an integrated conceptual framework. A newly global civilian public administration can do the same, if equipped with equivalent resources and mandate.

In some ways, however, such an enterprise could even surpass these models. It could avoid the lingering nationalist paranoia inherent in security policy, and it could rise above the blatantly materialistic goals of international business. The resulting globalism would call for worldwide research and cooperation in a vast array of social and humanitarian matters of concern to all nations and people. Perhaps our discipline, which began on a rather puny scale as a governmental reform movement in the boroughs of New York, can become associated with cooperative research and problem amelioration on a worldwide scale.

A Teacher of Governance

A final proposal for an emerging issue in the field is restricted to the United States.

In our country, we have thought of public administration as historically performing perhaps two major roles vis-à-vis the society. These are (1) implementer of statutes, the role defined by classical concepts of legislative rule in a democracy, and (2) servant of the chief executive, the role that emerged in successive Progressive eras and especially the New Deal. As we now approach the new century only a few years away, one wonders whether a third role should not now emerge—that of teacher of governance to society.

Those who are innately suspicious of government—whether free marketeers on the right or civil libertarians on the left—may wince at this teaching metaphor, for it implies a different and more crucial role for public administration than it has played in the past. The notion of teacher suggests the possession of superior knowledge and insight. It also implies a position of respect and influence. These inferences are deliberately intended in my choice of words, because it is my belief that American public administration will need to occupy a more elevated position in American society in the third millennium than we now customarily accept.

I am not speaking of a necessarily bigger bureaucracy, although that could be true as well. Also, I am not advancing the metaphor of teacher because the society is somehow becoming ignorant. Indeed, in terms of quantity and flow of information, the very opposite is true. Instead, the society will need more teaching because collective problems are becoming compounded in their complexity as technology advances and social interdependency increases; interest-group avariciousness and a self-regarding rights mentality are fracturing the capacity for political bonding and united action for common political goals; and the combined costs of arms, public services, and interest on the public debt are outrunning the society's political capacity to tax itself. This creates a permanent crisis of insufficient public resources.

What is needed from public administration, then, in such a society? A readiness to teach ongoing lessons of governance, I submit. I would, moreover, submit that public administration possesses a capacity to instruct society with respect to both the substantive knowledge and normative ideals of governance. In the realm of substance, such teaching will add to our collective understanding of intricate policy interconnectedness among the hard lessons of past governing experience, the long-term implications of present societal trends, and the full range of available public policy options. In the normative realm, this teacher will remind us of the need to accept duties as well as demand rights; sacrifice immediate self-interest to the extent necessary for a viable public order; concern ourselves with all the effects of proposed policy on others; and defend the interests of future generations, as well as our own.

It is true that other elements of society than public administrators already do much teaching to us. Political leaders set forth visions of the future and determine the policy directions of society, as they certainly should. Economic entrepreneurs provide the energy, vigor, and productive capacity that make the good life possible from a material standpoint. Reformers and clergy raise our moral sights, while scholars and intellectuals furnish new ideas and technologies.

Politicians, producers, and preachers are indispensable and should not be downplayed or dismissed. Their efforts have created the America we know today. Nevertheless, their combined teaching efforts will not be enough for governance in the twenty-first century. Politicians are limited by a time horizon fixed by the next election, even though the time implications of public policy are constantly extending. Entrepreneurs operate within an economic system where self-interest, not public-regardingness, is paramount. Reformers, religious leaders, and academicians contribute best as critics of government rather than partakers in governance. It is public administration alone that possesses the potential to teach society how to govern itself beyond the year 2000.

At the same time, public administration is probably not fully ready for this new role. Its potentiality for normative leadership must be further developed. Let me suggest three ways in which the discipline could begin to prepare for its impending responsibility.

First, we must establish the teacher's credibility. We must grope for ways to reverse the effects of our society's innate antibureaucratic biases. This task can begin by working out ways to demonstrate to the population the high levels of effectiveness that prevail within most public agencies. Not stopping at that, we must also continuously and visibly demonstrate that we are always attempting to improve agency effectiveness. Further, we must react to budgetary stringency, not with the rearguard tactics of trying to preserve programs at all costs, but instead with creative redefinitions of core agency missions.

For their part, academicians in the field can support the enhancement of credibility by supplementing their traditional preoccupation with adequate control of bureaucracy and turn to ways of legitimizing its lawful missions and operations. It is time that our theorists discuss bureaucracy's essential contributions to a democratic society as much as they do its dangers. Professional associations such as the American Society for Public Administration (ASPA) and the International City Managers Association (ICMA) must educate all of us—especially the public administration community itself—to a realization that we are not just another pressure group fighting for survival in a changing society, but a proud leadership cadre that is dedicated to making the ongoing process of change as constructive as possible.

Second, we must develop adequate forums in which to perform the teaching function—classrooms, if you like. These need to be acquired at two levels: (1) the interface between careerists and political appointees; and (2) at the level of citizenry as a whole. While present classrooms such as hearings, cooperative projects, training programs, college curricula, and the mass media are obviously vital as educational forums and should be retained, we can fashion additional ways in which teachers and learners come together in an atmosphere of trust.

At the level of careerist-appointee interface, the relation between lower political appointees and the federal Senior Executive Service (SES) would logically suggest itself as a setting for education. But the SES's size and flagging image may mean that more drastic reforms of the upper civil service are necessary. One idea to draw on may be the grand corps concept in French administration. A *corps* in this sense consists of high-morale professionals in a given substantive area who operate in all departments instead of just one. Thus they transcend the agency viewpoint, and can be accepted by incoming appointees as knowledgeable yet above the fray to some extent. Such corps members might thus succeed as administrative educators.

At the level of citizenry, we should think of forums where administrators have the opportunity to talk candidly and engage in informal interaction with citizens. Possibilities would be call-in talk shows broadcast on municipal cablevision; visits by administrators to schools and civic groups; public-sector plant tours; and administrative town meetings held in regional offices and city halls.

Finally, an improved language of dialogue should be fashioned for teaching governance. This is of critical importance, since the key words around which ideas cluster become symbols for the broader vision of what we are about. As the philosopher of language John Searle (1969) points out, the very fact that we employ certain words commits us to the underlying value premises embedded in these words (he calls these the constitutive rules of the institution). Our discipline should thus set out to promote verbal symbols that are adequate to public administration's teaching task. This will require not just coining cute phrases but building on language constructs of appropriate connotation already deeply rooted in our culture. One candidate here is the public interest (Flathman 1966). Although ridiculed by mostly academics, the term nonetheless directs dialogue to broad societal purposes and consideration of the interests of all affected parties (Wamsley, Goodsell, Rohr, Stivers, White, and Wolf 1987). Another possibility is high citizenship, which can be construed as imposing obligations of responsibility to the polity as well as a conferral of rights (Frederickson 1982; Frederickson and Chandler 1984). Further development of the symbolization of governance will be of major priority in the years ahead.

The Challenge Ahead

These five emerging issues are, as admitted earlier, not clear projections from present research or action agendas. They are a product of my world view. Nonetheless, each issue has also been raised by others, and none depart wholly from current concerns in the field.

Full emergence of the proposed issues will not be automatic or easy. Longstanding intellectual traditions in public administration create much resistance to each. The strong thread of scientism that runs through our field's history creates counterforces to the qualitative research contemplated by administrative ethnography, the humanistic research called for in administrative biography, and the reflective assessment of technology called for in an analysis of analysis. The field's continuing ethnocentrism argues against adopting a truly global perspective. Finally, our traditional dedication to a purely instrumentalist posture for public administration runs counter to the proposed teacher role.

At the same time, the field is by no means static intellectually. Indeed, one might argue that our emerging superdiscipline is filled almost to overflowing with paradigmatic diversity, conflicting cross-currents, and a continuing assault on all orthodoxies. We should be delighted that our field is not orderly and calm but turbulent and vital. This turbulence is what makes the five proposed issues not inconceivable as emerging lines of inquiry but ripe for serious dialogue. To illustrate, challenges from interpretivist and radical-humanist ontological-epistemological schools of thought are pushing aside the old monopoly once held by positivist social science on our research assumptions and procedures. The current low ebb but continuing survival of comparative administration studies is, quite possibly, preliminary to a vast new interest in the global perspective. A surge of interest in the normative dimensions of public administration is making good headway. The instrumentalist tradition of the field is being challenged by a call for elevating the public administration to the status of full partner in the process of democratic governance.

In short, one cannot be pessimistic about such a vital and dynamic discipline as our own. For an elderly centenarian, public administration is remarkably alive in mind and body. This gives us all an opportunity to participate in the field's constant reshaping as we move ahead.

References

Brown, Brack, and Richard J. Stillman. 1985. "A Conversation with Dwight Waldo: An Agenda for Future Reflections." *Public Administration Review* 45:459–67.

Burke, Frances. 1984. "Eleanor Roosevelt, 11 October 1884–7 November 1962—She Made a Difference." *Public Administration Review* 44:365–72.

Caldwell, Lynton K. 1984. "Land Use Policy as an International Issue." *Policy Studies Journal* 12:553–60.

Caro, Robert A. 1975. *The Power Broker.* New York: Random House.

Cleveland, Harlan. 1982. "The Character of the Institution." *Public Administration Review* 42:310–13.

Cleveland, Harlan. 1985. "The Twilight of Hierarchy: Speculations on the Global Information Society." *Public Administration Review* 45:185–95.

Deal, Terrence E., and Allan A. Kennedy. 1982. *Corporate Cultures.* Reading, Mass.: Addison-Wesley.

Doig, Jameson W., and Erwin C. Hargrove. 1987. *Leadership and Innovation: A Biographical Perspective on Entrepreneurs in Government.* Baltimore: Johns Hopkins University Press.

Doty, Pamela. 1983. "Values in Policy Research." In *Values, Ethics and the Practice of Policy Analysis,* edited by William N. Dunn. Lexington, Mass.: Heath.

Eveland, J.D. 1983. "Some Themes in the Interactions of Technology and Administration." *Policy Studies Journal* 11:409–19.

Flathman, Richard E. 1966. *The Public Interest: An Essay Concerning the Normative Discourse of Politics.* New York: Wiley.

Frederickson, H. George. 1982. "The Recovery of Civicism in Public Administration." *Public Administration Review* 42:501–8.

Frederickson, H. George, and Ralph Clark Chandler, eds. 1984. "Citizenship and Public Administration." *Public Administration Review* 44:99–209.

Goodsell, Charles T. 1981. "The New Comparative Administration: A Proposal." *International Journal of Public Administration* 3:143–55.

Goodsell, Charles T. 1986. "Charles A. Beard: Prophet for Public Administration." *Public Administration Review* 46:105–7.

Gladden, E.N. 1972. *A History of Public Administration.* London: Frank Cass.

Hansen, Susan B. 1983. "Public Policy Analysis: Some Recent Developments and Current Problems." In *Political Science: The State of the Discipline,* edited by Ada W. Finifter. Washington, D.C.: American Political Science Association.

Hart, David K. 1985. "The Federalist and the Public Service: Fame and Fame-Worthiness." Manuscript.

Jenkins-Smith, Hank C., and David L. Weimer. 1985. "Analysis as Retrograde Action." *Public Administration Review* 45:485–94.

Kaufman, Herbert. 1960. *The Forest Ranger.* Baltimore: Johns Hopkins University Press.

Kilmann, Ralph H., Mary J. Saxon, and Roy Serpa. 1985. *Gaining Control of the Corporate Culture.* San Francisco: Jossey-Bass.

Lasson, Kenneth. 1978. *Private Lives of Public Servants.* Bloomington: Indiana University Press.

Lawless, Edward W. 1977. *Technology and Social Shock.* New Brunswick, N.J.: Rutgers University Press.

Lewis, Eugene. 1980. *Public Entrepreneurship.* Bloomington: Indiana University Press.

Maynard-Moody, Steven, Donald D. Stull, and Jerry Mitchell. 1986. "Reorganization as Status Drama: Building, Maintaining, and Displacing Dominant Subcultures." *Public Administration Review* 46:301–10.

Meltsner, Arnold J. 1976. *Public Analysis in the Bureaucracy.* Berkeley: University of California Press.

Nachmias, David, and David H. Rosenbloom. 1978. *Bureaucratic Culture.* New York: St. Martin's Press.

Naisbitt, John. 1982. *Megatrends.* New York: Warner.

Nagel, Stuart. 1982. "Doing Better with Less." *Public Administration Times,* 1 and 15 September, 15 October, 1 and 15 November.

O'Brien, David M., and Donald A. Marchand, eds. 1982. *The Politics of Technology Assessment.* Lexington, Mass.: Heath.

Otway, Harry J., and Detlof von Winterfeldt. 1982. "Beyond Acceptable Risk: On the Social Acceptability of Technologies." *Policy Sciences* 14:247–56.

Peters, Thomas J., and Robert H. Waterman. 1982. *In Search of Excellence.* New York: Warner.

Riggs, Fred W. 1976. "The Group and the Movement: Notes on Comparative and Development Administration." *Public Administration Review* 36:648–54.

Rouse, John E., Jr. 1982. "Boundaries of an Emerging Superdiscipline." *Public Administration Review* 42:390–98.

Sathe, Vijay. 1985. *Culture and Related Corporate Realities.* Homewood, Ill.: Irwin.

Schein, Edgar H. 1985. *Organizational Culture and Leadership.* San Francisco: Jossey-Bass.

Searle, John R. 1969. *Speech Acts: An Essay in the Philosophy of Language.* Cambridge, England: Cambridge University Press.

Seidman, Harold. 1980. *Politics, Position, and Power.* 3d ed. New York: Oxford University Press.

Springer, J. Fred. 1985. "Policy Analysis and Organizational Decisions." *Administration and Society* 16:475–508.

Strachey, Lytton. 1918. *Eminent Victorians.* New York: Harcourt, Brace.

Taylor, Serge. 1984. *Making Bureaucracies Think.* Stanford: Stanford University Press.

Wamsley, Gary L., Charles T. Goodsell, John A. Rohr, Camilla M. Stivers, Orion F. White, and James F. Wolf. 1987. "The Public Administration and the Governance Process: Refocusing the American Dialogue." In *A Centennial History of the American Administrative State,* edited by Ralph Clark Chandler. New York: Macmillan.

Wildavsky, Aaron. 1979. *Speaking Truth to Power.* Boston: Little, Brown.

CONTRIBUTORS

JONATHAN BENDOR received his Ph.D. in political science from the University of California, Berkeley, in 1979. Since that time he has taught at the Graduate School of Business, Stanford University, and is currently associate professor of public policy and public management. His publications include *Parallel Systems: Redundancy in Government* and articles in *American Political Science Review* and *American Journal of Political Science.*

NAOMI CAIDEN is chair of the Department of Public Administration at California State University San Bernadino, where she has been professor since 1981. She received her Ph.D. in political science at the University of Southern California in 1978. She is the co-author, with Aaron Wildavsky, of *Planning and Budgeting in Poor Countries,* and has written many articles on budgeting. She is editor of *Public Budgeting and Finance.*

PHILLIP J. COOPER is professor of political science at the Rockefeller College of Public Affairs and Policy, State University of New York at Albany. He is the author of *Public Law and Public Administration* and *Hard Judicial Choices.* He received his M.A. and Ph.D. in political science at the Maxwell School of Syracuse University.

ROBERT B. DENHARDT is research professor of public administration at the University of Missouri (Columbia) and chair of the Governor's Advisory Committee on Productivity for the State of Missouri. He is a past president of the American Society for Public Administration. He is the author of *In the Shadow of Organization* and *Theory of Public Organization.*

JAMES W. FESLER is Alfred Cowles Professor Emeritus of Government at Yale University. He has served as vice president of the American Political Science Association and is a recipient of the Waldo and Gaus Awards for outstanding contributions to the professional literature in public administration. He has served on the staff of the President's Committee on Administrative Management and has been a consultant with the United Nations as well as various federal agencies. His published works include *Public Administration: Theory and Practice* and *American Public Administration: Patterns of the Past.*

PATRICIA S. FLORESTANO is vice chancellor for governmental relations for the University of Maryland and was formerly director of the university's Institute for Governmental Service. She is a past president of the American Society for Public Administration and a past chairperson of the Urban Affairs Association. Her publications include *The States and the Metropolis* and articles in *Public Administration Review, Presidential Studies, Urban Affairs Quarterly, National Civic Review,* and other journals.

ROBERT C. FRIED received his Ph.D. at Yale University and is professor of political science at the University of California, Los Angeles. His books include *The Italian Prefects, Planning the Eternal City, Comparative Political Institutions, Comparative Urban Politics,* and *Performance in American Bureaucracy.* His current work is in the field of comparative criminal justice systems.

ROBERT T. GOLEMBIEWSKI is research professor at the University of Georgia. He is an active organization development consultant and has contributed some 300 research pieces to several literatures. His latest books are *High Performance and Human Costs; Classics in Social Science;* a reprint of his 1965 *Men, Management, and Morality;* and *Phases of Burnout.*

CHARLES T. GOODSELL is director and professor at the Center for Public Administration and Policy, Virginia Polytechnic Institute and State University. He is the author of *The Social Meaning of Civic Space: Studying Political Authority Through Architecture, The Case for Bureaucracy: A Public Administration Polemic, American Corporations and Peruvian Politics,* and *Administration of a Revolution.* He edited *The Public Encounter: Where State and Citizen Meet.*

NICHOLAS L. HENRY is president of Georgia Southern College. Prior to that, he was professor of public affairs and dean of the College of Public Programs at Arizona State University. Among his books are *Public Administration and Public Affairs, Doing Public Administration, Governing at the Grass Roots,* and, with John Stuart Hall, *Reconsidering American Politics. Public Administration and Public Affairs* has been translated into Japanese and was published by Bunshindo Publishers of Tokyo under the title *General Theory of Modern Administrative Management Systems.*

HELEN INGRAM is acting director of the Udall Center for Studies in Public Policy. She is also a professor in the Department of Political Science at the University of Arizona and holds a joint appointment in the College of Law and the School of Public Administration and Policy. She is book review editor for *American Political Science Review.* Her most recent book is *Continuity and Change in Water Policy.*

HERBERT KAUFMAN, for many years a member of the Department of Political Science at Yale, and then of the Governmental Studies Program at the Brookings Institution, has written books and articles on public administration, urban government, and organization theory, including *The Forest Ranger, Governing New York City* (with Wallace S. Sayre), and, most recently, *Time, Chance, and Organizations.*

514

KENNETH L. KRAEMER is director of the Public Policy Research Organization and a professor in the Graduate School of Management and the Department of Information and Computer Science at the University of California, Irvine. Dr. Kraemer's research interests include the management of information systems and organizations; the organizational, social, and public policy implications of computing, and the strategic and political uses of computing. His most recent books are *Datawars, Wired Cities,* and *Managing Information Systems.*

VINCENT L. MARANDO is professor of government and politics at the University of Maryland. His books include *The Forgotten Governments* and *The States and the Metropolis.* He is the author of numerous articles on urban politics, policy, and administration. He received his Ph.D. from Michigan State University and was a Public Administration Fellow.

STUART S. NAGEL is professor of political science at the University of Illinois. He is the secretary-treasurer and publications coordinator of the Policy Studies Organization. His most relevant books include *Policy Evaluation: Making Optimum Decisions; Public Policy: Goals, Means, and Methods; Policy Studies: Integration and Evaluation,* and *Evaluation Analysis with Microcomputers.*

LLOYD G. NIGRO is a member of the faculty of the Institute of Public Administration at Georgia State University. He received his Ph.D. in public administration from the University of Southern California and has been on the faculties at USC and at Syracuse University. He is the co-author of *Modern Public Administration* and *The New Public Personnel Administration.* He has also authored numerous articles in the areas of public personnel and administrative thought. He was co-recipient of the Dimock Award for the best lead article in *Public Administration Review* in 1987.

JAMES L. PERRY is a professor in the School of Public and Environmental Affairs, Indiana University at Bloomington. His research focuses on public management and public personnel administration. He is the author or co-author of four books and over fifty articles appearing in journals such as the *Academy of Management Journal, Administration and Society, Administrative Science Quarterly, American Political Science Review,* and *Public Administration Review.*

MICHAEL B. PRESTON is currently chairman of the political science department at the University of Southern California, where he has been a member of the faculty since 1986. He does research in the areas of urban and black politics, public administration, and manpower politics. His books include *Race, Sex, and Policy Problems,* edited with Marian Palley, *The New Black Politics,* and *The Politics of Bureaucratic Reform.* His most recent publications deal with black politics in Chicago.

HAL G. RAINEY is professor in the Department of Political Science at the University of Georgia. His primary research interests and most recent articles concern the nature of public management, organizational design and incentive systems, political environments of organizations, and public perceptions of taxes and government services. He has served as chair of the Public Sector Division of the Academy of Management, and serves on the editorial boards of the *Academy of Management Review, Administration and Society,* and *State and Local Government Review.*

JOHN A. ROHR is professor of public administration at Virginia Polytechnic Institute and State University. His books include *Ethics for Bureaucrats: An Essay on Law and Values* and *To Run a Constitution: The Legitimacy of the Administrative State.* He is an associate editor of *Administration and Society* and recipient of the 1988 NASPAA/ ASPA Distinguished Research Award.

DEBRA W. STEWART is professor of political science and public administration and dean of the Graduate School at North Carolina State University. She is the author of three books and numerous articles, including works on equal employment opportunity policy, management ethics, and women in politics.

DWIGHT WALDO is Albert Schweitzer Professor in the Humanities, Emeritus, at Syracuse University. He is the author of more than fifty books and essays in the area of political science and public administration. He has held various administrative positions and offices in professional organizations and served for eleven years as editor in chief of *Public Administration Review.*

MAURICE C. WOODARD is professor of political science at Howard University. He has also served as a staff associate at APSA since 1975. He received his Ph.D. from the University of Kansas in 1969. His areas of specialization are public administration, American government and politics, and urban policy and black politics. He has published extensively in the area of minorities in higher education and has prepared two editions of the *Directory of Black Americans in Political Science* for APSA. "Minorities and Policy Problems: An Overview as Seen by the U.S. Commission on Civil Rights," which he co-authored with Edward R. Jackson, appeared in Marian Palley and Michael Preston's *Race, Sex, and Policy Problems.*

NAOMI B. LYNN is professor of public administration and political science and dean of the College of Public and Urban Affairs at Georgia State University. She is a past president of the American Society for Public Administration.

AARON WILDAVSKY is professor of political science and public policy at the University of California, Berkeley. He is also a former president of the American Political Science Association.

Index of Names

Index of Subjects

2450